Praise for
America's New Democracy

"The best, most affordable textbook for freshmen level American national government. Nothing is left out . . . and the students will gain so much from it."

—Cheryl A. Brown, *Marshall University*

"Rather than just focusing on decisions and events of history, this text provides examples of current involvement and, more importantly, how students as voters can influence the political process. It strives to create an educated and engaged citizenry."

—Nancy S. Lind, *Illinois State University*

"It's an informative, engaging book that offers both breadth and depth on the standard topics in American politics. The theme—that elections are at the center of American politics and have wide-ranging causes and consequences—is a natural one, both for teachers and students of American politics."

—Charles R. Shipan, *University of Iowa*

"The text provides a thematically driven, comprehensive review of American politics and government."

—Peter Watkins, *Saint Joseph's College*

"This is a thorough introductory textbook that is not just about politics—it also introduces students to political science. The major themes, debates, and conclusions of contemporary scholarship are discussed cogently but accessibly."

—David Campbell, *University of Notre Dame*

"This text covers the many aspects of American government. It is supported by excellent graphics and additional reading that entice a class to discussion."

—Sarah Miller, *Lourdes College*

"This book links the study of American government and politics with political science. It emphasizes explanation and description, and students become familiar not only with the substance of American politics, but also how political scientists go about their work. This is how we ought to teach American government."

—Daniel E. Ponder, *University of Colorado at Colorado Springs*

"The authors have gone to great lengths to include the most timely and up-to-date information that is available. I am also especially fond of the use of political cartoons as I feel strongly that this type of medium speaks directly to students in a way that the written word sometimes cannot do."

—Tomas J. Cioppa, *Brookdale Community College*

"This text does an excellent job not only introducing topics but also defining concepts and providing different perspectives. Table and figures are provocative and informative."

—Francisco Durand, *University of Texas at San Antonio*

"The chapter introductions were wonderful, each telling an interesting story that engages the reader and provokes further thought and interest. This text is an easy-to-read and engaging introduction to American politics and institutions."

—Debbi Daniels, *University of Minnesota*

MORRIS P. FIORINA is Professor of Political Science and Senior Fellow of the Hoover Institution at Stanford University. He received a B.A. from Allegheny College in Meadville, Pennsylvania, and a Ph.D. from the University of Rochester. Before moving to Stanford, he taught at the California Institute of Technology and at Harvard University.

Fiorina has written widely on American government and politics with special emphasis on representation and elections. He has published numerous articles and six other books: *Representatives, Roll Calls, and Constituencies; Congress—Keystone of the Washington Establishment; Retrospective Voting in American National Elections; The Personal Vote: Constituency Service and Electoral Independence* (coauthored with Bruce Cain and John Ferejohn); *Divided Government;* and *Culture War? The Myth of A Polarized America* (coauthored with Samuel Abrams and Jeremy Pope). He has served on the editorial boards of a dozen journals in the fields of political science, economics, law, and public policy, and from 1986 to 1990 he served as chairman of the Board of Overseers of the American National Election Studies. He is a member of the National Academy of Sciences.

In his leisure time, Fiorina favors physical activities, including hiking, fishing, and sports. Although his own athletic career never amounted to much, he has been a successful youth baseball coach for fifteen years. Among his most cherished honors is a plaque given by happy parents on the occasion of an undefeated Babe Ruth season.

PAUL E. PETERSON is the Henry Lee Shattuck Professor of Government and Director of the Center for American Political Studies at Harvard University. He received his B.A. from Concordia College in Moorhead, Minnesota, and his Ph.D. from the University of Chicago.

Peterson is the author of numerous books and articles on federalism, urban politics, race relations, and public policy, including studies of education, welfare, and fiscal and foreign policy. He received the Woodrow Wilson Award from the American Political Science Association for his book *City Limits* (Chicago, 1981). In 1996 his book *The Price of Federalism* (Brookings, 1995) received the Aaron Wildavsky Award for the best book on public policy. He is a member of the American Academy of Arts and Sciences.

It is not only when writing a textbook that Peterson makes every effort to be as accurate as possible. On the tennis courts, he always makes correct line calls and has seldom been heard to hit a wrong note when tickling the ivories.

Bert Johnson is Assistant Professor of Political Science at Middlebury College in Middlebury, Vermont. He received his B.A. from Carleton College and his Ph.D. from Harvard University.

Johnson has written on federalism, intergovernmental relations, and campaign finance and has published articles in journals such as *Social Science History* and *Urban Affairs Quarterly*. His analysis of President George W. Bush's first-term interactions with Congress appears in Steven Schier's edited volume, *High Risks and Big Ambition: The Presidency of George W. Bush* (Pittsburgh, 2004). When not investigating new ideas about American politics, he can be found exploring prime rock climbing spots throughout the United States.

D. STEPHEN VOSS is Assistant Professor of Political Science at the University of Kentucky. He received his Ph.D. from Harvard University, studying with Gary King, and specializes in voting and elections with a particular focus on racial politics in the U.S. South. A New Orleans native, Voss also has two bachelor's degrees from Louisiana State University—one in history and one in print journalism.

Voss has authored or coauthored articles in various political science journals, including the *American Journal of Political Science, Journal of Politics, Public Opinion Quarterly, State Politics and Policy Quarterly,* and *American Politics Research.* He also coauthored *CliffsQuickReview American Government* and is working on the Federal Elections Project with David Lublin of American University. Prior to entering academia, Voss was a political reporter for Gannett News Service and edited a top-selling travel guide, *Let's Go: USA.*

Voss spends his leisure time shooting pool, playing cards, enjoying warlike computer games, watching David Lynch videos, and listening to hard-edged music of all sorts. He used up his 15 seconds of fame while in graduate school, thanks to an unscripted cameo appearance as the blue spaceman in Phish's "Down with Disease" music video.

WILLIAM G. MAYER is an Associate Professor of Political Science at Northeastern University in Boston, having received his B.A. and his Ph.D. from Harvard University. He is the author of six books and numerous articles on topics such as public opinion, political parties, voting and elections, media and politics, and the presidential nomination process. More importantly, he is married to Amy Logan and the father of two children, Natalie and Thomas. He also teaches Sunday School to kindergartners at St. Jude's Catholic Church in Waltham, Massachusetts.

PENGUIN ACADEMICS

AMERICA'S NEW DEMOCRACY

PENGUIN ACADEMICS

AMERICA'S
NEW DEMOCRACY

FOURTH EDITION

MORRIS P. FIORINA
Stanford University

PAUL E. PETERSON
Harvard University

BERTRAM JOHNSON
Middlebury College

D. STEPHEN VOSS
University of Kentucky

WILLIAM G. MAYER
Northeastern University

PEARSON
Longman

New York San Francisco Boston
London Toronto Sydney Tokyo Singapore Madrid
Mexico City Munich Paris Cape Town Hong Kong Montreal

Editor in Chief:	Eric Stano
Executive Marketing Manager:	Ann Stypuloski
Supplements Editor:	Brian Belardi
Production Manager:	Savoula Amanatidis
Project Coordination and Electronic Page Makeup:	Electronic Publishing Services Inc., NYC
Cover Design Manager:	Nancy Danahy
Cover Image:	Copyright © Franklin McMahon/Corbis
Photo Researcher:	Anita Dickhuth
Senior Manufacturing Buyer:	Alfred C. Dorsey
Printer and Binder:	Quebecor World Book Services— Taunton
Cover Printer:	Phoenix Color Corporation— Hagerstown

For permission to use copyrighted material, grateful acknowledgment is made to the copyright holders on pp. 566–567, which are hereby made part of this copyright page.

Library of Congress Cataloging-in-Publication Data
America' s new democracy / Morris P. Fiorina . . . [et al.].—4th ed.
    p. cm. — (Penguin academics)
Includes bibliographical references and index.
ISBN 978-0-205-57248-9
1. Democracy—United States.   2. United States—Politics and government.   I. Fiorina, Morris P.
JK1726.F56 2008
320.473—dc22

                                                        2007024586

Visit us at www.ablongman.com

For more information about the Penguin Academic Series, please contact us by mail at Longman Publishers, attn. Marketing Department, 1185 Avenue of the Americas, 25th Floor, New York, NY 10036, or via the Internet at http://www.ablongman/feedback.

ISBN-13: 978-0-205-57248-9
ISBN-10: 0-205-57248-0

1 2 3 4 5 6 7 8 9 10—QWT—10 09 08 07

contents

PART FOUR Outputs from America's New Democracy 367

College-age people are instinctively skeptical when they approach the study of American government. Students do not struggle with the concept that institutions or practices may malfunction. Hidden motives, corrupt bargains, social injustice, rampant incompetence—these are precisely what many (if not most) undergraduates today expect to encounter. Of course, not all students react to bad news in the same way. Some smirk knowingly. Some thump their chests and demand radical reform. Most shrug or yawn. Precious few, however, gasp in surprise.

Many popular political science works reinforce the pessimism of the age, especially with regard to democratic politics. They downplay the importance of mass political behavior—and teach that elites actually run the U.S. government, with limited regard for the voting public.[1] This book, by contrast, offers a guardedly upbeat message, one that stresses the system's responsiveness. Our purpose is not to suppress healthy skepticism. Rather, it is to cultivate a mirror image of analytical techniques already in place—to get readers in the habit of looking beyond the surface when appearances are *negative*, not only when they are rosy. We encourage readers to approach sky-is-falling-down political rhetoric with the same critical eye that they automatically reserve for sunny optimism.

Admittedly, institutions or practices that seem to function effectively in fact sometimes do not. Yet sometimes institutions or practices that appear dysfunctional—those that draw on base motives, express questionable values, or seem to lack an underlying logic—actually perform surprisingly well. Ours is an even-handed orientation, one that seeks the virtues as well as the vices of American government. Such cautious optimism may sound alien to modern readers, especially those who have learned about politics primarily from journalistic sources. But it dates back to the Enlightenment "political science" of the nation's founders (in particular, James Madison) and is a dominant mode of thinking among several contemporary schools in the political science discipline.

The intellectual perspective described here motivates the book's central theme: Elections (and the anticipation of them) matter more in America's political system now than they have in the past, than they do in other industrialized democracies, or than other political writers usually recognize. Votes are the main currency in the political market, so influencing them motivates political behavior even when the connection is not obvious. Fiorina and Peterson first articulated this claim while writing a textbook in 1993, and at the time they expected the argument to meet with substantial resistance. Most of the developments they described were fairly recent. But the presidencies of Bill Clinton and George W. Bush have lessened the novelty of the argument—and, if anything, turned it into conventional wisdom.[2] This new book lies squarely in the mainstream of scholarly thinking about American politics.

A Unified Approach to American Government

Regardless of whether one accepts this book's central argument, it serves as a valuable organizing framework for learning about American government. The book's theme and its intellectual perspective link every chapter. An introductory chapter announces the emphasis on popular influence, especially as transmitted through democratic elections. The remaining 14 chapters then each deal with a subject conventionally covered by American government texts. Rather than consign culture, opinion, and electioneering to single chapters, however, we continue to trace their effects through American political institutions all the way to the shape of public policies.

Every chapter begins with a vignette that either illustrates the voting public's power or seems to contradict it. We then use the stories to draw larger lessons about popular influence on each component of the American political system. We emphasize the electoral incentives that political actors face, how those incentives shape institutions, and how the institutions translate competing pressures into public policy. Thus, the result is more a unified book than a textbook, albeit one written for newcomers to the topic.

Challenging Today's Student

This volume differs from an introductory textbook in one other sense as well. Instructors often operate on the implicit view that their students are not adequately motivated to undertake college work. They presume that undergraduates will not endeavor to learn new words or to think through complex ideas. This viewpoint has led some instructors to oversimplify their courses and some textbook authors to avoid sophisticated arguments. Having each taught American government for many years, we are not unsympathetic with the pressures these educators face.

Nevertheless, we suspect that the main problem for typical students is neither stupidity nor laziness but simple boredom. Our experiences as educators at both private and public colleges and universities suggest that most students who are engaged by a subject are perfectly willing to do the work necessary to learn, even if it means checking a dictionary occasionally or reading a paragraph a second time. Rather than blame students for their boredom, therefore, we hypothesize that political science textbooks need to do a better job of conveying why political science is both interesting and relevant to students who lack an inherent love of the subject.

Given our premise, this book intentionally challenges college undergraduates. We treat readers as mature and thoughtful people, curious about their world but impatient with authors who waste their time. To meet the requirements of this demanding audience, we have done everything possible to streamline the book's presentation and spice up the book's language without sacrificing substance. Each chapter is an extended essay told in a uniform authorial voice, not a series of disembodied topics. We tell stories. We emphasize meaning and significance, the "bottom line." We use the active voice, straightforward sentences, and nontechnical language whenever possible. We do not just define or describe; we interpret and sometimes provoke. Our hope is that readers will find this approach as satisfying an antidote for their boredom as our own undergraduate students have.

Features of the Fourth Edition

The first edition of this book grew out of a textbook by Fiorina and Peterson called *The New American Democracy*.[3] It is not just an "essentials edition" of that larger text, however. As part of the *Penguin Academics* series from Longman Publishers, *America's New Democracy* is an alternative for instructors and readers who want to move away from standard textbooks—those who prefer a learning tool crafted around an engaging narrative, available at an inexpensive price, and unified by a strong framework upon which to attach facts picked up along the way. We have adapted the book so that it differs substantially from the source, taking on its own distinct personality. The key features of this edition are as follows:

- Greater focus on the book's underlying theme, including transition sections (a) linking each introduction to the book's central argument and (b) explaining how the body of the chapter illustrates popular influence in the political system. Chapters are organized to work readers through the logic connecting each topic to electoral influences.

- Large sections of new or substantially revised material, including new introductions for most chapters.
- A reorganized table of contents, with the material broken up to facilitate use in a 15-week course. This is accomplished by offering larger, merged chapters on public opinion and the media, on elections (including presidential and congressional elections), on political factions (including parties and interest groups), and on public policy (including domestic, economic, and foreign policy).
- America's new democracy does not stand still for long, and any book that seeks to explain it to today's students must incorporate the latest developments in a variety of ways. In the years since the release of the third edition, Democrats won congressional elections, two new justices took their seats on the Supreme Court, Hurricane Katrina devastated the Gulf Coast, and the war in Iraq became increasingly controversial. We discuss all these developments in the pages that follow, as well as such matters as the continuing debate on immigration policy, the public's rapidly changing media consumption habits, Congress's failure to pass a budget in 2006, the "frontloaded" 2008 presidential primary calendar, the Jack Abramoff lobbying scandals, and the Bush administration's policies on wiretapping and other surveillance.

All of these updates, and the legion of others we have included in this edition are important. The Supreme Court's 2007 decisions to allow a ban on so-called partial birth abortion and to interpret the Clean Air Act as covering carbon dioxide emissions, for example, will have significant consequences both for public policy and for future elections.

As scholars, we have also done our best to include the most up-to-date political science research on the areas we cover. This includes new work on term limits (Chapter 3), media bias (Chapter 5), structural barriers to voting (Chapter 6), the effects of judicial elections (Chapter 12), and the polarization of Congressional voting (Chapter 15).

This new edition also attempts to respond even more effectively to the needs of instructors and students. Chapter introductions, illustrations, examples, figures, tables, photographs, and suggested readings have been revised, updated, and improved based on feedback from a dozen reviewers, various helpful fellow professors, and hundreds of our own students.

Furthermore, in this edition we have integrated a new feature—"Election Voices"—into the text of every existing chapter. Each "Election Voice" considers a concrete public policy debate concerning an issue related to the chapter topic. In Chapter 2, for example, we describe the debate over the constitutionality of the death penalty. In Chapter 8, we outline arguments for and against new restrictions on lobbying. And in Chapter 15, we delve into the complex matter of U.S. energy policy. We review each issue area, cite alternative arguments on each side, and encourage students to conduct further research on their own. By highlighting these ongoing policy debates, we hope to make abstract concepts concrete while also conveying the vitality and dynamism of America's new democracy.

We encourage instructors familiar with the earlier editions to request a copy of the instructor's manual (see the next section). It provides clear chapter-by-chapter detail on the changes in the new edition, thereby minimizing the amount of new course preparation necessary to make the transition to the revised book.

Supplements

INSTRUCTOR'S MANUAL & TEST BANK (DOWNLOAD ONLY)

This resource manual contains an overview of what each chapter tries to accomplish and how the material fits into an undergraduate classroom. For each chapter, it provides instructors with a list of learning objectives, suggests possible pedagogical strategies to assist with classroom use of the book, outlines in detail the arguments and evidence contained in the body of the book, and lists numerous test questions drawn directly from material found in the chapters. Available exclusively on the Instructor Resource Center (www.ablongman.com/irc).

COMPUTERIZED TESTING SYSTEM (DOWNLOAD ONLY)

This easy-to-master electronic supplement includes all the test items in the printed test bank. The software allows you to edit existing questions and add your own items. Tests can be printed in several different fonts and formats. Available exclusively on the Instructor Resource Center.

Study Site for American Government (http://www.longmanamericangovernment.com)

This online course companion provides a wealth of resources for both students and instructors using any of Longman's American government texts. Containing practice tests, flashcards, and Web explorations, the Study Site helps students quickly master the fundamentals, review a subject for understanding, or prepare for an exam.

MyPoliSciKit

A comprehensive interactive media tool for students and instructors using *America's New Democracy*, Fourth Edition, this Web site offers a rich battery of assessment tools and numerous interactive activities. MyPoliSciKit is available at no additional cost when packaged with the text. In addition to quizzes for every chapter, the following are just *some* of the other features it offers:

Simulations. Students are given a role to play—such a Congress member, lobbyist, police officer—experiencing the challenges and excitement of politics firsthand.

Visual Literacy Exercises. Students interpret data and work with graphs and charts dealing with intriguing political topics. Each activity begins with an interactive primer on interpreting graphics.

Participation Activities. Bringing the importance of politics home, and designed to encourage student participation, these activities appear in 3 types: (1) "Debates," (2) "Surveys," and (3) "Get Involved" activities.

Comparative Exercises. Students compare the U.S. political system with those of other countries.

"Test Yourself" quizzes. These 10-question multiple-choice quizzes at the end of every activity give instructors a quantifiable way to evaluate student performance and understanding of the material.

Research Navigator™. This database provides thousands of articles from journals—including nearly 50 of the most respected journals in political science—as well as popular periodicals like *Newsweek* and *USA Today*, giving students and professors access to both scholarly and topical content from a variety of sources.

Online Administration. Instructors can easily track students' work on the site and monitor their progress on the activities. The Instructor Gradebook ensures a seamless, efficient, and flexible experience for busy instructors.

MyPoliSciKit is available at no additional charge when an access code card is ordered bundled with a new copy of this book. Ask your Longman representative for details.

Acknowledgments

We want to thank the many people who helped out during the preparation of this book and the editions preceding it. Our editor, Eric Stano, as well as the political science editorial assistant, Donna Garnier, patiently guided the fourth edition to publication.

We also wish to express the deepest gratitude to those who have assisted with editions of the text from which this book draws. Bruce Nichols first argued the need for a new-century approach in introductory texts on American government. The Center for Advanced Study in the Behavioral and Social Sciences provided generous support for Peterson's work on the first edition during his academic year there. Harding Noblitt of Concordia College read the entire first-edition manuscript in search of errors of fact and interpretation, which saved the authors much embarrassment. In addition, portions were read by Danny Adkison, Sue Davis, Richard Fenno, Gary Jacobson, Barry Rabe, and Chris Stamm, whose comments helped with fact checking. Larry Carlton supplied important factual material. Rebecca Contreras, Alison Kommer, Shelley Weiner, and Sarah Peterson provided staff assistance. Research assistants included Ted Brader, Jay Girotto, William Howell, Donald Lee, Jerome Maddox, Kenneth Scheve, Sean Theriault, and Robert Van Houweling. Martin West of Harvard University and Sam Abrams of Stanford University performed a multitude of tasks to develop the second edition of *The New American Democracy*, from which the first edition of this book borrowed heavily.

Finally, we would like to thank the reviewers who provided comments on earlier editions to help us prepare the fourth: Cheryl A. Brown, Marshall University; Scott Buchanan, Columbus State University; David Campbell, University of Notre Dame; Tom Cioppa, Brookdale Community College; Debbie Daniels, University of

Minnesota; Fransico Durand, University of Texas of San Antonio; Jim Enelow, University of Texas at Austin; Gibbs Knotts, Western Carolina University; Christopher N. Lawrence, Millsaps College; Nancy S. Lind, Illinois State University; Sarah Miller, Lourdes College; Daniel E. Ponder, University of Colorado at Colorado Springs; Charles R. Shipan, University of Iowa; Fred Slocum, Minnesota State University–Mankato; James Toole, Indiana University; Peter Watkins, Saint Joseph's College; and Garry Young, George Washington University.

We regret that this edition could not reflect all of their useful suggestions. Nonetheless, any improvements in the fourth edition of *America's New Democracy* owe much to their extraordinarily helpful advice.

M. P. F.

P. E. P.

B. N. J.

W. G. M.

Foundations of America's New Democracy

Democracy in the United States

TEXAS GOVERNOR GEORGE W. BUSH BECAME PRESIDENT OF THE
United States in one of the most closely contested elections in American history—and
also one of the most controversial. Unlike any president in more than a century, Bush
received several hundred thousand fewer votes than the man he defeated, Vice
President Al Gore. He squeaked out a victory only because of the Electoral College, a
200-year-old method of selecting the nation's chief executive (see Chapter 7). Bush
picked up 271 out of 538 electoral votes, one more than he needed for victory.

Nor was Bush's victory simply a matter of old-fashioned rules giving him a bit of luck. The vote margin in Florida was so razor-thin that state law required a recount. Whoever won Florida was going to win the presidency, and it quickly became clear that Florida's electoral procedures were not precise enough to resolve such a close contest in a manner satisfactory to everyone. Bush came out on top weeks after the election, when a favorable ruling from the Supreme Court ended the vote counting.

In part because of this narrow and unusual victory, voters quickly polarized over the Bush presidency, with roughly half disapproving of the new chief executive. Bush could not take the American public for granted if he wanted to succeed. Despite promises that he would make "decisions based upon principle, not based upon polls or focus groups," Bush had to stay in campaign mode and constantly weigh policy choices for their likely political consequences. The White House reportedly polled voters twice a month.[1]

Bush received a huge burst in popularity after the 9/11 terrorist attacks. Indeed, his job approval ratings reached unprecedented levels. But Bush's father had attained similarly impressive ratings during the Gulf War without being able to sustain them long enough to win reelection. The younger Bush knew that his newfound popularity would fade. He moved quickly against two nations thought to harbor terrorists—Afghanistan and Iraq—and his administration took great pains to send upbeat messages back to the American people (see Chapter 5). Bush also worked quickly to set up a new Homeland Security apparatus, a dramatic change in the federal bureaucracy (see Chapter 11).

Numerous other White House policy decisions seemed to reflect political calculations. The Bush administration worked with liberal U.S. Senator Ted Kennedy to formulate bipartisan educational reforms. Bush agreed to raise barriers against foreign steel, contrary to Republican free-trade principles—in apparent recognition that the party needed votes in steel-producing states. Bush reluctantly agreed to farm-state demands for large agricultural subsidies, shoring up the rural vote. In short, Bush and his congressional allies never stopped campaigning for reelection.

Far from paranoia, this constant campaigning reflected a calculated response to the constant campaigning of Bush's Democratic rivals. Commentators began speculating on likely challengers before Bush even entered the Oval Office in 2001. No fewer than nine Democratic candidates had entered the presidential race by early 2003, only halfway into Bush's term. U.S. Senator John Kerry of Massachusetts, the eventual nominee, spent years campaigning in key nomination states such as Iowa and New Hampshire.

After Kerry won the nomination, liberal activists began working for his victory. New campaign-finance reforms had weakened the ability of the national parties to fund hard-hitting campaign ads on behalf of their candidates. Into this void appeared new organizations—called "527 Committees" after the tax code that defined them—that collected political donations and independently ran ads to influence the election. Anti-Bush 527 committees attracted the most money.

Senator Kerry, meanwhile, strove to connect with campaign audiences. He smiled a lot, took vacations that showed off his athleticism, and named a youthful running mate, Senator John Edwards of North Carolina. He sharpened his political positions, which had evolved from the intricacies of congressional politics, so that they would be easier to communicate. When Kerry's energetic wife, Teresa Heinz Kerry, seemed too outspoken for the delicacies of a national campaign, their large brood of well-mannered children spread out around the country to promote the Democratic nominee's message.[2]

Unlike in 2000, the 2004 contest did not leave the winner's identity in question: Kerry conceded defeat the day after the election. But the election produced only a brief hiatus in presidential campaigning. By the early spring of 2005, a pack of major Democrats, including John Edwards and Senator Hillary Clinton, were clearly starting to position themselves for the 2008 race. Republicans too, anxious at the prospect of an open nomination battle for the first time in eight years, were lining up to run national campaigns. Former New York City Mayor Rudolph Giuliani and 2000 presidential hopeful Senator John McCain began exploratory efforts. Pundits scrutinized Republican losses in the 2006 congressional races for any clues as to the outcome of the 2008 presidential contest. Meanwhile, a few political observers, evidently bored with speculation about 2008, began drawing up a rough list of politicians who seemed poised for a presidential run in 2012.[3]

It was the new American democracy at work.

The central theme of this book is that elections are the key to understanding contemporary American democracy. Elections not only matter, they are more important in the United States than in other democracies and more important today than they were in most earlier periods of U.S. history.

ELECTION NIGHT 2004
Bush aide Karen Hughes speaks with CNN during an election-night rally in Washington, D.C. *Do you think the recent spate of close elections has made the American public more cynical or less cynical about politics?*

By "elections," we mean more than just Tuesdays in November in even-numbered years. While the counting of votes is clearly critical, the many strategic calculations and decisions that precede Election Day are also fundamentally important. Bush and Kerry planned their presidential bids far in advance of the 2004 contest. They compiled proposals and worked hard to frame successful political messages. They cultivated the leaders of interest groups that voters join. They campaigned aggressively to win over unaffiliated voters, visiting cities and towns across the country. It was their joint sensitivity to public demands—their election-eering—that produced such a close contest. Overall, it was a presidential campaign of great energy, some positive, some negative.

Elections drive the modern political system because Americans have developed *a unique conception of democracy* that requires frequent citizen participation, with the result that *elections are plentiful* and *politicians are permanently campaigning.* The need to please a demanding electorate shapes the nation's institutions, both the formal ones set up by law and the informal ones—such as political parties, interest groups, and the mass media—that express public demands to elected leaders.

A Unique Conception of Democracy

Americans are more cynical than they used to be, although skepticism has always been part of the American character. They generally do not trust government as much as they did a generation ago.[4] Americans believe that government costs too much and delivers too little. They think politics is needlessly rancorous and often corrupt. They do not respect public servants, whether elected or appointed. They are unenthusiastic about major-party presidential candidates and yearn for a new style of leader. All of this discontent worries many civic-minded observers, who see it as a barrier to the many positive things that public policy might be able to accomplish.

Nonetheless, some suspicion of government is healthy. Governmental institutions by their very nature threaten human liberty because they hold a "monopoly of the legitimate use of physical force."[5] Government can take people's property, lock them up, or even kill them—and use the law to justify such actions. Of course, those who participate in politics usually want government to do good things, not bad ones. They hope government's vast powers will help them realize some vision of a better society. But what makes government so powerful is that it need not rely on voluntary cooperation, as charities and service organizations do. Government is a way to force everyone else to pursue the same vision. It is effective at resolving disagreements because it can back up society's decisions with violence if necessary. Such power is easy to abuse, and history is filled with examples of governments that have abused it. Citizens *should* be wary.

TRANSFER OF POWER
When government authority changes hands in many counties, it is a source of anxiety. Election "upsets" sometimes result in the end of democracy when leaders refuse to surrender power. Americans take for granted how casually power changes hands in their political system, even when rival leaders dislike or disrespect each other. Here, the Democrats celebrate their victories in the 2006 Congressional races. *Why do you think transfers of power occur more smoothly in the United States than elsewhere?*

Why do we accept the existence of governmental institutions at all, then? Thomas Hobbes, the great English political philosopher, blamed human nature. In a world without government, he argued, life would be "solitary, poor, nasty, brutish and short" because people would descend into "a war of all against all."[6] Most Americans agree with Hobbes that some form of government is necessary, but they've developed a unique conception of democracy that favors *weak governmental institutions* that are especially *responsive to public influence.*

Weak Institutions

British author Samuel Johnson once commented, "I would not give half a guinea to live under one form of government rather than another. It is of no moment to the happiness of an individual."[7] Johnson's comment is silly, at best. Lives can be saved or destroyed, depending on the type of government under which people live. The scope and structure of government are among the most critical decisions that a society must make. Aristotle recognized this fact 23 centuries ago, prompting him to work out a simple classification scheme for political institutions. He divided governments into three general categories: government by one person, by the few, and by the many.

Few Americans today support government dominated by a small number of people. When a single ruler such as an emperor or a tsar controls the state, that individual may put the people's welfare first, last, or anywhere in between. An absolute ruler answers to no one. Government by the few may appear slightly better, because members of a ruling class can compete with each other. They may try to improve social conditions as a means of attracting public support during internal disputes. But without periodic elections, a small ruling group generally can remain unified enough to exploit its position. Americans, therefore, overwhelmingly favor **democracy** (from the Greek word *demos*, meaning "people"), a form of government in which citizens share power.

Knowing that most Americans support "rule by the many" does not settle all questions regarding the form of government. Just about every democracy more complicated than a small town is a representative democracy, or **republic**; citizens elect leaders to govern them rather than choosing policies themselves. James Madison, architect of the U.S. Constitution, did not trust that government would wind up in the hands of virtuous representatives elected by wise and well-meaning citizens concerned with the public good. "If men were angels," Madison explained, "no government would be necessary."[8] Nor did Madison believe that written limits

HAIL TO THE CHIEF
Elected leaders have no monopoly on popular support. Dictators such as North Korea's Kim Jong Il use threats, intimidation, and propaganda to generate the appearance of public approval. *What sets apart government by a small number of people is how they treat citizens who do not support them.*

on government would prevent tyranny. Even if someone sketched out a list of actions forbidden to elected leaders, officials would easily be able to break through such "parchment barriers" once the restrictions became inconvenient to the wishes of a majority.

Madison therefore endorsed "buttressing" constitutional rules and citizen education with something firmer: a framework of counterbalancing political institutions that would divide up power among themselves. Each national office rooted its authority in the people, but it would receive its own **constituency** (a set of people entitled to choose the holder of that office), who then would choose their leaders at different times and within different places. Having been selected in varied ways, public officials would reflect different ideas and interests—leading them to keep an eye on rivals in other branches as a way to protect their own authority. In other words, self-interest would encourage leaders to check (that is, block) each other's abuses, resulting in a balanced system that protected voting majorities from the politically powerful.

Madison did not view majority rule as a foolproof solution to the dangers of strong government, however. Rather, the system of **checks and balances** promised one other benefit: It was a form of representation that placed clear limits on popular whims. It could prevent a minority from abusing governmental powers, but it also could frustrate a majority trying to abuse those powers. Electing representatives was a rather blunt instrument for manipulating public policy. Unless voters were fairly unified and fairly patient, the government responded sluggishly to public demands. This slowness kept American government weak.

Popular Influence

Political theorists disagree over how much popular control is desirable. Some prefer that citizens take a more active role in government. Democracy is more than just a decision-making procedure for them; it is also an educational forum. A citizenry improves itself while deciding the community's future.[9] Elections play a critical role in this *popular model of democracy* because they are the mechanism for instructing officials about public wishes.

Other theorists question whether the average citizen should take more than a passive role in government. Too much participation produces lots of talk but little action. It can make compromise difficult. Nor are citizens clearly capable of weighing policy proposals and choosing among candidates in that fashion.[10] These critics favor instead a *responsible model of democracy*, in which elected officials choose policies but must answer to the people afterward. Citizens seem better able to judge a candidate retrospectively—that is, by looking at past performance and voting out those who perform inadequately.*

---

* Some theorists, including James Madison, would reserve the term "democracy" for forms of government in which all citizens gather together in one place and make governmental decisions, as in ancient Athens or modern New England town meetings. We use the term more broadly, to include situations in which the people rule indirectly as well as directly.

In the real world, of course, all democracies combine popular and responsible features. Yet the principles of popular democracy have shaped American thought from the earliest days of the republic. Even President John Adams, who was relatively suspicious of the common people compared to many of his peers, nonetheless argued that citizens should have frequent opportunities to instruct and judge their representatives. "Where annual elections end, there slavery begins," Adams explained.[11] The system's responsiveness has only increased since then.

For this reason, one brand of American cynicism strikes us as particularly unhealthy. Many citizens believe they have little influence over government. Unlike the other forms of distrust, which are prudent given government's vast powers, we find this brand of pessimism discouraging because it is so misguided. Whatever the flaws of American government, inadequate opportunity for citizen input is certainly not one of them. The American political system allows frequent opportunities to give leaders feedback. We turn to that topic now.

Elections Are Plentiful

American politics has evolved over the course of two centuries to allow greater popular participation. The connection between representatives and the public has become increasingly direct. National institutions are less insulated from popular influence than they once were—in part because of the increasing number and frequency of elections, but also because of the more extensive campaigning that accompanies them. These trends have accelerated dramatically in recent decades, to the extent that calling the system America's "new democracy" is no exaggeration.

Half a Million Elected Officials, and Then Some

The United States has more elections than any other country on Earth. More than half a million people in the United States are elected officials, about one official for every 500 Americans. National elections, which determine the officials of the federal government, receive close media attention every two years, but these contests are just the tip of the iceberg. Voters select various public officials in statewide elections, not only the governor and one or two state legislators, but sometimes also a lieutenant governor, a treasurer, a state attorney general, an auditor, and perhaps some public utility commissioners. The quantity explodes when consideration moves to the local level, where cities, towns, villages, 3,000 counties, 16,000 school boards, and numerous special districts all must be filled. If all elected officials lived in one place, the population would exceed that of Cleveland.[12]

Even the judicial system—often viewed as insulated from political pressure—is permeated by elections. In 39 states, voters elect at least some judges. Altogether, Americans select more than 1,000 state judges and about 15,000 local court officers.[13] The result? Americans must vote constantly to stay involved. To take just one example, professors at the University of Houston estimated that a resident of Houston is represented by 126 elected officials, judges included.[14]

Although half a million elected officials sound like a lot, there are far more elections than there are elected officials. First, many officials must win two or more elections before they can take office. In the **primary election**, each party chooses a nominee, who then squares off against the other parties' nominees in the **general election**—which selects the officeholder. *Nonpartisan elections*, where candidates do not run with party labels, also sometimes use primaries to narrow the field of candidates. And occasionally, elected officials hoping to keep their posts must survive a **recall election**, in which dissatisfied citizens try to remove sitting officials during their terms. California Governor Gray Davis lost his position to activist and movie actor Arnold Schwarzenegger through a 2003 recall election.

Some elections do not choose officials at all. In 27 states and the District of Columbia, voters may influence public issues directly by making law at the ballot box.[15] This **direct democracy** operates through two different types of "propositions." Some states allow **initiatives** (proposed laws or constitutional amendments placed on the ballot by citizen petition). Some decide policy through **referenda** (laws or state constitutional amendments proposed by a legislative body that require voter

THE GOVERNOR OF CALIFORNIA Arnold Schwarzenegger won election in 2003 when voters recalled Governor Gray Davis. *Do celebrities have advantages over other candidates in popular democracies?*

approval before going into effect). These forms of direct democracy show little sign of losing their popularity. A few states, such as California, frequently have more initiatives and referenda on the ballot than elected offices to be filled.

Other countries do not have nearly so many elections. Consider Great Britain, which elected Tony Blair prime minister in 1997 and reelected him in 2001 and 2005. In each of these elections, Britons voted for only one person—a candidate for parliament. Between each election, Britons voted on only two other occasions, for only two offices—local councillor and representative to the European Union. United States citizens even vote a lot more often than other North Americans. A Mexican citizen votes at most four times in a four-year period: in presidential, congressional, state, and municipal elections. A Canadian votes at most three times (national, provincial, and municipal) in a four-year period, except for an occasional referendum, such as Québec's 1995 vote on sovereignty.

The Limits of Voting

Stressing the importance of elections may paint a rather rosy picture. To avoid any misunderstanding, therefore, we must emphasize three qualifications: (1) Elections involve more than what takes place in the voting booth. (2) Elections do not always express the popular will. (3) Elections are not the only important force in American politics.

First, our notion of electoral influence is very broad. We are referring not just to what happens in the voting booth, nor even just to what goes on during campaigns. Rather, when we write about the importance of elections, we include the anticipation of, and the preparation for, future elections. Political actors would be foolish indeed if they waited until Election Day to worry about what the public wants. Looking ahead affects what presidents propose, what they sign, and what they veto; what Congress passes and what it kills; whom groups support and whom they oppose; and what the media cover or ignore. Voters wield much of their power passively.

Second, when we stress the importance of elections, we are not making a naïve claim that "the people" rule. Just as the winner of an Olympic event may have been determined on the training fields years earlier, so the outcomes of elections may be determined far in advance of the actual campaigns. And once elections are underway, many potential voters choose not to participate (see Chapter 6). Failing to vote means that a citizen gives up any influence over which politicians advance their careers and which ones fade into obscurity. Sitting out a primary election means that the voter is more likely to get stuck choosing between two unappetizing candidates in the general election. Low turnout gives disproportionate influence to groups of people who vote at higher rates, such as the elderly.[16] In short, elections can be tremendously important without necessarily giving the public what it wants.

Finally, to say that elections are the driving force behind American democracy does not mean that other elements of the political system are unimportant.

Comprehending how elections operate within America's new democracy sometimes requires understanding the historical evolution of American government, the political behavior of individual Americans, the workings of the country's basic institutions, and the policies that the government produces. All of these topics thus receive thorough treatment in the chapters that follow. First, though, we consider one important drawback to a system driven by elections: the cost of the stressful contests themselves.

The Permanent Campaign

The new American democracy is marked by a **permanent campaign**.[17] The term literally means that campaigning never ends; the next election campaign begins as soon as the last one has finished, if not before. The dust from the 2004 elections had barely settled before discussion turned to which party would win control of Congress in 2006. Every action undertaken—or not undertaken—by the 108th Congress (2003–2004) was viewed as a potential issue in the upcoming presidential campaign. And even before the 2004 presidential campaign had run its course, pundits were speculating about who would run for president in 2008. The publisher emeritus of *Campaigns and Elections* magazine seemed to embody the dominant attitude when he wrote, in February 2005, "It has only been a few months since the last presidential election, but it is never too early to begin handicapping the next one."[18]

The deeper meaning of the term *permanent campaign* is that the line between campaigning and governing has disappeared. How an elected official governs is, in effect, just another strategic campaign decision. This change could be good or bad. On the good side, it might enhance democracy by encouraging leaders to consider

ALWAYS CAMPAIGNING
Even when elections are distant, electioneering is a mainstay of American politics. Here, President George W. Bush meets a patron of an Arlington, Virginia, donut shop while on a July 2006 visit to promote his immigration proposals. *Some countries limit the time allotted for candidates to campaign. Is this a good idea – or even feasible – in the U.S.?*

public desires throughout their time in office. On the bad side, injecting campaign tactics into government may result in short-term thinking, a more combative governing style, and more emphasis on image than on substance.[19] Either way, though, the permanent campaign has transformed the political system.

Causes of the Permanent Campaign

At least seven developments have moved American democracy in a popular direction by contributing to the permanent campaign. Some of these explanations receive more in-depth treatment in later chapters, but let's review them briefly here.

Separation of Elections   A century ago, public officials were all elected on the same day. Citizens in most states could cast votes simultaneously for local, state, and national offices. Over time, states began separating their elections from the federal contests. Many Americans now turn out to vote for president at one general election, for governor at another, and for mayor at yet another. Primary elections occur earlier in the election year. Initiatives and referenda may take place on still other occasions. There is very little "quiet time."

Decay of Party Organizations   The two major parties in the United States are the Democrats and the Republicans (or **GOP**, for "Grand Old Party"). These two parties have dominated the political system for a long time. The GOP started just before the Civil War and, ironically, the Democrats are even older. These parties give voters a choice by advocating different ideologies (see Chapter 4). Republicans tend to be conservative politically, which means they are "the right" or "right wing." Democrats tend to be liberal and are called "the left" or "left wing."* A party's issue positions shift only gradually, simplifying the choices a voter must make. Parties have weakened, however, meaning that a candidate cannot rely on party workers to staff a campaign office and cannot rely on party members to provide supportive votes (see Chapter 8). Today's politicians must build their own organizations almost from scratch, which takes extensive time.[20]

Spread of Primaries   A century ago, party leaders selected candidates for office. Or, in the language of reformers: Candidates were picked in "smoke-filled rooms" by party "bosses." To eliminate the corruption that often accompanied such deal making, reformers passed laws giving voters the right to select party nominees in primary elections (see Chapter 7). Primaries became the dominant mechanism for nominating presidential candidates after World War II (see

(text continues on page 16)

---

* *The origins of this terminology lie in the French Assembly that sat after the French Revolution (1789–1795). In the Assembly, conservatives sat on the right side of the chamber and liberals on the left (as you face the podium). The U.S. Congress and some other world legislatures follow a similar practice today.*

INITIATIVES AND REFERENDA

As we point out in this chapter, American politics has become more "popular" in recent years. Advances in polling, interest group lobbying, and new media technology, among other factors, have ensured that elected officials are continually in the public eye. As one consultant put it, "politicians have to assume they are on live TV all the time. You can't get away with making an offensive or dumb remark and assume it won't get out."[32]

But some activists argue that democracy works best when politicians are out of the picture altogether. They promote the institutions of direct democracy—initiatives, referendum, and recall—as a way to let the public make policies without the interference of flawed or corruptible elected officials.

In 27 states and in hundreds of local governments, citizens may alter the law through a direct popular vote. Rules vary, but measures can qualify for the ballot through a petition process (initiative) or via an act of the legislature (referendum) or through some combination of the two.[33] In 2005, voters in California rejected a 48-hour waiting period for minors seeking abortions; Maine voters approved spending $12 million on conservation, and Texas voters passed a measure banning gay marriage.[34] Direct democracy may be the antithesis of what we have called the "*responsible* model" of democracy, but its advocates argue that it does the best job of making government *accountable*. "One big difference between initiatives and elected representatives," says one activist, "is that initiatives do not change their minds once you vote them in."[35]

Voters oppose a series of initiatives in California.

Research shows that in certain cases, initiatives can educate voters, increase voter turnout, and force public officials to abide by the public's wishes.[36] But critics argue that any pluses are swamped by minuses. Skeptics charge that policies that result from initiatives and referenda are haphazard and contradictory, that wealthy special interests can overwhelm opponents by spending outlandish sums of money, and that majorities may use direct democracy to trample on minority rights.[37] Political commentator David Broder condemns direct democracy for being a "radical departure from the Constitution's system of checks and balances."[38]

WHAT DO YOU THINK?

1. Do initiatives and referenda enhance or detract from American democracy?
2. Are there certain kinds of issues that are better decided by initiatives and referenda, and certain kinds of issues that are better decided by elected officials? Which types of issues fall into each category?

(continued on next page)

INITIATIVES AND REFERENDA (continued)

For more on the **debate over direct democracy**, see the following Web sites:

PRO

www.hjta.org

www.ballot.org

The Howard Jarvis Taxpayers Association, a California group of fiscal conservatives, and the Ballot Initiatives Strategy Center, a liberal organization, view direct democracy as a powerful tool with which to change public policy for the better.

www.iandrinstitute.org

The Initiative and Referendum Institute at the University of Southern California documents all aspects of direct democracy in the U.S.

CON

www.ncsl.org/programs/legman/irtaskfc/IandR_report.pdf

The National Conference of State Legislators released a report in 2002 arguing that "representative democracy is more desirable than the initiative." The organization suggests reforms for states with existing direct democracy systems.

Figure 1.1). Each public office now requires twice as many visits to the voting booth as they once did, shortening the delay between elections. On August 8, 2006, for example, Representative Joe Schwarz (R-MI) was defeated in a primary scarcely 19 months after he had taken the oath of office.

Mass Communications   Today's candidates must exploit the mass media or their opponents will gain an advantage. They work to get their names in the papers and their pictures on television. Dozens of cable television channels enable candidates to communicate with small, well-defined audiences. C-SPAN provides continuous coverage of congressional debates, giving people outside Washington a chance to observe public officials directly. Radio talk shows have increased in popularity. Candidate and interest-group Web sites, Internet "blogs," and video sharing sites have proliferated, and conversation on the Internet (although often erroneous and conspiratorial) is perhaps the fastest-growing mode of political communication.

The effects of technological development have been intensified by changing journalistic norms. Media outlets demand content, and they do not shy away from criticizing political figures (see Chapter 5). Any move a politician makes might end up on television or on the Web. Partly as a consequence of the media's insatiable appetite for news, the distinction between public and private life has eroded. The financial and medical histories of elected officials are treated as public business, and reporters ask candidates almost any question imaginable, no matter how

FIGURE 1.1   The number of presidential primaries has increased greatly in the past three decades

Would party leaders select better standard bearers than the voters do?

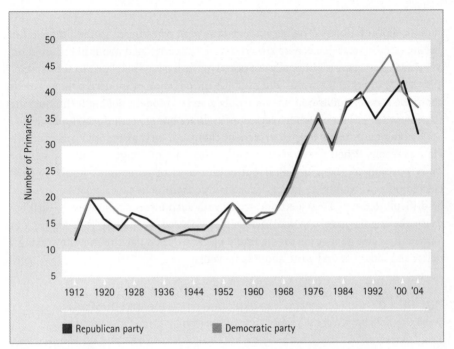

Source: Harold Stanley and Richard Niemi, *Vital Statistics on American Politics* (Washington, DC: CQ Press, 2000), p. 62, and data compiled by Sam Abrams.

tasteless or unrelated to government. Campaigning never ends because the public never stops watching.

Profusion of Interest Groups   The campaign organizations that today's candidates assemble are built in large part from the numerous interest groups created during the past generation (see Chapter 8). When political scientists wrote about interest groups at mid-century, they referred mostly to a few large business, labor, and agricultural organizations. Now there are thousands of generally smaller, more narrowly focused organizations. These groups monitor elected officials and report to voters about what the politicians are doing. They may post information on Web sites, send blanket e-mail to their members, or even buy television advertisements. The most recent development is for interest groups to run critical ads well before a campaign ever begins. For example, a conservative group called the Club for Growth ran a series of advertisements criticizing four moderate Republican senators who seemed poised to vote against President Bush's tax cut proposals in 2003.[21] Two of these senators would not have to face voters formally for another three years, but for them the campaign was already under way.

Proliferation of Polls   The permanent campaign owes much to the profusion of polling (see Chapter 5). Leaders always have been concerned about public opinion, of course. Politicians traditionally are portrayed as having their "ears to the ground" and their "fingers to the wind." But until the introduction of modern polling, beliefs about the state of public opinion were only guesses. Modern polling techniques are much more precise tools when elected officials are hungry for information.

Polling contributes to the permanent campaign by making opinions immediately available. When a new issue arises, politicians no longer wonder about the savvy position to take; they find out within days or sometimes hours. Even if elected officials wanted to make decisions free from political calculation, it would be difficult to do so. They are bombarded with such information at every turn because the media have become increasingly focused on polling (see Figure 1.2). Some critics charge that the media find it easier to "manufacture" news by taking a poll than to identify and write about real events.

FIGURE 1.2   Poll coverage has exploded since the mid-1960s
Do opinion polls serve a useful social or political function?

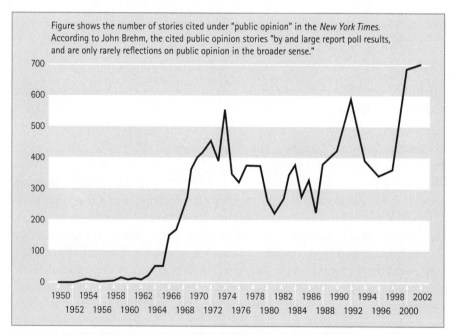

Figure shows the number of stories cited under "public opinion" in the *New York Times.* According to John Brehm, the cited public opinion stories "by and large report poll results, and are only rarely reflections on public opinion in the broader sense."

Source: 1950–1988: John Brehm, *The Phantom Respondents* (Ann Arbor, MI: University of Michigan Press, 1993), p. 4; 1988–2002, author's calculations based on *New York Times Index.*

Money Campaigning today is expensive. Polls, political consultants, and TV ads cost a great deal of money. Thus, the total cost of election campaigns has increased dramatically in the past three decades (see Figure 1.3). Victorious campaigns for the House of Representatives, for example, were nearly three and a half times more expensive in 2004 than in 1976, even after adjusting for inflation.[22] The quest for money is continuous. U.S. senators must raise more than $22,000 every week of their six-year terms to run for reelection.[23] In 2002's 36 governor's races, candidates spent a total of $833 million—a 41 percent increase over spending in the same states just four years earlier.[24] Such steep financial demands mean that public officials must be concerned with the next election even when it is years away.

More Democracy?

The United States pays a price for the pervasiveness of elections. Continuous electioneering creates a governmental system that is unattractive in many respects. Important social problems fester; delays and compromises undermine the effectiveness of public policies; inefficiency and stalemate are widespread.[25] Ironically, reformers disgusted with the American political system often call for more responsive institutions. Americans apparently believe, with John Dewey, that "The

FIGURE 1.3   The total costs of American elections have increased dramatically in the last five decades

Should Congress try to limit spending in election campaigns?

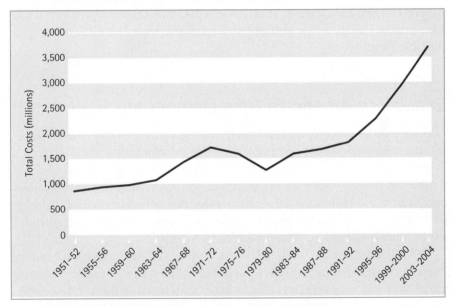

Note: All figures have been adjusted for inflation in terms of 2001 CPI constant dollars.

Sources: Common Cause, the Center for Responsive Politics, and respective volumes of Herbert E. Alexander, *Financing the 1951–1952* [and 1995–2000 vols.] *Election* (Washington, DC: CQ Press)

cure for the ailments of democracy is more democracy."[26] Such reforms overlook the tremendous popular pressure that political leaders already face.

Single-issue voters and other kinds of special interests at times do wield disproportionate influence. However, such groups lose much of their clout when a clear majority of the voters takes a strong interest in a highly visible subject. Elected officials cannot routinely support positions contrary to those of their voters and expect to escape the wrath of the electorate indefinitely. Moreover, majorities remain potentially powerful even when the public is uninformed about or unaware of an issue. Elected officials realize that the media spotlight may suddenly shine into what seemed to be a dark corner. Most of the time, incumbents think twice before taking actions in back rooms if those actions cannot be defended once the doors are opened.[27] Leaders are never sure which decisions will explode into campaign issues, so they tend to be cautious in handling all of them—which limits the power of well-connected special interests.

Political stagnation rarely results from unresponsive institutions. More often, the problem is that voters disagree with each other and political institutions cannot resolve their differences. America is a diverse country, after all, and the constituents who elect public officials reflect that diversity. If elected officials wish to follow their electoral incentives and remain in office, they must attend to the demands generated by these diverse constituencies. Reconciling so many demands requires compromise. It slows down progress and prevents common-sense solutions to national problems. Political leaders either must persuade their opponents or bargain for their support, a process that becomes harder when the public is more attentive and involved. Thus, reforms that shift American politics in a still more popular direction may worsen problems of stalemate and delay rather than eliminate them.

Evaluating America's New Democracy

Across the entire sweep of human history, most governments have been tyrannical. A government that did not murder and rob its subjects was about as good a government as people could expect. Tragically, tyrannical governments are not just a matter of ancient history. In the twentieth century alone, governments caused the deaths of 170 million people, a number that *does not include those who died in wars.*[28] The death toll has not ended: North Korea's government routinely tortures and summarily executes political dissidents, for example.[29]

When judged comparatively, democratic institutions have a nice track record. To quote the great American judge, Learned Hand, "Even though counting heads is not an ideal way to govern, it is at least better than breaking them."[30] To be sure, Americans should not set too low a standard for their political life. No one would seriously argue that Americans should be satisfied just because their country has avoided dissolving into chaos and their government does not torture or kill them.

But they must apply realistic standards when evaluating their political system. Citizens pay a cost for their ability to make political decisions together. Democracy is hardly perfect and rarely pretty. As former British Prime Minister Winston Churchill once remarked, "Democracy is the worst form of government except all those other forms that have been tried."[31]

Critics of the U.S. government selectively cite statistics showing that the country is worse than Canada in one respect, worse than Japan in another respect, worse than Sweden in some other respect, and so on. But can one conclude with confidence that any comparable national government works better on the whole? We think the answer is no. Only when comparing the United States with other countries do we see that American democracy, for all its faults, has an unmatched record of maintaining order, encouraging prosperity, protecting freedom, and redressing injustices. Citizens in the United States enjoy rights and privileges that citizens in other lands die to achieve. Not only can American citizens vote more often, but Americans also can speak their minds more freely, find out more easily what their government is doing, and deal with a government less likely to discriminate against them. On average, citizens of the United States are wealthier than citizens of any other comparably large country. They are better housed, better fed, and better clothed. Their physical environment is better protected against degradation. Their nation owes less money than most other industrialized countries.

Americans have been growing increasingly unhappy with a government over which they have more influence than ever before. Now that we have explained how thoroughly American majorities exercise their influence, it should be clear that the sour national mood is difficult to justify. Serious problems and unresolved conflicts certainly exist, but most are the natural result of an active and diverse voting public, not the result of an arrogant and inattentive government. More than ever before, and more than in other democracies, electoral influences drive politics in the United States. Elections have always played a central role in American political thought, because the framers relied on a system of checks and balances to protect freedom, but in practice the power of elections has grown. The number of elections has increased many times over, and public officials are permanently campaigning. The result is a responsive political system that, although imperfect, is still the envy of much of the world.

KEY TERMS

checks and balances, p. 9
constituency, p. 9
democracy, p. 8
direct democracy, p. 11
general election, p. 11
GOP, p. 14

initiatives, p. 11
permanent campaign, p. 13
primary election, p. 11
recall election, p. 11
referenda, p. 11
republic, p. 8

SUGGESTED READINGS

Bok, Derek. *The Trouble With Government.* Cambridge, MA: Harvard University Press, 2001. Comprehensive analysis of the pros and cons of modern government in the U.S.

King, Anthony. *Running Scared: Why Politicians Spend More Time Campaigning Than Governing.* New York: Free Press, 1996. Provocative study by a British political scientist who shows how elections shape contemporary American politics.

Schier, Steven E. *By Invitation Only: The Rise of Exclusive Politics in the United States.* Pittsburgh: University of Pittsburgh Press, 2000. Argues that parties, interest groups, and candidates have switched in recent years from broad-based mobilization of voters to targeted "activation" of select portions of the public.

Thurber, James A., and Candice Nelson, Eds. *Campaigns and Elections, American Style.* Boulder, CO: Westview Press, 2004. Political scientists and campaign consultants describe how modern political campaigns work.

ON THE WEB

For more on **U.S. democracy**, see the following Web sites:

DEMOCRACYNET
www.lwv.org
The League of Women Voters produces an online voter guide with state-specific information.

THE FEDERAL ELECTION COMMISSION (FEC)
www.fec.gov
This online portal of the FEC provides easy-to-use information regarding all aspects of elections—from electoral histories to campaign finance contributions.

PROJECT VOTE SMART
www.vote-smart.org
This richly informative site is supported by a nonpartisan group. It contains biographical histories, voting records, campaign finances and promises, and performance evaluations of elected officials and candidates.

The U.S. Constitution

THE SOLDIERS WHO STRAGGLED HOME AFTER AMERICA'S Revolutionary War often encountered desperate conditions upon their return. Many had abandoned their sources of livelihood for months or even years so that they could fight for independence, leaving businesses to dry up and farms to fall into disrepair. Some had contracted crippling diseases or suffered irreparable wounds on the battlefield. Others had lost their homes and families to the violence of war.

The new country's financial turmoil only added to whatever difficulties Americans faced trying to rebuild their lives. The national government entered peacetime deeply in debt, and initially it could not repay war bonds. It also could not pay veterans the wages and pensions they had been promised. Private finances were not much better. The states contained few mature industries. Restrictive European trade laws blocked access to the most desirable export markets, and the English did not show much interest in extending loans to their recent enemies. Little money circulated through the economy.

Four out of five New Englanders lived on family farms, a yeoman population that grew what it required to live and not much more.[1] The postwar economy hit them hardest of all. They relied on costly trade with Europe and the West Indies to provide essential household items such as gunpowder, glassware, basic medicines, and metal goods such as nails. Many needed to clear land, purchase seed, buy live-stock, and build new homesteads after the war—but the limited availability of credit meant that, to receive loans, they had to accept exorbitant interest rates. Not all of them could afford the interest payments.

By the late 1780s, rural America was suffering. Hundreds of farmers landed in debtor's court for failing to meet their financial obligations. Some saw their property auctioned off, at a fraction of its true value, to distant owners with no intention of farming the land themselves. Others, including Revolutionary War veterans, went to prison for days, weeks, even months. Conditions were worst in Massachusetts. In some western counties as much as a third of the population faced legal action because they owed money. Coastal merchants and bankers seized, through lawsuits, the same land that British troops could not overrun with guns. One farmer lamented, "Those who gloriously supported our independence now find their moveables vanishing like empty shades, their lands sinking under their feet."[2] Small farmers soon filled the prisons, often for failing to repay tiny sums.

New England's farmers gradually turned to violence as a way to protect their land. They harassed tax collectors and disrupted court hearings. Two hundred mili-tants shut down the New Hampshire statehouse for five hours, holding the gover-nor and state assembly as hostages. But the confrontation reached its peak in west-ern Massachusetts, where it took on the name **Shays' Rebellion.*** Rebels may have numbered as much as half the population in some counties, and a third of them were veterans. After the state started imprisoning people without trial, the rebels grew militant, raiding wealthy homes and even trying to seize a government ar-mory. Members of the militia deserted when ordered to crush the rebellion, and other states refused to send troops. Eventually a privately funded army, led by

---

* *Daniel Shays, a Pelham native and former Continental Army captain, helped lead part of the Massachusetts rebellion. But naming the confrontation after him exaggerates the extent of his influence over a wave of resistance that swept the region.*

members of a secret society of former revolutionary officers, took up arms for the government.* They found a cluster of rebels outside Sheffield and fired upon them at close range for six minutes, killing four, wounding 30, and effectively ending the resistance.

When Americans speak of their "founding fathers," they typically do not mean the defeated participants in this 1786 uprising, most of whom remain nameless or forgotten. Nor do they have in mind the many independent farmers who opposed ratification of the U.S. Constitution in 1789 or helped vote the party of George Washington, John Adams, and Alexander Hamilton out of office in 1800. Quite the contrary. Whether one takes the founders to include those who signed the Declaration of Independence, those who led the revolution against Britain, or those who wrote the U.S. Constitution, most of them lined up in opposition to these farmers and debtors.

Consider the role a few famous politicians played in Shays' Rebellion itself. Massachusetts Governor John Hancock, whose sweeping signature adorns the Declaration of Independence, ordered his troops to kill the Shaysites "if necessary." Sam Adams, the great rabble-rouser who once helped organize a party to dump British tea into Boston Harbor, now engineered a Riot Act to outlaw public gatherings. Violators faced 39 lashes and months of imprisonment. Nathaniel Gorham, who presided over the Congress, wrote a Prussian prince to ask whether the nobleman would be willing to assume kingly powers in America.[3]

The unrest in New England frightened national leaders, convincing them of the need for a strong federal government. The Constitution they proposed a year later was in part an act of self-defense, a legal tool to keep the unrest of 1786 from happening again.† Although the document contained rules to protect popular majorities from the government, including the scheduling of frequent elections (see Chapter 1), it also contained provisions to limit the political system's responsiveness and therefore to protect unpopular minorities—especially people like the framers.

At the same time, America's common people shaped the political system because they were a large portion of the framers' audience and of their potential opposition. Part of the influence was indirect. To ensure the Constitution's legitimacy across the countryside, its authors proposed a document strategically constructed to win approval. They did not just force it on the nation. They were clever politicians who developed constitutional provisions acceptable to state majorities, including many voters who were not wealthy.

Some of the yeoman influence was more direct. Many leaders from rural regions demanded that the U.S. Constitution contain a Bill of Rights to restrict governmental power. Provisions added to the document at their insistence have

---

* George Washington was the titular head of the group, which was known by various names (for example, the Order of Cincinnati). Membership was hereditary.
† Most states appointed their delegates to the Constitutional Convention only after Shays' Rebellion.

gained importance over time. Rural voters often jealously guarded the rights of state governments as well as American ideals of liberty and equality, which led them to elect leaders such as Thomas Jefferson (who vowed to exercise federal powers modestly) and Andrew Jackson (who embodied frontier populism and therefore a more open political system). In short, rural radicals who fought the growth of federal power were, in some ways, as much the "fathers" of America's new democracy as the more urbane founders we often know by name.

Influences on the U.S. Constitution

One reason the U.S. Constitution found an acceptable audience was that the framers wrote a document reflecting the political beliefs of the American public. The Constitution's specific provisions drew heavily on the nation's *inherited political traditions,* on *revolutionary experiences,* and on lessons learned during the *early years of independence.* We therefore briefly review those influences before showing how they flowered in the document itself.

Inherited Political Traditions

A small group of religious radicals, now remembered as "the Pilgrims," set sail for England's Virginia colony in 1620. To cover costs for the voyage, they loaded the ship *Mayflower* with passengers who did not share their beliefs, who simply wanted to seek their fortunes. The ship never reached its destination. Instead, the *Mayflower* arrived in what is now Provincetown, Massachusetts. Imagine the dismay of the ship's ambitious immigrants when they looked out and, instead of seeing rich tobacco fields, they saw New England's bare and rocky shoreline! The Pilgrim leaders knew that they would have to pacify disappointed passengers if they were going to found a new colony.[4] Before disembarking, therefore, the settlers formulated and signed the Mayflower Compact, the first document in which colonial Americans expressly agreed to create a new government. In keeping with radical principles held by the Pilgrims, it promised a communal framework that would allow individuals to decide religious and political matters for themselves.

Few English settlements began as social experiments. Most formed as "proprietary" colonies under companies or prominent English nobles. The proprietors founded such settlements, such as Virginia's Jamestown colony, almost exclusively for profit. Even these colonies indirectly promoted local control, though, because owners seldom tried to manage their lands directly. Elected assemblies made many important decisions, including the proper level of taxation. Thus, regardless of whether settlements began with democratic ideals or only developed democratic practices out of habit, the American colonies gravitated toward egalitarian political arrangements.

Americans eventually developed political principles to explain and justify their existing practices. Ironically, the ideals that encouraged American rebellion originally came from the mother country. Few Britons believed that their leaders ruled by *divine right*, by the command and authority of God. The English knew full well that their national legislature had set a new family line on the throne more than once—most recently in 1689, after the Stuart king, James II, threw his royal seal into the Thames River and tried to flee the country on a fishing boat. But if royal lines might come and go, Europeans needed some other explanation of why governments could exercise legitimate authority.

To grapple with this puzzle, political theorists such as Thomas Hobbes, John Locke, and Jean-Jacques Rousseau engaged in a thought experiment. They asked themselves, "What might life have looked like before government institutions existed, such that people would have invented them?" The three came up with varying answers, with Hobbes painting the most pessimistic picture of life's natural state and Rousseau imagining a savage existence of some nobility. But all three basically agreed that humans must have given up certain freedoms intentionally, as part of a contract with the rest of society, so that they could reap the benefits of living cooperatively. These theorists concluded, in short, that political authority must have been built on the consent of the governed.

Social-contract theory could imply a wide range of institutions, depending on exactly what the governed agreed to give up and what the government agreed to do in exchange for the right to rule. Locke, an English writer whose *Second Treatise of Government* (published in 1690) prefigured both the language and the ideas in America's Declaration of Independence, concluded that people must have entered communities as a means to protect preexisting rights to life, liberty, and property. They sacrificed some less crucial freedoms to ensure the continuation of more important ones.

Because Locke placed these **natural rights** at the center of the social contract, he sought a form of government that would not threaten people's health, freedom, or possessions. The best way to prevent such tyranny, the Englishman decided, was to set up institutions similar to those in his home country (which had a relatively long history of citizen independence). In particular, he endorsed dividing up the legislative and executive functions of government so that they did not reside in the same institution. Nearly 60 years later, the French philosopher Montesquieu added to this list a third governmental function—the judicial power—but the logic remained the same. A **separation of powers** would allow branches of government to check each other if one tried to grab too much influence, maintaining a healthy political balance and therefore preventing the need for a revolution (which is why it is sometimes called "a system of checks and balances").

Merely stacking up multiple branches of government to compete with each other does not ensure liberty, however. Not long after Locke wrote, the British system fell out of balance. The crown began using royal privileges to concentrate power in a small circle of ministers drawn from Parliament but appointed by the king. Thomas Paine, a radical British pamphleteer, popularized one method to prevent such corruption: requiring public officials to renew their right to rule. A political system with frequent elections would allow citizens to replace corrupt leaders with virtuous men from their own communities, removing the need for violent rebellion. American colonials avidly read Paine's essay *Common Sense* in the months leading to their insurrection. The seeds of democracy had taken root in the colonial soil.

The Revolutionary Experience

England and France ended 74 years of on-and-off war when they finalized the Peace of Paris in 1763. The English, led by the young and energetic monarch King George III, left the conflict with a vast new empire—including choice colonies in Asia and the Americas. But generations of warfare left the British government strapped for cash two years later. Looking for a source of new tax revenues, Lord of the Treasury George Grenville decided that Americans should help defray the British Empire's rising military costs.

Grenville did not consult colonial representatives before asking Parliament to create a Stamp Act, which imposed a tax on pamphlets, playing cards, dice, newspapers, marriage licenses, and other legal documents. Violent protests against "taxation without representation" spread throughout the colonies. A group in Boston called the Sons of Liberty looted homes and otherwise harassed the crown's colonial representatives. Parliament then switched to a tax on colonial imports, which was easier to collect but further ignited passions. Colonists avoided importing English goods, instead wearing homespun clothes and drinking native beverages such as hard cider.[5] In one memorable incident, a group of colonists dressed as Mohawks seized a shipment of imported tea and dumped it into Boston harbor. The Boston Tea Party of 1773 prompted Parliament to withdraw the Massachusetts colony's charter, close its elected assembly, ban town meetings, strengthen Boston's armed garrison, and blockade the harbor.

The following year, Americans organized a Continental Congress attended by delegates from 12 colonies. It issued a statement of rights and called for a general boycott of British goods, but stopped short of rebellion. Nonetheless, colonists began assembling guns and training volunteers for military exercises. To put down the rising insurrection, British soldiers marched from Boston into the countryside, where they clashed with 600 armed "patriots." The shots, according to Ralph Waldo Emerson, were "heard 'round the world." Delegates from all 13 colonies journeyed to Philadelphia for a second Continental Congress. They withdrew America's "united states" from the British Empire on July 4, 1776. Their formal announcement, a document written mainly by Thomas Jefferson and called the **Declaration of Independence**, denounced King George III in terms clearly borrowed from John Locke (see Table 2.1).[6]

The Revolutionary War lasted seven years. Numerous Europeans, excited by the radical ideals of freedom and equality behind the revolution, journeyed to the Americas to help with the war effort. Loyal colonists who opposed independence, meanwhile, lost their property and were imprisoned or exiled. Some 80,000 fled to

TABLE 2.1   Social-contract Theory and the Declaration of Independence

Although Thomas Jefferson denied that John Locke was a central reference for his draft of the Declaration of Independence, the ideas of social-contract theory clearly influenced America's revolutionaries. Here are just a few examples of parallel language between Locke and the Declaration. *Do you think such similarities could have resulted by accident?*

Liberal Principle	Declaration of Independence	Locke's Second Treatise of Government
Egalitarianism	. . . all men are created equal . . .	. . . all men are naturally in . . . a state . . . of equality . . . (Ch. II.4)
Consent	. . . deriving their just powers from the consent of the governed . . .	. . . all peaceful beginnings of government have been laid in the consent of the people . . . (Ch. VIII.112)
Unlikelihood of Rebellion	. . . mankind are more disposed to suffer . . . than to right themselves by abolishing the forms to which they are accustomed . . .	People are not so easily got out of their old forms . . . [T]he people, who are more disposed to suffer than right themselves by resistance, are not apt to stir . . . (Ch. XIX.223, 230)
Right of Rebellion	. . . when a long train of abuses . . . evinces a design to reduce them under absolute despotism, it is their right, it is their duty, . . . to provide new guards for their future security . . .	. . . if they see several experiments made of arbitrary power . . . if a long train of actions shows the councils all tending . . . to reduce them to slavery . . . it devolves to the people . . . to provide for their own safety and security . . . (Ch. XVIII.210 and Ch. XIX.222)

Note: The bulk of the Declaration (see this book's Appendix) lists specific injustices allegedly condoned by King George III. Many of these specific claims also echo Locke's language. Some mimic his specific examples of tyranny.

London, Nova Scotia, or the West Indies. In 1783, the British recognized American independence in the Treaty of Paris.

Americans had refined their political ideals during the war. In particular, their commitment to democracy strengthened. Eight of the 13 states eased property qualifications for voting, and five lowered them for candidates to the lower houses of state legislatures.[7] Over time, fewer state legislators possessed great wealth, especially in the North—giving new political opportunities to those from modest backgrounds. Six states limited the number of terms that governors could serve, and ten required that they face annual elections.[8] The seeds of democracy had sprouted.

Government After Independence

The new country faced an uncertain future after achieving independence. Certainly it contained abundant resources: fertile lands for farming, rivers and lakes teeming with fish, lush forests stocked with game for hunting or trapping, mountains and hills that one day would furnish valuable minerals and fuels. The nation's citizens, although spread thinly across the 13 states, were relatively young and ambitious. Soon they would be joined by equally capable immigrants, many fleeing poverty or oppression back home, as well as able-bodied African slaves imported by force.* The long-term economic prospects looked hopeful.

The military prospects did not look so promising, however. Threats surrounded the Americans (see Figure 2.1). Resentful English colonies challenged them from the north, and warships periodically dragooned U.S. sailors into British service. Ambitious Spanish colonies pushed upward from the south, creeping beyond the Florida border to claim large segments of what is today Alabama and Mississippi. Ruthless pirates ranged up and down the eastern shoreline, striking without warning and then retreating around jagged islands or up narrow rivers to avoid capture. Unpredictable Native American tribes roamed the lands to the west, and other tribal settlements dotted the interior of the United States itself. Even France, a revolutionary ally, blocked U.S. trade with its islands in the West Indies and demanded repayment of war loans.

Nor did the nation's government appear capable of dealing with the many sources of danger. The states were bound under the **Articles of Confederation**, a charter signed in 1781. It represented little more than a "firm league of friendship" in which "each state retains its sovereignty, freedom, and independence." The document provided for no independent executive and left most judicial functions with the states. States received equal representation within the Continental Congress, regardless of size. On all important issues, a supermajority of nine states (out of 13) had to agree before action could be taken. In fact, because the Congress frequently lacked a quorum (the minimum number who must be present for official business to take place), even minor issues were difficult or impossible to resolve.

The Articles granted the Congress limited power. Congress could declare war but could raise an army only by requesting states to muster their forces. Congress could not tax citizens; it had to rely on voluntary state contributions, so the government could not pay its debts. Perhaps most significantly, the Continental Congress could not promote commerce effectively. States coined their own money, flooding the country with multiple currencies. Constant quarrels over the relative worth of different state coins impeded trade. Congress could negotiate **tariffs** (taxes on imports and exports) with other nations, but so could each state. States also imposed trade barriers on one another. New York, for example, placed tariffs on New Jersey cabbage and Connecticut firewood.[9] The country lacked a centralized government that could provide political stability, mediate conflicts among the states, and defend the nation.

This is not to suggest that all slaves arrived after independence. The first Africans apparently arrived in 1619, before the landing of the Mayflower, and thousands of African descent took up arms during the revolutionary conflict, both for and against Britain. See George Brown Tindall, America: A Narrative History (New York: Norton, 1984).

FIGURE 2.1   Map of competing claims

This map shows only some of the competing claims being made in North America in 1787. Because the British had a superior navy and pirates sometimes ranged the coast, the United States was, in a sense, besieged on all sides. *Should a nation shape its Constitution on the basis of emergency conditions such as these?*

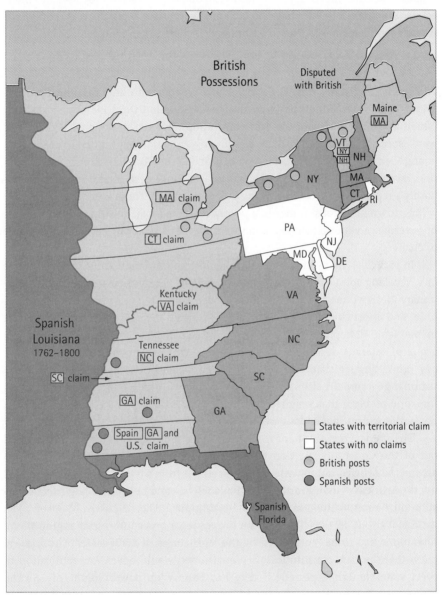

Source: Edgar B. Wesley, *Our United States: Its History in Maps* (Chicago: Denoyer-Geppert Co., 1965), p. 37.

The Constitutional Convention

A group of reformers met to discuss constitutional changes in 1786 at what became known as the Annapolis Convention, but only five state delegations attended. They proposed another meeting for the next year, one that attracted much greater interest in the aftermath of Shays' Rebellion. Every state legislature except Rhode Island's sent delegates to the Constitutional Convention in Philadelphia.

A Controversial Process

Few politicians happy with the Articles of Confederation attended the Constitutional Convention. Either they were uninterested or, in Patrick Henry's words, they "smelt a rat."[10] As a result, the 1787 convention attracted 55 national leaders who were especially frustrated with the current government. They tended to be wealthy, young "demi-gods," as Thomas Jefferson called them—bankers, merchants, plantation owners, bondholders, and speculators in land west of the Appalachians—hardly a representative sample of the U.S. population.[11] These ambitious men were willing to spend a hot summer in a poorly ventilated hall, debating the fine points of governance with no compensation, because they had strong convictions in favor of change.

In particular, many of the framers had noticed, with increasing anxiety, the rise of a "levelling spirit" among the common people.[12] From their perspective, revolutionary ideals of liberty and equality had been taken to an extreme, leading to disorder and unrealistic expectations. Citizens resisted the new government's policies in the same disruptive way they had protested British policies. For example, a group of veterans descended on Congress in 1783 to demand their rightful back pay, prompting legislators to flee to Princeton College. As the delegates sought a national government strong enough to grapple with peacetime problems, therefore, one problem that weighed heavily on their minds was the need to suppress political impulses that endangered their own interests.[13]

The framers were not above bending rules in order to get what they wanted out of the Constitutional Convention. State legislators had instructed them to amend the Articles, not to write a new document from scratch. Yet delegates tossed out the Articles on their fourth day in Philadelphia, and began working from a constitutional draft written in advance by Virginia delegate James Madison. The Articles were quite explicit about the proper legal procedure for changing them: Alterations had to be "confirmed by the legislatures of every state." The framers knew that the new constitution they envisioned would never win ratification in every state, though, especially if they had to give up power voluntarily. So the framers decided to change the rules. They wrote in the Constitution that it would take effect after receiving the approval of only nine states. And the vote would take place in newly elected constitutional conventions, not state legislatures.

These machinations caused no uproar outside the convention hall because the public did not learn about them. The delegates had agreed to a "gag rule" that allowed deliberations to proceed in secret.* And once the framers finished their handiwork, national leaders in the Confederation Congress gave the opposition little time to prepare for a fight. They submitted the Constitution to the states for approval just 11 days after the convention adjourned. Some of the most supportive states then moved swiftly to build up momentum behind the document, scheduling delegate elections before details could circulate. At any rate, many likely opponents of the Constitution among the yeomen population could not vote because of property qualifications.

Opponents of the Constitution protested that the whole process was unsavory. A group of discontented young politicians appointed to do a specific job instead ignored both their instructions and the law. They worked in secrecy to redesign the political system and then exploited numerous strategic advantages to win official approval for their plans. Was the country from its beginning therefore nothing more than a sham democracy? To reach such a cynical conclusion would require us to ignore why the Constitution managed to avoid widespread public opposition. The framers did not write the most desirable document they could dream up. Instead, they were good politicians.[14] They worked hard to anticipate objections that their Constitution might raise from regular Americans, and made the changes necessary to create a successful product.

A Successful Product

As wealthy and educated Americans interested in political change, the Constitutional Convention delegates shared many of the same principles. Furthermore, 10

---

* Most of our knowledge of the convention comes from Madison's notes, which he kept from the public until after his death.

CONSTITUTION WRITING
Delegates to the Afghan national assembly read copies of their new constitution in 2004. *Is Constitution writing naturally more difficult elsewhere, or do Americans have an unrealistic impression of what their own founding was like?*

skeptics abandoned the convention before the Constitution was completed, leaving only three who refused to sign the finished product. Yet the delegates did not agree on everything. Some disagreements were tactical. The framers disputed which sorts of changes voters would accept. Other disputes derived from genuine political differences. Delegates represented varied regions with conflicting interests: large versus small states, southern versus northern states, and so on.

The delegates therefore used numerous strategies to construct a plan on which they could agree and that voters might accept. On sharply drawn conflicts, the delegates *split the difference*, compromising between the two sides. When their ideal system was unlikely to win voter approval, they often *used vague language* that would allow flexibility of interpretation later. With other conflicts, they simply *delayed the decision*, either by giving someone else the authority to choose or by using language whose implications would be unclear until some time had passed.

Splitting the Differences   The delegates' differences were submerged during the opening weeks of the convention, when a spirit of unity and reform filled the Philadelphia hall. But as the four-month convention progressed, delegates pulled back from some of the more far-reaching ideas and began fighting over issues that divided their states. The convention leaders searched for compromises that would keep most delegates happy.[15]

Large and small states disagreed over how to structure the legislative branch. Madison had prepared a constitutional draft, with convention chair George Washington's active involvement, prior to the Philadelphia gathering. His **Virginia Plan** proposed two chambers, each with state representation determined by population. Delegates from smaller states countered with an alternative plan that gave each state equal representation, but a convention majority rejected the proposal, prompting delegates from the small states to consider leaving Philadelphia. The issue was turned over to a committee controlled by moderates. They brought back a compromise, brokered by the middle-sized state of Connecticut, that created a senate with equal state representation and a house with seats proportionate to population. The solution allowed both small states and large states to block legislation they opposed: small states in the senate, large states in the house.

The delegates also disagreed over rules for amending the Constitution. Small states wanted unanimous consent of state legislatures that would sharply limit amendments. Big states, on the other hand, believed that a unanimity rule would lead to stagnation and protracted conflict. The resulting compromise did not require unanimous approval, but nonetheless made changing the Constitution very difficult. Just proposing an amendment either requires two-thirds of the nation's state legislatures to call a new constitutional convention (which has never happened) or requires two-thirds of each congressional chamber to endorse an idea. To become constitutional law, proposed amendments then must win support from three-quarters of the states, either in ratifying conventions (a method used only once) or in the state legislatures. Only 27 amendments have cleared these hurdles:

the 10 amendments in the Bill of Rights and then 17 more, many intended to protect or expand voting rights.

The second major split divided the southern slave states from the northern states, whose economies relied on free labor. For example, the North and South were divided over taxes on imported goods; Southerners feared that tariffs would harm slave plantations and other farms. Northerners, meanwhile, wanted to end the international slave trade. The two sides compromised, with southern delegates accepting tariffs in exchange for a guarantee that Congress could not interfere until 1808 with the "importation of such persons as any of the states now existing shall think proper to admit."

Northern delegates did not want to count slaves when figuring state representation in the House. Southerners thought they should be counted. On the other hand, southerners did not want slaves counted for purposes of taxation, which northerners endorsed. The two sides came up with the **three-fifths compromise**, in which a state's slave population would be multiplied by three-fifths when determining both taxes and House seats. Although this computational device obviously has no practical relevance today, it may be the constitutional provision that most offends modern sensibilities, because it implies that the framers did not consider African Americans full people.

Using Vague Language Most of the framers desired a strong government but doubted that their ideal system would make it past voters. To help their cause, the framers often included vague language that later Americans could interpret broadly to give the federal government greater influence. For example, although the Constitution limited the powers of Congress to a specific list, it also gave Congress the flexibility to "make all laws which shall be necessary and proper" for exercising those powers. Later, when attitudes changed, the **necessary and proper clause** would be elastic enough to allow congressional influence to grow.

Many convention delegates wanted a strong executive.[16] Alexander Hamilton even proposed granting powers comparable to those of a British monarch. But the delegates knew that voters would reject a constitution that threatened the return of another King George III. Hence, they placed clear limits on presidential power, to please those who wanted an executive that was little more than a glorified clerk carrying out congressional orders, but left enough flexibility to allow the evolution of presidents who were strong political leaders. The president received numerous vague privileges, such as the authority to recommend legislation, that could increase the power of the executive office later.

Convention delegates also wanted a federal judiciary to settle conflicts among the states, but they apparently disagreed on whether federal courts should possess the controversial power of **judicial review**—that is, authority to strike down laws that violate the Constitution. So convention delegates simply inserted a clause binding judges to treat the Constitution as the "supreme Law of the Land." The **supremacy clause** allowed the Supreme Court, 16 years later, to claim powers of judicial review.

THE DEATH PENALTY

As we point out in this chapter, the founders made some parts of the Constitution vague so that they could more easily win ratification of the document. Some of these obscure phrases mean little to us today, but some have proved to be the pivot around which modern controversies revolve. One such phrasing is the prohibition against "cruel and unusual punishment" in the Bill of Rights.

The meaning of this clause in the Eighth Amendment depends on what we consider to be "cruel and unusual." When James Madison wrote the phrase, he borrowed the wording from the English Bill of Rights of 1689, which Parliament had passed in reaction to the excesses of the deposed King James II. There was no doubt that James had perpetrated cruel and unusual punishments – the disembowelment and beheading of his enemies had achieved wide renown.[21]

But what about the modern death penalty? Thirty-eight states currently provide for the execution of the most violent offenders, and federal law allows capital punishment for terrorists, traitors, and several other categories of criminals.[22] In 2005, 60 inmates were put to death and 3,400 sat on "death row" awaiting execution.[23] Is this "cruel and unusual"? Is the death penalty unconstitutional?

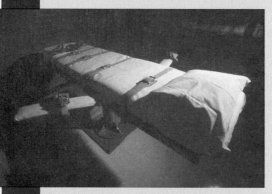

The death chamber in a Texas prison.

Some activists say "yes." Former Supreme Court Justice William Brennan, an eloquent opponent of the death penalty, argued that capital punishment is "degrading to human dignity" because it fails to accord sufficient value to human life.[24] What could be crueler? Others point to advances in DNA testing that have uncovered wrongful convictions in several death penalty states. Some studies have found that poor and minority criminals are more likely to be erroneously convicted.[25] Shouldn't this count as "unusual"?

Death penalty supporters respond that it serves a clear and justifiable purpose. "I support the death penalty," says President George W. Bush, "because I believe, if administered swiftly and justly, capital punishment is a deterrent against future violence and will save other innocent lives."[26] Problems with the way the death penalty is administered can be corrected, and today's lethal injection is a far cry from James II's gruesome methods.

Most voters agree with the death penalty's proponents, with some reservations. In 2006, polls found that two-thirds of Americans supported capital punishment.[27] But people are more cautious about executing minors or the mentally ill. Perhaps not coincidentally, the Supreme Court ended the execution of mentally retarded criminals in 2002, and banned the use of the death penalty for minors (those under 18 when they committed their crimes) in 2005.[28]

THE DEATH PENALTY *(continued)*

WHAT DO YOU THINK?

1. Should the constitutional guarantee against cruel and unusual punishment protect convicted criminals from execution, or does the Eighth Amendment only apply to brutal and sadistic violence?
2. What standard should officials use when determining what constitutes cruel and unusual punishment?

For more information about the death penalty debate, see the following Web sites.

Pro-Death Penalty

http://www.cjlf.org

The Criminal Justice Legal Foundation assists in a variety of legal cases.

www.prodeathpenalty.com

Justice for All is a victims'-rights organization that provides articles, links, and a database of crime victims.

Anti-Death Penalty

www.ncadp.org

The National Coalition to Abolish the Death Penalty provides reports, informational materials, and links to other organizations that share its views.

www.deathpenaltyinfo.org

The Death Penalty Information Center argues that there are serious practical difficulties with capital punishment.

Delaying the Decision   Many disagreements in the Constitutional Convention did not require single, definitive answers. As long as the Constitution provided some way to determine the proper procedure for resolving later disputes, it did not have to declare what the resolution would be. For example, the delegates differed over whether the Supreme Court needed lower federal courts to assist it, but they compromised by letting Congress decide whether to create lower federal courts. The first Congress established a system of lower courts whose essentials remain intact today.

The question of property qualifications for voting was a delicate one because Constitutional Convention delegates possessed different sorts of assets. Southern planters preferred limitations based on land ownership whereas northern merchants preferred limitations based on wealth. Rather than settle the dispute, the Constitution let states establish their own qualifications, as long as anyone eligible to vote for the lower chamber of a state legislature could vote in elections for the House of Representatives. The wording therefore allowed states to exclude poor citizens from voting however they liked, yet guaranteed the vote to everyone already eligible (that is, those who would decide whether to ratify the Constitution). This open-ended language later permitted states to extend the right to vote.

ELECTING THE PRESIDENT
About a month after Election Day,
members of the Electoral College
meet at statehouses around the
country to officially tally their votes
for president. Here, Texas electors
meeting in Austin cast their votes
for George W. Bush in 2000. *Why
did the founders create the
Electoral College?*

The method for presidential selection once again divided big and small states. The delegates compromised by constructing a two-stage **Electoral College** system with uncertain implications. The first stage lets each state select the same number of electors as it holds seats in Congress, a provision that favors large states. For example, Texas now picks 34 electors, because it has 2 Senate and 32 House seats, whereas a handful of states get only 3 (as does the District of Columbia). After their selection, the nation's electors all vote. If a candidate receives a majority of the Electoral College vote (50 percent plus 1 vote, or 270 votes today), that person wins. If no candidate receives a majority, the House of Representatives gets to decide who becomes president. This stage favors small states because each state delegation votes as a unit, but that has only occurred twice (in 1800 and 1824). The Constitution did not specify that voters would choose members of the Electoral College directly. Instead, the manner of selecting electors was left up to the states. Not until 1864 did the last state, South Carolina, give voters the power to select electors directly.[17]

The First National Election

The Articles of Confederation were unpopular, but ratification of the Constitution was hardly inevitable. Powerful state politicians such as New York Governor George Clinton did not want their powers handed over to a centralized government. Revolutionary war heroes such as Patrick Henry and Sam Adams, meanwhile, feared that the framers were throwing away the rights they had fought to create. "Before the meeting of the late Federal Convention at Philadelphia a general peace, and a universal tranquility prevailed in this country," Henry warned. But now, "I conceive the republic to be in extreme danger. Here is a revolution as radical as that which separated us from Great Britain."[18] And numerous constitutional provisions clashed with the sympathies and interests of America's inland farm population. These voters faced a difficult choice: either accept the new document, which seemed likely to favor the nation's commercial interests, or stick with an ineffective governmental framework.

Americans quickly polarized over the new proposal. The **Federalists**, who supported the Constitution, included many prominent national politicians and well-funded newspapermen. Benjamin Franklin, a soft-spoken elder statesman, promoted the Constitution in Pennsylvania. Alexander Hamilton, a hero at the decisive battle of Yorktown, emerged as a rising star during the New York ratification campaign. Especially important was General George Washington, America's revolutionary leader, whom everyone expected to become the first U.S. president after ratification.

The Federalists faced one of their toughest battles in the state of New York. A series of newspaper essays, written under the pen name "Publius," appeared there defending the provisions of the Constitution in great detail. The essays drew on history, philosophy, logic, and occasionally wit to counter the opposition; they are generally regarded as the finest essays on American political theory ever written. Three men wrote the *Federalist Papers*, as they are now called: Alexander Hamilton, James Madison, and diplomat John Jay. Hamilton wrote the greatest number, Madison the most influential (including No. 10 and No. 51, which appear in this book's appendix).

The **Anti-Federalists**, those who opposed ratification of the Constitution, lacked a leader of national stature. Thomas Jefferson, the one man who could have galvanized the opposition, bowed out. He strongly sympathized with the inland farmers and worried that the Constitution did not protect civil liberties adequately, but he admitted to his friend Madison that the document still deserved ratification.

JAMES MADISON (1751–1836), ONE OF THE AUTHORS OF THE *FEDERALIST PAPERS*
How did the Federalists respond to the Anti-Federalist claim that the new constitution would produce tyranny?

Aside from a few elder heroes, the burden of opposition therefore fell on local figures. They attacked the Constitution as a blueprint for national tyranny. Undercutting the states would take power from the people. The number of congressional representatives would be too small to include a wide variety of citizens, and repeated reelection would create a political aristocracy. Presidents would become virtual kings.

With energy and organization on their side, the Federalists easily won the first rounds in the struggle. Conventions in four states ratified the document by an overwhelming vote within four months of its signing (see Table 2.2). Pennsylvania also approved it quickly, thanks to some strong-arm political tactics. However, a vocal minority at the Pennsylvania convention opposed the Constitution. They distributed a stinging critique of both the document and the ratification process. Of all their criticisms, though, only one seemed powerful enough to derail ratification: The proposed Constitution did not mention important civil liberties such as religious freedom, free expression, or even rights against abusive law enforcement.

Silence on civil liberties was no mere oversight. Some delegates saw the protection (or limitation) of rights as a state issue, not a national one. Others felt that protecting certain rights in the Constitution might imply that other, unlisted, rights could be violated. The author of Virginia's famous statement of rights, George Mason, sat in the convention hall; he was one of three delegates who refused to endorse the final proposal. Delegates explicitly rejected South Carolina delegate Charles Pinckney's suggestion that the Constitution assure a free press.[19] The Federalists recognized their miscalculation during the fight over ratification in

TABLE 2.2 Voting of delegates after the first national election

Americans elected delegates in each state, who then voted on whether to ratify the Constitution. *At what point did the founders have enough states on board to start a feasible government?*

State	Date	Yes Votes	No Votes	Percentage Yes
Delaware	Dec. 7, 1787	30	0	100.0
Pennsylvania	Dec. 11, 1787	46	23	66.7
New Jersey	Dec. 18, 1787	38	0	100.0
Georgia	Jan. 2, 1788	26	0	100.0
Connecticut	Jan. 9, 1788	128	40	76.2
Massachusetts	Feb. 6, 1788	187	168	52.7
Maryland	Apr. 26, 1788	63	11	85.1
South Carolina	May 23, 1788	149	73	67.1
New Hampshire	June 21, 1788	57	47	54.8
Virginia	June 25, 1788	89	79	53.0
New York	July 26, 1788	30	27	52.6
North Carolina	Nov. 21, 1789	194	77	71.6
Rhode Island	May 29, 1790	34	32	51.5

Source: Lauren Bahr and Bernard Johnson, ed., *Collier's Encyclopedia*, Vol. 7 (New York: P. F. Collier, 1992), p. 239.

Massachusetts. They narrowly secured the state's support only after promising to amend the Constitution so that it would protect freedoms explicitly. Victories in Virginia and New York required similar guarantees—and North Carolina and Rhode Island withheld ratification until the Constitution's first 10 amendments, the **Bill of Rights**, passed through the Federalist-controlled Congress. This single temporary setback is instructive, because it clearly reveals how Federalist successes otherwise depended on anticipation of popular sentiment. The one time they ran directly against public opinion, they were forced to back down.

Evaluating the Constitution

American schoolchildren often learn a sanitized version of their nation's founding, one that hides the political maneuvering behind the U.S. Constitution and portrays early leaders as saints. It may seem unpatriotic to remind readers, as historian Joseph Ellis writes, "that all the Founding Fathers, before they were marbleized and mythologized, were considered fallible and controversial figures."[20] Why not allow people to hold on to rosy national legends created by wishful thinking and the passage of time? Won't acknowledging the gritty truth just add to modern cynicism? Not really. As Ellis recognizes, public discontent builds from a false sense that today's decision makers fall well below the caliber of leadership once available.

Flesh-and-blood public officials cannot compete with storybook figures. They naturally suffer from the unrealistic comparison, which fuels cynicism. It is therefore worthwhile to admit that the framers did not differ from the elected officials of today as much as modern Americans customarily suppose. The founders "played politics." They compromised to win the support of voters, like any effective politician in a democracy. They filled the Constitution with language that appeared to protect the privileged at the expense of the underprivileged—for example, provisions protecting contracts, ensuring the repayment of war bonds, banning wealth-based taxes, and preserving slavery. In short, the golden era that Americans feel they have lost actually never existed.

So does the story offer no heroes, nothing to inspire national pride? Certainly the founders, despite their imperfections, often behaved heroically, but perhaps the true antidote to modern cynicism should be the Constitution itself, which (like many movie heroes) rose from uncertain beginnings to achieve greatness. Evaluating the Constitution requires more than just an assessment of whether the founders had selfish motivations or whether the procedures they followed would be acceptable today. The Constitution was the product of a whole nation—not just the few names we remember today, but also the forgotten people who assisted them or who resisted them. What matters, ultimately, is whether the resulting document provided a sound, but flexible, framework of democratic government. The Constitution did that job, grounding all three branches of government in the people and allowing the system's openness to increase with time.

Even the Constitution itself is only a flawed hero. The most obvious blemish is the stain of slavery, which remains indelible. The Constitution validated the slave trade and counted each slave as three-fifths of a person. It required free states to return escaped slaves to the places from which they had fled. It also divided powers so well that, when a national majority turned against the tyranny of slavery, they could not end such an immoral institution peacefully. It is not easy to think how delegates could have designed a constitution that would have both freed slaves and won ratification by the voters of 1788, but the fact remains that they did not try very hard.

Nonetheless, the delegates wrote a document quite different from the Articles of Confederation (see Table 2.3). Their handiwork contributed solutions to three of the most immediate and pressing problems facing the United States. First, the new Constitution facilitated economic development by outlawing the chaos created by state currencies and tariffs. As a result, trade among states flourished, and the United States grew into an economic powerhouse. Second, the Constitution created a unified nation at a time when Britain, France, and Spain were all looking for a piece of the action in the New World. Instead of falling prey to European ambitions, the United States profited from European divisions by seizing the opportunity to

TABLE 2.3 Comparing the charters

The Articles of Confederation were a "league of friendship" and seldom allowed the national government to give orders to states. *Did the Articles have any advantage over the U.S. Constitution?*

Weaknesses of the Articles of Confederation	How Addressed in Constitution
Congress could not levy taxes.	Congress has power to levy taxes (Article I, Section 8).
States could restrict commerce among states.	States cannot regulate commerce without the consent of Congress (Article I, Section 10).
States could issue their own currency.	States are prohibited from coining money (Article I, Section 10).
Executive was not independent of Congress.	An independently elected president holds the executive power (Article II).
There was no national judicial system.	The Supreme Court was created, and Congress was granted the power to establish lower federal courts (Article III, Section 1).
Amendments to Articles had to have unanimous approval of states.	Large majorities are necessary to amend the Constitution, but there are several different ways to do so (Article V).

Source: Articles of Confederation; U.S. Constitution, articles listed. See Appendix.

make the Louisiana Purchase of 1803, which doubled the size of the country. Finally, the Constitution created a strong executive branch that could adapt to an increasingly complex world, taking on additional duties (such as budgeting and regulation) as well as mastering the duties that became increasingly complicated (such as defending the nation and organizing the government bureaucracy).

In the two centuries that have followed, the main lines of conflict have changed. People no longer worry much about the political divisions that captivated the framers. But the Constitution still allows the American political system to reconcile demands and opinions from many different groups and interests. In that sense, the true hero of the story lives on. Subsequent chapters discuss ways in which the compromises of 1787 have been redefined in response to changing political circumstances, allowing the U.S. Constitution to become the longest-lasting Constitution in the world.

CHAPTER SUMMARY

The framers intentionally proposed a government that would be acceptable to voters—not only those who happened to weigh in on ratification, but also those who would determine the legitimacy of the new institutions in the years that followed. Many powers that the founders wanted to claim for the government were left undeclared, couched in vague language that later Americans could interpret according to the needs and beliefs of their age. The Constitution left the state governments with their own authority and independence. The presidency did not receive royal prerogatives, and the Congress was restricted to a specific list of powers. Many compromises were necessary.

The U.S. Constitution certainly reflects the desire of the framers for a stronger, more-centralized national government than the one in place immediately following the Revolutionary War. It contained legal provisions that would protect people such as the framers and perhaps even promote their selfish interests. Yet it also reflects the values of their opponents and potential opponents, such as the Anti-Federalists who demanded a Bill of Rights (which contains amendments that have become more influential with time).

The opposition also helped change the meaning of the U.S. Constitution over time. Initially, they did so by forcing the framers to defend their handiwork in the *Federalist Papers*. These essays explained the meaning of various constitutional provisions in a way that contemporaries presumably found acceptable, grounding constitutional interpretation in the expectations of the audience. Later, framers such as Alexander Hamilton and John Adams fell from political favor, replaced by politicians more sympathetic to the values of the nation's yeoman majority. The national government organized under the Constitution eventually became a mixture of contrasting ideals, characterized primarily by the openness and the election-driven responsiveness that distinguishes America's new democracy.

KEY TERMS

Anti-Federalists, p. 39
Articles of Confederation, p. 30
Bill of Rights, p. 41
Declaration of Independence, p. 28
Electoral College, p. 38
Federalist Papers, p. 39
Federalists, p. 39
judicial review, p. 35
natural rights, p. 27

necessary and proper clause, p. 35
separation of powers, p. 27
Shays' Rebellion, p. 24
social-contract theory, p. 27
supremacy clause, p. 35
tariffs, p. 30
three-fifths compromise, p. 35
Virginia Plan, p. 34

SUGGESTED READINGS

Dahl, Robert. *How Democratic Is The American Constitution?* New Haven, CT: Yale University Press, 2003. A critical look at the Constitution from one of the country's most eminent political scientists.

Rakove, Jack. *Original Meanings: Politics and Ideas in the Making of the Constitution.* New York: Random House, 1996. Pulitzer Prize-winning examination of the ideologies and political factors behind the drafting of the Constitution.

Wood, Gordon S. *The Radicalism of the American Revolution.* New York: Knopf, 1992. Portrays the unleashing of a democratic ideology during the struggle for independence.

ON THE WEB

For more information about the U.S. Constitution, see the following Web sites.

www.archives.gov/national_archives_experience/constitution.html
The National Archives and Records Administration provides the full text of the Constitution, biographies of each of its signers, and high-resolution images of the document itself.

www.pbs.org/ktca/liberty
This companion site to a PBS series on the American Revolution, provides a comprehensive overview of the Revolutionary War, including time lines, accounts of battles, and biographies of key figures.

www.usconstitution.net
USConstitution.net, a privately-maintained Web site, provides a wealth of information about the Constitution and its historical lineage.

Federalism

"I HAVE NO IDEA WHERE MY 2-YEAR-OLD SON IS." NICOLE WILLIAMS, a new arrival to Houston's Astrodome, was trying to enlist the help of the media. On her T-shirt she had written "Please help me find my family." Not long before, she explained, she and four relatives had gathered with thousands of other displaced New Orleans residents at the interchange of Interstate 10 and Causeway Boulevard for evacuation. After she boarded a bus bound for Texas, Williams realized to her dismay that her family would not be allowed to join her. Nor did state troopers allow her to disembark. Now, like countless other victims of Hurricane Katrina, she had to cope not only with the consequences of the winds and floods, but also with a haphazard and disorganized federal, state, and local government response.[1]

Hurricane Katrina roared ashore near New Orleans on August 29, 2005. The scale of the disaster that followed in Louisiana, Mississippi, and Alabama is difficult to comprehend. At least 1600 people lost their lives,[2] 1.5 million were displaced, hundreds of thousands were thrown out of work, and estimates of property damage approximated $100 billion.[3]

Government at all levels had fair warning that such an event was possible. For years, experts had said that New Orleans, with its below-sea-level neighborhoods protected by a network of levees and canals, was particularly vulnerable to a large hurricane. Disappearing wetlands in the Mississippi delta had left the city even more exposed to devastation from a major storm.[4] Walter Maestri, a local emergency management official, said in 2001 that "Even though I have to plan for it, I don't even want to think about the loss of life a huge hurricane would cause."[5]

The 2005 hurricane was unusually severe, but what shocked most Americans was the incapacity of all levels of government to mount a swift and efficient response. For days, chaos and lawlessness gripped New Orleans as thousands of desperate disaster victims waited for rescue in the Superdome, at the city's Convention Center, at the I-10 cloverleaf, in hospitals and nursing homes, and on the roofs of their houses. Whatever plans each level of government had made for such a contingency seemed to be dependent on another level of government bearing most of the burden. New Orleans Mayor Ray Nagin said that the city had hoped to "Get people to higher ground and have the feds and the state airlift supplies to them—that was the plan, man."[6] Louisiana Governor Kathleen Blanco argued that the state couldn't provide enough aid without significant help from Washington. As her chief of staff put it, "This was a bigger natural disaster than any state could handle by itself, let alone a small state and a relatively poor one."[7]

Meanwhile, the federal government's response was curiously flat-footed. The Federal Emergency Management Agency (FEMA), newly incorporated into the

AFTER THE FLOOD
Days after Hurricane Katrina hit, a New Orleans woman waves at National Guard rescuers. *Can lines of responsibility be clearly drawn to prevent confused intergovernmental response to disasters?*

Department of Homeland Security, was slow to realize how serious the disaster was, and its bureaucratic rules held up the arrival of trailers, helicopters, and rescue workers to the affected area.[8] FEMA director Michael Brown (who was fired in the wake of the disaster) blamed the delays on bickering between the state and the city. "I very strongly, personally regret," Brown told Congress, "that I was unable to persuade Governor Blanco and Mayor Nagin to sit down, get over their differences and work together."[9]

Disaster planning and response has always been a joint effort among all levels of government. States and cities serve as critical "first responders" in times of crisis, but because they have limited resources, they must work smoothly with the national government and rely on federal largesse when they are overwhelmed. Hurricane Katrina shook the faith of the public and of many policy-makers that this process was working effectively. As Republican Senator Susan Collins put it, "If our system did such a poor job when there was no enemy . . . how would the federal, state and local governments have coped with a terrorist attack that provided no advance warning and that was intent on causing as much death and destruction as possible?"[10]

The Hurricane Katrina episode shows why the structure of intergovernmental relations—seemingly so technical—has been an intense source of conflict since the nation's founding. On the one hand, the story shows the important value preserved by letting cities and states do their own thing: they can make policies that fit the needs and interests of their local populations. At the same time, the story shows why some people argue that more responsibilities ought to be transferred to the national government alone. With so many officials at various levels vying to make policy, government actions can be slow, confusing, and inefficient. When fundamental values are at stake, fights over whether to make policy at the state level or at the national level can be especially heated. Are the benefits of divided power worth the costs? How do Americans decide which policies are national and which are local?

The Trend Toward Centralized Government

Deciding how much to centralize power has been a challenge since the country's founding. As a compromise between those who wanted a stronger national government and those who wanted to protect the states, the framers developed a principle called **federalism**—the belief that multiple sources of government authority could coexist, each with its own sphere of responsibility. The U.S. Constitution established a federal system, laying out the areas of law in which each level of government enjoyed unchecked (or "sovereign") authority (see Table 3.1). The result is a system of **dual sovereignty** with two formal units, the *national government* and the *state governments.**

---

* *Local governments are also important governmental units, but they are not fundamental units in the U.S. federal system. According to a long-standing legal doctrine known as Dillon's rule (after nineteenth-century Iowa judge John Dillon), local governments are in legal terms mere "creatures of the state" that a state legislature may alter or abolish at any time.*

TABLE 3.1 Constitutional division of power between national and state governments

Powers granted to the national government	Powers granted to the state governments
Conduct foreign affairs	
Raise armies and declare war	Maintain state militias (the National Guard)
Regulate imports and exports	
Regulate interstate commerce	Regulate commerce within the state
Regulate immigration and naturalization	
Establish and operate federal court system	Establish and operate state court systems
Levy taxes	Levy taxes
Borrow money	Borrow money
Coin money	
Provide for the general welfare	
Make laws "necessary and proper" to accomplish the above tasks	Exercise powers not granted to national government

Few nations follow the principle of federalism. Most have unitary political systems, in which all authority is held by national governments; any local jurisdictions are just administrative outposts lacking sovereignty. Yet federalism seems ideally suited to a nation characterized by geographic, ethnic, and cultural diversity (see Chapter 4). By allowing subdivisions to "do their own thing," it provides a useful way to resolve conflicts that can tear other countries apart. Federalism also promotes economic development, because it gives states the authority and interest to focus on local needs. As early as the 1830s, the keen French observer Alexis de Tocqueville noted, "One can hardly imagine how much division of sovereignty contributes to the well-being of each of the states that compose the Union."[11]

Nonetheless, the Constitution was a vague document open to numerous interpretations. American voters sometimes elected leaders who desired to expand the authority of the national government, and those leaders (along with the judges they appointed) found words in the Constitution that seemed to permit centralization of authority. These officials also realized that the national government's economic clout provided a way to exert additional influence. As a result of these two forces, permitted if not encouraged by modern voters, governance has become much more centralized than in the nation's past.

Federalism in the Courts

The Constitution does not say who should settle disputes between the national government and the states. Before the Civil War, some opponents of centralized power argued that states could nullify, or invalidate, national laws that infringed on their authority. The doctrine of **nullification** was seldom invoked, however. Instead, the Supreme Court granted itself the power to decide how the Constitution divided up sovereignty, in the sweeping 1819 decision *McCulloch v. Maryland*—among the most important the Court has ever made. This assumption of responsibility became accepted over time.

A few constitutional amendments attempted to protect state governments from federal encroachment. The Tenth Amendment, added in part to satisfy revolutionary hero Sam Adams, emphasizes that states retain "the powers not delegated" to the national government. The Supreme Court rarely invokes this provision, though. The Eleventh Amendment also protects states. It gives them **sovereign immunity** from suits filed under national law, a provision to which conservative members of the Supreme Court began giving teeth in the mid-1990s. For example, in a 2001 opinion written by Chief Justice William Rehnquist, the Court ruled that a woman suffering from breast cancer could not sue her employer—the state of Alabama—for discrimination under the federal Americans with Disabilities Act.[12] States cannot always rely on this constitutional protection, however. Rehnquist wrote another opinion in 2003 that opened states to suits filed under the Family and Medical Leave Act, explaining that the federal government's interest in preventing sex discrimination trumped state sovereignty.[13]

Federal judges have interpreted numerous phrases in the Constitution as permitting expanded federal power. Four are especially important: the **supremacy clause**, declaring national law superior to state law, the **necessary and proper clause**, giving Congress great flexibility in carrying out its enumerated powers, the **commerce clause,** giving Congress control over interstate trade, and the **spending clause**, giving Congress access to a very deep purse. Combined, these ambiguous phrases laid the groundwork for a significant centralization of power in the national government, to which the Fourteenth Amendment added after the Civil War (see Chapters 13 and 14).

The Supremacy Clause   The Constitution says that national laws "shall be the supreme Law of the Land . . . Laws of any State to the Contrary notwithstanding." The U.S. Supreme Court declared, in *McCulloch v. Maryland* (1819), that this language gives it authority to strike down state laws that violate the U.S. Constitution. The McCulloch case revolved around the Bank of the United States, an entity that commercial interests thought vital to economic prosperity but that many farmers and debtors resented. Responding to popular opinion, the state of Maryland levied a steep tax on the bank. James W. McCulloch, an officer of the bank's Maryland branch, refused to pay and took his case to the Supreme Court. The Court ruled in favor of McCulloch. Maryland could not tax a federal bank, Chief Justice John Marshall explained. The "power to tax involves the power to destroy."[14] If a state government could tax a federal agency, then states could undermine national sovereignty—which the supremacy clause would not allow.

The Necessary and Proper Clause   The Constitution gives Congress authority "to make all laws which shall be necessary and proper for carrying into Execution" the government's list of powers. Chief Justice Marshall analyzed these words in the McCulloch decision as well. Maryland argued that Congress had no authority to establish a national bank, because a bank was not *necessary* for Congress to carry out its delegated powers. But Marshall, an ardent Federalist, explained that the language does not mean *absolutely* necessary; it only means convenient. "Let the end be legitimate," he said. "Let it be within the scope of the Constitution, and all means which are appropriate, which are plainly adapted to that end, which are not prohibited, but consistent with the letter and spirit of the Constitution, are constitutional."[15] Since the *McCulloch v. Maryland* decision, courts have generally found that almost any means selected by Congress is "necessary and proper." As a result, the necessary and proper clause has come to be known as the **elastic clause**—it stretches to fit almost any policy, provided that the policy is related to a Constitutionally-delegated power.

The Commerce Clause   One of the most important of these delegated powers appears in the commerce clause. The Constitution gives Congress power "to regulate commerce . . . among the several states." In the nineteenth century, the courts understood *interstate* (between-state) commerce to mean trade across state lines. During the Great Depression, however, Franklin Delano Roosevelt (FDR) and the Democratic Congress wished to exert more control over the economy. FDR

WAVES OF GRAIN?
Before the New Deal, the Supreme Court ruled that the power of Congress to regulate commerce generally applied only to goods produced or processed in multiple states. But the New Deal court decided that Congress can prevent farmers from growing food even if their produce will never leave the farm. *Do you think the framers envisioned a national government with such power?*

initiated what he called the **New Deal**—a wide array of proposals expanding the federal government's power to stimulate economic recovery. The Supreme Court resisted at first, but after Roosevelt's landslide reelection in 1936 the justices moved toward an interpretation of the commerce clause that centralized government authority. In 1941, a farmer violated New Deal crop limits by sowing 23 acres of winter wheat on his own land to feed his own family and his own livestock. What took place entirely on his farm, he argued, bore no relation to commerce "among the several states." Yet the Supreme Court ruled against the farmer in *Wickard v. Filburn* (1942), reasoning that his actions affected interstate commerce. By declining to buy wheat and instead growing his own, the farmer was depressing worldwide wheat prices.[16] Such an expansive definition of interstate commerce greatly increased the reach of Congress.

The Spending Clause   The Constitution gives Congress authority to collect revenues and to use this money to provide for the "general welfare." The New Deal Supreme Court considered the meaning of this clause when it ruled on the constitutionality of the social security program enacted in 1935 that established pensions for senior citizens. A taxpayer had challenged the program as oriented toward the specific welfare of the elderly and not the general welfare. But the Supreme Court, in tune with FDR's enlarged conception of federal power, said it was up to Congress to decide whether any particular program was for the general welfare "unless the choice is clearly wrong."[17] So far, the Court has never found Congress "clearly wrong."

Not only has the Supreme Court refused to restrict the purposes for which Congress can spend money, it has also granted Congress the right to attach almost any rule to the money it distributes. For example, in 1984, Congress enacted the National Minimum Drinking Age Act, a law linking federal highway funds to state-set legal drinking ages. Under this law, states can adopt any drinking age that they prefer, but must forego 10 percent of their highway funding if they choose an age younger than 21.[18] When the state of South Dakota objected, calling this provision coercive, the Supreme Court ruled, in *South Dakota v. Dole* (1987), that Congress was within its rights to connect road maintenance and construction to the drinking age. South Dakota argued that a state's drinking age bore no relation to how it used highway funds, but the Supreme Court decided that both involve "highway safety."[19]

Authority to tax and spend has remained one of the broadest congressional powers because the federal government's scope expands every time it raises taxes. The more revenue that is extracted from state economies by federal taxation, the more that cash-strapped state governments need to get the funds back through federal grants—and therefore the more willing they must become to meet congressional stipulations. Some scholars consider the national government's spending authority "the greatest threat to state autonomy."[20] The next section therefore looks at how the national government distributes funds to state and local government.

Federalism and Government Grants

The classic understanding of federalism envisions levels of government as distinct and separate, each sticking to its own duties. As governmental interactions became more complicated after World War II, though, this conception seemed inadequate; different levels of government usually worked together in the same policy areas to solve problems. For example, in the area of disaster planning and response, the national Federal Emergency Management Agency (FEMA) must coordinate its efforts with state offices of emergency preparedness as well as with local first responders such as police departments and rescue squads.

Political scientist Morton Grodzins helped focus attention on the gap between how people viewed federalism and how it actually operated by using the contrast between two sorts of dessert. He compared the classic model of federalism to a traditional layer cake: stacked levels, with a strip of icing buffering one level from the next. Grodzins preferred an alternative, cooperative view of federalism in which government agencies worked together, intertwining their functions. As an image for this view of intergovernmental relations, Grodzins selected a dessert popular at the time he was writing: the marble cake, in which light and dark batters were swirled before baking to give the cake a mottled look like cut marble. This image has persisted.

Grodzins made clear that he favored **cooperative (or marble-cake) federalism** because it would accommodate a growth in government power. The national government should raise taxes, he suggested, and distribute the resulting revenue to state governments as an inducement for them to address important policy areas.[21] Grodzins got his wish. Congress enlarged the number, size, and complexity of programs funded in part by the federal government but administered more locally. Only $102.7 million was spent on grants to local governments in 1930, but these funds grew to $51.9 billion by 1962.[22] By 1982, they had more than tripled to $175.5 billion.* Spending seldom goes down—and when it does, the restraint never lasts. Senator John McCain drew attention to this point when he attacked his colleagues in 2003 for continuing to "spend money like drunken sailors."[23]

Most federal grants are **categorical grants**—grants with fairly specific regulations about how the money must be spent. These grants have become controversial because they impose so many limits on states. The "War on Poverty," a wide-ranging set of categorical grants enacted in 1964 to enhance economic opportunities for low-income citizens, in particular has come under sharp criticism. Many of the programs in that effort failed because they required so many participants, including both national and local politicians, that administrators rarely shared the same policy goals and rarely had enough resources to promote the goals they did share.[24]

Republicans typically criticize categorical grants because of the influence they give the national government at the expense of the states. They rarely vote to shrink federal spending, however. Instead, they endorse giving states more

Unless otherwise indicated, all amounts in this chapter are calculated in 2005 dollars.

flexibility by distributing funds through **block grants**—intergovernmental grants with a broad set of objectives, a minimum of restrictions, and maximum discretion for local officials. The federal government expanded block grants in three waves, each prompted by Republican victories: once after Richard M. Nixon's 1968 victory, once at the beginning of the Reagan administration, and once after the 1994 election when Republicans captured control of Congress.

Generally, however, Congress has shown little enthusiasm for reducing the size or number of categorical grants—regardless of whether Republicans or Democrats control the institution (see Figure 3.1). Once Republicans took charge in the late 1990s, they began approving categorical grant programs to spend money in ways supported by their party. For example, in 2001 President Bush enthusiastically signed into law a new education reform bill, the No Child Left Behind Act that required all states, in exchange for federal dollars, to test students annually so that their educational progress could be monitored. Schools that failed to keep up would face penalties.

FIGURE 3.1   Growth of federal grants to states and localities

Expenditures for intergovernmental grants continue to rise, and with decreasing flexibility for how states may spend the money. *Why would categorical grants rise and block grants fall at a time when the Republicans controlled Congress?*

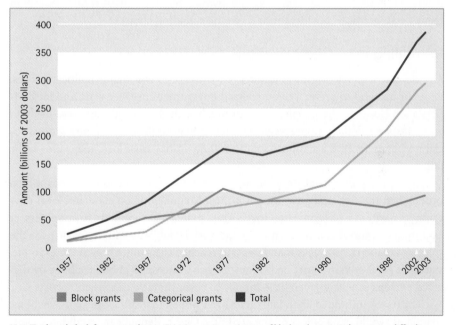

Block grants   Categorical grants   Total

Note: Totals exclude defense expenditures. Deriving precise estimates of block and categorical grants is a difficult undertaking. Here we have employed grants used mainly for developmental purposes as a proxy for block grants and grants used mainly for redistributive purposes as a proxy for categorical grants.

Sources: Paul E. Peterson, *The Price of Federalism* (Washington, DC: Brookings, 1995), Ch. 5; U.S. Bureau of the Census, *Federal Aid to the States for Fiscal Year 1998, 2002, 2003.*

Why are categorical grants so irresistible? Because members of Congress use federal spending to improve their chances for reelection. The precise rules accompanying categorical grants let the legislators control what the money buys. Constituents seeking funding must go to them rather than to local officials, and those who receive money give credit to the members of Congress. Aside from legislators, however, the current state of affairs satisfies few people. It frustrates Americans who oppose "big government," because they win electoral victories but the government still does not shrink. At the same time, the system frustrates those who support social-welfare policies—because the funds often are not distributed in a way that helps the needy.[25] The federal budget does not operate like Robin Hood, taking from the rich states and giving to the poor. Rich states receive more funding per person than anyone else (see Figure 3.2).

Centralizing welfare policies may help the poor in a different way: by overcoming state government's natural tendency to squeeze social programs. When states are not subject to federal regulation, they try to keep benefits low enough that they will not be "welfare magnets" that attract "other people's poor." Federal programs can prevent states from engaging in a "race to the bottom" by equalizing benefits nationwide. Even this defense of federal grants, however, only applies to welfare programs. States and localities customarily provide traditional services—such as transportation, sanitation, and education—regardless of whether they face federal pressure to do so. Congress, meanwhile, tends to invest money poorly in these areas; political considerations drive the spending choices.

Retreating from Centralization

The debate over federalism continues. It divides the two major political parties. Republicans tend to prefer a decentralized government because state and local officials are closer to the people, more in touch with their needs, and less likely to waste taxpayer dollars. Conversely, Democrats tend to think that many serious social problems require a national solution; they do not trust local majorities to be fair.

In the early 1990s, debate focused on the issue of **unfunded mandates**, which occur when the national government imposes regulations on state and local governments without covering the costs. This strategy is tempting to members of Congress because it allows them to "solve" social problems without paying for the solutions. By 1993, countless mandates had reached the statute books. For example, state and local governments had to ensure equal access to public facilities by disabled persons but were given little money to cover the new construction costs.

Critics of unfunded mandates had high hopes that after the 1994 elections, mandates would be a thing of the past. That year, Republican candidates campaigned in favor of governmental **devolution**, the return of governmental responsibilities to state and local governments. But Republican lawmakers soon proved that they were not immune to the practice. The Bush education bill required states

FIGURE 3.2 Richer states get more per capita aid

Richer states usually get more money than poorer states. *Is this unfair, or do rich states deserve more because they pay more to the federal government in taxes?*

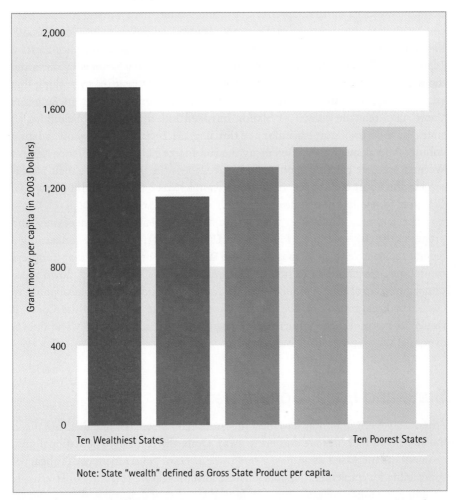

Note: State "wealth" defined as Gross State Product per capita.

Sources: Calculated by authors from U.S. Bureau of the Census, *Federal Aid to the States for Fiscal Year 2003*, September 2004, Table 1; *Statistical Abstract of the United States, 2004–2005*, Table 17; *Statistical Abstract of the United States 2006*, Table 654.

and school districts to set standards, but critics said it provided little money to help them do so. After 2001 new antiterrorism rules also placed severe strain on state and local governments, as law enforcement officials were required to step up their monitoring of potential terrorist targets around the country. "When we get federal mandates, where do we get the money?" one Kentucky mayor asked. "We would hope that the federal government would be more understanding."[26] Republican

Senator Lamar Alexander—a former Tennessee governor—lamented, "The conservatives are just as bad as liberals at passing new programs and expecting someone else to pay for it."[27]

Conservatives on the Supreme Court, meanwhile, have worked to scale back constitutional interpretations that promote centralized government. For example, the Supreme Court narrowed the scope of the commerce clause in *United States v. Lopez* (1995). Congress had attempted to set policy for public schools by declaring them gun-free zones—an effort the national government justified by arguing that education was a "business" that influenced interstate commerce, but the Supreme Court ruled that the federal legislation intruded into a policy area belonging to states. In 2000 the Court expanded the thrust of the *Lopez* decision by invalidating another federal law that justified using the commerce clause. The Violence Against Women Act gave battered spouses and rape victims the power to sue their attackers, but the Court did not see much connection between this law and the power of Congress to regulate interstate commerce.

The Supreme Court also tried to limit the elasticity of the necessary and proper clause. For example, in *New York v. United States* (1992), a case concerning a federal radioactive waste disposal law, the Supreme Court declared that Congress cannot give direct orders to states.[28] Five years later the Court struck down a national gun control law for similar reasons. If the law, which required local police to check the backgrounds of gun buyers, were allowed to stand, said the Court, it would "compromise the structural framework of dual sovereignty."[29] The debate over dual sovereignty clearly has not died.

State and Local Government

American government may have become more centralized, but that does not mean the states and localities are withering away. Quite the contrary. The national government has increased its authority, but lower levels of government usually bear responsibility for implementing policy. These lower levels are often the ones actually spending the funds collected through federal taxation and distributed via competitive grants or according to specific formulas. State and local governments are the ones hiring new bureaucrats to implement federal mandates (see Chapter 11). If "the devil is in the details," as the old saying goes, then it is often lower levels of government that administer the policies that emerge from America's new democracy.

State Government

The federal government's design was adapted from constitutions in many states. Thus, it is not surprising that the basic organization of most state governments bears a strong resemblance to that found in the U.S. Constitution. Just as Congress has the Senate and the House, legislatures have an upper and a lower chamber in all states except Nebraska (which has only one chamber). All states have multitiered court systems roughly comparable to the federal system (see Chapter 12). And every state has an independently elected governor, the chief executive of the state, whose responsibilities roughly parallel those of the president.

State governments differ in many important ways, however. State legislatures vary greatly in size. Most lower houses have around 100 representatives, but New Hampshire's lower house contains 400 legislators while Alaska's has only 40. Some state governments hold their elections in even-numbered years, in conjunction with federal races; others do not. In some states, administrative officers such as the secretary of state and the attorney general are elected, whereas in other states the governors appoint these officials.

State policies vary as well. One reason is that different states have populations with a variety of cultures, with varying voter preferences and varying traditions of conducting government. Cultural differences may explain why states vary significantly in how they treat abortion, assisted suicide, or social welfare. Another reason for policy variation is that states serve as "laboratories of democracy"—places where policy makers can experiment with solutions to social problems. If a solution works at the state level, other states may copy it or the federal government may try to imitate it at the national level.[30] Scholars have shown, for example, that states are more likely to establish state lotteries if their neighbors have their own lottery programs.[31]

Variation in Responsibilities   The size and range of state responsibilities have grown dramatically in recent decades. As a percentage of GNP, state expenditures increased by more than 60 percent between 1960 and 2003. States bear heavy responsibilities for financing education at all levels. They maintain parks, highways, and prisons. They manage welfare and Medicaid programs that serve low-income populations. They give grants to local governments to help pay for police, fire, and other basic governmental services.

The amount spent on governmental services varies from state to state. For one thing, wealthier states spend much more on public services. In 2003, the state and local governments in the 10 richest states spent an average of $5861 per person on public services, whereas in the 10 poorest states they spent, on average, about $4900 (although, of course, the purchasing power of a dollar may be greater in a poor state).[32] Federal grants have done little, if anything, to reduce fiscal inequalities. Expenditures are also affected by elections. Each party has its favorite type of public service. Democrats in the legislature tend to prefer high expenditures for social services. The more Republicans who win, the higher the expenditure for traditional government services such as national defense.[33]

As state government has become more complicated, state legislatures have also become more professional. That is, they have lower turnover rates, higher salaries, more staff, and longer sessions. In 2006, California's legislature was among the most modern. Its members remained in session throughout the year, enjoying $110,880 in salary, retirement benefits, and handsome daily expense payments, as well as the services of a full-time staff. Turnover rates were only about 18 percent. By contrast, Wyoming paid its legislators $125 dollars a day and limited its legislative sessions to a maximum of 40 working days in odd-numbered years and 20 days in even-numbered years. It had a turnover rate twice that of California.[34] In the 1990s, voters reacted against the professionalization of state government, as many states limited the terms of legislators, cut their staffs, and reduced their salaries and benefits. One expert argues that term limits, now in effect in 15 states, have produced a "crumbling of legislative power," weakening the legislatures and strengthening the other branches of state government.[35]

State Political Competition   Despite differences among states, state elections bear a strong resemblance to national elections. The same two political parties—the Republicans and Democrats—are the dominant competitors in nearly all state elections. A new trend toward competitive politics and divided government has developed in most states (see Figure 3.3). The voters may like this split in power: Each party can act as a check on the other, and government does not drift to either political extreme.[36]

Being governor of a medium- to large-sized state has become one of the best ways to prepare for a presidential run. Four of the last five U.S. presidents have been governors, and former governors have been major candidates in every presidential election campaign since 1976. George W. Bush's popularity as governor of Texas, coupled with the advantages of a well-known family name, quickly catapulted him into the presidential limelight.

FIGURE 3.3   States with divided government

Increasingly, the governor of a state belongs to a party different from the party that controls one or both houses of the state legislature. *Is this pattern an accident or the result of conscious decisions by voters?*

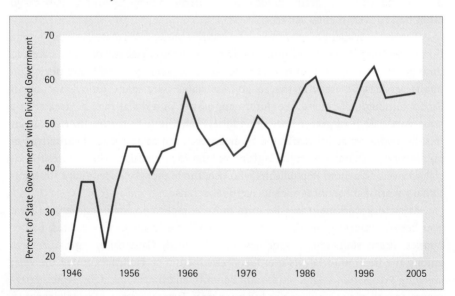

Sources: Morris Fiorina, *Divided Government* (Needham Heights, MA: Allyn and Bacon, 1996); *The Book of the States*, Vol. 32: 1998–1999 (Lexington, KY: The Council of State Governments, 1998).

Since 1950, many states have strengthened the office of governor by lengthening terms of office, reducing term limitations, and enhancing the governor's veto power over legislation. Most governors now have a **line-item veto**, a power that allows them to reject specific parts of a bill. Ten governors have a particularly strong form of the line-item veto that allows them to eliminate or cut particular spending items.[37] In part because of their newfound strength, governors have become influential players in national policy debates. For example, they lobbied Congress to increase spending on homeland security after the 9/11 attacks.[38]

Political competition in the states takes on an added significance every 10 years because of **reapportionment**, the periodic redrawing of state legislative and congressional district lines. Prior to the 1960s, many states declined regularly to redraw district boundaries, a neglect that led over time to state legislative districts with embarrassingly unequal populations. Since the Supreme Court ruled in 1962 and 1964 that districts must have similar numbers of residents,[39] regular battles have followed each decennial census, as Democrats and Republicans compete to draw boundaries in the way most favorable to their party.[40] During the round of redistricting that followed the 2000 Census, for example, a Colorado state representative complained that reapportionment was "submerged in a morass of partisan haranguing."[41]

Even though many politicians and activists have complained that the party that happens to be in power can unfairly manipulate district lines to their political advantage, the Supreme Court has declined to play the referee in such situations. In a 2006 decision regarding Texas's boundary lines, for example, the Court said that it could not identify a "reliable standard" for deciding whether a partisan manipulation of district lines was unconstitutional or not.[42]

State Economic Action   In the nineteenth century, state governments played an active role in state economies, granting charters to private corporations and investing their resources to assist in the development of key industries. After the New Deal, the states faded in importance, but many became active again in the 1980s and 1990s—seeking to reinvigorate their business climate through tax incentives, worker-training programs, and active recruitment of out-of-state firms.

States with large economies and significant international exports, such as California and Texas, often arrange trade missions to foreign countries. When Arnold Schwarzenegger won election as governor in 2003, one of his first meetings was with Mexico's secretary of foreign affairs.[43]

States are aggressive in seeking out economic opportunities because of their vulnerability to downswings in the economy. When times are bad, state tax collections plummet, making it hard for state governments to meet their obligations. Most recently, state budgets across the country collapsed in 2002 and 2003. Budget shortfalls were so bad that the executive director of the National Governor's Association declared that the crisis was the worst for the states since the War of 1812.[47] Governors and state legislatures needed to identify some combination of tax hikes and spending cuts that would balance their budgets—and, as they customarily do, the states dealt with their financial woes by scaling back programs for the young.[48] Indiana's Democratic governor cut a huge sum from the state's school for the blind and also closed campgrounds and pools. Tennessee scuttled a summer program for gifted and talented high school students. Oregon's legislators cut their school budget by $112 million in special session. Illinois planned to cut pre-kindergarten classes for low-income children.

What accounts for this dramatic financial crisis, and the programmatic cuts that followed? Part of the answer is that various laws prevent states from solving their own problems in hard times. State laws give governors and legislators little flexibility in budgeting. Some state constitutions limit certain taxes or make taxes harder to approve. Most states require balanced budgets, whereas the federal government can spend far more money than it actually collects. States often operate under unfunded mandates imposed by the national government. Federal court decisions and federal agency rules constrain the choices that state and local governments can make—forcing them to update facilities for handicapped access or to refurbish prisons, for example. Numerous federal programs, such as the Medicaid health insurance program for low-income people, require states to provide matching funds if they want to receive grant money. The overall impact of this maze of limitations and requirements is that state budgets cannot respond quickly to new priorities or rapid economic changes, and education is the one expensive policy area flexible enough to absorb the damage.

But that cannot be the whole story. All of those laws and restrictions ultimately do not prevent the states from funding major programs adequately if they really wish to do so. Not only could voters pressure the federal government to back off their states, they also could demand that their states overcome the difficulties of raising additional

HIGHER EDUCATION WOES
When states faced budget shortfalls in 2002, many chose to cut funding for state colleges and universities. *Why do you think states decided to cut education spending rather than raise taxes?*

funding. But voters are doing just the opposite. Reports indicate that states use taxes to make up only a third of their shortfalls and resort to cuts to compensate for the rest.[46]

Whatever survey respondents say about their values, the reality is that public opinion in America's new democracy does not allow states to maintain generous programs for the poor and the young. Two governors who did try to hike taxes significantly during the 2002 crisis (Democrat Mike Easley in North Carolina and Republican Don Sundquist in Tennessee) faced picketing demonstrators pumped up by radio talk shows. It is this reality that forces governors to plead with the federal government for aid and allows journalists to assume that the states cannot tap into the money that tax cuts and federal spending inject directly into their local economies.

Local Government

Local governments come in many varieties. They govern villages, towns, cities, counties, school districts, and even special districts with rather narrow functions such as garbage collection or mosquito abatement. The relative influence of these various institutions varies from state to state. For example, in some rural states, counties are extremely important. Residents may define their identity by the county where they grew up. Northeastern states, on the other hand, usually give little authority to counties. The important local policies are more likely to be organized around townships. For especially urbanized areas, meanwhile, municipal governments usually assume many of the responsibilities otherwise performed by counties.

The Impact of Local Governments   Regardless of how local government institutions divide up their tasks, they are the ones carrying out many of the public policies that affect everyday life. They maintain roads. They take care of parks and community centers. They provide police, fire, and sanitation services. They run schools and local welfare programs. Americans, therefore, often see firsthand the benefits provided by local institutions. The elected officials who run local government are relatively close to voters as well, not only because they tend to share the beliefs of the voters around them, but also because they are fairly accessible. They may give speeches before neighborhood associations or other community groups. At election time, they may go from door to door, shaking hands and distributing their own campaign literature. It may be relatively easy to get a local official on the telephone.

Citizens have comparatively little difficulty influencing the choices made by local officials. Part of their influence, as always, comes from elections. Turnout is not high in most local elections. The local electorate generally is about half the size of the presidential electorate, and officials represent relatively few constituents.[47] If a politician makes a local group unhappy, therefore, those angry voters can have a measurable electoral impact. Even politically inactive citizens can "vote with their feet." Americans are a mobile people. Each year more than 17 percent move, and (within the bounds of their financial resources) they can "shop" for the type of locality in which they wish to live.[48] They may choose where to live based upon the school system, the tax level, the job market, access to highways and airports, or the types of

FIGURE 3.4 Evaluations of federal, state, and local governments

Why do you think more people trust local government than trust other governments?

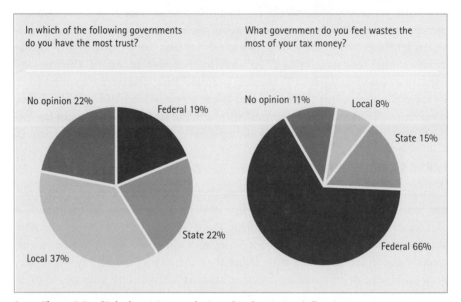

Source: Thomas R. Dye, "Federalism: A Return to the Future," *Madison Review* 1 (Fall 1995): 3.

recreation and entertainment available. Officials know that they must be responsive to community needs and effective at solving local problems or the local population will decline, dragging down revenues and property values. By giving people a choice, the diversity of local governments reduces conflict and enhances citizen satisfaction.

As a result, local governments are especially popular. According to survey results, fully 70 percent of Americans express "a great deal" or "a fair amount" of "trust and confidence" in their local government, while far fewer had a similar assessment of the national government.[49]

The Jobs Race   Local governments compete with each other to attract businesses that generate economic activity, sometimes pouring substantial resources into attracting and retaining employers. Although such competition has benefits because it keeps localities sensitive to the needs of their wealth producers, sometimes the competition can get out of hand. With state help, one county in Kentucky outbid its neighbors for a Canadian steel mill employing 400 people. The deal ended up costing the state $350,000 for every job created. Such bidding wars have spread across the country. As one Michigan official put it, "Right now, all we are doing is eating each other's lunch. At some stage we have to start thinking about dinner."[50]

Local businesses—and sometimes sports franchises—commonly threaten to move if they do not receive assistance from the cities where they are located. Sometimes companies move outside the United States altogether. It is a common, and increasingly controversial, problem faced by local governments.

Education Policy   Primary responsibility for education resides at the state and local level. Today, 95 percent of the cost of public education comes from state and local budgets, each contributing approximately half the cost (the exact percentage paid varies widely from one state to another). This decentralization means that taxes for education often go straight to the local community and so, aside from the occasional opposition of elderly voters, are not as unpopular as many other taxes.[51]

The public's commitment to local public schools is historically rooted. As early as 1785, Congress set aside revenue from the sale of land west of the Appalachian Mountains to help pay for the maintenance of public schools. Support for public schools intensified with the flood of immigrants that arrived in the nineteenth century, because these institutions helped build American democracy. Public schools fostered a common language among people from disparate parts of the world and reinforced a common American identity. They also educated the workforce to operate the new machines that eventually turned the country into an industrial power.

Nevertheless, public schools are not as popular as they once were. From 1973 to 2006, the percentage of Americans expressing "a good deal" or "quite a lot" of confidence in the public schools dropped from 58 percent to 37 percent (see Figure 3.5).[52] Part of the problem is simple self interest: Voters have become older and many do

(text continues on page 66)

FIGURE 3.5   Fewer Americans have confidence in public schools
Widespread criticism of public schools seems to have influenced public opinion. *What accounts for the decreased confidence in public schools?*

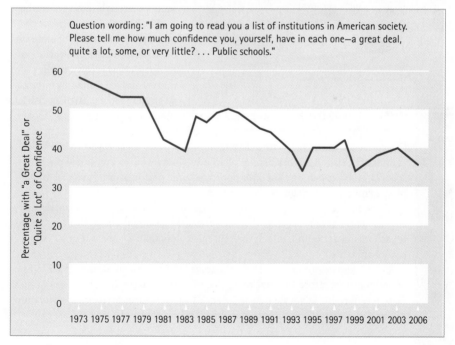

Question wording: "I am going to read you a list of institutions in American society. Please tell me how much confidence you, yourself, have in each one—a great deal, quite a lot, some, or very little? . . . Public schools."

Source: Gallup Poll, various years.

Election Voices

SCHOOL CHOICE

As we point out in this chapter, education is one of the most important policy areas that states and local governments handle. But some experts worry that states, cities, and school districts haven't done a good job in recent years. American students have only made modest—if any—academic advancements since the 1970s, even though spending on education has increased.[56] Nine-year-olds have improved their test scores in math, reading, and science, but these gains do not hold as they grow older.[57] What's more, schools in some urban areas are in desperate and lamentable condition. What can be done about these problems?

Some critics say that public schools have stagnated because they face no competition. The solution, they say, is to force public schools to compete against each other—and even against private schools—for students. School choice programs allow parents to send their children to a school other than the one assigned to them by the local school district. The most controversial forms of school choice are vouchers and charter schools.

Vouchers are simply scholarships that allow students to attend a private school. Under most voucher plans, students qualify for scholarships if they come from low-income families or attend chronically underperforming schools.[58] Since 1990, voucher programs have been established in Milwaukee, Cleveland, and the nation's capital.[59] During the 2005–2006 school year, 22,000 children were enrolled in private schools through these programs.[60]

Off to school.

Charter schools are privately managed schools that operate under a performance contract. Although they receive public money and are generally open to all students in a particular district, charters operate free from most regulations to which traditional public schools must conform. Consequently, charters are free to innovate and provide alternative curricula. In exchange for this freedom, states and local governments hold charter schools to a higher degree of accountability. Unlike traditional public schools, charters can be closed for poor academic performance, financial mismanagement, or inadequate enrollments.

Since 1991, 40 states and the District of Columbia have enacted some kind of charter school law. More than one million students attend one of the 3,617 charter schools in 2006; still, this figure represents less than 2.3 percent of all public school students.[61]

School choice proponents say that choice benefits the children of poor families who cannot afford to move to a better district or to pay private school tuition. As one civil rights advocate puts it, "inequity [in the current system] is a violation of the civil rights of the parents and children who are so afflicted by lack of income and by the mismanagement endemic to so many of the country's public school systems."[62] In addition, as traditional public schools compete to retain students—and the corresponding per pupil funds—they are bound to improve their performance.

Opponents contend that school choice programs drain public schools of money and talent, making it impossible for them to improve from competition. Moreover, critics say that voucher programs, in which sectarian private schools are allowed to participate, violate the separation of church and state (see Chapter 13). As one group argues, "Americans must be free to contribute only to the religious groups of their choosing. Voucher programs violate this principle by forcing all taxpayers to underwrite religious education."[63] In 2002, the Supreme Court ruled that voucher programs do not violate the federal Constitution, but opponents still contend that they violate many state constitutions that also establish a church-state boundary.

Public support for vouchers depends in part on the way the question is worded. In 2002, one poll asked the question about vouchers in two different ways and found that a majority supported vouchers if asked one way, but opposed it, if asked another way.[64] The same poll has found increasing support for charter schools over the last few years. Whereas in 2000, 42 percent of respondents favored charter schools, by 2005 support had increased to 49 percent.

WHAT DO YOU THINK?

1. Should state governments enact voucher programs that allow students to attend religious schools?
2. Do you think that competition among schools would spur higher performance? Or do you think public schools would suffer needlessly?

For more information on **vouchers and charter schools**, see the following Web sites.

Pro-School Choice
www.edreform.com
www.allianceforschoolchoice.org

The Center for Education Reform and the Alliance for School Choice are nationwide organizations that promote charter schools and voucher programs.

www.schoolchoiceinfo.org

School Choice Info is a Wisconsin-based group that produces research on school choice programs—especially Milwaukee's voucher system.

Anti-School Choice
www.aft.org

The American Federation of Teachers opposes school choice, arguing that such programs take resources away from public education.

www.nea.org

The National Education Association, a membership organization of public school employees, opposes vouchers for many of the same reasons.

www.au.org

Americans United for Separation of Church and State argues that vouchers violate the Constitutional prohibition against state support for religion.

not have children who benefit from schools. Part of the problem, however, is unhappiness with how public schools are performing. Critics argue that the schools are local monopolies that perform badly, pointing to weak performance by American students in reading, science, math, and geography.[53] Schools serve the interests of the adults teaching in and administering them, they say, not those of the students. Modern educators are more interested in making all children equal than in helping children reach their full potential. They no longer unify American children, instead advancing a multicultural agenda that undermines the nation's individualism.

All of these developments have added up to a loss of faith. Public schools have not benefited from the generous funding increases enjoyed by other government programs. Within the United States itself, financial support for public elementary and secondary education (as a percentage of gross domestic product) has increased only slightly over the past 15 years.[54] And teacher salaries, relative to the average wage in the United States, have declined since 1970.[55]

CHAPTER SUMMARY

Federalism divides sovereignty between the states and the national government. The Constitution does not define governmental powers clearly, however. As a result, the nature of American federalism has changed in response to numerous events, including both elections and court decisions. The national government has used its budgetary authority to help state and local governments overcome their own difficulties raising revenue—but at the cost of shifting power toward the level of government most distrusted by voters. States have also lost influence as they struggle to retain jobs, fund education adequately, and pay for unfunded mandates imposed by national institutions.

Despite the expansion of federal power, state and local governments remain vital components of the federal system. Nearly half of domestic spending by government ultimately comes out of state and local budgets, so these governments affect everyday life. Governors are well-known political figures, often positioned to seek the presidency, and legislatures affect both state and national elections by drawing district boundaries. Although few citizens participate in local elections, local governments are the most popular of all governmental levels, in part because people can "vote with their feet"—that is, they can choose local communities suited to their tastes.

The growing power of the national government in some ways represents a frustration of popular desires, because Americans generally trust their local officials more. They are annoyed by a federal bureaucracy that hands down orders, ignoring local needs. Yet support for the principle of federalism is not strong, and often the national government can find solutions for problems that voters do not allow state and local government to address. Frustration with centralized government should not conceal an important fact: The new balance in favor of national power has made it easier for popular majorities to change American social life rapidly, and voters often compel the national government to do exactly that.

Key Terms

block grant, p. 53
categorical grant, p. 52
commerce clause, p. 49
cooperative (marble-cake) federalism, p. 52
devolution, p. 54
dual sovereignty, p. 47
elastic clause, p. 50
federalism, p. 47
line-item veto, p. 59

reapportionment, p. 59
McCulloch v. Maryland, p. 49
necessary and proper clause, p. 49
New Deal, p. 51
nullification, p. 49
sovereign immunity, p. 49
spending clause, p. 49
supremacy clause, p. 49
unfunded mandates, p. 54

Suggested Readings

Conlan, Timothy. *From New Federalism to Devolution: Twenty-Five Years of Intergovernmental Reform*. Washington, DC: Brookings, 1998. Excellent analysis of changing federal policy.

Fiorina, Morris. *Divided Government*. New York: Macmillan, 1992. Explains why control of many state governments is divided between the Democratic and Republican parties.

Nivola, Pietro S. *Tense Commandments: Federal Prescriptions and City Problems*. Washington, DC: The Brookings Institution, 2002. Argues that national prescriptions and mandates are restricting cities' ability to respond to local needs.

Peterson, Paul E. *The Price of Federalism*. Washington, DC: Brookings, 1995. Contrasts the responsibilities of national, state, and local governments.

On the Web

www.nlc.org
National League of Cities

www.ncsl.org
National Conference of State Legislatures

www.nga.org
National Governor's Association

www.urban.org/center/anf/index.cfm
Several interstate governmental organizations provide information and policy priorities for state and local governments.

www.urban.org/center/anf/index.cfm
On this Web site, the Urban Institute's "Assessing the New Federalism" project presents information about the impact of programs devolving authority to state and local government.

www.federalismproject.org
The American Enterprise Institute's Federalism Project advocates devolution of more rights and responsibilities to the states.

Channels of Influence in America's New Democracy

American Political Culture

ALL 19 OF THE SEPTEMBER 11 TERRORISTS CAME FROM OTHER countries. Not one of them was an American citizen. In the aftermath of the attacks a few Americans chose to express their grief and anger by committing violent acts against people of Middle Eastern background living in the United States. Some incidents were as minor as bullying at school recess. Others were fatal. A Sikh was gunned down in a deadly instance of mistaken identity. A Yemeni shopkeeper, father of eight, was gunned down within sight of the American flag hanging in his store window. In all, Arab Americans faced an estimated 270 violent assaults within a month of 9/11—five resulted in deaths.[1] California alone recorded 73 official hate crimes against people perceived to be Arabs in 2001 (compared to only three the year before).[2]

These hostile acts, however, were carried out by a relatively small number of Americans acting on their own; none were official government actions. True, some members of the public called for the adoption of anti-Arab policies. Survey respondents overwhelmingly endorsed subjecting those of Arab descent to special security checks at airports. A majority favored requiring Arabs to carry special identification cards, and more than a third supported placing them under "special surveillance."[3]

The most dramatic policy changes occurred abroad, but tightened domestic security measures have prompted critics to protest that the authorities have unjustly singled out ethnic minorities for scrutiny. Many Arab Americans claimed to have been escorted off planes simply because of their ethnicity.[4] States beefed up their scrutiny of applicants for driver's licenses and other government documents.[5] Federal officials slowed the rate at which foreigners received permission to visit the United States and made the process more intrusive, such as taking fingerprints from applicants. They also reversed years of neglect by aggressively tracking down those who had overstayed their visas. They asked colleges to ensure that international students had their paperwork in order (one reason enrollment from abroad stagnated for two years running). In some cases, officials detained people for many months, denying them access to lawyers and even abusing them.[6]

Although some critics believe that such government actions are excessive, they pale in comparison to the treatment of perceived outsiders after previous national tragedies. Three generations ago, when Japan attacked Pearl Harbor, the government rounded up 120,000 Americans of Japanese ancestry and held them for up to three years in internment camps. Detainees often lost their property and their jobs. Citizenship offered them no protection.[7] A generation earlier, after the United States entered World War I, German Americans suffered considerable abuse.[8] In short, compared to the nation's historical experience, recent hate crimes have been isolated and any discrimination resulting from tightened security measures has been relatively mild.

Perhaps even more striking is the amount of effort that many Americans have devoted to dampening hostility toward Arab Americans. For every legislator who complained about Arabs running "all the convenience stores across the country," dozens increased their outreach to Arab American constituents who felt vulnerable as a result of the backlash.[9] President Bush called for unity and told Americans over and over again that Islam is a peaceful religion. The American media also declined to stir up ethnic hatreds, as they had during previous crises. Instead, journalists carefully documented injustices caused by new government policies. They also ran stories conveying a simple message: that the country's immigrant communities were filled with loyal Americans, just as horrified by the terrorist attacks as anyone else.

It is easy to take this insight for granted. "Of course Arabs can be good Americans," you might be thinking. "What does being an American have to do with race or religion?" This reaction makes perfect sense in the United States, but it would be far from obvious in most countries. Carl Friedrich, a professor who immigrated to the United States from Germany in the 1930s, wrote that "To be an American is an ideal, while to be a Frenchman is a fact."[10] Friedrich was pointing out that in most of the world citizenship is indeed defined by race or ethnicity. Nationality is a question of fact; either you are German or you are not. By contrast, an American may belong to any ethnic group. To be a "good American" refers not to a nationality but to a set of beliefs and values that people of any heritage may choose to embrace.

Yet Friedrich's comment hints at a strange contradiction. For all their diversity, Americans share a political "ideal"—a set of basic assumptions about the nature of a good society—more so than do citizens in other democracies. Certainly the United States has its share of controversy and disagreement, such as the political

UNITY IN DIVERSITY
How can Americans be so diverse, and yet so similar in their values concerning politics and government?
© 2001 Breen—Asbury Park Press

struggle between "liberals" and "conservatives" or between Democrats and Republicans. But it lacks major factions on the extreme left or the extreme right that might espouse a different set of fundamental ideals, a surprising political uniformity for such a diverse nation.

The mixture of *uniformity* and *diversity* found in the United States may seem puzzling, but this chapter shows that the two traits actually fit together. Historical experiences mold a citizenry's values, and they especially shape the fundamental beliefs about politics and government that some scholars call a nation's **political culture**. In the United States, immigration has been a dominant historical experience. The precise contents of America's political culture (the unity) developed out of the waves of people who have swept over the nation's shores (the variety). Early settlers brought distinct beliefs favoring individualism, freedom, and equality—values that later migrants helped reinforce and refine. The resulting world view forms the context for America's new democracy, the electoral environment that shapes its laws and its policies.

Social Diversity

John Jay wrote in the second *Federalist Papers* essay that Americans were "one united people; a people descended from the same ancestors, speaking the same language, professing the same religion." Such statements remind us that the *Federalist Papers* were primarily campaign documents, for Americans were not nearly so similar as Jay alleged, even in the 1780s. His exaggeration of American unity was a political tactic, an appeal to rise above serious divisions that threatened ratification of the Constitution.

Contrary to Jay's claim, the New World was not settled by "one united people." The British were especially numerous, of course, but they were not all of a kind. Puritans settled New England, while Virginians professed loyalty to the Church of England. Lord Baltimore invited his fellow Catholics to Maryland, while Pennsylvania welcomed Quakers. Moreover, after 1700, British immigration came increasingly from Scotland, Wales, and Ireland rather than from England.

Other nationalities settled in the American colonies. The Dutch founded New York—calling it New Amsterdam—and the Swedes established settlements in what are now Delaware and eastern Pennsylvania. The French were present on the northern and western borders, the Spanish in the south (although the latter never were very numerous). Indentured servants (who made up half the populations of Pennsylvania, New York, and New Jersey) included thousands of Germans, Scandinavians, Belgians, French, and Swiss. And these were only the voluntary immigrants; the involuntary immigrants—slaves—came from Africa.* Historians estimate that, in 1763, only 50 percent of the colonial population was English and nearly 20 percent was African American.[11]

---

* Native Americans, whose numbers had been decimated by wars and disease, were viewed as separate nations altogether.

You may react skeptically to this description of colonial variety. After all, a mixed group of Europeans and their slaves does not correspond to the modern-day notion of "diversity." Contemporary Americans might reserve this term for instances when people of color live peacefully among a white majority, when people who follow Christian traditions coexist with those who hold other religious beliefs, or when people with unconventional lifestyles enjoy the same rights and privileges as those who are more traditionally oriented. But diversity is relative to time and place.

Take the case of religious differences. In the sixteenth and seventeenth centuries, Protestants looked upon Catholics with no more understanding (and often with less) than that with which a Christian looks upon a Muslim today. Northern European Christians (Catholics, Calvinists, and Lutherans) pillaged, raped, and murdered each other on a monumental scale during the Thirty Years' War (1618–1648); one-third of the population of what is now Germany died during the conflict. Near the end of that period, Puritan dissenters from the Church of England fought Royalist defenders of Church and Crown in the English Civil War (1642–1653). Ultimately, both Charles I and the Archbishop of Canterbury lost their heads.

Nor has the United States been immune to bloodshed inspired by religion. The English Civil War echoed faintly in Maryland, where Catholics, Puritans, and Anglicans engaged in a "minor civil war."[12] Illinois Protestants murdered Mormon leader Joseph Smith in 1844 because, among other things, he taught that men could have multiple wives. Of course, like *Federalist Papers* author John Jay, Americans seeking peace in their communities often have tried to downplay the

A RELIGIOUS MARTYR
An Illinois mob murders Mormon prophet Joseph Smith in 1844. The diversity represented by his religion's polygamist practices was intolerable, especially in light of growing Mormon electoral influence. *When does a community have a right to enforce its morality, to enforce conformity rather than diversity?*

importance of internal differences. One myth holds that the nation is a melting pot, in which many peoples are melted down to form a new metal tougher than any of the ingredients.[13] The national motto, *E Pluribus Unum*, translates into a message of unity: "Out of many, one." But the simple truth is that, relative to the time and the place, the United States has always been especially diverse. And each wave of immigrants has faced uneasiness, fear, or even hatred from the citizens of their adopted country.

A Nation of Immigrants Then

The United States had an open-door immigration policy at the time of its founding, but not everyone was happy about it. One of the most cosmopolitan Americans of the time, Benjamin Franklin, expressed his resentment of Germans in various letters: "Why should *Pennsylvania*, founded by the English, become a colony of Aliens, who will shortly be so numerous as to Germanize us instead of our Anglifying them, and will never adopt our Language or Customs any more than they can acquire our Complexion?" [emphasis in original].[14]

Despite such misgivings, land was plentiful and labor scarce. The more rapidly the territory filled up, the more rapidly economic development would follow, so borders remained open. Immigration gradually increased, until by the mid-nineteenth century immigrants from England, Ireland, and Germany were arriving in numbers as high as 400,000 per year. Irish immigration became a major political controversy. Some Protestants feared that Catholics would put their allegiance to the Pope above their loyalty to the United States—and might even plot to overthrow the government on his behalf. Cartoonists of the period depicted the Irish as hairy, ape-like people. In the 1854 elections, an anti-Catholic party won 43 seats in the House of Representatives, almost a fifth of the chamber at the time.

Immigration increased considerably after the Civil War. The first of an eventual half-million French Canadians crossed the northeastern U.S. border in the 1860s and 1870s, and several million Scandinavians joined a continuing stream of English, Irish, and Germans (see Figure 4.1). Again, by today's standards such groups may seem alike, but their "ethno-cultural" differences often produced social conflicts.[15] Indeed, the era's political parties usually squared off over cultural issues. Northern Republicans appealed to native Protestants by calling for the prohibition of alcohol, for "blue laws" to restrict commerce on Sundays, and for regulations that would promote public schools at the expense of parochial or bilingual education. All of these proposals targeted the immigrant Catholic communities, where northern Democrats sank their roots.

German Lutherans were an important swing group in some Midwestern states. They generally voted Republican but swung to the Democrats when conservative Protestants within the Republican party attempted to legislate on cultural issues. In Wisconsin, for example, the Republicans lost only two statewide elections between 1858 and 1890. One came after the party raised liquor license fees, the second after it passed a measure requiring English-language instruction in the

FIGURE 4.1 Time Line: Immigration to the United States

The quantity and origin of immigration to the United States has changed sharply over time. *Why might interest in emigrating to the United States rise and fall?*

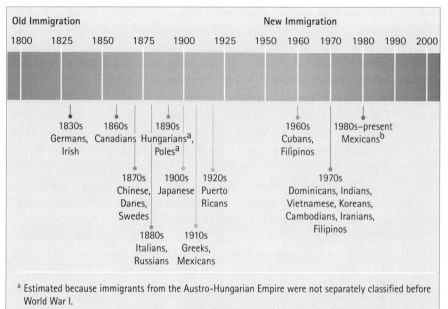

Old Immigration | New Immigration

| 1800 | 1825 | 1850 | 1875 | 1900 | 1925 | 1950 | 1960 | 1970 | 1980 | 1990 | 2000 |

1830s
Germans, Irish

1860s
Canadians

1890s
Hungarians[a], Poles[a]

1960s
Cubans, Filipinos

1980s–present
Mexicans[b]

1870s
Chinese, Danes, Swedes

1900s
Japanese

1920s
Puerto Ricans

1970s
Dominicans, Indians, Vietnamese, Koreans, Cambodians, Iranians, Filipinos

1880s
Italians, Russians

1910s
Greeks, Mexicans

[a] Estimated because immigrants from the Austro-Hungarian Empire were not separately classified before World War I.

[b] Mexican immigration first reached 100,000 in the 1910s. However, in terms of new immigration, Mexican immigration first peaked in the 1980s. Mexico remains the country of origin of the largest group of immigrants to the U.S.—Mexicans made up 14 percent of all legal immigrants in 2005.

Note: During these decades, immigration by the indicated nationality group first reached 100,000.

Sources: Stephanie Bernado, *The Ethnic Almanac* (Garden City, NY: Doubleday, 1981), pp. 22–140; U.S. Immigration and Naturalization Service (www.ins.gov). Department of Homeland Security, Office of Immigration Statistics, *2005 Yearbook of Immigration Statistics* (September 2006), Table 2.

schools. According to one historian, "Throughout much of Eastern Wisconsin, German immigrants jealously guarded what they regarded as their right to preserve many of the customs they brought with them from Europe."[16]

Immigration and Racial Fears The United States attracted millions of people from southern and eastern Europe beginning in the 1880s, an influx that encouraged anti-immigrant sentiments. Some of the criticisms echoed those heard in the past: Immigrants differed from "real Americans" because they spoke foreign tongues and worshiped in unfamiliar churches. By this time, though, the rhetoric shifted focus to emphasize genetic characteristics. "Real Americans" perceived Italians, Greeks, and other immigrants of the period to be people of color who threatened their nation's racial purity.[17]

Such sentiments were by no means limited to a small fringe of the population. A best-selling book by Madison Grant of the American Museum of Natural

History, published in 1916, warned that the United States was receiving "a large and increasing number of the weak, the broken, and the mentally crippled of all races drawn from the lowest stratum of the Mediterranean basin and the Balkans, together with hordes of the wretched, submerged populations of the Polish ghettoes."[18] Ethnic stereotypes even appeared within official government documents.[19]

The growing visibility of non-European peoples added urgency to racially charged political appeals. Asians began to immigrate on a significant scale—starting with the Chinese, thousands of whom participated in the California Gold Rush of 1849.* Later, more than 100,000 Chinese laborers helped build the transcontinental railroads. These "coolies" worked dangerous jobs for low wages, provoking complaints that they were undermining the American standard of living.[20] African Americans, meanwhile, began to play an active role in electoral politics after the Civil War, especially in the South, where a large population of former slaves could vote but many former rebels could not.[21] Employers, when challenged by their workers, often used black laborers to break strikes.

World War I strengthened anti-immigrant sentiments, especially after revolutionaries installed a communist government in Russia. The world seemed a frightening and unstable place, leading many Americans to question the wisdom of admitting immigrants who might subscribe to the same dangerous ideas that were tearing Europe apart. An anticommunist hysteria, the first "Red Scare," swept the United States. Religious bigotry also surged: Anti-Catholic and anti-Jewish sentiments spawned a second Ku Klux Klan in the 1920s that counted 25 to 30 percent of the adult male Protestant population in its membership.[22]

Outlawing Diversity   As public opinion turned against people of other races and ethnic groups, policy quickly followed. It initially focused on non-Europeans. To combat the "Yellow Peril," Congress passed the Chinese Exclusion Act of 1882, a ban on Asian immigration that was later expanded to include the Japanese and other nationalities. Around the same time, many state governments began depriving African Americans of fundamental social and political rights, a process completed by the turn of the century (see Chapter 14).

The backlash eventually spread. An immigration law adopted in 1917 required a literacy test that favored English speakers.[23] Law enforcement officials cracked down on immigrant communities during the Red Scare, perceiving them as incubators for radical politics. A series of laws passed in the 1920s restricted immigration and gave explicit preference to those from northern and western Europe.[24] By 1930, the era of the open door had ended.†

---

* Only two-thirds of the forty-niners were Americans, and only two-thirds of the Americans were white. Large numbers of Cherokee Indians and African Americans panned for gold. On the multicultural character of California after it was annexed to the United States, see Ronald Takaki, A Different Mirror (Boston, MA: Little, Brown, 1993), Ch. 8.
† Mexicans continued to enter the southwestern states to work in American agriculture (joining those who had been incorporated when the United States took the territory from Mexico), and after World War II, Puerto Ricans emigrated in significant numbers to New York City.

Before the United States closed its doors, more than 35 million people had left hearth and home to come to America. These newcomers and their children formed a large component of population growth in the United States, transforming a small country of 10 million inhabitants in 1820 into a nation of more than 100 million by 1920. The change did not come smoothly, however. Along the way, native-born Americans voiced strong and tenacious doubts about tolerating so many immigrants from countries and cultures different from their own.

Contemporary Americans may be dismayed by the ignorance and hatred that, historically, often greeted outsiders. But anti-immigrant anxieties reflected a truth easy to forget today, which is that no one really knew whether a democratic government could manage the conflicts spawned by a rapid influx of foreigners. Most of the world's multi-ethnic governments have been either short-lived (like Yugoslavia) or authoritarian (like the Austro-Hungarian and Soviet empires). For much of its history, by contrast, the United States has coped successfully with the risk of maintaining open political institutions while absorbing a population of unprecedented variety. Diversity is a critical, but often overlooked, component of America's democratic experiment.

A Nation of Immigrants Now

The Great Depression distracted Americans from their concern with ethnocultural politics. Several bigoted radio personalities commanded a large audience during that period of economic troubles, and discrimination against Catholics and Jews continued into the 1930s and beyond. But tensions were gradually dying down. The cumulative effects of economic troubles, World War II, revulsion against the Holocaust, the Cold War, and generational change led to a reduction in discrimination.

As soon as public policy opened American borders again, however, anti-immigration sentiment revived, indicating that the quiet period was only a brief interlude between the cultural conflict of yesterday and that of today. The Immigration Act of 1965 permitted the largest surge of foreigners since the 1890s. The 1965 legislation abandoned the national-quotas system, which had favored northern Europeans. As a result, immigration from Latin America and the West Indies increased rapidly. Many refugees from Fidel Castro's Cuba fled to Florida during this period. In addition, hundreds of thousands of new immigrants from Vietnam, Korea, Cambodia, India, Iran, the Philippines, and other countries became the first numerically significant Asian groups since the Japanese (see Figure 4.1).

In the 1990s the absolute number of immigrants—about 9.7 million—was higher than in any previous decade, though lower as a proportion of the population than it had been at the turn of the century.[25] Immigration levels have remained high in more recent years, although after 9/11 there was a temporary decline due to the new restrictions described at the opening of this chapter. In 2005, 1.1 million legal immigrants arrived in the U.S., of which about 160,000 were from Mexico. Another 176,000 were from countries in Europe, and 400,000 came from Asian nations.[26] These figures include only legal immigrants; between 10 and 12 million people now live in the United States illegally.[27]

As a result of this newest wave of immigration, by the 2000 census the proportion of population of European origin had dropped to less than 70 percent, and it is projected to fall to less than two-thirds in the next two decades. Whites of European origin have lost their majority status in California, as well as in many large cities. This dramatic shift in the U.S. population has fueled political conflicts over immigration that echo those from previous centuries.

Evaluating the New Immigration

In 1994, California voters overwhelmingly passed Proposition 187, an initiative that denied state services to illegal immigrants and their children. Support for the measure was high even in counties where very few immigrants lived.[28] Although courts later struck down this measure, the question of eligibility for governmental services has remained on the national agenda ever since. Welfare reforms enacted in 1996 denied legal immigrants access to food stamps, a measure that remained in effect until 2003. Critics in both parties objected to President Bush's proposed

(text continues on page 83)

A NATION OF IMMIGRANTS
Protestors at a 2006 rally in Chicago oppose stricter immigration laws. *Why has immigration often been the subject of political conflict?*

Election Voices

IMMIGRATION

In early 2006 political conflict over immigration once again boiled over. At issue were the 10 to 12 million "illegal" or "undocumented" immigrants in the U.S., most of them from Mexico. Months earlier, House Republicans had passed an "enforcement-only" bill that would have made unauthorized entry into the country a felony (later amended to a criminal misdemeanor), provided for more than 700 miles of border fencing, and imposed stiff penalties on employers of illegal immigrants.

Most Democrats and some Republicans support a version of President Bush's alternative proposal, often called "enforcement-plus." Strict border controls are part of this plan too, but so is a program that would allow undocumented immigrants to stay in the country and eventually gain citizenship. The Senate began considering the two rival plans in the spring.

On May 1, more than a million pro-immigrant demonstrators staged "mega-marches" in many American cities. Although senators continued to hold hearings on immigration, Congress delayed meaningful action until after the 2006 election.

The issues today are reminiscent of, but arguably more complex than, those of the past. Some studies conclude that immigrants benefit the economy; others, that they are a net cost. Few experts, however, contend that the benefits or costs are large compared to major government programs such as Medicare and Social Security.[56] Economists point out that not all immigrants are alike: skilled immigrants are a significant net gain to the economy, but unskilled immigrants depress the wages of low-skilled native workers.[57]

The Border Patrol arrests illegal aliens in Arizona.

Those sympathetic to immigration argue that low-skilled immigrants take jobs that Americans don't want. As a poultry industry executive commented, "Reality speaks and it says that, absent Hispanic workers, we could not process chicken."[58] State and local governments, meanwhile, complain that they spend a lot more on social services for immigrants—education, police, medical care—than they receive in taxes.[59]

Some immigration opponents worry that the greater homogeneity of today's immigrants poses a threat to U.S. culture, overwhelming the processes of assimilation that worked in the past.[60] Other observers think these fears are exaggerated. Under new laws, for example, Mexicans in the U.S. can register to vote in Mexico, but few take the opportunity.[61] Los Angeles Mayor Antonio Villaraigosa, whose parents were immigrants, explained: "Most of us don't want to go back to Mexico and we don't want any part of this country reverting to Mexico. We know we are a lot better off being Americans."[62]   (continued on next page)

A final complicating factor is security. Might Al Qaeda or other terrorists smuggle in chemical, biological or nuclear weapons through porous borders?

The immigration issue splits both parties, although disagreement appears greater among Republicans.[63] Democrats are traditionally favorable to ethnic minorities, but low-skilled Americans who compete directly with low-skilled immigrants tend to be Democrats.

Republicans are split into several factions. Many in the business wing of the party, like the executive quoted above, are sympathetic to immigration as a ready source of cheap labor. But many Republicans worry about the threats to national security and others are concerned about threats to American culture. Still others focus on law and order, arguing that people who enter the country without following the proper procedures should not be rewarded.

As usual, most Americans occupy a pragmatic middle ground. They split about evenly on whether immigrants are a net boon or burden, and on whether illegal immigrants contribute more to the country than they cost in services.[64] Still, more than 80 percent of Americans believe that illegal immigration is "out of control,"[65] and similar majorities say that it is unfair to grant rights to illegal immigrants while law-abiding would-be immigrants remain shut out.[66]

Americans agree with defenders of immigration that it is unrealistic to deport, or even punish, the unauthorized immigrants already here. Thus, public opinion seems generally supportive of the "enforcement-plus" plan. Americans say that illegal immigration is a serious problem, and that it must be stopped, but that those already here should be offered a path toward eventual status as legal residents or citizens.[67]

WHAT DO YOU THINK?

1. Is immigration today substantially different from past waves of immigration? Why or why not?
2. Should the principle of obeying the law be subordinated to the practical difficulties of doing anything about the illegal immigrants already here?
3. Should illegal immigrants be eligible for public services such as schools and medical care?

For more information on the **immigration issue**, see the following Web sites:

Government Sites

www.uscis.gov

U.S. Citizenship and Immigration Services

www.uscis.gov/graphics/shared/statistics/index.htm

Department of Homeland Security, Office of Immigration Statistics

The U.S. CIS (previously the Immigration and Naturalization Service (INS)) offers up-to-date information on immigration policy. The Office of Immigration Statistics produces annual reports and other publications containing useful information on historical and present-day immigration.

Immigrant Rights Sites

www.nclr.org

National Council of La Raza

Provides reports and information about Hispanic Americans, as well as about issues affecting immigrants.

www.nnirr.org

National Network for Immigrant and Refugee Rights

Opposes restrictive immigration legislation, such as the 2006 House bill.

Proponents of Stricter Immigration Policies

www.fairus.org

Federation for American Immigration Reform

Supports reducing immigration to less than 1/3 of current (legal) levels.

www.immigrationcontrol.com

Americans for Immigration Control

Supports deporting illegal aliens and strictly monitoring borders.

guest worker program for immigrants (which could lead to citizenship after a period of years). Some Democrats argued that low-wage immigrant labor would undercut the wages of U.S. workers, and some Republicans claimed that the program would reward lawbreakers. Immigration was a major issue in the 2006 congressional elections and remains a contentious topic in Congress.

Concerns about immigration are not new, but that does not mean they are totally groundless. There are at least three tangible reasons why immigration today differs from that encountered in the past. First, in contrast to earlier periods in American history, immigrants are not entering an economy hungry for unskilled labor. There is no exploding railroad industry to absorb today's immigrants as it absorbed the Irish and the Chinese. There is no expanding steel industry sending representatives to Eastern Europe to recruit workers. The American economy is moving away from manufacturing to a globally integrated service and information economy. Many Americans, especially those who lack technical skills, face severe difficulties in the transition. Research indicates that competition from immigrants undercuts the wages of low-skilled Americans who are already struggling to make ends meet.[29]

Second, levels of government do not share the burdens and benefits of immigration equally.[30] Studies show that immigrants strengthen the national economy. They pay nearly as much in taxes as they consume in government services. But most of the taxes paid by immigrants are federal income and social security taxes. This revenue does not go directly to the states and cities responsible for providing educational and social services to new migrants. In recent decades, more than 75 percent of new immigrants went to six states: California, New York, Texas, Florida, New Jersey, and Illinois. This disparity focuses the costs of immigration much more narrowly than the benefits. Heavy immigration forces local and state governments to cut services, raise taxes, and beg for money from higher levels of government—options that elected officials naturally view as unpleasant.

Finally, whereas late–nineteenth-century law barred a person "likely to become a public charge," the immigration law adopted in 1965 gives preference to those with relatives already in the country. Two-thirds of all immigrants today are relatives of those already present. In consequence, a higher proportion of dependent persons—especially older people—have been admitted in recent years than in previous eras.[31] Current U.S. immigration policy admits fewer taxpayers and more people in need of services than the law that gave first preference to productive workers. Even if immigrants as a group pay as much in taxes as they consume in services, many American taxpayers ask why they should admit *anyone* likely to be a drain on government programs.

These are all material explanations for opposition to immigration. Over and above economic costs, however, many opponents of immigration regard it as a threat to America's political culture. They believe that people who speak different languages, believe in different religions, and practice different customs could threaten American unity and possibly American safety. They fear a divided society, in which groups retain their own narrow identities and fight each other for power and influence. They urge the United States to close the door before too much *pluribus* destroys the *unum*.[32] To understand these fears, however, we need to know precisely what these Americans seek to defend.

Philosophical Unity

From the French visitor Alexis de Tocqueville in the 1830s to the Swede Gunnar Myrdal in the 1940s, visitors have claimed that Americans agree on a common core of values defining what it is to be American. These beliefs usually are described as "individualist," and the political culture they produce is generally referred to as a "liberal" one.[33]

Classical liberalism emerged in Europe after medieval thought disintegrated in the religious wars of the seventeenth century. Whereas earlier philosophies viewed human nature as sinful, requiring authority to keep it in check, liberalism empowered the individual. Authority does not come from God, according to liberal thinkers such as John Locke and Jean-Jacques Rousseau, but instead from a "social contract" conferring privileges and duties on everyone, both rulers and ruled (see Chapter 2).

The social contract preserves individual rights such as life, liberty, and property that are more fundamental than the hereditary privilege of the nobility or the religious privilege of the clergy. Having certain inviolable rights is necessary because liberal thinkers view altruistic sentiments—that is, the desire to "do good"—as too weak to provide a reliable basis for government. Human beings are willing to oppress (or at least mistreat) others if allowed, so rights are a necessary protection.[34]

Instead of viewing individuals as the product of political society, a view that goes back to the ancient Greeks, liberalism makes society the product of individuals. You might wonder what difference this makes. Consider Democratic President John F. Kennedy's famous exhortation: "Ask not what your country can do for you; ask what you can do for your country." Classical liberals shudder at these words. If society is nothing more than a collection of individuals, then any sacrifice demanded for the "greater good" is simply something taken away from one person for the benefit of another.[35]

What kind of political system follows from such a philosophy? A small government, one that treats everyone equally under the law and is limited by individual rights—rights to the exercise of religion, to free expression, and to their own property. Governments in such a system are merely instrumental, not ends or values in themselves. The political system exists to protect and serve individuals, and it may be retained or jettisoned depending on how well it meets these obligations.

The preceding words should have a familiar ring, for the ideas are the basis of America's political system. Indeed, the second paragraph of the Declaration of Independence (see the Appendix at the back of this book) is little more than a summary of liberal ideals: political equality, natural rights, and instrumental government. The Constitution and its Bill of Rights form an elaborate statement of the limits under which government should operate. For this reason, the American constitutional tradition often is called a liberal tradition.

Writers sometimes exaggerate America's level of philosophical agreement. A competing tradition, often called **civic republicanism**, existed at the time of the Revolution.[36] Civic republicanism placed more emphasis on virtue and the public good, less emphasis on individual freedom. Over time it lost ground to liberalism, but the tradition certainly has not disappeared—as indicated by the positive response to President Kennedy's message of self-denial.[37] Modern advocates use the label **communitarianism**, which emphasizes their belief that freedom comes not from individuals making the best choices for themselves but rather, from community members working together to make decisions about the common good.[38]

Other critics point out that the ideals exalted in the liberal tradition often did not extend very far in practice.[39] African Americans did not enjoy equal rights until a century after the Civil War. Full rights and privileges did not extend to women until even later, and the rights of other minority groups, such as homosexuals, remain matters of political controversy today. Nevertheless, there is plenty of evidence that Americans agree to certain basic liberal principles that set them apart from the citizens of other democracies.

American Individualism

Perhaps the most striking difference between Americans and people elsewhere lies in the emphasis Americans place on individual responsibility. Figure 4.2 reports the results of a survey conducted in 10 democracies that asked respondents whether they "completely agree" that "It is the responsibility of the state ('government' in the United States) to take care of very poor people who can't take care of themselves." Note that less than a quarter of the American respondents opted for governmental responsibility, a proportion that is only half as large as that in the next closest country (Germany).

Another survey of six long-established Western democracies found Americans to be similarly uniform in their belief that individuals are responsible for their own welfare. Less than a quarter of Americans supported a government-guaranteed income, disagreeing with majorities of Germans, British, Italians, and Dutch (see Figure 4.3). Fewer than one in three Americans agreed with the notion that government should reduce income inequality. And little more than one-third of Americans, compared to an average of two-thirds in the four European

FIGURE 4.2 Americans emphasize individual responsibility much more than people elsewhere

Why would an immigrant society be more likely to embrace self-sufficiency?

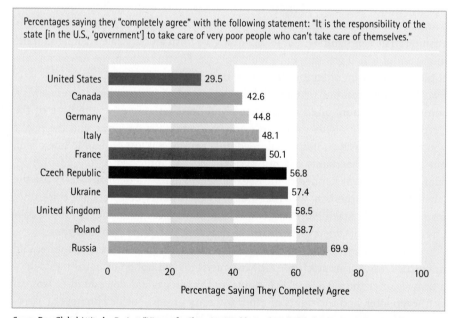

Percentages saying they "completely agree" with the following statement: "It is the responsibility of the state [in the U.S., 'government'] to take care of very poor people who can't take care of themselves."

Country	Percentage
United States	29.5
Canada	42.6
Germany	44.8
Italy	48.1
France	50.1
Czech Republic	56.8
Ukraine	57.4
United Kingdom	58.5
Poland	58.7
Russia	69.9

Percentage Saying They Completely Agree

Source: Pew Global Attitudes Project, "Views of a Changing World: Combined Global Attitudes Project Data," June 3, 2003, available at http://people-press.org/pgap/. The Pew Global Attitudes Project bears no responsibility for the analyses or interpretations of the data presented here.

FIGURE 4.3   Americans give top priority to freedom from government interference rather than to government guarantees of equality

Why is Canada closer to the United States than many European nations?

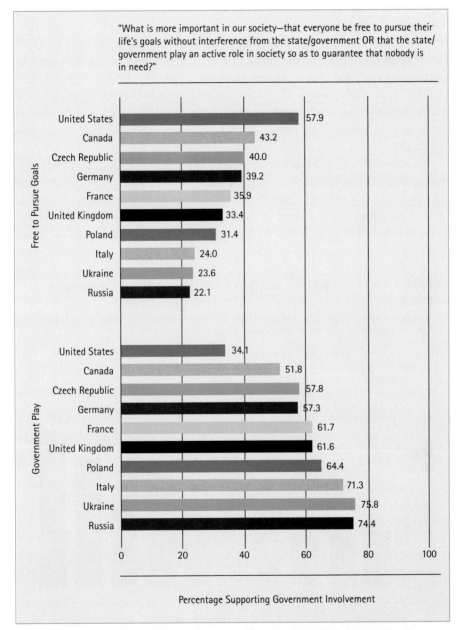

"What is more important in our society—that everyone be free to pursue their life's goals without interference from the state/government OR that the state/government play an active role in society so as to guarantee that nobody is in need?"

Free to Pursue Goals

United States	57.9
Canada	43.2
Czech Republic	40.0
Germany	39.2
France	35.9
United Kingdom	33.4
Poland	31.4
Italy	24.0
Ukraine	23.6
Russia	22.1

Government Play

United States	34.1
Canada	51.8
Czech Republic	57.8
Germany	57.3
France	61.7
United Kingdom	61.6
Poland	64.4
Italy	71.3
Ukraine	75.8
Russia	74.4

Percentage Supporting Government Involvement

Source: Pew Global Attitudes Project, "Views of a Changing World: Combined Global Attitudes Project Data," June 3, 2003, available at http://people-press.org/pgap/. The Pew Global Attitudes Project bears no responsibility for the analyses or interpretations of the data presented here.

democracies, believed that the government should guarantee a decent standard of living for the unemployed.

The American preference for individual responsibility is not simple stinginess. Rather, Americans are suspicious of government (see Chapter 1). They fear its power and doubt its competence. In political scientist Samuel Huntington's view, "the distinctive aspect of the American creed is its anti-government character."[40] People skeptical of government naturally have qualms about letting the state take their money and hand it out to others. At the same time, Americans believe that individual responsibility works. They consider hard work the key to success, whereas people elsewhere are less likely to put faith in personal effort. As a consequence, an overwhelming majority of Americans are optimistic about getting ahead (see Figure 4.4).

One would think that those at the bottom of the economic ladder would be far less optimistic than those at the top. In fact, the American belief in individual achievement bears little relation to personal success. Even the poorest Americans reject a government-guaranteed income, and only the very poorest feel that the government should reduce income differences. Americans at all income levels

FIGURE 4.4   Americans are much more optimistic about the benefits of hard work

Are Americans more optimistic because of their political beliefs or because they genuinely have more opportunity to improve their conditions?

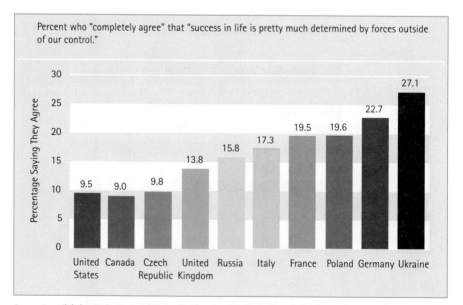

Percent who "completely agree" that "success in life is pretty much determined by forces outside of our control."

Source: Pew Global Attitudes Project, "Views of a Changing World: Combined Global Attitudes Project Data," June 3, 2003, available at http://people-press.org/pgap/. The Pew Global Attitudes Project bears no responsibility for the analyses or interpretations of the data presented here.

FIGURE 4.5   Even American minorities share the individualistic values of the larger society

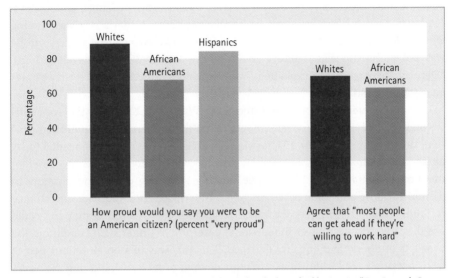

Source: "proud": Harris Poll, June 12, 2002; "get ahead": "The Black and White of Public Opinion," Pew Research Center, October 31, 2005, http://people-press.org/commentary/display.php3?AnalysisID=121, accessed September 9, 2006.

believe in the importance of hard work.[41] Poor Americans are as likely as others to embrace the "work ethic" and as likely to take personal responsibility for their condition.[42] The poor dislike the progressive income tax almost as much as the rich.[43]

Perhaps the most powerful illustration of American individualism lies in the attitudes of minorities. African Americans and Hispanics clearly share in the American Dream less often than white Anglos do. On average they earn less, work in less prestigious occupations, and suffer discrimination in many forms. It comes as no surprise, then, that they are a bit less likely than whites to embrace the American Dream. But it does come as a surprise that they embrace it as often as they do. African Americans and Hispanics are quite similar to white Anglos (see Figure 4.5). In sum, even those who face an extra burden in the American social order still support its basic premises.[44]

All People, Created Equal

Liberal philosophers once assumed that liberty and equality would reinforce each other, and they typically ranked equality right after liberty in their list of cherished values. They assumed that a free society would allow lots of people to generate wealth, therefore equalizing conditions compared to a society in which some of the people labored in chains. At the same time, a wide and nearly equal dispersion of wealth would spread political influence across the society, creating an independent population able to resist encroachments on their freedoms.

Early in American history, liberty and equality probably did go together. Citizens in the democratic United States enjoyed both more liberty and more equality than did their contemporaries in nations run by kings and queens. However, French observer Alexis de Tocqueville foresaw that a day was coming when Americans would have to choose between their two central values, and he was not optimistic that freedom could survive a clash with the leveling spirit. "Democratic peoples," he explained, "want equality in freedom, and if they cannot have that, they still want equality in slavery."[45]

The two ideals clashed after the Civil War, as a result of the Industrial Revolution. Technological developments raised the barriers to economic competition; the start-up capital for a factory greatly exceeded the resources needed to set up shop as a small-town craftsperson. Changes in finance, such as the development of stock markets and large-scale banking, allowed greater concentrations of wealth. Farming and trade relied on government-supported railroads and storage facilities, usually run by corporations that spanned many communities and could use their clout to overpower independent enterprises. Under such conditions, the concepts of liberty and equality diverged. The only way to stop ambitious people from working to collect profit was to regulate their property—inhibiting their ability to compete, limiting their production, or taking away their earnings. Conversely, maintaining liberty required accepting inequality after the Industrial Revolution, a dilemma that only increased with time.

Thus far, however, Tocqueville's worst anxieties about the frailty of liberty seem to have been unwarranted. The United States has maintained support for most freedoms, even when faced with growing financial disparities, because American political culture mandates only a certain kind of equality: equal treatment before the law. One person has the same rights as another, regardless of heredity, religious faith, or the whims of public officials. By contrast, Americans are not committed to economic equality, believing that intelligence and hard work should bring special rewards. They celebrate entrepreneurs who become rich by providing consumers with products or services they want to buy, seemingly agreeing with Madison that "diversity in the faculties of men" inevitably produces inequalities.[46]

Today it is customary to talk about this distinction in terms of the difference between "equality of opportunity" and "equality of results." Americans strongly support equality of opportunity. Everyone should have a fair chance to *pursue* happiness or success. No one has a right to *attain* those things, though, without earning them. Government need not, and maybe should not, use its power to ensure equality of results: similar jobs, similar houses, similar clothes, similar bank accounts. The dilemma between liberty and equality therefore is a false one—public policy need not crack down on personal ambitions to produce the brand of fairness that Americans demand.

However, the global economy continues to challenge how Americans think about equality. Large-scale economic activity obscures whether someone's wealth has resulted from personal accomplishments or from unequal opportunities. Corporations may succeed because of their political pull rather than because of their successful competition in the marketplace. Appointment to plum corporate offices can open up a world of vast financial resources, complete with tax-shielded expense accounts and exorbitant compensation—opportunities that few Americans share.

Discomfort with the ostentatious display of wealth—including gas-guzzling vehicles, aristocratic lifestyles, and giant homes of oriental splendor—grew during the last decade. A 2001 survey by Pew Charitable Trusts found that an increasing number of Americans considered the country "divided into 'haves' and 'have-nots.'"[47] But these attitudes crystallized into an issue on the political agenda after scandals erupted in 2002. Right in the middle of a devastating stock market slide, the American public learned of a whole series of corporate officers who banked millions by selling overvalued stock as their companies secretly approached financial ruin.

Great inequalities now exist in the United States, a situation that has not improved in six decades and in fact has worsened since the early 1970s.[48] Naturally, some Americans have become disillusioned with a political system that can tolerate such inequalities. It is not clear, though, whether public uproar will strengthen the future appeal of policies that equalize economic results. Reform movements typically focus on curbing the worst abuses of corporate power; they seldom attack the foundations of the economic system. Accordingly, the financial scandals of 2002 prompted legislation to improve corporate accounting practices, but did not produce a reform effort sweeping enough to threaten the current style of doing business.

In sum, current events only underscore that Americans consider equality of opportunity sufficient and do not demand equality of results. Success is up to the individual. This belief shows up in government policy. The United States spends a smaller proportion of its national income on social welfare than most other democracies do. But the United States historically has spent a larger proportion of its national income on education than other democracies have. Education is a means by which individuals improve their skills and make themselves useful, a policy that enhances opportunity—so it is one of the few areas of society that Americans want government to equalize (see Table 4.1).

Ideology, American Style

Readers whose primary knowledge of American government comes from observing current events may wonder how scholars can seriously propose that a philosophical unity governs national politics. News coverage constantly echoes with energetic, and sometimes vicious, attacks fired back and forth among political figures subscribing to different "ideologies." The clashes sometimes rise beyond personal squabbles, instead involving clear debates over the proper direction of government. These debates sometimes unite most members of one major political

TABLE 4.1   All policies are not created equal

Americans share a basic belief in the importance of equality, but their support for using policy to equalize social resources varies sharply depending on the particular policy area. *Are the policies with strong support for equalization distinct from those with lukewarm support?*

QUESTION: Do you believe it is the responsibility or isn't the responsibility of the federal government to make sure minorities have equality with whites in each of the following areas, even if it means you will have to pay more in taxes?

Policy Area	Percentage Saying "Yes"
Courts/police	73.0%
Schools	70.0
Health care	62.0
Housing	50.1
Jobs	47.0
Income	46.2

Source: Washington Post/Kaiser Family Foundation/Harvard Survey Project, 2001 Harvard Racial Attitudes Survey; 1995 Race Poll. Questions on courts/police, schools, health care, and jobs were asked in 2001, housing and income in 1995.

party against the other. If this is the sound of consensus, one reasonably might ask, what would real conflict sound like? How can we dismiss ideological disagreements that seem so real and so fundamental to the people participating in them?

Answering this challenge requires an understanding of political ideologies and how they operate. An **ideology** is the basic lens through which someone observes and evaluates government, the collection of orientations a person uses to impose order on a complicated political world. When a new conflict intrudes on the political agenda, citizens need some way to determine where they stand on the issue, and their individual ideologies can provide the shortcuts needed to formulate a quick opinion. Furthermore, to the extent that a candidate for office can convey his or her ideology, it aids voters in predicting how the candidate will react to unanticipated issues that do not spring up until after the election.

This is all quite abstract, but usually it works in a fairly straightforward way. Consider one example of an ideology: a person's basic perspective on the meaning of human conception. Some people believe that human life begins when an egg becomes fertilized, others that it occurs at some later stage of fetal development. This ideological difference will divide people on a host of political issues. The obvious one is abortion, because someone who considers a fertilized egg to be human life will find the procedure more objectionable than someone who does not. But these ideologies also speak to a host of other issues related to the origin of human life, such as cloning, stem-cell research, surrogate parenting, and even prenatal care. Voters can evaluate that whole gamut of specific issues in terms of their ideology toward human life, and they may be able to anticipate a candidate's positions if they know whether the politician is pro-life or pro-choice.

Ideologies are not equally encompassing, however. Political philosopher Karl Mannheim distinguishes an ideology according to how fundamentally it shapes one's political thinking.[49] Some ideologies are "particular," a way of thinking about politics that grows out of a specific set of interests or personal preferences. Other ideologies are "total," in that they refer to the very basis of one's existence, the entire mental apparatus that determines how someone relates to the world. The liberal ideology that unites Americans is the all-embracing, total sort of ideology. It grew out of the religious, economic, and scientific changes that characterized the Enlightenment period of European thought, which roughly corresponded to the eighteenth century.

Liberals differed fundamentally from people who believed in rule by kings (that is, monarchists). Economically, liberals tended to emerge from the capitalist economy developing at the time, so they stood out for their belief in the importance of property rights, their faith in contracts, and their sense that commercial relations should take place with limited government interference. In terms of religion, liberals emphasized the dignity of the individual human soul and the importance of observing nature's rules as a means of getting closer to religious truth. They thought that education and spiritual development shaped a person's character, downplaying the significance of heredity. The Enlightenment period was also a time of great mathematical and scientific advances, which encouraged people's faith in logic and careful observation—as well as their sense that individuals could work together, without direct coordination by a higher governmental authority, to produce a vibrant society. These impulses combined into a comprehensive world view, one that early settlers to the American colonies usually brought with them.

The relatively distinct perspective that united philosophical liberals allowed Thomas Jefferson's Declaration of Independence to call it "self-evident" that all individuals are created equal and enjoy unalienable rights. Such ideas were hardly evident to King George III or his ministers during the war for independence. Nor are they necessarily obvious to some of the modern rivals to liberal political theory, such as Marxists (who view religion, science, and politics as subordinate to economic relations) or theocrats (who believe truth comes primarily through religious leaders with a close connection to a higher power). For the most part, though, liberal ideals *are* taken for granted by the bulk of Americans today, which is why the United States lacks strong communist or religious political parties in the European mold. Political debate in the United States operates largely within the bounds of liberal philosophy, with all sides, however strident, endorsing their policies by invoking similar ideas of freedom, fairness, and individuality.

Some Americans do endorse conflicting "liberal" or "conservative" or "libertarian" political ideologies. But these are examples of Mannheim's "particular" ideologies, growing out of specific interests and preferences. They usually revolve around the best method for achieving social goals, rather than around what the goals ought to be. **Libertarianism** most closely resembles the beliefs of liberal political philosophy, in that it gives individualism a central place in political life and permits only minimal use of government power. But modern liberals and conservatives do not stray far from this perspective. They both have areas of life that they think government ought to leave alone—and in the areas for which they do promote heightened government activism, their reasons tend to be stated in terms of promoting freedom, equality, or individual rights more actively.

Any generalization about the political system usually has exceptions, but it is possible to describe how modern liberals and conservatives differ (see Table 4.2). American **liberalism** supports an active government in the economic sphere but permits a high degree of autonomy when citizens make moral choices. Liberals endorse using political institutions to address widespread social inequalities, such as those associated with race or gender, but not to promote other forms of good behavior. They prefer more international cooperation to solve world problems and look to foreign policy as a way of promoting freedom and equality worldwide.

Conservatism, meanwhile, endorses less government regulation of economic matters but favors public policies that will shape the nation's culture in a moral direction rather than an amoral one. Conservatives shy away from allowing government to intrude on people's private spheres of life—such as families, churches, clubs, or businesses—and may endorse taking steps to strengthen private institutions weakened by prior government policies. On many issues, they favor decision making at the state

TABLE 4.2   Typical issue preferences by ideology

No ideological grouping is completely uniform, but it is possible to offer a profile of the issue positions typically held by a proponent of each political ideology. *Are three ideologies adequate for capturing the issue preferences of most American voters?*

Issue	Classical Liberal (Libertarian)	Modern Liberal	Modern Conservative
Strong Federal Government	Against	For	Against
Higher Taxes, More Services	Against	For	Against
Aggressively Equalizing Wealth	Against	For	Against
Increasing Business Regulations	Against	For	Against
Affirmative Action	Against	For	Against
Gun Control	Against	For	Against
Generous Foreign Aid Payments	Against	For	Against
Legislation to Promote Morality	Against	Against	For
Incentives for Traditional Family Structures	Against	Against	For
Weakening Rights of the Accused	Against	Against	For
Strong, Aggressive Military	Against	Against	For
Religion in Public Schools	Against	Against	For
Subsidies to Help American Businesses	Against	Against	For
Laws to Regulate Internet Content	Against	Against	For
Removing Abortion Rights Guarantee	Varies	Against	For
Decentralizing Government Power to States	Varies	Against	For
Outlawing Capital Punishment	Varies	For	Against
Active Federal Judiciary	Varies	For	Against
Agricultural Subsidies	Against	Varies	Varies
Taxes on Imported Goods	Against	Varies	Varies
Ban on Flag Burning	Against	Varies	Varies
Greater Limits on Immigration	Against	Varies	Varies

and local level rather than at the national level. They see foreign and defense policy as a means for promoting the American way of life, so they endorse a strong military and an independent foreign policy focused on national security concerns.

In sum, liberals, conservatives, and libertarians all share a liberal political philosophy in the broader sense; they agree that freedom and equality are good things but differ on how best to protect and promote them.

Why a Liberal Political Culture?

We now return to the question posed at the start of the chapter. How can we explain the apparent contradiction: a population that is strikingly diverse in its ethnic, racial, and religious makeup but surprisingly uniform in the beliefs and values that constitute its political culture? How has American political culture survived waves of immigrants bred in different social environments?

Part of the answer lies in the way the nation formed. Early settlers in the United States, although ethnically and religiously diverse, nevertheless originated from a narrow economic slice of the European population. Impoverished peasants usually could not afford the costs and risks of transporting their lives to the American frontier, and the colonies held few attractions for European nobles.[50] Rather, the early settlers overwhelmingly came from what, looking back, we might call the middle class, the very group that embraced liberal ideas. They found nothing in the Americas to dispute such ideas because, as political scientist Louis Hartz emphasizes, the colonies lacked their own feudal tradition. There was no hereditary elite to provide the basis for the kind of aristocratic conservatism that persists even today in Europe. Nor was there an oppressed peasant class that might form the basis for radical agrarian parties.

Perhaps as important as what the United States lacked, however, is what it had. In particular, it had a great deal of land. North America was a sparsely populated continent over which the United States steadily expanded.[51] Some historians suggest that the frontier operated like a social safety valve: Rather than revolt against intolerable conditions (the only option in the settled countries of Europe), struggling citizens found it easier to pack up their belongings, move west, and start again—as did many of the rural protestors in Shays' Rebellion (see Chapter 2).

A plentiful supply of land and a scarcity of labor meant that ambitious individuals could and did succeed. The individualistic values that the early settlers brought with them were reinforced by conditions in the new country. Generations of radical scholars have plaintively asked, "Why no socialism in America?"[52] The simplest answer is that Americans never saw much need for it. Why risk trying to change the political system, as a strategy for personal improvement, when more direct methods are readily available? Individual effort usually has been enough to provide an acceptable life for most people.

Still, questions remain. The frontier closed more than a century ago, and labor shortages have not been of much concern for more than half a century. Even if historical conditions reinforced the beliefs and values of the early settlers, of what relevance is that today? The millions of immigrants who arrived after the Civil War were not from liberal societies. Most of them came from authoritarian states with established churches, and most had lived their lives in communal peasant societies that *did* have feudal traditions. Habit cannot explain their embrace of American political culture, nor can simple lessons taught in books or in American schools.

One possibility is that American institutions teach liberal political philosophy indirectly rather than just directly. Political scientist Sven Steinmo argues that American government is so fragmented that it rarely acts in a positive way to improve society.[53] Often it is "gridlocked," or unable to address social problems at all—and when it does act, it often does so via the exchange of political favors among special interests (see Chapters 8 and 9). In consequence, immigrants to the United States pick up on the same wisdom already possessed by natives: Look to yourself because you cannot look to government, and best keep government limited because it will usually act against the public interest. In short, American institutions may preserve the ideas that gave rise to them.

Immigrants may even be healthy for the liberal tradition. Rather than posing a threat to American traditions, as many feared, the flow of diverse peoples to America may have reinforced and strengthened American traditions. How could that be? The answer lies in what social scientists refer to as *self-selection*. With the tragic exception of African Americans, immigrants came to the United States voluntarily. It is possible that the sort of person most likely to leave family, friends, and village behind is exactly the sort of person most likely to adopt the liberal tradition.

Remember that through most of history, immigration was not a matter of taking a train to Dublin, Frankfurt, or Rome and catching a flight to New York. Before the Civil War, the journey usually took months, as immigrants walked to a port and then suffered through a long journey below deck on a sailing ship. Even after the Civil War, when steamships shortened the ocean voyage and railroads shortened the land journey, the trip still took weeks. Most of the people who booked passage knew that they would never see their relatives or their homes again.[54] What kind of people made such a decision?

In all probability, the people who migrated already were—relative to their own societies—unusually individualistic. They were willing to leave the communal order of their societies. They were more ambitious, more willing to run risks in the hope of bettering themselves. Bigoted as it was, even the Immigration Commission in 1911 recognized that "emigrating to a strange and distant country . . . is still a serious and relatively difficult matter, requiring a degree of courage and resourcefulness not possessed by weaklings of any class."[55] In short, although they had never heard of the liberal tradition, immigrants already displayed much of its spirit.

Today's immigrants seem no different. They have left their homes and families in Asia, Africa, Mexico, and South America. They have endured hardships to come to a new land with a different culture and language. In some extreme cases they have risked life and limb to emigrate, as with the boat people of southeast Asia who braved pirates, sharks, and storms, and with the Cubans who swam from rafts to the Florida coast. Such people display a kind of individual initiative that can fairly be considered "American," regardless of their nationality.

True, many come to the United States after they are pushed off their land, when crops fail, or when unemployment takes away their jobs. Emigration under such circumstances may not seem to have occurred by choice, such that it would select for individualists. Nevertheless, not everyone in poor or troubled countries chooses to try life elsewhere. Many remain in their homelands, enduring miserable conditions. The few who do emigrate, therefore, still exercise a politically meaningful choice. And those who dislike American values can always return to their home countries, as a third of all immigrants eventually do, so self-selection also shapes the ones who stay behind.

In sum, immigration and the resulting diversity should not threaten core American values. On the contrary, successive waves of immigrants should rejuvenate those values. People who are willing to endure hardships, eager to work hard, and convinced that they can create a better life are unlikely to demand an intrusive government. Rather, whatever their skills or education, these immigrants will be the kind of self-sufficient people that Americans themselves seek to become.

Chapter Summary

For more than two centuries the United States has been a study in contrasts. On the one hand, the nation always has been diverse socially, containing a wider array of ethnic and religious groups than most other lands. On the other hand, the diverse citizenry of the United States has long shown a higher level of agreement on fundamental principles than is found in other democracies.

FIRST MUSLIM IN CONGRESS Democrat Keith Ellison, of Minneapolis, Minnesota, was elected to Congress in 2006. A Muslim, he did not highlight his faith in his campaign, choosing to focus on more traditional campaign issues such as the Iraq War and health care reform.

America's fundamental political principles grew out of a classical liberal political philosophy that stressed the rights and liberties of individuals, while giving much less emphasis to their duties and obligations to the community. Today, that philosophy is reflected in a greater emphasis on individual responsibility and hard work, as well as greater suspicion of government, than is found in other countries.

Throughout American history, many native-born citizens have feared that immigration threatened the distinctly American political culture. Yet American political ideals have proved surprisingly resilient. In all likelihood, immigrants reinforce rather than weaken the spirit of individualism in the United States. The very fact of their mobility suggests that they have an ambitious, individualistic outlook compatible with the American political culture.

KEY TERMS

civic republicanism, p. 85
classical liberalism, p. 84
communitarianism, p. 85
conservatism, p. 94

ideology, p. 92
liberalism, p. 94
libertarianism, p. 93
political culture, p. 74

SUGGESTED READINGS

Borjas, George. *Heaven's Door: Immigration Policy and the American Economy.* Princeton, NJ: Princeton University Press, 1999. Argues that immigration has hurt the poorest native-born workers, especially African Americans. Calls for restricting immigration and limiting it to better-educated and more highly skilled people.

Hartz, Louis. *The Liberal Tradition in America.* New York: Harcourt, 1955. This classic, if at times impenetrable, discussion of the liberal tradition argues that the absence of feudalism allowed liberal ideas to spread without resistance in the United States.

Huntington, Samuel. *Who Are We? The Challenges to America's National Identity.* New York: Simon & Schuster, 2004. Controversial argument that Latino immigration threatens America's "Anglo-Protestant" values.

Lipset, Seymour Martin. *American Exceptionalism.* New York: Norton, 1996. The latest work on American political culture by an eminent senior scholar who has spent much of his career studying it.

Simon, Julian. *The Economic Consequences of Immigration,* 2nd ed. Ann Arbor, MI: University of Michigan Press, 1999. Argues that the U.S. economy would benefit from an increase in legal immigration.

ON THE WEB

IMMIGRATION AND NATURALIZATION SERVICE
www.uscis.gov
This comprehensive site, maintained by the U.S. Department of Justice, covers all facets of immigration in the United States. It provides statistical reports on the history of immigration to the United States, as well as information on the current guidelines for becoming an American citizen.

DIVERSITY INC
www.diversityinc.com
Sponsored by several major corporations and public interest organizations, this site provides original content on many groups in the American population, with a particular focus on diversity in the work force.

Public Opinion and the Media

Contrary to the impression we might get from popular mythology, American wars have often been controversial. The War of 1812, the Mexican War, the Civil War, World War I, Korea, Vietnam—all provoked substantial domestic opposition. Indeed, World War II may have been the only war in American history in which the country was united in its determination to fight the war through to victory.

Given that background, it should have come as no surprise that, as President George W. Bush prepared the nation for an invasion of Iraq in late 2002 and early 2003, the American public was divided about whether such a war was necessary or desirable. In every major prewar poll that was taken on the subject, a majority of Americans supported taking military action against Saddam Hussein, but a sizable minority always opposed it. ABC News and the *Washington Post*, for example, asked this question eight times between January and mid-March, 2003: "Would you favor or oppose having U.S. forces take military action against Iraq to force Saddam Hussein from power?" On average, 64 percent were in favor, 32 percent opposed.

As in past conflicts, once the fighting started, Americans closed ranks behind the military effort. Following the beginning of the conflict on March 20, surveys found that about three-fourths of the public supported the war, while just 20 percent opposed it. Polls also showed that 70 percent of Americans approved of the way Bush was "handling the situation in Iraq."

Had the war in Iraq ended the same way that the 1991 Gulf War did, with a clear U.S. victory followed by rapid withdrawal of American forces, there is little doubt that the second Gulf War would be regarded today as one of the signal achievements of George Bush's presidency. But the war didn't end with such a clear cut victory. Although U.S. forces captured Baghdad on April 9, 2005, pacifying and rebuilding Iraq has proved to be vastly more difficult than defeating Saddam Hussein's army.

In a classic study of public attitudes about the wars in Vietnam and Korea, political scientist John Mueller showed that Americans' opposition to both wars mounted in direct proportion to the number of U.S. casualties.[1] Slowly but steadily, the same thing has occurred in Iraq. The day Baghdad fell Gallup found that 76 percent of the American public said that it was "worth going to war." By 2006, amid media reports from Iraq of suicide bombings, roadside explosives, and roving militias, a narrow majority of Americans took the opposite position: 55 percent said the Iraq War had not been worth fighting and only about 40 percent of the public approved of President Bush's performance.[2]

The public's shifting positions on Iraq reflect a larger truth about America's new democracy: Voters have very high expectations of their leaders, and they often use election time to express their displeasure. Leaders must be careful to anticipate public demands, or they will not lead for long. To complicate matters, public opinion can be difficult to measure accurately and can also be unpredictable, shifting in response to current events. As the data on the Iraq War show, many Americans may come to oppose a policy that they themselves endorsed when the crucial decisions were being made.

Furthermore, most Americans derive their knowledge of government from media organizations that are themselves major players in both the U.S. economy and the U.S. political system. Although the media do not speak with one voice, the professionals who convey political news—and who disseminate news of public opinion to government officials—have their own interests and personal traits that influence how they carry out the critical function of keeping Americans informed.

For these reasons, elections capture the people's demands imperfectly. Elections drive American politics, but it is not always clear what drives voters.

Sources of Public Opinion

The reason for public opinion's importance is captured aptly by political scientist V. O. Key's definition: "those opinions held by private persons which governments find it prudent to heed."[3] Democratic governments find it "prudent" to heed the opinions of private persons, of course, because of elections. Note that in Key's conception, public opinion can, but need not, be expressed actively. Even if public opinion is silent, or "latent," public officials may act or fail to act because they fear arousing it. This is the so-called law of anticipated reactions, whereby elections influence government even though they do so indirectly and passively.[4] The common phrase "public opinion wouldn't stand for that" acknowledges that public opinion can exercise power subtly.

The opinions that people hold reflect numerous influences. Most of these sources are stable and personal: values, self-interest, education. But applying them to particular issues may not be straightforward. And some influences—such as the media—can shift rapidly. Thus, even a politician who tries to "give the people what they want" may be surprised come Election Day.

Children begin to form political attitudes at an early age. Research carried out in the 1950s and 1960s generally concluded that the single most important **socializing agent** was the family, and that within the family the mother was most important—she spent far more time with the children in that era. Studies found that many children identify themselves as Democrats or Republicans well before they have any idea what the parties stand for. And older children are very likely to share the party affiliation of their parents. A few scholars concluded, however, that schools were more important than family.[5] And the influence of family may have declined in recent decades, given increases in single parenthood, in the divorce rate, and in mothers working outside the home.

Socialization often works indirectly, by forming the *beliefs and values* on which individuals act later in life. For example, a very young child may learn fear of, or comfort with, nudity—and this psychological orientation may shape adult attitudes about such political issues as strip clubs restrictions or pornography bans. But sometimes socializing agents consciously try to activate political attitudes. The Catholic Church officially opposes abortion, for example, and rank-and-file Catholics are indeed less accepting of abortion than are mainline Protestants and Jews.[6] Whether the influences lie in the distant past or in the present, differences among people with different socialization experiences emerge regularly on all kinds of issues.

Although people form many of their attitudes in childhood, their political views continue to develop over the course of their lifetimes. Childhood socialization can be reversed by adult experiences, and especially by one's *self-interest*.[7] For example, blue-collar workers are more sensitive to a rise in unemployment that throws them out of work, whereas professionals and managers are more sensitive to a rise in inflation that drives up interest rates and depresses the overall business climate.[8] People often evaluate public policy by asking, "What's in it for me?"

Education shapes public opinion, but it belongs in a separate category because it works in varied ways. Schooling shapes the interests people have by determining their occupational choices as well as their tastes in entertainment. It shapes the beliefs people adopt, because teachers and college professors tend to hold political attitudes that differ from those of the general public and may consciously or unconsciously socialize students to see the world as they do.[9] Finally, the skills learned in colleges and universities may change how people think about the political world. Highly educated people tend to be willing to tolerate minorities or deviant groups,

FIGURE 5.1   Higher education is associated with greater tolerance of diversity

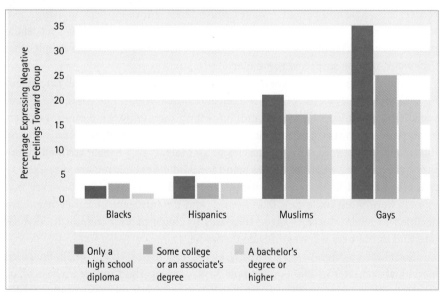

Source: American National Election Study, 2004.

for example, which may reflect how they analyze and adapt to diversity (see Figure 5.1).[10] Higher education also is associated with a greater sense of **political efficacy**—the belief that the citizen can make a difference by acting politically—which may be a result of the skills learned in school that make participation easier.

Measuring Public Opinion

In the nineteenth century, measuring public opinion was an art form. Politicians looked at informal straw polls, consulted community leaders, or scanned the newspapers' editorial pages to understand the public mood. But the process was less like science and more like "reading tea leaves."[11] The advent of modern survey research in the 1930s (pioneered by a former journalism professor named George Gallup) clarified public opinion, making it a much more powerful political force. The key to this change was the scientific design and administration of randomized surveys that have become a standard tool of the modern election campaign.

Most often researchers measure public opinion via telephone polls. Various firms and academic organizations contact individuals, ask them questions, and report the responses. Of these, Gallup is the most widely recognized name. Newspapers, magazines, and TV networks also sponsor regular polls—NBC News/*Wall Street Journal*, CBS News/*New York Times*, ABC News/*Washington Post*, *USA Today*/CNN—and base major stories on them.[12]

Sampling Error

The general public is sometimes suspicious of survey research, refusing to believe that fewer than 2,000 people can speak for an entire nation. They may be right to distrust polls, but the reason for skepticism is misplaced. Statisticians have demonstrated that the responses of a few thousand people usually mirror the opinion of 220 million adults quite well—so long as everyone has a roughly equal chance of being polled. That is, the small group needs to approximate a **random sample** of the population. For this reason, telephone surveys often use random-digit dialing; to equalize the odds of selection, a computer randomly selects which numbers to call within a given telephone exchange. People with unlisted numbers may be irritated when they answer their phones and hear pollsters, but no one has given out their numbers—the computer has found them by accident!

Even if an opinion poll based on a random sample could be conducted perfectly, it still would not get estimates of public opinion exactly right, because who participates in the poll would be a matter of chance. But the existence of such **sampling error**—the error that creeps into polls because of the necessity of taking a sample of the public rather than asking everyone—is not the main reason why polls are sometimes unreliable. On average, relatively small random samples will yield a correct picture of political attitudes, and the sample need not be very large before those estimates are consistently precise.

Consider a simple example to illustrate. Suppose that every reader of this book flipped a coin 1,500 times. The most likely result, the "right" answer in this instance, would be 750 heads—because a coin flip turns up heads half the time. But of course some of you would get a few more heads by chance, and some a few more tails—that's the sampling error. Statistical theory tells us precisely how much each experiment would bounce around the typical result. It is a statistical fact that 95 percent of the time we would find between 705 and 795 heads (between 47 and 53 percent). This range is what pollsters mean when they report that surveys have a "margin of error" of plus or minus 3 percent: 95 percent of the time their survey method would turn up an estimate within 3 points of the right answer.

In the real world, though, the calculated sampling error captures only one source of inaccuracy, probably a relatively minor one—although it can make more of a difference in polls that sample places, such as voting precincts, rather than individual people. Exit polls, polls taken on Election Day to project winners and estimate support for candidates among different demographic groups, must rely on this latter method. In the 2000 race, the main exit polling organization, Voter News Services, drew an unrepresentative sample of precincts in Florida, leading network news anchors to prematurely project a Bush win in the state. The main dangers with random-sample surveys are instead the inaccuracies that do not result by chance but, rather, occur because the survey method is biased away from the truth—either because of *selection effects* or because of *measurement error*. We discuss those two sources next.

Selection Effects

The key to getting an unbiased sample is to make sure that individuals cannot affect whether they are in or out of the sample. If we were to poll attendees at a hockey game, an opera, or even a political science lecture, our sample would be suspect, because the members of each of these audiences share a common interest—in hockey, opera, or political science—that brought them together. This common interest differentiates them from the American population at large, and it might do so in ways relevant to the survey questions being asked.

Errors in survey estimates caused by an unrepresentative method of selecting respondents is called a selection effect. Just as immigrants to the United States are not representative of citizens in their home countries because they elect to migrate (see Chapter 4), survey respondents will not be representative of the general public if they have control (directly or indirectly) over whether to participate. Similarly, a survey will be biased, and will produce consistently inaccurate results, if the researcher's sampling method consciously or unconsciously selects a certain kind of participant.

Using random telephone samples certainly does not solve the problem with **selection bias.** Some of these selection effects are small. For example, most telephone polls leave out citizens of Hawaii and Alaska and they all omit the small portion of the U.S. population without telephones. Some selection effects are more serious, though. Typically, more than half the original sample either never answer the phone or refuse to be interviewed.[13] Regardless of whether unavailability results from personality traits or lifestyle differences, the people whom surveys fail to sample may differ in politically relevant ways from those who participate. For example, research shows that surveys tend to underrepresent men, young people, whites, and the wealthy—all traits that are related to one's political attitudes.[14]

Selection bias will be even more severe for surveys in which broadcast stations or Web sites encourage any and all viewers to participate. These may be good ways to generate listener or viewer interest, but they have no more scientific value than letters to the editor or the feedback heard by elected officials at town meetings. People who take the time and trouble to participate are those who care the most. They are not representative of the much larger population. For example, in 2006 an online poll sponsored by the liberal blog DailyKos found that Wisconsin Senator Russell Feingold was respondents' top choice for president in 2008, with 30 percent of the vote.[15] Other polls taken at the same time showed Feingold in the low single digits, and the senator later announced he would not run.

Measurement Error

Opinions are difficult to gauge using surveys, which makes them subject to **measurement error**—to being measured improperly. Part of the problem is that opinions are not physical facts that can be measured objectively, such as the length of a rope or the weight of a candy bar. Beliefs and judgments may be hard to quantify, and answers may depend on the options provided for a particular question.[16] If a "don't know" option is not available, respondents' answers can be particularly random or ill-informed.

Also, people hold complex attitudes. Yet the speed necessary for opinion polls may not allow a detailed picture of those views. The questionnaire cannot take too long, or costs will be very high and respondents may stop cooperating. The answers have to be easy to code into a computer and summarize, or the results from a large sample will be too complicated to process and report to others. For these reasons, how people answer a poll depends very much on the wording of the questions: whether they are *confusing*, whether they are *value-laden*, and whether they are *too blunt* to capture the complex range of opinions people hold.

Confusing Questions   The Holocaust Memorial Museum opened in Washington, D.C., in the spring of 1993. Coincident with the dedication of the museum, the American Jewish Committee released startling data from a survey conducted a few months earlier by Roper Starch Worldwide, a respected commercial polling organization. The poll indicated that 22 percent of the American public believed it "possible . . . the Nazi extermination of the Jews never happened" and that another 12 percent were unsure. In total, one-third of all Americans apparently had doubts about whether the Nazis murdered 6 million Jews in World War II.

Editors and columnists jumped on the story. What was wrong with the American people? Had the educational system failed so miserably that in the short span of 50 years the worst genocide in history had become a matter of mere opinion? Was anti-Semitism so widespread and deeply ingrained in the population that Holocaust denials by the lunatic fringe were making headway? What did the Holocaust poll say about the American people?

Very little, it turned out. The Gallup Organization—a Roper competitor—soon demonstrated that the Roper poll was gravely mistaken, because Roper had asked a confusing question. The exact wording of Roper's question was

> *Does it seem possible, or does it seem impossible to you that the Nazi extermination of the Jews never happened?*

One of the first rules of survey research is to keep questions clear and simple. The Roper question fails that test because it contains a double negative (*impossible ... never happened*)—a grammatical construction long known to confuse people. Gallup conducted a new poll in which half of the sample was asked the Roper question with the double negative and the other half was asked an alternative question,

> *Does it seem possible to you that the Nazi extermination of the Jews never happened, or do you feel certain that it happened?*

This seemingly minor change in question wording made a great deal of difference. In the half of the sample that was asked the Roper question, one-third of the respondents again replied that it was possible the Holocaust never happened or that they were unsure, but in the half that was asked the alternative question, less than 10 percent of the sample were Holocaust doubters. Roper eventually retracted its initial poll results. The whole episode had been the product of a simple mistake.[17]

The point of the Holocaust poll example is that no one accused the Roper organization of choosing a bad sample or a sample that was too small. Rather, Roper asked a poorly constructed question that produced an inaccurate measurement.

Value-Laden Wording   What look like minor variations in question wording can produce significant differences in measured opinion. This is especially likely when the variations involve the substitution of emotionally or politically "loaded" terms for more neutral terms. A classic example comes from the controversy over social spending. Consider the following survey question:

> *We are faced with many problems in this country, none of which can be solved easily or inexpensively. I'm going to name some of these problems and for each one I'd like you to tell me whether you think we're spending too much money, too little money, or about the right amount.*[18]

When the public was asked about "welfare" in late 2004, the responses showed that a plurality of Americans believed that too much was being spent:

Too little   23%
About right   34%
Too much   40%

Conservatives might take heart from such a poll and use it to argue that public assistance to the poor should be slashed. But when the same people in the same poll were asked about "assistance to the poor," a large majority responded that too little was being spent:

Too little   69%
About right   23%
Too much   6%

Liberals might take heart from such a poll and use it to argue that welfare spending should increase.

Looking at these two questions together, though, it's hard to ascertain what the public really thinks. Both invoke the same policy, but different stereotypes. "Welfare" carries negative connotations; it seems to prompt people to think of lazy and undeserving recipients, so-called welfare cheats. But "assistance to the poor" does not seem to evoke these negative images. This is clearly a case where the careless (or clever) choice of question wording can produce contradictory findings on a major public issue.

Oversimplified Questions   The Supreme Court handed down the *Roe v. Wade* decision in 1973, striking down restrictions on a woman's right to terminate a pregnancy in the first three months (and limiting restrictions on that right in the second trimester). Since then, the abortion issue has never left the national agenda, so most Americans probably decided long ago where they stand on it. In fact, answers they give to similar questions about abortion are fairly constant over time.

Yet different survey questions appear to suggest very different conclusions about public opinion on the abortion issue. Some suggest that the United States is strongly anti-abortion, and others portray the United States as overwhelmingly pro-choice. If this variation does not result from uncertainty and does not result from variation over time, the difficulties must result from inconsistent measurement. The main problem is that most survey questionnaires are too limited to capture the complexity of attitudes toward abortion.

Consider the effects of question wording shown in two recent surveys. One 2004 poll prompted:

Please tell me whether or not you think it should be possible for a pregnant woman to obtain a legal abortion if the woman wants it for any reason.

By a substantial margin (58 percent to 38 percent), Americans thought it should not be possible.[19] As pro-life activists claimed, Americans were pro-life. Should Democratic campaign consultants have advised their clients to flip-flop to the pro-life side in anticipation of the next election? Well, probably not. The next year, a different survey asked,

> The 1973 Roe v. Wade decision established a woman's constitutional right to an abortion, at least in the first three months of pregnancy. Would you like to see the Supreme Court completely overturn its Roe v. Wade decision, or not?

By a resounding margin (63 percent to 30 percent), Americans said that *Roe v. Wade* should not be overturned.[20] As the pro-choice spokespersons claimed, America had a pro-choice majority. Should Republican campaign consultants have advised their clients to flip-flop to the pro-choice side?

Which poll was right? Probably neither. Upon close examination, both survey questions are suspect. Each contains words and phrases that predispose people to answer in one direction. The first question uses the phrase "for any reason." Most Americans are not *unconditionally* pro-choice, any more than their other political ideals are unconditional. If forced to choose yes or no, some genuinely pro-choice people will say no, believing that there must be reasons for an abortion that even they would consider invalid. The second question leans in the opposite direction. Some generally pro-life people might be hesitant to "completely" overturn a major Supreme Court decision. Thus, even on an issue where many people have stable, considered opinions, variations in question wording can make a big difference in the answers they give.

A survey also can skew answers by how it frames an issue, encouraging the respondent to answer questions from one point of view rather than another. For example, a CBS News/*New York Times* poll asked participants to respond to the following statement:

> Even in cases where I might think abortion is the wrong thing to do, I don't think the government has any business preventing a woman from having an abortion.[21]

By close to a 3-to-1 margin (69 percent to 24 percent), Americans agreed with that sentiment. Apparently, the country stands firmly in support of abortion rights. On the other hand, when another CBS News/*New York Times* poll asked people whether they agreed or disagreed with the stark claim that "abortion is the same thing as murdering a child," Americans were deeply split (46 percent agreed and 41 percent disagreed). Similarly, a majority of Americans regularly agrees that "abortion is morally wrong" (51 percent agreed, and 34 percent disagreed in the aforementioned CBS News/*New York Times* poll).[22]

The first question uses a *choice* frame. Individualistic Americans favor freedom of choice, especially when it involves freedom from governmental interference. The second question and the statement use an *act* frame. Many Americans who favor choice nevertheless are troubled by the act of abortion. Hence, even poll respondents with stable, well-defined positions on abortion might react differently to these variations in wording—depending on which values the interviewer seems to be asking them to endorse. It is no surprise that the pro-choice side of the debate consistently employs one frame, the pro-life side the other.

The National Opinion Research Center (NORC) uses an abortion question that illustrates clearly that the complicated relationship Americans have with abortion causes answers to be sensitive to what pollsters specifically ask:

> *Please tell me whether or not you think it should be possible for a pregnant woman to obtain a legal abortion if*
> 1. *the woman's health is seriously endangered?*
> 2. *she became pregnant as a result of rape?*
> 3. *there is a strong chance of serious defect in the baby?*
> 4. *the family has low income and cannot afford any more children?*
> 5. *she is not married and does not want to marry the man?*
> 6. *she is married and does not want any more children?*

For the most part, answers to each of these various conditions change little over time. After moving in a liberal direction in the late 1960s, opinion stabilized at the time of the *Roe* decision, and stayed remarkably constant thereafter (see Figure 5.2). Yet answers vary widely across the conditions. On average, Americans favor

FIGURE 5.2   Popular attitudes toward abortion have been remarkably stable since *Roe v. Wade* (1973)

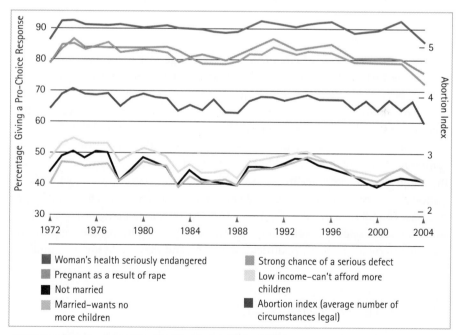

Woman's health seriously endangered
Pregnant as a result of rape
Not married
Married–wants no more children

Strong chance of a serious defect
Low income–can't afford more children
Abortion index (average number of circumstances legal)

Note: Respondents who answered "don't know" are included in the calculation.

Source: Calculated by the authors from the General Social Survey 1972–2004 Cumulative Data File.

FIGURE 5.3   Americans tend to favor abortion rights, but with restrictions

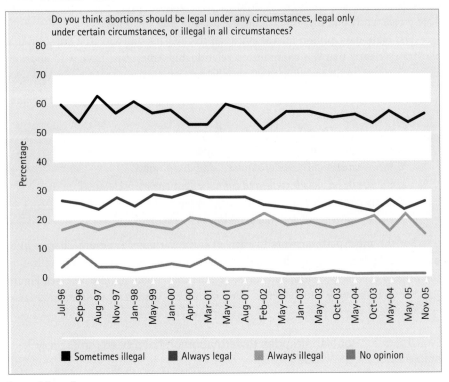

Source: Gallup polls.

legal abortion in half of the circumstances, with large majorities supporting abortion in the first three ("traumatic") circumstances, but more people regularly opposing abortion in two of the second three ("elective") circumstances.[23]

Consistently inconsistent, Americans are pragmatic, not ideological, on the abortion issue. They favor the right to choose, but not an unconditional right to choose in every possible circumstance—a complexity that the shorter, and more common, abortion questions fail to tap. Surveys show that rape, birth defects, and threats to the mother's health are overwhelmingly viewed as justifiable circumstances, but personal convenience and gender selection are not. The mother's age, financial condition, and marital status divide the population deeply. For this reason, Americans oppose overturning *Roe*, but as Figure 5.3 shows, they approve of laws that make abortion more difficult to obtain, and they oppose public funding.

Governing by Public Opinion?

Public opinion is very sensitive to how it is measured, but knowledge about survey techniques has increased greatly over time. The more leaders learn about precisely what the public wants, the more potential they have to respond to those desires. In general, as this book argues, leaders commonly do that. However, the limits on "governing by public opinion" do not all result from imperfections in how pollsters measure public attitudes. Leaders may choose to ignore public opinion polls for other reasons. Public attitudes may not be a reliable basis for choosing good policies—or even for choosing policies that will make voters happy in the long run. And most elected officials do not represent the nation as a whole; they represent a specific set of constituents whose opinions vary in their intensity.

The Limits of Public Opinion

Polls offer a snapshot of public opinion, but the demands that voters express at election time may not reflect the answers that they will provide a stranger who knocks on the door or who calls on the telephone. Poll results are vulnerable to how people approach political life since, on most issues, people are *uninformed, unconstrained* by ideology, and *unpredictable* because of their inconsistency.

Americans Are Uninformed   Americans are an accommodating people. If a pollster asks a question, many will cooperate by giving their best answer, even if they have never thought about the question or have no basis for deciding what their answer is. A 1989 survey provides an extreme example. People were asked to rate 58 ethnic and nationality groups. Although one group included in the list ("Wisnians") was fictitious, 29 percent of the sample ranked them anyway.[24]

On many issues, people have little or no information. The extent of popular ignorance is most obvious when surveys pose "factual" questions. As shown in Figure 5.4, only a third of adults older than age 26 could identify the political party controlling their state legislatures in 2003. Less than a quarter could identify the Speaker of the U.S. House of Representatives; more than a third could not even identify the political party in charge. Young adults did even worse.

Elections are not standardized tests, of course; voting intelligently does not require knowing the answers to all sorts of factual questions. But widespread ignorance extends to important matters of government and public policy. During the 2004 election campaign, for example, two-thirds of 18- to 29-year-olds said that one or both presidential candidates favored reinstating the draft, when both President Bush and his challenger John Kerry had repeatedly stated their opposition to such a measure.[25]

Why do people have so little knowledge of basic facts and issues? The answer is that most people seldom pay attention to politics. News magazines sell far fewer copies than entertainment and lifestyle magazines do. Far more Americans love *Raymond* than watch *The NewsHour with Jim Lehrer*. Far more care about who becomes the next "American Idol" than care about who becomes their next U.S. senator. Upon learning the full extent of popular ignorance, some politically involved students react critically, jumping to the conclusion that apathetic Americans are irresponsible people who fall far short of the democratic ideal. Such reactions overlook the reasons why people pay so little attention to public affairs.

FIGURE 5.4 Americans are not very knowledgeable about the specifics of American government

Young people know even less about government than relatively ill-informed older Americans.

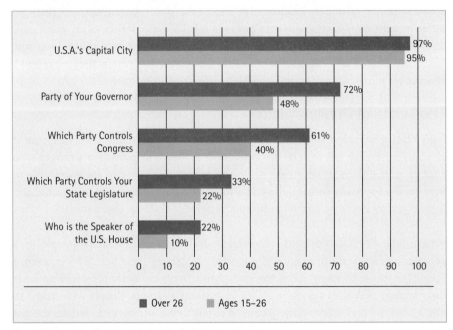

Source: Representative Democracy in America Project, 2003.

The simple fact is that most people have little time for politics; it is something of a luxury interest. They work hard to take care of the "necessities"—paying the bills, caring for their families, and nurturing personal relationships. They may not have time or energy for the *New York Times* and C-SPAN after dropping off and picking up children, commuting, working, and housekeeping. The effort required to stay informed competes with human necessities such as recreation and relaxation.

Those who criticize ordinary citizens for paying little attention to public affairs often have jobs that enable them to stay informed with little effort. For example, in a university environment, political conversation is a common diversion, and for many professors and students, being informed is relevant to academic pursuits. Likewise, many journalists have jobs that involve following politics: If they are not informed, they are not doing their jobs. But most Americans do not have these incentives, a fact that critics in academia and the media tend to forget. Nor is it clear what such people would do with their knowledge of public affairs if they were able to obtain it.

The general point is that gathering, processing, and storing information is neither effortless nor free. For most Americans, bearing such **information costs** brings them little tangible return.[26] Few citizens believe that they have enough power to influence how conflicts in Afghanistan, Sudan, or Iraq will resolve. And when faced with a costly activity that has no obvious benefit, many of them quite rationally decide to minimize their costs. Thus, from a logical standpoint, the puzzle is not why so many Americans are ill-informed; the puzzle is why so many are as informed as they are.[27]

Of course, information costs do not fall equally heavily on all people. Education makes it easier to absorb and organize information; thus, it comes as no surprise that more-educated Americans are better informed than less-educated ones (see Figure 5.5). In addition, the benefits of information are not the same for all people on all issues. Most people will be better informed on issues that directly affect their lives. Parents and teachers are more knowledgeable than other citizens about school operations and budgets. Human services providers are more knowledgeable about welfare and other public assistance policies. Such **issue publics** are different from the large mass of citizens in that their members' occupations make information cheaper to obtain, as well as more relevant, interesting, and valuable.[28]

In addition to varying across people and issues, the costs and benefits of being well informed may vary over time. When major events make it seem worthwhile to be better informed, information levels surge. During the fall of 2001, for example, after an unknown terrorist mailed envelopes containing the deadly disease anthrax

FIGURE 5.5 Higher education is strongly associated with greater knowledge of politics and government

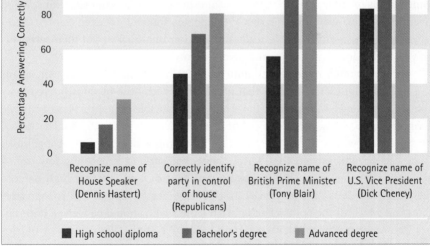

Source: National Election Studies, 2004.

to members of Congress and the news media, nearly 80 percent of the American public correctly responded to the question, "As far as you know, which form of anthrax is more often fatal: the skin form, the inhalation form, or do you think they are equally likely to be fatal?"[29] After such burning issues are resolved and the controversy subsides, however, information levels return to normal.[30]

Of course, some people consider it their duty as citizens to be informed, so they stay attuned to public affairs simply because they believe it is the "right thing" to do. Other people find politics to be intrinsically interesting, in the same way that some enjoy sports or the arts. For such people, staying informed is a matter of taste or values, not the result of any tangible benefit from being informed. What others view as costs, they see as a source of satisfaction.[31]

Americans Are Unconstrained   Another characteristic that makes it easy to misinterpret public opinion is that even when people have reasonably firm views on issues, those views often are surprisingly unconnected to each other. That is, the American people are not constrained by political ideology.

People who are deeply interested and involved in politics, whether as activists or as office holders—such people are traditionally called **political elites**—tend to have well-structured **ideologies** that unite their positions on policy issues. To know that such a person is a "liberal" or a "conservative" is to know a good deal, because underlying principles and political alliances mold their system of belief (see Chapter 4). Ordinary citizens—traditionally called the **mass public**—are another matter.[32] Rather than believing consistently in either activist or minimal government, an important trait that distinguishes liberals and conservatives, ordinary citizens generally favor federal spending in some areas but oppose it in others. They favor regulation in some areas but oppose it in others. They favor toleration for some groups in some situations, but not for other groups in other situations. When given the option, about one-quarter of the population will not even classify themselves on a liberal–conservative scale, and another one-quarter put themselves exactly in the middle: "moderate, middle of the road."[33]

Pessimists often interpret the nonideological thinking of ordinary Americans in a negative light and presume that preferences with little obvious interconnection are somehow less valid than those with a predictable structure. Here again, we disagree. In our view, American political ideologies are as much *social* as logical constructions, which is why they change in meaning over time. Personal views aside, can anyone explain the logical connection among supporting low capital gains tax rates, being pro-life, opposing gun control, and favoring high defense spending? Positions on such issues may go together for liberal and conservative elites, but why? Maybe political elites are the ones who should be viewed critically.

The American people have a strong pragmatic strain. Perhaps views unconstrained by ideology should be taken as evidence of American common sense. Whether you regard ideological thinking as good or bad, however, bear in mind one point: Because they presume that ideological thinking is the norm, party and issue activists, media commentators, and many public officials tend to conclude too much on the basis of opinion polls and voting returns. Support for one variety of government action may indicate nothing about support for another, seemingly similar government action. Support for a candidate's position on one issue may suggest little or nothing about that candidate's "mandate" to act on seemingly related issues. In short, the nonideological nature of people's issue preferences means that elites often hear more than the voters are saying.

Public Opinion Is Inconsistent   Given that people often have not thought about issues or the connections among them, it should come as no surprise that the public sometimes sends contradictory messages. Opinions with little basis are not likely to abide when survey questions change emphasis or as time passes. For example, in 1980, when Ronald Reagan defeated Jimmy Carter and the Republicans made striking gains in Congress, many in the media interpreted the election results as a "resurgence of conservatism" or a "turn to the right" in American politics. The evidence, however, was confusing.[34]

A poll taken in 1978 reported that an overwhelming 84 percent of the citizenry thought the federal government was spending too much money. A smaller majority thought that the federal government had gone too far in regulating business. Popular sentiments such as these appeared to foretell the Reagan victory that followed. Then again, the same poll asked the same people which domestic programs they favored cutting and which areas of business activity they favored deregulating. Surprisingly, majorities often indicated that most domestic activities deserved *higher* funding or *more* regulation—hardly a conservative resurgence!

Obviously, such contradictory views confuse political debate, distorting whatever message voters try to send during an election. President George W. Bush pushed a tax-cut plan early in his administration that a majority of voters supported in polls at the same time they endorsed increased spending on social security and education. In each case, both parties could refuse to compromise or to adapt their platforms, firm in the belief that public opinion supported much of what they stood for.[35]

Why is public opinion so inconsistent? Obviously, ignorance is part of the explanation. People are unaware of how little is being spent on programs such as "welfare" and foreign aid. Thus, they believe, erroneously, that cutting such unpopular programs will free up sufficient funds to maintain popular ones. Some voters also believe that waste and inefficiency are so pervasive that simply streamlining government operations would allow painless spending increases.

Not all examples of inconsistency reflect insufficient and inaccurate information, however. Citizens so consistently contradict themselves when applying general principles to specific cases that other explanations must be at work. We have seen that people favor cutting spending in general but not specific programs. They also oppose amending the Constitution but favor amendments to require a balanced budget, limit congressional terms, and ban flag burning. And, perhaps most interesting of all, they support fundamental rights but regularly make numerous exceptions.[36] As Figure 5.6 shows, virtually all citizens say "people should be allowed to express unpopular opinions"—but then half refuse to extend this right to people who offend racial or religious groups.

It is easy to label such inconsistencies hypocrisy, and some do. Or such inconsistencies may indicate that ordinary people do not have a clear understanding of rights, and perhaps they do not. But there are other, more positive interpretations as well. To the law professor, the newspaper editor, or the political activist, rights

FIGURE 5.6   Americans tend to endorse general principles but make numerous exceptions to them

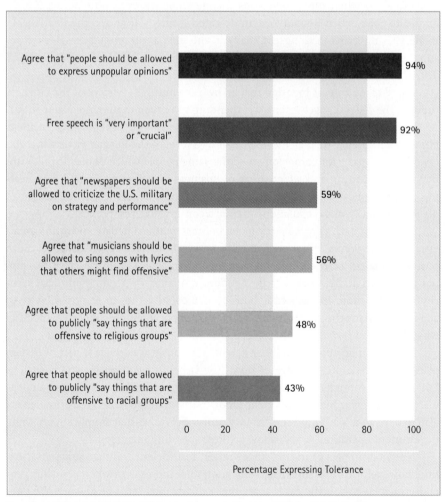

Source: "unpopular opinions": Gallup Poll, June 12–July 5, 2002; "free speech": Gallup Poll, November 10–12, 2003; "religious groups," "military," "musicians," "racial groups,": *State of the First Amendment, 2005*, First Amendment Center, www.firstamendmentcenter.org, accessed September 17, 2006.

may be viewed as absolutes. Letting government infringe on guaranteed protections leaves open the possibility that government will water them down until they are meaningless. But Americans tend to be pragmatists. Few distrust their elected government so much that they are unwilling to bend the rules once in a while. The absolutist language of rights is foreign to the problem-solving American way of thinking. Rights are good things, but they must be balanced against other values.[37] Americans may feel no contradiction in advocating a right while simultaneously endorsing significant exceptions.[38]

The Role of Representation

Never before have politicians been so well equipped to measure and interpret public opinion. Indeed, critics regularly complain that policy is too "poll driven." During the 2000 presidential campaign, George W. Bush promised that he would end the permanent campaign. "A responsible leader ... makes decisions based upon principle, not based upon polls or focus groups," he told an audience in Michigan. Six months into his presidency, though, observers noted that the Bush White House was polling about twice a month.[39] The permanent campaign seems inescapable. The presidency aside, however, there is no guarantee that public policy will follow public opinion even when preferences are clear. The reason is that although individual politicians may be highly responsive to public opinion, the system of representation as a whole may not be.

The Columbine tragedy provides an illustration. On April 20, 1999, two male students at Columbine High School in Colorado killed 12 of their peers, a teacher, and wounded more than 20 others. The killers used two shotguns, a semiautomatic pistol, and a semiautomatic rifle in their murderous spree. This was the fourth school shooting in little more than a year. Other young males had shot teachers or students in West Paducah, Kentucky; in Jonesboro, Arkansas; and in Springfield, Oregon. Whether because of the cumulative impact or the sheer scale of the rampage, the Columbine shootings energized elected officials into action. In particular, antigun members of Congress decided to revive a stalled juvenile-crime bill so that they could use it as a vehicle for passing new gun control laws.

One controversial measure was a Senate proposal to require background checks on potential customers at gun shows. The measure initially had failed because many Republican lawmakers saw it as an undue burden on gun consumers, but the inflamed state of public opinion following the school shootings gave some of them second thoughts. After still another shooting (in Conyers, Georgia), the Senate reconsidered its earlier decision and narrowly approved the proposal. By much wider margins, the Senate adopted other provisions mandating trigger locks on, or lock boxes with, every handgun sold, outlawing imports of high-capacity ammunition clips, and raising the age at which juveniles could buy handguns and assault weapons. The amended bill passed the Senate by a comfortable margin and then went to the House of Representatives.

House Republican leaders also thought that the aroused state of public opinion required some response. Speaker Dennis Hastert (R-IL) commented that "This is one of those rare times when the national consensus demands that we act" and promised that the House would pass a gun control measure.[40] But the issue was now thoroughly entangled in partisan politics. Vice President Gore obviously believed that his highly visible gun control stance would aid his presidential bid, and congressional Democrats hoped to use the issue to help regain control of the Congress in 2000. The key target group was suburban voters—especially women, whom polls showed favored gun control more than men did.[41] To appeal to them, Democrats framed the issue as one of protecting children.

The Democrats were not united, however. A senior House Democrat, John Dingell of Michigan, was an avid hunter and a former National Rifle Association (NRA) board member. Dingell worked with Republican leaders to develop an amendment that would weaken the Senate's gun show restrictions. Forty-five Democrats followed Dingell and joined Republicans to pass the weaker provision. Then, angry liberal Democrats who believed the legislation did not go far enough joined angry conservatives who felt it still went too far. Together, they defeated the bill. Gun control was dead.

At first glance this story seems to be one of irresponsible or even corrupt behavior by the Congress. Certainly, that is the way the media portrayed it. The story line offered by the media was simple: Public opinion counted less than the campaign contributions and arm twisting of the NRA. But this account is too simplistic. Members of Congress do not get reelected by opposing an aroused majority of their constituents in exchange for an interest-group endorsement or a $5,000 PAC contribution. Rather, the failure of the House to pass gun control measures shows the imperfect connection between aggregate public opinion and national public policy.

Members of Congress typically represent districts of 630,000 people, their **constituents**. These voters may hold opinions quite different from those of the country as a whole. The national distribution of opinion is of little importance to members of Congress unless they happen to be considering a run for the presidency; the distribution of opinion in their districts is what counts. And what counts even more is the distribution of opinion among the voters who elected them. So it is no surprise that the minority of Democrats who followed Dingell's lead came mainly from rural and mixed districts, where guns tend to be a more important part of daily life. Many representatives who voted against gun control followed the sentiments *in their districts*.

Still, given the high level of support for the gun control provisions, it is likely that some representatives did vote against district majorities. Was this the NRA at work? To some extent, probably yes, but remember that interest-group endorsements and campaign contributions don't vote. There have to be voters in the district who will act on the group's support. The problem for gun control activists is that their supporters are much less likely to act on their convictions than are their opponents, who see government attempts to limit access to guns as an attack on their way of life. Even Democratic Minority Leader Richard Gephardt (D-MO) conceded, "The 80 percent that are for gun safety just aren't for it very much. They're not intense."[42]

Indeed, although most polls registered a high level of support for gun control, the same polls indicated that the public did not regard it as one of the more important issues facing the country. One national poll indicated that gun control ranked twelfth in importance as a voting issue in the next election.[43] Not many supporters of gun control are intense, **single-issue voters** (if they vote at all), but the opponents of gun control certainly are.

Does Public Opinion Matter?

American voters often fail to provide clear and useful signals to politicians, because people's views are uninformed, unconstrained by ideology, and therefore unpredictable. Nor is it certain that a good politician should make decisions based on national opinion, even when it is clear—both because people's views vary in intensity and because no one except the presidential administration represents the entire nation. Despite all these limits, however, leaders do tend to "govern by public opinion" inasmuch as voters usually get what they want in the long run. Benjamin Page and Robert Shapiro, for example, analyzed a huge collection of surveys and concluded that American public policy follows public opinion. When trends in opinion are clearly moving in one direction, public policy follows. The more pronounced the trend, the more likely policy is to follow (especially when the public moves in a liberal direction).[44]

The reason why public opinion can serve as a guide, despite all its flaws, is that what individuals do is not directly connected to what groups do. People individually may serve as poor guides for policy making, but public opinion in the aggregate possesses many virtues that individual's opinions lack. Public opinion as a whole operates in a fashion that is fairly rational and fairly consistent. This may seem like a difficult idea, but it makes sense intuitively, as indicated by the common maxim "The sum can be greater than the parts." Think of a grade school orchestra. Individually, the young musicians are so unsteady that it is difficult to identify the tune each is playing; but put them all together, and the audience can make out "Twinkle, Twinkle Little Star." So it is with public opinion.

Most of the public is not ideological, but the public at large certainly understands that the Democrats are to the left of the Republicans on most issues.[45] So even if individual voters do not know a candidate's ideology or party affiliation, many people do know this, and even the less-informed voters will tend to back the appropriate candidate by taking advice from other voters or organizations that share their perspective.[46] The same process works with individual issue preferences. Any one person's opinions may contain some random elements caused by lack of information or lack of reasoning, but the general direction or "mood" of the public is easier to detect, and voters act on their shifting moods in a predictable fashion.

Political scientist James Stimson shows, for example, that if hundreds of survey questions are analyzed together, they indeed yield a portrait of an electorate that was turning to the right in the years leading up to Reagan's election.[47] Given these views, voters sensibly showed greater inclination to select a Republican.

In short, the process of aggregation may cancel out individual error and enable the central tendency to emerge. That is why, if one looks at the general direction of policy as shaped by the electoral system, public opinion emerges as a critical influence on the government.

Media Influence on Public Opinion

Public opinion on the whole responds predictably and rationally to the information available to it. For many critics of the American political system, though, this begs a very important question: How good is the information available to the overall public? A public that reacts sensibly to poor or distorted information could still be a hindrance in a democratic society. Following popular opinion might even be dangerous because it would be open to manipulation.

Concern with the quality of the nation's information providers is a legitimate source of anxiety. Very few Americans experience national politics first hand. Most learn about the national government through **mass media**—affordable communications technologies capable of reaching an extensive audience. They rely on newspapers, magazines, broadcast stations (for television or radio), Web sites, or at least on word-of-mouth political commentary from friends and relatives who form part of the mass-media audience. Yet the country contains a small number of major media organizations, so the sources for political information could be narrow.

Furthermore, the men and women who staff these organizations do not form a random sample of the U.S. population. People choose whether to enter journalism and that creates another selection effect. The attitudes of people who enter the journalistic profession inevitably will be unrepresentative of what Americans typically believe.

On the other hand, news reporters and editors generally try to perform their jobs in as "unbiased" or "balanced" or "objective" a way as possible. They may fail on occasion, but news coverage is not as distorted as media critics customarily suggest—at least not in obvious ways, such as favoring one political party or ideology. And even if media organizations occasionally distribute a biased product, it is doubtful that these distortions make much difference for American attitudes. Audience members are both sophisticated and stubborn; they recognize unfair news coverage and resist opinions different from their own.

Which Information Sources Do Americans Use?

Communication is a two-way street. No one can make people read newspapers, listen to the radio, watch TV, or visit a Web page. Citizens are free to consume or ignore any message. These choices affect what information becomes available, because media companies are profit-making enterprises. Their growth or decline reflects the tastes of the popular audience.

Surveys show that TV supplanted newspapers as the public's principal source of information in the early 1960s and has remained on top ever since. In one 2006 poll, 57 percent of Americans indicated that they saw TV news "yesterday," while only about 40 percent could say the same about newspapers or radio (the Internet lagged far behind).[48] Figure 5.7 shows that most Americans also view TV news as the most trustworthy. In short, TV is America's dominant information provider, although people still turn to newspapers in large numbers when they wish to learn about state and especially local elections.[49]

While television is still the medium of choice, the public's overall pattern of media consumption is becoming more diverse, as Figure 5.8 indicates. As recently as 1993 the nation regularly tuned in to nightly network news broadcasts, but today no nationwide source of news can command the attention of a majority of Americans.

Individuals vary not only in the types of news they watch, but also in their absorption of information.[50] Well-educated or older individuals are particularly likely

FIGURE 5.7   Contemporary Americans consider TV their most credible source of news

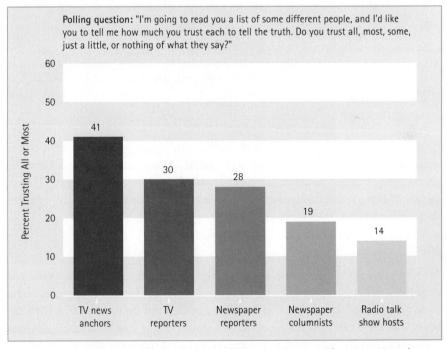

Source: Center for Survey Research and Analysis, University of Connecticut, Newspaper Editors Survey, September 12–October 1, 2003

FIGURE 5.8   Americans are relying on a wider range of news sources

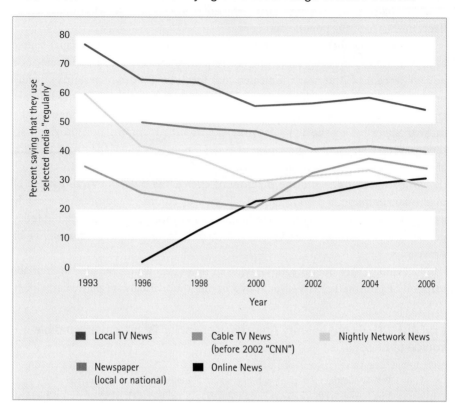

Source: Pew Research Center for the People and the Press, "News Audiences Increasingly Politicized; Online News Audience Larger, More Diverse,"Washington, D.C.: Pew Research Center, June 8, 2004, p. 5; Pew Research Center for the People and the Press, "Online Papers Modestly Boost Newspaper Readership, Washington, D.C., Pew Research Center, July 30, 2006, p. 1. Pew Research Center polls for CNN data.

to rely on newspapers, as are whites. Newspaper supporters argue that print is more informative than TV, but research fails to uphold that argument once the characteristics of the audience (such as education) are taken into account.[51] That is, people of comparable background tend to learn about the same amount, whether they rely on print or television.

Media Biases

Modern journalists strive to be objective. They are supposed to report events and describe conflicts accurately so that voters can make informed judgments about their government. If reporters and editors usually lived up to this ideal, then the small number of established news sources would not be much cause for concern. But news organizations and other media corporations represent an important player in the political system—essentially an institution with its own interests, values, and operating procedures. The people who staff these organizations differ from the general public. The mass media therefore might threaten democracy's operation by providing skewed information or even by trying to manipulate popular opinion.

Many observers believe that the media do skew the news. The most common charge is that the media show political bias, but most academic critics believe that other sorts of bias are even more serious.

Ideological Bias   Conservatives often complain about the "liberal media." There is no doubt that liberal viewpoints are overrepresented among practicing journalists. Numerous studies report that journalists are more Democratic than the population at large. A 2004 survey of the national press corps found that only 7 percent identified themselves as "conservative," while 33 percent of the electorate at large did so.[52] More detailed analyses indicate that journalists hold views that are even more liberal than those of other college-educated professionals, especially on social issues such as abortion, crime, and gay rights.[53]

But do such biases show through in the news? Some studies find evidence of partisan bias on the part of reporters. One sophisticated analysis that statistically matched media coverage with the views of similar members of Congress estimated that most major media outlets hold positions close to those of a moderate Democrat.[54] On a less serious note, another study found that George W. Bush was the butt of about 20 percent more late-night jokes than John Kerry during the 2004 election campaign.[55]

Although journalists do deviate from objectivity and Republicans suffer more than Democrats, lapses are not as common as media critics imply. In the 2004 election campaign, Democrat John Kerry received a considerable amount of negative coverage, interrupted only briefly for generally positive news about the Democratic convention in July. The media tend to be hard on incumbents, losers, and those caught up in scandals—even when they are Democrats. Similarly, late-night TV hosts usually focus on whoever offers the best material. Bill Clinton, who left the presidency in 2001, still pops up from time to time in comedians' monologues.

Although they are less vocal, critics on the left of the political spectrum also charge that the media are ideologically biased—only *they* see a conservative slant. Whatever the personal views of rank-and-file journalists, they work for profit-making enterprises that rely on corporate advertising. They cannot afford to emphasize ethical or environmental abuses perpetuated by business, because to do so would offend potential advertisers. Media celebrities also attract generous honoraria from corporate interests who invite them to give speeches, leading critics to call them "buckrakers" rather than muckrakers.

Some defenders of the journalistic profession point to the contradictory critiques as evidence that no real ideological bias exists. If one group says the news is too liberal and another says it is too conservative, they imply, then coverage must be just right. This response rules out the possibility that *both* criticisms may be correct. News professionals resemble others who share their social status: progressive reformers with left-wing social views who nevertheless reap the solid incomes and generous retirement benefits that go with being on a corporate payroll.[56] Just as John Kerry in 2004 could be both too left-wing for the Republicans and too comfortable with big business for the Greens, so it is possible for the typical journalist to be biased in a way that will prompt different critics to use different terminology.

The weakening of the dominance of the big-three networks should reduce any existing bias. Local news and public affairs programs are more likely to reflect community sentiments and less likely to represent the biases of network news operations headquartered in New York, Washington, and Los Angeles. Cable channels broadcast programs produced by conservative and evangelical groups. Columnist John Leo even notes the rise of comedy that showcases "anti-liberal humor," including HBO's Dennis Miller, "blue collar comic" Larry the Cable Guy, and the irreverent Comedy Central cartoon *South Park*.[57] Talk radio has a conservative slant. The Internet is open to all points of view, and libertarians are especially well represented there.

Biased Story Selection   Periodically, frustrated citizens write to editors to complain that all their newspapers ever print is bad news. These readers are criticizing the professional norms that journalists use to define what is "newsworthy." People working hard and contributing to their communities are not news; the kidnapping of a little girl is. A government program that works well is not news; one that is mismanaged, corrupt, or a failure is. This negative tone has only become more prominent over time, with reporters today exhibiting what some media critics consider a "junkyard dog" mentality—attacking anyone who comes within range.[58]

Newsworthiness also favors things that are new, especially those that are exciting and unusual. Sudden events make better news than gradual developments or persistent conditions. A crisis lends itself to the kind of hit-and-run coverage favored by contemporary media. Heroes and villains, not abstract social and economic developments, form the ingredients of a good story. This bias is particularly characteristic of TV, which is even more fast-paced than print. TV needs dramatic events, colorful personalities, bitter conflicts, short and snappy comments (sound bites), and, above all, compelling pictures. A frequently heard maxim is "If it bleeds, it leads."

A media tendency to favor sudden, short-term developments can have serious political implications. Stories that do not fit media needs may receive insufficient, or at least distorted, treatment.[59] For example, journalists lionized Private Jessica Lynch of West Virginia after she was injured, captured, and then rescued during the war in Iraq (to the point that critics charged that reporters were helping the U.S. military fabricate "shamelessly trumped-up claims"). They paid far less attention to other members of the Army's 507th Maintenance Company, some of whom died, some of whom fought heroically, and some of whom (including another young woman, Shoshana Johnson) spent two weeks longer in captivity. Rarer still were articles examining the broader question of why and how a navigational error led a maintenance company right to the front lines.

Professional Bias   A third kind of media bias arises from the demands of the journalism profession itself. A few journalists are experts who work specific beats— business reporters, education reporters, health reporters, Supreme Court reporters, and so on. But most reporters and journalists are generalists who lack specific substantive expertise. They operate on tight deadlines and must start from scratch on each new story. Thus, on many subjects more complex than scandals and conflicts, they are dependent on experts and other outside sources for information and interpretation.

Ironically, despite the familiar image of the investigative journalist, reporters uncover only a small fraction of the scandals they report—probably less than one-quarter.[60] Government agencies expose the lion's share, and they generally do so officially, not through surreptitious "leaks." Moreover, as journalists themselves recognize, the news media have increased their emphasis on entertainment.[61] Especially in the case of TV, looks and personalities are more important today than a generation ago, but even serious newspapers have become more like tabloids.

The lack of internal expertise and the competitive pressure for ratings and sales contribute to an unattractive feature of modern political coverage: "pack journalism," in which reporters unanimously decide something is The Big Story and stampede after it. Comedian Jon Stewart prefers a different image: Small children playing soccer, all clumped together and thoughtlessly chasing a ball.[62] The recent war in Iraq has increased concerns about whether American journalists are "shirking their duty" to keep an eye on government. "Regardless of their own views on the war," according to Mark Weisbrot, co-director of the nonpartisan Center for Economic and Policy Research, "American journalists became the Bush administration's major means of promoting it."[63] Beginning in about mid-2003, however, the tenor of most American war reporting became sharply more critical, leading to criticism from Republicans that the media were unfairly emphasizing setbacks over positive developments.

Political News

The mass media play an important role in democratic politics. Ideally, they transmit information about problems and issues, helping voters make intelligent choices among the candidates who compete for their votes. Many critics believe that the general biases we have just discussed can cause media coverage of elections and government to fall far short of the ideal.

Emphasis on Personalities   The president is a single individual with personality and character; therefore, the presidency is inherently more interesting than a

(text continues on page 127)

SHOULD FREEDOM OF THE PRESS BE LIMITED TO PROTECT NATIONAL SECURITY?

The First Amendment says "Congress shall make no law . . . abridging the freedom of speech, or of the press . . . ." On its face, this seems like a straightforward declaration. But does the freedom of the press extend to cases in which national security is stake? While democracies thrive on free information, sometimes secrecy is necessary to the conduct of an effective foreign policy—especially in times of war. This tension between secrecy and democratic accountability has yet to be fully resolved.

Prior restraint—forcibly preventing media outlets from reporting on an issue—is among the most drastic steps the government can take. Many legal scholars argue that the First Amendment clearly prohibits it, but the U.S. government in rare cases has tried to halt publication of sensitive information.

The most celebrated case of attempted prior restraint was the 1971 publication of the Pentagon Papers. A Defense Department consultant named Daniel Ellsberg, convinced that the Vietnam War was misguided, leaked a copy of a classified government history of the conflict to several newspapers. The *New York Times* and later the *Washington Post* published portions of that history, now known as the Pentagon Papers, for several days until lower courts—at the urging of the government—ordered them to stop. The Nixon administration argued that publication of the secret document would "result in great harm to the nation," including "the death of soldiers, the destruction of alliances, the greatly increased difficulty of negotiation with our enemies, [and] the inability of our diplomats to negotiate."[101] The newspapers disagreed, and appealed to the Supreme Court.

A woman sells newspapers in Manhattan.

In a 6–3 decision released only four days after oral arguments, the Court sided with the newspapers, allowing publication to continue. While the justices left open the possibility that prior restraint might be allowed in certain extreme circumstances, they said the government had a "heavy burden of showing justification for . . . such a restraint."[102] And the Nixon administration, in the Court's view, did not meet that burden.

This is an unusual case. More common are situations in which media outlets themselves must decide when it is appropriate to print previously-secret information. An interesting case of this kind occurred in 2006, when the *New York Times* published details of a secret program, begun shortly after 9/11, in which counterterrorism officials had gained access to transaction records from an international financial database that included banking information on many

SHOULD FREEDOM OF THE PRESS BE LIMITED TO PROTECT NATIONAL SECURITY? *(continued)*

Americans. The Bush administration viewed the program as a "vital tool" in the war against terrorism, saying that it had played "a hidden role in domestic and foreign terrorism investigations . . . and helped in the capture of the most wanted [al] Qaeda figure in Southeast Asia."[103]

Administration officials had asked the paper not to publish the article, saying that "disclosure of the . . . program could jeopardize its effectiveness." But the *Times* refused to halt publication. As Bill Keller, the newspaper's executive editor, summed up his conclusion, "We remain convinced that the administration's extraordinary access to this vast repository of international financial data, however carefully targeted use of it may be, is a matter of public interest."[104]

WHAT DO YOU THINK?

1. How should courts decide whether an issue is serious enough to merit prior restraint? What kinds of evidence should the courts expect from the government that would fulfill the "heavy burden" of justification? What if the government felt that by presenting such evidence in court, national security would be endangered?
2. Did the *New York Times* make the right decision in publishing its story on the administration's use of financial data to track the activities to terrorists? Do you agree with Keller's argument that the *Times* should publish stories that are "a matter of public interest," despite government pleas for secrecy?

For more on government secrecy and journalism, see the following Web sites:

www.cjog.net

The Coalition of Journalists for Open Government promotes government transparency.

News Organizations

http://abcnews.go.com/sections/politics
www.cnn.com
www.latimes.com
www.foxnews.com
www.washingtonpost.com

These industry leaders provide thorough coverage of political news.

collective such as Congress or an abstraction such as the bureaucracy. The president receives the lion's share of media coverage.[64] And not only does Congress play second fiddle, coverage of the institution has declined in recent decades.[65]

The problem, of course, is that the president is only one part of the government, a part with fairly limited powers (see Chapter 10). Thus, the media can cause citizens to focus on the president to a degree that is disproportionate to the office's powers and responsibilities.

This focus of the media on personalities seems to be a universal tendency. Note that it is similar to building sports coverage around superstars, such as

WAR HERO
Former POW Jessica Lynch drew widespread media coverage, even as she tried to focus attention on her comrades. *Why does even war coverage tend to focus on a few personalities?*

baseball slugger Barry Bonds or ace pitcher Pedro Martinez. An effective governmental team, like a winning sports team, requires a strong group, but the media find individual heroics and failures more compelling. Such media coverage encourages citizens to think about government in terms of the heroic exploits and tragic failures of individuals rather than in terms of institutions and processes.[66]

Emphasis on Conflicts, Scandals, and Mistakes   Reporters focus on conflict, and they really swoop down on a story when it contains a whiff of scandal. The Clinton administration was dogged with repeated scandals, some sexual and some financial. George W. Bush, too, faced a number of controversies that generated waves of negative coverage, including charges that his administration falsely manufactured the reasons for going to war in Iraq, and that his political advisers had leaked the name of a CIA operative because her husband had criticized the war effort. Reports that military police had tortured detainees in Iraq's Abu Ghraib prison also spawned weeks of critical press attention.

The focus of congressional coverage has changed as well. From 1972 to the mid-1980s, policy stories outnumbered scandal stories by 13 to 1, but since then the ratio has plunged to 3 to 1.[67] It is doubtful either Congress or the White House has gotten that much worse.

Campaign Coverage   Nowhere do critics of the mass media find more to criticize than in the media's coverage of political campaigns. The media provide little coverage of policy proposals, which voters might use to pick among candidates. Nor do they spend much time covering formal party events, such as the national

AMERICAN PRESIDENT WITH
AMERICAN IDOLS
President Bush meets with 2006
American Idol contestants. *Is
media coverage too focused on
entertainment at the expense of
"hard news"?*

conventions at which the major parties select their presidential nominees (see Figure 5.9). Instead, reporters focus on "character" issues that have little to do with the ability of candidates to govern. Thus, the press dwells on issues such as whether President Bush dodged military service as a young man or whether Senator Kerry earned his military commendations in Vietnam.

FIGURE 5.9   The networks increasingly ignore the national political conventions

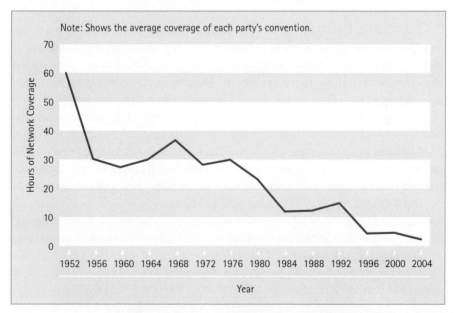

Source: Adapted from Harold Stanley and Richard Niemi, *Vital Statistics of American Politics,* 5th ed. (Washington, DC: CQ Press, 1995), p. 69; "Vanishing Voter Poll: Interest Lagging in Political Party Conventions," Harvard University, John F. Kennedy School of Government, July 22, 2004.

Journalists ignore policy positions because their main goal is to handicap the race. Coverage focuses on which candidate is leading, which candidate is dropping back, which one is coming up on the rail, what the latest polls say, who got what endorsement, and how a new announcement on a key issue will affect the polls. Candidate qualifications receive little attention, and issue positions are evaluated for their success as tactical moves. In short, reporters treat democratic elections as little more than horse races.

This tendency toward **horse-race coverage** has become much more pronounced over the past generation, and the attention devoted to substance has declined.[68] Increasingly, journalists interpret what candidates say rather than allowing candidates to speak for themselves. Studies that compare network newscasts from the late 1960s with those today find that the average sound bite for presidential candidates who appeared on the news has fallen from 43 seconds to less than 8 seconds in length.[69] Even high-profile candidates receive little time to explain their positions on complex issues.

As a result, most candidates seek ways to communicate with voters directly, such as appearing on television talk shows, setting up Web sites, and paying for phone banks that contact potential voters. Establishment reporters complain that candidates are trying to insulate themselves from the hard questioning of seasoned political reporters. But if "hard questioning" is only going to produce snippets on the evening news, then it cannot be doing much for the democratic process. Candidates may simply value the opportunity to talk about issues rather than the trivia so fascinating to journalists.

The Presidential Debates   Although political coverage exhibits many shortcomings, the material going out over the airwaves is not always negative. One of the high points of modern presidential campaigns is the series of debates between the two—sometimes three—major candidates. No other campaign events earn such high ratings. In fact, more people watch the debates than vote.

The first televised debates were held during the 1960 campaign between candidates Richard Nixon and John Kennedy. One of the surprising findings in studies of the debates was that people who listened to them on the radio evaluated Nixon's performance more favorably than people who watched them on TV did, an indication that visual images could influence voter perception.[70] No debates took place in 1964, 1968, or 1972, but they have been held in every election since. The format and arrangements continue to be matters of considerable controversy, but presidential debates have become an institution. Studies show that performance in the debates can sway the undecided voter.

As in campaign coverage generally, the first question journalists raise about debates is "Who won?" Most observers agreed that President Bush lost the first debate in 2004, missing an opportunity to gain a clear advantage over his opponent and turning the race into a neck-and-neck battle. Senator John Kerry failed to press his debating advantage in the two clashes that followed—Bush held his own in the town hall format of the second debate and Kerry seemed too tired and ill-focused to sway voters in the final showdown. While neither candidate gained an advantage in overall support from the debates, surveys showed that voters had learned a great deal about their policy positions, a fact that reiterates the effectiveness of an unmediated message.[71]

Prospects for Change   Americans are not happy with the press corps. Popular evaluations of the media have declined sharply since the mid-1980s. Growing percentages believe that the media are unprofessional, uncaring, immoral, and even harmful to democracy (see Table 5.1). Yet the American public gets what it pays for. News executives use focus groups and other measures of audience interest to determine what impresses their consumers: what they will read, what they will watch, what they will buy.[72] News coverage may fall short of what public-spirited critics would like to see, but only because it provides more of the sort of "news" that the audience wants. As humor columnist Dave Barry gently mocks, "You don't want to read about the economy. You love to read about sex. Everybody does."[73]

Media Effects

Media organizations may offer a biased product, but do distortions in political journalism influence how Americans think about their government? Are advanced communications technologies something to worry about?

People once feared mass media as a great danger to democratic politics. The rapid spread of radio in the 1930s coincided with the rise of fascism in Europe. Some scholars worried that this was more than coincidence. Before 1930, political leaders had communicated with constituencies indirectly, speaking and writing to lower-level leaders who in turn communicated with the grassroots. But demagogues such as Hitler and Mussolini spoke directly to their audience, sparking fears that radio created a "mass society" of lonely individuals susceptible to charismatic hate mongers.[74]

TABLE 5.1   Negative evaluations of the media are on the increase

News organizations generally . . .	1985	2003
Are moral	54%	45%
Are immoral	13	32
Care about the people they report on	35	31
Don't care about the people they report on	48	56
Are highly professional	72	62
Are not professional	11	24
Protect democracy	54	52
Hurt democracy	23	28
Care about how good a job they do	79	68
Don't care about how good a job they do	11	22

Source: Pew Research Center for the People and the Press polls.

Stimulated by such concerns, researchers conducted numerous studies of the media's ability to persuade. Contrary to expectations, though, research on the effects of mass communication turned up negative results. Americans were remarkably resistant to propaganda; media messages seldom altered the audience's views. Listeners apparently engaged in **selective perception**, absorbing information consistent with their predispositions and discounting the rest. Thus media exposure tended to reinforce what people already believed.[75]

By 1960, many scholars accepted the idea that mass media had a minimal impact on American public opinion.[76] Younger generations of researchers took a new look at the subject, however, after the rapid spread of TV. This newer research has documented important media effects, more subtle than the kind of mass persuasion that earlier studies had sought to discover.

Agenda Setting   The media set the agenda, even if they cannot determine how issues get resolved. By focusing on an issue or event and whipping up concern, news coverage induces people to think about a particular problem. Catastrophes in Third World countries, for example, go largely unnoticed unless the media—particularly television—turn their attention to such events. Famine struck Ethiopia in 1984, resulting in numerous front-page articles in powerful U.S. newspapers such as the *New York Times* and *The Washington Post*. The Associated Press (AP) wire service carried 228 stories.[77] But it was not until television stations beamed heartrending footage into their living rooms that a great number of Americans became aware of the problem and supported governmental efforts to help.[78] Similar responses followed media coverage of Somalia, Rwanda, and the devastating 2004 tsunami in the Indian Ocean. Media analysts have even given responses such as

THE CNN EFFECT
News coverage of major world disasters such as famine, war, and the 2004 Indian Ocean tsunami has at times shaped the political agenda. *Why do the news media focus attention on some disasters and not others?*

these a nickname: the "CNN effect," after the tendency for a problem to be addressed once CNN covers it. In short, the media may not tell people *what* to think, but they do tell people what to think *about*.[79]

Agenda setting is well documented, although much of the evidence is inconclusive.[80] Researchers face a dilemma trying to sort out what causes what. Do the media cover what the public wants, or does the public respond to what the media cover? Some careful studies suggest that the independent impact of the media has been exaggerated; astute government officials use the media to publicize problems that they already wish to address.[81] Nevertheless, experimental studies that raise viewer concern about subjects *not* high on the national agenda have been able to provide some evidence of agenda setting.[82]

Priming and Framing   President George H. W. Bush's approval ratings soared in 1991 after an American ground offensive drove Iraqi forces out of Kuwait. His popularity ratings reached unprecedented levels (near 90 percent). Yet within a year they had plummeted. What happened? Journalists turned to other stories after the war ended, chiefly the struggling economy. Gradually, Bush's ratings became dependent on his handling of the economy, which was viewed far less positively than his handling of the war.[83] His son also faced a foreign policy crisis: the 9/11 attacks. Although the extended coverage of 9/11 allowed George W. Bush's popularity to remain high for much longer than his father's did (see Figure 5.10), negative coverage of the economy, and the Iraq War ultimately deflated Bush's approval ratings.

These are examples of **priming**—in the elder Bush's case, news coverage prompted people to evaluate him according to his handling of the war in February 1991, but later coverage led people to evaluate him in terms of the economy. Obviously, the media do not have full control over which criteria Americans use to evaluate their presidents. War pushes everything else off the agenda of public opinion: All other concerns seem minor when husbands and wives and sons and daughters are in danger. After the war ends, both the media and the public turn to other concerns.

Framing and priming are related notions.[84] Earlier in the chapter, we explained that Americans tend to shift their reported issue preferences depending on how pollsters phrase a question. How issues are framed shapes more than just survey results, however; it also molds how public opinion thinks about issues more generally. For example, if crime is framed as a problem that presidents can and should do something about, it is more likely to have a political impact than if it is framed as an uncontrollable by-product of social breakdown.

Evaluating Media Effects   Media organizations can affect the political agenda—what people think about. They can prime people to think about certain issues and frame how they evaluate them. But the strength of these media effects depends on both the audience and the message. People who are uninterested in and uninformed about politics are most susceptible to agenda setting, holding other things

FIGURE 5.10   Wartime presidents, father and son

George H. W. Bush's, extraordinarily high approval rating declined steadily after the media shifted its focus to the economy (rather than Desert Storm). His son, George W. Bush, saw an enormous jump in approval ratings after September 11. It subsequently eroded, but not before the 2002 elections where the Republicans gained in both the House and the Senate.

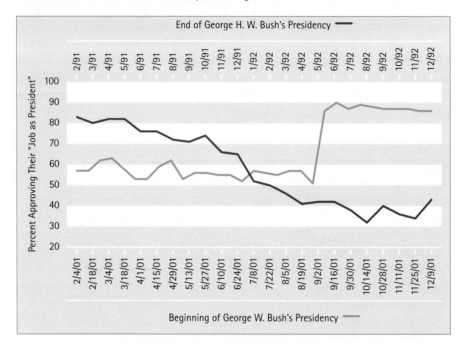

equal. For example, political independents are more likely to be uninformed, so their concerns shift from one issue to another with changes in the intensity of media coverage that they see. Partisans are already primed to think in terms of issues at the core of their party's concerns, so their attitudes prove more resistant to change.[85] On the other hand, the uninformed and uninterested are not as likely to pay close attention to the media, a factor that makes them less likely to be swayed by media messages.[86] CNN can't change what you think is important if you're not watching CNN! The fact that the most persuadable people are often the least engaged may make the overall effects of the media smaller.

The characteristics of the information being communicated are at least as important as the composition of the audience. When a problem or event is far away—well beyond personal experience—the mass media provide the only information available. During the Vietnam conflict, for example, Americans supported the war early on, when journalists did not criticize it, but turned against the war when journalists started publicizing American failures. Media influence diminishes, though, when information is closer to home and people have some personal basis for arriving at opinions.[87] American voters are not mere slaves of the mass media when it comes to the domestic policies that most closely affect their daily lives.

Mass Media and the Election Connection

Mass media have existed for less than two centuries. The political news they provide does contain some bias, and sometimes the resulting distortions do affect public opinion. However, the overall trend in their development has not been to undermine democracy, but to strengthen it. Indeed, mass media are a critical component of America's new democracy. The more that voters know about the actions of their governmental leaders, the more they can exert popular influence. Knowledge is power, and more political information is available now than ever before. Politicians must adapt to the information-rich environment, part of a never-ending struggle to shape how their constituents perceive them.

Newspapers

At the time of the American Revolution, most of the colonies' newspapers were weeklies; the first daily paper in the United States began publication in Philadelphia in 1783.[88] These early papers were published by printers who, like Benjamin Franklin, also published books, almanacs, and official documents. They reprinted material from European newspapers and from each other, as well as letters and essays from their readers.

As party politics developed, both fledgling parties realized the importance of having a means of communicating with their constituents. Hamilton and the Federalists established a "house" paper, the *Gazette of the United States*, and the Jeffersonians responded with the *National Gazette*. These newspapers were unabashedly one-sided: They printed the party line, viciously attacked the opposition, and depended for economic survival on government printing contracts. Thus, although early presidents did not speak in their own voices, they have been "going public" to the extent that technology allowed since the beginning of the republic.[89]

Improvements in the manufacturing of paper and type and the invention of the steam-driven printing press made it cheaper and easier to publish papers. In 1833 the *New York Sun* began daily publication, selling for a mere penny. (Before that time the going price for a newspaper was an exorbitant six cents!) The rise of the penny press marks the birth of the mass media in the United States. Millions of ordinary people could purchase and read newspapers. Within two years the circulation of the *Sun* was third in the world, behind only the two largest London newspapers.

As readership expanded, newspapers began to acquire their modern characteristics. One is sensationalism. Then, as now, crime and sex sold newspapers. Politics and economics were left to the older weeklies. Still, the new penny papers were overwhelmingly partisan. According to the 1850 census, only 5 percent of the country's newspapers were neutral or independent.[90] Politicians worked hand in hand with the editors of friendly papers and withheld information from those allied with the opposition.

After the Civil War, an independent press began to develop. One-sided editorial positions remained common, but many publishers saw little point in alienating a large portion of their potential audience. Nor did political leaders need party organs any longer. This was the heyday of the political machine, when party bosses used their own networks of volunteers to communicate with constituents (see Chapter 8). Patronage jobs and government contracts, not editorials, cemented political alliances.

The trend toward independence continued into the turn of the century, when many newspapers became large enterprises. Hearst, Scripps, and other companies bought up independent papers and consolidated them into great chains. Thus, the typical paper no longer was the voice of a lone editor. Journalists became more professional and even less partisan. Some newspapers were important participants in the Progressive movement, publishing "muckraking" exposés of shocking conditions in American industry and of corruption in government.

The most important development in the modern newspaper industry has been the decline in diversity. Afternoon newspapers have all but disappeared. Mergers have resulted in most cities being served by one or two papers, compared to several half a century ago, and chains such as Gannett (which owns 100 newspapers in the U.S.)[91] have continued to gobble up independent newspapers. Moreover, some media conglomerates own TV and radio stations—even networks—not just newspapers. Some observers worry that the mass media are losing their value as they face increased pressure to generate corporate profits.

Radio

In the 1930s, the print monopoly of mass communications began to erode. The first radio stations appeared in the 1920s, the first radio news agencies in the 1930s. Politicians quickly made use of this exciting new technology. President Calvin Coolidge (1924–1928) was known as "Silent Cal," but to reach voters he took to the airwaves. Franklin Roosevelt helped calm a worried nation in the 1930s with his famous "fireside chats." Radio demagogues, such as the hateful Father Coughlin, exerted a less calming influence during the same period.

Radio spread rapidly throughout the country. Today there are approximately 16,000 radio stations that reach nearly 85 percent of the population at some time on an average day. Virtually every household has at least one radio; the average is more than five. And, of course, there are millions of cars on the road, nearly all of which contain radios. The growth in radios and radio stations has not produced a comparable growth in media voices, however. Media mergers have undercut diversity in radio programming just as they have eliminated variety in the print media. Less than a decade ago, the two largest radio chains owned 115 stations. By 2003 they owned 1400. Five owners reap more than half of all the revenues spent on local radio.[92]

Probably the most important political development in radio communications is the rapid increase in talk shows. The talk format is very popular, trailing only country-western and adult contemporary music programs in total listeners. Sometimes local chat radio can wield dramatic political power. When Tennessee Governor Don Sundquist attempted to establish a state income tax in 2002, talk-show hosts helped generate massive protests against the proposal, a "tax war" they eventually won. Satellite technology and low long-distance telephone rates have allowed national talk shows as well. Rush Limbaugh's radio show is perhaps the best-known example. This conservative commentator began broadcasting nationally in 1988 and in 2006, reached about 14 million listeners per week on more than 600 stations.[93]

Television

To most people today, the term *mass media* means television. There are more than 1,500 television stations in the United States, and about 99 percent of all households have at least one TV set, the average being four. Like radio, TV is close to being a universal medium of communication.

The first TV station went on the air in 1939, but TV grew very slowly during World War II. Afterward it spread rapidly; by 1960, 90 percent of all households had TVs. Three large networks initially dominated the industry: NBC, CBS, and ABC. The networks pay local affiliates to carry programs the networks offer. The affiliates, in turn, make advertising time available for the networks to sell. Of course, the profit that networks make from their advertising time depends critically on the popularity of their shows—which is why ratings are such an important consideration when it comes to programming decisions.

It was the Kennedy administration that first elevated TV above the print medium and used it effectively to communicate political messages. During his short presidency, Kennedy held regularly televised press conferences that enabled him to go over the heads of the Washington press and communicate directly with voters. Kennedy once commented to a reporter, "When we don't have to go through you bastards we can really get our story to the American people."[94]

When network TV reached its height, about 85 percent of stations were affiliated with ABC, CBS, or NBC. But the network system began to fray after government deregulated the cable industry in the 1970s. The percentage of households with cable increased from 20 percent in 1980 to nearly 67 percent in 2005, while prime-time network news lost nearly half its audience.[95] Critics complained that the networks have responded to falling ratings by neglecting their news responsibilities. For example, executives in charge of ABC and CNN negotiated in 2002 to merge their newsroom operations, which could have saved $100 million but elicited widespread opposition. Still, the network news broadcasts continue to draw an audience of about 27 million people on an average weekday.[96] Network TV is still the largest single source of information available to Americans.

New Media

Cable TV is the most widespread example of the **new media**, although the term also includes satellite TV, DVD players, cellular phones, MP3 players, and especially anything connected with the Internet. The Cable News Network (CNN) appeared in 1979. Younger viewers often receive their political news laced heavily with satire by entertainers such as Jon Stewart on cable's Comedy Central. Stewart's "fake news" program, *The Daily Show*, not only featured interviews with 2004 presidential contenders but also was specifically invited to cover the Democratic National Convention.[97]

Aside from cable TV, few Americans use the new media for political information. While surveys indicate that about 73 percent of the American population had access to the Internet by 2006, few of those with Internet access pay much attention to political Web sites. One survey conducted during the height of the 2004 primary season found that only 24 percent of Internet users had ever visited a candidate's Web site, a figure far lower than the number who had seen a candidate on network TV's evening news or even CNN.[98] Those who do use the Internet for political information often read the online version of mainstream news outlets such as CNN, the *New York Times*, and *USA Today*.[99]

But the political importance of the Web has been growing. Neither presidential candidate had an official Web site in 1992 whereas, by 2004, Web sites were standard in campaigns as far down as the local level. Use of the Web for raising money has grown rapidly in recent campaigns as well. Online contributions became very important during the Democratic primary for 2004, as Howard Dean broke records in online fundraising, and John Kerry later followed his example.[100]

Chapter Summary

Public opinion is a basic element of democratic politics, but measuring public opinion is an inexact science at best. The question wording, the sample, and the complexity of the issues make designing good public opinion polls tricky. Public opinion exerts its influence largely through the calculations of public officials, who understand that they can be challenged in free elections and must consider the distribution and intensity of views on any issue. Elected officials clearly hesitate to defy the will of an aroused public, but even unexpressed public opinion may influence the actions of politicians who fear arousing it.

Despite the importance of public opinion, governing by opinion poll is difficult and perhaps undesirable. Citizens tend not to be well informed; their views are not firmly held, can change quickly, and often are not connected to other, seemingly related views. For these reasons, poll results often are misleading and often are misinterpreted by politicians and journalists. In the long run, American democracy follows public opinion, but public policy does not always respond to shifts in public opinion over the short term.

In recent years many people have expressed concern that *mass media* are increasingly shaping public opinion. Overall, little evidence supports the worst fears of media critics. Nevertheless, under some circumstances, the media can move public opinion—if not directly, then by determining how values, interests, and education come together to shape individuals' political beliefs. Such effects depend on people's predispositions and on their outside sources of knowledge.

Frequently, critics charge the media with one or another form of bias. Journalists certainly appear to be establishment liberals, progressive reformers who support capitalism but endorse liberal social change. More important, norms of newsworthiness and pressures on the news-gathering process distort coverage of political issues, prompting critics to assail the way the news industry presents both elections and the process of governance. Nevertheless, the mass media are less than two centuries old, and the spread of political knowledge permits voters to use their influence more effectively. If knowledge really is power, then media organizations form an important political institution that has expanded popular influence in America's new democracy.

KEY TERMS

agenda setting, p. 133
constituents, p. 118
framing, p. 133
horse-race coverage, p. 130
ideologies, p. 114
information costs, p. 112
issue publics, p. 113
mass media, p. 120
mass public, p. 114
measurement error, p. 105

new media, p. 138
political efficacy, p. 103
political elites, p. 114
priming, p. 133
random sample, p. 103
sampling error, p. 103
selection bias, p. 104
selective perception, p. 132
single-issue voters, p. 119
socializing agent, p. 101

SUGGESTED READINGS

Cook, Timothy. *Governing with the News: The News Media as a Political Institution*, 2nd ed. Chicago: University of Chicago Press, 2005. Argues that, like other political institutions, the media have a set of cohesive rules of conduct and affect public policy.

Iyengar, Shanto, and Donald Kinder. *News That Matters*. Chicago: University of Chicago Press, 1987. An exemplary experimental study that demonstrates the existence of agenda setting and priming.

Jacobs, Lawrence, and Robert Shapiro. *Politicians Don't Pander: Political Manipulation and the Loss of Democratic Responsiveness*. Chicago: University of Chicago Press, 2000. Provocative argument that today's politicians follow their own strongly held preferences and that polls are only a tool used to determine how best to frame the positions that the politicians personally favor.

Page, Benjamin, and Robert Shapiro. *The Rational Public*. Chicago: University of Chicago Press, 1992. Monumental study of public opinion from the 1930s to the 1990s. The authors argue that, viewed as a collectivity, the public is rational, however imperfect the individual opinions that members of the public hold.

Stimson, James. *Public Opinion in America: Moods, Cycles, and Swings.* Boulder, CO: Westview Press, 1991. Statistically sophisticated examination of American public opinion from the 1960s to the 1990s, in which the author finds that public opinion was moving in a conservative direction in the 1970s but reversed direction around the time of Reagan's election.

Zaller, John. *The Nature and Origins of Mass Opinion.* New York: Cambridge University Press, 1992. An influential reinterpretation of public opinion findings that argues that people do not have fixed opinions on many subjects. Rather, their responses reflect variable considerations stimulated by the question and the context.

ON THE WEB

For more on public opinion, see the following Web sites:

AMERICAN ASSOCIATION FOR PUBLIC OPINION RESEARCH
www.aapor.org

An academic association interested in the methods, applications, and analysis of public opinion and survey research. This site offers access to the *Public Opinion Quarterly* index and its contents.

THE ROPER CENTER FOR PUBLIC OPINION RESEARCH
www.ropercenter.uconn.edu

An academic, nonprofit center for the study of public opinion that maintains the world's largest archive of public opinion data.

THE NATIONAL OPINION RESEARCH CENTER
www.norc.uchicago.edu

Based at the University of Chicago, this social science data site provides access to survey history, a library of publications, links, and information on general social survey methodology.

THE PEW RESEARCH CENTER FOR THE PEOPLE AND THE PRESS
www.people-press.org

This site reports on surveys of American public opinion, particularly as related to the media and the way they cover campaigns and government.

Individual Participation

"You CAN'T ALWAYS GET THEM WITH THE PHONE. YOU DON'T always get them with the mail. That's why we go to the door." That's how one party activist explained what he was doing during the unusual voter turnout campaign of 2004.[1] That year, the two major political parties devoted an extraordinary amount of effort and resources to getting their voters to the polls, whereas in the past most efforts had been geared toward persuading independents. "Get-out-the-vote" drives used to be only a secondary concern.

The roots of this reversal go back to the 2000 election. George Bush led Al Gore in the polls throughout October, but ultimately lost the popular vote. Bush advisors blamed this last-minute surprise on the Republican party's failure to get its voters to the polls as effectively as the Democrats had. In addition, looking ahead to 2004 Republican strategists felt that most voters had formed strong impressions of President Bush; hence, the number of voters in the middle—the so-called swing voters—would be unusually small. Under these conditions victory would likely go to whichever party could mobilize its supporters more effectively.

The result was a Republican "72-Hour Plan," a detailed get-out-the-vote strategy that would be set in motion during the final three days of the campaign. The Republican National Committee field-tested the plan in a few states during the 2002 midterm elections, and then widened the effort in 2004, painstakingly building an extensive, grass-roots field organization in every major state that was expected to be competitive. In Ohio, for example, the 2000 Bush campaign had 16 paid staffers, supplemented by 22,000 volunteers, and was never organized at the precinct level. By contrast, in August of 2004 the *Columbus Dispatch* reported that the Bush organization already had 45 full-time staffers, 58,000 volunteers, and a chairperson in each of Ohio's 12,132 precincts.[2]

The Republican get-out-the-vote drive was organized by their national and state party organizations. The Democrats, in contrast, largely "outsourced" their voter turnout effort, relying on the volunteers and organizational capabilities of labor unions and liberal activist groups such as *MoveOn.org* and *America Coming Together*. The result was, as the *New York Times* put it, "the most expensive and successful voter drive in history."[3] Each party claimed to have a million volunteers. The Republicans said they had contacted 18 million voters; the Democrats said they had made 23 million phone calls and knocked on 8 million doors.[4] While these claims may be exaggerated, surveys found that many more Americans reported hearing from a political party in 2004 than in 2000.[5]

What effect did all this work have on the actual voting? The answer remains uncertain. In 2004, 60.7 percent of the eligible electorate voted, the highest turnout in 36 years and 6.4 percentage points higher than turnout in 2000. But it is unclear how much the party field organizations had to do with this surge. A significant portion of the increase no doubt reflected the emotion and energy generated by the controversy over the war in Iraq and other issues. Even in the "non-battleground" states, which were conceded to one candidate or the other and thus saw little organizational activity, turnout increased by 5.4 percent.[6]

Finally, the fact remains that despite a close election, hotly contested issues, and a massive get-out-the-vote effort, 40 percent of eligible Americans sat out the election. Even under highly favorable conditions, U.S. voter turnout still lagged well behind the levels routinely recorded in other democracies. In the 2006 congressional elections, voter turnout dropped back down to more typical levels.

Voting is widely regarded as the fundamental form of democratic participation. If little more than a majority votes, how representative are the public officials it elects, and how legitimate are the actions these officials take? Political theorist Benjamin Barber charges that "In a country where voting is the primary expression of citizenship, the refusal to vote signals the bankruptcy of democracy."[7] Not everyone is so concerned about low voter turnout, though. Unlike a century ago, some point out, there are no poll taxes, literacy tests, gender barriers, or property requirements to block access to the voting booth. Voters *choose* to stay away. If nonvoters decline to participate, why badger them to do so? What would these apparently disengaged people bring to an election?[8]

Whether or not one is concerned about low participation, it presents a puzzle. The United States is a rich country, with citizens who have high levels of education. Usually democracy thrives in such a setting, and voting is the *only* form of democratic participation for the great bulk of the population. Yet turnout is inconsistent in presidential contests and can be quite low in other elections, even if they feature close contests.

Low voter turnout is interesting for one other reason. It threatens our claim that elections drive American politics. Why would voter participation be significantly *lower* if elections had a *greater* impact on politicians in America than in other countries? Americans presumably have enough common sense to decide whether an activity is worth their effort. Surely most would vote if they learned from observation that elections were important. Therefore, maybe Americans do not vote because their experience contradicts our interpretation.

Certainly some Americans stay out of politics because they doubt their ability to make a difference. But this chapter will show that most explanations for why Americans do not vote have very little to do with the importance of elections or who wins them. Americans actually vote at a higher rate than the statistics imply, and—leaving aside voting—they participate in politics more often than citizens in other countries. To the extent that voter participation is lower, it generally results from the laws governing elections and does not undermine the relevance of voting itself. Before defending these claims, however, we will review the history of the **franchise**, or right to vote, in the United States. Equipped with this background, you will be ready to understand why many people do not participate actively in America's new democracy.

A Brief History of the Franchise in the United States

A single political party, the Democratic–Republicans, dominated the United States in the early nineteenth century. The party's members in Congress met in a caucus before each presidential election to nominate their candidate, who invariably won. But in 1824 the caucus could not unite behind a single nominee. As a result, four candidates vied for the office; the main contenders were Secretary of State John Quincy Adams (son of the second president), War of 1812 hero General Andrew Jackson, and Speaker of the House Henry Clay of Kentucky.

Although Jackson received the largest share of the popular vote, no one managed a majority in the Electoral College. The election went to the House of Representatives, as specified in the Constitution. There, Speaker Henry Clay delivered the victory to Adams, who in turn appointed Clay secretary of state, a position once considered the stepping-stone to the presidency. Jackson, the popular favorite, was shut out.

The Birth of Mass Democracy

Ironically, this instance of popular frustration produced one of the nation's most dramatic moves toward full democracy. Jackson's supporters were so outraged by the "corrupt bargain" between Adams and Clay that they redoubled their efforts for the next presidential election. They linked local political organizations together across the country, and they spread their campaign outward to the newly settled West. They pressured for change in election laws, sometimes successfully. For example, four states transferred the right to choose presidential electors from their legislatures to the voters. Turnout increased in all the other states. In total, more than three times as many men voted for electors in 1828 as had voted in 1824, and that year Jackson easily defeated Adams.[9]

Despite the tripling of voter turnout between 1824 and 1828, only about 56 percent of the adult male population voted in 1828. The problem was not necessarily lack of interest. Many men had no choice. Property qualifications for voting varied from state to state and were very unevenly enforced, but in various forms they continued into the 1830s. Most states restricted the franchise to taxpayers until the 1850s.[10] Only upon the eve of the Civil War could it be said that the United States had universal white male **suffrage** (another term for franchise).[11]

Not all voter qualifications were economic. Until the 1830s, a few states limited voting to those who professed belief in a Christian god. Jews were not permitted to vote in Rhode Island as late as 1830. Blacks generally could not vote until after the Civil War, and they lost their rights again a generation later by means of poll taxes, literacy tests, white primaries, and other discriminatory procedures (see Chapter 14). Only modern electoral reforms, such as the Voting Rights Act of 1965, effectively expanded the franchise to African Americans.

Women briefly enjoyed the right to vote in New Jersey after the Declaration of Independence. They lost it in 1807, though, and more than 60 years passed before another state granted women voting rights. Wyoming became the first state to extend the franchise to women in national elections in 1890. Eleven other states, mostly in the West, had followed by 1916. Finally, in 1920, the suffrage movement won its crowning victory when the Nineteenth Amendment was ratified (see Figure 6.1).

The last major extension of the franchise came with the adoption of the Twenty-sixth Amendment. Prior to 1971, most states did not grant the vote to those under age 21. This restriction became an embarrassment during the Vietnam War, however, because it implied that soldiers mature enough to die in Asian jungles were not mature enough to choose political leaders. Even Republican President Richard Nixon supported extending the suffrage to include those 18 and older, despite the certainty that most young voters of the era would oppose both him and his party.[12]

FIGURE 6.1   The right to vote in the United States has been steadily expanded

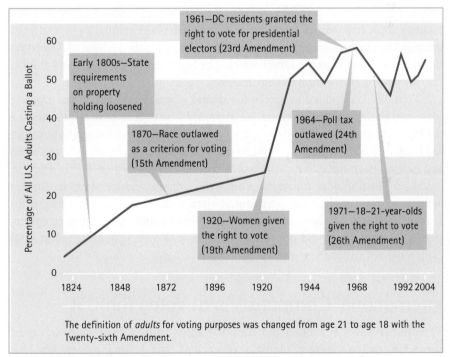

The definition of *adults* for voting purposes was changed from age 21 to age 18 with the Twenty-sixth Amendment.

Note: Extending the franchise to new groups does not always result in better turnout.

Source: Adapted from Harold W. Stanley and Richard G. Niemi, *Vital Statistics on American Politics 1999–2000* (Washington, DC: CQ Press, 2000), p. 12.

Women's Suffrage and the Importance of Elections

The uneven expansion of the franchise illustrates the overwhelming power of free elections to make a society even more democratic over time. Elected leaders naturally want to expand the influence of social groups that support them. And once a few members of a social group achieve political power, no politician wants to explain why others like them should remain powerless. Promising to give a group more influence in future elections is a fairly cheap way to attract its support, or at least forestall its opposition. This dynamic operated to expand voting rights for blacks and the young, but it was most apparent in the case of women's suffrage.

Fewer than a dozen states allowed women to vote in 1916. Many influential Democratic politicians opposed giving them the franchise. They believed that women were more likely to support Republican reformers. Women would vote against labor unions, against liquor interests, and against machine politicians—all key Democratic constituencies. Moreover, southern Democrats worried that granting voting rights to women would raise African American aspirations for similar rights.

Democratic President Woodrow Wilson, who was running for reelection that year, did not have a clear position on women's suffrage. Indeed, he once dodged the issue by saying that the question had never come to his attention. But Wilson was in a difficult spot. He had won the 1912 election in a three-way race, receiving only 42 percent of the popular vote. His 1916 opponent, Republican Charles Evans Hughes, supported women's suffrage, and one-sixth of the country's electoral votes belonged to states where women could vote. If Wilson came out against a constitutional amendment to expand the franchise, he risked moving Hughes one-third of the way toward an Electoral College majority.

Thus, Wilson decided to ignore the wishes of many Democrats and signaled his moderate support for the cause. He promised to vote in favor of a 1916 women's suffrage referendum in New Jersey, his home state. Partly on the strength of this moderate position, Wilson was able to carry 10 of the 12 women's suffrage states and narrowly win reelection. Other politicians quickly jumped on the bandwagon, passing a constitutional amendment through Congress and the states in time for women to vote in the 1920 presidential election nationwide. Interestingly, the United States was far ahead of most of the world in granting full rights of citizenship to women. France did not allow women to vote until 1945, and the last Swiss canton did not enfranchise women until 1990![13]

International Comparisons of Voter Turnout

The United States expanded the franchise more quickly than other advanced democracies. Today, every mentally competent, law-abiding citizen who has reached the age of 18 may vote. Elections are a central institution of American politics. It is therefore puzzling (and perhaps a bit embarrassing) that Americans participate at particularly low levels. The truth is not quite as dire, however, as the statistical comparisons imply (see Table 6.1). Procedures for calculating turnout

TABLE 6.1   Americans are less likely to vote than the citizens of other democracies

Figures represent turnout as a percent of registered voters in the most recent election for the lower house of the legislature or parliament. Note that the United States' turnout in 2002 was 69 percent of **registered** voters, while it was only 46 percent of **eligible** voters.

Country (year)	Turnout as percent of registered voters	Country (year)	Turnout as percent of registered voters
Malta (2003)	95.7	Costa Rica (2006)	65.1
Australia (2004)	94.3	Canada (2006)	64.9
Luxembourg (2004)	91.7	Czech Republic (2006)	64.5
Belgium (2003)	91.6	Hungary (2006)	64.4
Iceland (2003)	87.7	Portugal (2005)	64.3
Denmark (2005)	84.5	Israel (2006)	63.5
Austria (2002)	84.3	Ireland (2002)	62.6
Italy (2006)	83.6	New Zealand (2005)	61.6
Sweden (2002)	80.1	United Kingdom (2005)	61.4
Netherlands (2003	80	France (2002)	60.3
Brazil (2002)	79.5	India (2004)	57.7
Germany (2005)	77.7	Estonia (2003)	57.6
Norway (2005)	77.4	Venezuela (2000)	56.6
Greece (2004)	76.6	Bulgaria (2005)	55.8
Spain (2004)	75.7	Russia (2003)	55.7
Latvia (2002)	71.2	Lithuania (2004)	46.1
United States (2002)	69	Switzerland (2003)	45.4
Japan (2005)	67.5	Poland (2005)	40.6
Finland (2003)	66.7		

Source: For international data, International Institute for Democracy and Electoral Assistance, www.idea.int, accessed September 25, 2006. For U.S. data, "Voting and Registration in the Election of November 2002," United States Department of Commerce, Bureau of the Census, July 2004, p. 2.

differ from country to country, and the differences systematically downgrade American turnout figures relative to those in other democracies.

Turnout would seem simple enough to measure. It should be the proportion of those able to vote who actually do so. The U.S. Bureau of the Census calculates official turnout in presidential elections as the number of people voting for president divided by the number of people in the voting-age population. This definition seems straightforward, but it lowers American turnout as much as 5 percent relative to other countries.

Consider the numerator, the number of people voting for president. If an American believes that all the candidates are bums and either does not vote for president or does not pick a recognizable candidate, that citizen is not counted as having voted. Other countries are more flexible. In France, for example, unhappy voters have long scribbled an offensive suggestion across their ballots (the English translation has initials "F.Y."). French election officials count such ballots, whereas most American officials would not.[14] Furthermore, if someone casts a "frivolous" write-in vote (in 2004, for example, six people in Rhode Island voted for "Mickey Mouse"),[15] election officials in many jurisdictions ignore that vote rather than tabulating it as "other." The decision to exclude some ballots lowers U.S. turnout figures by 1 to 2 percent per election.[16]

More important are factors that affect the denominator, the number of people in the voting-age population. The **voting-age population** is the number of people older than the age of 18, a number that includes some groups legally ineligible to vote: felons, people confined to mental or correctional institutions, and (most important) noncitizens. Counting the entire voting-age population rather than only the eligible voting-age population lowers U.S. turnout figures by another 3 percent.[17] The underestimate is getting worse because the numbers of felons and immigrants are rising.[18]

Other countries use a different denominator in their turnout calculations: the registered population. More than 30 percent of the American voting-age population is unregistered. When turnout is measured as the number voting among **registered voters**—those who have signed up according to the requirements prevailing in their states and localities—U.S. figures jump to the mid-range of turnout in industrial democracies, as Table 6.1 shows.

Because registered American voters turn out at levels typical of other democracies, it is tempting to conclude that registration requirements are part of the problem. Voter registration is automatic in most of the world, a function performed by the central government. American practice differs in making registration entirely the responsibility of the individual, and one-third of the eligible population does not bother to register. It is not clear whether simplifying registration would make a significant difference, though. A few states have no registration, and others let voters register at their polling stations on Election Day, yet turnout still falls well below the levels in many European countries.[19] Activists tried to increase voting by pushing 1993's "motor voter" law, which required motor vehicle offices to double as voter registration offices—but evidence suggests that this reform did not make much difference.[20] Statistical simulations suggest that liberalizing registration procedures would increase national turnout figures by only about 9 percent.[21]

How American Institutions Lower Turnout

Registration requirements may not explain low voter turnout, but other legal differences between Europe and the United States do. Voting is compulsory in some countries.[22] Greek electoral law provides for imprisonment of nonvoters for up to 12 months. That penalty is never applied, but other democracies do penalize nonvoters, at least sometimes. Australian law allows for fines of up to $50 for not voting (without a valid excuse), and 4 percent of nonvoters apparently must pay.

Turnout is almost 15 percent higher in democracies with compulsory voting than in other democracies.[23] No doubt turnout in American elections would

(text continues on page 150)

SHOULD VOTING BE COMPULSORY?

Despite the high voter turnout in 2004, America's pattern of low turnout will probably continue. Studies of younger generations newly entering the electorate indicate that they are less likely to follow news about politics, and therefore less likely to know or care much about elections, than their parents and grandparents were when they were at a similar age.[59] If you don't know or care, you're less likely to vote.

For years, experts argued that the obvious solution was to make it easier to register. Americans voted less, the argument went, because registration rules were complex, obscure, and onerous. So states and local governments—sometimes at the prodding of Congress and the courts—dutifully changed the rules to make the voters' burden less severe. They eased deadlines, reduced the amount of documentation required, and allowed citizens to register at more locations. Yet these changes have had little discernible effect on turnout.

If making it easier to vote hasn't worked, what about making it hard *not* to vote? Why not enact a law (or a constitutional amendment) that would require all eligible citizens to cast a ballot and that would impose some kind of penalty—

A voter casts a ballot in a Swiss election.

probably a small fine—on those who don't? Anyone who was disgusted with all of the candidates or had a principled reason for not voting would be free to leave their ballot blank.

Compulsory voting has never been tried in the United States, but a number of other democracies use it, including Australia, Belgium, and Luxembourg. A check of Table 6.1 reveals that these countries rank near the top in voter participation rates. Historical evidence confirms this impression that compulsory voting laws are effective.[60]

Proponents of compulsory voting say that it fulfills a democratic ideal by ensuring that all citizens have an equal voice. Such a prescribed minimum level of participation, they say, would lead to more equitable representation.[61] While most political scientists find that the policy views of voters and non-voters are similar, it is wrong to say that there are *no* differences whatsoever. Even 100 percent turnout rates would not have altered the results of presidential elections in landslide years such as 1984—but they might have made a difference in close elections such as 2004.[62]

Opponents of compulsory voting say voting is a right—and inherent in every right is a person's capacity to decide not to exercise it. The right to free speech also entails the right to keep silent if one chooses. The right to an attorney means that one can also waive that right. Forcing people to go to the polls is a violation of each person's right not to participate in an election.

(continued on next page)

149

SHOULD VOTING BE COMPULSORY? *(continued)*

Opponents also question the desirability of pushing apathetic people to vote. Women and African Americans who were disenfranchised in earlier periods of history clearly wanted to vote, but were legally prohibited from doing so. Today's nonvoters, by contrast, almost certainly could vote if they wanted to. They just don't seem to think that it is worth the effort. So what does the country gain by canvassing the views of the disengaged?

The public seems to agree with these criticisms, at least for now. A 2004 ABC News poll asked, "In a few countries every eligible citizen is required by law to vote in national elections. Those who don't have a good excuse for not voting are subject to a small fine. Do you think this would be a good law or a poor law to have in this country?" Only 21 percent said it was a good law, versus 72 percent who thought it a poor law.

Thus, there is little chance that the United States will adopt compulsory voting any time soon. Yet history has shown that it is possible to change the public's mind. Were a significant number of political scientists and civic groups to decide that compulsory voting is the only way to deal with the country's chronic turnout problem, perhaps, in time, most Americans would come to share this view.[63]

WHAT DO YOU THINK?

1. Is voting a right or is it a duty?
2. Is society better off if we encourage or require disengaged people to vote?
3. Would compulsory voting affect the outcomes of American elections? If so, which party would benefit most?
4. Besides compulsory voting, what are some other ways to encourage groups such as young people and the poor vote at higher rates?

For more information on voting and participation, see the following Web sites:

www.idea.int/vt/

International Institute for Democracy and Electoral Assistance (IDEA)

IDEA keeps meticulous records of voter turnout in countries around the world, and lists nations that have compulsory voting.

increase if the government punished those who abstained! But it is not clear that, to Americans, the ideas of democracy and forced voting go together.

Several additional institutional variations raise the costs of voting for Americans. Elections in America are held on Tuesdays, an ordinary workday. In most of the rest of the world, either elections are held on Sundays or election days are proclaimed official holidays. In Italy, workers receive free train fare back to their places of registration, usually their hometowns, so in effect the government pays for family reunions.

Also, keep in mind that the United States conducts more elections than other countries do (see Chapter 1).[24] In most European countries, citizens vote only two or three times in five years—once for members of Parliament, once for representatives to the European Union, and perhaps once for small numbers of local officials. The burden is much less than American voters face, so turnout statistics for a single American election are not comparable with those for a single European election. Some have suggested, not completely tongue in cheek, that turnout in the United States should be calculated as the percentage who vote at least once during a four-year period. This number would be closer to turnout figures for other countries.*

Finally, some states use voter lists to select people for jury duty. Although serving on juries is an important right, established to protect citizens from out-of-control government prosecutions, many Americans consider it an annoying disruption of their private lives; they will forgo voting to avoid the responsibility. One study concluded that turnout is 5 to 10 percent lower where jury selection targets voters.[25] And this calculation leaves out the many Americans who do not register because they mistakenly believe that they live in such jurisdictions.

All in all, both intentionally and accidentally, American practices raise the "costs" of voting relative to those in other countries. When some citizens understandably react to those costs by failing to vote, editorialists criticize them for their lack of public spirit. Scholars, meanwhile, are puzzled that turnout is so low in such a wealthy, educated country, where civic attitudes encourage popular participation. But the nation's laws are not equally encouraging. Political scientist Bingham Powell estimates that differences in electoral institutions, chiefly registration systems, depress American turnout between 10 and 15 percent relative to that in Europe.[26] In sum, it costs Americans more to vote, and they receive less support for voting than citizens in most other countries.

Why Americans Vote Less Often Than in the Past

For many people the puzzle is not only that turnout levels are lower in the United States than in other advanced democracies, but also that turnout has fallen over time. In the 1880s and 1890s, turnout rates in presidential elections typically hit 75 or 80 percent. The declines continued during the past generation, hitting a half-century low in 1996 (see Figure 6.2). In off-year elections, turnout has declined more erratically, but it is significantly lower now than it was a generation ago. Other forms of electoral participation—such as working in campaigns, attending political meetings, or signing petitions—may have declined over the last generation as well.[27]

To many observers, these declines in popular participation suggest that something is terribly wrong with American politics. Their concern was reinforced in the late 1970s when analysts noted that participation was declining at the same time

---

* Interestingly, Switzerland also asks voters to turn out frequently, and the turnout rate there is comparable to the American rate.

FIGURE 6.2   Turnout in the United States seldom reaches 1960s levels

What are the causes of declining turnout? Why the difference between presidential and off-year elections?

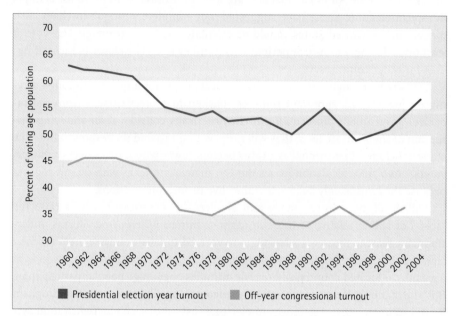

Source: The Committee for the Study of the American Electorate and the Census Bureau.

that trust in government was declining. Many feared that declining trust threat-ened the entire political system and that declining turnout was but an early symp-tom of a coming crisis. Research soon showed, however, that the two trends were largely unrelated. That is, turnout declined among the trusting and the cynical alike, and the former were no more likely to vote than the latter.[28]

What makes the decline in turnout all the more puzzling is that two other de-velopments in the past three decades led to an expectation of *rising* turnout. First, court decisions, federal legislation such as the Voting Rights Act and its amend-ments, and the Twenty-fourth Amendment to the Constitution have removed nu-merous impediments to voting. For example, poll taxes and literacy tests were abolished, state and local residency requirements were shortened, registration was made simpler and more convenient, bilingual ballots were permitted, and absentee voting was made easier. Such reforms were especially effective in the South, where they helped overcome the legacy of racial discrimination.

Second, socioeconomic change should have raised turnout in the post-1964 period. Education is the single strongest predictor of turnout. Higher educational levels produce a keener sense of civic duty and help people deal with the complex-ities of registering and voting. Researcher Ruy Teixeira estimates that, other things being equal, the net effect of socioeconomic changes, chiefly education, should have been to raise national turnout by about 4 percent.[29]

What, then, explains the decline in turnout? There is less agreement here than on the explanations for turnout differences between the United States and other democracies. Journalists often take voters to task for being lazy and uninvolved, while criticizing the candidates for being uninspiring and unworthy. But the question of why some people vote while others abstain is certainly more complicated than newspaper editorials usually imply.

For one thing, although citizens of other democracies generally vote at much higher levels than Americans, turnout is on the decline elsewhere as well. In 17 of 19 advanced democracies around the world, turnout in the 1990s was lower than in the 1950s.[30] Hence, the sources of declining turnout cannot be unique to the United States. Political scientists Steven Rosenstone and John Mark Hansen divide the reasons for voting into two general categories: individual motivations and outside mobilization.[31]

The Decline of Individual Motivations to Vote

Individual motivations reflect the personal costs and benefits associated with voting. If you are paid by the hour and you take time off in order to vote, you lose a portion of your wages. If you are a parent who cares for small children, you must pay a sitter or drag the kids along in order to vote. Even if you are a professional with flexible hours, you do less work on election day if you take the time to vote.

Moreover, not all costs are tangible. When you spend time on political activity, you have less time to spend on other, perhaps more attractive or fulfilling, activities. For some people with little education or information, the entire voting situation is confusing and uncomfortable; staying home enables them to avoid such discomfort. If you are surprised that such minor considerations could lower turnout, consider that turnout generally falls when the weather is unpleasant.[32]

There also can be benefits to voting, of course. One reason, though not the only one, why historical turnout levels were so high (sometimes more than 75

153

DILBERT'S PHILOSOPHY OF REPRESENTATION
Some Americans, like Dilbert in the accompanying cartoon, consider voting a duty rather than merely a right.
Voting is the central act of participation, one these Americans find personally gratifying. Other Americans
neglect voting and seek representation through protests or other focused activities.
Dilbert reprinted by permission of United Features Syndicate, Inc.

percent outside the South) is that many people were paid to vote. For example, scholars estimate that the going price of a vote in New York City elections in the 1880s ranged from $3 to about $7.50 (expressed in 2005 dollars) and that prices soared as high as $37 in particularly competitive circumstances.[33] Material rewards are a much rarer benefit of voting today, but direct payments for voting (sometimes called "walking around money") still surface here and there.

And for some citizens, elections still directly affect their material interests. For example, local government employees vote in low-turnout local elections at higher rates than people employed in the private sector, and government employees in general vote at higher rates, other things being equal.[34] For such individuals, elections give them influence at picking their own bosses.

Today, however, most of the material benefits of voting have faded. The incentives are primarily psychological. Some people take civic norms to heart and feel a duty to vote; they avoid guilt by voting. Others take satisfaction in expressing their preferences for candidates or positions on issues, much as they might enjoy cheering for athletic teams. These "psychic" benefits of voting are important, because it is very rare for elections to approach a tie.[35] With a small committee, every member has the potential to tip the scale, but in an election, any single voter is relatively insignificant. About 120 million Americans voted in the 2004 presidential election, and thousands of votes separated the two candidates even in the most closely divided states. In the 2006 elections for the U.S. House of Representatives, an average of 175,000 citizens voted in each congressional race. A voter would have been unreasonable to think the outcome depended on whether he or she voted.[36] The personal benefits of voting cannot exceed the costs, and this has dismal implications for turnout if an individual vote makes no difference.

Thus, psychic benefits are critical. They do not depend on whether a voter affects the outcome. A voter with a strong sense of duty, who takes considerable satisfaction in expressing a preference, gets those benefits just by casting a vote. These incentives have declined over time, however. Americans once expressed their political preferences by marching around in uniforms or attending festivals. Now they do so in the privacy of a voting booth, simply coloring in an arrow or punching out a chad or tapping a computer screen. Such an anonymous manner of expressing preferences gives many potential voters little satisfaction. And, as we noted in Chapter 4, Americans are individualistic; they are unlikely to respond to civic duty alone. The result is that Americans today are disengaged from the electoral process.[37]

Another political factor that has lowered the benefits of voting is that elections have become less competitive. As we will see in Chapter 7, the advantage of incumbency in congressional elections increased greatly after the mid-1960s, and a similar process occurred more slowly in state legislative elections. Many presidential elections in the 1970s and 1980s were landslides, and gubernatorial elections became less competitive as well. Rosenstone and Hansen find that in states with competitive gubernatorial campaigns in presidential election years, turnout is 5 percent higher, other things being equal.[38] In a result consistent with such arguments, national turnout dropped 5 percent in 1996 when Bill Clinton led Bob Dole by a comfortable margin from start to finish, but increased in the much closer 2000 and 2004 contests.

The Decline of Outside Encouragement to Vote

Parties, groups, and activists are often concerned about the **mobilization** of their potential supporters (although they are less so in uncompetitive elections). Campaign workers provide babysitting and rides to the polls, thus reducing the individual costs of voting. They apply social pressure by contacting citizens who have not voted and reminding them to do so. Various groups and social networks to which individuals belong also exert social pressures, encouraging the feeling that one has a responsibility to vote.

For a long time, parties neglected their mobilizing efforts, instead focusing on media strategies. Polling and advertising are probably not good substitutes for the kind of pound-the-pavement, doorbell-ringing workers who once dominated campaigns. Voters may be motivated by the coaxing of a campaign worker standing at the front door or telephoning late in the afternoon on election day, but those same voters may not be motivated by an impersonal TV spot or a taped telephone message. In fact, political parties trying to attract additional votes recently have started returning to the old methods of voter mobilization, such as phone calls and personal visits from politically active neighbors.[39]

As we noted at the beginning of the chapter, late in the 2000 presidential campaign, intensive get-out-the-vote efforts helped Al Gore mobilize a large urban electorate and win the popular vote—a success that prompted both parties to reconsider their priorities and focus increased resources on mobilization in 2004. Recent campaign-finance reforms have helped revive mobilization practices as well, because they included a loophole allowing state and local parties to fund get-out-the-vote activities that assist candidates for federal office. Many of these mobilization efforts have been highly targeted to competitive states, however, so their potential to raise overall national turnout is somewhat suspect.

The Decline of Social Connectedness

A final explanation for declining turnout falls somewhere between personal and outside motivations. Stephen Knack raises the possibility that common thinking about voting is misconceived. Rather than voting being the fundamental political act, voting may instead be a social act—a way to be part of the community. Voters may take pleasure from having an excuse, once in a while, to gather in a local building and make contact with their neighbors. Voting is related to giving blood, donating to charities, doing volunteer work, and other forms of community involvement.[40]

Voters would respond to these incentives only if they felt socially connected to those around them. **Social connectedness** is the extent to which people are in fact integrated into society—their families, neighborhoods, communities, churches, and other social units. Social connectedness may well have declined over time. Older Americans grew up in a simpler age, when Americans were less mobile and more trusting of their fellow citizens. They may be more connected than are younger Americans, who have grown up in a highly mobile society where cynicism about their fellow citizens is widespread.

Certainly young people seldom vote, and not simply because of their stage in life. Rather, political scientist Warren Miller has shown that declining voter turnout is a result of what social scientists call a **compositional effect:** a change in the people who compose America's potential electorate, rather than a change in behavior.[41] Turnout is declining because of the simple fact that older Americans, who have always been accustomed to voting at high rates, are dying and being replaced by younger Americans who have never voted much.

It is less clear whether social connectedness explains turnout directly. Investigators have examined the possibility, but they are stuck using relatively crude indicators of social connectedness, such as marriage rates, home ownership, church attendance, and length of residence in a community. Nevertheless, such studies find that decreased social connectedness accounts for as much as one-quarter of the decline in presidential election turnout.[42] One telling fact that supports this argument is that although turnout is not related to trust in *government*, it is significantly related to trust in *people*.[43]

SOCIAL CONNECTEDNESS
These 1940s league bowlers were closely connected to their community, but many Americans today may not be. *Why might levels of general community involvement explain levels of political participation?*

Is Low Turnout a Problem?

Low voting rates probably would not stimulate as much discussion as they do if all social and economic groups in America exhibited the same rates. But people differ in their ability to bear the costs of voting, in the strength of their feeling that voting is a duty, and in how often they are the targets of mobilization. Consequently, turnout rates differ considerably across social groups (see Figure 6.3).[44]

Highly educated people are far more likely to vote than people with little formal education. Education instills a stronger sense of duty and gives people the knowledge, analytic skills, and self-confidence to meet the costs of registering and voting. Over and above education, income also has a significant effect. The wealthy are far more likely to vote than the poor. Affluence, too, reflects a set of skills and personal characteristics that help people overcome barriers to voting.

FIGURE 6.3   Group differences in turnout, 2004

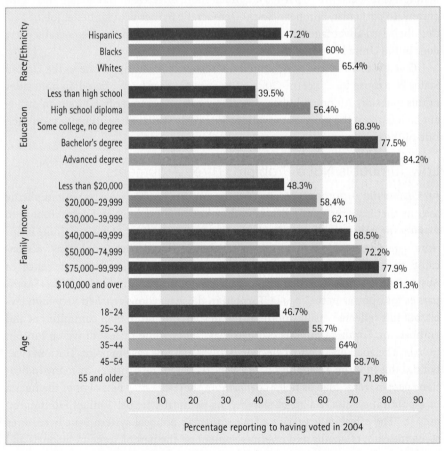

Source: Voting and Registration in the Election of November 2004, United States Bureau of the Census, Current Population Reports, P20-556, March 2006, Table B, p. 4.

Studies of turnout in the 1970s concluded that once differences in education, age, and income were factored out, blacks were at least as likely to vote as whites.[45] But more recent research finds that blacks are still somewhat less likely to vote, even taking into account socioeconomic differences.[46] Other minorities, such as Latinos and Asians, face language barriers that depress their participation levels.[47]

Turnout increases with age until one becomes very old, when the trend reverses. People presumably gain experience as they age, experience that makes it easier for them to overcome any barriers to voting. They also become more socially connected, as well as more settled in a life situation that clarifies their political preferences. But at some point, poor health and limited mobility intervene.

Interestingly, the relationships between socioeconomic characteristics and turnout are consistently stronger in the United States than in other democracies. Indeed, in some countries there is almost no relationship between education and income on the one hand and voting on the other.[48] The reason is not that in other democracies education and income have effects different from those in the United States; it is that elsewhere parties are much more effective at mobilizing their supporters. In particular, European Social Democratic parties do a far better job of getting their less-advantaged potential voters to the polls than the Democratic party does in the United States.

Given who votes and why, should the relatively low turnout rate in the United States be a cause for concern? Quite a few answers have been offered on both sides of this question. Among scholars, differing views on turnout often hinge on different beliefs about the motives for voting. We briefly sketch three arguments on each side of the debate.

Low Turnout Is Not a Problem: Three Arguments

An Optimistic Argument   Many of those concerned about low turnout implicitly assume that high turnout indicates enthusiasm about politics and commitment to making the political order work. Maybe that assumption is not correct. Some skeptics suggest that high turnout may indicate tension or conflict. People may vote because they believe losing would be unacceptable. Consider the experience of Austria and Germany as their democratic governments crumbled and the Fascist parties took power in the 1930s.[49] Turnout in those elections reached very high levels, but this reflected disillusionment and desperation more than commitment and enthusiasm. Similarly, pundits claimed that "angry white males" drove up turnout in 1994. The 2004 presidential election is a less extreme case in point. Turnout rose, but did this indicate a healthier political system? On the contrary, by many indications people were "mad as hell." Low turnout therefore may be a sign of the health of a political system, a sign of stability. As political scientist Samuel Huntington puts it, "The effective operation of a democratic political system usually requires some measure of apathy and noninvolvement on the part of some individuals and groups."[50]

An Elitist Argument   On average, nonvoters are less educated than those who do vote. Studies also show nonvoters to be less informed, less interested in politics, and less concerned about it. Citizens with less education may be more susceptible to getting caught up in political fads. They may be vulnerable to deceptive political advertising, or even outright manipulation. Not voting may represent an admirable display of restraint, an awareness on the part of uninformed citizens that they should stay out of a contest they know little about. Social theorist David Reisman once remarked, "Bringing sleepwalkers to the polls simply to increase turnout is no service to democracy."[51] Columnist George Will is even more succinct. "Smaller is smarter," he says.[52] Of course, if the process of encouraging people to vote also informed them and raised their interest in politics, this would not be the case.

A Cynical or Radical Argument   Some radicals contend that it is not the nonvoters but the voters who are a cause for concern. According to this viewpoint, elections don't matter—they are charades. Real decisions are made by power elites far from the popular arena. If so, voting is merely a symbolic act that makes the masses feel content. Anyone who turns out has been duped. Of course, we disagree strongly with this argument. As we illustrate throughout this book, elections matter a great deal—in some cases, too much. They have enormous impact on public policies that directly affect the quality of American life.

Low Turnout Is a Problem: Three Arguments

Low Turnout Reflects a "Phony" Politics   Low turnout may reflect disgust with an American politics that does not address "real" issues of concern to those who vote less, such as minorities and the poor. What are real issues? Basically, they involve economics: jobs, health care, housing, income distribution, and education. Instead, the parties debate "phony" social issues relevant to the upper-middle class: rights of free expression, gun control, feminism, animal rights, capital punishment, and gay rights.

Basic public opinion data seem to reinforce this criticism. A Gallup Organization poll from April 2004 asked respondents what they considered the most important problem faced by the United States. Economic issues topped the list; 43 percent of respondents mentioned unemployment, the economy's overall performance, or some other economic worry. Another 39 percent selected the war in Iraq or terrorism as the nation's most important problem. Very few people listed the hot-button issues that often dominate partisan debate, such as gun control or racism (targeted by liberal politicians) or gay marriage, abortion, and other morality issues (targeted by conservative politicians). Nor is concern with economics and foreign affairs unique to recent times. Since Gallup began asking the question in 1935, one of those two issue areas has almost always ranked at the top—foreign affairs during wartime, economic issues in times of peace.[53] In short, typical Americans usually worry about more practical concerns than the symbolic battles that make up the lifeblood of electoral competition, so it is hardly surprising that they perceive politics as a luxury interest irrelevant to their daily lives. This perception could drive down voter participation.

Low Turnout Discourages Individual Development   Classical political theorists from Aristotle to John Stuart Mill emphasized that political participation educates citizens, stimulating their individual development. Participants become better human beings, which in turn enables them to take society to a higher level. From the standpoint of this argument, low turnout signifies a lost opportunity. The argument is most persuasive when applied to participation in intensive, face-to-face processes such as local council sessions or town meetings.[54] It seems less relevant to impersonal processes such as voting in a national election. Nevertheless, it reminds us that voting may shape more than just an election. It may shape the voters themselves and help determine what manner of people they are.

The Voters are Unrepresentative   The most obvious concern arising from low turnout is that it produces an unrepresentative electorate. The active electorate is wealthier, whiter, older, and better educated than the potential electorate. However, numerous studies suggest that voting patterns do not bias election results. The policy views and the candidate preferences of nonvoters differ little from those of voters. Some studies have even found that at times the conservative candidate was more popular among nonvoters.[55]

How can this be? First, although minorities and the poor vote less often than whites and the affluent, the difference is only a matter of degree. Thus, blacks are less likely to vote than whites, but only about one-eighth of all the nonvoters are black. Similarly, the more highly educated are more likely to vote, but 25 percent of the nonvoters have some college education. Nonvoters are not all poor, uneducated, or members of minority groups. Plenty of nonvoters are affluent, well educated, and white—particularly those who have relocated and have not taken the time to change their registration. According to the U.S. Bureau of the Census, nearly one in five Americans moves during the two-year interval between national elections.[56]

Second, few groups are as one-sided in their political inclinations as African Americans, who voted Democratic roughly 9 to 1 in the 2004 presidential election. If turnout among most other groups were to increase, the Democrats might get more than half the additional votes, but the Republicans would get a fair proportion as well.

Does Turnout Matter?

Our view is that nonvoters and voters have diverse motives. Some nonvoters are content while others are alienated, and the same goes for voters. High turnout can indicate either high approval of the political order or serious dissatisfaction with it. Nonvoters don't have much information, but as we saw in Chapter 5, neither do many voters. Low turnout does make the actual electorate somewhat less representative than the potential electorate, but not as much as critics often assume. Some potential voters undoubtedly are discouraged by a politics focused on social issues, but other citizens turn out to vote precisely because of their concern with such issues. And although participation fosters citizenship, we doubt that the impersonal act of casting a vote fosters it very much. In short, we find some validity in each of the arguments presented; we reject in its entirety only the argument that elections do not matter. Low turnout is a cause for concern, yes, a cause for despair, no.

Outside the Voting Booth

Americans turn out at lower levels than citizens in other democracies. Moreover, they are significantly less likely to participate in politics and government in other ways than they are to vote. Only one-fifth of Americans report having contacted a government official in the last year, and even fewer report having signed a petition about a political or social issue during the same period. Substantially fewer have made financial contributions to a party or candidate, attended a political meeting or rally, or worked in a campaign. Two-thirds of Americans participate in no way beyond voting.[57]

It is a bit surprising, then, to learn that Americans are *more* likely to engage in these less common forms of participation than are the citizens of some countries where turnout is much higher. Even though only a small number of Americans work in campaigns or contact public officials, the numbers are even lower elsewhere (see Figure 6.4). Why would Americans vote less often, but participate frequently in other ways? Explanations vary.

- Because there are far more offices and government bodies in the United States, there are far more opportunities to contact officials, attend board meetings, and so forth. Even if Americans were less likely to take advantage of any particular opportunity, the sheer number of chances would result in a higher level of political participation than in other countries, where opportunities are more limited.
- America's individualistic political culture, with its emphasis on rights and liberties, encourages Americans to contact public officials and to protest government actions. In contrast, the political cultures of most other democracies are more deferential to authority and discourage ordinary citizens from taking an active role in politics. Citizens elsewhere are less likely to protest government decisions, and when they do, their governments are more likely to ignore them.

FIGURE 6.4   Americans are more likely than citizens in other democracies to participate in ways more demanding than voting

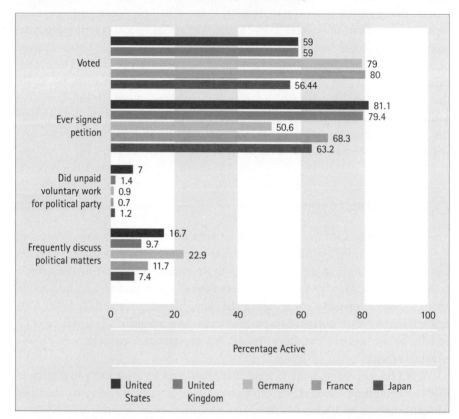

Source: Voter turnout figures: United States, Committee for the Study of the American Electorate; United Kingdom, 2001 parliamentary election figures as reported in International Institute for Democracy and Electoral Assistance (IDEA), "Voter Turnout in Western Europe Since 1945, A Regional Report," Stockholm, Sweden, 2004; Germany, 2002 parliamentary election figures as reported by IDEA; France, 2002 presidential election figures as reported by IDEA; Japan, 2001 parliamentary elections as reported by IFES, www.ifes.org/eguide/turnout2001.htm, accessed February 23, 2005. Petition, voluntary work, political discussion figures: World Values Survey, 1999–2002 dataset, ICPSR 3975, January 2005.

- Finally, many Americans participate in politics indirectly by joining or supporting interest groups. These groups encourage activism by soliciting signatures or contributions from their members, sponsoring political meetings, and so forth. There are far more groups and associations active in politics in the United States than in other countries, so there are far more opportunities for participation through groups. Groups are particularly likely to be the source of "unconventional" or "contentious" participation: protests, demonstrations, and civil disobedience.

POLITICAL PROTEST
Americans may not turn out to vote quite as much as citizens in other nations, but protests are common in Washington, D.C., and elsewhere. *Under what circumstances do you think protests are most likely to have an effect on policy-makers' decisions?*

CHAPTER SUMMARY

Most of the American electorate stays away from the polls in most elections. To some extent this pattern results from barriers to participation. Registration is left to the individual, voting is less convenient than elsewhere, and citizens are called on to vote often. In addition, mobilizing agents, such as parties and unions, are weaker in the United States than in other modern democracies; hence, Americans get less encouragement from larger organizations than do citizens of other democracies. Nevertheless, turnout statistics exaggerate the difference between the United States and other democracies—and Americans are more likely to engage in other forms of participation than citizens of democracies elsewhere.

The declining rates of participation in the United States since the 1960s are more difficult to understand, especially because other democracies have experienced a similar trend. Reforms have lowered the costs of voting, and educational levels have gone up, but Americans seem less interested in politics than ever. The explanations for such disenchantment are a matter of much debate. But for our purposes, low turnout appears to be less relevant. Evidence is thin that low turnout alters the election results. Nonvoters are not all the same, and they do not differ from voters as much as is usually presumed. Elections do not matter less just because some voters choose to stay home.

KEY TERMS

compositional effect, p. 156
franchise, p. 143
mobilization, p. 155
registered voters, p. 148

social connectedness, p. 155
suffrage, p. 144
voting-age population, p. 148

SUGGESTED READINGS

Keyssar, Alexander. *The Right to Vote.* New York: Basic Books, 2000. A comprehensive history of the evolution of the suffrage in America.

Rosenstone, Steven, and John Mark Hansen. *Mobilization, Participation, and Democracy in America.* New York: Macmillan, 1993. Comprehensive statistical study of electoral and governmental participation from the 1950s to the 1980s, with particular emphasis on the decline in turnout.

Verba, Sidney, Kay Schlozman, and Henry Brady. *Voice and Equality: Civic Volunteerism in American Politics.* Cambridge, MA: Harvard University Press, 1995. Fascinating discussion of the development of political skills in nonpolitical contexts, such as churches. Strong on attention to differences involving race, ethnicity, and gender.

Wattenberg, Martin. *Is Voting for Young People?* New York: Longman, 2006. Documents the decline in voting and general political engagement among young people—not only in the United States but in other developed democracies. Calls for compulsory voting.

ON THE WEB

THE LEAGUE OF WOMEN VOTERS
www.lwv.org
A nonpartisan political organization, the League of Women Voters encourages the informed and active participation of citizens in government.

PROJECT VOTE SMART
www.vote-smart.org
This wide-ranging site is supported by a nonpartisan group that gathers and distributes biographical histories, voting records, campaign finances and promises, and performance evaluations of elected officials and candidates.

National Elections

Tension ran high in the days before the 2004 election. The contest between President Bush and Senator John Kerry looked close, "too close to call" as the journalists like to say, leaving many Americans fearful of an election fiasco resembling the one that occurred in 2000. Wall Street's stock market was stagnant as investors fearful of a crisis held back their funds.[1]

Opinion polls in the months before the election only added to the confusion. Even the last-minute surveys gave little guidance—some put Bush ahead, some put Kerry ahead, but in every case the predicted margin of victory was so tiny that the polls were, in the words of the *Washington Post*, "meaningless in attempting to predict the outcome."[2] As if to reiterate this point, the respected polling organization Gallup announced that its final prediction was for a tie: 49 percent for Bush to 49 percent for Kerry.[3]

Because the polls seemed to be no help, pundits scrutinized campaign events for some clue as to the outcome. Kerry supporters pointed to their candidate's solid performance in three presidential debates, and argued that Bush's shaky demeanor in the first contest had hurt the president. Bush partisans countered that the president had scored points by highlighting several curious statements by Kerry, such as that he had voted in favor of an $87 billion spending package for the Iraq war "before I voted against it," and that a U.S. intervention in another country needed to pass a "global test" before it would be justifiable.[4]

A second set of "issues" seemed even less relevant to the future of the country, and sometimes approached the bizarre. Rumors raced across the internet that a bulge in the back of Bush's jacket indicated that he had been wearing an earpiece during the first debate (the Secret Service later said the bulge had been a protective device). Photos of Kerry windsurfing and snowboarding were supposed to show that he was out of touch with regular Americans. A group of angry Vietnam Swift Boat Veterans claimed that Kerry hadn't deserved some of his service medals, and a CBS news program produced a document, later shown to be a forgery, that alleged that Bush had not lived up to his obligations as a National Guardsman in the 1970s. These were the topics that dominated press coverage of the campaign. Could the world's most powerful democracy possibly choose its leader on the basis of such "issues"?

In the final few days, media organizations appeared to decide that the balance of these issues, along with a few other hints, pointed toward a Kerry win. Turnout would surge, many observers argued, and this would favor Kerry. Last-minute voters would break for Kerry. Kerry had dedicated volunteers in Ohio and Florida. Kerry had overcome organizational confusion within his campaign and now had momentum. In previous campaigns, Kerry had always been strongest near the finish line.

This pro-Kerry burst of conventional wisdom continued well into Election Day, when preliminary exit poll figures appeared to show the Massachusetts senator doing well. When Bush's victory became clear late on election night, conservative CNN analyst Tucker Carlson admitted his surprise. Virtually "all smart people in Washington on both sides thought Kerry was going to win," he said.[5]

Contrast this flurry of anxious last-minute second-guessing with how political scientists approached the election. Using statistical models refined over several presidential elections, scholars committed themselves to predictions long before most of the remarkable campaign events took place. Some of the most sophisticated attempts at forecasting the election came out in July and August, for example, around the time of the national party conventions and long before the first presidential debate.

Of the seven forecasts, only one described the election as too close to call. The other six predicted a Bush victory. In fact, one pair of scholars predicted in August that Bush would receive 51.7 percent of the major-party vote. He received 51.5

percent. What might seem even more remarkable is that these political science models were based on such factors as yearly economic growth, unemployment rates, overall presidential approval, and the amount of time that the party in power has controlled the White House. They incorporated no information on debate performances, attack ads, internal campaign turmoil, or misstatements. No mysterious earpieces; no windsurfing photos; no Swift Boat Veterans for Truth.

In general, the political scientists gave much clearer and much earlier predictions than all of the pundits, and they basically got it right.

The case of the 2004 campaign underscores the difference between how journalists approach elections and how political scientists understand them. Looking back, both sets of professionals can offer a story to explain why the 2004 elections turned out the way they did, but the two stories have very little in common. Journalists emphasize personalities and short-term campaign strategies. They focus on how much money the candidates raised or how clever their ads were. They trace small shifts in the polls to recent campaign events. After each contest, reporters wipe the slate clean and start speculating on the next election.

Our story, though, emphasizes the long-term regularities that shape voting. Research indicates that much of electoral behavior is predictable in advance. The public enters an election period with attitudes and loyalties mostly in place (although it may take some time to sort out their priorities and apply them to the options at hand).[6] The most important question for voters is how close the candidates' values and preferences are to theirs, and this favors candidates who seek the political center.

Nor can candidates simply pick the message Americans want to hear. They enter an election constrained by their own political histories and by the alliances they have formed. Their prospects depend on the quality of the opponents they face—assuming that they face any opposition at all, because anticipation of inadequate voter support may convince a potential candidate not to run. Thus, once the cast of characters stabilizes, for most voters their choice is obvious. This predictability makes elections look less important than they are.

Some reformers seek radical change in the political system because they think elections do not give regular Americans much influence. They are discouraged by the performance of political institutions, and they suppose that legal changes to open up the electoral system—for example by limiting campaign spending or by making election laws fairer—would correct the flaws. Our sense, by contrast, is that elections and public opinion matter more in the United States today than they ever have, so we are naturally skeptical of remedies based on the opposite diagnosis!

The difference between how journalists and political scientists view national elections is not just a quibble between two sets of professionals. The journalistic approach helps explain why Americans might be cynical about the system, blaming bad candidates or unfair media coverage or campaign-finance abuses for results they dislike. But short-term election strategies matter less than people commonly think and rarely influence the final showdown.

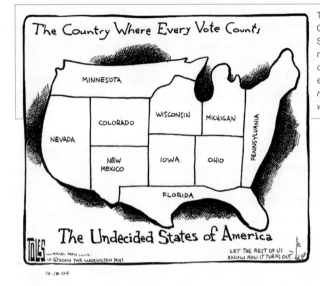

The Country Where Every Vote Counts

MINNESOTA

COLORADO   WISCONSIN   MICHIGAN

NEVADA   PENNSYLVANIA

NEW   IOWA   OHIO
MEXICO

FLORIDA

The Undecided States of America

LET THE REST OF US
KNOW HOW IT TURNS OUT.

10-18-04

THE UNITED SWING STATES OF AMERICA
Some reformers argue that too much attention gets paid to close states in presidential elections. *But can politicians really afford to ignore voters in whole regions of the country?*

Once one realizes that the main force guiding elections is the abiding dispositions of American voters, a different culprit for poor institutional performance emerges. The problem is not that Americans lack influence, but that their electoral system is oriented toward giving even a divided public what it wants.

Voting Behavior: The Importance of Elections

Citizens exhibit considerable continuity in voting behavior. This "electoral inertia" explains why presidential candidates know ahead of time that they will probably lose some states and win others. It is also why some congressional districts feature hard-fought campaigns, while in others no one challenges the sitting representatives. Elections sometimes are uneventful not because voters are powerless but because they exercise their power in ways that political actors can plan around.

Many people decide how they will vote before a campaign begins. In presidential elections, typically one-third to one-half of the electorate decides how to vote *before the primaries*. According to American National Election Studies surveys, one-half to two-thirds of the electorate decides how to vote before the fall campaign gets under way. The figure was 54 percent in 2000, when no incumbent ran, and 79 percent in 2004, when Bush sought reelection.[7] Hence, strategy cannot influence most voters.

How can people make up their minds before candidates debate their policies and programs? The answer is simply that Americans have a longer time horizon than the considerations that dominate news coverage. Voter preferences accumulate for years, long before a single contest gets under way. They emphasize party loyalties and government performance, not policy proposals or candidate personalities.

Party Loyalties

About two-thirds of the American electorate view themselves as Democrats or Republicans. Political scientists call this allegiance **party identification**, or party ID.[8] Party ID was once thought to be much like a religious affiliation: learned in childhood, resistant to change, and unrelated to the group's actual doctrines.[9] In fact, partisanship does respond to events and ideas, but only gradually.[10] Party ID thus ensures strong continuity from election to election.

For example, the Civil War and Reconstruction created many yellow-dog Democrats in the South—people who wouldn't vote for a Republican if the Democratic nominee were a yellow dog. Eventually, white southerners began to vote Republican in national elections, but they took much longer to switch party labels. Similarly, the Great Depression left many northerners intensely committed to the New Deal Democratic party of Franklin Roosevelt.

Party ID makes most elections quite predictable, even before candidates decide whether to run or how to manage their campaigns. Certain groups consistently vote Democratic, others steadily Republican (see Table 7.1). African Americans, urbanites, and Catholics have traditionally been Democratic groups. The wealthy, rural residents, southerners, and white Protestants—especially evangelicals—tend to vote Republican. The increase in political independents has not

TABLE 7.1   Groups differ in their support for the parties

				Percentage Voting Republican		
Population category	Bush 2004	Bush 2000	Dole 1996	Bush 1992	Bush 1988	Reagan 1984
White	58	54	46	40	59	64
Hispanic	44	31	21	25	30	37
African American	11	8	12	10	12	9
Poor ((< $15,000/year)	36	37	28	23	37	45
Affluent (< $50,000/year)	56	52	48	44	62	69
Union	38	37	30	25	42	46
White Protestant	n/a	63	52	47	66	72
Catholic	52	47	37	35	52	54
Jewish	25	19	16	11	35	31
Big-city resident (population > 500,000)	39	26	25	28	37	n/a
Suburban resident	52	49	42	39	57	61
Rural resident	59	59	46	40	55	67
Lives in the East	43	39	34	35	50	53
Lives in the Midwest	51	49	41	37	52	58
Lives in the South	58	55	46	43	58	64
Lives in the West	49	46	40	34	52	61

Source: "Portrait of the 2000 Electorate," *New York Times* (December 20, 2000). Available at time of publication at www.nytimes.com/images/2000/12/20/politics/elections/nwr_portrait_education.html; 2004 Exit poll, CNN.com, accessed November 3, 2004.

undermined this predictability. Even the growing number of self-professed independents usually find themselves closer to one party than to another.[11]

A "gender gap" has also sprung up, dividing the political preferences of men and women—a gap that has been growing stronger (see Figure 7.1). John Kerry might have won the 2004 election if no men had voted! Gender differences in voting do not result from so-called women's issues, such as abortion, which men and women view similarly.[12] Rather, the gap appears to stem more from long-standing gender differences over the use of force and the responsibility of government to address social ills (see Table 7.2).[13] It is not clear whether such differences grow out of childhood socialization, biology, self-interest, or some combination of factors.[14] The political preferences of women are not all the same, though; married women tend to have preferences much closer to those of men.[15] The electoral gap flows naturally from each gender's political preferences.[16]

Politicians are aware of how various groups differ politically. For the strongest partisans, the campaign is irrelevant; come hell or high water, they will vote their party IDs. Because potential candidates know how many members of each group appear in a given state or congressional district, they can strategize around such data. They usually need not wait for the formal election to respond to known voter preferences.

FIGURE 7.1   Since 1980, women have consistently voted more Democratic than men

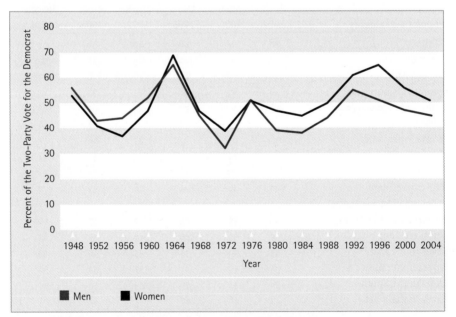

Source: The Gallup Organization; 2004 Exit Poll, CNN.com, accessed November 3, 2004.

TABLE 7.2   Women's and men's attitudes

	Women	Men
Role of Government		
Consider self conservative	50%	56%
The less government the better	36	47
Favor school vouchers	28	33
Favor Bush tax cuts	32	43
Favor allowing Social Security funds to be invested in market	39	47
Force/Violence		
Iraq War was worth the cost	37	41
Extremely important to have strong military	53	60
Government should make it more difficult to buy a gun	66	46

Source: 2004 National Election Study [dataset], Ann Arbor, MI: University of Michigan, Center for Political Studies, 2005.

Government Performance

Not every voter consistently supports the same political party. Swing voters typically react to the performance of current elected officials, though, and not so much to personalities or campaign promises.[17] Assessing performance does not require hours watching C-SPAN or reading the *New York Times*. Rather, voters can judge economic conditions from their own experiences and from word-of-mouth stories. They can judge other social conditions by observing their communities, schools, and workplaces.

Sometimes voters are upset about a problem and eager for government to do *something* about it. Thus, candidates talk about the need to "get tough on crime," or "fix the health care system," or "get guns out of the hands of children." These are important political issues, to be sure, but they do not evoke specific policy solutions. Such appeals merely tap into a general judgment of government performance.

The 1984 presidential election provides a classic illustration of how voters look toward past performance (this tendency is often called **retrospective voting**). Surveys showed that on many issues, voters were closer to the Democratic nominee, Walter Mondale, than to President Reagan. A majority considered tax increases inevitable (Mondale's position), were skeptical about "Star Wars" (the missile defense system dear to Reagan's heart), rejected Reagan's call for increased defense spending, and disliked Reagan's policies toward Central America.[18] Nevertheless, Reagan carried 49 states. Policy differences aside, most voters approved of the nation's overall direction since 1980.

Voters can hardly be blamed for adopting shortcuts such as retrospective voting. They are not equipped to judge among policy proposals, and candidates may not keep their promises anyway. Good performance by government suggests

HORSE RACE
Senator George Allen, Republican of Virginia, campaigns for reelection in 2006. *Do you believe Americans voted retrospectively in 2006?*

competent leadership, so voters reasonably choose not to "fix something that ain't broke."[19] Bad times, on the other hand, add credibility to any claim that someone else ought to get a shot at running the government. A campaign can "spin" an administration's record creatively, but it is difficult to make virtues out of a bad economy or an unpopular war—no matter how clever the media experts or how expensive their advertisements.

Policy Proposals

Policies and programs are the essence of elections for the most politically active citizens. These voters view campaigns as long-running debates—opportunities for candidates to educate the electorate about alternative paths the country might choose and to persuade voters to follow one of them. However, voters seldom use policy proposals to determine their choice among candidates.[20] One reason is that policy debates often are complex, and people have limited information. To cite one example, the Medicare bill enacted in 2003 that added a prescription drug benefit to the program required 416 printed pages. How could voters possibly be expected to evaluate such complex issues?

Moreover, voters often are unsure where the candidates stand. Research on the 1968 election, for example, found that views on U.S. policy in Vietnam were mostly unrelated to the presidential vote. How could that be true, when disagreement about the war was tearing the country apart? The answer is that the candidates gave voters little basis on which to choose. The Democratic nominee, Hubert Humphrey, kept wavering. The Republican, Richard Nixon, refused to reveal his position, because to do so would undermine his "secret plan" to end the war. In the end, befuddled voters assessed both candidates as though they supported the same policy.[21]

One occasional exception is a social or cultural policy, such as gun control or abortion. Such issues are "easy" in the sense that voters generally know where they stand. Moreover, the desired outcome and the policy that achieves it are one and the same: allow gun ownership or ban it; stop abortions or permit them.[22] Yet even these "hot-button" issues allow candidates to equivocate. In 2004, Kerry tried to distance himself from gun control, espousing the rights of hunters and taking time for a goose-hunting excursion during the fall campaign. Bush sounded a moderate tone on abortion: "I understand there's great differences on this issue..." said Bush in one debate, "but I believe reasonable people can come together and put good law in place that will help reduce the number of abortions."[23]

Candidate Qualities

Not surprisingly, the individual candidates are a major source of *change* in how people vote from election to election.[24] In a country that exhorts voters to "support the person not the party," the nature of the candidates is a major influence on how people vote. But it is important to keep in mind several cautions.

First, personality is seldom the most important candidate quality. In fact, detailed analysis of what people like and dislike indicates that most of the traits they mention are relevant to governing: intelligence, integrity, and experience.[25] Voters may admire a president open enough to smooch with his wife on national television. They may not relish the prospect of spending four years listening to a stumbling speaker or hearing lectures from an arrogant one. But these considerations sway few voters.

Second, after the election there is a tendency to downgrade the loser's personal qualities and upgrade the winner's. Journalists reinforce this tendency by habitually explaining politics in personal terms. Many Democrats praised John Kerry as a dignified Vietnam War hero before the 2004 election, and criticized him as indecisive and aloof afterwards. Kerry hadn't changed, but many in the Democratic party found it easier to blame their messenger than to admit that the electorate had rejected their message.

PUBLIC DISPLAY OF AFFECTION Al Gore's aggressive kiss reportedly surprised wife Tipper at the 2000 Democratic National Convention. Whatever her reaction, "The Kiss" electrified some pundits, who gave it credit for Gore's bounce in the polls. But humorist Dave Barry thought Gore resembled an alien depositing an egg sac. *Is it important to have an affectionate national leader, or is that relevant only to a personality contest?*

FIGURE 7.2   The Democratic advantage in party identification has eroded

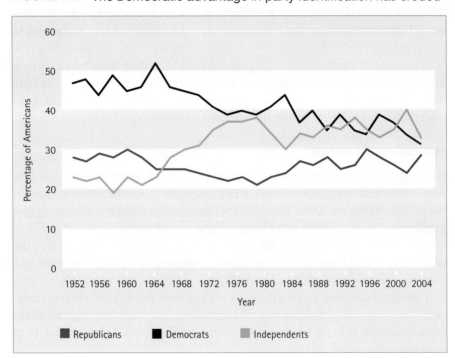

Source: American National Election Studies.

Finally, we should remember that what people think about a candidate is based partly on political compatibility—whether they belong to the same party (see Figure 7.2), whether the politician has performed well, and whether the politician espouses similar values. Thus candidates are important, but there is a tendency to misunderstand how. Personality looks much more influential than it really is.

The Incumbency Advantage

It is not hard to see how presidential elections might ensure public influence. The contests are nearly always energetic ones, covered heavily in the media. Voters pay attention and participate at relatively high rates. The importance of congressional elections may seem less obvious, though, for they are seldom competitive. Sitting members of Congress, called **incumbents**, often do not face serious opposition. And even when they do encounter real opponents, incumbents rarely lose.

The true measure of voter strength is not how often they replace elected officials, however. Low congressional turnover is itself a symptom of how much voters matter. Party has long been and continues to be the dominant factor in winning House elections, just as it is in presidential elections. Partisan control of the House seldom changes, and House incumbents seldom lose, because many House districts are **safe seats**. Voter preferences are so one-sided that these districts are almost certain never to elect representatives of a different party. Serious candidates from the minority party rarely challenge the incumbent, because they know they will lose.

One reason why party remains the most important factor in House elections may be that many voters know little, if anything, about specific candidates. Only a third of the citizenry can recall the names of their incumbents, and even fewer can remember anything they have done for their districts. Only 10 percent or so can remember how incumbents voted on a particular bill. Challengers are even less known. Lacking information, many people simply pick the party with which they generally sympathize. The importance of partisanship explains why the Democrats could maintain unbroken control of the House of Representatives between 1954 and 1994, despite the departure of all but three of their 1954 incumbents during the period.[26] In House elections, 70 percent or more of all party identifiers typically stick with their party's candidate.[27]

Incumbents do win reelection at a very high rate, a trend that has increased while the effect of party has declined. Statistical studies of House elections have found that the **incumbency advantage**—the electoral benefit of being an incumbent, after taking into account other relevant traits—has grown from about 2 percent before 1964 to as high as 12 percent in some recent elections.[28] The increase has not been smooth; rather, the incumbency advantage surged in the late 1960s, bounced around that high level until 1986, and then slipped in the 1990s (see Figure 7.3). This development need not betray a decline in voter influence, however.

FIGURE 7.3   The advantage of incumbency surged in the mid-1960s

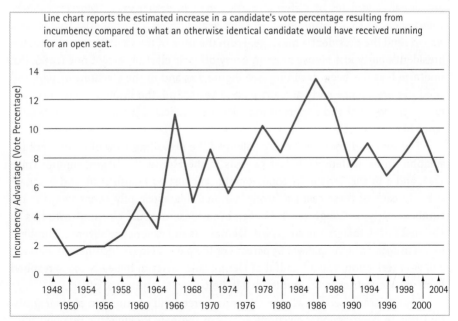

Source: Calculated by the authors using the Gelman–King method. See Andrew Gelman and Gary King, "Estimating Incumbency Advantage Without Bias," *American Journal of Political Science* 34 (November 1990): 1, 142–164.

One reason why incumbents seem to do so well is that politicians have more information about voters than they did in the past. Incumbents usually know when they are in trouble, and endangered incumbents frequently decide against running for reelection—which pumps up the success rate of the ones who try to keep their seats.[29] Also, members of Congress work very hard to maintain good relations with their constituents. Their continued success in large part reflects their efforts at pleasing district voters (see Chapter 9). When members of Congress do not behave in the manner desired by their constituents, strong candidates rise to challenge them, and no automatic advantage of incumbency saves them from defeat.

National Forces

Former Speaker of the House Thomas P. "Tip" O'Neill (D-MA) once commented that "all politics is local." O'Neill's remark partly reflected the parochial politics of Massachusetts, but it also is a reminder that members of Congress ultimately must answer to people in thousands of separate localities. During O'Neill's heyday—the 1970s and 1980s—national political forces generated by presidents, parties, and economic conditions had reached a low point in their influence on congressional races. Since the late 1980s, however, national factors have reemerged as significant in races for Congress, becoming at least as important (although not necessarily more important) as local factors.[30]

Presidential **coattails**—the tendency of presidents to carry their own party's candidates for Congress into office—declined in strength in the latter half of the 20th century.[31] More voters today split their tickets, voting for presidential and congressional candidates of different parties than in earlier eras.[32] Moreover, fewer voters seem to treat voting in an election year without a presidential contest as a way to send the president a message. From the time of the Civil War until 1998, the president's party lost House seats in every off-year election except one (1934). But **midterm loss** has been declining (see Figure 7.4), and in the elections of 1998 and 2002 the president's party actually gained seats. Still, the limited connection between presidential and congressional elections indicates the independent importance of each contest.

The 1994 and 2006 elections challenged the prevailing view of incumbent insulation. In 1994, Democrats lost 52 seats in the House, the largest rupture since 1946, and 8 in the Senate. In 2006, Republicans lost 30 House seats and 6 Senate seats. In each of these cases, a strong national tide apparently swept away the incumbent party in Congress.[33] However, even these unusual elections owe less to national forces than many supposed. Democrats did experience severe incumbent losses in 1994, for example; yet 85 percent of the party's House incumbents who ran still won reelection, and a handful of Democratic losses in the early 1990s resulted from unique district changes intended to help elect minorities to office.[34]

Experts are uncertain whether national forces will continue to play a significant role in congressional elections. Many of the new Republicans retained their

FIGURE 7.4   Incumbent administrations do not lose as many House seats in midterm elections today as they did in the past

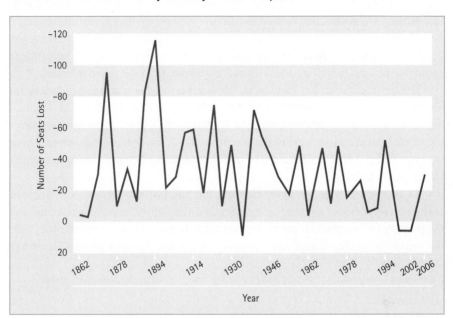

Source: Norman J. Ornstein et al., eds., *Vital Statistics on Congress, 1995–1996* (Washington, DC: Congressional Quarterly, 1996), p. 55.

seats in 1996 by using the same time-honored localism once used by their Democratic predecessors: avoiding controversial stands and highlighting district activities.[35] Democrats who won in 2006 are likely to behave the same way.

To the extent that national forces are regaining strength, it may be because political parties have become more active. Parties control more campaign resources that candidates wish to attract; the national parties raised nearly $1.5 billion in 2004.[36] The congressional parties are more unified than they were a generation ago, and the differences between Republicans and Democrats are greater.[37] Congress contains few moderates. Thus, voters today usually are presented with a clear choice between two candidates who hold distinct positions on national issues. Such clear differences can overwhelm local factors or the candidate's personal traits.

Interest groups help link congressional elections through issue advocacy. In 2002, for example, the United Seniors Association, an organization funded by the pharmaceutical industry, spent $8.7 million on ads.[38] Indeed, groups may run ads without the knowledge of (and sometimes in defiance of the wishes of) their candidates. Campaign-finance reforms passed in 2002 imposed some limits on how interest groups may advertise, but they hindered the parties even more—so interest groups were able to gain even greater ability to force candidates to address national issues.

The Senate Paradox

The founders intended the House of Representatives to be highly sensitive to popular wishes. However, they viewed the Senate differently. The Constitution originally provided for senators to be chosen by state legislatures, not elected by the people. According to Madison, the insulated Senate would proceed "with more coolness, with more system, and with more wisdom, than the popular branch."[39]

Neither institution has evolved in the manner Madison and the founders expected. The House as a whole is not very responsive to changes in the national mood, because most members succeed at constructing political identities satisfying to their local constituencies. On the other hand, the Seventeenth Amendment (adopted in 1913) exposed senators to popular election.* Senators must stay sensitive to public opinion.

Of course, elections are never far from the mind of any member of Congress. Members of the House put their fates on the line every other November, not counting the primary campaigns that are under way scarcely more than a year after they take the oath of office. But if anything, the situation is worse for senators (see Figure 7.5).

* Many states adopted various popular-voting procedures for their senators as early as the mid-nineteenth century.

FIGURE 7.5   Representatives get reelected more often than Senators

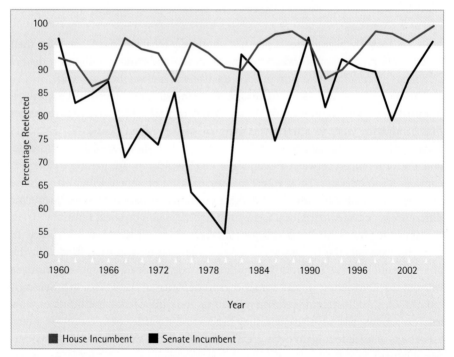

Source: Norman J. Ornstein et al., eds., Vital Statistics on Congress, 1995–1996 (Washington, DC: Congressional Quarterly, 1996), pp. 60–61, election results.

Not only are one-third elected every two years, but Senate campaigns, which must reach voters across whole states, are so expensive that incumbents must typically raise an average of just over $20,000 every week of their terms.[40] This time-consuming, psychologically draining activity keeps all of them aware of their need to maintain political support. Plus, senators represent more diverse constituencies, who are therefore harder to please. And because their offices are more powerful and have a higher visibility—they are covered much more often by the national media and by big-city newspapers—senators are more likely to face strong opponents.[41]

Evaluating the Importance of Campaigns

The importance of the campaign is exaggerated. Contrary to what the media imply, many presidential elections are decided before the campaign begins. Conditions in the preceding four years and the government's response to those conditions generally determine the outcome. Political scientist James Campbell has calculated that between 1948 and 2000, the campaigns probably were decisive in 1948 and 1960, two exceedingly close elections. The campaigns may have been decisive in 1976, 1980, and 2000. In the other nine elections, the outcome was largely predetermined.[42] Certainly campaigns matter, but only when the electorate is otherwise closely divided.[43]

Campaigns are shaped by what takes place long before the election. A card game provides a good analogy. Who wins often depends on the deal of the cards. No matter how skillfully one plays, skill may not overcome a bad hand. In politics, some cards are dealt years, even decades, before the election. Good economic conditions are aces dealt to the incumbent party; poor conditions are aces dealt to the opposition. International embarrassments and costly wars also may serve as trump cards. Media coverage seldom mentions the luck of the draw, because most of this is "old news." Journalists praise and criticize campaigns, as though strategic decisions operate on a level playing field; they forget that social and economic realities often dictate how the game is played. In short, journalists generally neglect the main explanations for who wins, the topic on which they expend so many words and so much ink.

Did the fact that Massachusetts Governor Dukakis lost to Vice President George H. W. Bush in 1988, while Arkansas Governor Clinton beat Bush four years later, indicate that Dukakis ran a poor campaign and Clinton a brilliant one? Dukakis surely could have done some things better, and Clinton certainly found his way out of a few tight spots.[44] But a recession made the George H. W. Bush administration a much fatter target in 1992 than the Reagan–Bush administration was in 1988. As Clinton's adviser, James Carville, said, "It's the economy, stupid!"

The importance of the campaign emerges in close contests. If a race is about even when the election begins, then any minor event or clever ploy can tip the balance among the few swing voters. Biased media coverage or a few extra advertisements may make a difference. But then, so can any sort of happenstance—trying to

THE IMPORTANCE OF CANDIDATES?
Political scientists tend to believe broad trends such as the state of the economy are decisive in elections. *Was the 2004 election an exception that hinged on the candidates' personalities?*

pinpoint the "cause" of victory or defeat becomes futile. Nor does the rarity of such close contests justify the attention that campaign strategy receives in the news.

Can Reforms Improve the System?

Thus far, we have been very optimistic about the importance of elections in American politics. Despite the media's emphasis on campaigns and character, these are mostly short-term, frivolous factors that operate at the margins. Most voters choose among candidates in a sensible manner, following their long-term party loyalties and medium-term evaluations of government performance. If elections seldom seem very close, this is partly because good candidates know how to anticipate voter behavior and adjust their own career decisions accordingly.

Despite this optimism, three topics worry many would-be reformers: (1) the role of money in national politics, (2) the apparent unfairness of some electoral institutions, and (3) the haphazard nature of the nomination process. In each case, critics exaggerate distortions in the nation's democratic process. Further, the practices and laws that most bother reformers sometimes provide underappreciated benefits. What would result after fixing specific flaws in the electoral system might not be better—and could be much worse—than what the United States has now.

Campaign Finance: The Role of Money

National officeholders generally must win two stages of election: a nominating campaign in which they become the standard bearer of a particular political party, and a general election in which they defeat the other parties' nominees to win the office. The process usually requires large sums of money, some of which the federal government collects. The money comes from voluntary checkoffs on Americans' income tax returns and is distributed by the Federal Elections Commission (FEC).

Financing Nomination Campaigns   Qualifying presidential candidates (who raise small amounts of money in each of 20 states) may have their fund raising matched, dollar for dollar, as long as they agree not to exceed a spending limit, and as long as they continue to do well in successive state primaries.[45] In 2004, the FEC spending limit for the nomination campaign was $37.3 million. From 1976 to 2000, almost every major candidate for president accepted these **matching funds**, but in 2004, both George W. Bush and John Kerry chose to forgo the federal money, opting instead to raise all their money privately and thereby avoid the spending limit. As a result, each campaign raised and spent more than $200 million before the general election campaign had even begun. Experts anticipate that few serious candidates will accept public funding in the future, because changes in campaign-finance law have doubled the size of contributions that candidates may accept from individual donors.[46]

Financing Presidential Campaigns   Under the terms of the 1974 Federal Elections Campaign Act (FECA), the general-election campaign is publicly funded. The FEC gives major-party candidates subsidies (Bush and Kerry received approximately $75 million each in 2004), and in return the candidates agree not to raise and spend any more. Beginning in the 1990s, however, campaigns increasingly relied on funding that was not subject to federal regulation (see Figure 7.6). Unlike the hard cash provided to an individual candidate, this unregulated **soft money** never reached the nominee's hands, but was largely expended by political party organizations. So much soft money flowed through the political system (a total of almost $400 million in 2000) that reformers focused their efforts on limiting its influence, finally eliminating most soft money in 2002. The absence of soft money may make the publicly funded general election system less attractive to candidates, increasing the chances that future presidential nominees will reject the public funds and raise unrestricted amounts of money, as the major primary candidates did in 2004.[47]

FIGURE 7.6   In the 1990s reliance on soft money in presidential elections increased dramatically

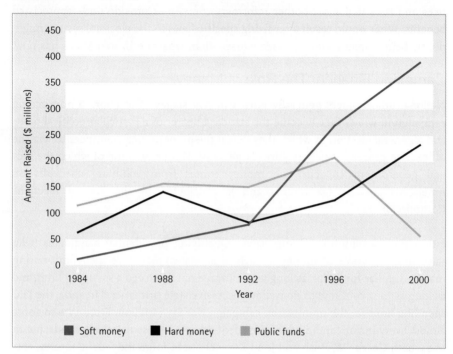

Source: The Federal Election Commission. Note that the Federal Election Commission began requiring the parties to disclose their soft money in 1991. Figures for 1991 through 2000 are from the FEC. Figures for the 1984 and 1988 cycles are based on voluntary disclosures by the parties and on published estimates. Public funding declined in 2000 because Bush, Forbes, and the Republican party did not accept federal matching funds.

Spending in the General-Election Campaign   Labor Day traditionally is the official start date for the fall campaign, although today's nominees take shorter breaks after the summer conventions than in the past. From the start of the campaign until Election Day (the first Tuesday after the first Monday in November), the candidates maintain an exhausting pace, and the campaign dominates the news.[48]

Campaign consultants oversee the expenditure of the large sums of money raised. These specialists in modern, candidate-based campaigns have replaced party leaders, who supervised strategy in earlier eras. Modern campaigns retain pollsters expert in measuring surges and slumps in public opinion. Media consultants schedule the candidate's time, design campaign ads (or spots), and stage media events that attract the interest of reporters. Derided by critics as "handlers" or "hired guns," some campaign consultants have become celebrities.

The most important category of general-election spending is for what the FEC calls electronic media—TV and radio advertising—and the lion's share goes to television. In 2004, 56 percent of Kerry's general election spending and more than 70 percent of Bush's was for electronic media.[49] Although campaign advertising is widely criticized, studies have consistently found that it is informative; those exposed to ads know more about the candidates and where they stand. The issue content of ads actually has increased in recent years.[50] The emphasis on issues has come with a cost, however; ads are increasingly negative in tone. Rather than make positive cases for themselves, candidates offer memorable criticisms of their opponents.[51] There is also evidence that ads become more negative near the end of the campaign, when voters are paying the most attention.[52]

Financing Congressional Campaigns House elections have become increasingly expensive: Average spending in a House race was more than half a million dollars in 2004, with 53 candidates spending more than two million.[53] Moreover, the gap between incumbents' spending and that of their challengers is wide and has grown wider since 1980 (see Figure 7.7). For many of today's reformers, the explanation for the advantage of incumbency is simple and self-evident: money.

Money certainly affects candidate visibility, and congressional challengers are seriously underfunded. Furthermore, attracting so much campaign cash requires

FIGURE 7.7 The spending gap between incumbents and their challengers

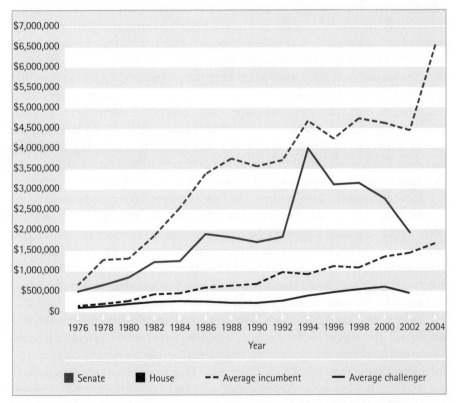

extensive effort from elected officials, a chore they often dislike. Nevertheless, research on congressional election financing paints a surprisingly complicated picture. Although money contributes to the electoral advantage that incumbents enjoy, its contribution is less than is often supposed.

Researchers have found that campaign spending yields what economists call *diminishing returns*: The more a candidate spends, the less impact each additional dollar will have. For an incumbent who already has perquisites of office worth as much as a million dollars a year, an extra $100,000 has less impact than it would if it were spent by a challenger who lacked taxpayer-provided resources. For this reason, campaign-finance reforms that make it more difficult to raise or spend money should lessen electoral competition by hurting challengers, who most need money so that they can compensate for the incumbents' name recognition and perks.[54]

Incumbents may receive so much money in part because they are so likely to win, rather than the reverse. The mid-1960s' surge in the incumbency advantage *preceded* the explosion of congressional campaign spending. Moreover, the growth of political action committees (PACs) took place only after the adoption of campaign-finance laws in 1974, by which time incumbents had already developed a significant advantage. Heavy spending by an incumbent generally signals that the incumbent is in trouble.[55] Of the 10 highest-spending representatives in 2004, six received 55 percent of the vote or less. The great majority of incumbents probably would still be reelected if campaign spending were slashed.

Perhaps the most discouraging impact of campaign spending today is one that is difficult to observe, let alone measure. Because it takes so much money for a challenger to mount a serious campaign—$600,000 in the estimation of political scientist Gary Jacobson—many potential challengers never enter the race. Why invest so much money for what is at best a long shot? Thus, amassing substantial campaign funds may be most important as a deterrent: Money can't buy the candidate love, but perhaps it can scare off rival suitors.[56]

In recent years the topic of campaign-finance reform has received enormous attention. Many citizens view the system as little more than bribery. Columnist Dave Barry writes, "Basically, our campaign finance system works this way: Donors give money to politicians, who then use the government to do favors for the donors."[57] Although this probably exaggerates the current system's negative effects, there is no question that citizens are disgusted with it. They are cynical about government, suspecting that politicians care only about what wealthy interests have to say.

Even if the campaign-finance system is fundamentally flawed, however, it is not certain what sort of electoral reform would improve matters. Spending is heavily regulated in other democracies. In Britain, neither parties nor individual candidates for office are permitted to buy broadcast time to communicate directly with potential voters. They are limited to a small number of publicly financed addresses by national party leaders. In Germany, the law restricts parties to the free air time provided by TV networks; they may not buy additional ads.[58] Such restrictions on campaign messages do not appear consistent with the First Amendment or with American values in favor of free expression.

Many other democracies provide at least some degree of public financing.[59] But using government money to subsidize campaigns requires some method of determining eligibility and deciding how much money to give. The country could not turn over millions of dollars to any person or party that chose to throw a hat into the ring. The typical solution is to look back at the previous election. For example, in many countries the parties receive public subsidies in proportion to the number of votes they received in the previous election or the number of seats they hold in parliament.* It is hard to see how a system geared toward rewarding past successes would make either incumbents or dominant parties any less secure than they are now.

The Role of Electoral Institutions

The United States operates on the principle that everyone should have equal influence over government. This commitment fuels widespread distaste for the role of money in national elections, for example, and undergirds the one-person–one-vote legal doctrine. Systems of representation never give everyone equal influence in practice, however. Full equality is impossible to implement, if for no other reason than the fact that an electoral system must accommodate other social goals—including efficiency, individual autonomy, protection of minorities, and fidelity to tradition.

Inequality may open election laws to criticism. Certainly alternative arrangements could equalize influence compared to the current system. On the other hand, reforms also often carry costs, including possible unanticipated consequences. Weighing the costs and benefits of political change requires analyzing how current institutions actually work. We focus here on two institutions in the U.S. system that cause voter influence to vary—the electoral college in presidential elections and legislative districts in congressional elections.

The Electoral College   The presidential candidate who garners the most votes—the so-called **popular vote**—does not necessarily win. Four times in American history, the candidate who came in second became president, including George W. Bush in 2000.† The reason for this discrepancy is the electoral college. Each state possesses a certain number of **electoral votes** and selects the rules that determine which candidate(s) will receive them. If a candidate wins more of the battles for electoral votes, then the total quantity of individual votes received nationwide is irrelevant.

The electoral college distorts popular preferences by unequally distributing the electors who cast electoral votes. Each state picks one elector for each House

---

* Examples include Austria, Belgium, Denmark, Finland, Germany, Mexico, Sweden, and Turkey.
† The other three were John Quincy Adams in 1824, Rutherford B. Hayes in 1876 and Benjamin Harrison in 1888.

and Senate seat in Congress (with an additional three electors assigned to the District of Columbia under the terms of the Twenty-third Amendment). Because every state has two senators, influence is not proportional to population; small states get a numerical advantage. The smallest states receive yet another advantage because of the guarantee that they will each get at least one House member no matter how small their populations. For example, with two senators but only one seat in the House, Wyoming has three electoral votes—approximately 1 electoral vote per 165,000 residents. With two senators but 53 seats in the House, California has 55 electoral votes, approximately 1 vote per 617,000 residents—a ratio only one-quarter as large as Wyoming's. Using figures from the 2000 census, a candidate theoretically could become president with the electoral votes of states containing only 45 percent of the U.S. population.

Large states have tried to compensate for their disadvantage by assigning all of their electors to the candidate receiving the most votes. This **winner-take-all voting** system is used in all states except Maine and Nebraska. Because large states have so many electoral votes to distribute, they are often the most attractive targets for campaign activity. And because large states tend to be diverse, they are usually competitive electoral arenas, another trait that draws candidate attention.

Experts disagree about whether, on balance, the electoral college favors large states, favors small states, or balances power. Their disagreements usually hinge on rather technical differences in how they evaluate influence.[60] But the small-state advantage helped President Bush tease out a victory over former Vice President Gore, because many Bush states were small ones. And the winner-take-all system explains why candidates often win big electoral college majorities despite modest advantages in the popular vote. In 1996, Clinton won 49 percent of the popular vote but 70 percent of the electoral vote.

For more than a century the popular and electoral vote winners were the same, so the electoral college received little attention. The 2000 election changed that. At first many observers thought Al Gore might win the presidency with a minority of the popular vote. Bush seemed quite strong in the Republican "L" (depicted in Figure 7.8), a cluster of heartland states that consistently vote for the GOP. Yet Gore seemed capable of tipping the balance in enough swing states to win without a popular majority. Concentrating his efforts in rural states would have cost Bush the election. As it turned out, Gore's policy proposals played well in coastal areas, and urban voters mobilized heavily behind him, so that he trounced Bush in a handful of densely populated states. But he lost the electoral vote.

Norms of equal influence have become very strong. It seems unjust, in America's new democracy, for the majority to find its desires frustrated.[61] It is therefore worth considering what useful role the electoral college might play. Breaking up votes by state requires that a candidate have broad appeal. Winning a state overwhelmingly is not as useful as winning lots of different states. The 2000 election illustrates this dynamic. Gore crushed Bush in California and New York, so

FIGURE 7.8   The Republican "L"

The base on which GOP majorities were built in presidential elections in the 1970s and the 1980s was a wide swath of states called the Republican "L." It takes in the Rocky Mountain region, the Plains states, and the entire South. With Alaska thrown in, these states have a total of 233 electoral votes (270 are needed to win). Bill Clinton cracked the "L," but it reemerged in 2000.

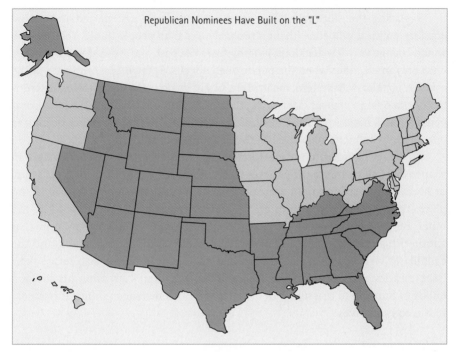

Republican Nominees Have Built on the "L"

Source: "Republican Nominees Have Built on the "L,"" *Congressional Quarterly Guide to the 1996 Republican National Convention* (August 3, 1996): 9.

he won the popular vote. (Remove either state and Gore lost handily.) But Bush squeaked through in the electoral college because he won a larger variety of states. The system therefore discourages politicians from adopting a strategy that unites a minority of the country (whether Southerners or city dwellers or anyone else) while dividing the majority. Divisiveness does not pay off.

The electoral college also may reduce the importance of money. It allows candidates to focus their resources on undecided states. Candidates still can choose to spend vast sums, blanketing battleground states with ads, but these excessive expenditures bring diminishing returns more quickly. The major-party candidate with fewer resources therefore does not suffer as much under the current, more-focused system.

Finally, the electoral college may reduce corruption. Presumably electoral misbehavior is easiest in states where partisanship is most one-sided. Public officials are more likely to share interests, and citizen opinion on who should win the presidency is most uniform. Under the current system, the potential for statewide corruption peaks where it is least likely to make a difference. The electoral college ensures that vote totals matter only as a state becomes less lopsided, when the competing sides are better able to demand fair and honest procedures.

Replacing the electoral college with a popular-vote system certainly would equalize political influence (though probably less than people think). Yet doing so would change very few elections, judging from the past, and it could make a difference only in elections when the public does not clearly favor one candidate or the other. A popular-vote system, meanwhile, might bring costs: encouraging discriminatory campaign appeals, forcing candidates to find resources adequate to compete for votes nationwide, and rewarding states that can find ways (fair or foul) to pile up overwhelming majorities for their candidate of choice.

Whatever happens to the electoral college, it is clear that the current system shapes campaign strategy. If you were a citizen of Kansas or Utah, of Mississippi or Massachusetts, you might scarcely have known the 2004 election was taking place. Your states were written off by one party and taken for granted by the other. But if you were a citizen of Florida, Ohio, Pennsylvania, West Virginia, or another "battleground" state, you were bombarded with campaign ads, and the candidates visited your state numerous times. The candidates also recast their issue positions to appeal to the swing states, with Kerry stressing his lifelong hobby of hunting to reassure gun owners, and Bush distancing himself from extreme conservatives.

Apportionment of Congressional Districts

Using electoral districts to determine the nation's legislators also frustrates the will of the majority. This is obvious for the Senate. The Constitution gives every state two senators, regardless of population.* The House presents a more complicated picture, because representatives run in election districts that shift periodically. The Constitution requires a census every decade. After each census, the 435 seats in the House are apportioned among the states according to their populations, a process called **reapportionment**.

Currently, six states have populations so small that they get only one representative each, a minimum guaranteed by Article I. After the smallest states receive their single representatives, the remaining congressional districts must be of almost precisely equal population. This provision applies both within states and, to the extent possible, across them. Nationally, the shift in congressional districts from state to state has favored the GOP in recent decades. States in the Northeast and Midwest have lost House seats to the South and Southwest, as population has shifted to the predominantly Republican Sun Belt.

Once states learn their allotments, they set to work **redistricting**—drawing the boundaries of the new districts to equalize population. In most states the legisla-

*This provision can be amended only with the consent of every state (Article 5).

FAIR WEATHER FOR THE SOUTH
Population growth in the heavily Republican Sun Belt has outpaced that in the North, causing congressional districts to migrate southward. The Detroit area of Michigan, where this cartoon was first published, has been especially hard hit. *Do you think it is harder for a region to recover economically if it loses political power after a decline?*
Source: Thompson-Detroit Free Press 2000

ture does the work, but in five states bipartisan commissions do the job, and several others have a more complicated process. Redistricting is often highly contentious, because political careers depend on which voters get placed in which districts. Politicians often accuse each other of **gerrymandering**—that is, of drawing the lines to benefit a certain group. The courts may be pulled into the process. But every district still ends up with the same population.

Aside from voters in a few small states, therefore, everyone receives about the same amount of House representation. The prime source of inequality is the winner-take-all process of electing one member per district and granting the seat to the person who wins the most votes—called the **single-member, simple-plurality (SMSP) system**. The system disadvantages voting minorities. Candidates win nothing if they do not receive the most votes, even if the second-place finisher gets 49 percent. Any minority spread over many districts will remain unrepresented unless it becomes dominant in at least one place.

Recognizing these realities, critics occasionally question the electoral system itself. Some suggest that the United States should shift to **proportional representation**, in which a party receives congressional seats according to its share of the vote. Certainly, such a system would equalize influence, compared to the current method. Yet it could undermine the ombudsman role served by legislators (see Chapter 9). The current system assigns each locality a particular member of Congress, responsible for defending that area's interests before the national government. An alternative system that pooled votes over a large geographic area or even over the nation as a whole would sever this direct link between legislator and voter.

Proportional representation systems also carry a risk. They might assist fringe parties dedicated to undermining the political system.[62] Even parties with few supporters could garner enough votes to win at least one seat, so the incentive to choose mainstream politicians would diminish. The party system might splinter enough that social conflicts would all have to be settled within the halls of government, among combative representatives, rather than through the coalition building that candidates often require to win elections in a district-based system.

The Nomination Process

The role that incumbent war chests play in chasing off qualified challengers is not the only problem with the manner in which candidates for office are recruited and nominated. If any segment of the electoral system dampens popular influence, and in a fashion that is difficult to justify, it is a nomination process that limits the range of choices voters can express.

Presidential Nominations   The United States is unusual among world democracies for its lengthy, participatory process of nominating candidates for chief executive. One British correspondent calls it "a bizarre ritual."[63] In most democracies, party activists and leaders choose nominees. But in the United States every citizen, whatever the depth of his or her commitment, may participate in selecting among possible candidates for the two major parties. Barriers are minimal for participation in a **caucus**—a meeting of candidate supporters—or a **primary election**—a preliminary election. At the presidential level, nearly three-quarters of the states choose their delegates in primary elections, and the remainder choose them in caucuses. Because caucus states tend to be smaller, most of the nation's delegates are chosen in primaries.

The caucus is a rather time-consuming process. Supporters of the respective candidates meet in each voting precinct to start the process of delegate selection. Generally, they gather in public places, such as town halls or public schools, but sometimes they meet on quasi-private property, such as restaurants. These precinct gatherings are only the beginning, however, because the process has a number of stages. For example, the Iowa caucuses are the first major test for candidates, because they occur very early in the election year. But these caucuses only choose delegates to the county conventions held in March, which then choose delegates to the May congressional district conventions, who move on to state conventions held in June!

Democratic caucuses are constrained by national-party rules that require proportional representation for the supporters of different candidates, as well as equal numbers of male and female delegates where possible. Any registered Democrat is eligible to participate. Republican caucuses are less open. Some limit participation to party officials and workers. Some use variants of proportional representation, and some continue to use winner-take-all voting procedures.[64]

Caucus turnout is extremely low—typically in single digits. About 6 percent of the voting-age population participated in the 2004 Iowa caucuses despite a close contest between Democrats John Kerry, John Edwards, and Howard Dean. This figure was not unusually low; the 12 percent turnout in the 1988 Iowa caucuses, when both parties had competitive contests, is believed to be the highest caucus turnout ever recorded. Caucus participants of both parties are unrepresentative of the general population in terms of income and education, and ideologically they tend to be more extreme than their party's broader base of party identifiers.

Primaries take many forms across the states. In **closed primaries**, only party members can vote—and only in the primary of the party in which they are registered. Some primaries are only "semiclosed" because they allow independents to select party primaries and vote as well. **Open primaries** allow any registered voter to select one party's primary and vote in it, even if that person is a member of another party. Most of the southern and upper Midwestern states have open primaries.

Evolution of the Nomination Process   The direct primary is an American invention, a reform that swept across the states in the early twentieth century. Despite their adoption at the state and local levels, however, primaries did not determine presidential nominations for another half-century.[65] As late as 1968, Vice President Hubert Humphrey won the Democratic nomination without entering a single primary. Primaries simply served as beauty contests used by particular candidates to show party leaders their popular appeal. These leaders—mayors, governors, and other public and party officials—actually controlled the delegates to national conventions.

The Republicans were the first to begin moving toward greater popular participation in their nominating process. In 1964, Senator Barry Goldwater, an insurgent from Arizona, won the nomination by edging out the party's establishment candidate in the California primary.[66] But the real push to openness came after Humphrey's presidential nomination. Many liberal activists had supported "peace" candidates Eugene McCarthy and Robert Kennedy, who opposed the war in Vietnam.[67] These candidates won most of the year's primaries, driving President Lyndon Johnson from the race in the process. Their supporters thus were outraged that the nomination went to Johnson's vice president. The party adopted its current process to mollify the antiwar movement.[68]

The past two decades have seen much tinkering with the rules, but the broad outlines of the system have not changed. In 2004, all of the Republican delegates and about 80 percent of the Democratic delegates were chosen in primaries and caucuses.* The general pattern today is for candidates to build extensive organizations in the states where the first caucuses and primaries are held. Here the emphasis is on "retail politics," face-to-face contact with voters.[69] An early victory can lead to greater support and more news coverage in the caucuses and primaries that follow.

Strengths and Weaknesses of the Nomination Process   Despite its participatory nature, many observers are critical of the presidential nomination process.[70] Their concerns fall into two broad categories, one procedural, the other political.

The nomination process is sequential: Candidates organize and campaign in one state, then pack up and move on to the next. The problem, critics complain, is that the process starts before citizens are interested in the election and outlasts citizen endurance.[71] A poll taken in June 2004, as the candidates shifted gears from the nomination process to the general election campaign, revealed that 52 percent of the respondents felt that the campaign is too long.[72] A candidate debate in the early days of the 2004 campaign, carried by CNN in prime time, drew an audience of 1.8 million. That was slightly smaller than the audience for the WB network's soon-to-be-cancelled situation comedy *Run of the House*, and far behind top-rated *CSI*, which drew 26.5 million viewers on the very same night.[73] Many candidacies therefore die before voters are tuned in to the campaign.

The long process may bore ordinary voters and leave the nominees "damaged goods" when they finally emerge from the grueling process. Yet it shines a bright light on candidates, revealing a great deal of information about them that Americans choose to consider when they vote. Is it better for voters to be ignorant of personal shortcomings or the questionable activities of a public servant, flaws that often went unknown before the modern nomination process? Opinions differ. The scrutiny may expose bad leaders, but the lack of personal privacy also may drive away some good leaders. Indeed, some have suggested (jokingly?) that anyone willing to expose every aspect of his or her life to media scrutiny is not the kind of person who should be in power.

And so the procedural argument goes, back and forth. The structure of the nomination process has positive and negative qualities, and any change is soon criticized. For example, in 2000 and 2004 the primaries were "front-loaded"; many states moved their primaries to early dates in hopes that the nomination contests would be decided more quickly and the winners would have more time to unify their parties and plan

(text continues on page 194)

---

* *The Democrats generally reserve about 20 percent of their slots for elected officials and party leaders who are called superdelegates.*

Election Voices

SHOULD THERE BE A NATIONAL PRIMARY TO NOMINATE PRESIDENTIAL CANDIDATES?

Of all the proposals for restructuring the presidential nomination process, the national primary is both the simplest and the most radical. It is also one of the oldest: The Progressive party endorsed the idea in 1912 and President Woodrow Wilson recommended it in his first annual message to Congress in 1913.

A national primary would scrap the current system of staggered individual state primaries and caucuses and instead hold a primary election in all 50 states at once. According to one version of the plan, the winner of that election would then automatically become his or her party's presidential candidate. In another variant, the winner would become the nominee only if he or she won at least 40 percent of the total vote. If no candidate achieved that threshold, a second, runoff election would be held between the top two finishers in the first election.

According to its proponents, a national primary has several advantages. First, it is much simpler than the current system. Instead of the complexity of 50 different state contests spread over three or four months, each with its own set of election laws and delegate selection rules, the national primary would substitute one or at most two decisive elections, both of which, presumably, would be governed by a single system of rules.

Hillary Clinton campaigns in New Hampshire.

Second, a national primary would treat all states equally. The current process gives a much greater voice to states that happen to vote early. Two states in particular, Iowa and New Hampshire, have an outsized role in selecting presidential candidates. Besides violating basic considerations of equity, most people admit that Iowa and New Hampshire are, in important ways, unrepresentative of the country as a whole. Neither state, for example, has a significant number of African-Americans or a large city.

Third, a national primary would almost certainly increase the number of people who participate in the presidential nomination process. Under the present system, voter participation rates vary widely according to when a state holds its primary. In the 2000 Republican race, for example, 52 percent of the eligible electorate turned out for the New Hampshire primary on February 1. But in the 23 primaries held after March 9, when George W. Bush and Al Gore had wrapped up their nominations, the average turnout was just 16 percent.[84] By ensuring that all people would go to the polls while the race was still undecided, a national primary would almost certainly increase participation.

But the national primary also has its opponents. The worst aspect of a national primary, according to these critics, is that it would limit the presidential

(continued on next page)

SHOULD THERE BE A NATIONAL PRIMARY
TO NOMINATE PRESIDENTIAL CANDIDATES? *(continued)*

nomination process to candidates who are already well known and/or well financed. Only someone who was famous before the race began or who had an enormous amount of money to spend could run a full-scale, national campaign. Trudging through the snows of Iowa and New Hampshire to meet individually with voters may be taxing, but it requires less money and name recognition.

A national primary might also lead to the nomination of a candidate who is supported by a small and zealous minority, but is considered unacceptable by most of the party. A single extremist with only 30 percent of the vote could win if a number of other candidates split the moderate vote. The sequential nature of the current primary system, by comparison, generally prevents this sort of problem from occurring. A fringe candidate may win some early primaries, but the mainstream of the party will usually coalesce around a more acceptable alternative.

It is precisely to avoid this problem that most recent national primary proposals require the winner to receive some minimum percentage (usually 40 percent) and call for a runoff election if no candidate crosses that threshold. Yet, runoffs carry problems of their own. Interest and participation in runoff elections are usually lower than they are in the first election.[85] And because most recent national primary proposals call for the first-round primary to be held in the last half of August or the first week in September, Americans might face the prospect of holding three national elections over a period of just 70 days.[86] Voter fatigue might be a real problem.

Electoral reform is not, to say the least, atop the list of priorities for most Americans. But when they do think about such matters, Americans seem to support the national primary. On fifteen occasions between 1952 and 1988, the Gallup Poll asked a national sample if they favored having "presidential candidates chosen by the voters in a nationwide primary election instead of by political party conventions as at present." On average, 67 percent supported the national primary; only 21 percent opposed it.

WHAT DO YOU THINK?

1. Proponents say the national primary is better because it is simpler. Is simplicity really an advantage in the design of political institutions?
2. Is there an advantage to having one or two small states lead off the delegate selection process, or would we be better off if all 50 states voted at once?

Although there is no major Web site devoted to the national primary controversy, the following sites contain detailed information on the 2008 nomination calendar.

www.thegreenpapers.com
www.rhodescook.com
www.nass.org

for the fall election campaign.[74] As Figure 7.9 shows, these hopes were fulfilled. But then critics charged that this front-loading gave an advantage to well-known, establishment candidates who could raise large sums of campaign money quickly.

A second set of criticisms focuses on the *politics* of the nomination process. Reformers who instituted primaries claimed they were giving "power to the

FIGURE 7.9   In 2000 and 2004, the presidential nominations were decided earlier than ever

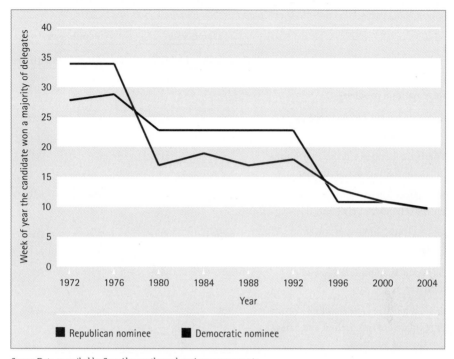

Source: Data compiled by Sam Abrams through various news reports.

people"—the new procedure would empower ordinary citizens at the expense of the party bosses. In fact, other elites rose up to be the new bosses: political activists and the media.

Political activists have always exerted more influence than ordinary citizens, because they participate. Caucus turnout is extremely low, and although primary turnout is higher, it is still much lower than that in general elections. Of the 18 states that voted while the nominations were still undecided in 2000, 12 set turnout records, but the average turnout was only 13.6 percent![75] Even more important, activists work in campaigns and give money to candidates; they help mobilize others.

None of this would be cause for concern if the activists were like everyone else. But activists differ in politically relevant ways. Not only are their views more *intense*, but party activists' positions are more *extreme* as well (see Table 7.3). Candidates often must conform to these policy positions if they wish to win nominations. Consequently, the primary process may force candidates to take positions far from the center of the political spectrum where the mass of Americans are located. Democratic candidates generally are more liberal, and Republican candidates generally more conservative, than the average voter.[76]

Another consequence of the enhanced influence of activists in the nominating process is that they skew the political debate. To someone following the process, it

TABLE 7.3   Party activists are not moderates

Surveys find that on most issues, Democratic activists tend to be more liberal than Democratic identifiers, and Republican activists more conservative than Republican identifiers. Here is how national convention delegates compared to their parties' supporters in 2004.

Issue	Democrats		Republicans	
	Delegates	Identifiers	Delegates	Identifiers
Government should do more to solve nation's problems	79%	48%	7%	35%
Government should do more to promote traditional values	15%	26%	55%	61%
The United States did the right thing in taking military action in Iraq	7%	21%	96%	78%
New government anti-terrorism laws excessively restrict civil liberties	77%	53%	15%	25%
Abortion should be permitted in all cases	64%	37%	8%	13%
Gay couples should be allowed to marry	44%	36%	3%	11%
Federal government should do more to regulate environmental and safety practices of business	85%	71%	15%	45%

Source: *New York Times*/CBS News Poll, 2004 Democratic National Delegate Survey, conducted June 16–July 17, 2004; *New York Times*/CBS News Poll, 2004 Republican National Delegate Survey, conducted August 3–23, 2004.

may seem that the most important issues facing the United States are so-called hot-button issues, such as abortion and gun control. Although issues such as these are important, ordinary voters do not view them as crucial.[77] So they may prefer that the spotlight turn to bread-and-butter issues, such as education, medical care, and prosperity.

The media are the second group that gained influence from the nomination process, because journalists are the ones responsible for interpreting primary and caucus developments for the American people. Some critics claim that the press trivializes elections by emphasizing matters other than policy and performance (see Chapter 5). The press reports the horse race—who is ahead and by how far, who is "coming up on the rail," and who is fading from contention. This emphasis has increased over time such that, for the last couple of decades, four-fifths of election coverage focuses on the horse race aspect.[78]

The media warp public perception of elections in other ways. For example, Iowa, the first caucus state, and New Hampshire, the first primary state, receive a disproportionate share of news coverage. Some critics ask whether two sparsely populated, rural states should play such an important role in determining candidate viability or, indeed, in determining who is the front runner.[79] For the 2008 race, Democrats tried to address this criticism at the cost of continuing the front-loading trend. Party officials moved the Nevada caucus and South Carolina primary to the beginning of the calendar to lessen the influence of Iowa and New Hampshire.[80]

Finally, some observers complain that the media no longer merely report the nomination process but also have become important players in it. News stories have grown overwhelmingly interpretive, rather than simply factual.[81] For example, in every campaign there is a widely publicized "expectations game." The question is not so much whether candidates win or lose but how they perform relative to "expectations." And who sets these expectations? The media.

The classic example occurred in 1972, when Senator Edmund Muskie's campaign never recovered from his showing in the New Hampshire primary. Muskie won the primary over George McGovern 46 percent to 37 percent. But New Hampshire was next to Muskie's home state of Maine, so the media expected him to do well. They thought that, comparatively, McGovern's showing was unexpectedly strong for a native of South Dakota and brought him extensive publicity as a result. The momentum that McGovern took out of his New Hampshire loss carried him to the Democratic nomination!

The media are more influential in the primaries than in the general-election campaign. Voters cannot use party cues to decide among candidates in primaries, because they all belong to the same party. Nor is presidential performance of any use. Normally, all the candidates in the incumbent party's primaries defend the president's record, whereas all the candidates in the other party's primaries criticize that record. Consequently, citizens use other information to choose among the candidates, and in most cases the media provide it. In particular, the electorate usually wishes to know which candidates are serious, and campaign coverage gives that signal. None of these sources of media influence appears in the general election.

Whatever your view of the pros and cons of the American nomination process, it is now well established and, therefore, unlikely to change except in marginal ways for the foreseeable future. Many of the problems that bother critics originate not in national law, but in the combined decisions of political parties, individual states, and media organizations. Even if reformers did succeed at changing the process, the alternatives might be worse than the current system.

Who Nominates the Vice President?   Before the establishment of the contemporary nomination process, the conventions chose the vice-presidential as well as the presidential candidates. Today, the choice is completely in the hands of the presidential nominees. The presidential nominees simply announce their choices, and the conventions accept them. Usually they attempt to select a nominee who will help the ticket (or at least not hurt it).[82]

Bush's choice of Dick Cheney in 2000 offset his inexperience with national politics; Cheney was a widely respected former Cabinet secretary and congressman. In 2004 John Kerry chose Senator John Edwards, a southerner who had performed surprisingly well as a presidential candidate in the primary campaign. Recent choices for vice president have, as often as not, been better respected nationally than the men who chose them.

The Congressional Nomination Process The congressional nomination process is much simpler than the presidential one: A nominee for the House or Senate must win at most one primary election, not a sequence across many states. In a few states, party conventions can nominate candidates, but in most states primary voters do the job.

The dates of **filing deadlines** and primary elections vary widely across states.[83] The filing deadline is the latest date on which a politician who wishes to be on the ballot must file official documents with, and/or pay fees to, state election officials. In 2006 the dates ranged from December 19 (2005!) in Illinois to August 11 in Louisiana. The primaries started on March 7, and the last was held on September 23. Thus, some candidates know whether they will have opponents, and who those opponents are, as much as nine months earlier than others.

The hardest-fought primaries occur when a seat becomes "open" because an incumbent dies, retires, resigns, or opts to run for another office. If both parties have strength in the area, the primaries in both parties are hotly contested. If only one party is strong, its primary will be a donnybrook, because the winner is viewed as the next member of Congress. **Open seats** are critical to political change within a party because few incumbents lose primaries. In the 10 elections held since 1980, a total of 50 House incumbents and six Senate incumbents were defeated in primaries, and not many more faced tough races. This record does not prove that primaries are unimportant. Incumbent primary successes probably indicate the same

THE CHOICE
Presidential nominees try to select running mates that will help the ticket. John Kerry may have selected John Edwards because of his southern heritage and perennial optimism. *Was this a wise strategy, or should Kerry have chosen an older, more experienced vice presidential nominee, as President Bush did in his choice of Dick Cheney?*

thing as general-election successes do: Incumbents behave in such a way as to keep their constituencies satisfied and preempt a strong challenge.

CHAPTER SUMMARY

Many traits that reformers dislike about the American electoral system result from the quantity of popular input, rather than from the limits on it. For example, incumbency advantages in congressional elections largely result from the effort that incumbents put into satisfying voters back home. Even senators must campaign continually to retain their power, contrary to what the founders originally expected. They cannot simply ride national political forces to victory.

The American nomination process is far more open than the nomination processes of other democracies. It gives rank-and-file voters more influence in the United States than they have in other countries, and it gives "outsider" candidates a chance by enabling them to pull off upsets in early primaries and caucuses. If the system has any serious flaw, it is probably the way campaign finance laws, party activists, and the media can run off or shut out candidates before ordinary voters have had adequate time to consider them. But even this influence may be exaggerated, and at any rate no obvious reform is available to fix it.

Campaigning is often misunderstood. It is not an independent force that determines election outcomes. Rather, the campaign itself is shaped by events and conditions in the years leading up to the election. The reason why campaigns are limited in their impact is that most voters do not make up their minds on the basis of campaigns. People vote for the parties they favor, vote against leaders when they dislike the government's performance, consider policy differences when these are easy to compare, and weigh candidate traits relevant to governance. Only a minority decide how to vote late in the campaign, by using knowledge of particular candidates or the particular things they say.

KEY TERMS

caucus, p. 190
closed primaries, p. 191
coattails, p. 176
electoral votes, p. 185
filing deadlines, p. 198
gerrymandering, p. 189
incumbency advantage, p. 175
incumbents, p. 174
matching funds, p. 181
midterm loss, p. 176
open primaries, p. 191
open seats, p. 198

party identification, p. 169
popular vote, p. 185
primary election, p. 190
proportional representation, p. 189
reapportionment, p. 188
redistricting, p. 188
retrospective voting, p. 171
safe seats, p. 174
single-member, simple-plurality (SMSP) system, p. 189
soft money, p. 181
winner-take-all voting, p. 186

Suggested Readings

Abramson, Paul, John Aldrich, and David Rohde. *Change and Continuity in the 2004 Elections.* Washington, DC: CQ Press, 2006. This quadrennial publication provides a comprehensive overview of voting behavior in national elections.

Fenno, Richard. *Home Style.* Boston: Little, Brown, 1978. Influential study of how House members interact with constituents, earning their trust.

Fiorina, Morris. *Congress—Keystone of the Washington Establishment,* 2nd ed. New Haven, CT: Yale University Press, 1989. A critical look at the implications of constituency service for national policy making.

Holbrook, Thomas. *Do Campaigns Matter?* Thousand Oaks, CA: Sage, 1996. A scientifically rigorous study of the impact of presidential campaigns.

Mayer, William, ed. *In Pursuit of the White House 2000: How We Choose Our Presidential Nominees.* Chatham, NJ: Chatham House, 2000. An informative collection of essays covering all facets of the contemporary nominating process.

Mayhew, David. *Congress—The Electoral Connection.* New Haven, CT: Yale University Press, 1974. Influential work that shows how much of congressional structure and behavior can be explained by the assumption that reelection is the most important goal of members.

On the Web

THE UNITED STATES ELECTORAL COLLEGE
www.archives.gov/federal_register/electoral_college/electoral_college.html
A detailed explanation of the electoral college as well as an historical database of presidential election data. The site is maintained by the National Archives and Records Administration and has links to other government data sets pertaining to elections on all levels of government.

FEDERAL ELECTION COMMISSION
www.fec.gov
The Federal Election Commission is the government agency that tracks campaign spending and writes campaign finance regulations. Their site includes a searchable database of candidate and donor information.

AMERICAN NATIONAL ELECTION STUDIES
www.umich.edu/~nes
Probably the single most important source of data for students of American elections. This impressive collection of election surveys, conducted from the 1950s to the present, is the source of many of the figures and tables that appear in this book.

Political Parties and Interest Groups

AMERICANS ARE UNHAPPY WITH THE STATE OF THEIR MEDICAL care.[1] Per citizen, they pay far more for care than citizens in other industrialized countries— over twice as much as in the United Kingdom, for example.[2] Yet health access and health outcomes in the United States are no better, and often worse, than in countries with lower costs. Almost 16 percent of the population lacks health insurance.[3] Life expectancy is shorter: 77.5 years compared to 78.6 years in Germany and more than 82 years in Japan.[4] Infant mortality is higher. Seven out of every thousand children born in the United States in 2003 died, more than in comparable countries.[5] It is no surprise, then, that Americans rate health care costs as "the most important financial problem" facing their families, and that as voters prepared to go to the polls in 2006, 80 percent said health care was a "very important" or "extremely important" issue.[6]

Two major efforts to address public concerns about health care have occurred since the early 1990s. In 1993, it seemed as though the political system was going to respond to voters' demands by enacting a thorough reform. President Bill Clinton promised to "take on the health care profiteers" after his election.[7] He appointed a task force, led by his wife Hillary, to propose an omnibus reform bill that could limit medical costs and expand coverage to the uninsured. The administration eventually suggested a massive reorganization of the health-care system. But interest groups descended on Congress and fought an all-out war over the reform bill—"the most expensive lobbying battle in history."[8] Spending estimates for this effort ranged as high as $300 million, including $50 million in campaign contributions from interests both for and against the reforms.

One opposition group ran an especially popular series of ads against the Clinton Plan, featuring two characters named Harry and Louise. The ad warned that Americans would have to "pick from a few health care plans designed by government bureaucrats." It then delivered the punch line: "There's got to be a better way." The Clinton Plan died, but so did every other reform proposal; no one found the "better way" that Harry and Louise sought. Interest-group lobbying apparently denied Americans the fundamental changes they wanted.

Fast forward a decade to the 2002 congressional elections. A new health care issue had come to dominate the political landscape: rising prescription drug costs for the elderly. Pharmaceutical companies release new drugs every year, and sometimes these brand-name drugs represent significant advances in medical treatment. Companies naturally want to profit from developing medicines and moving them through the risky governmental approval process, but the high prices charged for such products do not sit well with an aging population. Seniors began to clamor for government assistance to help them afford costly brand-name drugs—and, because the elderly are a numerous and politically active group, neither the Democrats nor the Republicans could refuse. Candidates from both parties promised during the 2002 election campaigns that they would use taxpayer money to cover senior prescriptions.

Once again, politically influential voices demanded fundamental change. This time, however, powerful groups scrambled to influence legislation rather than block it. The battle quickly formed along party lines and it was partisan bickering rather than interest-group obstruction that seemed to jeopardize action. Republicans wanted to provide the assistance through private health insurers whereas Democrats insisted on extensive coverage through Medicare, and each side attracted a host of interests favorably inclined toward their approach.[9] An entire year went by without progress.

Finally, one of the most powerful interest groups in Washington, the 35-million-strong American Association of Retired Persons (AARP), broke the logjam by agreeing to help pass a Medicare bill supported by President Bush.[10] The group normally sides with Democrats, but Republicans enticed them across party lines with a plan officially estimated to cost at least $400 billion over 10 years. The proposal still did not move quickly. It was caught between conservatives disgusted that a Republican president would endorse huge spending increases and liberals upset with a bill they thought would increase corporate profits for the pharmaceutical industry. Democratic presidential candidates in particular excoriated the AARP for delivering President Bush a policy victory so soon before the 2004 elections. But the group's active involvement helped free this fundamental policy shift from the gridlock created by party disputes, giving the public what it apparently wanted.

James Madison warned against the "mischiefs of faction"—against the danger of allowing self-interested pressure groups to take over the reins of government. Yet to many Americans, Madison's worst nightmares appear to have been realized. The 1990's paralysis on health-care reform illustrates the perceived ills of interest-group democracy. It shows special interests using their powers of persuasion to prevent change when most of the public believed that some kind of change was necessary. In other words, it indicates why Americans think that the system does not listen to what voters have to say.

On the other hand, the successful enactment of prescription drug legislation shows that the role of interest groups in American politics is not simple. Interest groups need not stand in the way of public wishes. Indeed, sometimes they are effective tools that force parties and politicians to be responsive

What stands out about modern parties and interest groups is not the extent to which they clog up the system. It is how much both sorts of organizations have opened up to public influence over time. Of course, sometimes parties and interest groups will block change, especially when the public itself is divided. At other times, however, these institutions serve as important conduits through which voters communicate with their government in between elections. The factions in politics today resemble the rest of America's new democracy because they have opened up to public participation.

Political Parties: A Necessary Evil?

When George Washington left office in 1796, he warned his fellow citizens against forming political parties. "The spirit of party," he warned, "agitates the community with ill-founded jealousies and false alarms, [and] kindles the animosity of one part against another." Washington's warning came too late. Thomas Jefferson and James Madison had already begun laying the foundations for an electoral alliance against Washington's successor, President John Adams. Jefferson, who regularly glorified the small farmer, began to reach out to urban interests. He and Madison concluded an alliance with New York's Republicans, giving them access to a clever New York City political operative named Aaron Burr. Burr delivered New York's 12 electoral votes to the coalition in the 1800 election, giving Jefferson the edge to defeat Adams and win the presidency. Thus, the second president of the United States was cast from office after losing a two-party presidential race.

The Constitution contains not a word about political parties, but they have been active in U.S. national politics ever since. It is hard to imagine a government without them. Political parties serve as the main connection between ordinary citizens and the public officials they elect. Parties nominate candidates for office, shape the electoral process, and mobilize voters. And after elections have determined the winners, parties also coordinate the actions of elected officials in the government. Despite the presence of parties almost since the country's founding, however, Americans have not always accepted the role they play in the political system. Periodically, voters have grown unhappy with the major parties available to them and have expressed their displeasure by supporting new organizations (see Table 8.1).

Political Parties in U.S. History

Two major parties have dominated elections for national office throughout American history. Americans therefore understandably regard a two-party system as a natural state of affairs. However, most democracies support more than two parties. The two-party system probably results from how the United States translates popular votes into control of public offices. American elections take place within geographic units (states, congressional districts, city wards, and so on), and the candidate who attracts the most votes—the one who is "first past the post"—wins the electoral unit no matter how many other candidates are in the race or how close the finish. Thus, winning is everything. Finishing in any position except first gets nothing. Citizens view voting for a smaller party as "wasting" their votes.[11]

Third parties regularly arise but they nearly all disappear quickly, either because they are a reaction to a particular problem that fades in importance or because one of the major parties co-opts their main issues. Ross Perot's populist, fiscally conservative Reform Party faded in the mid-1990s, for example, after President Clinton agreed to help eliminate huge federal deficits and after congressional Republicans embraced the drive for term limits—two concerns that had motivated party activists. Only once has a new group risen to become a major political party: the Republicans in the 1850s.

The United States may have always sustained two parties, but the system has altered significantly over the course of American history. Change usually occurs gradually. Individuals float in and out of the electorate, or from one party to

TABLE 8.1   Third parties in U.S. history

Candidate (party, year)	Showing	Subsequent Events
Theodore Roosevelt (Progressive Party, 1912)	27.4% 88 electoral votes	Party supported GOP nominee in 1916
H. Ross Perot (Independent Party, 1992)	18.7% 0 electoral votes	Perot formed new party (Reform) to take part in 1996 and 2000 presidential elections
Robert M. La Follette (Progressive Party, 1924)	16.6% 13 electoral votes	La Follette died in June 1925
George C. Wallace (American Independent Party, 1968)	13.5% 46 electoral votes	Wallace ran in Democratic primaries in 1972 until he was injured in assassination attempt
Martin Van Buren (Free Soil Party, 1848)	10.1% 0 electoral votes	Party drew 5 percent in 1852; supporters then merged into supporters then merged into Republican Party
James B. Weaver (Populist Party, 1892)	8.5% 22 electoral votes	Party supported Democrat William Jennings Bryan in 1896
H. Ross Perot (Reform Party, 1996)	8.5% 0 electoral votes	Perot adopted a lower profile
John B. Anderson (National Unity Campaign, 1980)	6.6% 0 electoral votes	Anderson withdrew from elective politics
Ralph Nader (Green Party, 2000)	3% 0 electoral votes	Nader failed to qualify for federal funding in 2004
Strom Thurmond (States' Rights Democratic Party, 1948)	2.4% 38 electoral votes	Democrats picked slate acceptable to South in 1952
Henry A. Wallace (Progressive Party, 1948)	2.4% 0 electoral votes	Party disappeared
Patrick Buchanan (Reform Party, 2000)	> 1% 0 electoral votes	Buchanan appeared to be finished in national politics

Note: The list excludes many third-party candidates who received less than 2 percent of the popular vote. Other third parties that won at least 2 percent of the vote include the Liberty Party (1844); the Greenback Party (1880); the Prohibition Party (1888, 1892); and the Socialist Party (1904, 1908, 1912, 1916, 1920, 1932).

Source: Adapted from Kenneth Jost, "Third-Party Prospects," *The CQ Researcher* (December 22, 1995): 1148. Updated with 1996 and 2000 election returns.

another—actions that cause election results to vary—but the system as a whole remains fairly stable. The same people usually vote for the same parties each time. The same parties usually win in the same places. Occasionally, however, some sort of dramatic event can shock the political system, resulting in changes that are more sudden or more sweeping. Whole groups may enter or leave the electorate, or may swing their support from one party to another. Republican areas can become Democratic ones, and vice versa.

Realignment scholars have tried to formalize the study of political change by breaking American political history into a series of distinct electoral eras, or "party systems."[12] Each era features stable party alignments. The minority party rarely wins the presidency, for example, unless it can find a military hero to nominate or it identifies some other temporary opportunity. But at some point a crisis disrupts the tidy arrangement of voters.* Rivals within the major parties may start fighting each other, or strong third parties may arise. Voter turnout surges in response to the excitement. Finally, a **critical election** (or realigning election) alters the existing electoral alignment altogether. New groups enter the electorate, or influential groups switch parties for good, solidifying the terms of political conflict for a generation or more.

Although defining "critical elections" or "electoral eras" is a tricky business, and some scholars doubt that it is possible to do so without oversimplifying political history,[13] the party-systems interpretation nevertheless provides a useful way to remember how American political parties have changed over time (see Table 8.2).

---

* Some scholars suggest that realignments naturally occur about once a generation, as society drifts away from the conditions that initially produced a party system.

TABLE 8.2   The party-systems' interpretation of U.S. electoral history

First Party System (Jeffersonian): 1796–1824*

7 Democratic—Republican presidential victories
1 Federalist victory

Second Party System (Jacksonian Democracy): 1828–1856

6 Democratic victories
2 Whig victories

Third Party System (Civil War and Reconstruction): 1860–1892

7 Republican victories
2 Democratic victories

Fourth Party System (Industrial Republican): 1896–1928

7 Republican victories
2 Democratic victories

Fifth Party System (New Deal): 1932–1964

7 Democratic victories
2 Republican victories

Sixth Party System (Divided Government): 1968–??

7 Republican victories
3 Democratic victories

* Years are approximated.

The First Party System (Jeffersonian)   Some historians date the first party system from the early 1790s to about 1824. Commercial interests in the young republic, especially those located in New England, supported the Federalists. The party's initial leaders included President John Adams and Treasury Secretary Alexander Hamilton. Agricultural interests in the South and West, including many voters outraged by Hamilton's tax on whiskey, gravitated to the Democratic–Republicans. Those averse to a strong executive also supported the opposition, which was centered in the Virginia congressional delegation. Thomas Jefferson defined the party's public image, but James Madison also played a prominent role in its development.

The overriding issue during this period was the establishment of a national government and the delineation of its power. Jeffersonians wished to keep the national government small and, although Jefferson made an exception to allow the Louisiana Purchase, they generally interpreted the Constitution to limit federal power. Federalists preferred that government exert more authority. They supported higher taxes, government assistance for local industries, a centralized military, and ambitious public improvements such as roads and bridges. The two parties were also divided over foreign policy. Federalists favored strong ties with the English, whereas Jeffersonians leaned toward the French.

In some ways, partisan competition has never been as bare-knuckled as it was early in this party system. Both embryonic parties had their own newspapers, which they used to revile each other. The Federalists essentially tried to shut down Jefferson's 1800 presidential campaign by passing the Alien and Sedition Acts of 1798, which (among other things) allowed them to jail people who criticized incumbent Federalist leaders. Some prominent Federalist sympathizers even accused Jefferson of conspiring with Jesuit priests and hash-eating Arab assassins as part of a secret society called the Illuminati. Their alleged purpose was "to root out and abolish Christianity, and overthrow all civil government."[14] These scurrilous efforts backfired. The Jeffersonians became the dominant political party, winning the presidency seven consecutive times from 1800 to 1824. The Federalist Party withered so badly after the War of 1812 that most political competition consisted of behind-the-scenes struggles among Democratic–Republican factions. The system splintered when General Andrew Jackson was denied the presidency in a "corrupt bargain" after winning both the popular vote and the electoral vote in 1824 (see Chapter 6).

The Second Party System (Jacksonian Democracy)   After his defeat in 1824, General Jackson and his allies laid the groundwork for another presidential campaign. In particular, they sought to mobilize more of their potential support. The strategy succeeded with a vengeance: Between 1824 and 1828, turnout in the presidential election tripled, sweeping Jackson into office.

The Jacksonian Democrats were the world's first mass party. One of their party's principal architects, Martin Van Buren, is sometimes called the father of parties. The Jacksonians openly passed out government jobs and contracts as a way to consolidate their hold on power. The Whigs, another mass party, formed to oppose "King Andrew" and his successors. They often used the same tactics. But the Democracy lost only two presidential elections to the Whigs, each time against a war hero (William Henry Harrison in 1840, Zachary Taylor in 1848). Democrats also controlled Congress through much of this period.

Many conflicts from the previous alignment persisted in the second party system, especially those over the proper power of the federal government. The Jacksonians vigorously opposed having a national bank and otherwise limited the growth of federal power. As a charismatic military leader, General Jackson might have built the presidency into a much stronger office, but he devoted most of his energies to other tasks—and the Democrats who followed Jackson showed little inclination to aggrandize their post. The Whigs, led by Kentuckian Henry Clay, endorsed programs of internal improvement funded by the national government. Forces also clashed over rates of taxation on imported goods.

The party system could not contain sectional differences. Dissatisfied citizens began running for office under third-party banners. The Free Soilers opposed the expansion of slavery into the territories.* The Whigs collapsed first, replaced by a new Republican party after 1854. Then the Democrats splintered in 1860, nominating both northern and southern candidates for president. Together with the Constitutional Union candidate, they received nearly 60 percent of the popular vote—but Republican candidate Abraham Lincoln led the race with nearly 40 percent, which was enough to give him an electoral college majority.

The Third Party System (Civil War and Reconstruction) War seldom enhances democracy, but the Civil War realignment produced the most competitive electoral era in American history.[15] The Democrats maintained a base in the House of Representatives during the Civil War and then took control in 1874, following the South's readmission to the Union. The Republicans maintained control of the Senate, though, because the wartime government had admitted several sparsely populated western states that dependably elected Republican senators.[16]

At the presidential level, the third party system became known as "the period of no decision." From 1876 to 1892, no presidential candidate received as much as 51 percent of the popular vote. In two elections (Rutherford Hayes in 1876 and Benjamin Harrison in 1888), the electoral college chose a president who had come in second in the popular vote. The dominant issue at the beginning of the period was reconstruction of the South, but economic issues took center stage after 1876. Industrialization, the rise of large business organizations, and a long agricultural depression generated the political issues of this party system.

During this era, party organizations reached their high point. Bitter memories of the Civil War left many people committed to the party of the Union

---

* Another third party, the Know Nothings, opposed immigration, especially of Catholics.

(Republicans) or of the rebels (Democrats), and these citizens voted a straight party line. Indeed, independents often were viewed as traitors. With feelings so strong and politics so competitive, the parties exerted tremendous effort in campaigns.[17] Parties reached such a high level of organization in many cities that they were referred to as **machines**.

The depression of the 1890s plunged much of the country into misery. Agricultural protest, common throughout the period, gave rise to the Populist movement—which seriously challenged the major parties in the South and West. Eventually Populists fused with the Democrats at the national level; they attempted to form a worker-farmer alliance.* The new strategy was doomed from the start. Cultural issues sharply divided urban Catholics and rural Protestants, as did questions such as taxation and immigration. Many of the impoverished voters who might have joined the alliance were African Americans, who remembered their debt to the "Party of Lincoln." In 1896, the Democrats nominated William Jennings Bryan for president, a man who encapsulated the economic and social frustrations of rural America. His nomination undermined Democratic support in urban areas. The "period of no decision" was over; Americans had decided.

The Fourth Party System (Industrial Republican)   The critical election of 1896 inaugurated a period of Republican dominance. The Democrats contracted to their base in the old Confederacy. The Republicans lost the presidency only twice during the fourth party system, in 1912 and again in 1916—both times to Democrat Woodrow Wilson. Wilson's unique success owed much to a factional split within the GOP. The Republican party included two wings, the old guard of pro-business conservatives and a progressive wing that wanted to reform American institutions. In 1912, progressive former President Theodore Roosevelt split from the Republicans to challenge his party's old guard nominee, President William Howard Taft. Roosevelt's campaign under the Progressive (or Bull Moose) Party label ultimately attracted more votes than Taft did, the only time a third-party candidate has picked up more support than a major-party nominee, but the practical effect was to put the Democrat in the White House.

This temporary rift within Republican ranks did not end the fourth party system, however. Wilson won reelection in 1916 on a platform of keeping the United States out of World War I, which he subsequently failed to do. He lost both his prestige and his health during this second term, and troubles in both economic and foreign policy hurt the image of his party. Ohio Senator Warren Harding, the Republican candidate in 1920, promised to quiet the turmoil of the World War I years. "America's present need is not heroics, but healing; not nostrums, but normalcy," he explained.[18] This message played well, not only to men but also to the millions of women who would be participating in their first presidential election.

---

* At the local level, Populists sometimes fused with Republicans. The Fusion ticket in Louisiana linked Populists with southern Louisiana Republicans (both blacks and sugar cane planters).

Harding won by an unprecedented landslide, and two more successful Republican presidential candidates followed him.

Two forces eventually undermined their dominance. One worked slowly. Growing urban populations increasingly preferred Democrats—a pattern that crystallized when Al Smith of New York won the Democratic presidential nomination in 1928, the first time a major party had run a Catholic for president. The disastrous stock market crash of 1929 was a more sudden force, and more damaging to the GOP. The Great Depression of the 1930s resulted in unemployment levels over 20 percent. A third of the nation's banks failed; a quarter of families lost their savings.[19] The Republican party lost the House in 1930, and the Democratic party established a new party system starting in 1932.

The Fifth Party System (New Deal)   The fifth party system was a class-based alignment like those found in modern European democracies. Especially after Franklin D. Roosevelt's first term, the Democrats became the party of the "common people" (blue-collar workers, farmers, and minorities), whereas the Republicans became, more than ever, the party of established interests. The Democrats therefore enjoyed strength in numbers. Only Republican war hero Dwight D. Eisenhower was able to crack the Democratic monopoly on the White House, and only from 1952 to 1954 did the Republicans control Congress as well.

The South formed a major component of FDR's coalition early on, but Democratic politicians struggled to reconcile the region's expectations with those of liberals and African Americans in northern cities. Gradually, party leaders began weaning themselves off the southern white vote. FDR won repeal of the 104-year-old "two-thirds rule," which required that the Democratic nominee receive a two-thirds majority of delegates to the national convention. With that rule's elimination in 1936, southerners no longer could veto unacceptable presidential candidates—which meant that they could not resist the growing national pressure for racial change. In 1948 the Deep South bolted the party rather than vote for President Truman, who had begun taking steps toward racial equality. Then southerners—along with other voters upset with the pace of social change—left in droves when President Lyndon B. Johnson pushed an aggressive civil rights agenda through Congress in the mid-1960s. Republican Richard Nixon's presidential victory in 1968 signed the death warrant for the New Deal party system.

The Sixth Party System (Divided Government)   Most commentators believe that the New Deal party system is gone, but they are in less agreement about what sort of party system has replaced it—or even if one has. The electoral alignments that developed around Richard Nixon's presidency have puzzled scholars for much of the past generation because they do not resemble realignments of the past.

The end of the New Deal party system did not lead to dominance by either major party, as happened after voters rejected William Jennings Bryan in 1896 or abandoned the Republican Party during the Depression. Instead, Nixon's victory initiated decades of split election outcomes. The Democrats lost seven of the ten presidential elections from 1968 to 2004, but controlled the House for forty years straight (1954–1994) and the Senate for most of this period as well. Although Republicans won Congress in 1994 as well as the presidency in 2000 and 2004, victory margins remained slim and Democrats recaptured the Congress in 2006. Democrats also continue to maintain an advantage in nationwide party identification (see Figure 7.2). Voters have exhibited a high rate of **ticket splitting**—supporting candidates of different parties in the same election. Three presidential elections in a row gave the White House to a candidate who lacked a majority of the popular vote: Clinton in 1992 and 1996, then Bush in 2000. Some scholars interpret this evidence as an indication that American parties have grown too weak to create a new party system.

Nor can scholars identify a critical election of the sort that initiated previous realignments. The 1964 presidential election offers one possibility, because it marked the end of Democratic dominance in the South. Wedge issues such as race, religion, crime, and war led white southerners into the arms of Republican Senator Barry Goldwater. Yet the only effect of that election was to increase Democratic strength in Congress and return Lyndon Johnson to the White House—hardly a critical shift in the partisan control of American institutions. The 1968 election,

PREACHING TO THE CHOIR

Democratic candidate John Kerry made a strong effort to turn out the African American vote late in the 2004 election campaign, including this appearance at an African American church. His attempt continued a long party tradition of courting minority voters. Democrats locked up the African American vote starting in the 1960s through aggressive appeals, including an ambitious social welfare agenda as well as support for race-conscious policies, such as affirmative action. But their strong civil rights stand may have ended the New Deal party system by driving away white southerners and the urban working class.

meanwhile, exhibits other features of a critical election. It occurred during a period of crisis, for example, following urban riots and protests against the Vietnam War— as well as the assassinations of civil rights leader Martin Luther King, Jr., and presidential candidate Robert F. Kennedy. The election switched party control of the presidency. But Richard Nixon, the winning candidate, exploited the new wedge issues only indirectly and imperfectly. Instead, it was Alabama governor George Wallace's third-party campaign that thrived on racial and cultural resentments.

The inability to pin down a clear realignment has led many scholars to question the usefulness of a party-systems approach to political history. They cannot agree whether the current, sixth period of electoral history reflects a weak and confused realignment, or no durable set of alignments at all. Even supporters of the party-systems approach must concede that today's electoral patterns do not fit well into the framework that they have popularized (although they argue that the right issue or leader could realign voters in a way that resembles earlier party systems).[20]

Nevertheless, the United States entered a distinctly different electoral era after the 1960s, one unlike any that had preceded it. Independents and swing voters enjoy an unprecedented amount of political influence, and elections matter more than they have historically. Party control of the White House fluctuates more. Like previous party systems, however, the era exhibits distinctive party alignments. Republicans tend to attract the support of small-town and rural voters. They thrive in the West and, increasingly, in the South. As former Senator Zell Miller of Georgia described the situation, "Democratic leaders are as nervous as a long-tailed cat around a rocking chair when they travel south."[21] Democrats dominate cities, university communities, and the Atlantic and Pacific coasts, and receive solid support from racial and ethnic minorities. These patterns receive detailed attention in Chapter 7 but, for convenience, we can think of today's confusing and election-driven period as the sixth party system.

Evaluating American Political Parties

Americans do not regard parties as a fundamental institution of democratic governance. Mostly they are indifferent, but many Americans think government would be better off if no parties existed at all.[22] Political scientists typically challenge that conventional wisdom. E. E. Schattschneider devoted much of his life to the task, arguing that "modern democracy is unthinkable save in terms of the parties."[23] Professional organizations in political science at times have called openly for stronger parties.[24] What critical functions do strong parties carry out?

The Plus Side of Strong Parties Without political parties to *organize political life*, it is likely that democracy would be too disorganized to operate except at the local level. Parties coordinate the actions of thousands of public officials. At each level of government, executives count on the support of their fellow partisans in the legislature, and legislators trust the information they get from their fellow partisans in the executive branch. Parties also coordinate activities across levels of government—as when, in 1995, Democratic governors convinced some Democratic members of Congress that they should support far-reaching welfare reform proposals.

Party members correctly believe that they will be judged according to their collective performance.[25] This belief gives them an incentive to *fashion a party record worth defending* at the polls. Parties need to maintain unity, or their "brand names" will not mean anything. President George W. Bush was able to rely on congressional support for his controversial tax-cut proposals, for example, in part because other Republicans recognized the need for his administration to create a record of accomplishment. Parties identify social problems, publicize them, and advance possible solutions. The competitive struggle for power motivates them to educate the public and fashion a policy agenda. Like predators, party leaders seek to identify vulnerable members of the other side. They may make a special effort to recruit candidates who can challenge those potential victims, candidates who might improve the party's image (as the Republicans did in 2002 by trying to expand their pool of black candidates).[26] Where parties are weak, as they were in the American South during the first half of the twentieth century, politics degenerates, taking on a more personal quality as factions contend for private benefits.[27]

Parties help *synthesize societal demands into public policy*. Not all social problems can be solved by clever policy proposals. Occasionally interests conflict, and some sort of compromise becomes necessary. And even if satisfying every specific interest were possible, the end result might detract from the general interest. For example, granting every individual's spending demand can lead to deficits,

BLOWING IN THE WIND?
Bush campaign officials mocked John Kerry's windsurfing hobby in 2004, arguing in one ad that Kerry's issue positions depended on the "way the wind blows." *Are such campaign attacks effective, or do voters make up their minds based on other factors?*

inflation, high interest rates, and other national costs. Because parties compete nationwide, they offer a mix of benefits and burdens to everyone. Yet they must do so in a way that appears beneficial to the general interest, or they suffer at the polls—as the Democrats did in 2004 or the Republicans did in 2006.

Imagine that no parties helped *winnow the field of candidates*. Rather than choosing between two candidates for most offices, voters would be faced with many more. The candidates would lack party labels, so voters would have to learn about each set of candidates to determine their preferences. And if elections usually had more than two serious candidates, officials would frequently enter office with a minority of the vote. Politics thus would become much more complicated than it is now.

The Minus Side of Strong Parties

The Minus Side of Strong Parties   Americans hold political parties in relatively low esteem, despite the valuable functions they can perform, for two reasons. First, parties do not always provide the valuable services of which they are capable. Politicians do not form parties to promote the public good. They want to win elections and gain power; organizing politics happens to be a good way to do that. Public officials devote real effort to maintaining their parties, but only because parties help them govern. A second and more important reason why Americans are suspicious of political parties is that party influence is a double-edged sword. Parties strong enough to organize politics are also strong enough to abuse their power. Each of the positive functions that parties can perform may be corrupted.

A strong party that controls its members can become the equivalent of an elected dictatorship, a charge the Progressives leveled at urban machines. They can force voters to select between two stark choices, even on issues for which more than two options (should) exist. They may recruit celebrities, or party hacks good at winning elections, rather than qualified people good at administering government.

Parties may choose to suppress issues rather than address them. For example, the parties avoided the slavery issue during the first half of the nineteenth century, and the Democrats suppressed issues of racial equality in the first half of the twentieth.

The parties may attempt to confuse responsibility so that they can escape any blame for bad times and win undeserved credit for good ones. Worse, rather than helping to solve a public problem, opposition parties may concentrate on blocking the governing party's attempts to do so. The temptation to torpedo the other party's initiatives is especially strong when **divided government** exists—when one party holds the presidency but does not control Congress—because then voters will be unsure who is responsible for lingering social problems.[28]

The Balance Sheet

The Balance Sheet   On balance, then, are parties good or bad? Scholars value parties because they answer important political needs. Academics generally do not evaluate parties in isolation; their focus on institutional performance forces them to question the merits of a party-driven system compared to the available alternatives. Reformers, on the other hand, can emphasize the failings of political parties: that they often do not make useful contributions and, indeed, often abuse their power. Reformers can advocate reforms without specifying what alternative institution will evolve to take on the responsibilities once shouldered by parties. Regardless of which side is right, it is clear which side has won: The reformist impulse successfully spawned legal changes that have weakened the political parties over time.

Why Are American Parties So Weak?

Parties have never been as strong in the United States as they are in other industrialized countries. In most of the world, major parties are fairly unified organizations. People join parties the same way they join clubs: They pay dues, receive official membership cards, and have a right to participate in various party-sponsored activities (such as nominating candidates). Americans who travel abroad often are surprised to find that parties elsewhere run newspapers and television stations. Party members in other governments are much more united than they are in the United States, and parties run much more coordinated campaigns than those seen in the candidate-centered politics of the United States.

Historically, the United States did not have true national party organizations. Rather, the state parties briefly joined together every four years to elect a president. Similarly, party members in government have not been terribly cohesive. Both parties (but especially the Democrats) have suffered from regional splits, and both parties have incorporated conflicting interests—agricultural versus commercial, and so forth.[29] Because parties lack unified memberships, modern American commentators often discuss parties primarily in terms of adherents to the parties in the electorate, ordinary citizens who identify themselves as Democrats or Republicans.

For most of the twentieth century it appeared that political parties in the United States—whatever concept of party one used—were in decline. Reforms wounded state and local organizations first; then changes after World War II undercut the national associations. Party cohesion and presidential support in Congress declined.[30] The number of adherents to the two parties began dropping in the mid-1960s as well, to be replaced by self-professed "independents." But by the mid-1980s, the first two of these trends reversed: Party organizations became more active again, and parties became more important in government.

Party Organizations Under Fire Party organizations were at their strongest near the end of the nineteenth century. But a progressive reform movement arose in the 1890s in the wake of rapid industrialization and urbanization. Although Progressives accepted popular democracy in theory, they were outraged by some democratic practices—particularly the activities of urban party machines. They instituted elitist reforms that would limit the voting rights of immigrants and the poor, such as requiring potential voters to pass a literacy test first, as well as measures of direct democracy such as primaries and citizen initiatives that would allow voters to undercut elected bodies. Parties went into decline at all levels of government because of the reforms the Progressives promoted at the state and local levels.

The two principal resources that parties depend on are control of **patronage**— the dispensation of government jobs and contracts—and control of nominations for office. Progressive reforms limited both of these. Patronage was gradually eliminated by regular expansions of civil service protection (see Chapter 11). After World War II, unionization of the public sector also gave government workers a layer of protection from partisan politics. Today, the president controls fewer than 4000 appointments.[31] At the height of the spoils system—and with a much smaller federal government—presidents controlled well over 100,000.[32] Similarly, governors and big-city mayors who once controlled tens of thousands of jobs control only a few thousand today. Meanwhile, party control over nominations was greatly weakened by the spread of the direct primary, an important Progressive reform (see Chapter 7).

Deprived of their principal resources, modern American parties have few sticks and carrots with which to work. Electoral defeat did not mean that people would lose their jobs, so voters were less inclined to support parties unquestioningly. Similarly, outsiders could challenge parties for their nominations—and if they won, the parties had no choice but to live with the result. Controlling neither the livelihoods of ordinary voters nor the electoral fates of public officials, party organizations atrophied.

However, deliberate political reforms are not entirely to blame for the weakening of American parties. Other factors also contributed to their decline. For one thing, the communications revolution lessened the need for traditional parties. Candidates can reach voters directly with ads. And in the United States, political parties do not control communications outlets the way they do in some European countries. The post–World War II increase in mobility—social, economic, and residential—also undercut parties. Better-educated voters have less need of parties to make sense of politics.

The Revival of Party Organizations?   It was clear by the 1980s that creative politicians had found new uses for party organizations. Parties began using direct-mail technology to raise large sums of money. They hired full-time political operatives who were campaign experts. They retained lawyers who knew how to exploit loopholes in campaign-finance law, as well as specialists skilled in computers and other technologies. They made these consultants and services available at low cost to candidates nationwide. Congressional campaign committees began actively recruiting candidates for office, a level of national intervention that would have been unthinkable half a century earlier. In 2006, both national parties even launched online social networking services, reminiscent of the popular Facebook and MySpace sites, to build connections among partisans, recruit volunteers, and spread information.[33]

National organizations are no longer the weakest level of party organization, as they were through most of their 150-year history. Today, the national committees are active and well financed, and they have been joined by senatorial and congressional campaign committees. The national committees have helped rejuvenate lower-level party organizations.[34] Most state parties, meanwhile, now have permanent headquarters and employ full-time staff. Many conduct statewide polls. They provide campaign aid and recruit candidates more actively than they did a few decades ago. The parties have built up some strength again, although not the same powers they once exercised.

Parties Versus Interest Groups

Parties once served important functions. They provided the channel of communication between voters and their government. They brought like-minded citizens together into institutions that could work for their interests and their policy preferences. They gave candidates electoral resources and delivered votes. When reforms undermined the strength of parties, these basic political needs remained. Voters still needed a way to communicate with government. Citizens still sought to unite in organizations that would promote their interests and policy preferences. Candidates still needed to find resources so that they could win elections. To fill the political void, therefore, citizens created private associations to carry out the tasks for them.

Special-interest groups rose up from the ashes of the party-dominated system. These groups differ from parties in that they seldom seek mass membership and they do not try to win political offices themselves. Rather, they tend to collect people according to relatively narrow political interests: by occupations, by industries, by leisure activities, by preferences on a single public-policy issue. Interest groups proliferated in the Progressive era, when reformers systematically attacked the parties. They surged again in the 1960s and 1970s, when American parties reached their low point.

The decline of parties and rise of interest groups appear linked. For this reason, some political theorists suggest that there is a necessary trade-off between parties and interest groups.[35] If parties do not fill the political vacuum, interest groups must. Logically, then, the real alternative to party domination of the electoral process is not some ideal form of popular control, but a different system of skewed influence. As the next section shows, the contemporary political system that replaced party-dominated government is not clearly better or worse than the one it replaced.

Interest Groups: A Biased Chorus?

Many Americans participate in politics indirectly by joining or supporting private associations—organizations that are made up of people with common interests and that participate in politics on behalf of their members. Although only half the adult population votes in presidential elections, more than three-quarters of Americans belong to at least one interest group. On average they belong to two, and they make financial contributions to four.[36] Americans are joiners, more so than citizens in other nations.

Of course, not all the groups with which people are associated are political groups. Many are social clubs, charities, service organizations, church groups, and so forth. But there are literally thousands of groups that do engage in politics, and even seemingly nonpolitical groups often engage in political activity. For example, parent-teacher organizations often are active in school politics; neighborhood associations lobby about traffic, crime, and zoning policies; and even hobby or recreation groups mobilize when they perceive threats to their interests—witness the National Rifle Association.

Development of the Interest-Group System

Americans have a long-standing reputation for forming groups. In his classic book *Democracy in America*, Alexis de Tocqueville, the celebrated nineteenth-century French author and statesman who visited the United States in 1831, noted this tendency. "Americans are forever forming associations," he wrote. "At the head of any new undertaking, where in France you would find the government or in England some territorial magnate, in the United States you are sure to find an association."[37]

However long-standing the American propensity to form associations, there are more political groups today than ever before. Nor has group formation in the United States been a steady process. Rather, it has occurred in several waves. Before the Civil War, few national organizations existed; life revolved around "island communities" unconnected by social or economic links.[38] As the railroads connected the country after the Civil War, though, a national economy developed—and national associations, such as labor unions, were not far behind. Another major wave of group organization occurred during the Progressive era, roughly 1890 to 1917. Many of today's most broad-based associations date from that era; the Chamber of Commerce, the American Farm Bureau Federation, and the National Association for the Advancement of Colored People (NAACP) are examples.

The greatest wave of group formation in American history occurred in the 1960s and 1970s. In fact, one study found that 40 percent of the associations with Washington offices were formed after 1960.[39] This last wave was by far the most diverse. Thousands of additional economic groups formed, but they tended to be narrower than earlier ones; the American Soybean Association and the Rocky Mountain Llama and Alpaca Association are two examples. Similarly, in commerce and manufacturing, numerous specialized groups joined the older, more broad-based ones. "Government interest groups" formed to represent public-sector workers. All kinds of specialized occupational associations formed as well, such as the National Association of Student Financial Aid Administrators.

Innumerable shared-interest groups have also formed in recent decades. Some are actively political, working for particular points of view. Liberal groups, such as the National Organization for Women (a feminist group) and People for the American Way (a civil liberties group), are deeply involved in politics, as are such conservative groups as the Christian Coalition (which promotes traditional morality) and Operation Rescue (an anti-abortion group). Many "citizens" groups, such as Common Cause (a political reform group), Greenpeace (an environmental group), and the National Taxpayers' Union (an antitax group) are little more than a generation old. Such groups often have a narrow focus, in which case they are called "single-issue groups." Other groups are not primarily political. But under the right circumstances, almost any group may become involved in politics. A sports association for snowmobilers and mountain bikers may seem as apolitical as a group can get, but when government threatens to restrict their use of public lands, then such organizations gear up for a political battle.

Not all active interest groups have elaborate formal organizations with membership dues, journals, meetings, conventions, and so forth. Some are little more than addresses for teams of lawyers to whom sympathizers send contributions. Some large corporations maintain their own Washington offices, as do hundreds of state and local governments and even universities.

The explosion of groups was partly reactive; the expansion of government activity gave people more reasons to form them. Business groups, for instance, may form in reaction to governmental regulations or because they see opportunities to procure government subsidies. Group formation also responds to opportunities; groups expand whenever a change in communications or transportation technology enables them to do so. Computer databases, for example, permit the generation of all kinds of specialized mailing lists. People with common interests can communicate easily and cheaply via the Internet. And once a group forms on one side of an issue, its opponents usually need to get organized or lose the fight.

Forming and Maintaining Interest Groups

That so many Americans belong to so many associations often leads people to overlook the difficulties that groups face. Women's groups contain only a small fraction of the female population. Few blacks join the NAACP. Most gun owners do not belong to the NRA. As these examples suggest, millions of people do not join or support associations whose interests they share.

Supporting a group requires the investment of personal *resources*. Contributing money or paying dues is the most obvious cost, but the time required for group activities can be significant too. One commits resources when the *incentive* to do so—

the expected benefit—justifies the investment. Incentives take many forms, though, and different groups rely on different incentives. Political scientist James Q. Wilson divides incentives into three categories.[40] The first he calls *solidary*. Some people join a group for social reasons. They simply wish to associate with the particular kinds of people who join the group, so membership is an end in itself. Most of these groups are nonpolitical, though, such as Greek organizations on a college campus.

A second category of incentives is *material*. Some people join a group because membership confers tangible benefits. Microsoft does not belong to various trade associations so that managers can socialize with other computer executives; they have plenty of other opportunities to do that. Microsoft belongs because the trade associations are seen as a way to protect and advance corporate interests. Material incentives also play a role in some political groups. Workers may join a politically active union because it gives exclusive access to some jobs. Interest groups oriented toward material benefits such as unions have declined in influence, however.

Finally, some people join groups for *purposive* reasons. They are committed to the group's purpose, such as fighting climate change or ending abortion. But interest groups that work only to improve government policy often experience the greatest difficulty attracting active members. The **free-rider problem** hinders their efforts.

The Free-Rider Problem   Groups, no matter how popular their cause, find themselves struggling to attract members and contributions. The group's achievements

SOLIDARY BENEFITS
Political groups often choose protest tactics because they lack access to more conventional resources. But protesting can be a lot more exciting than other forms of interest-group activity. These cheerleaders, for example, have found a way to express their opinions while having a good time with like-minded activists. *Does conventional political participation have to be boring?*

may fall far short of what they could accomplish if everyone who believed in the group's purpose lent a hand. This unsupportive behavior can frustrate political activists. Why in the world, they ask, would people do nothing to promote a goal in which they really believe? Why would they accept results far less satisfying than what they could obtain, when all they would have to do is work together—that is, to engage in collective action? Something must be wrong with people. Their "apathy" seems so irrational. What is rational for a group of like-minded people, though, is not the same as what is rational for an individual.

If you donate several hours of your time to march for the end of hunger, does your contribution measurably reduce the amount of malnutrition in the world? Does it reduce your chances of starving to death? Although most well-meaning people are reluctant to admit it, in each case the truthful answer is no. If your personal sacrifice makes no measurable difference, why contribute? Furthermore, most policy changes and social improvements are **public goods**. You cannot walk into a store, buy them, and consume them yourself—as you can pizzas or TV sets. Individuals receive the benefit whether they contribute or not. When world hunger declines, everyone lives in a safer world. So if groups cannot deny you the fruits of their labor, why contribute? When a group works to change policies, people enjoy roughly the same level of benefits whether or not they contribute. Even if someone genuinely wants the world to change, therefore, inactivity is not irrational; political activism is.[41]

Most interest groups suffer the free-rider problem in one form or another, but it is less likely to plague smaller groups and those promoting fairly tangible goals. If a few neighbors pool their efforts to clean up a nearby vacant lot, it is easy to identify the slackers and pressure them. It would be unthinkable, however, for a large city to rely on volunteers to maintain city parks. At the same time, cleaning up a vacant lot is more satisfying than cleaning the atmosphere. Feeding the poor in a soup kitchen is more satisfying than reducing world hunger. This is why bumper stickers often urge socially concerned individuals to "Think globally, act locally."

The most important implication of the free-rider problem for democratic politics is that "special" interests will be able to overcome it more easily than "public" interests will. Other things being equal, small groups organized for narrow purposes have an organizational advantage over large groups organized for broad purposes. For example, a small number of agribusinesses seeking millions of dollars in farm aid will find it easier to organize an association than the millions of consumers whose grocery bills might each go up an extra dollar a month as a result.

Overcoming the Free-Rider Problem   The tactics that interest groups use to compel cooperation are not always pretty. Labor unions may rely on threats—and sometimes even outright violence—to enforce a decision among workers to strike. Milder forms of coercion are widespread. For example, professional and occupational associations lobby governmental jurisdictions to hire, approve, or certify only their members. Such requirements are ways of coercing potential free riders into joining the associations that represent their trades and professions.

An alternative strategy is to try to maximize the perceived impact of an individual contribution – in essence, arguing that one person can make a noticeable difference after all. For example, the United Nations Children's Fund (UNICEF) often focuses its publicity not on large abstract problems like "world hunger," but on the specific, concrete effects of small contributions. Sixty dollars, claims one UNICEF affiliate, "can provide enough vaccine to immunize 60 children with polio."[42]

Many groups develop **selective benefits** available only to their members. They may publish journals containing useful information. They may provide consulting services, giving members a place to call when they need help. The AARP offers the most notable example of this strategy for overcoming the free-rider problem. For a mere $12.50 per year, members gain access to the world's largest mail-order pharmacy (where volume buying keeps prices low); low-cost auto, health, and life insurance; discounts on hotels, air fares, and car rentals; and numerous other benefits. Even a senior citizen who disagrees with the AARP's political positions finds it hard to forgo membership!

Many groups owe their existence to **political entrepreneurs**, activists who take the lead in promoting collective goals.[43] Motives vary for why someone would allow others to free-ride on them. Sometimes being a leader offers personal advantages: power, excitement, money, sex appeal. Sometimes individuals are not powerless. Your $20 contribution to improve health care in the Third World may have no measurable impact, but if Microsoft founder Bill Gates contributes $6 million, he certainly will observe the effects of his generosity. Sometimes individuals, institutions, or corporations have such a large stake in the group goal that they are willing to bear more than their share of the effort. They let others free-ride on them to give the appearance of broad-based support. For such large actors, political activity is simply a good business decision.

One organizer that is often overlooked is the government itself. As the role of government expanded in the 1960s and 1970s, activists needed new ways to implement programs within a decentralized federal system. One strategy was to stimulate and subsidize organizations. Once formed, local groups could help develop standards and regulations, publicize them, and carry them out. To those trying to build a stronger welfare state, these groups were politically useful as well because, once established, they would be able to fight against shrinking government. Not surprisingly, associations that receive federal funds are more than twice as likely to support expanded government activity—and, by implication, elected officials who expand it—as groups that do not.[44] The government subsidized political groups who would then help it grow bigger.

Despite the prevalence of free-rider problems, people do not always evaluate their political activities from a self-interested standpoint. Sometimes individuals simply get caught up in a **social movement** and jump on the bandwagon. Few abolitionists or civil rights marchers ever received benefits equivalent to the costs they paid, but they resisted the urge to free ride because they were caught up in the emotional and moral fervor of their movement. Still, social movements typically mobilize only a small proportion of their possible constituencies. Moreover, most people cannot sustain political passions for long, especially once demands for reform get bogged down in the tedious details of legislation and bureaucratic regulations. Movements have a tendency to lose momentum. For a social movement to exert continued influence, it must find a way to "institutionalize" itself—to spin off formal associations that face the same free-rider pressures as other interest groups.

How Interest Groups Influence Government

The groups, associations, and institutions that make up the interest-group universe engage in a wide variety of political activities.

Lobbying   Many interest groups attempt to influence government the old-fashioned way: by lobbying public officials. **Lobbying** consists of attempts by group representatives, known as lobbyists, to influence the decisions of public officials. Lobbyists draft bills for friendly legislators to introduce, testify before congressional committees and in agency proceedings, meet with elected officials and present their cases (sometimes at posh resorts where the officials are the guests), and provide public officials with information.

Lobbying to ensure favorable national policies and prevent unfavorable ones has become a massive American industry. Spending on lobbying activities has spiraled upward; it reached $200 million per month by the end of 2005. Corporations account for the lion's share of traditional lobbying. Health-care industries alone spent $356 million in 2005. Lobbying operations vary widely in scope. The U.S. Chamber of Commerce and its Institute for Legal Reform together spent $20 million in 2005. The largest lobbying firm, Patton, Boggs, reported spending $36 million that year. Miller Brewing Company, in contrast, spent less than $3 million, even though it spent more than any other beer company. Other lobbyists and lobbying groups spend almost nothing at all.[45]

There are federal and state laws that require lobbyists to register with government agencies, but because of disagreement about what lobbying is and who is a lobbyist, as well as lack of enforcement, those who register are only a fraction of those engaged in lobbying.[46] In 2005, there were nearly 35,000 registered lobbyists in Washington, D.C., a figure that many say understates the number of people working to influence government.[47]

The profession labors under a negative image (we doubt many parents dream that their children will grow up to be lobbyists). Movies, novels, and even the newspapers often portray lobbyists as unsavory characters who operate on the borders of what is ethical or legal—and often step across them. This characterization is an exaggeration. To be sure, there are notable examples of shady behavior by lobbyists, such as the case of Republican operative Jack Abramoff, who pled guilty to fraud in 2006 and helped implicate several powerful congressmen in corruption

SHOULD LOBBYING BE RESTRICTED?

Some 35,000 lobbyists are registered to do business in Washington, D.C. As we discuss in this chapter, they spend much of their time tracking public policy issues, monitoring Congress, and meeting with representatives and senators. When the public hears about lobbyists, the news usually isn't good. In 2006, lobbyist Jack Abramoff, a Republican, pleaded guilty to fraud and apparently agreed to cooperate with federal law enforcement officials in their investigation of one or more members of Congress. In an unrelated incident, a lobbyist and former aide to Congressman William Jefferson (D-LA), pleaded guilty to bribing the congressman in exchange for favorable treatment of a client. An FBI raid discovered a suspicious $90,000 in cash in Jefferson's freezer, wrapped in aluminum foil.[70]

Such incidents stoke outrage among public interest groups, and evidence does suggest that some policies designed to keep track of lobbying need improvement. One study, for example, found that almost 14,000 disclosure files were missing from the Senate Office of Public Records. Nearly every major lobby firm has failed to file at least some of the required documentation in recent years.[71] Other practices are legal, but may seem fishy. Retired members of Congress often immediately begin second careers on K Street, the Washington corridor known for its heavy concentration of lobbying firms.

Checking email messages in the halls of Rayburn House Office Building.

In the wake of the 2006 scandals, advocates proposed a variety of possible reforms. The mildest simply called for improved disclosure rules and better record-keeping. But others argued that new, more stringent rules had to be put in place. Some proposals included: bans on former members of Congress taking lobbying jobs for a period of years; prohibition of members of Congress from trying to place their aides in such jobs, restrictions or bans on travel paid for by outside organizations, tighter regulation of so-called "grassroots lobbying," and bans on campaign contributions from lobbyists.[72]

Proponents of such proposals argue that they would reduce corruption and place ordinary citizens back on a more level playing field with organized interests. But critics worry that these policy changes – especially the more stringent ones – would deprive lobbyists of their first amendment right to "petition the government for a redress of grievances." Furthermore, they argue, tight regulations on lobbying would reduce the amount of information available to lawmakers and detract from the quality of legislative debate. As illustrious a figure as President John Kennedy once observed, "there is no more effective manner of learning all important arguments and facts on a controversial issue than to have the opposing lobbyists present their case."[73]

WHAT DO YOU THINK?

1. Do lobbyists pose a threat to effective democracy, or do they help Congress make better decisions by adding information to the legislative process?

2. Do lobbyist disclosure rules deprive lobbyists of their first amendment rights? How about bans on lobbying by former members of Congress? Bans on campaign contributions from lobbyists?

For more on lobbying and lobbyists, see the following Web sites:

www.opensecrets.org

The Center for Responsive Politics offers a comprehensive database of lobbyist expenditure information, and advocates lobby reform.

www.publicintegrity.org

The Center for Public Integrity has investigated existing lobbyist disclosure rules and found them wanting.

www.allcd.org

The American League of Lobbyists, a professional association for registered lobbyists, maintains a lobbying code of ethics, and insists that lobbying is part of the first amendment tradition.

scandals. But such transgressions are hardly the norm, and corrupt behavior by interest-group lobbyists is less widespread today than it was in previous eras of American history. Numerous conflict-of-interest laws and regulations, along with an investigative media ever on the lookout for a hint of scandal, make outright corruption in today's politics relatively rare.

For the most part, lobbyists supply public officials with information and arguments to support their political goals. They tend to deal with officials already sympathetic to their positions, providing them with ideas and support. Lobbyists have little incentive to distort information or lie. To do so would mislead their allies and undermine their credibility. "One of the perceptions about lobbying is that you go out drinking, and the guy's your buddy so he does you favors," one lobbyist explains. "Those days are long gone. That sort of thing may work on tiny things like a technical amendment to a bill, but on big, important issues personal friendships don't mean a thing."[48] Many political scientists think that lobbyists serve a useful purpose, injecting valuable information into the legislative process.

Grassroots Lobbying Interest groups supplement their Washington lobbying with public-outreach activities, trying to persuade the "grassroots." Whereas lobbying consists of attempts to influence government officials *directly*, grassroots lobbying consists of attempts to influence officials *indirectly* through their constituents, the "troops in the field." Organizations such as the conservative Christian Coalition and the liberal MoveOn.org send regular emails to millions of members, urging them to contact their representatives about major issues.[49] This sort of lobbying is not new. The Anti-Saloon League, a prohibition group, included more than 500,000 names on its mailing list nearly a century ago—long before dependable long-distance telephone service, let alone computers, Web sites, and e-mail![50] But grassroots lobbying is especially effective now that Congress is decentralized through the committee system (see Chapter 9). Inside-the-beltway strategies worked when only a few leaders required persuasion, but government is generally more open than in the past. It is not so easy for Washington insiders to make private deals; it is more important than ever to show popular support for their groups' positions. Moreover, the availability of cheap communications technologies makes grassroots lobbying much easier.

Electioneering and PACs   Personal and grassroots lobbying influence public officials on specific matters. Another way to promote a group's goals is to influence who gets elected in the first place.

Political action committees (PACs) are specialized organizations for raising and spending campaign funds. Many are connected to interest groups or associations. They come in as many varieties as the interests they represent. Some, such as the realtors' RPAC and the doctors' AMPAC, represent big economic interests. Others are smaller. Beer wholesalers, for example, have SixPAC. Not all PACs serve economic interests, and politicians sometimes form their own.[51]

There is widespread public dissatisfaction with the role of PACs in campaign finance. It is therefore ironic that the proliferation of PACs is partly an unintended consequence of previous campaign-finance reforms.[52] They sprang up in the early 1970s as a direct response to reforms, and have enjoyed explosive growth in the past few decades. From a mere handful in 1970, they proliferated rapidly in the 1980s (see Figure 8.1).

PACs have played an increasingly prominent role in congressional campaign finance. They tend to give instrumentally, which means that they donate to incumbents regardless of party, especially to the members of key committees. (See Table 8.3, p. 228) In the final weeks of the 2006 congressional campaign, when business leaders calculated that the Democrats were headed for significant victories, PAC donations to Democratic candidates surged.[53]

Like interest-group corruption in general, the PAC problem in particular may be somewhat exaggerated by the popular media. Most PAC contributions are small and are intended as a way to gain access to public officials. Most research has failed to establish any significant relationship between contributions and votes.[54] Evidence even suggests that politicians extort PACs, pressuring them to buy tickets to fund-raisers and otherwise make contributions as a condition of continued access. For example, a former congressional staffer told one of us the following story:

> In our office we loved the FEC [Federal Election Commission] reports. We'd comb through them and list all the business groups who had contributed to our opponent.

FIGURE 8.1 PACs formed rapidly after the 1974 Federal Election Campaign Act (FECA) reforms

Campaign-finance reform had unintended consequences unwelcome to reformers. Can you think of other reforms that may have backfired?

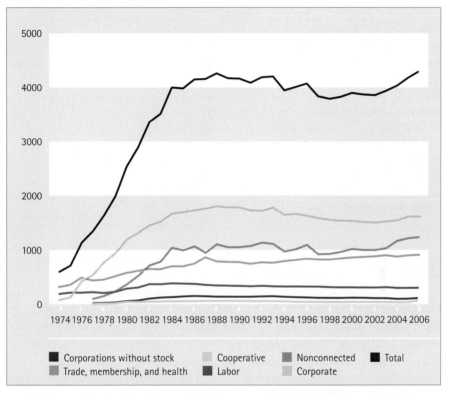

Source: Paul Herrnson, *Congressional Elections*, 2nd ed. (Washington, DC: CQ Press, 1995), p. 106; Federal Election Commission, www.fec.gov.

> Then we'd call them up and say, "Hey, we noticed that you contributed to our oppo-
> nent's campaign. The Congressman just wants you to know that there are no hard
> feelings. In fact, we're holding a fund-raiser in a few weeks; we hope you'll come and
> tell us your concerns."

Persuading the Public In recent years, independent groups have sought to influence public opinion in election campaigns in an effort to defeat those who do
not share their issue positions or (less often) to support their allies. So-called "527
groups," named for the section of the tax code under which they are formed, spent
over $480 million in the 2004 election cycle on everything from television com-
mercials, to public opinion polling, to paid grassroots organizers who went from
house to house knocking on doors.[55] Spending by these independent groups has

TABLE 8.3   Business PAC contributions tend to follow political power

	Contributions to Republicans Jan.–Feb. 1993 (Democratic majority)	Contributions to Republicans Jan.–Feb. 1995 (Republican majority)
American Dental Association	27%	90%
American Bankers Association	52	87
American Hospital Association	53	81
Ameritech	35	79
AT&T	36	79
American Institute of CPAs	45	87
Home Builders	45	71
Realtors	75	91
RJR Nabisco	69	81
United Parcel Service	55	78

Source: Jonathan Salant and David Cloud, "To the 1994 Election Victors Go the Fundraising Spoils," *Congressional Quarterly Weekly Report* (April 15, 1995): 1057.

grown dramatically, perhaps because rules governing political party expenditures have become much more strict since 2002.

Interest-group advocacy has become increasingly aggressive. Elected officials today rarely have the luxury of "down time" between campaigns. They never know when a group might launch an issue-advocacy campaign against them even if an election is far away. For example, during the California energy crisis in the spring of 2001, a group representing energy companies and Republicans ran attack ads against Governor Gray Davis, even though Davis was barely halfway through his term. They were attempting to "soften him up" before he even faced a Republican opponent. Davis won his reelection bid, but the critical ads may have contributed to his low popularity—which eventually resulted in a recall election that booted Davis from office in 2003.

One technique allowed by modern electronic communications is **direct mail**. Groups compile computerized mailing lists of people who may look favorably on their leaders or causes and then send out printed or computer-generated materials soliciting contributions. Often, an attempt to scare or provoke recipients into contributing to the mailing exaggerates the threat the group faces. Some groups depend almost completely on direct-mail fund-raising for their budgets. The citizen's group Common Cause, for example, prides itself on its dependence on small contributions.[56] Once again, the rise of the Internet has made the direct-mail strategy both easier and cheaper.

Finally, any group likes to have favorable media coverage for its activities and points of view. Thus, groups are always on the lookout for opportunities to get such coverage—opportunities to plant stories, to associate themselves with popular issues and candidates, and to position themselves as opponents of unpopular issues and candidates. For some groups, however, the sorts of actions necessary to attract attention come with a cost: They make the group look irresponsible or frightening to American voters.

Litigation   Many groups impatient for social change either do not wish to wait for the public to get behind them or doubt that they will ever persuade enough people. Instead, they file lawsuits and concentrate on persuading the legal community of the rightness of their causes.[57] Liberal groups tend to be more active in the courts, but conservative groups use litigation strategies as well. Not all legal tactics involve direct lawsuits. Some groups stage demonstrations in front of courthouses to influence judicial decision making. Others file *amicus curiae* (a Latin term meaning "friend of the court") briefs in cases in which they are not otherwise directly involved.

Naturally, legal action is not a strategy oriented toward democratic majorities. The growth of lawsuits may be the most significant limit on popular influence in America's new democracy. On the other hand, lawsuits are a way for individual citizens to challenge entrenched government officials and force them to be responsive. Thus, the growth of litigation limits the popular will in some ways but enhances it in others.

Direct Action   The United States has a long history of citizens engaging in direct action to influence government policy. From the Revolutionary War itself, to abolitionist raids before the Civil War, to urban riots and violent strikes, "unconventional politics" is as American as apple pie.[58] Forms of direct action are often used by social movements, whose members previously have not been organized, who lack access to power, and who lack the resources to use other strategies. The media—TV in particular—find direct action newsworthy and thus communicate the protests to locales far beyond where they occur.

How Influential Are Interest Groups?

The answer to this question is a matter of enormous disagreement. On the one hand, some critics believe that interest groups dominate American politics. One critic charges that the United States suffers from "demosclerosis," a condition in which interest groups clog the veins and arteries of the body politic.[59] Another claims that Americans have the best Congress "money can buy."[60] Certainly the volume of interest-group activity and their massive expenditures of resources amount to strong circumstantial evidence that groups are influential. On the other hand, academic research yields less clear conclusions. There are so many groups, and so many *opposing* groups, that their efforts tend to cancel each other out. Particular interests were more influential in the past, however. Changes in American politics undermined the classic "iron triangles" that once governed areas of policy.

Iron Triangles   Observers of American politics in the 1940s and 1950s noted that a collusion of congressional committees, executive agencies, and interest groups dominated many policy areas.[61] These three actors worked hand in hand to form a subgovernment that was almost entirely responsible for the particular policy in question. A congressional committee provided an agency with budgetary support. The agency produced outcomes favored by the interest group. The interest groups provided campaign support to the members of the congressional committee. Some of these three-way alliances were so tight, and therefore so hard to penetrate, that they received the name **iron triangles.**

The preconditions once necessary to sustain iron triangles are almost gone. Congress has changed, making the committees weaker. Interest groups have proliferated, so most associations have rivals who will not leave their influence unchallenged. In particular, citizens groups representing consumers, environmentalists, and taxpayers can oppose the excesses of special-interest politics. And the media are less likely to ignore examples of special-interest profiteering. In the spring of 2002, for example, a bill authored by Senator Paul Sarbanes of Maryland that would place greater restrictions on corporate accounting practices appeared to be near death, as financial services lobbyists waged a fierce battle against it. But within weeks, news of accounting scandals at the communications giant WorldCom created a public outcry that gave the bill new life.[62] Today companies must abide by Sarbanes' rules. As this episode illustrates, iron triangles melt in the glare of publicity.

Issue Networks   Many scholars believe that a new form of policy environment has arisen. The new **issue networks** are bigger, broader, and much looser connections of interest groups, politicians, bureaucrats, and policy experts.[63] Indeed, calling the collection of people in a policy area a "network" may exaggerate the actual degree of organization and stability that characterizes interest-group activity in Washington today.[64] Modern groups are most capable when they act on low-profile issues, when they attempt to block action rather than originate it, when no other groups directly oppose them, and when they have plentiful resources.[65] Otherwise, they face significant limits. The real world of American democracy is more complicated than many popular commentators suggest.

Evaluating Interest Groups

Participation is easier for people who have more resources. Thus, it is no surprise that the affluent contribute more than the poor and that two-worker families with small children participate less than those whose family situations leave them more free time.[66] More generally, a large institution or corporation has more resources to contribute than a solitary citizen. Furthermore, the free-rider problem gives an advantage to narrow interests. Economic groups and funding recipients benefit, at the expense of the broader population of consumers and taxpayers. Americans therefore hold interest groups in low regard.[67] They seem to violate the American principle that everyone should enjoy equal influence on government.

On the other hand, equal influence can never be more than an ideal. Party-dominated government did not give Americans equal influence either. Political scientists thus have not held interest groups in as low regard as ordinary citizens have. They recognize that American politics often consists of an interplay of numerous interests organized into competing associations—and interplay that can lead to compromises and other positive outcomes.

Unfortunately, rival interest groups do not always check and balance each other. Sometimes rival groups choose to cooperate, demanding a mixture of higher prices and tax breaks at the expense of the national economy.[68] Their involvement also sometimes makes American politics more negative. Ordinary citizens have multiple attachments and affiliations. A retired couple, for example, naturally favors higher social security and Medicare expenditures. But they might demand less for themselves, knowing that the result would be higher taxes on their children or lower government expenditures on their grandchildren's schools. Leaders of interest groups for the elderly, by contrast, typically see their job as maximizing group benefits. They have no incentive to be reasonable or to balance competing social goals.

This crowding out of moderate demands by more extreme ones is reinforced by the tendency of group activists and leaders to be more zealous in their views and more committed to group goals than nonmembers (see Table 8.4). It is doubtful that most regular men and women who supported the Equal Rights

TABLE 8.4   The extremism of group activists and leaders

One study compared the views of 100 top leaders in environmental groups with the views of scientific experts—in this case, cancer researchers. Both sets of people were asked to rate various cancer risks on a scale of 1 to 10, with 10 being the highest. Relative to expert judgments, environmentalists consistently overstated the risks of cancer from environmental causes.

	Risk of Cancer	
Carcinogen	Environmentalists	Scientists
Dioxin	8.1	3.7
Asbestos	7.8	6.5
EDB	7.3	4.2
DDT	6.7	3.8
Pollution	6.6	4.7
Dietary fat	6.0	5.4
Food additives	5.3	3.2
Nuclear power	4.6	2.5
Saccharin	3.7	1.6

Source: Stanley Rothman and S. Robert Lichter, "Environmental Cancer: A Political Disease," Annals of the New York Academy of Sciences 775 (1996): 234–235.

Amendment (ERA) wanted to force female soldiers into combat. But activists pushing the ERA argued that "combat duty, horrendous as it might seem to all of us, must be assigned to persons on a gender-neutral basis."[69] Most Americans prefer a satisfactory compromise on abortion or the environment, not the extremes posed by the organizations they may join to promote one side or the other. In the end, the general interests of a moderate population can get lost amid the bitter fighting of intense and extreme special interests.

But what can be done? As the critics look over the experience of democratic governments, they see only one means of controlling group demands that is both democratic and effective. Ironically, it is the institution that George Washington warned the country about—political parties. Americans thus may face a difficult choice: determining which is the lesser evil, particularized groups that give more weight to those with money or general groups that distort individual influence in haphazard and potentially dictatorial ways.

Chapter Summary

Although the Constitution makes no mention of them, political parties have been part of American politics from the early years of the republic. Indeed, American political history has exhibited a series of party systems, wherein each party has dependable support among particular social groups so that elections tend to be similar. The basic reason why parties have played such an important role in American history—as well as in the histories of all modern democracies—is that they perform essential organizing functions. Yet most Americans do not hold parties in especially high regard. Parties struggle for power and, therefore, often act in self-interested ways contrary to the general interest. To prevent such behavior, the nation passed a series of reforms aimed at undercutting the power of political parties.

Americans have turned to a different source of influence on government: interest groups. There has been a major increase in the number of interest groups since 1960. These groups are an important mechanism for increasing popular influence, because more than ever they use strategies of electioneering, grassroots lobbying, and public persuasion. Although interest-group activity is constitutionally protected, many worry about its effects. Special interests seem better represented than general interests.

No doubt the United States could choose to reverse course, strengthening the political parties and weakening interest groups. The result would not be a return to some golden era of individualistic politics; the parties did not give Americans equal influence any more than interest-group democracy does. But one thing is clear. Regardless of which mechanism for popular influence becomes dominant in the future, both sorts of groups have become better at representing popular demands than they were in the past.

KEY TERMS

critical election, p. 206
direct mail, p. 228
divided government, p. 214
free-rider problem, p. 220
iron triangles, p. 230
issue networks, p. 230
lobbying, p. 223
machines, p. 209

patronage, p. 216
political action committees (PACs), p. 226
political entrepreneurs, p. 222
public goods, p. 221
realignment, p. 206
selective benefits, p. 222
social movement, p. 222
ticket splitting, p. 211

SUGGESTED READINGS

Aldrich, John. *Why Parties?* Chicago: University of Chicago Press, 1995. Wide-ranging rational-choice account of how and why politicians form and transform political parties.

Baumgartner, Frank, and Beth Leech. *Basic Interests.* Princeton, NJ: Princeton University Press, 1998. Comprehensive review, critique, and synthesis of literature on interest groups.

Green, John C., and Paul Herrnson, eds., *Responsible Partisanship? The Evolution of American Political Parties Since 1950.* Lawrence, KS: University Press of Kansas, 2003. Comprehensive analysis of how well the political parties have served the American electorate, spread out over essays by some of the most influential researchers on the topic.

Skocpol, Theda. *Diminished Democracy.* Norman, Oklahoma: University of Oklahoma Press, 2003. Describes the evolution of groups from mass membership associations to top-heavy, professionally-managed organizations, and considers the consequences for American democracy.

Walker, Jack. *Mobilizing Interest Groups in America.* Ann Arbor: University of Michigan Press, 1991. Describes the state of the Washington interest-group universe. Noted for discussion of outside support for the establishment of groups.

ON THE WEB

233

ON THE WEB

For more on political parties, see the following Web sites:

THE MAJOR PARTIES
www.democrats.org
www.republicans.org

The Internet home of the two major political parties. These sites offer information on virtually all aspects of the two parties—from their beliefs to their structure.

THE NATIONAL COMMITTEES
www.rnc.org
www.dnc.org

Party Web sites that solicit contributions, attack their opponents, and advocate party policies.

The Institutions of America's New Democracy

The Congress

"LOCAL GOVERNMENT MUST BE THE FIRST LINE OF DEFENSE ON the home front," argued Baltimore Mayor Martin O'Malley in congressional testimony just months after 9/11.[1] Congress seemed to agree, and aid to state and local "first responders" soared: In the first year after the attacks, the national government increased its preparedness assistance tenfold to $20 billion. Still, critics argued that spending should be much higher. Democratic presidential candidate John Kerry warned that the Bush administration was doing too little to close the "preparedness gap," and a Council on Foreign Relations Study called "Drastically Underfunded, Dangerously Unprepared" recommended upping the spending by $100 billion.[2] Lawmakers responded enthusiastically. Between 2001 and 2006 Congress allocated more than $200 billion for homeland security.

An odd spending pattern began to emerge, however. A reasonable observer might expect grants to be the highest in big cities because the potential loss of life and the amount of property damage are much greater there. Similarly, you might expect most funds to go toward activities such as inspecting airline and shipping cargo, providing security for nuclear plants, and guarding key bridges and tunnels. The reality is quite different.

Rural Wyoming, for example, gets five times as many federal dollars per capita as do California and New York.[3] Devil's Tower and historic Fort Laramie are impressive, to be sure, but are they more likely to be terrorist targets than the Golden Gate Bridge or the Empire State Building? This is not an isolated case—in fact, of the 10 cities classified by the Department of Homeland Security (DHS) as most at-risk, only Washington, D.C. (where members of Congress spend much of their time), is among the top 10 in federal assistance.

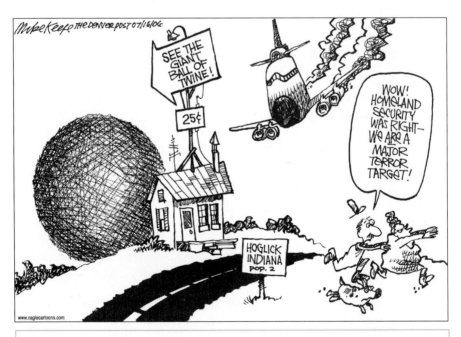

A TERROR TARGET?
Critics charged that homeland security grants were spread far and wide, rather than being directed exclusively at areas that had the highest risk of attack.

Moreover, wherever the money is spent—rural or urban—homeland security expenditures appear curious, if not silly. For example, Santa Clara County, California, bought Segway scooters for its bomb squad; the Princeton, New Jersey, fire department purchased Nautilus equipment and a Bowflex machine; and Columbus, Ohio, ordered Kevlar vests for its police dogs.

Even when spending seemed worthwhile, it was often not obviously related to terrorism, such as forest fire claims in New Mexico and a federal child pornography tip line.[4] Some purchases that did appear more related to homeland security, such as chemical weapons suits for the city of North Pole, Alaska (population 1,646; motto: "Where the Spirit of Christmas Lives Year-Round") seem to be low priority expenditures. What is going on?

The answer has to do with how Congress works. Lawmakers—keenly aware of each state's equal representation in the Senate—adopted a funding formula for homeland security grants that guaranteed each of the fifty states at least 0.75 percent of the total funds. That minimum largely explains why Wyoming, with 0.17 percent of the American population, receives 0.85 percent of the grants.

But the guarantees to each state still leave 60 percent of the funding available for allocation on the basis of "risk assessment." If this is true, what accounts for the examples above that appear to have little to do with risk? Here the explanation probably has to do with the structure of the congressional committee system. Homeland security agencies fall under the jurisdiction of 88 different congressional committees and subcommittees.[5] The members of these panels authorize programs, appropriate funds, and oversee the operation of the agencies. These responsibilities provide numerous opportunities for legislators to influence where the money goes. Even representatives whose districts contain no plausible terrorist target demand a share of homeland security funds.

Homeland security is not atypical. A look at agriculture policy, transportation policy, trade policy, and other issue areas shows a similar picture. Congress is structured to serve its individual members, which means addressing their reelection goals. But because Congressional institutions and rules are designed this way, they may lack the capacity to act coherently in the national interest. Although individual representatives and senators often care deeply about serving the nation, they can do nothing to address societal problems if they do not remain in office. Members therefore tend to view issues in terms of the needs of their own particular constituencies, whether they live in New York City, Laramie, Wyoming, or North Pole, Alaska. Dedication to satisfying voters, as America's new democracy requires, need not produce results that will gratify the nation as a whole.

The Organization of Congress

Article I of the Constitution sets out the structure and powers of a national elected assembly, called the Congress. The U.S. Congress differs from elected assemblies in other advanced nations. Most world democracies are *parliamentary* in form, with the elected assembly choosing a chief executive from among its members. In parliamentary systems, the assembly usually does little more than rubber-stamp proposals from the executive it has selected. Indeed, assemblies are rarely called legislatures, because they do little legislating; instead they are called parliaments, because they do a lot of parleying (that is, talking). The United States is one of the few world democracies with a *presidential* form of government—a government in which the chief executive is elected directly by the people rather than chosen by the legislature. Legislatures are more independent, and therefore ultimately more powerful, in presidential systems.*

Like many of the world's parliaments, Congress is **bicameral**, consisting of two chambers: an upper chamber called the Senate and a lower chamber called the House of Representatives. Splitting Congress and constituting each chamber differently makes the legislative branch change policies slowly. For example, the House of Representatives passed tax cuts in 2001 and 2003 that were much larger than the Senate preferred. Negotiations between the two houses produced the compromise legislation that ultimately became law.

The House and Senate are not undifferentiated collections of people who sit in their seats all day debating and voting as the urge strikes them. Like other large decision-making bodies, the two chambers have developed traditions that advance their work: (a) the committee system, which is an extensive division of labor; and (b) a party leadership structure, which effectively organizes large numbers of people to make decisions. Because of its large size, the House places more importance on internal organization.

The Congressional Parties

Political parties help organize the legislative branch (although not to the extent they dominate parliaments in other democracies). In practice, the House's majority party selects the **Speaker of the House**, a constitutional officer. Until a century ago, the Speaker was the only formal party leader in the chamber, often rivaling the president as the most powerful public official in the United States. Powerful Speakers decided who would sit on all House committees and who would chair them, an effective system of reward and punishment for commanding loyalty. Moreover, as chair of the Rules Committee, which determines legislative procedure, the Speaker controlled the **floor** of the chamber. Speakers ruled.

A folksy Republican called "Uncle Joe" Cannon was the last of the dictatorial Speakers. Cannon dominated the House in the first decade of the twentieth century, but he could not suppress the Republican party's growing progressive wing. Imposing party discipline on House members he considered "traitors" led Cannon to an increasingly punitive use of his powers.[6] Dissident Republicans who chafed

---

* A few countries, such as France, have hybrid systems.

under the Speaker's iron rule eventually joined with Democrats in a revolt that stripped Cannon's office of its most important resources. From 1910 to 1911, the Speaker lost the power to make committee assignments and was removed from the Rules Committee. Procedural reforms also guaranteed ordinary members some right to have their proposals considered.[7] The office of Speaker has never regained the powers removed at this time. Committee slates, for example, now are identified in party steering committees, then elected within meetings of the entire party membership (called the party *caucus* for the Democrats and the party *conference* for the Republicans).

Next in line to the Speaker is the majority leader, also elected by the full membership of the dominant party. The majority leader is responsible for day-to-day operations, such as scheduling legislation, coordinating committee activity, putting together the coalitions needed to pass legislation, and negotiating with outside institutions. The majority leader also plays a significant role in the party by working to prevent minor spats and internal quarrels from developing into destructive feuds.[8] The opposition party elects a counterpart, the minority leader, to provide similar services.

Both party's leaders are assisted by **whips**, a group of around two dozen members (it varies by party) who serve as links between leaders and the parties' rank and file—explaining positions, outlining strategies, counting votes, and occasionally whipping party members into line.* The chief whip position is a desirable one for members hoping to lead their party, so maneuvering for these posts can become aggressive. For example, U.S. Representative Nancy Pelosi of San Francisco became the Democratic party's chief whip in 2001 after a 118–95 vote in the Democratic caucus—but only after a behind-the-scenes campaign that involved lots of arm-twisting and interest-group lobbying. As part of her effort, Pelosi helped raise $3.9 million on behalf of other Democratic congressional candidates, whereas her rival only raised $1.5 million. Pelosi served in the position for only a year before becoming minority leader, and became the first woman Speaker when Democrats took over the House in 2007.[9]

The Senate leadership is simpler. The vice president is officially the president of the Senate, and has the constitutional right to break ties. The Constitution also provides for a president pro tempore, who oversees the chamber in the absence of the vice president (which is most of the time). This office has little power and ordinarily goes to the most senior member of the majority party. The real leadership comes from the Senate's majority and minority leaders and whips, but they are not as powerful as the officers in the House. One of the main jobs of the leaders is negotiating **unanimous-consent agreements**, so called because all senators with any interest in proposals agree to them. Generally these agreements specify the terms of debate: what sort of amendments will be in order, how long they will be debated, when votes will be taken, and so forth.[10]

The title derives from "whippers-in" of the hounds in a fox hunt, although coercion is actually rare.

Unanimity is helpful because of the Senate's tradition of careful deliberation. According to present rules, a single senator can talk for as long as she or he desires, paralyzing the chamber. When senators oppose a bill or a presidential nominee but lack the votes to win a floor fight, they may vow to **filibuster**—to keep talking until the other side gives up. Often the threat of a filibuster is enough to force a compromise. The Senate majority can end a filibuster, but only by adopting a **cloture** motion. A vote for cloture requires the support of 60 senators, so a coalition of 41 senators may stop the Senate from acting on any issue. The Senate's old-fashioned debating rules are one important reason why voting majorities often fail to get their way.

The filibuster has become increasingly controversial. Nothing in the Constitution guarantees that a minority of senators may block action; the custom only exists within the Senate rules. Yet the filibuster has become a powerful weapon for opposition parties hoping to stop change when they hold neither the White House nor a congressional chamber. Republicans hindered President Clinton from 1993–1995 as a minority party, and Democrats returned the favor during the first six years of President Bush's administration. For example, Democrats blocked 10 of Bush's appellate court nominees during his first term.

The Committee System

Congress does most of its work through committees. Since 1980, for example, 6000 to 8000 bills have been introduced in each two-year session of the House of Representatives, but only 10 to 15 percent eventually passed. A few unsuccessful proposals died on the floor, but most of the 85 to 90 percent that failed never made it out of committee.

To accomplish their work, both the House and the Senate utilize several kinds of committees. **Standing committees** have fixed memberships and jurisdictions, and they persist from one Congress to another. The Appropriations, Commerce, and Foreign Relations committees are examples. **Select committees**, by contrast, are temporary committees created to deal with specific issues. For example, the House established a Select Committee on Homeland Security in June 2002 that became a permanent committee three years later. Both houses of Congress had standing committee systems in place by 1825.[11] More than half a century later, the Legislative Reorganization Act of 1946 gave the committee system the shape it largely retains today. In the 110th Congress (2007–2008) there were 20 standing committees in the House and 17 in the Senate (see Table 9.1). These "full" committees are subdivided into more than 150 subcommittees. There also are four "joint" committees with membership from both houses, and a small number of select committees.

House committees fall into three groups by level of importance. Both parties agree that the Rules, Appropriations, Energy, and Commerce, and Ways and Means Committees are highest in importance. The Rules Committee is the "right arm" of

TABLE 9.1 Standing committees of the 108th Congress

Committee	Size (party ratio)	Number of Subcommittees
Senate		
Agriculture, Nutrition, and Forestry	21 (D11/R10)	5
Appropriations	29 (D15/R14)	12
Armed Services	25 (D13/R12)	6
Banking, Housing, and Urban Affairs	21 (D11/R10)	5
Budget	23 (D11/R11/I1)	0
Commerce, Science, and Transportation	23 (D12/R11)	7
Energy and Natural Resources	23 (D11/R11/I1)	4
Environment and Public Works	19 (D9/R9/I1)	6
Finance	21 (D11/R9/I1)	5
Foreign Relations	21 (D11/R10)	7
Health, Education, Labor, and Pensions	21 (D10/R10/I1)	3
Homeland Security and Governmental Affairs	17 (D9/R8)	5
Judiciary	19 (D10/R9)	7
Rules and Administration	19 (D10/R9)	0
Small Business and Entrepreneurship	19 (D10/R9)	0
Veterans' Affairs	15 (D7/R7/I1)	0
House		
Agriculture	46 (D25/R21)	6
Appropriations	66 (D37/R29)	12
Armed Services	62 (D34/R28)	7
Budget	39 (D22/R17)	0
Education and Labor	49 (D27/R22)	5
Energy and Commerce	57 (D31/R26)	6
Financial Services	70 (D37/R33)	5
Foreign Affairs	50 (D27/R23)	7
Homeland Security	34 (D19/R15)	6
House Administration	9 (D6/R3)	2
Judiciary	40 (D23/R17)	5
Natural Resources	49 (D27/R22)	5
Oversight and Government Reform	41 (D23/R18)	5
Rules	13 (D9/R4)	2
Science and Technology	46 (D24/R22)	5
Small Business	33 (D18/R15)	5
Standards of Official Conduct	10 (D5/R5)	0
Transportation and Infastructure	75 (D41/R34)	6
Veterans' Affairs	29 (D16/R13)	4
Ways and Means	41 (D24/R17)	6

Source: Respective committee Web sites at the House homepage (www.house.gov) and the Senate homepage (www.senate.gov).

the Speaker; it controls the flow of legislation to the floor and the conditions of debate. The other three possess broad powers that enable them to affect nearly everything government does. Committees at the second level of importance deal with nationally significant policy areas: agriculture, armed services, energy, civil rights, and so forth. The least important committees include governmental "housekeeping" committees and committees with narrow policy jurisdictions such as Veterans' Affairs. The Budget Committee has a special status. Members can serve for only six years in any 10-year period, and its membership is drawn from other committees and from the leadership.

The Senate committee system is simpler than that of the House; it has only major and minor committees. Like their House equivalents, Appropriations and Finance are major committees, but the Senate Rules Committee has far less power than its House counterpart (the Senate leadership itself discharges the tasks performed by the House Rules Committee). Instead, Budget and Foreign Relations are the other major committees, the latter because of the Senate's constitutional power to provide advice and consent on treaties and ambassadorial appointments.

Committee power in the Senate is widely distributed: Chairs of major committees cannot chair any other committee or subcommittee, and chairs of minor committees can chair only one other panel. Each senator can serve on one minor and two major committees, and every senator gets to serve on one of the four major committees named above. On average, senators sit on more committees than representatives do—in part a simple reflection of size difference: The Senate has nearly as many committees as the House but less than one-fourth as many members. Also, senators represent entire states, so many more issues concern their constituents. As a result, senators' legislative lives are not so closely tied to particular committees as are the lives of representatives.

Committees as Party Tools   The committee system is formally under the control of the chamber's dominant party. Party committees nominate members for assignment, and party members gather in caucus to approve those assignments. Each committee thus has a partisan balance at least as favorable to the majority as the overall division of the chamber. The more important committees are especially stacked in favor of the majority party. In the 110th Congress, for example, the Democrats had a 9–4 advantage over the Republicans on the House Rules Committee, a ratio far greater than their 233–202 edge in the chamber. In contrast, the party ratio on the less important Science and Technology Committee was 24–22.

The parties customarily choose committee chairs based on **seniority**; the majority-party member with the longest continuous service on the committee is usually its chair. This norm for selecting committee chairs evolved in the Senate in the 1880s and migrated to the House after the 1910 revolt. The parties also normally do not remove members from committees once they have been assigned to them. Because these customs are rarely violated, the committee leadership enjoys some autonomy from the parties.

Committee chairs began to exercise so much power by the 1950s, in fact, that members of Congress began to question their authority. The Democrats who controlled some of these committees behaved autocratically, closely controlling staff and budgets and even refusing to call meetings or to consider legislation they opposed. Some manipulated the subcommittee structure, creating and abolishing the smaller units, varying subcommittee jurisdictions, and monopolizing their chairmanships. To make matters worse, because members from safe southern seats had built up considerable seniority, Democratic chairs tended to be notably more conservative than their party's rank and file.[12]

The Democrats picked up a large number of new seats in the wake of Watergate. The party caucus, fortified by this contingent of younger and more liberal members (the "class of '74"), deposed three moderate committee chairs known for their overbearing style. For example, one of their victims, House Armed Forces committee chair F. Edward Hebert (D-LA), had addressed the new members as "boys and girls" when speaking before them.[13] The Democrats also weakened the committee positions themselves. A caucus resolution passed in the early 1970s allowed House committee chairs to lead only one subcommittee. A "subcommittee bill of rights" protected the jurisdictions, budgets, and staff of the smaller units. The Senate moved in the same direction as the House, spreading power more evenly across the membership.[14]

Decentralizing authority to 250 standing committees and subcommittees restored party influence. The Republicans took control of the House in 1995 and their leaders acted to restrict subcommittee independence, but they still jealously guarded the authority of the party leadership. For example, they relaxed the seniority system. Speaker Gingrich passed up the most senior committee members when he named the Republican chairs of the Appropriations, Commerce, and Judiciary committees. The Republican conference also adopted a three-term limit on committee chairs, first enforced in 2000. When Democrats regained control of the House in 2007, they retained these terms limits.

The policy influence of committees themselves also remains questionable. Some scholars argue that committees are simply tools of the congressional parties.[15] They point out that parties are so concerned with controlling public policy that they stack committees with loyal members, and argue that party leaders shape committee jurisdictions so that the reliable members write and revise important legislation. Although sometimes called the "partisan theory" of committee formation, this view essentially suggests that the committee system has little independent influence.

Theories of Committee Formation   Not everyone agrees that committees lack independent power, however. There are many exceptions to the pattern of party influence. Sometimes committees behave in a bipartisan fashion. Furthermore, the process of defining committee jurisdictions is extremely complicated, and not clearly under the direct control of the leadership.[16] Scholars have offered other interpretations of the committee system that assign them an independent influence on public policy. We mention two here: the distributive theory and the informational theory.

The **distributive theory** notes that members choose committees relevant to their districts. For example, members from urban districts seek membership on committees that deal with banking, housing, or labor; members from rural districts opt instead for committees that deal with agriculture and natural resources. The committee membership gets first crack at legislation in their issue area, and other members of the chamber go along with the committee in exchange for similar deference on bills they have shaped. This **logrolling** ensures that Congress will deliver benefits to each participant's constituency. Studies document that districts and states receive a disproportionate share of government grants if their representatives sit on the relevant committees.[17]

An alternative interpretation is that committees primarily serve a knowledge-gathering function.[18] This **informational theory** stresses that members frequently are uncertain about the outcomes that proposed laws will produce. Hence, they wish some members to become experts in each subject area and to share their knowledge with the broader membership. One way to do this is to give committees disproportionate influence, subject to the condition that they do their job conscientiously. Committee members gain power over a policy area only to the extent that they specialize in it and give the chamber useful, reliable information.

Studies of committees are not conclusive about which perspective—distributive (or logrolling), informational, or partisan—is the best way to explain the purpose and behavior of the committee system. Committees likely fit all three at one time or another as members strive to balance their competing needs: to serve their local constituencies, to gain reliable information about public policy, and to accomplish partisan goals. It also may be that the type of committee matters a great deal. For instance, committees that hand out money for public projects or fund important programs seem to behave in distributive fashion. Other committees that deal with complex public policies such as environmental or telecommunications regulation may serve an informational function. Finally, some committees—such as the Rules Committee that controls the agenda and floor debate—seem dominated by the party leadership.

Other Sources of Organization

In recent years voluntary groupings of members with common interests have become increasingly common. Called **caucuses,** but smaller than a party caucus, these groupings cross party, committee, and even chamber lines. As of 2006, there were nearly 300 such groups, ranging from long-standing ones such as the Congressional Black Caucus and the Northeast–Midwest Congressional Coalition, to newer ones such as the Sportsmen's Caucus, the Shellfish Caucus, the Internet Caucus, and the Gulf Coast Rebuilding and Recovery Caucus.[19]

(text continues on page 248)

AN EXPLOSION OF EARMARKS

Pork barrel politics is almost as old as Congress itself. The pejorative term refers to members' efforts to procure various benefits for their districts and states. Originally, these benefits were mostly construction projects that brought government money and jobs to constituents—dams, roads and bridges, public buildings, military bases. But as the size and scope of government expanded, so did the kinds of benefits. Today all manner of projects, grants, and subsidies are considered part of the pork barrel.

In recent years, so-called 'earmarks' have aroused the ire of critics. This term generally refers to congressional instructions that direct government activity or money to a specific project or activity in a particular location. Most such instructions are not actually included in the laws that pass Congress, but are contained in the committee reports or the floor managers' explanatory statements that executive agencies rely on to implement the legislation.[52] Although such provisions are not legal mandates, agencies ignore them at their peril, because they rely on Congress for their budgets.

A pig makes a guest appearance at a Capitol Hill news conference on government waste

Earmarking has exploded in the past decade. In 1991 a major transportation bill included 538 earmarks, but in 2005 a similar bill contained more than 6,300.[53] In this latter bill, nearly half a billion dollars was designated for the notorious Alaskan "bridges to nowhere." One bridge would have linked Ketchikan to a remote island with a population of 50 people. Another would have linked Anchorage to Port MacKenzie, a rural area with one resident.[54] Not coincidentally, Alaska Representative Don Young was chair of the House Committee on Transportation and Infrastructure at the time, and Alaska Senator Ted Stevens chaired the Senate Appropriations Committee. After a torrent of ridicule from Washington think tanks, talk show hosts, and even comedian Jay Leno, the earmarks were withdrawn, but the money for Alaska was left in the bill and Alaskan officials decided to build the bridges anyway.

On first thought it might appear that pork barrel spending is indefensible. But not everyone sees it that way. For one thing, relative to the federal budget the sums at stake are small potatoes. The Congressional Research Service estimates that earmarks accounted for about $53 billion dollars in the 2004 budget.[55] That sounds like a lot of money, but in a budget of more than $2 trillion, earmarks were less than 3 percent of the total. In that light, earmark reform hardly seems worth the effort. Critics retort that this money could always be spent on more worthwhile programs or simply applied to the deficit to lower the burden on future generations.

(continued on next page)

AN EXPLOSION OF EARMARKS *(continued)*

A second defense of earmarking is that earmarks pave the way for legislation to pass. Even a policy change that is highly desirable from a national standpoint can create losers as well as winners, and one way to get losers to go along with the change is to use pork barrel benefits to compensate their constituents for losses.[56] Skeptics respond that political and party influence is behind pork much more often than good policy is.

At the time of this writing only one in five Americans approves of the job Congress is doing. But approval of individual members remains much higher. Fenno's paradox still lives: we like our member of Congress much more than we like Congress itself. To Jay Leno's audience, the Alaskan bridges to nowhere are a comic travesty, but to the constituents of Representative Young and Senator Stevens the bridges and associated jobs and spending are benefits stemming from the hard work of their representatives in Washington. As long as constituents reward their members for activities such as earmarking, such activities will continue.

WHAT DO YOU THINK?

1. Should the U.S. Representative from your congressional district and the senators from your state earmark legislation to benefit your district and state?
2. Some fiscal conservatives have urged the president to "stop us before we spend again" by instructing executive agencies to ignore any earmarks that are not actually written into legislation (more than 90 percent of all earmarks). If you were a presidential adviser, would you recommend this action?

For more information on *earmarks and pork barrel spending,* see the following Web sites:

Citizens Against Government Waste
www.cagw.org

This organization keeps careful track of alleged pork barrel spending, and compiles an annual "Pig Book" to publicize it.

United States Senate and United States House of Representatives
www.senate.gov
www.house.gov

The official Web sites of many members of Congress (accessible through the main House and Senate sites) present local projects in the best light.

Caucuses are extremely varied in their concerns, their activities, and their effects. They can support the efforts of party or committee leaders, but they also can pressure party or committee leaders to act or not act on particular issues. Similarly, they can be a vehicle for cooperation across chambers, across parties, or across committees; or they can obstruct the proposals of chambers, parties, or committees because of some special interest they feel is being slighted or dealt with unfairly (e.g., wine, potatoes). Some caucuses are lavishly financed by outside interests while others subsist with modest contributions of office space, money, and staff from their members. The Sportsmen's Caucus, for example, had a 2003 budget of $860,000 provided by donations from the National Rifle Association and manufacturers and sellers of sporting equipment. There are few studies of caucuses and their activities as yet, but they appear to be increasingly important actors in the congressional process.[20]

Not all organizational resources available to the congressional membership involve reorganization of the members themselves. The legislative branch is much larger than the 535 elected members of the House and Senate. The members have personal staffs that total more than 7,000 in the House and 4,000 in the Senate, and each chamber hires thousands of staff members to support the committees. Many of these staffers are clerical workers, and others are policy experts who play an important role in shaping legislation. Additional employees help coordinate partisan legislative proposals.

Thousands of other staff members work in various support agencies of Congress. The Library of Congress employs thousands. So does the Government Accountability Office (GAO), the watchdog agency of Congress that oversees the operation of the executive branch. A smaller number of people work for the Congressional Budget Office (CBO). This agency provides Congress with expert economic projections and budgetary information. In total, the legislative branch of government consists of some 30,000 people.[21]

How a Bill Becomes a Law

Every civics class teaches that Congress "makes the law" governing the United States. However, this tidy phrase is inadequate to describe the complex process by which a bill becomes a law. Passing a single statute requires steering it through two chambers, organized into about 250 committees and subcommittees, and usually requires the support of members of two political parties and numerous interest groups. Although no flowchart could possibly convey the complexity of getting a major bill through Congress, we will outline the stages through which important legislation must pass (see Figure 9.1).

To start things off, a bill or resolution is introduced by a congressional **sponsor** and one or more cosponsors. The initial wording may be the legislator's own work or a proposal offered by a constituent, but most often it is provided by legislative staff at the member's direction. The presiding officer then refers the proposal to an appropriate committee. Because legislation has become more complex, recent House Speakers have used **multiple referrals**, sending the bill simultaneously to more than one committee or dividing it among several committees.

Once the bill goes to committee, the chair gives it to an appropriate subcommittee. There, if the subcommittee chair and sponsor give the bill a high priority, the staff schedules hearings at which witnesses will speak in favor of the bill or in opposition to it. Sometimes hearings are genuine attempts to gather information.

FIGURE 9.1 How a bill becomes a law

There's a bit more detail involved than passage by Congress and a presidential signature. *With such a complicated process, can voters ever be sure that their representatives are working hard?*

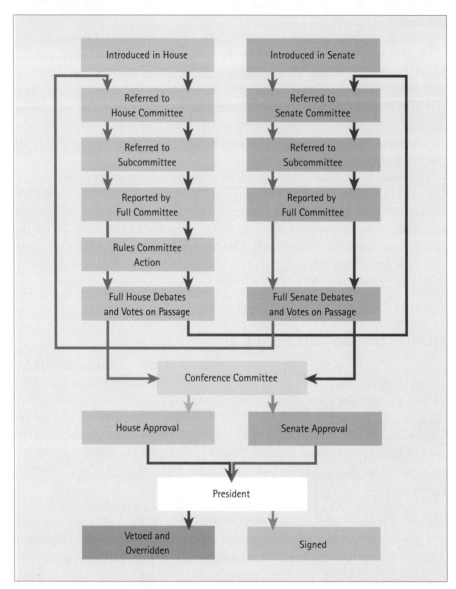

More often, they are carefully choreographed: The subcommittee staff stacks the witness list with legislators, bureaucrats, interest-group leaders, and ordinary citizens who favor of the position of the subcommittee chair. As one study observed, "committees neither seek nor receive complete information. Rather, they seek to promote certain views of their issues to bolster their abilities to produce favorable legislation."[22]

After hearings, the subcommittee begins **markup** of the bill—revising it, adding and deleting sections, and preparing it for report to the full committee (assuming that a majority of the subcommittee supports the final product). The full committee may repeat the process, holding its own hearings and conducting its own markup, or it may largely accept the work of the subcommittee. If a committee majority supports the bill after committee markup, the bill is nearly ready to be reported to the floor—but not quite.

When Bills Go to the Floor

Let's consider first what happens in the House. Bills that are not controversial, either because they are trivial or because they have extremely narrow impact, can be called up at specified times and passed unanimously with little debate. Somewhat more important bills are considered under a fast-track procedure called **suspension of the rules**. Upon being recognized, the committee chair moves to consider a bill under suspension. If a two-thirds majority of those voting agrees, the bill will be considered on the floor. Debate is limited to 40 minutes, no amendments are in order, and a two-thirds majority is required for passage. There is some risk in considering a bill under suspension because it needs two-thirds support. Even if a majority backs the legislation, it might fail under the higher threshold. Indeed, opponents of a bill sometimes support the motion to suspend the rules precisely so that they can raise the required number of votes.

Legislation that is especially important, and therefore usually controversial, goes to the Rules Committee before going to the floor. The Rules Committee may hold its own hearings, this time on the type of **rule** it should grant. In these hearings only members of Congress may testify. The rule specifies the terms and conditions of debate. A rule specifies the time that the supporters and opponents will be allowed to speak. It also may regulate the introduction of amendments, prohibiting them (a *closed rule*) or specifying the amendments that are in order (a *restrictive rule*). In recent years three-quarters of all bills coming from the Rules Committee have been granted restrictive rules.

Assuming that the Rules Committee recommends a rule, the floor then chooses to accept or reject the rule. Rules rarely are rejected, but that does not mean the floor goes along with anything the Rules Committee proposes. Rather, in shaping the rule, the committee anticipates the limits of what the floor will accept. Sometimes committee members miscalculate and are embarrassed when a floor majority rejects their rule. Otherwise, the bill is finally under consideration by the chamber. After debating a proposal and voting on amendments, the floor then decides whether to adopt the bill.

In the Senate, the process is a bit simpler. For uncontroversial legislation, a motion to pass a bill by unanimous consent is sometimes all that is necessary. More important and controversial legislation will require the committee and party leaders to negotiate a unanimous-consent agreement, which is a complicated bargain analogous to a rule granted by the House Rules Committee. Assuming that they succeed and thereby avoid a filibuster, the bill eventually comes to a floor vote.

If a majority votes to adopt the bill, are we at the end of the process? Not at all. Before the bill can be sent down Pennsylvania Avenue for the president's signature, it must pass both chambers in identical form. The bill may have started in one chamber before going to the other, or it may have proceeded simultaneously through both. In either case, it is extremely unlikely that the House and Senate will pass exactly the same bill. In fact, their versions of the legislation may be in serious conflict.

For major legislation, each chamber appoints some of its members to participate in a **conference committee** that tries to reconcile the two versions of a bill. In theory, each chamber's conferees are committed to their chamber's version of the legislation and will negotiate a compromise as close as possible to their chamber's desired solution. In practice, this is not likely. Conferences for some complex bills involve hundreds of members who support some parts, oppose other parts, and care little about still other parts. This context makes the situation ideal for bargaining. When a majority of each chamber's conferees agree to the final draft, the compromise bill is reported back to the parent chambers, where another floor vote in each chamber is required for passage.[23]

Budgetary Politics

Now, you may think that we have finally reached the end of the legislative process. Technically, this is true, but passage of a bill does not guarantee that it will be implemented. The reason is that we have been describing only the **authorization process**. Before the government actually can carry out the activities that Congress authorizes, funding must be approved for them.

The Constitution grants Congress the power of the purse and makes the House the lead actor: All tax bills must originate in the House, and by custom and tradition, all appropriations bills do too. The **appropriations process** parallels the authorization process. Specialized appropriations subcommittees in each chamber hold hearings and mark up a budget bill (the subcommittee chairs are commonly referred to as "the Cardinals of Capitol Hill").[24] The full committees may do the same, but usually they defer to their subcommittees.

In the House, appropriations bills are *privileged*; they take precedence over other legislation, and a motion to take up an appropriations bill can be offered at any time. But in practice, appropriations bills, too, usually pass through the Rules Committee. Thus, appropriations subcommittees in both chambers must report bills, the rank and file in both chambers must pass them, and a conference committee must agree on every dollar before the government actually has any money to spend. The necessity of getting budget bills through the process, and their privileged status, sometimes tempts members of Congress into tucking other laws and regulations inside of them. These legislative **riders** may have a better chance of passing than a separate bill because of the chaotic nature of the budgetary process. For example, anti-smoking advocates were able to float through the budgetary process a ban against smoking on commercial airline flights, and environmentalists used budget negotiations to limit logging harmful to spotted owls.[25]

The Congressional Career

Legislators are extremely sensitive to their constituents' wishes, more so than members of Congress from earlier eras. The reasons are straightforward: (1) Elected officials are more likely to think of politics as a job and wish to retain office. (2) Technological changes have made elected officials less able to hide their actions and better able to determine what voters want. (3) Elected officials remain in office longer if they cater to the tastes of local voters and provide the services that constituents demand. (4) Electoral fortunes are less likely to rise or fall on the basis of ties to national political parties.

The Growing Electoral Incentive

Until the late nineteenth century, many more congressional representatives quit than were defeated. Job conditions were not very attractive. The national government was weak, and the District of Columbia was little more than a swamp.[26] Ambitious politicians, especially outside the South, often found state government a better outlet for their energies.[27] Even those members willing to serve multiple terms sometimes were prevented from doing so by rotation practices, whereby political factions in a congressional district "took turns" holding the congressional seat. Abraham Lincoln, for example, stepped down from the House of Representatives in 1848 after serving only one term.[28] Average service in the House did not reach three years until after 1900. The early Senate was equally unstable. In the first 10 years of the republic, more than one-third of the senators failed to serve out their terms. Before 1820, more senators resigned during their terms than were denied reelection by their state legislatures![29]

Today things are quite different. The Congress is the world's foremost example of what political scientists call a professional legislature. Its members are full-time legislators who stay for long periods. Relatively few members quit voluntarily, and many intend to remain in Congress indefinitely. This professional interest in retaining their jobs prompts representatives to be electorally sensitive, if not hypersensitive. Contemporary incumbents fare so well precisely *because* they are so electorally aware; they anticipate threats to their reelection and act to avoid them.

Channels of Communication

More congressional decisions are public now compared to a generation ago. Until 1971, House members often cast votes by standing, speaking (aye or nay), or depositing colored cards (called tellers) into boxes—procedures that camouflaged each member's position. But rule changes that year made it easy to demand a **roll-call vote**—in which each member declares a vote on the record—and the number of roll calls in an average session more than doubled. Recorded votes are risky because they are available to interest groups or opposition researchers seeking campaign issues. Damaging votes need not be highly visible ones. Even an obscure vote can come back to haunt a member years later.

Compensating for this increased scrutiny is the improved information that members of Congress have about their constituents. Not only do their offices have fax machines, e-mail, and Web pages—technologies undreamt of a few decades ago—but travel subsidies and other perks have expanded greatly. Indeed, critics argue that Congress has become more polarized in part because many members are "perpetual commuters" who do not socialize with each other.[30] Members were reimbursed for only three trips to their districts in 1960. By 1976 the yearly limit had increased to 26, and today there is no limit except the overall budget allocated to each member. Members travel to their districts 30 to 50 times a year! Important business is rarely scheduled for Mondays or Fridays, because so many members travel on those days. Moreover, members can afford to conduct surveys if they want a scientific way to learn the views of constituents.[31] Thus, one reason why fewer incumbents are defeated is that fewer give their constituents reasons to defeat them.

Members of Congress also can compensate for increased scrutiny by communicating with constituents directly. Congressional use of the **frank**—free postage for official business—has grown, and computerized mailing lists make the resource more useful. Not surprisingly, congressional mailings to constituents are more frequent in election years (although newsletters cannot be mailed within 90 days of an election).

Constituency Service

You may think of members of Congress primarily as *lawmakers*. Making laws is their principal business and main constitutional responsibility. But members of Congress do much more than legislate. The official title of House members is "representative," and most people's view of representation involves a wide range of activities.[32]

One chore that demands a great deal of the time and effort is district service—making sure that congressional districts get a fair share (or more) of federal programs, projects, and expenditures.[33] Legislators therefore customarily seek generous spending bills that allow them to spread money around widely and perhaps wastefully. Critical observers compare the process to standing around a barrel of pork and handing the meat around lavishly, leading them to call it **pork-barrel spending**. Sometimes budget bills are larded with fat. For example, the budget bill that went to President Bush in early December 2004 squeezed numerous federal agencies as a way to curtail deficit spending, but it still had expensive projects on behalf of particular states and districts—such as $350,000 for Cleveland's Rock and

Roll Hall of Fame and $335,000 to help North Dakota protect its sunflowers from blackbirds.[34]

Even Americans who disapprove of pork-barrel legislation usually applaud when their representatives and senators bring home the bacon, and they reward them at the ballot box for it.

Another activity to which modern representatives devote a great deal of attention is constituent assistance, or "casework." Citizens, groups, and businesses frequently encounter difficulties in qualifying for government benefits or in complying with federal regulations. When their problems are not solved through normal channels, they appeal to members of Congress for assistance. About one in six voters reports having contacted a representative for information or assistance. In overwhelming numbers, they were satisfied with the resolution of their problems and, again, showed their gratitude at the polls.[35]

Members of Congress hire large staffs to help with the chore. Each House member heads an office system—one part in Washington and one or more parts in the district—and directly employs an average of 18 personal staff assistants, more than 40 percent of whom are assigned to district offices.[36] Indeed, it has been said that Capitol Hill is the headquarters of 535 political machines.* Such was not always the case. In 1950 the average representative had three staff employees. But the number of citizens who reported contacting their representatives for this purpose tripled between 1958 and 1978, as the size of government grew and the size of the congressional staff grew with it.[37] Staff jobs can be extremely demanding, because they require balancing both lawmaking needs and political needs. One staffer described his job this way: "I have to worry about what's going on on the legislative side, what's going on politically back home. You want to make sure the press releases are going out, the service operations are going well. You're always juggling a bunch of balls."[38]

District service and constituent assistance often are included together under the general term **constituency service**. Service takes up a growing amount of legislators' time, and for good reason: It helps them please voters and therefore makes reelection easier. When members of Congress take positions on issues, they please some groups and antagonize others. On controversial issues, their positions may lose them as many votes as they gain. But when incumbents provide valued services to constituents, nearly everyone approves. Small wonder that, by a 5–1 margin (judging from one survey), House administrative assistants consider constituency service the most important factor helping their employers stay in office.[39]

The Decline of Party

Voters are not as loyal to the political parties as they once were. Although 70 percent of voters select their parties' candidates in congressional elections, that figure is low by historical standards—encouraging candidates to court voters of all

---

* Senators have larger staffs than House members. The size depends on a state's population.

parties.[40] In particular, sitting members of Congress have found that they can win the loyalty of other party members through constituency service. Since the late 1960s, the rate at which voters support incumbents of a different party has often been close to 50 percent.[41] But the decline of partisanship does not give elected officials a free ride. Representatives cannot take votes for granted; they must offer voters personal reasons to support them.

At one time, parties were powerful enough to bully members of Congress into sticking with the leadership, even if it meant casting votes that would damage them in their districts. Fewer constraints exist now to prevent legislators from acting on the electoral incentives they face and the information they have. Legislators can support the interests of their district—liberal or conservative, with the president or against, and so forth—except under unusual circumstances. This flexibility tends to make voters in a district happier with their representative.

Of course, parties in Congress have become more powerful recently. Parties have grown more unified in their roll-call voting, as Figure 9.2 illustrates. However,

FIGURE 9.2 The congressional parties are more unified today than a generation ago

The graph shows the percentage of all recorded votes on which a majority of voting Democrats opposed a majority of voting Republicans. Numbers for each year have been averaged over each Congress. Is party unity in Congress good or bad?

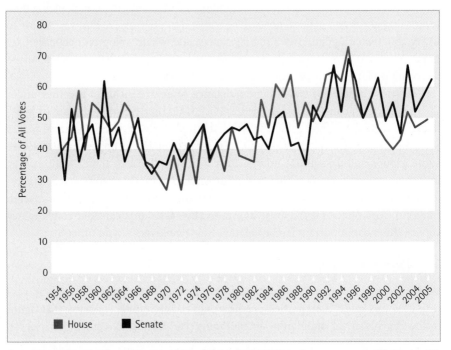

Source: Norman Ornstein, Thomas Mann, and Michael Malbin, *Vital Statistics on Congress, 2001–2002* (Washington, DC: CQ Press, 2002), p. 172; *CQ Weekly* vote studies, various years.

modern party unity does not threaten individual members of Congress. One important reason why the parties have grown more unified is that the electoral incentives faced by their members are more similar. Whereas southern Democrats once differed greatly from their northern counterparts, by the 1990s they had become a liberal, urban party in both regions (especially their House members). Republicans, meanwhile, have become an identifiably conservative, suburban and small-town party. Members are willing to give more power to party leaders because their leaders are much more likely to want the same things they do; they need not fear the electoral consequences of sticking with the team.[42]

Furthermore, members of Congress gain an electoral advantage from helping their parties. Strong leaders can help a party produce better outcomes than the party would get if the members all worked independently. Passing an imperfect bill may be better than passing no bill at all, so members may sacrifice some influence over particular details. Even when party members are unhappy with policies desired by their leaders, they have some incentive to stick together. Electoral success is partly linked to the successes of their political parties, the party images as a whole, and the performance of their presidential candidates. Congressional parties are also increasingly active in campaign funding, causing members to feel indebted to the leadership.[43] But members of Congress occasionally do tire of the compromises required by leadership, especially when the other party's beliefs seem more compatible. Sen. James Jeffords of Vermont abandoned the Republicans in 2001, early in President Bush's administration, at a time when the Senate was evenly divided between the parties. He became an independent and switched his support to the Democratic party, giving it control of the Senate until the 2002 elections.

HELPING THE PARTY
New York Senator Hillary Clinton helped raise large amounts of money for the Democratic party and its candidates in 2004 and 2006. *What do you think Clinton had to gain from helping her party?*

Evaluating Congress

It is easy to get so wrapped up in the details of Congress and its operations that one loses sight of the reason for our interest in the institution. The reason, of course, is that Congress is the first branch—arguably the most powerful and most important of the three branches of government. As columnist George Will writes, "There is little a president can do if a determined congressional majority opposes it."[44] Congress is the branch that bears primary responsibility for representing the needs and values of the American public and for developing legislation to improve their well-being. How well does Congress meet its responsibilities? The most common criticism of the congressional process is obvious: *It is lengthy and inefficient.* Legislation may take months or even years to wend its way through the process, with lots of duplicated effort—both within and across the chambers. Moreover, after all is said and done, Congress often produces a compromise that satisfies no one. Of course, this is what the framers intended. They wanted to ensure that laws would pass only after thorough deliberation.

But that raises a second criticism: *The congressional process works to the advantage of policy minorities, especially those content with the status quo.* Proponents of legislation must build many winning coalitions—in subcommittee, full committee, appropriations committee, conference committee, and on the floor—in both chambers. Opponents have it much easier. A minority that controls only a single stage of the process may be able to block action.

Given that members are trying to please constituencies, *they continually are tempted to use their positions to extract constituency benefits,* even when important national legislation is at stake. The distribution of homeland security funding we described at the beginning of this chapter is a perfect example. Every member, even one from a district with little objective "need," wants a "fair" share of the federal pie—by which the legislator usually means "as much as possible." Such a process defeats, distorts, and otherwise damages national interests while promoting members' parochial interests.

Indeed, sometimes the act of passing such legislation ensures that it will not work; the compromises necessary to get legislation through Congress may spread available resources too thin. Taken to extremes, this tendency can be almost comical. Consider, for example, the Economic Development Administration created in the 1960s to subsidize the construction of infrastructure—roads, utilities, industrial parks, and so forth—in depressed areas. By the time the program was killed by the Reagan administration, it had been repeatedly expanded by Congress to the point where more than 80 percent of all the counties in the United States were officially classified as "economically depressed" to make them eligible for federal subsidies.[45]

This type of distortion of priorities does not result because Congress ignored the demands of voters. Quite the contrary: It results because members of Congress, ostensibly working in their constituents' interest, spread resources so broadly and thinly that they have little impact.

Fenno's Paradox

More than people in other democracies, Americans are proud of their political institutions. They revere the Constitution, honor the law, and respect the presidency and the courts. But the prominent exception to this generalization is the Congress. Congress is often the butt of jokes. Humorist Mark Twain once observed that "there is no distinctly native American criminal class except Congress." Even former members of the institution sometimes pile on. Former congressman Bob Dornan of California described the politicians he saw in Washington as "annoying little guys who ran for class president in fifth grade and lost and ran again in eighth grade and lost again and now they're policy wonks and all they want is power."[46]

Disparaging quips such as these reflect popular sentiments. Surveys report that only a minority of Americans trust Congress to do what is right or have confidence in Congress, and they view members as having ethical standards only a bit higher than those who sell cars (see Figure 9.3). The reputation of Congress has

FIGURE 9.3   The public rates members of Congress lower than those of other occupations

What do the occupations with low rankings have in common with politicians? What sets the ones with high rankings apart?

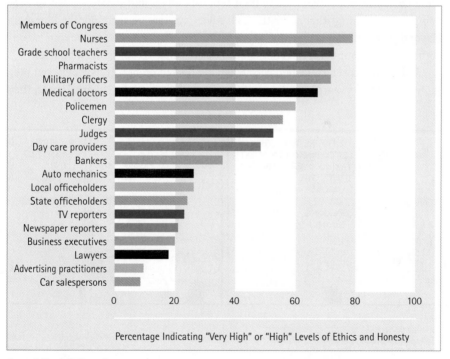

Percentage Indicating "Very High" or "High" Levels of Ethics and Honesty

Source: Gallup Poll, November 19–21, 2004.

been repeatedly tarnished by scandals. Ironically, this most electorally sensitive institution is the one whose image is the most negative.[47]

This negative perception of Congress contrasts with the generally positive view Americans have of their particular senators and representatives. After all, voters reelect 90 percent or more of all the incumbents who run. This gap between electoral approval of individual members and unhappiness with the collective Congress is so striking that political scientists have given it a name: Fenno's paradox. Professor Richard Fenno first publicized the fact that citizens invariably rate their members of Congress far more favorably than they rate the Congress as a whole.[48] Members take advantage of this disparity by adopting an unusual electoral strategy: "Members run *for* Congress by running *against* Congress."[49] They criticize the institution and claim that they are different from the members who cause problems.

Fenno's observations are not puzzling in light of a good understanding of the operation of Congress and the incentives underlying congressional operations. Americans dislike Congress but nevertheless reelect the great majority of their senators and representatives because they judge the collective Congress and the individual member by different standards.[50] They judge the Congress by how well it meets the challenges the country faces. Judging from opinion polls, Americans think Congress rarely does a good job, and they take an equally dim view of how they think Congress operates—sluggishly, conflictually, inefficiently, and sometimes corruptly. But citizens judge their representatives and senators positively for doing the very things that make the collective Congress perform poorly. Members respond to the narrow interests that are part of their constituencies, looking for opportunities to channel them benefits or to exempt them from general policies.

Voters may resent such behavior when conducted on behalf of others, but they shower electoral rewards on the elected officials who do it for them. That is, they

AMERICANS LOVE TO HATE CONGRESS
Although Americans dislike Congress as a whole, they tend to approve of their own representatives.

would prefer other people's representatives to be **trustees**—legislators who use their own judgment to decide what is right—but demand that their own representatives serve as mere **delegates**—legislators who carry out the precise wishes of their constituents back home regardless of what they personally believe policy ought to be. However, because voters demand roughly the same sort of responsiveness everywhere, Congress as a whole often fails to work for the national good. An old saying states that "if you want to make an omelet, you've got to break some eggs." Voters want lots of omelets and reward legislators who deliver them to the table, but they curse the kitchen for all the eggs it breaks in the process of feeding everyone. Widespread disgust with Congress, therefore, does not stem from a breakdown in the connection between constituents and representative; it grows from the responsiveness required by an especially strong connection.

The Moneyed Interests

Gobs of money flow into congressional elections every two years, and most of that money goes to the Democrats and Republicans who already hold office. Interest groups consistently fatten the campaign coffers of senators and representatives at the same time that these politicians are voting on issues of public policy critical to lobbyists. Usually the favored legislators vote the way their contributors wish them to vote.

The whole system, when observed from a distance, reeks of political bribery. Humor columnist Dave Barry describes the way most popular observers view the campaign-finance system: "Sleazeballs who want government favors give money to politicians, who give it to consultants, pollsters, advertising agencies, and television stations, who get you to elect the politicians, who thus get more money from sleazeballs. Do you see what's morally wrong with this, voters? That's correct: Your government, the government that your Founding Fathers fought and died for, is being sold over and over like a used mobile home, and *you're not getting a cut.*"

But political scientists who actually dig into the flow of cash often come away with a sharply different story. Neither the pattern of giving nor the pattern of accepting interest-group donations looks the way it should if cynics are right.

Take the suspicion that lobbyists buy votes with their weighty checks. "How in the world," one might wonder, "could politicians vote against people who have dropped thousands of dollars into their laps?" This logic seems persuasive—but if donors are trying to buy votes, their strategies are incredibly foolish. Interest groups do not give the bulk of their money to swing legislators. Rather, generous donations usually go to the members of Congress most likely to support a group in fair weather or foul. Agricultural associations favor rural representatives. Medical associations favor doctors. Trial-lawyer associations favor trial lawyers. Why would lobbyists try to buy the votes they could have had for free?

Perhaps contributors do not try to buy new votes but, instead, try to buy elections for their firmest supporters. Maybe money, in other words, disrupts the election connection between rulers and ruled. "If interest groups are doling out money to keep their friends in office," critics ask, "is that really democracy?" Problem is, the pattern of donations contradicts this straightforward logic as well. Interest-group money does not flow to the politicians most in danger of losing their jobs. Quite the contrary, often the biggest checks go to the most stable members of Congress, including some who expect no opposition at all when they run for reelection. Money also flows to party leaders who have gained influence precisely because of their ability to hold on to power for many terms, leaders who enjoy so much influence that their constituents are unlikely to sacrifice it by voting them out of office. Smart contributors would not invest precious funds in elections where they were least likely to make a difference.

If they are not buying votes or elections, what do political action committees get for all that money? Political scientists Rick Hall and Frank Wayman propose a compelling answer. After interviewing staff members and probing the bill histories for three congressional committees, Hall and Wayman discovered that the main effect of campaign contributions is that special interests get extra work out of members. They are not buying legislative votes or legislative seats; they are just buying time.[51]

Contributors reward those who perform important services to them in the halls and committees of Congress. Campaign cash helps mobilize legislators on a group's behalf, making up for the time they spend attending committee meetings, fine-tuning legal language, or marshaling votes before a congressional showdown. The money might lure legislators away from rival activities, such as working on other legislation or doing casework for constituents.

To reformers, this alternative story may evoke just as much cynicism as the more direct tale of political bribery. "Legislators are supposed to use their precious time working for the people," a critic might charge, "not for those with the deepest pockets!" True enough. But it is not exactly clear what a member of Congress would do if freed from the obligation of working to pay back supportive interest groups.

Legislators who lacked demanding contributors might choose to skip more meetings, pass the shaping of legal provisions off on unelected staff members, or let crucial votes shape up haphazardly—because these are the sorts of activities that voters back home seldom monitor. Lacking the money to buy advertisements, representatives might focus less time on legislating and more on campaigning or on scraping together smaller contributions. They might just work less! In short, special interests may have purchased "the best Congress that money can buy," but it is not clear they purchased anything that voters otherwise would have owned themselves.

CHAPTER SUMMARY

Members of Congress work as full-time professional legislators, and most (at least try to) serve for many terms. They have strong incentives to please the constituencies who must reelect them. This pressure shapes Congress itself. Members organize the committee system not only to deal efficiently and effectively with major national problems but also to enable them to concentrate on issues important back home. Members hesitate to give the party leadership enough power to mount efficient and effective responses to national problems, in part because that power might be used to prevent them from serving constituency interests or even to force them to oppose constituency interests. The structure of Congress is an uneasy compromise between what it takes to get the job done and what it takes to get reelected.

The result is that Congress is slow and inefficient, and the laws that emerge from the complex legislative process may not be very effective policy. Citizens hold Congress in much lower esteem than they hold their individual representatives and senators, whom they reelect regularly. Critics fail to see, though, that the problem is not a lack of democratic responsiveness—caused, for example, by large interest-group donations—but rather an excess of it. It is precisely the efforts of representatives to serve their supporters that make it so difficult for Congress as a whole to serve the national interest.

Key Terms

Suggested Readings

Arnold, R. Douglas. *The Logic of Congressional Action*. New Haven, CT: Yale University Press, 1990. An excellent discussion of how the incentives that motivate members interact with characteristics of public policy problems to shape legislation.

Cox, Gary, and Mathew McCubbins. *Setting the Agenda*. New York: Cambridge University Press, 2005. Important work that shows how the majority party in Congress operates through its control of the agenda.

Kingdon, John. *Congressmen's Voting Decisions*, 3rd ed. Ann Arbor: University of Michigan Press, 1989. Classic study of how representatives decide to vote on the floor.

Ornstein, Norman, Thomas Mann, and Michael Malbin. *Vital Statistics on Congress, 2005–2006*. Washington, DC: American Enterprise Institute, 2007. This biennial compilation of congressional statistics is to Congress watchers what *The Bill James Baseball Sourcebook* is to baseball fans.

Schickler, Eric. *Disjointed Pluralism*. Princeton, NJ: Princeton University Press, 2001. Focuses on the historical development of congressional rules and procedures.

ON THE WEB

For more information on the U.S. Congress, see the following Web sites:

ROLL CALL ONLINE AND *THE HILL*
www.rollcall.com
www.thehill.com

Roll Call and *The Hill* publish news for and about Congress. *Roll Call* requires a subscription to access; *The Hill* does not.

THOMAS ONLINE: LEGISLATIVE INFORMATION ON THE INTERNET
http://thomas.loc.gov

THOMAS is the most comprehensive congressional Web site. It posts the full text of all congressional proceedings and contains historical information on Congress from its inception to the present.

CONGRESSIONAL QUARTERLY
www.cq.com

Congressional Quarterly is extremely successful in its mission to "project the highest levels of accuracy, comprehensiveness, nonpartisanship, readability, timeliness and analytical rigor."

The Presidency

THE LAST WEEK OF FEBRUARY 2006 WAS GOING TO BE THE WEEK when President George W. Bush would focus the country's attention on energy policy. In his nationally televised State of the Union address nearly a month earlier, Bush had announced the Advanced Energy Initiative, a program designed to help break a dependency on foreign oil that the president described as an "addiction."[1] On visits to high-tech development centers around the nation, Bush touted the new research funding and business tax credits that were part of the proposed program. "There's a lot of needless politics in Washington, D.C.," the president said. "And of all the issues, becoming less dependent on foreign sources of energy is an issue that we ought to be able to unite and show the American people we can work together to help advance the technologies that will change the world in which we live."[2]

But few elected officials in Washington were inclined to spend that week working on energy policy. Instead, a sudden furor erupted over the sale of six major U.S. ports to a company owned by the government of the United Arab Emirates, a Middle Eastern ally of the U.S. An inter-agency task force had approved the sale of port operations in New York, New Jersey, Baltimore, New Orleans, Miami, and Philadelphia to the company, Dubai Ports World, and the Bush administration defended the sale as a typical business transaction that posed no threat to national security.

Politicians from both political parties disagreed, arguing that foreign ownership of port operations would make the nation vulnerable to attack. "Our ports are major potential terrorist targets," said Senator Christopher Dodd (D-CT). "I strongly urge the administration to thoroughly investigate this acquisition." Senator Tom Coburn (R-OK) went further, questioning the United Arab Emirates' commitment to anti-terror policies: "Handing the keys to U.S. strategic ports to a regime that recognized the Taliban is not a sound next step in the war against terror."[3]

Only three years before, Bush and his aides might have had little trouble in muting congressional opposition, or at least in arriving at a face-saving compromise. During his first term as president, Bush achieved near-record backing from lawmakers, winning on congressional votes about 80 percent of the time.[4] But now, with the war in Iraq dragging on, the disaster of Hurricane Katrina fresh in the public mind, the president's approval rating below 40 percent, and a congressional election less than a year away, Bush could count on no such support. On the contrary, Senate Republican leader Bill Frist and Republican House Speaker Dennis Hastert hastily broke with Bush and called on him to reconsider the deal. The president threatened to veto any effort to halt the sale, but critics remained just as vocal and, as one columnist put it, "astonishingly bipartisan."[5]

By early March, Dubai Ports World realized the futility of continuing to fight and decided to give up its effort to buy the U.S. facilities. An upset President Bush warned in a March 11 speech that the dispute could send a negative "message to our friends and allies around the world, particularly in the Middle East."[6]

Bush also spent five paragraphs of that speech talking about energy policy, but few journalists or members of Congress seemed to notice. "It's always the same story," one former administration official told a reporter. "They have a plan—an elaborate plan of the president's message day by day. But there's something in the system that has a hard time coping with the unexpected."[7]

Political scientists have long observed that presidential power is shaped by the context within which presidents operate. This is because public expectations of the

FIGURE 10.1 "Rally 'round the flag" effects

Presidents' gains in popularity average 7 percentage points in the months following crises.
Why do you think President Clinton did not experience as large a boost in public support as
his predecessors after foreign policy crises?

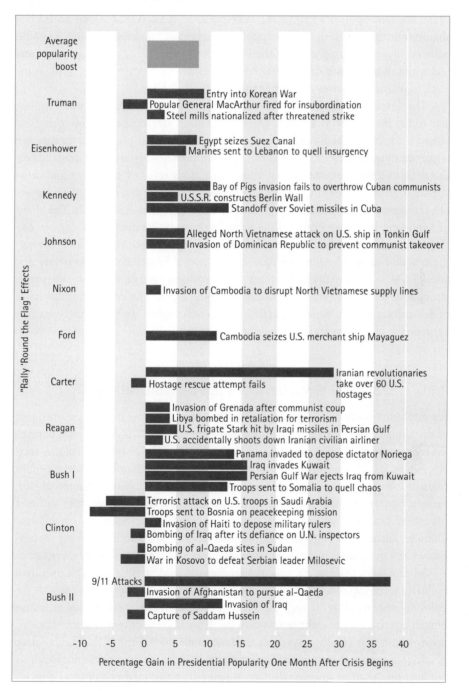

president largely define how voters and the Washington community judge the nation's chief executive.[8] If presidents meet public expectations, their prospects for reelection—and their clout with Congress—increase. If presidents exceed expectations, so much the better. But if presidents fall short, their authority can quickly evaporate. During Bush's first term, his response to the 9/11 attacks and his leadership in waging the war in Iraq met public expectations for decisive action. By 2006, however, the continuing war and the Hurricane Katrina disaster changed the context within which Americans evaluated the president. It became more difficult for Bush to maintain control over his agenda.

This lesson about expectations applies not only to individual presidents, but also to the presidency as a whole. Over time, voters, seeking more from their government, have required a more aggressive and politicized presidency to manage highly complex institutions. But at the same time, they have imposed demands on Congress and the bureaucracy that make institutions resistant to change and insulate them from presidential action. The president lacks strong constitutional powers, relying on persuasion and negotiation to accomplish political goals. The chain of command is a loose one, and the president's administrative duties may exceed the capacity of an elected official. The resulting inefficiencies slow down government action backed by the president. Sometimes they make progress nearly impossible. As with so many institutions in the political system, therefore, the presidency may disappoint voters by failing to produce desirable results, but the cause of difficulty is not a desire to resist the popular will. Rather, the president often fails because the public got what it asked for.

The President's Growing Responsibilities

For most Americans, one person embodies the entire executive branch: the president of the United States. Certainly the president is an influential public official, perhaps the most powerful person in the world. But very few of the changes in culture, society, nature, or even government trace back to the decisions of individual people. Markets follow their own economic logic, dictated by the behavior of numerous consumers, businesses, and countries. Cultures evolve new habits, new tastes, and new modes of family or religious life through the individual decisions of millions. Climates fluctuate, diseases develop, the earth's crust shifts without asking permission of any mortal. Even the most powerful person in the world faces severe limits.

It may seem that the national government should be different. The president is clearly at the top of any flowchart of power. Changes in government must be the ultimate responsibility of the "big boss," right? In theory, yes. But as executive branch specialist Paul Light points out, the federal government is a multifaceted organization that employs nearly 13 million people.[9] It is not just the combination of advisers, agency directors, and civil servants under a presidential administration, but also the "shadow government" of independent contractors and local government employees who carry out federally funded programs.[10] Such a massive and complicated executive branch would be beyond the close management of any one person, even if he or she did not have to share power with other public officials.

The president faces an unresolvable dilemma when trying to change government in response to public desires. Folk wisdom suggests, "If you want something done right, you'd better do it yourself." But of course, a president cannot do the work of millions. Someone else has to perform most governmental tasks, and the president's dilemma is finding a way to get good performance from employees who may not share the same values as the president. With any effort to exercise authority, therefore, the president faces a difficult choice. The less detailed the instructions, the less likely government employees will carry them out exactly as desired. But more-detailed instructions reduce efficiency. Creating them requires the White House to spend lots of time and money gathering information about a policy area, so that rules passed down the chain of command provide clear guidance. And such rules may defeat their initial purpose, too, by preventing government employees who are trying to perform a job from using their own skills and judgment.

One way to increase the political responsiveness of government workers is to find employees who share a president's values or who subscribe to clear and predictable professional norms. The more someone thinks as you do, the more you can trust that person to perform a task the way you would do it. Within the executive branch, though, many employees can resist presidential pressure. The less control a president has over who holds a position, the less likely it is that a particular government employee will share the goals of the boss—and thus the less true control the president is likely to exercise. The president still selects and influences top-level appointees, but other administrators require an endorsement by members of Congress before they can take their jobs. Other rules, meanwhile, insulate rank-and-file government employees from a president's political desires, and many federal tasks are carried out by private companies, by independent government agencies, or by state and local governments that the executive branch controls indirectly if at all. The whole structure of the federal system sharply limits what the White House may accomplish.

Presidents do have a unique political asset: They fill the only position elected by a national constituency. Only presidents can claim to represent the country as a whole. This enhances their authority. On the other hand, this broad responsibility also creates problems. In the eyes of the voters, presidents are the focal point of the U.S. government. The public routinely blames presidents for events and conditions over which they have little control. Presidents are expected to conduct foreign policy, promote desired legislation, respond to disasters, manage the government, and address an endless variety of real and imagined social problems.[11]

Although presidents sometimes take credit for prosperity and success, they more often attract the blame when things go wrong. President George H. W. Bush, for example, enjoyed a succession of foreign policy triumphs equaled by few of his predecessors. His tenure saw the fall of the Berlin wall, the collapse of the Soviet Union, and a spectacular victory in the Persian Gulf War. Yet when the economy faltered, Bush was drummed from office.

Presidents also serve as the highest-ranking elected officials in their political parties. They must be sensitive to how their actions shape their parties' images. They must retain the support of their parties' most active members and contributors. If they do not satisfy their party constituencies, they may encounter difficulties with the party faithful in presidential primaries. In the 2004 primary campaign, when Democratic Party activists considered Senator John Kerry too moderate on the subject of the Iraq war, many turned to former Vermont governor Howard Dean. This sort of defection is a common problem, because party activists are generally more extreme than typical voters are (see Chapter 8). Presidents have to find ways to balance the demands of their ardent supporters with those of the electorate at large.

The President's Limited Powers

Even if presidents can balance their national and party constituencies, they usually cannot take action on their pledges without considering their level of support in Congress. Accommodating congressional demands is particularly important because of the fundamental division of power between the executive and legislative branches written into the Constitution. Those who wrote the Constitution ensured that presidents would govern only with the help of Congress. The result is a government of "separated institutions sharing powers."[12] Presidents are seldom in a position to force members of Congress to support them; they usually have to coax, beg, plead, and compromise to gain the necessary votes. More than 80 percent of the time, presidents either fail to secure passage of their major legislative agendas or must make important compromises to win congressional approval.[13]

Presidents find their position particularly exasperating because the public expects them to take decisive action. The expectations they face have increased much more quickly than the powers they have to meet such expectations. A thorough review of constitutional powers shows how little has changed to meet the increased expectations that presidents face in America's new democracy—and how many of the president's powers depend on congressional cooperation (especially in domestic affairs).

The Power to Persuade

Perhaps the most important presidential power receives no direct mention in the Constitution. Modern presidents rely on hundreds of public speeches each year to set forth their visions of the country's future. They use their high profiles, as well as their responsibility to spread information about the government, as opportunities to persuade Congress and the public at large to support their policies. Congress cannot check presidential propaganda, only reply to it—and members of Congress risk incurring either public or presidential wrath if they ignore the message.

The power to persuade is used much more openly today than it was in the early years of the republic (see Figure 10.2). Early presidents seldom spoke in

FIGURE 10.2   Growth in presidential speech making

Presidents started giving more public addresses with the Progressive Era presidencies, from Theodore Roosevelt to Woodrow Wilson, but a big surge followed the spread of broadcast media.

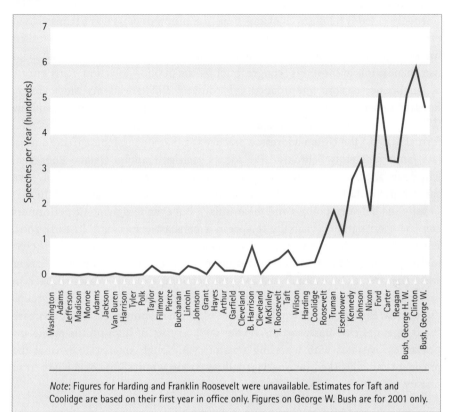

Note: Figures for Harding and Franklin Roosevelt were unavailable. Estimates for Taft and Coolidge are based on their first year in office only. Figures on George W. Bush are for 2001 only.

Sources: Data on Washington through McKinley are taken from Jeffrey Tulis, *The Rhetorical Presidency* (Princeton, NJ: Princeton University Press, 1987), p. 64; for Theodore Roosevelt, see Robert V. Friedenberg, *Theodore Roosevelt and the Rhetoric of Militant Decency* (New York: Greenwood Press, 1990); for Taft, see *Presidential Addresses and State Papers of William Howard Taft*, Vol. 1, 1910 (New York: Doubleday); for Wilson, see Albert Shaw, ed., *Messages and Papers of Woodrow Wilson*, Vols. 1 and 2 (New York: Review of Reviews Corporation, 1924); for Coolidge, see Claude M. Feuss, *Calvin Coolidge: The Man from Vermont* (Hamden, CT: Archon Books, 1965); for Presidents Truman through Reagan, see Roderick Hart, *The Sound of Leadership* (Chicago: The University of Chicago Press, 1987); for Hoover, George H. W. Bush, Clinton, and George W. Bush, information is taken from *The Public Papers of the President*, various years.

public, and when they did, their remarks were of a general nature. The Constitution requires that presidents report on the state of the union annually, but Thomas Jefferson and his immediate successors met this obligation through written messages to Congress. Early presidents usually avoided open involvement in day-to-day politics, and when they did get involved, they seldom used public speeches to do so.[14] Jefferson, a master politician, invited members of Congress to the Executive Mansion (later called the White House) for dinners, at which he attempted to persuade them to support his political agenda.[15] He also communicated his views through friendly newspaper editors.

The first moves toward a vocal presidency came early in the twentieth century, during the Progressive Era. Perhaps more than any other president, Theodore ("Teddy") Roosevelt changed the definition of what was permissible in presidential rhetoric. Roosevelt liked to achieve results by using what he called the **bully pulpit**.* Roosevelt suggested that, like a preacher, the president could use his position to move his "congregation"—the public—to action. Early efforts at public persuasion often failed, of course.[16] But presidents since Teddy Roosevelt have increasingly used the bully pulpit to persuade others.[17] Woodrow Wilson addressed a joint session of both houses of Congress in 1913 to deliver a formal **State of the Union address**, a practice that has since become traditional in late January or early February.[18] Presidents such as Franklin Delano Roosevelt, who gave "fireside chats" over the radio, and Ronald Reagan, a former actor, have seemed particularly effective at persuasion because they understood that there is "a thin line between politics and theatricals."[19] But even less dynamic performers can use their national visibility to spread a persuasive message. In early 2003, President George W. Bush proposed a "jobs and growth" plan that had as its centerpiece a cut on the taxes that investors paid on corporate dividends. "Lower taxes and greater investment will help the economy expand," reasoned Bush in his state of the union address.[20] Although Democrats and liberal interest groups argued that Bush's tax cuts would be harmful to the economy and would increase the budget deficit—Bush carried the day after a series of high-profile public appearances in states with wavering senators.[21] Although smaller than what the president initially asked for, the $350 billion tax cut was still one of the largest in history.

The Power to Recommend

Presidents who served before the Civil War seldom developed or promoted policies of their own.[22] They stayed out of the explosive slavery issue—a principle of silence that extended to other issues as well, especially after deliberations over legislation started on Capitol Hill.[23] Yet the Constitution explicitly encourages the president to recommend for congressional "consideration such Measures as he shall judge necessary and expedient." This power expanded rapidly after the end of the Civil War. The country was growing swiftly, and many social and economic problems broadened in scope.

The power to recommend gives presidents an ability to initiate debate, to set the political agenda.[24] Presidents can shut down old policy options, create new possibilities, and change the political dialogue. Bill Clinton proposed broadening health care coverage, reforming welfare, and reducing class sizes in public schools.

---

* Bully was nineteenth-century slang for "good" or "excellent," as in the old-fashioned phrase "Bully for you!"

George W. Bush placed tax cuts, education reform, and social security reform on the policy agenda.

However, this power does not go unchecked. Congress can—and often does—ignore or greatly modify presidential recommendations. Congress rejected Clinton's health care proposals and made significant changes to his proposals on welfare reform. It trimmed Bush's tax cuts. Nor is the power to initiate limited to the president. In 2007, House Democrats capitalized on their recent election victories by passing a "100-hour agenda" that included many measures designed to set the terms of debate for the next two years.

Presidents have the best opportunity to initiate policy in the first months after their election. For this reason, presidents make most new proposals at the start of their terms (see Figure 10.3). "You've got to give it all you can that first year," one of Lyndon Johnson's top aides noted. "You've got just one year when they treat you right."[25] The 75-day **transition** period between Election Day and the inauguration of a new president is critical. Incoming presidents do not yet have the burdens of office, but they have the time, resources, and importance to prepare for power. The transition period is typically followed by the presidential **honeymoon**—the first several months of a presidency, when reporters are kinder than usual, Congress more inclined to be cooperative, and the public receptive to new approaches.[26] Presidential popularity is at its peak, and public interest is high.

FIGURE 10.3   The presidential legislative agenda

Presidents offer their largest agenda during their first terms. *Why do presidents try to get the most done in their first year in office?*

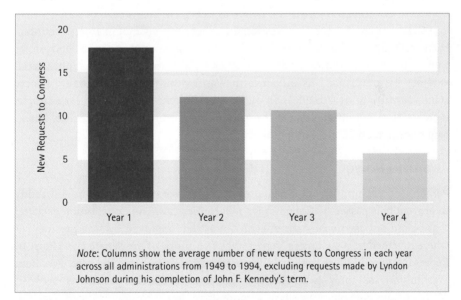

Note: Columns show the average number of new requests to Congress in each year across all administrations from 1949 to 1994, excluding requests made by Lyndon Johnson during his completion of John F. Kennedy's term.

Source: Calculations are based on data drawn from Lyn Ragsdale, *Vital Statistics on the Presidency* (Washington, DC: CQ Press, 1996).

The Budgetary Power

Before 1921, every federal agency sent its own budget to Congress for examination by an appropriations subcommittee. No one, not even the president, knew whether agency requests exceeded government revenues. President Woodrow Wilson asked for a bureau to coordinate these requests, but Congress at first refused to create one, saying it would encroach on congressional authority. However, when federal deficits ballooned during World War I, Congress relented.

Originally known as the Bureau of the Budget, the agency is now called the **Office of Management and Budget (OMB)**, a name that reflects its enlarged responsibilities. Although development of the president's budget is still its most important job, OMB also sets personnel policy and reviews every piece of proposed legislation that the executive branch submits to Congress to ensure that it is consistent with the president's agenda. Agency regulations, too, must now get OMB approval. One bureau chief claimed that OMB has "more control over individual agencies than . . . [the departmental] secretary or any of his assistants."[27]

OMB was once considered a professional group of technicians whose only goals concerned efficiency in budgeting. But OMB became more political during the 1980s and 1990s, when budgetary priorities starkly defined the differences between Democrats and Republicans.[28] Clinton's first OMB director, Leon Panetta, had been a Democratic member of Congress and later became the White House chief of staff, an admittedly political office. George W. Bush's first OMB Director, Mitchell Daniels, drew criticism for his advocacy of big tax cuts, and his second OMB director, Josh Bolton, helped negotiate congressional approval of a controversial $87 billion reconstruction package for Iraq.[29] Both Daniels and Bolton later took jobs in politics—Daniels as Governor of Indiana and Bolton as George W. Bush's chief of staff.

Congress created the Congressional Budget Office (CBO) in 1974 to counterbalance OMB's influence somewhat. The CBO evaluates presidential budgets as well as the budgetary implications of other legislation. The CBO's sophisticated analyses have enhanced its influence in Washington to the point where it now stands as a strong rival to OMB. In the 1994 health care policy debate, for example, it proved to be a "critical player in the game," whose estimates of the costs of health care reform doomed most proposals.[30]

The Veto Power

Perhaps the most important *formal* presidential power is the **veto**, a limited ability to prevent bills passed by Congress from becoming law. The Constitution declared that before any law "shall take effect," it must be "approved by" the president— whereas vetoed bills die unless "repassed by two-thirds of the Senate and House of Representatives." Before the Civil War, presidents seldom used the veto. President Washington cast only two. The average number cast by presidents between Madison and Lincoln was slightly more than four. Presidents from Franklin Roosevelt on have been much more willing to use the veto power (see Figure 10.4).

FIGURE 10.4 Trends in presidential use of the veto power

Presidents today use the veto less than they did at mid-century but more than they did in the 1800s. *Why did presidents become more assertive?*

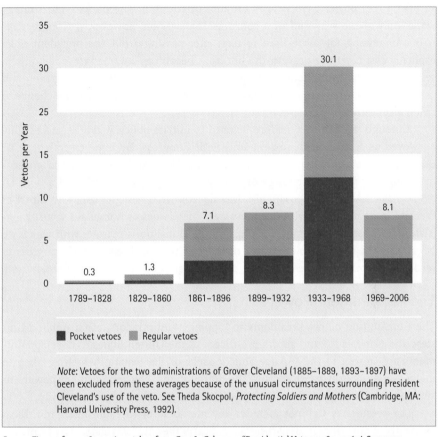

Pocket vetoes   Regular vetoes

Note: Vetoes for the two administrations of Grover Cleveland (1885–1889, 1893–1897) have been excluded from these averages because of the unusual circumstances surrounding President Cleveland's use of the veto. See Theda Skocpol, *Protecting Soldiers and Mothers* (Cambridge, MA: Harvard University Press, 1992).

Sources: Figures from 1789–1996 are taken from Gary L. Galemore, "Presidential Vetoes, 1789–1996: A Summary Overview," *Congressional Research Service Report for Congress*, 97-163 GOV; figures from 1997–2006 are taken from "Presidential Vetoes: 1789–Present," Office of the Clerk, U.S. House of Representatives, http://clerk.house.gov/art_history/house_history/vetoes.html, accessed January 22, 2007.

Congress usually fails to muster the two-thirds vote that is necessary in each chamber to **override** a veto. Since the Kennedy administration, Congress has over-turned approximately one out of every ten.[31] Only two of President Clinton's 37 ve-toes were overridden. The main check on the veto is simply its negative nature; it can stop policy change but not initiate it. During the energy crisis of the late 1970s, President Carter wanted an energy policy that was the "moral equivalent of war," but when confronted with opposition from oil-state senators, he was forced to sign a law much altered from his original proposals. Carter could have vetoed the legis-lation, but his desire for action required him to take what Congress was willing to give.

If Congress enacts a law 10 days before it adjourns, a president may exercise a **pocket veto** by simply not signing the bill into law. Nearly all of President Reagan's vetoes were pocket vetoes. Congress has no opportunity to override a pocket veto, so use of this power gave Reagan an aura of strength. The pocket-veto strategy works only at the very end of a congressional session, however; if Congress remains in session for more than 10 days after passing a bill, the president must explicitly cast a veto to prevent the bill from becoming law. Congress remains in session virtually throughout the year, now that the lines between governing and campaigning have blurred, so the last few presidents have rarely had the chance to cast pocket vetoes.

Although the veto can seldom be used to initiate policy, it can be successfully employed as a weapon in negotiations with Congress. By mid-2007, George W. Bush had issued only two vetoes: against a bill that would have allowed government funding for a wider range of embryonic stem cell research and a bill that would have set dates for troop withdrawals from Iraq. Still, he used the threat of the veto in negotiations with Congress over such issues as homeland security legislation, reconstruction funds for Iraq, and the Dubai ports episode with which we began this chapter.[32] In the first two instances, the veto threat forced Congress to reconsider its plans; in the latter case, the president's opponents were not deterred.

The Appointment Power

The Constitution allows presidents to "appoint Ambassadors, other public Ministers and Consuls . . . and all other Officers of the United States." These appointments are subject to the "Advice and Consent of the Senate," which is taken to mean that a majority must approve the nominations. The appointment power enables presidents to place thousands of officials in positions of responsibility.

The president's **Cabinet** includes key members of the administration. Most are heads of government departments and carry the title "secretary." The terms are left over from the days when a *secretary* was a confidential assistant who kept secrets under lock and key in a wooden *cabinet*. Originally, the president's Cabinet had but four departments, and the secretaries met regularly with the president. It was in Cabinet meetings, for example, that Abraham Lincoln developed his strategy for fighting the Civil War.

Over the years, government began to perform a much broader range of functions. As the number of departments grew from 4 to 15 and interest groups gained influence over them (see Table 10.1), the Cabinet lost its capacity to provide confidential advice to presidents. "Cabinet government is a myth and won't work," President Richard Nixon explained. "No [president] in his right mind submits anything to his cabinet."[33] Today the Cabinet meets only occasionally, primarily for ceremonial purposes. But Cabinet jobs are still an excellent way for presidents to reward influential political supporters or to improve the administration's professional reputation by bringing in respected people.

TABLE 10.1   Establishment year and interest-group allies of each cabinet department

Cabinet departments created after the nation's founding have specific issue domains and therefore fairly well-defined interest-group constituencies. Why would outer Cabinet departments form alliances with interest groups?

Department	Year	Interest-Group Allies
Inner Cabinet		
State	1789	
Treasury	1789	
Justice (attorney general)	1789	
Defense	1789 (as War Department)	
Outer Cabinet		
Interior	1849	Timber, miners, ranchers
Agriculture	1889	Farm bureau, other farm groups
Commerce	1913	U.S. Chamber of Commerce, other business groups
Labor	1913	Labor unions
Health and Human Services	1953	American Association of Retired Persons
Housing and Urban Development	1965	National League of Cities, Urban League
Transportation	1966	Auto manufacturers, truckers, airlines
Energy	1977	Gas, oil, nuclear power interests
Education	1979	Teachers' unions
Veterans Affairs	1987	American Legion, Veterans of Foreign Wars
Homeland Security	2003	State and local government, airlines, unionized public-safety providers
Environmental Protection Agency	Not an official department	Sierra Club, other environmental groups

Treaty Power

Presidents may negotiate **treaties**—official agreements with foreign countries—but they do not take effect without approval by a two-thirds Senate vote. This supermajority requirement limits presidential flexibility when negotiating with foreign countries. Prior to 1928, the Senate did not endorse 14 percent of the treaties brought before it.[34] A president who cannot get Congress to approve a treaty after negotiations conclude loses credibility in international politics.

No president was more frustrated by this constitutional check on presidential power than Woodrow Wilson. During negotiations to end World War I, President Wilson pursued one objective above all others: establishment of the League of Nations, an international organization to settle international disputes. Wilson believed that such an organization could prevent future world wars. But the Senate perceived the League of Nations as a threat to U.S. sovereignty and voted against joining. Shocked and dismayed, Wilson lost both his political efficacy and his personal health.

Because a small number of senators can block a treaty, presidents often negotiate **executive agreements**, legal contracts with foreign countries that require only a presidential signature. Nothing in the Constitution explicitly gives the president power to make executive agreements, but the practice has a long history. President James Monroe signed the first executive agreement with Great Britain in 1817, limiting the size of both countries' naval forces on the Great Lakes.

The Supreme Court affirmed the constitutionality of executive agreements in 1937.[35] Since then, presidents have turned to the device regularly. Most executive agreements either are extensions of treaties ratified by the Senate or involve routine presidential actions otherwise permitted by Congress. But presidents sometimes use executive agreements to implement major foreign policy decisions. For example, President George W. Bush relied on an executive agreement to set standards of official treatment for U.S. soldiers and other personnel in Afghanistan in the aftermath of the fall of the Taliban government in 2001.[36] In recent years, about 20 executive agreements have been signed for every treaty submitted to the Senate (see Figure 10.5).

The Power as Commander-in-Chief

The Constitution declares the president "commander in chief of the army and navy," a title that conveys significant authority over foreign affairs. Yet the Constitution gives Congress the power to declare war and to govern the armed forces. It did not settle which branch ultimately would control the nation's war power. Prior to the Civil War, presidents seldom acted on their own in military matters. For example, President James Madison refused to attack Great Britain in 1812 until Congress declared war.

Faced with a national emergency, Abraham Lincoln was the first to give an expanded interpretation to the role of commander in chief. When the southern states seceded from the Union, Lincoln proclaimed a blockade of southern ports and enlisted 300,000 volunteers before Congress convened. A few decades later, Theodore Roosevelt acted similarly, and in a much less urgent situation. He sent naval ships to Japan even though Congress refused to appropriate money for the trip. Congress, if it wished, could appropriate enough funds to get them back—which, naturally, members of Congress felt compelled to do! Following the lead of Lincoln and Roosevelt, modern presidents have often initiated military action without congressional approval. President Truman fought the Korean War without

FIGURE 10.5 Presidential use of executive agreements

Executive agreements are replacing treaties. *Why have presidents increasingly turned to executive agreements? Does this behavior deny the Senate its constitutional role in foreign policy?*

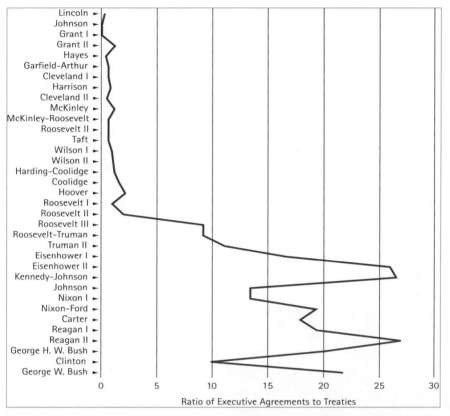

Sources: Gary King and Lynn Ragsdale, *The Elusive Executive: Discovering Patterns in the Presidency* (Washington, DC: CQ Press, 1988), 131–140; Harold Stanley and Richard Niemi, *Vital Statistics on American Politics, 2001–2002* (Washington, DC: CQ Press, 2001), 334; Data for George W. Bush calculated by authors from data on treaty actions available at Department of State, Office of the Legal Adviser, www.state.gov/s/l/index.htm, accessed June 19, 2006.

any congressional declaration whatsoever. More recently, President Clinton ordered the bombing of Kosovo without securing congressional approval.

Two major Supreme Court decisions have set the boundaries within which presidents exercise their authority as commanders in chief. In *United States v. Curtiss-Wright* (1936), the Court considered whether Congress could delegate to the president power over arms sales. Justice George Sutherland wrote that presidents were "the sole organ of the federal government in the field of international relations." The president has "a degree of discretion and freedom," he wrote, "which would not be admissible were domestic affairs alone involved."[37] This description seems to grant presidents wide latitude indeed.

The Court limited presidential power in a later case, *Youngstown Sheet & Tube Co. v. Sawyer* (1951). Trade unions in the steel industry had gone on strike during the Korean War. Claiming that the industry was crucial for national defense, President Truman ordered the federal government to seize control of the steel mills and commanded the strikers to return to work. In doing so, Truman ignored alternative procedures recently enacted by Congress for handling strikes, thereby attracting a constitutional challenge from the steel companies. Justice Robert Jackson wrote that presidents could not use their foreign policy authority to grab power at home. When a president "takes measures incompatible with the expressed or implied will of Congress, his power is at its lowest ebb," Jackson explained.[38]

The issue of executive authority arose again during the Vietnam War. In the summer of 1964, North Vietnamese torpedo boats attacked several U.S. destroyers stationed in Tonkin Bay off the coast of Haiphong, Vietnam's second-largest city. President Lyndon Johnson denounced the action as an unlawful attack on U.S. ships sailing in international waters.* Congress overwhelmingly passed the Tonkin Gulf Resolution, which effectively entered the United States into war with Vietnam

Only much later was it revealed that Johnson had misled Congress; the destroyers had invaded North Vietnam's territorial waters.

COMMANDER IN CHIEF
Here President Bush visits the USS Abraham Lincoln on May 1, 2003. *Why have presidents asked Congress to support military action, even as they question the legality of the War Powers Resolution?*

by giving the president authority to "take all necessary measures" to repel any attacks and to "prevent further aggression."[39]

The experience of a long and discouraging war in Vietnam prompted Congress to rethink the president's authority over military action. In 1973 Congress passed, over President Nixon's veto, the **War Powers Resolution**, which required that a president formally notify Congress any time U.S. troops are sent into harm's way. The resolution further specifies that troops must withdraw unless Congress approves the presidential decision within 60 days of receiving notification. Presidents generally question the War Powers Resolution's legal standing and sometimes ignore it. Nevertheless, recent presidents have sought congressional approval for their military actions, either formally or informally. After 9/11, Congressional approval proved to be an important vehicle by which President George W. Bush mobilized support on behalf of military action against the Taliban, al Qaeda, and Saddam Hussein. Prior to the wars in Afghanistan and Iraq, Congress overwhelmingly passed resolutions giving the president authority to use force.

Inherent Executive Power

The Constitution declares that "the executive power shall be vested in a President." Some claim that this statement adds nothing to presidential power; it simply summarizes the specific rights granted to the president. But many presidents have found in this clause the basis for a claim to additional rights and privileges. Presidential claims to inherent executive power have been invoked most frequently in making foreign policy, but presidents have asserted inherent executive power on other occasions as well.

One way in which presidents use their inherent executive powers is by issuing **executive orders**—directives to government employees that carry the weight of law unless they contradict acts passed by Congress. The Supreme Court ruled in 1936 that executive orders are constitutional, and since then they have increased in frequency and importance.[40] Truman used an executive order to desegregate the armed forces, Lyndon Johnson instituted the first affirmative action program, and George W. Bush sharply curtailed public access to the papers of former presidents.

Executive orders must not violate congressional legislation, and Congress may choose to overturn them after the fact. However, presidents rarely worry about their executive orders being overturned, because passing a bill through Congress is so difficult and time-consuming (see Chapter 9). Modern presidents have sharply increased the use of executive orders.[41]

The most controversial invocation of inherent executive powers has been the doctrine of **executive privilege**, the right of the president to deny Congress information it requests. George Washington was the first to invoke executive privilege when he refused to provide Congress information about an ill-fated military expedition on the grounds that "disclosure ... would injure the public."[42] Ever since, presidents have claimed authority to withhold information on executive decision making from Congress.

The Watergate affair in 1972 (see the section on scandals later in the chapter) brought this question before the Supreme Court. Prosecutors sought to review recordings of oval office conversations that President Nixon had held with his advisors, but the White House resisted, claiming that executive-branch policy discussions should be confidential. On the one hand, the Supreme Court sanctioned the doctrine of executive privilege, saying that confidential conversations between the president and his aides were "fundamental to the operation of government and inextricably rooted in the separation of powers under the Constitution."[43] Yet they ruled unanimously against Nixon after reviewing the communications, explaining that he lacked sufficient privilege to frustrate a criminal investigation.

The executive privilege issue came up again in 2002, when Congress's Government Accountability Office (GAO) sued to obtain records of White House energy-task-force meetings. Critics argued that the task force, headed by Vice President Cheney, had granted undue access to the scandal-ridden energy company Enron when formulating the administration's energy policy. The White House fought the suit and won, arguing that "the GAO intends to intrude into the heart of executive deliberations . . . which the law protects to ensure the candor in executive deliberations necessary for effective government."[44]

The Power as Chief of State

Presidents often symbolize the United States to foreigners, including their political leaders. The Constitution anticipated this ceremonial role, indicating that presidents "shall receive Ambassadors and other public Ministers . . . and shall Commission all the Officers of the United States." This clause seems to say little more than that presidents may welcome visitors and administer oaths of office. Yet the words endow presidents with an invaluable resource: the capacity to act with all the dignity that countries accord heads of state.

According to Walter Bagehot, a nineteenth-century analyst of British politics, governments have both "efficient" and "dignified" aspects.[45] The efficient aspect of government involves setting policy, administering laws, and settling political disputes. This is the nuts and bolts of policy making, the kind of activity performed by prime ministers in England or France. It is also hard work that often generates conflict. But government has a dignified aspect equally important to its long-term effectiveness. Governments must express the unity of the people, their values and hopes. Monarchs often symbolize their nation, as in England, whereas in France an elected president (separate from the prime minister) plays this ceremonial role. In the American system, the executive must perform both jobs—as seen by President

Bush's activities after terrorists attacked the United States, comforting the nation and formulating antiterrorism measures at the same time.

The dignified aspect of the presidency has always seemed somewhat inconsistent with America's egalitarian ideals. One of the issues discussed in the very first Congress was how to address George Washington. A Senate committee recommended "His Highness the President of the United States of America and Protector of Their Liberties," whereas the House, objecting to royal language, pushed the simpler title preferred by Washington: "the President of the United States."[46]

Presidents differ in their level of comfort with the pomp and circumstance of office. Ronald Reagan emphasized the dignified aspect of the presidency—overseeing formal parties and appearing frequently at ceremonial events, but delegating day-to-day policy concerns to others. Bill Clinton initially took quite the opposite tack, becoming known as a "policy wonk." Eventually, however, he distanced himself from the efficient side of governing, cultivating a strong but sympathetic image.

George W. Bush faced an agonizing conflict between the efficient and dignified aspects of the presidency on September 11, 2001. After the attacks on the World Trade Center and the Pentagon, security officials whisked Bush onto Air Force One from a Florida elementary school where he had been speaking, keeping his location secret for hours. Secret Service and military aides insisted that the president be kept safe to ensure a clear chain of command. But the nation clearly needed a dignified president to reassure the public and provide a sense of unified national response to the terrorism. Accordingly, Bush returned to the White House at 7 P.M. and delivered a televised address 90 minutes later. The symbolism of the White House address was as important as its substance.

As presidents have become increasingly engaged in policy, they have found it harder to maintain dignity—especially given increased media scrutiny. Some have received assistance from their families. First Lady Jacqueline Kennedy, for example, invigorated Washington's artistic and cultural scenes and restored the White House.

But presidential family members can be a liability as well as an asset. First Ladies Eleanor Roosevelt and Hillary Clinton angered conservatives by working for left-wing social policies,[47] and Nancy Reagan often attracted the scorn of liberals for her expensive gowns and purported reliance on astrologers for advice. Clinton in particular may have redefined the role of first lady, parlaying her position into a successful run for one of New York's U.S. Senate seats and (later) a presidential campaign of her own.[48] When Laura Bush became First Lady in 2001, however, she restored to the role its traditional emphasis on reinforcing the dignified aspect of the presidency. She took no public stand on controversial issues, instead emphasizing her former career as a public school librarian by expressing support for teachers and for education in general.

MEN OF THE PEOPLE
President Jimmy Carter often dressed in comfortable sweaters, even when meeting world leaders. President Andrew Jackson was a war hero known for his plain speaking and rough-hewn appearance. And while President George W. Bush usually maintains a formal appearance in the nation's capital, he dresses down for the cameras during retreats to his ranch in Crawford, Texas.

The vice presidency once served a primarily ceremonial function, another potential source of dignity for an administration, but the job has become more politicized in the last several decades. Perhaps because of the greater awareness that the vice president may one day gain the highest office, the role of the vice president has steadily broadened. For example, Vice President Albert Gore played a key role in shaping the Clinton administration's environmental policy. Dick Cheney, George W. Bush's vice president, helps direct national security policy; he served as Secretary of Defense in George H. W. Bush's administration.

The Impeachment Threat

Presidents may be impeached by a majority of the House for "high crimes and misdemeanors." The president must leave office if the Senate convicts by a two-

thirds vote. Nothing better clarifies the subordination of presidents to Congress than the fact that legislators can remove the executive at will. Although seldom used, the constitutional power of **impeachment** is no dead letter—as indicated by a sex scandal that tarnished the Clinton presidency.

The president's misconduct became a political issue when Paula Jones, an Arkansas public employee, sued Clinton for sexual harassment. She claimed that, while governor, Clinton had exposed himself to her in a Little Rock hotel room and requested sexual favors. Lawyers for Jones probed Clinton's romantic life while building their case, hoping to establish a pattern of inappropriate contact between Clinton and his employees and acquaintances. Under oath, Clinton denied having sexual relations with numerous women, including a young White House intern named Monica Lewinsky.

Evidence later appeared suggesting that Clinton and Lewinsky had indeed engaged in various forms of sexual conduct, including oral sex. Former solicitor general Kenneth Starr, who had been appointed as a special prosecutor to investigate Clinton land deals in the Whitewater affair, learned of this evidence that contradicted the President's sworn testimony. Starr expanded his investigation to include possible charges of perjury and obstruction of justice, and he eventually issued a report for Congress to use in hearings. The House voted (along mostly partisan lines) to impeach Clinton on December 19, 1998, making him only the second U.S. chief executive to face possible conviction.

The Senate decided in early 1999 to acquit Clinton after his trial. The president eventually owned up to deceiving investigators, but claimed his denial was not technically perjury because the Lewinsky affair did not include "sexual relations" as he understood the term. Public reaction to the explanation was hard to read.

Clinton remained popular, and some attributed Republican losses in 1998 congressional contests to a perception that the GOP had tried to overturn the 1996 election. At the same time, Democrats apparently suffered in the 2000 elections because of the administration's poor image.

The Lewinsky scandal illustrates that Congress's impeachment power operates under an implicit check. The Constitution requires a two-thirds vote to remove a president after impeachment, so it would nearly always require bipartisan effort. That effort will not arise in politically motivated impeachments, because members of Congress will not vote to remove an executive from their own party unless they feel they must. Impeachment is feasible only when a president's actions fundamentally violate the norms of American politics, as Richard Nixon's apparently did during the Watergate scandal.

Yet Clinton's scandals altered the American presidency in one important respect: They may have ended the use of **independent counsels** (also known as special prosecutors), investigators appointed to look into reports of executive-branch wrongdoing. Starr was able to spend huge sums of money investigating Clinton's sexual misdeeds because a judicial panel had appointed him in 1994 to look into an unrelated controversy, Whitewater. Many observers decided afterward that giving roving investigators so much power and resources threatened the independence of the executive branch. The law authorizing use of special prosecutors expired in 1999, with few members of Congress favoring renewal and even Starr testifying against it. Ethics investigations are now the province of the attorney general's office, part of the executive branch.[49] This change may make high-profile investigations less likely.

The Presidential Advisers

The modern president's closest advisers are White House aides who deal in matters of utmost confidentiality. At one time the president's personal staff was small and informal. Abraham Lincoln had just two young assistants. Even President Franklin Roosevelt originally had only a handful of personal aides.

To address organizational problems caused by the growing size of the federal government, Roosevelt in 1936 asked a committee of three specialists in public administration (headed by Louis Brownlow) to consider ways to improve federal government organization. Concluding that "the President needs help," the Brownlow Committee recommended sweeping changes throughout the government, including additional appointments to the president's personal retinue.

Congress rejected most of the Brownlow recommendations, but did agree to enlarge the White House staff.[50] The president's staff has steadily evolved in size and complexity.[51] The number of aides has grown from 48 in 1944 to more than 400 today. These aides generally fill the **White House Office**, part of a much larger collection of presidential advisers and coordinating agencies called the **Executive Office of the President (EOP)** (see Table 10.2).

Selecting Advisers

In Franklin Roosevelt's day, no single person headed the White House staff. Although Presidents Eisenhower, Nixon, and Ford had aides that directed a centralized White House office, as late as the Carter administration this structure was considered optional. Carter began his presidency using an alternative arrangement, with aides working together as "spokes in a wheel," each having direct access to the president. Today, however, presidents almost always place one person in charge.[52] This person, the **chief of staff**, meets with the president several times a day and communicates decisions to other staff, Cabinet officers, and members of Congress.

The best chiefs are usually Washington insiders. Although seldom acclaimed, Ronald Reagan's chief from 1987 to 1988, Howard Baker, was one of the most powerful and effective. A former Senate majority leader and presidential aspirant, Baker served at a time when he had forsaken all political ambition. Baker's skill at reaching compromises helped boost Reagan's popularity, despite the fact that the aging president had lost much of his former vitality.

Newcomers to Washington are usually less successful. Typically, they become lightning rods—people to be blamed when things go wrong. John Sununu, former governor of New Hampshire, was forced to leave the job of chief of staff when he was blamed for urging President George H. W. Bush to sign an unpopular tax increase.[53] Thomas McLarty from Arkansas resigned when he was blamed for the Clinton administration's poor start.[54]

TABLE 10.2   Executive Office of the President, budget and staff levels

	Budget (millions)*	Staff*
White House	$207	836
Office of Management and Budget	68	484
Office of National Drug Control Policy	29	111
Office of the U.S. Trade Representative	41	212
Office of Science and Technology Policy	5	29
Office of the Vice President	5	23
Council on Environmental Quality	3	21

Note: "The White House" includes National Security Council staff, Office of Administration, Office of Policy Development, and Council of Economic Advisers, in addition to White House Office and Executive Residence.

Source: Executive Office of the President, *Budget of the United States Government, Fiscal Year 2007*, Appendix, pp. 1039–1048.

*As of 2005.

Although Brownlow expected White House aides to have "no power to make decisions," modern presidents regularly use their staffs to shape their public policy proposals.[55] Within the White House staff, more than anywhere else, presidents can count on the loyalty of those around them simply because, unlike the careers of other bureaucrats (see Chapter 11), those of staff members are closely intertwined with those of the presidents.

The White House staff is more potent than ever, in part because presidents have more need for political help. Presidents today need pollsters and consultants who can keep them in touch with changes in public opinion. Many observers criticized George W. Bush's reliance on domestic policy adviser Karl Rove, whose primary experience was in campaign politics. Critics charged that Rove had too much power, and one disgruntled White House aide even complained that "everything, and I mean everything, [is] being run by the political arm."[56] White House officials insisted that chief of staff Andrew Card, and later his successor, Joshua Bolton, were really in charge of day to day affairs.

Presidents also need assistants who can help them communicate with the media, interest groups, and members of Congress. Once a major bill arrives for consideration on the chamber floor, White House aides are in regular contact with many legislators. So intense is the work inside the White House that most staff jobs demand 7-day, 100-hour work weeks. As a result, many positions go to young energetic people, and even they get tired after years on the job. By 2006, one longtime White House staffer admitted, "We're all burned out."[57]

In short, presidential advisers are indispensable if the president hopes to exercise agenda-setting powers such as recommending policies, proposing budgets, persuading legislators, sustaining vetoes, and attracting support for nominees.

WHITE HOUSE STAFF
Here press secretary Tony Snow, counselor to the president Dan Bartlett, communications director Nicole Wallace, national security adviser Stephen Hadley, and chief of staff Josh Bolton listen to President Bush as he holds a press conference. *What qualities make a good White House staff member?*

Quite apart from the president's genuine need for lots of political help, the White House staff is an excellent place to reward loyal supporters. Those who carry a candidate into office expect something in return after their candidate wins. The White House Office is a convenient place for the president to put campaign volunteers, because the president has exclusive control over appointments to his personal staff. No staff appointment needs Senate confirmation, not even the chief of staff. The public's limited understanding of executive branch organization prevented Republicans from getting much mileage out of Clinton's broken campaign promise.

Scandals in the White House Office

The highly personal and partisan nature of the White House staff can be a weakness as well as a strength. A White House full of personal friends and fellow partisans has at times so shielded presidents from external criticism that chief executives have lost touch with political reality. And sometimes staff members have used the power of the presidential office for improper, even illegal, purposes—paving the way for momentous scandals that tarnished both the sitting president's reputation and that of the presidency as an institution.

Scandals are hardly new to American politics. When lawmakers discovered that Abraham Lincoln's wife and her assistants outspent housekeeping funds, Lincoln successfully pleaded with Congress to appropriate more money secretly rather than to carry out an investigation.[58] But the intensity and significance of White House scandals have escalated in recent decades.[59] In addition to the Lewinsky scandal, two major and many more minor scandals have captured the attention of the nation and carried the potential for impeachment.

The most serious was the Watergate scandal during the Nixon administration. In 1972, at the instigation of members of the White House staff, five men broke into Democratic party headquarters at the Watergate condominium complex in Washington, D.C., apparently to obtain information on Democratic party campaign strategies. They were caught. Nixon's chief of staff, Bob Haldeman, knew that the burglars had received "hush money" so that they would not reveal White House involvement. When tapes of Nixon's own conversations indicated that the president himself had been involved in the cover-up, the House initiated impeachment proceedings, which convinced the president to resign.

In the Iran–Contra scandal, staffers in the Reagan White House illegally sold arms to the Iranian government and gave the profits, also illegally, to a group of guerrillas known as Contras who were fighting to overthrow a left-wing government in Nicaragua. White House aides faced prosecution and some Democrats talked of impeachment, but no direct evidence implicating the president turned up. Both scandals illustrate that presidents insulated from policy making by their advisers are often at risk.

The Two Presidencies

Put foreign affairs first, the sixteenth-century Italian thinker Nicolò Machiavelli advised his prince. If you fail at foreign policy, nothing you do in the domestic sphere will matter.[60] American presidents often wish to ignore foreign affairs, because voters pay more attention to domestic policies that influence their daily lives. Yet international politics has a way of forcing itself onto a president's policy agenda, and domestic successes generally will not save a president who flubs a foreign policy crisis. Machiavelli's advice still holds in America's new democracy.

Just as the public demands a strong economy and punishes the president for failing to provide one (see Chapter 7), the public also expects the president to keep the nation strong internationally. These policy areas differ in one important respect, however. The president clearly must share power with Congress on fiscal policy (see Chapter 15) and must work through the Federal Reserve Board to influence monetary policy (see Chapter 11), but in foreign affairs the president exercises more personal influence. The main limits on presidential action in this arena come from foreign leaders and global trends, not from U.S. politicians.

For this reason, foreign and defense policies provide a rare opportunity for presidents. They exercise more authority when dealing with other nations than when dealing with domestic policy. Many foreign policy duties are ceremonial and therefore give the executive chances to look presidential—while avoiding the political squabbles that often plague domestic policy. Foreign affairs allow an executive to tap into deep-seated patriotic emotions, to inspire deep loyalty in voters with military ties, and to gain respect worldwide. The government's international performance can play a significant role in electoral calculations.

In a classic essay, political scientist Aaron Wildavksy developed the **two-presidency theory**, which explains why presidents usually will exert greater power over foreign affairs.[61] Foreign policy requires fast action and focused responsibility, and neither interest groups nor members of Congress compete with the president as much over foreign affairs as over domestic affairs.

Foreign policy questions often require a rapid response, and not only because voters demand it. Sometimes options disappear as a crisis develops. Sometimes, sluggishness at resolving a conflict can allow disputes among nations to escalate—for example, if foreign powers misunderstand the American position. Moreover, foreign policy success often relies on secrecy. Military operations may be more successful when they are surprises, and sometimes ignorance of a nation's strategic position can lead foreign negotiators to give up more than necessary. Presidents are better equipped to streamline decisions for speed and secrecy. Partly for this reason, members of Congress sometimes follow a "self-denying ordinance" on foreign policy. They may not think it is their job to determine the nation's defense posture.[62] This was particularly true in the years immediately after World War II.[63]

(text continues on page 293)

THE U.S. POLITICS OF THE ARAB-ISRAELI CONFLICT

As we point out in this chapter, presidents usually have wider latitude to conduct foreign policy than to promote domestic initiatives. But the Arab-Israeli conflict may represent an exception. Here, the presence of powerful interest groups in the United States, combined with a long-standing, seemingly intractable conflict, has created a situation that has repeatedly frustrated U.S. leaders.

When Israel became a nation in 1948, the U.S. was the first country to recognize it. Arab states in the region, however, were upset by the creation of a Jewish nation on land that until the twentieth century had been occupied mainly by Arabs. After a provisional Israeli government declared itself to be a sovereign state, six Arab nations invaded Israel. Israel won that war, gained more territory than it lost, and then expanded the territory under its control in three later wars with its Arab neighbors. As a result, many Palestinians fled Israel to live in refugee camps in neighboring countries.

These Palestinian Arabs resented their status and objected to Israel's establishment of Jewish settlements in historically Arab areas. Control of the religiously significant city of Jerusalem was still another point of controversy. Many Palestinians engaged in strikes, civil disorder, and (in recent years) suicide bombings and other terrorist attacks to advance their cause. Meanwhile, Israel continued to occupy Palestinian regions captured in the wars, and refused to allow millions of displaced Palestinians to return to their ancestral lands.

A concrete barrier separates Jerusalem from the West Bank village of Abu Dis

Since 1976, Israel has been the number-one recipient of U.S. foreign aid. American presidents have also often backed Israel in the United Nations, where it otherwise might have been outvoted by Arab states. In recent decades, however, the U.S. alliance with Israel has become an uneasy one. Many critics in the United States and abroad have objected to the Israeli government's "aggressive behavior" in its responses to the suicide bombers. These responses have included such tactics as assassinating terrorist leaders, bulldozing the homes of terrorists' families, constructing a 450-mile "security fence" that would restrict travel between the West Bank and the rest of Israel, and engaging in retaliatory military incursions into Palestinian cities.[72]

In 2006, tensions worsened when the militant group Hamas, an organization that experts believe is responsible for at least 350 terrorist attacks,[73] won parliamentary elections in the semi-autonomous Palestinian Authority. The United

(continued on next page)

States, the European Union, and Israel promptly cut financial ties with the Palestinian government.

There are at least three options for U.S. leaders, each of which has drawbacks:

1. Support Israel's crackdowns on Palestinians. But would this position alienate Arab allies of the United States, such as Saudi Arabia, and complicate the situation in Iraq and efforts to combat terrorism?
2. Support the rapid creation of a Palestinian state. But would this position send the message that terrorist bombings are effective?
3. Force the two parties to the bargaining table, taking a hands-on role in negotiations and in the implementation of whatever peace plan might result. But would such an effort waste U.S. diplomatic energy, taking attention away from the nation's other international responsibilities?

Some in Congress have criticized President Bush for doing too little to resolve the conflict. Whatever the merits of the issue, it can be perilous for U.S. elected officials to appear to be anti-Israel. Although Jewish Americans make up only 2 percent of the population,[74] several key interest groups are extremely well-organized advocates for Israel. In particular, the American Israel Public Affairs Committee (AIPAC) has more than 100,000 members, meets with members of Congress more than 2,000 times a year, and is active on many college campuses.[75] Two prominent foreign policy scholars have gone so far as to argue that "the overall thrust of U.S. policy in the region is due almost entirely to U.S. domestic politics, and especially to the activities of the 'Israel Lobby.'"[76] Other academics dismiss this perspective as "paranoid and conspiratorial."[77]

When asked whether they sympathize with Israelis or Palestinians, Americans have consistently expressed support for Israel. Nevertheless, they also feel that a Palestinian state is justified—especially if terrorist groups pledge to end the suicide bombings.[78]

WHAT DO YOU THINK?

1. Should Americans become deeply involved in bringing the two parties to agreement, or would this waste energy that could be better expended elsewhere?
2. Should the fact that Israel is a democracy affect our foreign policy decisions related to the country? Why or why not?
3. Should elected officials pay much attention to public opinion on this issue, or are Americans' views on foreign policy too vague and ill-informed to be meaningful?

For more information on the Arab-Israeli conflict, see the following Web sites:

Pro-Israel

www.aipac.org

The American Israel Public Affairs Committee (AIPAC) is the largest pro-Israel lobby in Washington, and conducts many outreach activities in the rest of the country as well. Browse its issue papers for a detailed defense of the Israeli perspective.

THE U.S. POLITICS OF THE ARAB-ISRAELI
CONFLICT *(continued)*

www.ajc.org

The American Jewish Committee publishes a variety of briefings and issue papers on the Arab–Israeli conflict and other issues.

Pro-Palestinian

www.aaiusa.org

The Arab American Institute is a lobbying and outreach organization concerned with the Middle East conflict and with other issues of concern to Arab Americans.

www.palestinecampaign.org

The Palestine Solidarity Campaign is an activist organization dedicated to an independent Palestinian state.

Special interests occasionally influence American foreign policy. For example, the United States has refused to recognize the legitimacy of Cuba's regime, in part because hundreds of thousands of people who live in Florida come from families who fled Castro's revolutionary government in the 1950s. The conflict between Israel and Palestine is "a perpetual fixture of domestic politics," according to former Secretary of State James Baker, in part as a result of "the political power of the American Jewish community."[64] Israel receives one sixth of all U.S. foreign aid.[65] Yet few areas of foreign policy contain such strong and vitally interested domestic constituencies. Most nationality groups are not large enough, concentrated enough, or sufficiently attentive to events overseas to have a decisive effect on U.S. foreign policy. The interest-group structure is "weak, unstable, and thin."[66] This makes the policy environment easier for a president to negotiate.

Evaluating Presidents

Presidents are expected to be strong, yet presidential powers are limited. As a result, presidents seldom satisfy the hopes and aspirations of the voting public. Presidential successes are quickly forgotten, whereas their failures are often magnified by time. Presidents thus must work hard and exhibit impressive political acumen to convert their position into a source of continuing influence. Presidents add to their effectiveness by building up a strong professional reputation and extensive popular support—both of which are more difficult to achieve because of the intrusive nature of presidential news coverage.

Presidents who are competent and reliable are more likely to gain the cooperation of Congress and other **beltway insiders**, the politically influential people who live inside the highway that surrounds Washington.[67] Presidents also need to maintain their popularity with the general public. As Abraham Lincoln shrewdly observed, "With public sentiment, nothing can fail; without it, nothing can succeed."[68] Popularity is now quite easy to assess; pollsters ask respondents about presidential performance every week!

All presidents experience fluctuations in their popularity over the course of their terms. Their support rises and falls with changes in economic conditions and in response to foreign policy crises. But in addition to these external factors, presidential popularity tends to decline over time as public expectations go unfulfilled.[69] A study of the first term of eight recent presidents indicates that, apart from any specific economic or foreign policy events, their popularity on average fell by nearly 8 points in the first year and by 15 points by the middle of the third.[70] Their popularity recovered in the fourth year, when a presidential campaign was under way—either because presidents worked to communicate positive news about their administrations or because presidents start to look better when compared to their competition. Presidents regain popularity when reelected, but those bounces soon trail off. George W. Bush's popularity, which was about 50 percent at the time of the 2004 election, declined to the mid-30s by 2006.

If presidential leadership is so difficult—requiring a strong professional reputation, robust public popularity, and the cooperation of numerous self-interested individuals—why are some past executives remembered as "Great Presidents"? What allows some presidents to succeed, even in periods of crisis, when most fail? The simplest answer is that past presidents did not face the same expectations as today's executives, nor did they have to manage a mammoth government whose policies extend into all areas of public and private life. The federal government has, as the saying goes, "bit off more than it can chew."

Journalists typically discuss presidential performance in terms of personality traits: how clever the officeholder is, prior experiences in other political offices and the lessons those experiences taught, or how upbringing shapes the executive's world view. This emphasis on the identity of the president does receive support from some scholars. Political scientist James Barber, for example, proposes that effective presidents will be the ones who both like their job and readily adapt their policies to changing circumstances.[71] Presidents Lyndon Johnson and Richard Nixon failed, Barber suggests, because they saw the office as a burden rather than a blessing, and hence were willing to stick with failed policies even after public opinion turned against them. President Eisenhower missed the list of top presidents because, although he enjoyed the job, he waited for others to propose solutions for the nation's problems and so was too passive as a policy maker.

STRIKING OUT
President Richard Nixon is shown here
bowling. *What did Nixon's personality have
to do with his performance as president?*

As tempting as explanations based on personality might be, they ignore the extent to which presidential performance depends on the conditions under which the officeholder must act. We cannot say what Jimmy Carter would have achieved with the overwhelmingly Democratic Congress that Franklin Delano Roosevelt enjoyed, or how FDR would have grappled with the conservative Congress that his successor Harry Truman had to face. We do not know how FDR might have extracted himself from the Vietnam quagmire into which circumstances thrust Lyndon Baines Johnson, or what greatness LBJ might have achieved if faced by the evil of Nazi Germany. But the most recent evidence of how chance events can shape a presidency comes from President George W. Bush, as discussed in the chapter opening. The increased power that Bush enjoyed after 9/11, juxtaposed with the later decline in his ability to control the agenda, only underscores that, however much presidential personality and congressional party balances might shape what a president can do, public opinion is the real power behind the throne in America's new democracy.

Chapter Summary

Americans often wonder forlornly why the United States no longer elects great presidents who meet public expectations. They seem to believe that the failure is somehow one of insufficient public control over the political system. Yet most sources of frustration with the executive branch trace back to the demands of the public, or at least to the demands of elected officials who are then rewarded by voters for their behavior.

One reason why modern presidents fail is that they are expected to do so much. The institutions presidents must run and the problems they must solve have grown, yet their formal powers have changed very little. They still rely on cooperation from Congress. Passive presidents receive little praise but much scorn, and a president who preaches patience in the face of social problems risks reprisal from voters at the polls—even though presidents lack the opportunity to leave much of a stamp on government unless they are elected at the right political time.

Electoral considerations help account for the fact that presidents dominate policy making in foreign affairs more than on domestic issues. Voters expect presidents to take the lead, and they support presidents early in a crisis regardless of the actions taken. Only later, if things do not turn out well, do voters penalize poor choices. Voters defer to the president on foreign policy for good reason. The president has an expansive array of analysts and advisers from whom to draw advice. Having so much help allows the president to move quickly and secretly to resolve a crisis. If a president seems less capable in domestic policy, it is not due to disregard for public desires and is probably not due to personality quirks. Rather, the limits are imposed primarily by legislators closely tied to diverse voter preferences, the people with whom a president must share power.

Key Terms

beltway insiders, p. 294
bully pulpit, p. 272
Cabinet, p. 276
chief of staff, p. 288

Executive Office of the President (EOP), p. 287
executive agreements, p. 278
executive orders, p. 281

Suggested Readings

Barber, James. *The Presidential Character: Predicting Performance in the White House*, 4th ed. Englewood Cliffs, NJ: Prentice-Hall, 1992. Argues that presidential character affects presidential success.

Jones, Charles O. *The Presidency in a Separated System*, 2nd ed. Washington, DC: Brookings, 2005. Examines the role of the president under divided government.

Kernell, Samuel. *Going Public: New Strategies of Presidential Leadership*, 4th ed. Washington, DC: CQ Press, 2007. Describes the increasing tendency of presidents to use popular appeals to influence legislative processes.

Mayer, Kenneth. *With the Stroke of a Pen: Executive Orders and Presidential Power*. Princeton, NJ: Princeton University Press, 2001. Study of how presidents use executive orders to make policy.

Neustadt, Richard E. *Presidential Power and the Modern Presidents*. New York: Free Press, 1990. Modern classic on the limits to presidential power.

Rudalevige, Andrew. *Managing the President's Program: Presidential Leadership and Legislative Policy Formulation*. Princeton, NJ: Princeton University Press, 2002. Examines how presidents design policy initiatives.

Silverstein, Gordon. *Imbalance of Powers: Constitutional Interpretation and the Making of American Foreign Policy*. New York: Oxford University Press, 1996. Argues that the president's constitutional authority over foreign policy has not been ceded to Congress.

Skowronek, Stephen. *The Politics Presidents Make: Leadership from John Adams to George Bush*. Cambridge, MA: Harvard University Press, 1993. Provocative analysis of the historical development of the presidency.

On the Web

For more information on the presidency, see the following Web sites:

THE WHITE HOUSE
www.whitehouse.gov

The official Web site of the White House offers current and historical information about U.S. presidents.

CENTER FOR THE STUDY OF THE PRESIDENCY
www.thepresidency.org

The Center for the Study of the Presidency publishes *Presidential Studies Quarterly* and showcases academic information and links.

NATIONAL ARCHIVES AND RECORDS ADMINISTRATION
www.nara.gov/nara/president/address.html

The National Archives and Records Administration provides information about and links to presidential libraries.

The Bureaucracy

THE UNPRECEDENTED 9/11 TERRORIST ATTACKS PROVOKED FEEL-
ings of shock, anger, and vulnerability that many Americans had never experienced
before. But in the aftermath of the attacks, some channeled their reactions into a
much more familiar mood: U.S. government agencies had failed to do their jobs
well.

Such criticism contained more than just an element of truth. Prior to September 11, the Immigration and Naturalization Service (INS) didn't have the resources to keep track of millions of foreign nationals who were overstaying their visas in the U.S., including three of the 9/11 hijackers.[1] The Central Intelligence Agency (CIA), in charge of gathering information about foreign threats, and the Federal Bureau of Investigation (FBI), the organization that investigates crimes within the U.S., had done a poor job of coordination and information sharing about terrorists from abroad who were able to slip into the country. Finally, the National Security Agency (NSA), which monitors communications all over the world, fell far short of the number of analysts needed to make sense of the 2 million messages per hour that flowed into each of its many listening posts.[2] One former FBI official called the 9/11 incident "the greatest counterterrorism screwup in U.S. history. ...Billions and billions of dollars are spent on this, and if we can't get it, there's something very, very wrong."[3]

The public didn't have to be told that things were amiss. American leaders knew that they had to take immediate steps to prevent another serious terrorist attack.

As part of the administration's response, George W. Bush proposed reforming the way law-enforcement agencies conduct the business of domestic security. In doing so, the president moved to implement recommendations of a blue-ribbon commission that in February 2001 had called for greater coordination and planning among dozens of government organizations. His plan was different from that of the commission in one respect, however: Whereas the panel had called for a "significant organizational redesign"—namely, a new Cabinet-level agency charged with securing the U.S. from terrorism[4]—Bush's plan was much more modest. He created a new White House Office of Homeland Security, headed by former Pennsylvania governor Tom Ridge.

Ridge, with his small staff of 100 operating from a corner of the Executive Mansion, was expected to coordinate the activities of agencies as diverse as the FBI in the Justice Department, the U.S. Customs Service in the Treasury Department, the Federal Aviation Administration (FAA) in the Department of Transportation, and the Federal Emergency Management Agency (FEMA), an independent entity. These agencies—and dozens of others that Ridge was supposed to keep track of— all had separate budgets, separate directors, and separate organizational cultures. One national security expert likened the task to "getting a 40-mule team...pulling in the right direction."[5] In his public appearances, Ridge admitted that the job was as large as "building the transcontinental railroad, fighting World War II, or putting a man on the moon."[6]

After eight and one-half months of trying to manage the domestic security apparatus from the White House, and as members of Congress and the public expressed alarm at new revelations about pre-9/11 intelligence failures, the president conceded that he needed to do more. In June 2002, Bush asked Congress to create a Cabinet-level Department of Homeland Security that would have direct authority

TRANSPORTATION SECURITY
The Transportation Security
Administration (TSA), part of the
Department of Homeland Security,
is in charge of staffing airport
checkpoints. *What kinds of groups
and individuals do you think might
exert pressure on the TSA?*

over nearly 170,000 government workers that were then spread across eight departments. The Border Patrol, the Coast Guard, the Transportation Security Administration, and even the Secret Service would all be moved to the new organization. In a televised address to explain his reversal of course on this issue, Bush admitted that a more effective, unified structure was needed: "Right now, as many as a hundred different government agencies have some responsibilities for Homeland Security, and no one has final accountability."[7]

As obvious as their decision to reorganize might have been, Bush and Ridge faced a difficult task if they really wanted to create a new department. The last time the United States underwent a significant national security reorganization was in the late 1940s, after what President Truman called a "long hard battle" that had lasted more than four years.[8] In other words, Bush and Ridge were attempting to win approval for the largest federal government shakeup in more than five decades.

The eventual White House proposal was not the first one that administration officials tested. Ridge circulated two modest proposals before the final draft, both of which attracted vigorous objections from the agencies and interest groups involved. President Bush knew that the real proposal would need some method of overcoming "bureaucratic inertia."[9] He settled on secrecy. The final plan emerged from clandestine meetings conducted by Ridge with three high-ranking presidential aides: the top budgetary officer, the chief legal adviser, and the White House chief of staff. Few administration officials even learned of the plan until days before its public debut, so potential opponents could not nibble it to death with minor complaints.

The Bush administration's proposal led to the creation of a huge new agency, with 169,000 employees and a $37.5 billion budget. It became the third largest federal department, behind Defense and Veterans' Affairs. But Bush's advisers selected the agencies to incorporate into the department very carefully, choosing those with little political clout. Examples included (1) the Federal Emergency Management Agency (FEMA), which hires few employees; (2) the new Transportation Security

Adminstration, which lacked deep roots in its department; and (3) the Coast Guard, which had changed departments before. Bush did not try to touch the politically influential agencies—such as the Federal Bureau of Investigation (FBI), with its long history inside the Department of Justice. The stronger bureaucracies thus did not marshal their resources against Bush's plan.

Congress still could have blocked the sweeping Bush proposal. The White House estimated that 90 congressional committees and subcommittees exerted some jurisdiction over homeland security, a system of oversight that eventually would have to be simplified to deal with the consolidated department. But both chambers streamlined the legislative process—the House by creating a special committee of leaders to deal with the issue, the Senate by debating Bush's proposal on the floor of the chamber itself. Former senator Warren Rudman explained congressional cooperation this way: "Are you going to tell 280 million American people, if something bad happens, that you voted against this reorganization because you wanted to be sure that you had your subcommittee on carrots and lettuce?"[10]

One obscure provision did end up creating controversy. It allowed the secretary of Homeland Security to bypass ordinary civil-service rules and use a promotion system based on merit. Ridge argued that he would need such flexibility to assemble a "motivated, high-performance, and accountable workforce."[11] But leaders of the public employee unions strongly opposed giving department management so much influence over employees, many of whom enjoyed greater insulation from their bosses under the status quo. Democrats, the unions' usual allies, initially vowed to delay Bush's plan until Homeland Security employees received stronger job guarantees in the legislation.

Yet the 2002 elections were rapidly approaching. Critics claimed that a Democrat-controlled Senate was holding public safety hostage on behalf of their corrupt union allies. Bush himself charged that Senate Democrats who were opposing his executive reorganization were "not interested in the security of the American people." Senate Majority Leader Tom Daschle denounced Bush's remarks as outrageous,[12] but his fellow Democrats rightly feared the result of a popular president appearing in their states questioning their Democrats' patriotism. According to one observer at the time, "Bush is positioned to inflict grave political damage."[13] Democrats ultimately stood aside, allowing the homeland security bill to move swiftly toward passage.

Some political scientists believe that, in the United States, major governmental changes are no longer possible. Entrenched bureaucracies, allied with interest groups and key congressional committees, can block any comprehensive changes that would threaten their power or their resources.[14] Admittedly, Bush's proposal succeeded in part because it offended few powerful or entrenched interests. But being inoffensive is not enough to propel major bureaucratic reorganizations through the difficult legislative process described in Chapter 9.

The battle over creating a new Department of Homeland Security in 2002 proved that, under certain conditions, major change is possible. One important condition, of course, is public dissatisfaction. Voters need to believe that something is wrong with government. The 9/11 attacks left few doubts about that. But something more than dissatisfaction is required.

Voters also need to have a fairly clear idea what sort of changes would improve government's problems. In this case, the public exhibited special unity on Bush's proposal. Less than a quarter of the American public apparently opposed consolidating the agencies.[15] Most Americans believed that the Department of Homeland Security would make them safer. Such unified opinion provided Democrats little leverage to demand technical changes in the legislation. They still dragged their feet, but the unavoidable result was that opponents could brand them as opponents of change. Like any elected official who does not give voters what they want, Senate Democrats suffered for their unresponsiveness in the elections that followed.

To say that the new department was successfully created is not to say that its operations have met with universal acclaim. On the contrary, in its short lifespan, it has been criticized as ineffective and even dysfunctional by such diverse sources as think tanks, members of Congress, monitoring agencies, and its own inspector general.[16] Even as the Senate overwhelmingly confirmed Michael Chertoff to succeed Tom Ridge as secretary of Homeland Security in early 2005, Senators voiced a variety of complaints about distribution of grant funds, border protection, and the coherence of the overall homeland security strategy.[17]

In this chapter, we argue that Americans should not be surprised when government institutions fail to accomplish their missions, because that is the nature of bureaucracy. Government institutions tend to be inefficient because of how they are organized, and the U.S. government is even less effective than other governments.

Is our argument, then, that Americans should shrink the national government and "stop throwing good money after bad"? Not necessarily. Our point is that both the successes and disappointments of American institutions come from the same source: the responsiveness of government to elections, to public opinion, and to political pressures. The same responsiveness to political goals that causes American institutions to fail also allows them to respond quickly when the public is aroused—as illustrated by the massive reorganization of American law-enforcement and security agencies that followed the 9/11 attacks. Americans may not always like the performance of their government, but they nonetheless usually receive the type of government they ask for.

Structure of the Federal Bureaucracy

The president of the United States serves as the chief executive of the government, the person who bears primary responsibility for implementing the nation's laws. However, the nation's legal code is labyrinthine, and the tasks necessary to execute its laws are far more complicated than one person could hope to carry out—or even to oversee. Nor could the president's few immediate advisers do an adequate job. Implementing the country's rules and regulations requires an extensive network of federal workers living in every state, as well as a giant concentration of employees in Washington, D.C. The name for this structure of employees is the federal **bureaucracy**.

The federal government encompasses hundreds of agencies, most grouped under one of 15 **departments**, collections of federal agencies that report to a secretary who serves in the president's Cabinet. Between 60 and 70 **independent agencies**, such as the Central Intelligence Agency and the Environmental Protection Agency, are free-standing entities that report either to the president or to a board.[18] Finally, there are around three dozen **government corporations**, independent organizations that fulfill business-related functions.[19] Examples of government corporations include the Federal Deposit Insurance Corporation, which insures bank deposits, and the National Railroad Passenger Corporation, which runs Amtrak.*

Bureaucrats, the people who staff government bureaus and agencies, do not run for election, nor does the Constitution grant them any formal authority. Yet the decisions they make in applying laws to real-life circumstances give them a unique political power, to the point where scholars often treat the bureaucracy as though it were a separate branch of government. An exasperated President Harry Truman once said, "All the president is, is a glorified public relations man who spends his time flattering, kissing, and kicking people to get them to do what they are supposed to do anyway." He was especially frustrated "when it comes to these bureaucrats."[20] Presidents have a difficult time managing the bureaucracy because it is filled with inexperienced political appointees and low-prestige civil servants. Two other barriers also stand in the way of presidential influence over the bureaucracy. First, by law, many policy-making agencies in the executive branch need not answer directly to the president. Second, the president is seldom the only "boss" that bureaucrats have. They also answer to Congress, to special interests, and (at least indirectly) to the voting public. Dividing responsibility in this fashion means that bureaucrats often can ignore the boss or play one boss off against the others.

Why the Bureaucracy Is Unresponsive

Bureaucracies are essential to governmental action. Laws become effective only when an agency implements them. Without some kind of organization, government cannot build roads, operate schools, put out fires, fight wars, distribute social security checks, or do the thousands of other things Americans expect. Ideally, a bureaucracy is organized to carry out assigned tasks efficiently. Staff members are

---

* Because the dividing line between independent agencies and government corporations is sometimes difficult to pinpoint, the number of each type of agency is necessarily inexact.

selected for their ability to do their jobs. Each reports to a superior, and ultimate authority is exercised by the head of the agency. The bureaucracy provides each worker with the supplies necessary to get the job done. When all works perfectly, that is, bureaucracies exhibit unity, focus, and power.[21]

Yet, Americans often express frustration that the federal bureaucracy is arrogant and unresponsive. Most Americans think "people in the government waste a lot of money we pay in taxes" (see Figure 11.1). The bureaucracy is the big-government monolith that many disparage and some fear: the regulators, the tax collectors, and the social engineers. It is the villain of novels, movies, and television shows. Several presidents won office by campaigning against the government, promising to get the bureaucracy under control. Ronald Reagan's message was perhaps the most stark, as in this oft-quoted line: "Government is not the solution to our problem. Government *is* the problem."[22] But the size and power of government almost never shrinks, and the sense of public vulnerability seldom diminishes.

Ironically, the public is partly to blame for their own sense of helplessness. The number of functionaries has greatly increased with the expansion of federal government responsibility, but few of these workers answer directly to elected national leaders. Most employment growth has occurred at state and local levels (see Figure

FIGURE 11.1   The public thinks there is a lot of waste in government

Survey respondents were asked the following question: "Do you think that people in the government waste a lot of money we pay in taxes, waste some of it, or don't waste very much of it?" *What do you think? Is the public justified in its belief that the government wastes a lot of money?*

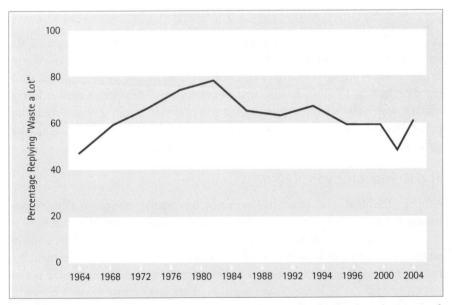

Source: National Election Study, Cumulative Data File, conducted by the Center for Political Studies at the University of Michigan.

FIGURE 11.2 Government employment, 1946–2005

The number of state and local employees has increased, but the number of federal employees has remained about the same. Note that federal government employment figures include civilians only. Active-duty military personnel appear in a separate category.

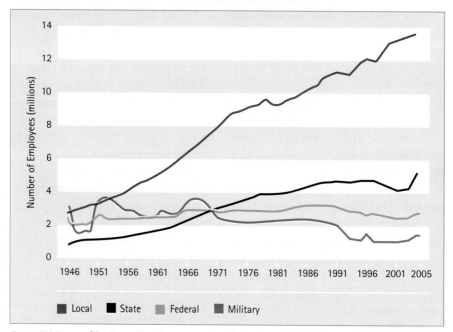

Sources: U.S. Bureau of the Census, *Historical Statistics of the United States: Colonial Times to 1970* (Washington, DC: GPO, 1975), pp. 1100, 1141; *Statistical Abstract of the United States, 2007*, Tables 450, 481; 499.

11.2). Because these positions often grow out of federal mandates or programs, the bureaucrats are not fully answerable to elected officials at any specific level of government. Many private contractors also perform tasks funded by government agencies. The decision to construct this "shadow government," over which elected federal officials exert only indirect influence, is a policy choice resulting from conflicting public demands. The voting populace opposes growth in the federal bureaucracy but still expects national leaders to accomplish an increasing number of tasks.

The Bureaucracy Problem

Although the ideal bureaucracy has tremendous potential, many forces inhibit perfection. Some of these flaws are inherent in all bureaucracies: They are slow to change, they have a tendency to expand, and performance is difficult to measure by outsiders. Other flaws, however, reflect the demands imposed on government bureaucrats through democratic elections: They often work under impossible expectations or debilitating limits. Taken together, these flaws create what is known as the "bureaucracy problem."[23]

Slow to Change   Any large governmental organization has standard decision-making procedures. Standardization is essential if large numbers of people are to coordinate their work toward some common end. Otherwise, staff would be so confused they soon would be unable to do anything. Institutional habits are hard to break, though, so bureaucracies are slow to adapt.[24] Despite massive increases in the use of energy in the United States, the Federal Energy Regulatory Commission has changed its approach to regulation of the electricity grid very little over the course of four decades.[25] After a catastrophic blackout in the northeastern U.S. during the summer of 2003, former Energy Secretary Bill Richardson complained, "We're a superpower with a third world grid."[26] As one humorist observed, "Bureaucracy defends the status quo long past the time when the quo has lost its status."[27]

Expansionary Tendencies   Once bureaucracies are created to address problems, they generally try to expand so they can address them better. Government agencies nearly always feel they need more money, more personnel, and more time to perform effectively.[28] The head of the Forest Service once exclaimed to a congressional committee: "Mr. Chairman, you would not think that it would be proper for me to be in charge of this work and not be enthusiastic about it and not think that I ought to have more money, would you? I have been in it for thirty years, and I believe in it."[29]

Difficulty Measuring Performance   Measuring the performance of government agencies from the outside is difficult, sometimes almost impossible. One might observe the social conditions agencies must address, but it is hard to know either (1) what conditions would be like without the agency's actions or (2) what an agency reasonably could accomplish given its resources.

The streets and parks in a city may be strewn with litter, but are garbage collectors to blame for performing badly? Is City Hall to blame for funding garbage collections inadequately (and if so, is the problem low taxes or waste elsewhere in the budget)? Or are inconsiderate citizens to blame for spreading more trash than residents in other cities do? Not even an agency's immediate supervisors may be able to make these sorts of judgments without expensive studies, perhaps of garbage collection in other cities or of the citizenry's sanitation habits. An elected official even further removed from collection efforts, who has less familiarity with street-level behavior, is almost helpless. In 2003, for example, many Californians criticized the U.S. Forest Service because its firefighters failed to stem the initial spread of the devastating Cedar Fire near San Diego that destroyed more than 2,000 homes and caused 14 deaths. Forest Service officials argued that they had done the best they could under the worst of possible circumstances, the sort of claim whose merits an elected official with limited expertise in fire prevention would be unable to weigh.[30]

Impossibility of Tasks   Most governmental tasks are difficult to accomplish. If they were easy, someone other than the government would have undertaken the job! Tasks are usually complex, funds limited, and goals vague.[31] Americans expect schools to teach their children—but many people disagree about what exactly should be taught. Commuters expect transportation agencies to achieve smoothly flowing traffic—but to avoid all bottlenecks, construction crews would have to pave almost everything. The Environmental Protection Agency is supposed to combat pollutants—but nearly all human activity pollutes, and citizens resist inconvenient measures that would limit their own waste. With such conflicting responsibilities, agencies may have no hope of satisfying everyone.

Red Tape   British bureaucrats once bound government and legal documents in a sticky, reddish tape, so that anyone who wanted to access a file would have to cut through the wrapping first. Today, the phrase *red tape* refers to any delay imposed by a government agency, the proverbial "forms filled out in triplicate" and "bureaucratic runaround" about which so many people complain.

Obviously, individuals experience numerous delays and must surmount numerous barriers when they seek assistance from government. These inconveniences often lead regular citizens to conclude that agencies are unresponsive to the public, and perhaps even malicious. To an extent, this perception may be correct. Certainly, there are times when an agency creates red tape so that a limited number of people can take advantage of a program or so that individual officials can "cut through the tape" quickly in exchange for rewards ranging from gratitude all the way to political favors or even bribes.

But this sort of chicanery is almost certainly the exception rather than the rule. Complaints overlook the fact that most red tape comes from elected officials, who require detailed documentation to explain spending and who force elaborate agency practices to promote political goals. As one analyst has observed, "One person's red tape may be another's treasured procedural safeguard."[32] Bureaucracies seem unresponsive to individual members of the public precisely because they are excessively responsive to public demands expressed through elected officials.

People often complain, for example, that it takes forever to get a bridge repaired. But bridge repair can be politically complicated. The design of the replacement bridge must be acceptable to neighbors. If the bridge has been designated an historical landmark—as have a surprising number of bridges—the local historical commission must approve the repairs. The agency responsible for the repairs, when getting contracts, must advertise the job and allow time for companies to submit bids. To avoid accusations of political favoritism, published criteria must guide the choice of contractors. And regulators must supervise the repairs themselves—not only to ensure quality, but also to ensure worker safety or to avoid environmental damage. Once again, a common bureaucratic problem is caused not by malice but by political demands that trace back to the public.

Bureaucracy in America

The bureaucracy problem exists in all countries, but American bureaucracies have special problems that are rooted in the country's unusual political history. United States bureaucracies had a difficult beginning. They were built with patronage and modernized slowly through "bottom-up" civil service reforms.

Difficult Beginnings American bureaucrats lack the noble heritage of their counterparts in other industrialized countries, where government departments evolved out of the household of the king, queen, or emperor. The lineage of federal bureaucrats in the United States is far less distinguished. Few American parents dream of the day when their children will grow up to be bureaucrats! The framers could not even agree on where to put the people who would run the new national government. Finally, as part of a compromise, they agreed to locate the home of the federal government, the District of Columbia, on the Maryland–Virginia border. The land Congress had chosen was swampy and miserable. Visitors complained that it was thick with "contaminated vapour," which produced "agues and other complaints."[33] If the government were to attract quality workers, location would not be its main selling point.

Mountains of Patronage President Andrew Jackson's administration pioneered the use of federal jobs as a political reward, or source of **patronage**. The practice of hiring workers on the basis of party loyalty became known as the **spoils system** when New York Senator William Marcy attacked Jackson for seeing "nothing wrong in the rule that to the victor belong the spoils."[34]

Politicians in both parties quickly saw that the spoils system suited their needs, because it allowed them to use tax revenue as an indirect payment to campaign workers who took on arduous jobs such as passing out pamphlets, organizing rallies, and getting people out to vote.[35] The New York machine politician George Washington Plunkitt explained the logic in this way: "You can't keep an organization together without patronage. Men ain't in politics for nothin'. They want to get somethin' out of it."[36] Patronage also made it easier for parties to raise large amounts of cash to fund campaigns. Government workers would receive open requests for political donations, knowing that failure to contribute their share could result in dismissal.[37] Politicians considered these practices a natural and legitimate part of politics.

Looking back on American political history, many scholars have found much to praise in the old spoils system.[38] For one thing, it helped immigrants adjust to the realities of urban life in the United States. "I think there's got to be in every ward somebody that any bloke can come to—no matter what he's done—and get help," said one Boston politician. "Help, you understand; none of your law and your justice, but help."[39] Some help took the form of jobs. Irish immigrants were particularly good at using politics to get ahead. In Chicago, the percentage of public school principals of Irish background rose from 3 percent in the 1860s to 25 percent in 1914. In San Francisco, it climbed from 4 percent to 34 percent over a similar period.[40] Today's affirmative action programs work much the same way; they allow disadvantaged groups to use their political leverage to gain a toehold in the economic and social mainstream.[41]

The spoils system nonetheless undermined the image of American bureaucracies. Education, training, and experience counted for little, and jobholders changed each time a new party came to power. As one Democratic leader joked after his party had been in power for years, a bureaucrat was "a Democrat who holds some office that a Republican wants."[42] The many decades of patronage politics have left an antibureaucratic legacy that continues to the present day. Not only do Americans consider government wasteful, they also do not grant federal workers much credibility.

Bottom-Up Reform   Civil service reformers gradually eroded the spoils system. In the 1880s, these reformers—a group of professors, journalists, clerics, and business leaders—went under the unflattering name **mugwumps**.* The reformers argued that government officials should be chosen on the basis of merit, not political connections. Mugwumps refused to back either political party, preferring to endorse reformers in both—leading to the quip that their "mugs" peered over one side of the fence while their "wumps" stuck out over the other.

The mugwumps won a succession of victories that gradually changed the system. Their first major breakthrough came in 1881 when President James Garfield was assassinated by a mentally disturbed man said to be a disappointed office seeker. Public scrutiny focused on the new president, Chester A. Arthur, who had once served as New York's customs collector and seemed to personify the spoils system. But the demand for reform swept the country, so in 1883 Congress passed—and Arthur signed—the **Pendleton Act**, creating a Civil Service Commission to set up qualifications, examinations, and procedures for filling jobs.

Civil service reform occurred from the bottom up. Requirements initially applied mainly to lower-level, less-skilled jobs—those who swept the floors and typed government forms. Gradually, higher-level positions fell under the civil service system. Such additions were especially plentiful when the party in power expected defeat in the next election. By making a job part of the civil service, soon-to-be-ousted presidents blanketed in the position, making it impossible for their successors to replace an unsupportive employee. Reform became nearly complete when, in 1939, Congress passed the **Hatch Act** that barred federal employees from campaigning and solicitation. The mountains of patronage were all but worn away.

Patronage still survives in the American political system, but primarily among the most prestigious jobs. Those include most members of the White House staff,

---

* Originally a sarcastic term of abuse, the name is a modification of a Native American word meaning "great man" or "chief."

the heads of most departments and agencies, and the members of most government boards and commissions. Political appointees also predominate in the upper levels of individual agencies and departments, inhabiting offices that bear such titles as deputy secretary, undersecretary, deputy undersecretary, assistant secretary, deputy assistant secretary, and special assistant. The estimated number of these top-level agency appointees grew from less than 500 in 1960 to nearly 3,400 by the George W. Bush administration.[43] Add the White House staff, and the total number of high-ranking patronage positions is probably close to 4,000.[44]

The president's ability to recruit political allies for the top levels of government has both advantages and disadvantages. On the positive side, it allows newly elected presidents to enlist people with innovative ideas, people who embrace their values and will lead agencies with these political goals in mind. For example, think-tank experts and business leaders helped design President Bush's dramatic tax cut plans and education initiatives.

Yet the simultaneous arrival of so many new faces complicates the coordination of government. European and Japanese governments are marked by close, informal, long-time associations among leading administrators. In the United States, the average presidential appointee leaves office after only a little more than two years; almost a third leave in less than 18 months.[45] Experienced career bureaucrats, on the other hand, often lack the political authority to make policy changes. In 2003, a bipartisan commission on reforming the government workforce found that, as a result, "Leadership responsibilities often fall into the awkward gap between inexperienced political appointees and unsupported career managers."[46]

With rapid change in personnel, governmental memory becomes as limited as that of an antiquated computer. One Japanese trade specialist who negotiated with the United States observed that "in the case of the United States, almost all of their negotiators seem like they came in just yesterday."[47] Worst of all, the denial of most top-level positions to regular civil servants makes government work an unattractive career for intelligent, ambitious young people. In Japan, many of the top students graduating from the country's most prestigious law schools know that eventually they can reach the highest levels of government through bureaucratic service. But the upper echelons of the U.S. government are not part of the career ladder. Not surprisingly, when asked what kinds of careers they are contemplating, fewer than one in four young people say they are "very" or "fairly" likely to consider working for the federal government.[48]

Outside Influences on the Executive Branch

The federal bureaucracy is difficult to control from the White House because of the way it was and is structured. However, presidents also struggle to direct the bureaucracy because political actors outside the executive branch influence agency behavior. In particular, government employees are also responsive to members of Congress, to influential interest groups, and to public expectations.

Congress and the Bureaucracy

Everyone knows that no one should have more than one boss. When two or more people can tell someone what to do, signals get confused, delays ensue, and accountability suffers. It also becomes possible for employees to play one boss off against the other. However, the separation of powers ensures that every federal bureaucrat has many bosses. Presidents may appoint federal employees and otherwise execute policies, but Congress formally creates and funds government agencies. With Congress divided into House and Senate, and each chamber divided into many committees, bureaucrats often find themselves reporting to multiple bosses, each one demanding and politically astute. This clamor for responsiveness from so many quarters means that the bureaucracy need not always give in to presidential demands or to congressional ones.

The Confirmation Process   Congressional influence begins with the selection of executive department officers. The Senate's advice-and-consent power has long given Congress a voice in administrative matters. One mechanism for exercising influence is the practice of **senatorial courtesy**, an informal rule that sometimes allows senators to block potential nominees for positions within their states or regions. This practice allows senators to protect their political bases by controlling patronage and gives them indirect control over administrative practices.

Confirmation battles sometimes receive extensive media attention and so have become a new form of electioneering. Little-known senators can rise to national attention through their advocacy or opposition exhibited in confirmation hearings. Votes on whether to confirm a particular nominee also can become a campaign issue. For this reason, senators demand greater influence than that permitted by traditional courtesies. Senators now want public assurances that presidential nominees will take acceptable policy positions, do not have conflicts of interest that will prevent successful performance of their public duties, and have not acted contrary to laws or conventional moral norms.

The Senate forced Bill Clinton to withdraw the nomination of Zoe Baird as attorney general because she had not paid the required social security taxes for her housekeeper. Alberto Gonzales, attorney general under George W. Bush, faced tough questions during his confirmation hearings about memos he wrote as White House counsel that argued that the Geneva Conventions on the humane treatment of prisoners of war did not apply to Taliban and al Qaeda detainees.

The Senate still rarely rejects presidential nominees. Yet the new, more election-driven confirmation process has had important consequences for administration. To decrease the likelihood of rejection, the White House must interview potential nominees at length, ask the FBI to undertake extensive background checks, and defend nominees against exhaustive senatorial scrutiny. When John Kennedy was president, the average nominee was confirmed in less than two and a half months. Today, presidents sometimes wait up to three times that long (see Figure 11.3).

Agency Reorganization   Congress often interferes with agency organization—for example, by opposing presidential proposals to reorganize executive departments. Congress resists change because each agency reports to a specific congressional committee, and these committees are frequently protective of their power, which allows them to serve constituencies back home. They therefore typically resist reorganization, no matter how redundant or antiquated existing organizational structures might be. For example, in the Clinton administration, Vice President Gore proposed shifting the law-enforcement functions of the Drug Enforcement Administration (in

FIGURE 11.3   Average time it takes presidential appointees to be confirmed

It has taken longer in recent years for presidential appointees to be confirmed. *What role might elections have played in this trend?*

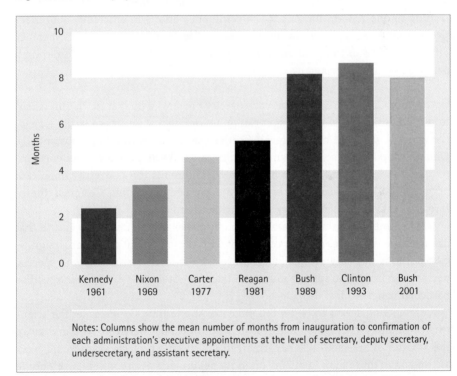

Notes: Columns show the mean number of months from inauguration to confirmation of each administration's executive appointments at the level of secretary, deputy secretary, undersecretary, and assistant secretary.

Source: Paul Light, *Thickening Government* (Washington, DC: Brookings, 1995) p. 68; and Brookings Institution Presidential Appointee Initiative Press Release, "Critical Posts in the Bush Administration Remain Vacant as Congressional Session Nears End," December 18, 2001.

the Department of Justice) and the Bureau of Alcohol, Tobacco and Firearms (in the Department of the Treasury) to the Federal Bureau of Investigation. Although the idea seemed logical because the agencies had similar functions, opposition from Congress and the agencies themselves killed the proposals.[49]

Legislative Detail Congress sometimes writes detailed legislation outlining an agency's specific legal responsibilities. Even legislation proposed by the president or by a specific agency will be revised extensively by Congress, mainly by the relevant committees.[50] Sometimes Congress invites an agency's clients to sue if they are discontented with their treatment. American bureaucracies therefore have limited authority over the jobs they do.

Legislative politics can produce absurd results. For more than a decade, critics have ridiculed laws that give the Agriculture Department authority to regulate sausage pizzas but give the Food and Drug Administration authority to regulate cheese pizzas. Agriculture receives its mandates from the House and Senate Agriculture committees, while the FDA operates under legislation authored by the House Energy and Commerce Committee and the Senate Health, Education, Labor and Pensions Committee. No committee wants to give up its slice of the pizza pie, so the odd division of agency responsibilities remains unresolved. The result, according to one report, "hinders the government's efforts to efficiently and effectively protect consumers from unsafe food."[51] The confusion also makes it rather difficult for a voter to figure out whom to blame if she gets sick after ordering a pan pizza with sausage and extra cheese!

Budgetary Control Every year, each agency prepares a budget for the president to submit to Congress. That budget can go up or down at any stage in the legislative process, and with limited revenues, the fear is that it will drop substantially. One or two powerful congressional enemies can make an agency's experience unpleasant, and an agency whose budget request ignores the desires of important players in the appropriations process may jeopardize its funding. Congress, therefore, indirectly influences agency spending decisions.

Sometimes Congress influences agency policies more directly. To ensure that agencies spend monies in ways consistent with congressional preferences, significant portions of many agency budgets are subject to an earmark, a very specific designation for how to spend funds (see Chapter 9). Some legislation even specifies particular congressional districts.

Earmarking seems to be on the increase. At one time Congress let the scientific community decide national research priorities, but between 1980 and 2003, the amount of research dollars earmarked for specific projects skyrocketed from $11 million to more than $2 billion, often for pet projects at a representative's home university.[52] The greatest "earmarker" of all time may be the former chair of the Senate Appropriations Committee, Robert Byrd of West Virginia, beloved by constituents for his generosity with federal funds. For example, he once slipped into an emergency bill a provision that shifted the 2,600-employee FBI fingerprinting center from downtown Washington to Clarksburg, West Virginia.[53]

Legislative Oversight   Committees sometimes hold hearings to ensure that agencies are not straying from their congressional mandates. In recent decades, the increase in such oversight hearings has expanded committee control over administrative practice. The number of days each year that committees hold oversight hearings nearly quadrupled between the 1960s and the 1990s.[54] Although the number of oversight hearings fell as a result of reforms instituted in 1995, they still far outnumber hearings called to consider specific legislation.[55] At these hearings, members of the administration must testify about agency experiences and problems. Witnesses representing outside groups either praise or criticize the bureaucrats. Through the oversight process, committees decide whether to revise existing legislation or modify agency budgets.

Yet, congressional influence is limited. Congress can enact general policies, but it cannot construct specific rules for every possible circumstance. Congress may decide to provide benefits to the disabled; but it is up to a bureaucrat to decide whether a particular handicap precludes employment, and it is up to the courts to determine whether the bureaucrat made the decision lawfully.[56] Often the difficulties of passing legislation will produce a compromise bill even vaguer than the policy area required. Thus, Congress and the president both face the same problem when dealing with the federal bureaucracy: Exercising formal power can be terribly difficult because bureaucracies will always exert substantial influence over policy because of the need to grant them administrative discretion, the power to interpret mandates from elected officials.

Interest Groups and the Bureaucracy

The purpose of many Cabinet agencies is to provide interest-group access to the executive branch of government. The Interior Department's job was originally to regulate the use of federal land, particularly in the West. Today, it maintains close ties to ranchers, timber companies, mining interests, and others who depend on federal lands for their livelihood.

Presidents exercise their control over the Cabinet departments primarily by appointing political allies to top positions. But once they become agency heads, allies often identify more closely with their turf than with the president's program. This tendency to "go native" is particularly pronounced when appointees already have close ties to interests connected to the department and hence are part of the issue network over which they suddenly gain responsibility.

The connections between departments and interest groups can change overnight, however. Nowhere was this more evident than in the case of the corporate accounting scandals that arose in 2002. Companies such as energy

(text continues on page 317)

HAS THE DEPARTMENT OF HOMELAND SECURITY BEEN A SUCCESS?

Is government reorganization an effective way to tackle policy problems? Or do bureaucratic battles, congressional turf wars, and other disruptions make such efforts more trouble than they are worth? The battle over creating a new department of homeland security in 2002 (described at the beginning of this chapter) provides proof that major change in the structure of government can occur, at least under certain circumstances. But policy experts are still debating whether the reorganization has changed the government for the better.

Although Americans supported the new department when it was first proposed, over the next few years critics charged that the Department of Homeland Security (DHS) had little to show for itself, and public opinion began to become more negative. Complaints about the agency's color-coded terror warning system prompted an internal review.[104] The department's isolation from the FBI and other intelligence agencies led one former homeland security official to admit that DHS had too often "been on the outside of the intelligence community with

Officials put a truck through a gamma radiation screening device prior to the Super Bowl

its nose pressed against the glass."[105] Worst of all, after the disastrous intergovernmental response to Hurricane Katrina in 2005, many experts argued that the Federal Emergency Management Agency (FEMA) should never have been absorbed into a department that was primarily concerned with terrorist threats. "As long as you require the FEMA director to go through two and three layers of bureaucracy to get a decision from the president, you're going to have a major problem," argued one former FEMA director.[106] By 2006, polls showed that most Americans thought the homeland security system needed major changes.

Optimists argue that the case of the Homeland Security Department shows that government can adapt to changing circumstances and, in so doing, act in the public interest. Problems exist, but they are the growing pains of a new organization, not fundamental weaknesses. Homeland Security Secretary Michael Chertoff put it this way:

> [W]e've got to finish the job of integrating, rather than reverse course and go back to the old fragmented...system. ...Understandably, each agency is proud of its heritage, and we don't want to obliterate that legacy. [107]

But others argue that the new department represents more of the same: Bureaucratic squabbling limited the department's initial scope, the agency was slow to improve communications with state and local governments, and has even had trouble coordinating its message on terrorism with that of other departments and agencies.[108]

> *No one says merging 170,000 employees from 22 different agencies should have been easy. But, even allowing for inevitable transition problems, DHS has been a disaster: underfunded, undermanned, disorganized, and unforgivably slow-moving....DHS has failed to address some of our most serious vulnerabilities, from centralizing intelligence to protecting critical infrastructure to organizing against bioterror.[109]*

WHAT DO YOU THINK?
1. Was the creation of the new Homeland Security Department a substantive change or just a superficial one?
2. Does this case study show that the politics of elections do not interfere with effective government? Or does it illustrate the reverse?

For more information on the new Homeland Security Department, see the following Web sites.

www.dhs.gov
www.ready.gov

The Department of Homeland Security's official Web sites.

http://hsc.house.gov
http://hsgac.senate.gov

The House of Representatives created a new committee to handle most homeland security matters, while the Senate divided oversight responsibilities among existing committees. These two links lead to the House Committee on Homeland Security, and to the Senate Homeland Security and Government Affairs Committee.

conglomerate Enron and telecommunications giants Global Crossing and WorldCom had engaged in bookkeeping trickery to hide losses and inflate apparent earnings. The CEOs of these companies had traveled on Commerce Department-sponsored trade missions and enjoyed access to high-level policy makers.[57] When the scandals broke, however, Commerce Department officials distanced themselves from the now-bankrupt firms and took the lead in crafting President Bush's proposed corporate policy reforms.[58]

Elections and the Bureaucracy

For more than a century, reformers have tried to separate politics from administration. Government should serve the people, they argue, not the special interests. Departments should make decisions according to laws and regulations, not in response to political pressure. Agencies should treat every applicant alike, not respond more favorably to those who contribute to political parties.

These reform principles are worthy of respect. When politics interferes, agencies can be inefficient and ineffective. The post office, long a patronage reserve, is said to deliver "snail mail." The Department of Housing and Urban Development, always a political thicket, has at times so badly mismanaged property that it had to blow up buildings soon after constructing them. Turf battles between the FBI and CIA may have prevented them from sharing critical information that could have prevented the September 11 terrorist attack.[59]

Many of the more effective federal bureaucracies are less politically charged. The National Science Foundation, protected from political pressures by an independent board, is known for the professional nature in with which it allocates dollars among competing scientific projects. Compared to many state agencies, the Federal Bureau of Prisons does a better job maintaining security without depriving prisoners of rights; it has succeeded in part because members of Congress, respectful of the agency's leadership, have left it alone.[60]

But even though agency autonomy has worked in some instances, electoral pressures also have played a positive role and, in any case, are an essential feature of modern bureaucracies.[61] Public pressure exerted through elections has affected the way bureaucracies keep secrets, enforce the law, manage their budgets, and make decisions. In the end, elections create pressures that force many agencies to balance competing interests by striking compromises.

Bureaucratic Secrecy   Bureaucracies like to protect their secrets. Inside knowledge is power. Secrecy can cover mistakes. Electoral pressures have sharply curtailed the amount of secrecy in American government. In the view of one specialist, "secrecy has less legitimacy as a governmental practice in the United States than in any other advanced industrial society with the possible exception of Sweden," in large part because "Congress has done a great deal to open up the affairs of bureaucracy to greater outside scrutiny."[62] Under the Freedom of Information Act of 1967, citizens have the right to inspect unprotected government documents. If the government believes the requested information needs to be kept secret, it must bear the burden of proof when arguing its case before a judge. The "Government in the Sunshine Act," passed in 1976, required that federal government meetings be held in public, unless they involve military plans, trade secrets, or personnel questions.

Bureaucratic Coercion   Bureaucracies are often accused of using their coercive powers harshly and unfairly. Police officers stop young drivers for traffic violations that are often ignored when committed by older drivers. Bureaucratic zealots trick sales clerks into selling cigarettes to heavily bearded 17-year-olds. Landowners cannot drain puddles off their property because environmental authorities have declared the soggy mud a "wetland." Although such abuses occur, they happen less frequently because agencies are held accountable to the electorate.

In 1998, for example, Republican senators sensed popular discontent with the Internal Revenue Service (IRS), the government's tax collection agency. The Senate Finance Committee held a series of hearings that brought to light a litany of agency failings. The IRS had lost $150 billion in 1995 because of mistakes, unreported income, or improper deductions. Taxpayers were overbilled an average of $5 billion per year.[63] The technology the agency used was so outdated that even IRS Commissioner Charles Rossotti admitted, "I have never seen a worse situation in a large organization."[64] As a result of the hearings, Congress enacted a law restructuring the agency, making it harder for the IRS to accuse taxpayers of wrongdoing and bringing its tax collection systems up to date.[65]

Agency Expansion   Although agencies generally try to increase their budgets, elections brake such tendencies, if only because politicians get blamed for raising taxes. "As a general rule," says analyst Martha Derthick, "Congress likes to keep bureaucracy lean and cheap."[66] The number of people working for the federal government, as a percentage of the workforce, has declined (review Figure 11.2), in good part because elected officials are under public pressure to cut bureaucracy.

Administrator Caution   Federal agencies are sometimes accused of going beyond their legislative mandates. But most federal agencies err on the side of caution. The worst thing any agency can do is make a major mistake. As one official explained, "The public servant soon learns that successes rarely rate a headline, but government blunders are front-page news. This recognition encourages the development of procedures designed less to achieve successes than to avoid blunders."[67]

In 1962 doctors discovered that thalidomide, a sedative available to pregnant women in Europe, increased the probability that their babies would be born with serious physical deformities. Congress immediately passed a law toughening the Food and Drug Administration's procedures for regulating prescription drug distribution.[68] Decades later, in keeping with this policy, the FDA refused to approve the sale of several experimental drugs to terminally ill people suffering from AIDS. When the FDA's refusal to allow experimentation became a public issue, the agency began to allow AIDS patients to try the untested drugs, this time loosening regulations in response to potential electoral pressures.

Compromised Capacity   Agency effectiveness is often undermined by the very terms of the legislation that created it. For legislation to pass Congress, a broad coalition of support is necessary. To build this support, proponents must strike deals with those who are at best lukewarm to the idea. Such compromises, demanded by members of Congress to shore up their electoral support, can cripple a program.[69]

Policy Implementation

Bureaucrats possess no independent constitutional authority. Instead, bureaucrats are employees who fall under laws passed by Congress, executive orders distributed by the president, and demands articulated by voters through elections and through the interest groups they join. In practice, however, government employees are the ones who must decide exactly how to enforce specific laws or presidential orders. They also are the ones who deal face-to-face with American voters and who decide when it is necessary to accommodate public demands. Because they exercise so much discretion, the bureaucracy as a whole possesses significant power.

It is not feasible to talk about bureaucratic policy making as conducted by every agency and in every policy area. Nor is it clear where, for any one policy area, some influences on government programs stop and other influences start. The reality is complex, with different contexts shaping each policy area. Thus, this chapter selects three particularly important areas of policy and sketches out the bureaucratic structure in each: (1) regulation, (2) foreign policy, and (3) monetary policy. The discussion of each case illustrates the way bureaucracies ultimately set policy within the bounds placed on them by the public and by the elected branches of government.

Regulation

Not all domestic policy involves redistributing tax dollars (see Chapter 15). The national government imposes numerous rules—called regulations—on private companies (as well as on lower levels of government). Regulations are attractive to politicians because their costs do not come out of the federal budget. They usually come indirectly, through higher prices paid by consumers (or through taxes paid to state and local governments). Voters reward elected officials for promoting social goals and blame someone else for the costs.

Regulations illustrate the important role of both bureaucracies and popular influence on domestic policy. Congress passes many regulations because they are a cheap way to curry favor with voters. When an industry's performance becomes unpopular, Congress can respond by adding rules for which consumers must pay. But most laws expanding the government's regulatory power are vague enough that Congress need not take responsibility for their implementation. Someone else has to give them teeth, and that unsavory task usually falls to bureaucrats who need not face reelection.

Members of Congress are more eager to approve rules than they are to fund regulatory agencies, and the rules they write are sometimes not closely related to real-world problems. The result can be a false sense of security. Americans may think that government is protecting them from a particular catastrophe when, practically speaking, effective rules are not really in place. Later, a well-publicized incident can get the public's attention and result in a new round of regulation. For example, Americans were startled in 2003 when the United States Department of

Agriculture (USDA) announced that meat from a Washington State cow diagnosed with deadly "mad cow disease" had entered the food supply. While regulators assured the public that the parts of the cow that carried the fatal disease—the brain and spinal cord—had been destroyed and posed no threat, the public demanded quick action to ensure the future safety of U.S. beef. The USDA then took steps that activists and some scientists had been recommending for years, stepping up inspections, banning the use of sick cows for food, and implementing several other safeguards.[70]

The History of Regulation   The basis for federal regulation is found in the U.S. Constitution, which gives Congress authority "to regulate Commerce." The first commerce clause regulations targeted the railroad industry. They expanded briskly during three periods in the country's history: (1) the Progressive Era, from the 1890s to the early 1900s, when muckraking journalists aggressively exposed the abuses of industrialization; (2) the New Deal period, when the national government targeted practices thought to have caused the Great Depression; and (3) the Great Society period, when the national government expanded its scope to influence numerous areas of American life.

Since the New Deal, the Supreme Court has almost always found regulatory policies constitutional.[71] Regulations now influence everything from civil rights to national insurance standards. Three situations frequently motivate policy makers to regulate industries: (1) when small numbers of companies provide products or services and could take advantage of their market dominance at the expense of consumers; (2) when companies might be tempted to engage in undesirable actions that would not cost them anything, such as polluting the environment to reduce production costs; and (3) when evaluating the quality of products or services would require more time or expertise than regular consumers are likely to bring to the task.

The Politics of Regulation   Electoral pressures influence when and how regulations are imposed. Members of Congress often create regulations or regulatory agencies to escape criticism when things go wrong. After a series of accounting scandals at companies such as Enron and WorldCom, for example, Congress passed the Corporate Accountability Act of 2002, which more strictly regulated corporations and corporate auditing firms. The need to respond to each high-profile crisis often results in overlapping or even contradictory regulations.[72]

Because telling people what to do can upset or anger them, members of Congress usually try to disguise their actions. Congress may not write a detailed set of rules, instead passing the job to an agency. The Clean Air Act of 1990, for example, did not raise gasoline taxes or alter emissions standards for high-pollution vehicles; it simply stated goals for reducing pollution levels and let the Environmental Protection Agency (EPA) figure out how to get there. Forcing agencies to determine regulations lets legislators distance themselves from rules that prove unpopular.[73]

The autonomy afforded to regulatory agencies is not limitless. There exists a zone of acceptance—a range within which Congress will accept that whatever an agency decides is the correct interpretation of the statutes.[74] When an agency extends beyond what Congress will permit, political opposition arises, and Congress forces the agency to backtrack. The courts also may help determine how far regulations go. Although regulatory policies are enacted by Congress and executed by agencies, federal courts interpret the meaning of congressional statutes and decide whether agencies apply them properly (see Chapter 12). Courts exercise considerable discretion when performing this role, because they are often asked to interpret vague laws.

Court interpretations of the 1973 Endangered Species Act illustrate how federal judges influence public policy. The law protects any species on federal lands that the U.S. Fish and Wildlife Service considers at risk of extinction. The natural habitats of species must be safeguarded from any human activity that threatens them, no matter what the economic consequences. The push for this legislation grew from the fear of extinction for politically popular animals, such as wolves, whooping cranes, and eagles. However, the Fish and Wildlife Service declared nearly 1,000 species to be in danger of extinction, including such little-known species as desert kangaroo rats, tiny snail darters, and spotted owls—an interpretation that federal courts have upheld.

Deregulation   Regulation is expensive. Salaries for bureaucrats, lawyers, and investigators generate an annual price tag that runs to billions of dollars. Regulatory policies also may limit the ability of businesses to compete effectively. The additional paperwork, inspections, procedures, and mandates imposed by regulatory agencies can make the difference between a business that thrives and provides good jobs to Americans and one that cannot compete with foreign firms.

Regular voters usually do not connect higher costs and business failures to government action, but sometimes policy analysts do—and they frequently join businesses in calling for a reduction in regulation. Congress sometimes responds to their calls by backing off from rules that govern industries. It has systematically authorized the partial deregulation of the trucking, banking, and communications industries.[75]

Perhaps the most celebrated deregulation occurred in the airline industry. At one time, a government agency oversaw the airfare set for every route commercial planes flew. Critics charged that the regulators used their authority to limit price competition for customer fares, driving up profits for the few carriers in the industry. Alfred Kahn pushed the issue forward when President Carter appointed him chair of the Civil Aeronautics Board. Kahn stripped away many of the pricing regulations that had governed the airline industry for decades.[76] His initiative led to enactment of the Airline Deregulation Act. Many of the policy outcomes were favorable: lower fares, more service to remote areas, and fewer deaths per passenger mile. Yet many experts argue that many regulations must remain in place to ensure that airline companies, in their eagerness to make a profit, do not cut corners too closely. Furthermore, even the most committed deregulators backed government assistance to the airline industry after the 9/11 attacks.[7] In this, as in many industries, complete deregulation is unlikely, because the public will always expect government to act in the wake of disasters or to prevent costly externalities.

Independent Regulatory Agencies   Not all agencies are part of Cabinet departments. Some of the most important, the independent agencies, have quasi-judicial regulatory functions meant to be carried out free from presidential interference. These agencies are generally headed by a board or commission appointed by the president and confirmed by the Senate. Independence from the president, which is considered desirable to insulate such agencies from partisan politics, is achieved by giving board members appointments that last for several years (see Table 11.1). For a number of agencies, a president may be unable to appoint a majority of board members until well into the second term.

Congress established most independent agencies in response to widespread public pressure to protect workers and consumers from negligent or abusive business practices. The Federal Trade Commission (FTC) was created in 1914 in response to the discovery of mislabeling and adulteration in the meat packing industry. The FTC was given the power to prevent price discrimination, unfair competition, false advertising, and other unfair business practices. Congress formed the Securities and Exchange Commission in 1934 to root out fraud, deception, and inside manipulation on Wall Street after the stock market crash of 1929 left many Americans suspicious of speculators and financiers.

TABLE 11.1   Independent agencies and their interest-group allies

Independent Agency	Board Size	Length of Term (years)	Interest-Group Allies
Federal Reserve Board	7	14	Banks
Consumer Product Safety Commission	5	5	Consumers Union
Equal Employment Opportunity Commission	5	5	Civil rights groups
Federal Deposit Insurance Corporation	5	3[*]	Banks
Federal Energy Regulatory Commission	4	4	Oil/gas interests
Federal Maritime Commission	5	5	Fisheries
Federal Trade Commission	5	7	Business groups
National Labor Relations Board	5	5	Unions
Securities and Exchange Commission	5	5	Wall Street
National Credit Union Administration	3	6	Credit unions
Tennessee Valley Authority	3	9	Regional farmers and utilities

* One member, the comptroller of the currency, has a 5-year term.

When originally formed, most regulatory agencies aggressively pursued their reform mandates. But as the public's enthusiasm for reform faded, many agencies found that their most interested constituents were members of the very community they were expected to regulate. Thus, the independent commissions have tended to become connected to organized interest groups.[78] In one instance, a regulator's legal fight to keep his job was financed by those subject to his regulation![79]

Regulation of the Electronic Media Freedom of the press is closer to being an absolute doctrine in the United States than in other countries. In theory the press has wide latitude in its ability to report on and even criticize government. For this reason, regulating media business poses different sorts of problems than regulating other sorts of businesses. Politicians do not routinely dictate policy to any significant media outlet—unlike the situation in some democracies.

Radio and TV, however, lack some press freedoms because they use the public airwaves. Government has used its power to regulate broadcast media, embodied in the Federal Communications Commission (FCC), as a justification for weighing in on media content—an argument accepted by federal courts. One outgrowth of this regulatory power is that politicians have ensured that media owners cannot use their property to favor some candidates over others. Legislation creating the FCC established an **equal-time rule** specifying that if a station sells time to a legally qualified candidate, it must be willing to sell time to all such candidates. Later, the rule was expanded so that, for example, when the networks carry the president's State of the Union speech, they also must carry a reply from the opposition.

From 1949 to 1987, the FCC also enforced a **fairness doctrine** that required stations to devote a reasonable amount of time to matters of public importance and to air contrasting viewpoints on those matters. Eventually, the doctrine also required stations to give public figures who were attacked an opportunity to reply. But communications technologies expanded so much that they undercut some of the rationale for government regulation. In 1987 an FCC staffed by Reagan appointees repealed the fairness doctrine. Despite a general trend toward deregulation, though, the fact remains that FCC regulations determine what American media organizations may do or say. After Janet Jackson bared a breast during the 2004 Super Bowl halftime show, complaints about indecency filed with the FCC skyrocketed from 111 in 2000 to more than a million in 2004.[80] In response, the FCC became more aggressive in issuing fines, and many in Congress called for increased penalties for broadcasters who aired offensive material.[81]

Recent years have seen a rise in the number of proposals for regulation of the Internet, a technology that does not use the public airwaves but does use electronic connections built up with assistance from government. Some people would like to regulate content, for example by banning pornographic, hate-filled, violent, or otherwise objectionable Web sites. The courts probably will rule against most such attempts to restrict content transmitted over the Internet.

Foreign Policy Institutions

The institutions responsible for American foreign policy took shape at the onset of the **Cold War** (1946–1989). This conflict between the United States and the Soviet Union sprang up in the wake of World War II. The Soviets first took over East Germany, and in short order, they also converted Poland, Hungary, Bulgaria, and Romania into satellite nations. Finally, in 1948, Soviet-backed communists seized control of Czechoslovakia. Together, these East European countries formed a buffer between the Soviet Union and Western Europe. Armed barriers prevented movement across borders—a line that came to be called the **iron curtain**.

President Truman mobilized bipartisan support for a strategy of **containment**. This policy, designed by a State Department specialist named George Kennan, called for stopping the *spread* of communism but otherwise allowing the ill-considered system to collapse on its own.[82] The Truman administration therefore greatly modernized and expanded America's diplomatic and espionage capabilities. Truman also assembled an impressive team of foreign policy advisers to help the United States resist Soviet expansion.

State Department The Cold War forced the United States to modernize its diplomatic institutions. Ever since then, the secretary of state usually has been the president's central foreign policy adviser and chief diplomat. For example, in her first two months as Secretary of State under George W. Bush, Condoleezza Rice traveled to eight European countries, Mexico, Israel, and the Palestinian Authority to shore up alliances and work toward a resolution to conflicts in Iraq and Israel.

Reporting to the secretary of state are **ambassadors**, who head the diplomatic delegations to foreign countries. Ambassadors manage U.S. **embassies**, which house diplomatic delegations in the capital cities of foreign countries.

INFORMAL DIPLOMACY
State Department employees bear the primary burden of U.S. diplomacy, but many other government officials and even private citizens sometimes act as informal national ambassadors. Here, actress Angelina Jolie, a United Nations goodwill ambassador, meets with refugees in India.

Consulates are maintained in important cities that are not foreign capitals. Although embassies and consulates help American tourists and businesses, their most important political responsibility is to gather detailed information on the government, politics, and social conditions of the host country. The ambassador also conveys to the host country the views of the U.S. government, as instructed by the State Department.

Negotiating with foreign powers is extremely challenging. As former Secretary of State George Marshall once commented, "In diplomacy, you never can tell what a man is thinking. He smiles at you and kicks you in the stomach at the same time."[83] Because the diplomatic corps is critical to American foreign policy, the staff managing U.S. embassies and consulates is organized into the **foreign service**. Dean Acheson, President Truman's secretary of state, worked hard to improve the service's professional caliber. A reporter at the time declared, "For the first time in the memory of living man, the American foreign office comes somewhere near being adequate to the needs of the country."[84]

Defense Department   Since the first decades of the country's independence, Americans have worried about the ill effects of a large military. Congress and the president have always made certain that the military was controlled by civilian appointees. As one analyst puts it, freedom "demands that people without guns be able to tell people with guns what to do."[85] The Cold War posed new challenges for this ideal of civilian control. To ensure the country's continued international leadership and carry out the policy of containment, Congress provided for the largest military establishment in the nation's history.

The military went through several major organizational changes. The 1947 National Security Act created a single Department of Defense that contained within it the departments of Army, Navy, and Air Force, each with its own civilian secretary appointed by the president. The secretaries for the army and the air force are responsible for their respective branches of the armed services. The secretary of the navy is responsible for both the naval forces and the marines. All three secretaries report to the secretary of defense, the president's chief civilian adviser on defense matters and overall head of all three departments.

Subordinate to the civilian leadership of the secretary of defense and the other three appointed secretaries, military professionals direct the armed forces. At one time, each armed force had its own leadership, and they acted more or less independently of each other. To achieve better coordination, Congress formally created the **Joint Chiefs of Staff** in 1947. The Joint Chiefs consist of the heads of all the military services—the army, navy, air force, and Marine Corps—together with a chair and vice chair nominated by the president and confirmed by the Senate.

The post-Cold War era offers a number of serious challenges for the Defense Department. After 9/11, many experts began to rethink basic war planning, which since Vietnam had been characterized by large-scale attacks with hundreds of thousands of ground troops. George W. Bush's first defense secretary, Donald

Rumsfeld, sought to reduce the use of such overwhelming attacks, and instead favored elite specialized technical forces, where possible. He also called for "flexible, light, and agile" deployments from the regular armed forces.[86] Although in the late 1990s, the Pentagon estimated that an attack on Iraq would require up to half a million troops,[87] in 2003 the U.S. invaded with about 130,000, plus 30,000 British allied forces.[88] These troops quickly swept north through the desert, subduing the enemy forces with apparent ease.

But al-Qaeda terrorists remain scattered over the globe, and a swift and successful war to depose dictator Saddam Hussein gave way to a costly occupation in Iraq, during which congressional critics complained that technology and agility were no substitutes for the larger numbers of troops needed to keep the peace. Afghanistan, too, remained dangerous and unstable years after the 2001 U.S. invasion. While the Bush administration pointed to encouraging signs, such as the successful free elections in both countries, skeptics argued that the new approach to fighting wars had failed.

The proper approach to military conflict may be disputed for some time, but what is clear is that the national defense has become more expensive in recent years. To pursue the campaign against terrorism and the Iraq War, the Bush administration sought and received more Congressional funding for national defense. This reversed a decline in military spending that had been underway since the end of the Cold War. In the 1950s, the United States spent 10 percent of its total gross domestic product (GDP) on defense. But with the end of the Cold War, Congress began to cut the defense budget, responding to the decline in public concern about the communist threat. By 1999, as Figure 11.4 shows, defense expenditures had dropped to 3 percent of GDP—the lowest level since before World War II. The campaign against terrorism brought this downward trend to a halt.

Central Intelligence Agency   Spying is an ancient and honorable practice, but its organization into an independent agency is of fairly recent vintage. The need for better-organized intelligence became clear during World War II, but it was not until the Cold War began that Congress established a systematic, centralized system of intelligence gathering. The National Security Act of 1947 created the Central Intelligence Agency (CIA)—the institution primarily responsible for gathering and analyzing information about the political and military activities of other nations—as a separate agency, independent of both the Department of State and the Department of Defense. Although State and Defense (as well as other departments) continue to have their own sources of intelligence, the 1947 law made the CIA the main intelligence collection agency.

It also gave the CIA the authority to conduct secret operations abroad at the request of the president, a controversial mandate. One especially notorious covert operation was an ill-fated attempt to dislodge communist leader Fidel Castro from Cuba.[89] In an effort to overthrow Castro, the CIA helped Cuban exiles plan a 1961 invasion on the shores of Cuba's **Bay of Pigs**. President Kennedy approved the

FIGURE 11.4   The Defense budget during and after the Cold War

Defense expenditures declined as a percentage of GDP from 1950 to 1999.

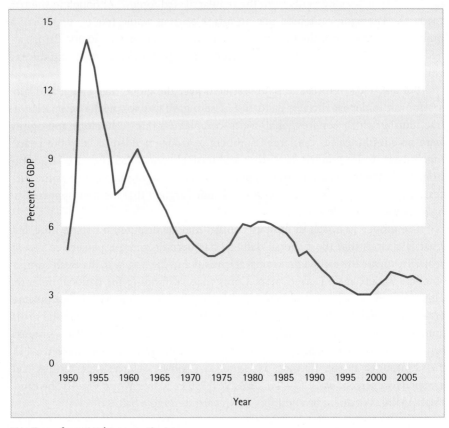

Note: Figures for 2006 and 2007 are estimates.

Source: Office of Management and Budget, Budget of the United States Government, Fiscal Year 2007, Historical Tables, Table

invasion, hoping that it might foment a popular insurrection, but refused to give it naval or air support. The effort failed, leaving in doubt the CIA's ability to conduct large-scale military operations. CIA covert operations in Chile in the early 1970s and in Nicaragua in the 1980s also drew criticism.

Nevertheless, the CIA has become one of the pillars of the foreign policy establishment.[90] The agency helps identify and squelch potential terrorist operations, assesses the threat of nuclear proliferation, and helps monitor other nations' compliance with arms control agreements.

The CIA director has traditionally had a close relationship with the president, briefing him regularly and playing a coordinating role with other agencies. In response to the intelligence failures that led to the 9/11 attacks, Congress created a new position of National Intelligence Director in 2004. This new office is designed to oversee the many federal intelligence agencies, including the CIA, the NSA, and the Defense Intelligence Agency, as well as to coordinate their activities. It remains to be seen whether the national intelligence director will effectively supplant the CIA director as the president's chief intelligence adviser.

National Security Council The National Security Council (NSC), created by Congress in 1947 and placed inside the Executive Office of the President, is responsible for coordinating foreign policy. Meetings of the NSC are generally attended by the president, the vice president, the secretaries of state and defense, the national intelligence director, the chair of the Joint Chiefs of Staff, the president's chief of staff, and such other persons as the president designates.[91] They help resolve competing foreign policy viewpoints.

The council is assisted by a staff located in the White House under the direction of the National Security Adviser (NSA). The NSA has often played a coordinating role, reconciling interagency disagreements or, if that proves impossible, reporting them to the president. But inasmuch as the NSA has more access to the president than any member of the foreign policy team, the adviser can wield great influence. During the Nixon administration, National Security Adviser Henry Kissinger even overshadowed the secretary of state.

The NSA has not escaped controversy. In what is called the **Iran–Contra affair**, the NSA office attempted, in the 1980s, to conduct a covert operation, selling arms to Iran and then diverting the funds to rebels in Nicaragua known as the Contras. Because Congress had forbidden such aid, the Iran–Contra affair developed into a bitter confrontation with President Ronald Reagan, who had privately asked National Security Adviser Robert McFarlane to "assure the Contras of continuing administration support."[92] Hearings and investigations followed, although no convictions withstood court appeals.

Setting Monetary Policy

The **Federal Reserve System** (or "the Fed") manages the government's monetary policy. Created in 1913, the Fed is headed by a board consisting of seven governors appointed by the president and confirmed by the Senate. Each Fed governor holds office for 14 years. The chair of the system serves a four-year term. The Fed acts on the economy through the operations of its 12 regional banks, each of which oversees member banks in its part of the country.

The agency is formally independent of both politics and external pressure groups.[93] Long terms ensure that presidents may not appoint majorities of the board until they have been in office six years. Members of Congress also seldom get a crack at the Fed's board members. Furthermore, monetary policy is too arcane to engage the general public, so Fed-bashing is not a very effective campaign tactic. The Fed maintains a professional image, not a political one—a self-preservation tactic enhanced by the tendency to hire qualified specialists to staff the agency.

SECOND MOST POWERFUL MAN IN AMERICA?
Ben Bernanke's role as chairman of the Federal Reserve Board gives him great independent influence. *What are the sources of his sway over economic policy?*

Because the Fed is small and relatively independent of other government officials, it can change monetary policy quickly—interest rates can fluctuate on a monthly, weekly, or even daily basis if the need arises (although the policy outcomes may take months to appear). The most important decisions affecting the day-to-day workings of the economy are made by the Fed's Open Market Committee (FOMC). This committee considers whether interest rates are too high or too low and what adjustments should be made. The committee consists of the seven governors, all of whom vote, and the 12 regional bank presidents, only five of whom have votes (the New York bank president always has a vote; the remaining four votes rotate among the other 11 banks). When the national economy slowed early in 2001, and then confidence collapsed after the September 11 terrorist attacks, the FOMC responded with a series of nine interest-rate cuts by October 2.[94]

The chair of the Federal Reserve Board ranks among the most powerful people in government. The chair's great power derives from close ties to the president, direct access to up-to-date economic information supplied by Fed staff, and the power to approve the appointment of the 12 presidents of the Federal Reserve banks (upon the recommendation of the member banks in each region). The current Fed Chair, Benjamin Bernanke, is an economist and former chairman of President Bush's Council of Economic Advisers. He succeeded the popular and successful Alan Greenspan in 2006, whose management of the economy in the 1990s won bipartisan praise.

Who Controls the Fed?   Buying Treasury bonds is a necessary part of the Fed's job. It is one way the Fed influences the amount of money in the economy. Fed investments earn billions of dollars (about $29 billion in 2005).[95] The Fed keeps about a tenth of this money for its own operations, turning the rest over to the Treasury.[96] This economic independence means that Congress cannot pressure the Fed by using its budgetary powers. Once the Senate approves nominees to the Fed, they become insulated from electoral pressures expressed through the legislative branch.[97]

The president—who appoints or reappoints the Fed's members, including the chair—has a great deal more influence than Congress.[98] The Fed must not stray too far from presidential demands, or it might tarnish its apolitical image. Ironically, this sensitivity to appearances allows politics to influence monetary policy. Republicans tend to dislike inflation, so the Fed attacks it more aggressively when Republicans hold the presidency. Democratic constituencies include lots of working-class voters whose jobs are insecure, so the Fed combats unemployment more aggressively when Democrats sit in the White House.[99]

Nevertheless, few citizens like either inflation or unemployment, so Fed behavior does not fluctuate very much with the party of the president. Presidents particularly dislike economic troubles during an election year. Some skeptics even argue that presidents deliberately manipulate the economy to engineer their reelections. They tolerate slow growth, even recessions, early in their terms of office so they can step on the gas and "rev up" the economic engine when payoffs are greatest. Richard Nixon's 1972 reelection campaign provides the classic example; his administration pulled out all the stops to achieve a huge increase in household income that year.[100] Yet neither Jimmy Carter nor George H. W. Bush presided over active economies during their reelection campaigns. At best, economic growth picks up only slightly in an election year, calling into question the extent to which presidents really manipulate monetary policy.

Many liberal critics argue that the banking industry controls the Fed and leads its members to fight inflation much more vigorously than they combat unemployment.[101] When jobs are plentiful and people are spending freely, the Fed typically responds by raising interest rates and slowing down the economy. As one critic put it, "Just when the party gets going, the Fed takes away the beer."[102] Certainly bankers enjoy some influence over monetary policy. They influence the appointment of the Board of Governors, and they nominate the Federal Reserve bank presidents, who cast five votes on the FOMC. But the Fed has not consistently fought inflation, as indicated by the 1970s, when it mistakenly allowed inflation to get out of control.

The Fed's Hold on Monetary Policy   The Fed is able to operate with a considerable amount of independence, in large part because it tries to achieve what nearly everyone desires: steady, stable economic growth. The president, in particular, requires solid economic performance and therefore usually can afford to leave the Fed alone. A case in point is the relationship President Clinton had with Fed chair Alan Greenspan. Ronald Reagan first appointed Greenspan as Fed chair, but Clinton retained him in 1996 to reassure financial markets.[103] Members of Congress also know that they would undermine confidence in the U.S. economy if they encroached too much on the Fed's domain.

The position of the Federal Reserve System in America's new democracy therefore is a rare case in which popular moods play little role in determining policy. Yet it is "the exception that proves the rule" of public opinion's influence. The election connection usually does not sway monetary policy precisely because of a conscious choice to insulate the money supply from the tides of political fortune. Just as a dieter might padlock the refrigerator as a defense against moments of weakness, Americans apparently do not trust themselves to weigh in on monetary policy. They respect—and even revere—the distant body of experts who try to fine-tune the economy without giving in to shortsighted impulses.

Policy Environments: A Summary

Scholars usually divide public policy into three areas: domestic policy, economic policy, and foreign and defense policy (see Chapter 15). We have now reviewed three rough policy areas, one in each category. Regulation is an important domestic policy. The foreign policy apparatus provides the president with information to use when dealing with other nations. And monetary policy is the main approach to adjusting the U.S. economy. Although each topic is unique—with its own policy environment, its own bureaucratic organization, and its own direct or indirect connection to public opinion—the main purpose of the discussion is to illustrate what they have in common.

First, the president may sit at the top of each bureaucratic flow chart, but numerous other political actors and outside influences shape institutional behavior and so limit what a president may accomplish. Second, Congress is seldom far from the bureaucracy. Lawmakers set the regulations, fund the defense and intelligence agencies, and confirm most of the various appointees. Third, orders from Congress and the president are seldom so clear that bureaucrats lose their discretion; they still usually set the precise rules and regulations under which Americans must operate, and in some instances they are protected by rules that explicitly establish their independence when setting policy. But, finally, most of these policy areas ultimately respond to public opinion. The government regulates an industry after high-profile scandals, accidents, or abuses of public trust—and then deregulates when the rules become too costly. The government shifts the money supply to find a proper balance between inflation and unemployment—but sometimes allows monetary policy to float so that it corresponds with the needs of elected leaders. And different portions of the foreign policy apparatus gain and lose power depending on the needs of elected legislators as well as the expectations for foreign affairs that members of the public hold. In short, policy implementation does not stray far from the pressures of elections and public opinion in America's new democracy.

CHAPTER SUMMARY

All bureaucracies exhibit certain operational flaws, but American bureaucracies have specific troubles that can be attributed to the electoral climate in which they have evolved. Moreover, the president must share influence over the bureaucracy with numerous other players, including Congress, interest groups, and the voting public. Bureaucracies do enjoy some discretion in implementing laws, but their actions generally fall within the bounds of what elected officials and the public demand of them. Both the inefficiency and the responsiveness of government bureaucracy, therefore, ultimately derive from political impulses—as illustrated by the failure and subsequent reform of national security agencies at the time of the 9/11 terrorist attacks. In short, the unelected employees who manage the day-to-day affairs of government respond to the elections so prominent in America's new democracy.

KEY TERMS

ambassadors, p. 325

Bay of Pigs, p. 327

bureaucracy, p. 304

civil service, p. 310

Cold War, p. 325

containment, p. 325

departments, p. 304

equal-time rule, p. 324

embassies, p. 325

fairness doctrine, p. 324

Federal Reserve System, p. 329

foreign service, p. 326

government corporations, p. 304

Hatch Act, p. 310

independent agencies, p. 304

Iran–Contra affair, p. 329

iron curtain, p. 325

Joint Chiefs of Staff, p. 326

mugwumps, p. 310

patronage, p. 309

Pendleton Act, p. 310

senatorial courtesy, p. 312

spoils system, p. 309

SUGGESTED READINGS

Kettl, Donald F. *The Transformation of Governance: Public Administration for Twenty-First Century America.* Baltimore, MD: Johns Hopkins University Press, 2002. Discussion of the challenges facing modern bureaucracies.

Light, Paul. *Thickening Government: Federal Hierarchy and the Diffusion of Accountability.* Washington, DC: Brookings, 1995. Identifies and explains the growth in higher-level governmental positions.

Melnick, R. Shep. *Regulation and the Courts.* Washington, DC: Brookings, 1983. Case studies of the central role the courts play in interpreting government regulations.

Niskanan, William A. *Bureaucracy and Representative Government.* Chicago: Aldine-Atherton, 1971. Develops the argument that government bureaucracies seek to maximize their budgets.

Wilson, James Q. *Bureaucracy: What Government Agencies Do and Why They Do It.* New York: Basic Books, 1989. Comprehensive treatment of public bureaucracies.

Young, James. *The Washington Community 1800–1828.* New York: Harcourt, 1966. Engaging, insightful account of political and administrative life in Washington during the first decades of the nineteenth century.

On the Web

For more information on the U.S. bureaucracy, see the following Web sites:

THE FEDERAL RESERVE
www.federalreserve.gov

The Federal Reserve System maintains an informative Web site, complete with publications, congressional testimony, and economic data.

FEDWORLD
www.fedworld.gov

OFFICE OF MANAGEMENT AND BUDGET
www.whitehouse.gov/OMB

The Office of Management and Budget offers copies of budget documentation, testimony before Congress, and regulatory information.

CONGRESSIONAL BUDGET OFFICE
www.cbo.gov

The Congressional Budget Office provides copies of its reports on the economy, the budget, and current legislation.

GOVERNMENT ACCOUNTABILITY OFFICE
www.gao.gov

The Government Accountability Office, the investigative arm of Congress, assists Congress in its oversight of the executive branch.

The Judiciary

"THE SUPREME COURT OF THE UNITED STATES IS AT STAKE IN
this race, ladies and gentlemen."[1] Whatever their political convictions were, activists
agreed with this statement by presidential candidate John Kerry in 2004. By the following June, the nation had gone for more than a decade without a Supreme Court
retirement. Because the Court rules on controversial issues such as affirmative action,
gay rights, and perhaps most visibly, abortion, activist groups on the left and the right

saw the Court as critically important. As summer began in the nation's capital, these groups sensed that they would not have to wait much longer for a new nomination.

Sure enough, on July 1 2005, Justice Sandra Day O'Connor, the first woman to serve on the Court, sent a brief letter to the president: "This is to inform you of my decision to retire from my position as an Associate Justice of the Supreme Court effective upon the nomination and confirmation of my successor."

Groups sprang into action. Those affiliated with the Democratic Party, fearing that the president would name a conservative to replace O'Connor, readied television advertisements, grassroots letter-writing efforts, and lobbying campaigns to oppose the new nominee. The National Abortion and Reproductive Rights Action League emailed a network of 800,000 activists within 15 minutes of hearing of O'Connor's retirement.[2] A conservative organization, Progress for America, announced within hours that it would spend $18 million to counter the efforts of liberals.[3] It looked as if the fight over the next justice would be vicious and partisan. As one former Justice Department official put it, the nomination process could be the most "bitter and depressing" in history.[4]

But that was before anyone knew who the nominee would be. On July 19, President Bush nominated Appeals Court Judge John G. Roberts for the position. Amiable and well-spoken, Roberts accepted the honor in the White House as his tow-headed four year old son, clad in a suit and short pants, danced near the podium, seemingly oblivious to the momentous event.

While Roberts was certainly on the conservative side of the spectrum (he had worked in the Reagan and George H. W. Bush administrations), he seemed squarely in the mainstream to most Americans, and not just because of his charming family. His appeals court decisions were mild and measured, and his professional record gave his opponents little ammunition.

After **Chief Justice** William Rehnquist succumbed to cancer in early fall, Bush proposed to have Roberts replace him at the head of the Court. Still, because Roberts had argued 39 cases before the Supreme Court, few questioned his qualifications for even this prestigious position.

In Senate hearings, he projected encyclopedic competence without revealing his opinions on the most controversial issues. Democrats at times seemed frustrated by his refusal to pin himself down. Senator Charles Schumer likened his reticence to a confusing discussion of movies:

> It's as if I asked you, "What kind of movies do you like? Tell me two or three good movies." And you say, "I like movies with good acting. I like movies with good directing. I like movies with good cinematography." And I ask you, "No, give me an example of a good movie." You don't name one. . . . Then I ask you if you like Casablanca, and you respond by saying, "Lots of people like Casablanca." You tell me it's widely settled that Casablanca is one of the great movies.[5]

Frustrations aside, Roberts' impressive performance in the hearings and his sterling professional record took the wind out of liberal activists' sails. Pollsters found that solid majorities of the public favored Roberts' confirmation.[6] Bush's opponents all but conceded defeat. Even Patrick Leahy, the senior Democrat on the Senate Judiciary Committee, announced that he would support the nominee. "Justice Roberts," said Leahy, "is a man of integrity."[7] The Senate confirmed Roberts by a vote of 78 to 22.

The Roberts nomination succeeded precisely because the president picked a candidate that Americans could support. Roberts' experience, his calm expertise on judicial matters, and even his photogenic smile won the backing of voters. Without controversial statements or a record of incompetence, activists on the left found little support for a fight. "I think history will say that George W. Bush knocked it out of the park when he selected John Roberts to be chief justice of the United States," said Republican Senator Lindsey Graham.[8]

Despite the judiciary's status as an unelected branch of government, it is not unusual for the courts to become embroiled in electoral politics. On the contrary, in recent decades, the judiciary has become tied ever more closely to electoral influences. Presidents are more likely to consider policy goals when selecting their nominees to the federal courts, and especially to the Supreme Court. If Senate committee chairs dislike a president's choice, they are more likely to delay or even refuse to schedule confirmation hearings. Individual senators openly ask nominees about how they might rule on various types of issues, even though no specific cases sit before the potential justices. If the nominee takes a clear position on a particular issue, or has written on the topic in law reviews and judicial rulings, senators and interest groups mobilize opposition based on their policy disagreements.

None of this maneuvering to influence the judiciary fits with how the framers viewed the courts. They hoped that judges would remain free from public pressures, relative to other political institutions, so that they could interpret written law neutrally. Judges were to protect individual citizens from governmental tyranny, even when an electoral majority endorsed restricting freedoms. But if current practices violate how the founders envisioned the political system functioning, they are fully consistent with trends in America's new democracy—which have spread public influence to even the most insulated institutions.

The Federal Court System

The Supreme Court provides the linchpin for the nation's judicial system, resolving difficult questions of federal law. (States have their own legal systems, which we discuss briefly at the end of this chapter.) Most of the day-to-day work of the federal judicial branch takes place at lower tiers. Indeed, the Supreme Court generally hears fewer than 100 cases per year, and the vast majority of those cases start in lower federal courts or in the state courts. These lower courts are less visible institutions, but they are no less affected by political and electoral forces. Thus, understanding how elections influence the federal judiciary, as well as how they impact civil liberties (see Chapter 13) and civil rights (see Chapter 14), first requires understanding how the federal court system works.

Organization of the Federal Courts

The Constitution established a Supreme Court but allowed Congress to decide on the shape of any lower courts (see Chapter 2). The first Congress enacted the Judiciary Act of 1789. That legislation still provides the basic framework for the modern federal court system, which is divided into three basic layers: trial courts, appeals courts, and the Supreme Court.

Trial Courts   Most federal cases initially appear in one of the 94 **district courts,** the lowest tier of the judicial system. A variety of high-profile cases are heard in the district courts. In 2007, for example, Vice President Dick Cheney's former chief of staff, I. Lewis Libby, was convicted in district court of charges related to the leak of the name of a covert CIA officer. Most federal cases begin and end in these district courts, which are also called trial courts (see Figure 12.1).

FIGURE 12.1   Federal and state court systems

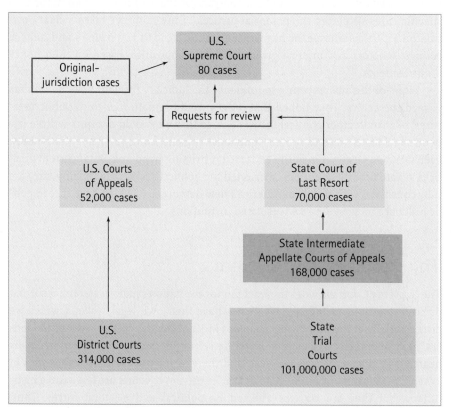

As this name suggests, the main responsibility of district courts is to hold trials. In all trials there are two sides: the **plaintiff**, the party bringing the suit, and the **defendant**, the party against whom the complaint is made. Trials settle alleged violations of the civil and criminal codes.

The **civil code** regulates the legal rights and obligations of citizens with regard to one another. Individuals ask the court to award damages and otherwise offer relief for injuries they claim to have suffered. Medical malpractice suits are one example of a civil action; the patient sues a hospital or a doctor for improper treatment. People cannot be imprisoned for violating the civil code (although they can be imprisoned for not complying with a court order resulting from a civil suit).

Violations of the **criminal code** are offenses against society as a whole. The government enforces criminal law, acting as plaintiff and initiating charges against suspects. If convicted, the criminal owes a debt to society, not just to the injured party. The debt may be paid by fine, imprisonment, or, in the case of capital crimes, execution. Table 12.1 summarizes the differences between civil and criminal cases.

The same action can violate both codes simultaneously, so the defendant may have to fend off accusations more than once. After a jury acquitted former football star O. J. Simpson in the murder of his ex-wife, Nicole Brown Simpson, her relatives filed a civil suit seeking compensation for pain and suffering caused by her wrongful death. Their tactic might sound foolish. Why should Simpson pay Nicole's family for their loss if he was not guilty of her murder? The plaintiffs were hopeful that they might win a civil suit, despite losing the criminal trial, because the burden of evidence is weaker. In a criminal trial, one is "innocent until proven guilty" beyond a reasonable doubt, but in a civil suit the jury needs only to decide whose case has the preponderance of supporting evidence. Also, a plaintiff cannot compel the accused to testify in a criminal trial because of the Fifth Amendment, but the accused in a civil action cannot refuse to respond without suffering consequences. The plaintiffs thus were able to secure a guilty verdict in the civil suit and a monetary award against Simpson of $33.5 million.

TABLE 12.1   Differences between civil and criminal trials

	Criminal Trial	Civil Trial
Plaintiff	The government	Private person or group
Issue	Duty of citizens to obey the law	Legal rights and obligations of citizens to one another
Type of wrongdoing	Transgression against society	Harm to private person or group
Remedy	Punishment (fine, imprisonment, etc.)	Compensation for damages
Standard of proof	Beyond a reasonable doubt	Preponderance of the evidence
Can defendant be forced to testify?	No	Yes

The Federal Bureau of Investigation usually looks into suspected violations of the federal criminal code, although other federal agencies (such as the Secret Service and the Bureau of Alcohol, Tobacco and Firearms) also exercise investigative powers. They turn over evidence to prosecutors in the office of a **U.S. attorney**, one of 93 litigators appointed by the president and confirmed by the Senate. If persuaded that a prosecution is warranted, the U.S. attorney asks a grand jury (consisting of 16 to 23 citizens) to indict, or bring charges against, the suspect. This stage is not a formal trial, just a decision to proceed with one, so the grand jury usually follows the U.S. attorney's advice. As one wit observed, "Under the right prosecutor, a grand jury would indict a ham sandwich."[9]

U.S. attorneys have a particularly high political profile. They usually share the president's party affiliation and may be sensitive to the needs of their own political careers. U.S. attorneys do not handle routine law enforcement. Often they concentrate on attention-grabbing activities that can lead to a candidacy for higher office. Former New York Mayor Rudolph Giuliani achieved prominence as a federal attorney after successfully prosecuting Wall Street inside-trader Ivan Boesky and tax-evading hotel magnate Leona Helmsley. Supreme Court Justice Samuel Alito also served as a U.S. Attorney in New Jersey in the late 1980s, where he earned a reputation as a confident, if low-key, leader.[10]

Appeals Courts   Federal district courts are organized into 13 circuits, including 11 regional circuits, a District of Columbia circuit, and a federal circuit (which includes the specialized courts such as the U.S. Court of International Trade). Each has a **circuit court of appeals**, the court empowered to review all district rulings (see Figure 12.2).* Appeals courts contain between six and 28 judges, depending on the size of the circuit. The senior appeals court judge assigns three judges, usually chosen by lot, to review each case. In exceptionally important cases, the appeals judges may participate in a **plenary session**, which includes all of them. Courts of appeals ordinarily take as given the facts of the case, as stated in the trial record and decided by district judges. They do not accept new evidence or hear additional witnesses but, rather, confine their review to points of law under dispute. Most appeals court decisions are final.

The Supreme Court in Action

The Supreme Court sits atop a massive pyramid of judicial activity. Each year prosecutors and private citizens bring more than 27 million criminal trials and civil suits before the state and federal courts.[11] Yet during the 2005–2006 term, the nation's high court heard only 74 cases. Through these few cases, the Court's chief justice and eight associate **justices** exert substantial influence.

---

* Originally, appeals court judges literally traveled a circuit, going by stagecoach from district to district to hear appeals hence—the name.

FIGURE 12.2 Courts of appeals circuit boundaries

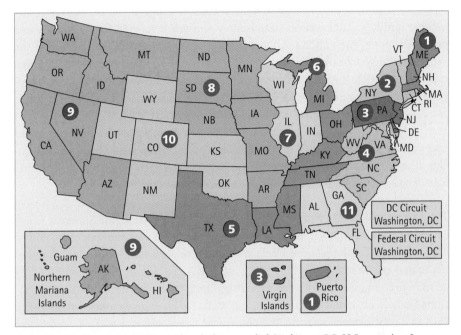

Source: Robert A. Carp and Ronald Stidham, *The Federal Courts*, 2nd ed. (Washington, DC: CQ Press, 1991), p. 18.

Certs   At one time the Supreme Court was, by law, forced to review many appeals. The workload became so excessive that, in 1925, Congress gave the Court power to refuse almost any case it did not want to consider. Today, nearly all cases argued before the Court arrive because at least four justices have voted to grant what is known as a **writ of *certiorari*** (or "cert").* When a cert is granted, it means the Court has agreed to consider the case and requests to be informed of the details.[12] The Court receives 8000 to 9000 petitions each year, denying approximately 95 percent of them.[13] Reviewing these petitions is a lot of work. "You almost get to hate the guy who brings the cert petitions around," a Supreme Court clerk once explained. "He is a really nice guy, but he gets abuse all the time."[14]

The number of certs granted by the Supreme Court has fallen markedly in recent decades. In the 1970s the Supreme Court decided as many as 400 cases annually.[15] The current Court seems to want to reduce its visibility in American politics; certs are granted only for those cases that raise the most important legal or constitutional issues.

The case for cert is strongest if two lower courts have reached opposite conclusions on similar cases. The Supreme Court feels a responsibility to clarify and

---

*Certiorari *is a Latin phrase that means "to be informed of."*

therefore standardize the law. In 1998, for example, the Wisconsin Supreme Court upheld a state law establishing a school voucher program in Milwaukee. Low-income families could receive state money and use it to send their children to a private school of their choice. Although many religious schools participated in the program, the Wisconsin court ruled that the law did not violate the constitutional clause prohibiting the establishment of religion (see Chapter 13). But a federal appeals court later found a similar program in Ohio to be unconstitutional. Because two lower courts had decided the same issue in contrary ways, the Supreme Court accepted the Ohio case in early 2002. In a landmark ruling, a slim majority found that vouchers did not violate the establishment clause because parents could decide whether the money went to religious institutions. Such a program of "true private choice," said Chief Justice Rehnquist, passed the constitutional test.[16]

The Decision-Making Process   Before reaching a decision, the Supreme Court considers **briefs**—written legal arguments submitted by the opposing sides. (Unfortunately for the justices, briefs are seldom really brief!) The justices then listen to oral arguments from contending attorneys in a plenary session, attended by all nine justices, the chief justice presiding. Open to the public, these plenary sessions are held on Mondays, Tuesdays, and Wednesdays from October through May. During a controversial hearing, the courtroom overflows, and outside, "protesters square . . . off at the courthouse steps, chanting, singing and screaming at each other."[17]

During the half-hour allotted to each side to present its case, attorneys often find themselves interrupted by searching questions from the bench. Former law professor Antonin Scalia is especially known for his willingness to turn the plenary session into a classroom seminar. Court reporters usually analyze the questions asked by justices to find clues indicating how each intends to vote on the case. Yet it is not always clear how closely the justices attend to the responses. As Chief Justice John Marshall said many years ago, "The acme of judicial distinction means the ability to look a lawyer straight in the eye for two hours and not hear a damned word he says."[18]

After hearing oral arguments, the justices usually reach a preliminary decision that same week in a private conference presided over by the chief justice. There are "three levels of elbow room about the conference table." The most ample is for the chief justice and senior associate justice, who sit at opposite ends. The next best is grabbed by the three most senior justices sitting on one side, leaving the four most junior crowded together across from them. No outsiders, not even a secretary, are permitted to attend. The only record consists of handwritten notes taken by individual justices.

Justices use the private conferences as opportunities to signal where they stand on each case—which way they are leaning and which points of law or politics decided their position. The justices usually formalize their preferences in a vote, taken in order of seniority. When in the majority, the chief justice chooses which justice may write the court's opinion; otherwise, the senior associate justice in the majority does so.[19]

That the justices "vote" on the case does not mean they decide policy issues the same way a legislature might. Indeed, both clerks and justices become uncomfortable when their colleagues openly approach a decision with political considerations in mind.[20] Instead, courts are expected to follow the principle of **stare decisis**. The phrase is Latin for "let the decision stand." Judges should adhere to **precedents**—prior decisions—including the written justifications known as **opinions of the court** that explained past decisions.

Stare decisis is a powerful judicial principle, ignored only at the risk of the legal system's stability and credibility. Consistent court decisions enable a country to live under a rule of law, because then citizens know what they are expected to obey. "We cannot meddle with a prior decision," one judge explained, unless it "strikes us as wrong with the force of a five-week-old unrefrigerated dead fish."[21]

The principle also helps maintain the almost-sacred relationship between Americans and their Constitution. It preserves the image of judges as impersonal specialists applying a tangible body of law, rather than a tiny, unelected elite telling legislatures what they may or may not do. But having to follow precedent can annoy judges who dislike the choices of their predecessors. One Utah judge got a bit carried away expressing his frustration: "We feel like galley slaves chained to our oars by a power from which we cannot free ourselves."[22]

When reaching a decision that seems contrary to a prior decision, courts try to find a legal distinction between the case at hand and earlier court decisions, usually by emphasizing how the facts of the current case differ. The process at times can strain credibility. An attorney once bragged, "Law school taught me one thing: how to take two situations that are exactly the same and show how they are different."[23]

The justice assigned responsibility for preparing the court's opinion circulates a draft version among the other eight. Comments received from them usually lead to revisions. Sometimes the comments are only suggestions, but sometimes they are demands; a justice will refuse to join the opinion unless certain changes appear in future drafts. On rare occasions, the justice writing the opinion has "lost a court"—that is, so many justices change their minds that the initial author no longer has a majority. To keep a majority, the justice writing the opinion may produce an extremely bland statement that gives little guidance to lower-court judges. In a 1993 sexual harassment case, *Harris v. Forklift Systems*, for example, the majority hardly created any precedent at all, saying only that courts should look at the "totality of the circumstances" to decide whether harassment has occurred.[24]

Justices who vote against the majority may prepare a **dissenting opinion** that explains their disagreement. Any member of the majority who is unhappy with the Court opinion may write a **concurring opinion** that provides different reasoning for the decision. Two hundred years ago, when John Marshall was chief justice, the Court usually issued unanimous judgments and Marshall wrote most opinions.

Today, the Court is less often unanimous in its judgments; justices are sufficiently concerned with public policy that they choose to write either dissenting or concurring opinions explaining their own preferences. Often a case produces so many separate opinions that it is difficult to ascertain exactly what the majority has decided (see Figure 12.3). It is not uncommon for the Court's opinion to describe the full judgment of only one justice, with everyone else either dissenting or concurring.

Once the Court reaches a decision, it usually sends, or **remands**, the case to a lower court for implementation. Because the Supreme Court regards itself as responsible for establishing general principles and an overall framework, it seldom becomes involved in the detailed resolution of particular cases. This procedure leaves a great deal of legal responsibility in the hands of lower courts.

If a court finds that an injury has been suffered, it is up to the court to fashion a **remedy,** the compensation for the injury. Often the remedy simply involves monetary compensation to the injured party. But a judge may also direct the defendant

FIGURE 12.3   Number of Supreme Court dissents

This graph shows the rising number of dissenting opinions written by members of the Supreme Court over the decades. Why do you think dissents have increased? Do dissenting voices make the Court look more or less useful in your view?

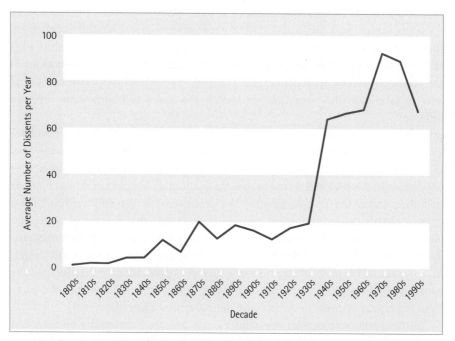

Sources: Data from Gregory Calderia and Christopher J. W. Zorn, *Of Time and Consensual Norms on the Supreme Court,* Inter-University Consortium on Political and Social Research, Study No. I01142; see Gregory Calderia and Christopher J. W. Zorn, "Of Time and Consensual Norms on the Supreme Court," *American Journal of Political Science* 42:3 (July 1998): 874–902.

to alter future behavior. To overcome racial segregation in schools, courts have ordered school boards to institute magnet schools (specialized schools that draw students from a large surrounding area), to set up special compensatory programs, or to bus children from one part of a city to another. As a Nixon appointee, Justice Lewis Powell, once put it, courts have the right, if racial segregation is sufficiently severe, to "virtually assume the role of school superintendent and school board."[25]

The Role of the Chief Justice The chief justice has only one vote, and many of the chief's tasks are of a ceremonial or housekeeping nature. For this reason, leading the court provides limited additional power. It may not even guarantee any special respect from the other justices, who sometimes may be arrogant and temperamental people. Chief Justice Charles Evans Hughes received a rude awakening on this score when he attempted to convene a session of the Court and noticed that Justice James C. McReynolds was absent. He sent a note along summoning McReynolds, but the independent-minded judge sent a reply back via the same messenger: "Justice McReynolds says to tell you that he doesn't work for you."[26]

Certain responsibilities do give the office added influence, however. Perhaps the most important power is the one mentioned earlier: the power of the chief justice, if voting with a majority, to decide who will write the majority opinion. This assignment power can have far-reaching consequences, because it influences the explanations given for a ruling and the tone of the Court's judgment. The chief can frustrate a particular justice by refusing to give him or her important cases. Chief Justice Warren Burger often angered his colleagues by switching to the majority side late in a case, presumably so that he could choose the opinion author.[27]

The Role of the Solicitor General A powerful figure who appears before the Supreme Court regularly is the **solicitor general**, a government official responsible for airing the presidential administration's views before the Court. The solicitor general presents the government's case whenever it is party to a suit and, in other cases, may submit *amicus curiae* briefs—literally, briefs submitted by a "friend of the court" explaining its position.*

Involvement of the solicitor general is a signal that the president and attorney general have strong opinions on a subject, raising its visibility and political significance. Some call the occupant of this office "the tenth justice," because the Court accepts about 60 percent of the solicitor general's cert petitions.[28] When the office of the solicitor general files an *amicus curiae* brief, its position is on the winning side approximately three-quarters of the time, a batting average envied by even the most successful private attorneys.[29] Some solicitors general eventually join the Court, as did four during the twentieth century.

---

* Amicus curiae *briefs can also be submitted by others who wish to inform the court of a legal issue presented by a particular case.*

The Role of Clerks   Much of the day-to-day work within the Supreme Court building is the job of **law clerks**—young, influential aides hired by each of the justices. Recently out of law school, most will have spent a year as a clerk with a lower court before being asked to help a Supreme Court justice. Each justice employs between two and four law clerks.[30]

The role of the law clerk has grown in recent years. Not only do clerks initially review certs, they also draft many opinions. Clerks have become so important to the Court's routine that some view the true "Supreme Court" of today as nothing more than a junior collection of bright but unseasoned attorneys, unconfirmed by the Senate or anybody else. The clerks' defenders reply that well-trained graduates of the country's most prestigious law schools may be better judges than aging titans who refuse to leave office well beyond the age of normal retirement. The truth probably lies between these two extremes: The enthusiasm of the young clerks and the experience of the justices are likely better in combination than either would be alone.[31] As Chief Justice Rehnquist said of the system, "The Justice may retain for himself control not merely of the outcome of the case, but the explanation for the outcome, and I do not believe this practice sacrifices either."[32]

Litigation as a Political Strategy

Interest groups increasingly use the federal court system to place issues on the political agenda, particularly when elected officials have not responded to group demands. To advance an issue, advocacy groups often file **class action suits** on behalf of all individuals in a particular category, whether or not they actually participate in the suit. For example, in the late 1990s groups of former smokers in several states filed class action suits against the major tobacco companies for lying to consumers about the health hazards caused by smoking. In one such case, a jury ordered the five major tobacco companies to pay millions of dollars in damages to up to 500,000 ill Florida smokers.[33]

Class action suits are justified on the grounds that the issues affect many people in essentially the same way. It should not be necessary for each member of the class to bring an individual suit to secure relief. But the main motive may be less to benefit the supposed clients than to profit the attorneys, because the amount won by each member of the class may be relatively small whereas the lawyers' fees approved by the court may be astronomical. A class action suit filed against the city of Chicago in 2001 on behalf of 5000 homeless people who claimed to have been harmed by the city's anti-begging law resulted in an average payment of less than $20 per plaintiff.[34] The lawyers received $375,000.[35]

Critics of the judicial system's power also fear that lawsuits have become a tactic for circumventing the democratic process.[36] Lawyers can use the courts as an indirect way to punish unpopular groups or to ban controversial products such as cigarettes or handguns—driving up their costs or driving their manufacturers out of business.

The Politics of Judicial Appointments

The judicial system is supposed to be politically blind. Justice, like the rain, is expected to fall equally on rich and poor, on Democrat and Republican, on all ethnic groups, and so forth. Judges are appointed for life so that they may decide each case without concern for their political futures. Chief Justice Warren E. Burger expressed this ideal when he claimed that judges "rule on the basis of law, not public opinion, and they should be totally indifferent to pressures of the times."[37] At one level these ideals are clearly a myth in America's new democracy.

Political influences play a major role in the selection of federal judges. Most share the same partisan identifications as the presidents who nominate them; 87 percent of Bill Clinton's nominees were Democrats, and 90 percent of George W. Bush's nominees have been Republicans (see Figure 12.4). Presidents before them were equally partisan.[38] The convention known as **senatorial courtesy** requires that a judicial nominee be acceptable to the senior senator of the state or region involved who shares the president's political party.

Judicial decisions reflect the political orientation of the president who appointed each judge. According to one study, George H. W. Bush's and Ronald

FIGURE 12.4   Partisan affiliation of district judges, 1968–2003

Republican presidents usually appoint Republican judges, and Democratic presidents usually appoint Democratic judges.

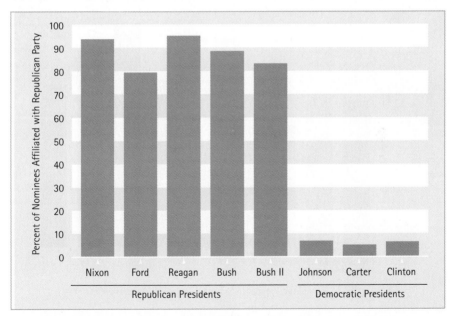

Source: Sheldon Goldman, "Reagan's Judicial Legacy: Completing the Puzzle and Summing Up," *Judicature* 72 (April–May 1989): 321–322; Sheldon Goldman, Elliot Slotnick, Gerald Gryski, and Sara Schiavoni, "W. Bush Remaking the Judiciary: Like Father Like Son?" *Judicature* 86 (May–June 2003), pp. 282–309.

Reagan's district court appointees were significantly tougher toward those accused of crime than were Clinton-appointed judges.[39] More generally, judges appointed by Democratic presidents are more likely than those appointed by Republican presidents to hand down liberal decisions (see Figure 12.5).

For at least the first half of the twentieth century, the idealistic view of judicial decision making guided the process through which the Senate confirmed nominees. Senators approved presidential selections as a matter of course. Most nominees did not even testify before congressional committees first. Earl Warren, for example, an Eisenhower appointee who dramatically changed the tenor of the Supreme Court as chief justice, was confirmed without testifying before the Senate.[40]

This longtime separation of Supreme Court nominations from political disputes owed a great deal to the efforts of William Howard Taft. Taft was the only person ever to serve both as president (1909–1913) and as chief justice of the Supreme Court (1921–1930). Before Taft, political factors openly affected the confirmation decisions; the Senate rejected a third of the presidents' nominees in the nineteenth century.[41] But Taft worked hard to enhance the quality of nominees, minimize the significance of confirmation procedures, and elevate the prestige of

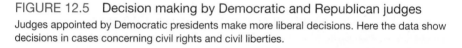

FIGURE 12.5   Decision making by Democratic and Republican judges

Judges appointed by Democratic presidents make more liberal decisions. Here the data show decisions in cases concerning civil rights and civil liberties.

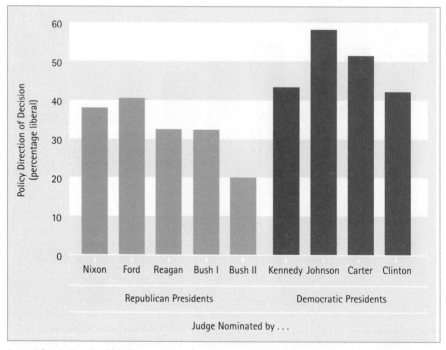

Source: Robert A. Carp, Ronald Stidham, and Kenneth L. Manning, *Judicial Process in America*, 6th ed. (Washington, DC: CQ Press, 2004), Table 7-1, p. 163.

the Court. He also made sure that the new Supreme Court building, eventually completed in 1935, was designed to resemble a Greek temple, so that Americans would respect their laws with the same reverence with which the ancient Greeks venerated their gods.

Taft was so successful that until 1968, the Senate confirmed every twentieth-century nominee except one, most without significant dissent. The Senate has regained some of its power in the past 40 years, however, and the judicial-selection process has become increasingly political. In 1987 the Senate rejected Reagan nominee Robert H. Bork after many interest groups and Democratic senators objected to Bork's conservative legal views. The 1991 nomination battle over Justice Clarence Thomas became an important issue in the following year's elections, after many women's groups claimed that Senators had not taken sexual harassment allegations against Thomas seriously enough. Finally, Bush nominee Harriet Miers withdrew her nomination in 2005 after many conservative interest groups objected that she had little judicial experience and that her credentials as a conservative were insufficient.

Justices are nominated by the president, evaluated by the Senate Judiciary Committee, and confirmed by a vote of the full Senate largely on the basis of their policy views. The procedure guarantees a voice in who holds judicial office to numerous politicians, interest groups, and the media—few of whom are equipped to evaluate the nominees for their legal expertise. Instead, these players pay close attention to the electoral and policy consequences of judicial appointments. The Senate's propensity to reject presidential nominees has increased.

Most lower-court nominees win confirmation. Rejections usually result from financial or personal problems uncovered during the confirmation process. However, in recent decades even lower-court confirmations have become politicized. Opposition-party senators are most likely to exert their power by refusing to bring

A JUDICIAL QUESTION
Activists protest as the Supreme Court hears a case on school desegregation in 2006. Why have Supreme Court nominations become increasingly politicized?

nominations to a vote. In the late 1990s, partisan conflict over judicial nominations became bitter and vocal, as President Clinton complained of congressional foot-dragging and Republicans criticized his judicial nominations as too liberal. Democrats used similar tactics to delay and block some of President George W. Bush's nominees, who they saw as "extreme conservatives."[42]

Presidents sometimes avoid confirmation battles by choosing moderate judges or nominees with unknown views. In 1990 President George H. W. Bush nominated David Souter, a New Hampshire state supreme court justice; unlike the ill-fated Robert Bork, Souter had never written an opinion or treatise on any major constitutional question. While this "stealth strategy" worked in Souter's case, it backfired fifteen years later in the case of Harriet Miers, whose lack of a record made President George W. Bush's allies nervous.

Most Supreme Court nominees also tell senators that they cannot comment on specific issues that might come before the Court. Legal scholars lament such conflict avoidance. One law professor protested that to sidestep a political firestorm, "no president will nominate anyone who has written anything very interesting."[43] The successful appointment of Samuel Alito, who Bush nominated after Miers withdrew, may temper this stark assessment somewhat. While Alito had a well-documented conservative record, his extensive testimony convinced most senators that he was, in Democratic Senator Robert Byrd's words, "an honorable man who loves his country, loves his Constitution, and will give of his best."[44] Alito was controversial, but succeeded in the end.

The United States is unlikely to go back to the apolitical way of selecting federal judges. Modern methods of communication—televised hearings, fax machines, toll-free numbers, radio talk shows, and the Internet—ensure that senators and interest groups can conduct detailed evaluations of each appointee. Presidents have no choice but to select judges with an eye to the public controversies they might create. Electoral considerations will continue to affect judicial selections.

The Power of Judicial Review

Policy-oriented senators scrutinize nominees closely because the Supreme Court's vast political authority includes the power of **judicial review**. Federal courts regularly declare laws of both Congress and the state legislatures unconstitutional, meaning that they are null and void. The Supreme Court is the court of last resort on such judgments. Exercising this power is controversial because it gives judges, appointed for life, the authority to negate laws written by elected representatives. Senators hesitate to surrender so much power, and the public seems to share their caution. By a margin of 5 to 1, Americans agree that the "Senate should carefully scrutinize a presidential nominee."[45]

Although the Constitution claims to be the "supreme Law of the Land," it says nothing explicit about judicial review. From what little they said at the

Constitutional Convention, it seems the delegates did not expect the Court to be powerful. Alexander Hamilton, writing as Publius in the 78th *Federalist Papers* essay, initially seemed to claim review powers for the judiciary, but then he backed off his aggressive posture three essays later. "The United States began its history," political scientist Robert McCloskey once observed, "with a Supreme Court whose birthright was most uncertain."[46]

Origins of Judicial Review

The Supreme Court first asserted judicial-review powers in 1803, as part of the *Marbury v. Madison* judgment. Many consider this opinion the most significant Supreme Court decision ever rendered, so it is worth understanding how the case evolved and why even those skeptical of judicial review tolerated the ruling.[47]

Marbury v. Madison followed one of the most contentious elections in U.S. history and the first peaceful transition of power from a president of one political party to that of another. Federalist President John Adams lost the 1800 election to Thomas Jefferson, candidate of the arch-rival Democratic–Republicans (see Chapter 8 for a discussion of these parties). Congressional elections that year also produced widespread Federalist losses, costing them control of both chambers. Adams and his supporters feared that the Jeffersonians would usher in a period of dangerous radicalism. They were determined to leave their mark on the U.S. government before stepping down.

The best means of resistance seemed to be to stock the judiciary with Federalist sympathizers, who would enjoy lifetime appointments. So in the last days before Adams left office, he nominated numerous judges, including 42 new justices of the peace for Washington, D.C. The Senate approved the appointments a day afterward, and that evening, as the skies grew dark in the nation's capital, Secretary of State John Marshall stamped their official commissions with the Great Seal of the United States. The appointments had been arranged so hastily, however, that administration officials failed to deliver the commissions. Jefferson's supporters found them when they arrived.

The Jeffersonians decided that appointees had no right to their posts until they received commissions—and so refrained from delivering them. But appointee William Marbury did not believe that the Jefferson administration could deny him a position simply because the official notification had not gone out. A law passed by Congress in 1789, the Judiciary Act, specified how jilted appointees might challenge denial of their posts. They could request a writ of *mandamus* (a court order) directly from the U.S. Supreme Court. Accordingly, Marbury sued Jefferson's secretary of state, future president James Madison.

Ironically, John Marshall, who had prepared Marbury's commission, was the Court's chief justice by 1803. Indeed, it was a Federalist-dominated court. Marbury seemed certain to win. Yet Marshall saw a rare opportunity in the case. Installing a few extra justices of the peace might offer the Federalists a short-term victory, but nothing more. And there was no guarantee that Madison would honor a Court ruling on Marbury's behalf. For Jefferson's administration to ignore the Court would weaken the judiciary over the long term. Instead, Marshall decided to give the administration its way, but to do so by declaring a constitutional principle that Jefferson opposed.

Marshall read his opinion to an anxious, crowded audience on February 24. His initial statement chastised the Jeffersonians for denying Marbury his rightful position. But then Marshall asked a crucial question: Was the Supreme Court the proper place to address Marbury's complaint? His stunning conclusion was that it was not. The Judiciary Act of 1789, Marshall explained, had violated the Constitution by giving the Court original jurisdiction over cases involving the Secretary of State. Marbury lost on a technicality.*

Marshall asserted the power of judicial review to explain why the Supreme Court could overturn offending portions of the Judiciary Act and deny Marbury's appeal. His reasoning was simple and straightforward: The Constitution is the highest law of the land, established by the people in convention before the national government even existed. No entity, not even Congress itself, can enact legislation that contravenes this higher law. Federal judges, who are responsible for interpreting the Constitution, are the ones who must declare when a law runs afoul of the Constitution's restrictions. They could void unconstitutional laws.

Marshall's brilliant decision had transformed a situation sure to sap the Court's power into one that strengthened it tremendously. Madison and Jefferson could not refuse to win their own case simply because they disliked the reasoning used to decide it! They would have looked ridiculous and would probably have lost credibility. Marshall had gained more power for the Court—a Federalist goal— through his willingness to lose a minor political battle. By invoking the power of judicial review for the first time, and in a manner that insulated it from challenge, Marshall ensured that the judiciary would always be an authoritative force.

Three Theories of Constitutional Interpretation

The justification for judicial review makes sense when one views a court's role as a technical one. If someone must examine laws and compare them to a higher written law, reconciling situations in which two rules plainly contradict, then judges seem a logical choice for the task. They have the training to interpret legal phrasing and the political independence to do it fairly if they wish. However, very few judgments of constitutionality are simple, because few provisions are precise. What should justices do when a law seems as though it might violate the meaning of the Constitution but does not do so in a manner so plain that anyone schooled in the law would see it?

To address this dilemma, judges have developed three distinct theories of constitutional interpretation: the plain meaning of the text, the original intent of the

---

* One of the great mysteries of American history is why Marbury never tried to go through proper judicial channels to attain his commission. Marshall left no doubt that Marbury would win if he followed legal procedures.

text, and the living-constitution approach. The approach most appealing to common sense is to go by the *plain meaning* of a constitutional provision's words. The law is whatever the written law says. After all, the words are what people voted on, not anything else, so only they can lay out the law. Plain meaning has two clear advantages: (1) it is the approach least open to judicial abuse, because courts must restrict their attention to the laws before them, and (2) it calls upon judges to perform the task for which they are best trained, which is to decipher the meaning of legal language.

But plain-meaning theory has limitations. The Constitution is a very short document that left many issues undecided and many phrases unexplained. For example, the First Amendment bars Congress from passing any law "respecting an establishment of religion." Legal experts disagree over how to give teeth to this prohibition—since to do so requires figuring out what the framers actually banned. What makes something a "religion" or not? At what point has a law moved too close to "an establishment" of one? And what does the "respecting" forbid that the word "establishing" alone might have allowed? The phrase is hardly plain, and the confusion it engenders is not just a rare exception.

Furthermore, words do not always have a clear legal definition. Vocabulary changes over time, and words that persist often alter in meaning. This transformation occurs regularly and swiftly in conversational English. The word *jazz* once served in New Orleans brothels to describe the transaction between prostitutes and their clients; now an interior decorator might offer tips to help you "jazz up" a bedroom. A "cool" teacher may be friendly or laid back, not coldly formal and aloof as once was the meaning of the term. Words used in legal terminology change in the same way, though perhaps more slowly. The word *man* at various times has referred to a male of any age, to an adult male, to an adult of any gender, or to humankind. The House may impeach a president for committing "high Crimes and Misdemeanors," but the Constitution's authors did not intend that phrase to include the minor legal violations we call misdemeanors today.

Sometimes social changes take the law outside any context anticipated by those who first wrote the provisions. The Second Amendment may grant a "right to bear arms," but does this include nuclear bombs and tanks or only hunting rifles? The word *arms* provides little guidance about which sorts of weapons citizens have a right to possess. Those who write laws often leave out details because they assume readers will understand what they mean, not anticipating that one day Americans will lack their cultural perspective. Early Americans may have understood what the Bill of Rights meant by "unreasonable" searches or "excessive" fines or "cruel and unusual" punishments, but today's readers lack the same point of reference.

A second approach, the theory of *original intent*, also tries to remain true to inherited law—but helps the authors a bit by filling in the meaning of words. Judges who take this approach must perform historical research to ascertain the intentions of those who approved constitutional provisions. Very little solid evidence exists to determine what the typical voter believed, but at least scholars can assess the intentions of the framers. Judges may examine such documents as the notes that James Madison wrote down at the Constitutional Convention, the *Federalist Papers*, and the speeches made during the ratifying campaign in 1787 and 1788. They also look at the laws commonly in effect when an amendment originated. Justice Thomas, for example, favors overturning *Roe v. Wade* because the words used to justify a right to abortion joined the Constitution at a time when many states outlawed the practice.

Original-intent theory has its own problems. Those who wrote the Constitution did not contemplate many issues now before the courts. Nor could they anticipate the many social complexities added, for example, by advances in travel and communications. Judges can abuse the practice of determining intent. They may sift through the evidence selectively to find examples or arguments supporting their political preferences, and even a sincere judge is not trained in social science or historical methods. Furthermore, those who supported provisions often did not agree on the meanings themselves, so even trained historians cannot settle what voters thought they were endorsing in these instances.

Faced with the difficulty of figuring out what inherited words mean, or were supposed to mean, some judges prefer to assess the law according to the sentiments of their own time. Societies evolve, and even fundamental law can evolve with them. This *living-constitution* theory allows judges to update the meaning of laws in light of the entire history of the United States as a nation. They can go beyond the literal meaning of laws or the opinions expressed at the time of their passage and incorporate the moral lessons Americans have learned since then. In the words of Justice Oliver Wendell Holmes, Jr., constitutional questions must be "considered in the light of our whole experience and not merely in that of what was said a hundred years ago."[48] Presumably, the passage of another century since Holmes served on the Court only makes his logic more compelling.

The living-constitution theory is practical in one important way: It gives the political system extreme flexibility when adapting law to situations alien to the framers. Laws, especially constitutional provisions, are slow to change through the democratic process. Judicial interpretation is a quicker method of adaptation. However, it is also the approach most susceptible to judicial abuse. Reading history's moral lessons is a highly personal endeavor. It takes judges farthest from their area of expertise, requiring as it does insights drawn from numerous fields (including sociology, political science, psychology, history, theology, and perhaps natural science). Many question the wisdom of giving this power to judges, who are appointed for life almost solely from the legal profession.

These three approaches—plain meaning, original intent, and living Constitution—are useful conceptually. A justice occasionally will develop the reputation for espousing a particular view of constitutional interpretation. The late Justice Hugo Black endorsed a literal reading of the Constitution, refusing in principle either to read rights into the language or to water down those stated starkly in the document. The late Justice William O. Douglas emerged from the "realist" school of law, which endorsed incorporating a judge's observations of the real world when interpreting legal phrases.

The labels are also useful as a form of shorthand in political discussion. During the 2004 presidential election debates, President Bush promised to appoint "strict constructionists" to the bench—meaning judges who would stick to the plain meaning of written law. Listeners attuned to the political buzzwords knew that most judges fitting this description would oppose abortion rights and loosen constitutional restrictions on government accommodation of religion. John Kerry, by contrast, said he would appoint judges likely to support abortion rights because they would believe in a living Constitution.

Concepts break down somewhat when describing the actual voting behavior of particular judges. Outsiders often point to Justice Antonin Scalia as the prime example of a strict-constructionist judge, but Scalia rejects the label. "I am not a strict constructionist," he told a law school audience in Wisconsin. "You shouldn't be a strict constructionist—you should be reasonable."[49] He does tend to read the religious-freedom clauses of the First Amendment narrowly, in that he allows the government wide latitude before finding a violation of either clause (see Chapter 13). But he allows occasional flexibility in the same amendment's free-expression clauses; for example, he includes symbolic gestures, such as flag burning, as instances of protected "speech."

Voting on the Supreme Court

The three legal approaches to constitutional interpretation are useful conceptually, but few justices have ever fit cleanly and consistently into one category or another. Nor do justices reveal a consistent and predictable allegiance to or disregard for precedents—another legal criterion for choosing sides in a case— although, of course, justices vary in their levels of caution. This flexibility leads some court watchers to question whether judicial opinions really derive, first and foremost, from legal criteria.

Scholars have proposed a variety of alternative explanations for judicial decision making, criteria that are personal and political rather than legal. Judges might vote according to their political ideologies, their policy preferences, their party affiliations, or their personal backgrounds. It can be difficult to parse these various explanations out from each other, because they overlap so much. Conservative judges usually prefer conservative policies, for example, and may have a personal background that would cultivate a conservative orientation. What the explanations have in common is a sense that judicial decision making will be predictable based on information about who the judges are, not just about their relationship with legal interpretation. In short, the Supreme Court is largely a political entity.

Predictability   Most of the time, justices vote along lines anticipated by those who nominated and confirmed them. By the time lawyers rise in prominence sufficient to warrant Supreme Court appointments, they usually have a track record of opinions, speeches, law review articles, and political activism to indicate likely future voting patterns. According to one study, information about the political views of Supreme Court justices at the time they were being confirmed allows one to anticipate the justices' decisions in civil liberties cases more than 60 percent of the time.[50] This predictability enables elected officials—both presidents and senators—to shape the future direction of the Supreme Court, thereby maintaining some degree of popular control.

Not every prediction of future behavior is correct, however. President Nixon appointed Justice Harry Blackmun, expecting him to follow in the footsteps of his conservative fellow Minnesotan, Chief Justice Warren Burger. Instead, Blackmun shifted decidedly to the left over the course of his career, and by 1992 he was the Court's most liberal justice.[51] On the present Court, Justice Souter also has disappointed conservatives, compiling a record as liberal as that of Clinton appointee Breyer.[52]

Policy Making Justices of the Court fall into quite predictable voting blocs. While Chief Justice John Roberts and associate Samuel Alito are still establishing their place on the court, the remainder of the current justices can be divided into three fairly well-defined blocs. Even Justice John Paul Stevens, "long . . . considered a maverick," has found himself almost constantly on the left in recent years. The most liberal justices, Stevens and Clinton appointee Ruth Bader Ginsburg, favor a certain amount of **judicial activism**, meaning that they are willing to overturn precedents to advance a vision of what the Constitution has come to mean (or ought to mean). Souter and the other Clinton appointee, Stephen Breyer, usually join the liberal bloc, especially when it comes to continuing the enforcement of activist judicial precedents from the Warren and Burger eras.

THE ROBERTS COURT

In this composite, the justices of the Supreme Court as of 2005 are pictured from left to right according to their judicial philosophies. On the left are John Paul Stevens, Ruth Bader Ginsburg, Stephen Breyer, and David Souter. In the middle is moderate Justice Anthony Kennedy. On the right are Chief Justice John Roberts, Samuel Alito, Antonin Scalia, and Clarence Thomas. *Do you think that justices time their retirements so that they are likely to be replaced by justices with similar judicial philosophies?*

A second bloc of conservative restorationists—including Thomas and Scalia—also frequently endorse overturning earlier court decisions. They think liberal judges have undermined the original meaning of the Constitution, and they will strike down precedents to restore older legal traditions. Although Scalia in particular often favors allowing elected representatives to decide thorny issues such as abortion, the conservative bloc also shows a certain willingness to strike down liberal-minded legislation that they see as invasive of the private spheres of American life: family, church, club, and neighborhood.

Anthony Kennedy usually serves as a crucial swing vote on the court, as did his recently-retired colleague Justice Sandra Day O'Connor. Unlike the conservative and liberal activists, Kennedy often promotes **judicial restraint**, forcing the majority to soften written opinions or weakening those opinions by writing a softer concurrence. He also writes more than his share, because often the only way a majority can hold together is to conform to the preferences of its least enthusiastic members. One outgrowth of this restraint is that Kennedy often avoids overturning prior court decisions, sometimes sticking with precedents contrary to his conservative inclinations. He emphasizes the importance of maintaining the Supreme Court's integrity as a judicial body rather than a legislative one. "Do I make policy?" Kennedy once asked. "Was I appointed for life to go around . . . suggesting answers to the Congress? That's not our function."[53]

Ironically, it is often the moderates who produce the decisions most frustrating to those who must stay within the bounds of constitutional law. "Ruling from the center" often requires rather fine legal distinctions. Justice O'Connor allowed government bodies to erect Christmas holiday displays—but only if they do not appear to endorse Christianity.[54] She considered nude dancing a protected form of expression—but allowed a requirement that strippers wear partial covering as a means of limiting the negative social effects that crop up around strip clubs.[55] Sometimes the twists and turns of a moderate voting record can produce such a complicated body of constitutional law that it creeps disturbingly close to the type of policy detail customary in legislation.

Nevertheless, it is also striking how closely the Court's swing voters track the preferences of public opinion and how much their reasoning carries the flavor of common sense (although dressed up in a legalistic vocabulary). The moderate judicial position on abortion, for example, matches the ambivalent opinions expressed by the American public surprisingly closely (see Chapter 5). The moderates do not mind some religious influences in schools, as long as schools are not pushing religion on students. They do not mind if government considers race when shaping university admissions policies, as long as the process does not resemble racial quotas. It may be no coincidence that these are the sorts of compromises that one often hears proposed by regular voters. As Justice Kennedy once told an audience of European judges, "If you're interpreting phrases like 'liberty,' you have to do it in a way that commands the allegiance of the people."[56]

Evaluating Judicial Review

Disagreements about theories of judicial review or judicial activism are not just academic, despite the occasional inconsistency of particular judges. The manner in which a court interprets the Constitution can have serious consequences. The second time the Supreme Court declared a law of Congress unconstitutional, the 1857 case *Dred Scott v. Sandford*, helped precipitate the Civil War.

Liberals unhappy with the active application of judicial review like to point to the Supreme Court's role at blocking reform early in the twentieth century. *Lochner v. New York*, decided in 1905, struck down a New York state law limiting the number of hours bakers could work. A string of such decisions around that time helped limit state governments as a force for social change. After Franklin Delano Roosevelt became president in 1933, several conservative Supreme Court decisions helped slow the New Deal. *Schechter Poultry Corp. v. United States* (1935), for example, struck down the National Industrial Recovery Act, which managed labor and competition in the private sector.[57] Called the "sick chicken" case, it placed the Supreme Court squarely at odds with the president and Congress, creating a constitutional crisis.

If anything, conservatives unhappy with an aggressive judiciary find even more to criticize. Earl Warren's tenure on the Supreme Court, from 1953 to 1969, offers numerous controversial applications of judicial review—especially in criminal justice and federalism. Many critics blame the 1973 abortion case, *Roe v. Wade*, for igniting a political controversy that has plagued American politics ever since and wreaked havoc in both electoral and judicial politics.

The many examples of failure and controversy have led some voices in both politics and academia to argue that the country should abandon judicial review as undemocratic. Despite the debate, however, judicial review has become a well-established practice in American government. It survives in part because it is seldom used to defy the strongly held views of national leaders. Between 1803 and 2004, the Supreme Court decided that a federal law was unconstitutional on only 159 occasions.[58] Most of these decisions affected old laws that were no longer supported either by a majority of Congress or by the president. The Supreme Court spends much more time striking down state laws unpopular with a large segment, if not a majority, of the American public. The period after the "sick chicken" case mentioned above provides an extreme example of the Court bowing to electoral majorities. In the wake of a series of anti-New Deal decisions in the mid-1930s, President Roosevelt proposed to expand the size of the Court, appointing one new justice for each current justice over the age of 70. This "court-packing plan," which would have allowed FDR to stack the Court with his allies, provoked outrage among even the president's friends in Congress and was rejected. Still, beginning in 1937 the Court shifted its position and stopped striking down New Deal programs as unconstitutional.

Research indicates that changes in Supreme Court policy generally parallel swings in national public opinion. These policy shifts are not so pronounced as those in Congress, but justices still seem to pay "attention to what the public wants."[59] Unpopular decisions are the exception, not the rule. Bartender Mr. Dooley, an Irish cartoon figure, was not wide of the mark when he observed years ago that "th' supreme court follows th' illiction returns." Federal judges are key players in the election-driven political system.

Statutory Interpretation

Judicial review is only the most sweeping and controversial of judicial powers. The courts also engage in **statutory interpretation**, the application of the laws of Congress to particular cases. American courts have great discretion in exercising this power. For example, in 2007, the Supreme Court ruled that the Clean Air Act grants the Environmental Protection Agency the authority to regulate CO_2 emissions, which most scientists believe have contributed to global climate changes.[60]

Approaches to statutory interpretation parallel those for constitutional interpretation. Judges may stick to the written law, because this is what a legislature formally approved. They may use congressional speeches, the claims of a bill's authors, and the record of amendments accepted or rejected to determine a bill's intent. Or they may read legislation expansively, to keep the meaning current with modern sentiments. This latter approach is often as controversial as the parallel theory of constitutional interpretation; it means that a bill can clear Congress with few members endorsing the sweeping application to which federal courts will put it.

Checks on Court Power

Although court decisions have great impact, their consequences can be limited by other political actors. "Judicial decision making is one stage, not the only nor necessarily the final one," political scientist Jack Peltason explains.[61] Other branches of government can alter or circumscribe court decisions in two important ways: by changing the laws that courts interpret or by neglecting to implement their rulings.

Changing the law is difficult in constitutional cases. It requires amending the U.S. Constitution, which is an arduous process (see Chapter 2). Troublesome statutory interpretations are easier to address, because Congress can simply change the law or clarify it. In the case of *Wards Cove Packing Co. v. Atonio*, for example, the Supreme Court narrowly interpreted a law banning race and gender discrimination—requiring those bringing a complaint to prove they suffered mistreatment. Congress responded in 1991 by passing a law shifting the burden of proof to the accused, effectively overturning the Court's judgment. Even this approach to constraining court power is a limited one, however, because passing laws through Congress is so hard. Statutory interpretation favoring one side in a dispute gives that side the political advantage, because it is easier to block a bill than to pass one (see Chapter 9). The difficult process for passing new legislation may allow faulty statutory interpretations to persist for decades.[62]

The political branches also can check court decisions by ignoring them. When told of a Supreme Court decision he did not like, President Andrew Jackson reportedly replied, "Justice Marshall has made his decision, now let him enforce it."[63] Although outright refusal to obey a judicial decision is unlikely today, legislatures may drag their feet on enforcing rulings. After the Supreme Court declared Bible reading in public schools unconstitutional, for example, the practice continued unchanged in many southern school districts.[64]

State Courts

Every state has its own judicial arrangements. In most states the basic structure follows the same three tiers found in the federal system: trial courts, courts of appeals, and a court of last resort, usually called the state supreme court. State courts perform the same basic tasks as federal courts: interpreting state laws and determining when they contradict the state constitution. Decisions of state supreme courts may be appealed to federal courts, but generally only when a question of federal law appears in the case.

Trial Courts: The Judicial Workhorses

Most judicial activity takes place within state trial courts under the control of state and local governments, and these courts go by many different names in the various states (district courts, county courts, courts of common pleas, and so forth). In fact, 99 percent of all civil and criminal cases originate in these courts.

Going to Trial   The process of bringing civil and criminal cases before state and local courts is comparable to the federal process. In civil cases, most states follow rules similar to the federal code of civil procedure. Criminal cases, meanwhile, rely on state attorneys and law enforcement officers to bring perpetrators to justice.

Upon receiving information from the police on criminal wrongdoing, prosecutors in the office of the local **district attorney** determine whether the evidence warrants presentation before a grand jury for prosecution. In large cities, the district attorney has enormous responsibilities. In Los Angeles, for example, the district attorney's office prosecutes close to 300,000 cases a year.[65] Many prosecutors earn recognition that wins them election or appointment to the judiciary. Around one-third of state supreme court judges were once prosecutors.[66] Many local district attorneys are interested in moving to other elected offices as well.

In early 2000, Paul Howard, a Georgia district attorney, was up for reelection. He pressed for the arrest and trial of Baltimore Ravens football star Ray Lewis after two murders outside a suburban Atlanta bar. But prosecutors could find no evidence linking Lewis to the crime, and Lewis's attorney criticized them for "indicting before investigating."[67] After prosecutors dropped charges and released Lewis, some observers blamed the botched investigation on the district attorney's desire for notoriety. "Because Howard tried to ride to fame on the back of Ray Lewis," one critic wrote, "he has damaged—not enhanced—his chances for reelection."[68]

Elected Judges   State courts are influenced by political factors at least as much as are federal courts. In 39 of the 50 states, both appellate and trial judges are subject to election. In the remaining states, judges are appointed by the state legislature, the governor, or a governmental agency. Exactly which judges are elected varies from state to state. In New York, trial court judges are elected but appellate judges are appointed.[69] In Georgia, it is the reverse. Studies show that, at least on a few issues, elected state judges are more likely to follow closely the opinions of their constituents.[70]

Although many state judges are subject to election, most judicial campaigns "are waged in obscurity, with the result that most voters are unfamiliar with the names, not to speak of the issues, involved in the campaign."[71] As a result, judicial elections have traditionally been dominated by organized groups and party politicians interested in controlling court patronage.

Interest groups have also had a growing influence on judicial elections, especially as the cost of running campaigns for judgeships has increased. In Illinois in 2004, for example, the two candidates for a state supreme court seat raised and spent a total of $9.3 million.[72] Much of the money to fund judicial races is donated by single-issue groups, which some observers claim has resulted in intensified battles over rights and justice.

Relations Between State and Federal Courts

For the first few decades under the Constitution, the relationship between state and federal judicial systems remained vague. Then, in an early key decision, *McCulloch v. Maryland* (1819), the Supreme Court made it clear that the power of judicial review applied to state laws (see Chapter 3).[73] However, federal courts usually defer to how states choose to interpret their own laws and constitutional provisions. They rule only on whether the state's approach squares with federal requirements.

Over the decades, the Supreme Court has found more than 1,100 state and local statutes and constitutional provisions contrary to the federal Constitution.[74] It is not hard to see why the Supreme Court would have an easier time overturning state laws than it does tossing out congressional acts. Congressional legislation generally enjoys the support of a national majority, or at least a majority among national political leaders. Court action casting out a recent law will anger a large segment of elites in the other branches of government. By contrast, state laws reflect the tastes or preferences of a state majority, but the nation as a whole may not think much of regional opinion. The Supreme Court can undo such laws without

(text continues on page 363)

Election Voices

SHOULD JUDGES BE ELECTED?

Federal judges are appointed for life. Many state judges are appointed by governors and state legislatures without a ripple of public notice. But their rulings affect many of the most important and controversial issues in American politics, such as abortion, education policy, the rights of those accused of crimes, and even the conduct of anti-terrorism efforts. Should voters be more involved in the selection of state and national judicial branches?

Advocates of judicial elections say yes. They argue that elections increase the accountability of the judicial branch and make it less likely that judges will issue rulings that depart from common-sense interpretations of the law.[76] As evidence, they point to studies that show that, on at least several issues, elected state judges are more likely to mirror the opinions of their constituents.[77] Public outrage at state judicial rulings on issues such as same-sex marriage and education funding seem to support this perspective.

But advocates of judicial appointment object to this analysis, arguing that most elections for judgeships fail to attract the attention of the public, and therefore cannot help the court system become more accountable. Most judicial campaigns "are sedate and cordial," and voter turnout is low.[78]

A judge reviews her notes

Finally, judicial elections present a special problem for candidates for office. On the one hand, they must give the public some useful information with which to make a voting decision, but on the other hand, it would be wrong to comment on future cases that might come before the courts. Even raising money from interest groups and private citizens risks the appearance of impropriety if these groups or citizens might one day become litigants. "It raises a lot of ethical questions that are not there for the average person running for election," says one elected California judge.[79]

Defenders of elections respond that politics is always an issue in the selection of judges. When the president nominates a new justice to the Supreme Court, when a governor appoints a new judge to the state bench, and even when so-called "nonpartisan" commissions choose judges, political considerations are always present. At least if judges are elected, the public will have a say—not just interest groups and backroom deal-makers.

WHAT DO YOU THINK?

1. Should judges be appointed or elected?

2. All federal judges are appointed, but some judges in 39 states are elected. Are elections a better idea on the state level than they would be at the federal level?

3. Which types of rulings do you think would be the most affected by judicial elections, if any?

For more information on judicial elections, see the following Web sites:

National Center for State Courts
  www.ncsconline.org
The National Center for State Courts, an organization of state judicial officials, provides evaluations and reports on judicial selection.

American Judicature Society
  www.ajs.org
The American Judicature Society promotes merit selection of judges.

angering most of the country and, indeed, may even please those outside the region in question. One reason why the Supreme Court could take an active role promoting civil rights, for example, was that they primarily angered leaders in the South; most of those elsewhere felt little attachment to the southern system of race relations (see Chapter 14).

The same act can simultaneously be a violation of both state and federal laws. Although the Fifth Amendment to the Constitution forbids **double jeopardy**—being tried twice for the same crime—something very close to double jeopardy can occur if a person is tried in both federal and state courts for the same action. In 1897 the Supreme Court permitted dual prosecutions, saying "an act denounced as a crime by both national and state sovereignties is an offense against the peace and dignity of both."[75] In recent years, the chances for such prosecution have been rising, because Congress, under pressure to do something about crime, has passed new laws essentially duplicating state laws.

Most of the time, federal and state officials do not prosecute a case simultaneously; rather, they reach an agreement allowing one or the other to take responsibility for prosecuting a crime. (From this comes the popular phrase "Don't make a federal case out of it.") For example, the 1995 bombing of a federal building in Oklahoma, which killed 168 people, constituted a violation of both state and federal laws. Although state officials began the investigation, federal investigators quickly took charge, and Timothy McVeigh and Terry Nichols were convicted in federal courtrooms for the crime. State prosecutors jumped back on the Nichols case only when he failed to receive the federal death penalty. The 2002 "Tarot Card Sniper" case that terrorized people around Washington, D.C., set off a legal battle between the federal government and two states (Maryland and Virginia) over who would get to prosecute the arrested suspects, John Allen Muhammad, 41, and John Lee Malvo, 17. The two were eventually convicted of murder in both Maryland and Virginia.

CHAPTER SUMMARY

The courts are the branch of government most removed from political influence. Federal judges are appointed for life. They are expected to rely on legal precedents when reaching their decisions. Nevertheless, the courts are not immune to electoral pressures. The day-to-day work of the judiciary is carried out by state and lower federal court judges. Many state judges and district attorneys are elected officials.

Political factors even influence the way Court justices use their powers of constitutional and statutory interpretation. When justices are selected for the bench, both presidents and Congress closely evaluate their judicial philosophies. Once appointed, most Supreme Court justices decide cases in ways that are consistent with views they were known to have at the time of their selection. If court decisions challenge deep-seated political views, they may be modified by new legislation, stalled at the implementation stage, or even reversed by legislators. For all these reasons, popular influences reach even the most insulated branch of government in America's new democracy.

KEY TERMS

briefs, p. 342
Chief Justice, p. 336
circuit court of appeals, p. 340
civil code, p. 339
class action suits, p. 346
concurring opinion, p. 343
criminal code, p. 339
defendant, p. 339
dissenting opinion, p. 343
district attorney, p. 360
district courts, p. 338
double jeopardy, p. 363
judicial activism, p. 356
judicial restraint, p. 356
judicial review, p. 350

justices, p. 340
law clerks, p. 346
Marbury v. Madison, p. 351
opinions of the court, p. 343
plaintiff, p. 339
plenary session, p. 340
precedents, p. 343
remands, p. 344
remedy, p. 344
senatorial courtesy, p. 347
solicitor general, p. 345
stare decisis, p. 343
statutory interpretation, p. 359
U.S. attorney, p. 340
writ of *certiorari*, p. 341

SUGGESTED READINGS

Agresto, John. *The Supreme Court and Constitutional Democracy*. Ithaca, NY: Cornell University Press, 1984. Makes a powerful case against judicial review.

Carp, Robert A. and Ronald Stidham, The *Federal Courts*, 4th Edition. Washington, DC: CQ Press, 2001. Lucid description of the federal court system and its political context.

Epstein, Lee and Jeffrey A. Segal. *Advice and Consent: The Politics of Judicial Appointments*. New York: Oxford University Press, 2005. Timely and comprehensive study of federal judicial appointments.

Melnick, R. Shep. *Between the Lines: Interpreting Welfare Rights.* Washington, DC: Brookings, 1994. Insightful analysis of the Court's role in the interpretation and elaboration of statutory law.

Simon, James F. *The Center Holds: The Power Struggle Inside the Rehnquist Court.* New York: Simon & Schuster, 1995. Describes the recent split between conservative and moderate justices.

ON THE WEB

For more on the courts, see the following Web sites:

SUPREME COURT
www.supremecourtus.gov

The official Web site of the U.S. Supreme Court contains information on the Court's docket, the text of recent opinions, the rules of the Court, and links to related Web sites.

LEGAL INFORMATION SITE
www.findlaw.com

This all-purpose legal-information site includes various searchable databases and links.

FEDERAL JUDICIARY
www.uscourts.gov

The Federal Judiciary home page provides a concise guide to the federal court system, a regular newsletter, and annual reports on the state of the judiciary written by Chief Justice William Rehnquist.

DEPARTMENT OF JUSTICE
www.usdoj.gov/osg

The Solicitor General's Office in the U.S. Department of Justice offers copies of briefs it has filed in federal court cases.

Outputs from America's New Democracy

CHAPTER 13

Civil Liberties

WHEN MOST PEOPLE THINK OF GOVERNMENT SURVEILLANCE and spying, they think of the Central Intelligence Agency (CIA), based in Langley, Virginia, on the outskirts of Washington, D.C. But the largest U.S. spy agency is actually a 45-minute drive northeast, in a boxy, obsidian building in Fort Meade, Maryland: the National Security Agency (NSA).

Created in 1952, the NSA is charged with breaking enemy codes and eavesdropping on suspicious communications around the world. Its 30,000 employees are more likely to be experts on mathematics and cryptography than they are to be adept at disguise or misdirection.[1] They use these skills to sift through a mind-boggling 650 million intercepted communications per day, searching for patterns, contacts with suspicious persons, and other "red flags" that would signal terrorist plotting, espionage, and other threats against the United States.[2]

While Americans have always accepted the need to spy on those who might threaten the country, they have also been wary of allowing espionage agencies to operate unchecked. Zealous pursuit of foreign plotters can easily evolve into a determination to apprehend American criminals, and in turn lead to surveillance of innocent Americans. A cautionary tale on this note occurred in the 1960s and early 1970s, when the NSA and other agencies spied on such "subversives" as folk singer Joan Baez and civil rights activist Martin Luther King Jr.[3]

IS BIG BROTHER WATCHING?
The National Security Agency's Threat Operations Center monitors communications from around the world.
Should the government have the power to track communications between American citizens? What if time is of the essence?

Since that time, spy agencies have been prohibited by law from monitoring Americans without obtaining a warrant from a secret federal court, established under the Foreign Intelligence Surveillance Act (FISA) exclusively to handle such sensitive cases.

But in the age of terrorism, things may be changing. In late 2005, the *New York Times* revealed that, pursuant to an executive order from the Bush White House, the NSA had been wiretapping many (perhaps millions of) communications between American citizens and foreigners abroad without obtaining a warrant.[4] Grounding his justifications on Congressional enactments that authorized steps to be taken against al Qaeda terrorists, the president said "there's no doubt in my mind it is legal."[5] Months later, more press reports claimed that the NSA had worked with major telephone companies such as Verizon, AT&T, and BellSouth to compile a massive database of billions of domestic telephone records to be used in so-called "network analysis" that might reveal patterns that could lead to the uncovering of terrorist plots.[6]

Is this kind of monitoring acceptable? Some experts argued that it was essential in the new terror war, and did not unduly intrude into Americans' lives. "The architect of [the telephone records] program deserves our thanks and probably a medal," wrote one authority on terrorism, stressing that the phone records the NSA used were stripped of information that could easily identify individuals.[7] President Bush insisted that "the privacy of ordinary Americans is fiercely protected in all our activities."[8] Others argued that the White House and the NSA had gone too far. The telecommunications company Qwest said it had refused to hand over its records to the government because of privacy concerns.[9] Senator Hillary Clinton (D-NY) said she was "deeply disturbed" by news of the program.[10] Facing a legal challenge in 2007, the Bush administration changed course, saying it would submit future surveillance to the review of the special FISA court.

Many Americans—voters and government officials alike—seemed to need more time to consider whether programs such as this violated privacy guarantees. As Senator Arlen Specter put it, "We're really flying blind on the subject [right now] and that's not a good way to approach ... the constitutional issues involving privacy."[11] With continuing threats from terrorism, these issues seemed likely to linger on the public agenda.

The American public's apparent ambivalence about the domestic surveillance programs reflects a deeper tension between a desire to be firm in the punishment of transgression while at the same time preserving the liberties that were enshrined in the Bill of Rights. Americans dislike any tendency to "coddle" terrorists or criminals who face justice, and they fear that the presumption of innocence makes proving guilt so difficult that many dangerous offenders go free. The American system sets such a high barrier against tyranny that even clear-cut cases exact serious costs—whether measured in time, money, or emotional trauma. Those who supported the NSA wiretapping claimed that without new governmental surveillance, terrorists might use cell phones, the Internet, and other tools to carry out their schemes to commit murder on a massive scale. The cost of protecting civil liberties in this case seemed high indeed.

This debate over one aspect of liberty—the treatment of the accused—mirrors the debate over civil liberties more generally. Some critics complain that judges undermine popular will by abusing the Constitution's freedoms. They allow individuals to exploit their rights. By contrast, this chapter argues that constitutional rights seldom protect individuals from a committed majority. Rights can deteriorate in response to political demands. Federal judges often shift the meaning of constitutional guarantees to suit the times. Especially in America's new democracy, courts seldom step far out of line from what voters expect from their government.

Origins of Civil Liberties in the United States

The U.S. Constitution never mentions the concept of **civil liberties**—fundamental freedoms that protect a people from tyranny. Nor did those who drafted the Constitution include explicit protection for most individual liberties. When delegate Charles Pinckney offered a motion at the Constitutional Convention to guarantee freedom of the press, a majority voted the measure down—on the grounds that states should be responsible for regulating speech and the press.[12] Federalists only later agreed to protect civil liberties, when ratification of the Constitution seemed in danger (see Chapter 2).

Conversational English sometimes refers to these fundamental freedoms as "rights." Indeed, the first 10 amendments to the U.S. Constitution—which list some of the most cherished civil liberties—are called "The Bill of Rights." Do not confuse these freedoms with *civil rights* (considered in Chapter 14). Civil liberties promise *freedom from government interference*, whereas civil rights guarantee *equal treatment by the government*. The Supreme Court has shaped the scope and meaning of both civil rights and civil liberties over time, as have political debates and election outcomes.

Selective Incorporation

Initially, the Bill of Rights did not apply to state governments (or to the local institutions that states establish). Sometimes the limitation was explicit. The First Amendment, for example, focused solely on the national government, saying that "Congress shall make no law" restricting speech or religious freedom. State governments could do whatever their voters permitted. As a result, for example,

Massachusetts, Connecticut, and New Hampshire continued to support Congregationalist ministers with tax money for several decades.[13]

Many other provisions failed to mention the level of government to which they applied. For example, the Fifth Amendment said that "no person shall . . . be deprived of life, liberty, or property, without due process of law." But deprived by whom? Chief Justice John Marshall ruled, in *Barron v. Baltimore* (1833), that "These amendments contain no expression indicating an intention to apply them to the state governments. This court cannot so apply them."[14] The city of Baltimore had harmed Barron's Wharf by filling the water around it with debris and thereby preventing large ships from docking there, but Marshall declared that the **due process clause** of the Fifth Amendment only protected Barron's property from the national government.

Civil liberties expanded over time. The first step came in the aftermath of the Civil War, when the Constitution picked up three new **civil rights amendments**: the Thirteenth, which abolished slavery; the Fourteenth, which redefined civil rights and liberties; and the Fifteenth, which guaranteed voting rights to all adult, male citizens.* Most important for civil liberty was the due process clause of the Fourteenth Amendment. This clause applied the language of the Fifth Amendment to the states, saying that they could not "deprive any person of life, liberty, or property, without due process of law."

Of course, the due process clause is rather vague. States cannot take away freedoms "without due process," but does this mean they can do so "with due process"? In other words, can states restrict freedom as long as they follow a fair procedure? Or does the due process clause contain political substance, such that even a fair procedure may never revoke certain natural privileges?

Most federal justices have hedged on these questions. Initially, the Supreme Court limited the impact of the new due process clause, ruling that it restricted only state actions that were fundamentally unfair. Starting in the 1920s, however, the Supreme Court began "incorporating" various liberties into the meaning of the due process clause. The Court has never accepted the theory, promoted by justices such as John Marshall Harlan of Kentucky and Hugo Black of Alabama, that states must respect all civil liberties mentioned in the Bill of Rights. But over time it has applied most of those guarantees to state governments anyway, an approach known as **selective incorporation.**

States may still ignore a few provisions of the Bill of Rights, such as the Second Amendment's right to "bear arms." But the due process clause gave federal courts a strong new weapon to wield against state laws unpopular elsewhere in the country. In particular, federal courts have limited what state governments may do in the areas of (1) *free expression*, (2) *religious freedom*, (3) *privacy*, and (4) *criminal justice*.

---

* *Southern voters likely would not have passed these amendments given the choice, but ratification was one condition for rejoining the union, and occupation governments controlled many Southern states.*

Freedom of Expression

Of all the liberties listed in the Bill of Rights, one trio is paramount: freedom of speech, press, and assembly. These three rights, although distinct, are closely intertwined. They all promise that Americans may express political ideas freely.

Free expression is vital to conducting elections in a democratic society, because vibrant campaigning is impossible without it. Free expression is also necessary for social change, because otherwise citizens cannot present their visions of the good life or debate where society should go. Yet even elected governments sometimes infringe on free expression, especially if voters are intolerant themselves. The First Amendment therefore protects free expression against the intolerance of both ruler and ruled.

The classic defense of free speech was provided by English civil libertarian John Stuart Mill, who insisted that in the free exchange of ideas, truth eventually would triumph over error. But must society tolerate the spread of offensive or hateful views? Even in such cases Mill defends free expression, both to prevent scurrilous ideas from gaining strength under the cloak of secrecy and to remind people why they believe what they do. Mill's logic has not convinced everyone, though—Americans often have been punished, directly or indirectly, for expressing controversial thoughts.

The Evolution of Free Speech Doctrine

The Supreme Court generally has not protected speakers and writers from political majorities. Instead, the Supreme Court's view of what free speech entails has moved along at about the same speed as—or perhaps a little slower than—that of the rest of the country. Initially, free expression guaranteed only that a speaker or writer could deliver a message without officials censoring it first (the **prior restraint doctrine**). Nothing prevented the government from punishing the speaker or writer after the fact. Indeed, the source of a hostile message could be convicted for bringing the government's "dignity into contempt," even if the criticisms were true!

Clear and Present Danger   The first major Supreme Court decision affecting freedom of speech arose when the United States started conscripting soldiers to fight in World War I. Socialist Charles Schenck distributed a mailing urging draft-age men to resist their conscription into the armed forces. A jury convicted Schenck of violating the 1917 Espionage Act, which made it illegal to obstruct military recruitment. A unanimous Supreme Court accepted Schenck's conviction in *Schenck v. United States* (1919). Justice Oliver Wendell Holmes explained that free speech did not extend to messages posing a "clear and present danger" to the U.S. war effort. To justify speech restrictions, Holmes drew a famous analogy: No person, he explained, has the right falsely to cry "Fire" in a crowded theater.

Although the **clear and present danger doctrine** initially developed to justify censorship, it also implicitly limited what government might do. Congress could not regulate speech *unless* it posed a clear and present danger. The doctrine thus provided a foundation on which a tradition of free expression could build. Indeed, after facing widespread criticism for *Schenck*, Holmes was one of the first to liberalize his views. The Court heard a parallel case called *Abrams v. United States* (1919) less than a year later. Left-wing protesters, angry at the United States for intervening in Russia's revolution, had thrown antiwar leaflets to munitions workers from an upper-story window. This time Holmes split with the majority, no longer seeing sufficient danger in a "silly leaflet by an unknown man."

During the 1930s, when the public became more tolerant of dissenting opinion, the Supreme Court changed with the political climate. Two cases decided in 1931, *Stromberg v. California* and *Near v. Minnesota*, were particularly important in this regard. Yetta Stromberg had encouraged children attending a camp operated by the Young Communist League to pledge allegiance to the flag of the Soviet Union, a violation of California's "red-flag" law.[15] And the Minnesota legislature had shut down a newspaper for publishing "malicious, scandalous and defamatory" material. In both cases the Court endorsed free expression. Neither Stromberg nor the Minnesota newspaper constituted a clear and present danger, the Court explained.

Balancing Doctrine   The tolerance that emerged during the 1930s did not survive World War II. Congress responded to public outrage against fascism by enacting a new censorship law in 1940, the Smith Act. Instead of acting as a bulwark against majority tyranny, the Supreme Court again started endorsing limitations on free speech. Nor did the end of World War II automatically restore civil liberties. Instead, the nation went through a second "Red Scare" (see Chapter 4 for a discussion of the first one). People regarded as pro-Soviet suffered harassment by government officials. Senator Joseph McCarthy of Wisconsin gained political popularity by accusing artists, teachers, and government officials of having ties to the

MODERN WITCH HUNT
Senator Joseph McCarthy (at right) built a career in the 1950s on investigating alleged Communist sympathizers. *His methods outraged many and frightened many more, but should civil liberties be balanced against other important governmental interests, such as national security?*

Communist party. Anyone who wished to receive a student loan or work for the federal government had to take an oath swearing loyalty to the United States.

It was not judges, but elected leaders, who resisted the threat that McCarthyism posed to the country's civil liberties. A disgusted President Eisenhower refused to act on McCarthy's most outrageous accusations, and McCarthy's Senate colleagues finally inquired into the senator's methods of operation, later censuring him for his inappropriate conduct. The courts, on the other hand, showed little interest in protecting minority dissidents. Instead, the Supreme Court enunciated a **balancing doctrine**, which allowed courts to "balance" freedom of speech against other public interests. In *Dennis v. United States* (1951), 11 nonviolent Communist party leaders faced prison sentences for spreading writings that espoused the revolutionary overthrow of government. The Court ruled their convictions constitutional, arguing that the "balance . . . must be struck in favor" of the governmental interest in resisting subversion.

Fundamental Freedoms Doctrine   Public opinion eventually became more supportive of free-speech rights, even for radicals and communists (see Figure 13.1). Reflecting these changes in public opinion, the Supreme Court gradually developed the **fundamental freedoms doctrine**, the principle that some civil liberties are basic to the functioning of a democratic society and require vigorous protection.

The doctrine had rather modest origins. It appeared, almost as an aside, in a footnote to an unrelated 1938 Supreme Court opinion written by Justice Harlan Stone. His *Carolene Products* footnote said that some freedoms, such as freedom of speech, might deserve a "preferred position" in the Constitution because of their central importance to an electoral democracy. Any law threatening these liberties should receive strict scrutiny from the Supreme Court.[16]

The fundamental freedoms doctrine became the Supreme Court's governing principle during the Vietnam War. Under its guidance, the Court was more effective at defending dissenters against government repression than it had been in any previous war. As one civil libertarian wrote in 1973, "The truly significant thing in recent years has not been the attempt of the current administration to suppress criticism, but rather the marked inability of the administration to do so effectively."[17]

In virtually every case that came before it, the Court ruled against efforts to suppress free speech. For example, it would not allow the University of Missouri to expel a student for distributing a cartoon of a policeman raping the Statue of Liberty. Said the Court, "The mere dissemination of ideas—no matter how offensive to good taste—on a state university campus may not be shut off" in the name of decency.[18]

The Nixon administration inadvertently helped expand civil liberties by trying to grab too much power. It tried to justify censoring publication of a Defense Department report criticizing the war effort, but it could not convince a single Supreme Court justice that national security required prior restraint of the document.[19] Commonly called the *Pentagon Papers case*, this decision greatly advanced

FIGURE 13.1 Percentage opposed to allowing extremist groups to make a speech

The public has become more willing to grant rights even to extremists. *Do you believe that this is a sign that people are becoming more tolerant? Or is their changed attitude merely a reflection of the end of the Cold War?*

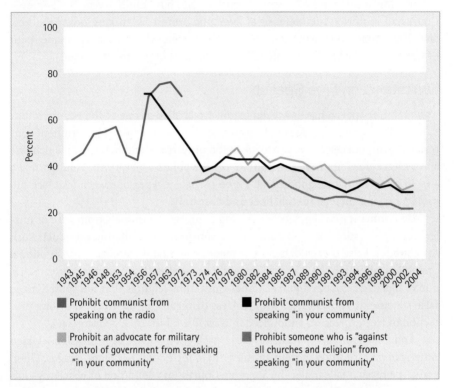

Prohibit communist from speaking on the radio

Prohibit an advocate for military control of government from speaking "in your community"

Prohibit communist from speaking "in your community"

Prohibit someone who is "against all churches and religion" from speaking "in your community"

Sources: Benjamin L. Page and Robert Y. Shapiro, *The Rational Public: Fifty Years of Trends in Americans' Policy Preferences* (Chicago: University of Chicago Press, 1992), p. 87; National Opinion Research Center, General Social Survey.

freedom of the press. In subsequent years, the Nixon administration's entanglement in the Watergate scandal served to reinforce both public and judicial support of civil liberties.

Symbolic Speech   Nothing better illustrates the contemporary Supreme Court's strong commitment to fundamental freedoms than its flag-burning decisions, which have enjoyed the support of both liberal and conservative justices.[20] During the 1984 Republican national convention in Dallas, a young radical named Gregory Johnson was arrested for burning an American flag to protest Reagan administration policies. Five years later, Johnson's case came before the Supreme Court. The Court, in *Texas v. Johnson* (1989), overturned his conviction, saying the principal purpose of free speech is to invite dispute; the mere burning of the flag was "expressive conduct" that did not breach the peace.[21]

Unlike earlier court decisions, the Supreme Court in the flag-burning case went well beyond popular opinion of the day. President George H. W. Bush angrily called for a constitutional amendment to prohibit flag desecration, and more than 70 percent of the public supported him. Almost immediately, Congress passed a law making it a federal offense to burn the flag, but within a year the Supreme Court had reaffirmed its defense of symbolic protest by striking down the new law.[22] The proposed constitutional amendment, meanwhile, has never made it out of Congress, although the Senate fell one vote short of passing it in 2006.

Limitations on Free Speech

Although free speech has now been firmly established as one of the country's fundamental freedoms, this does not mean that all speech is free of government control. Government certainly may regulate the time, place, and manner in which one speaks. One does not have the right to express political views with a bullhorn at 3 A.M. in a residential neighborhood. Three particular types of speech also lack full protection: commercial speech, libel, and obscenity.

Government may regulate advertising to protect consumers from false or misleading information, or to discourage the consumption of harmful products such as cigarettes. False speech defaming someone's reputation also lacks constitutional protection, although the standard depends on whether the victim is a private or a public figure. For public figures, a **libel** conviction requires that the source made false statements knowingly or with reckless disregard for the truth—a strong protection of free expression announced in *New York Times Co. v. Sullivan* (1964).

And the Court gives relatively little protection to sexual expression—which American culture finds more disturbing than, for example, violent images. Often sexual expression falls under the Supreme Court's 1973 definition of **obscenity**—offensive communications with no redeeming social value other than titillation. This determination, according to *Miller v. California* (1973), depends in part on local community standards.[23] Constitutional law provides, at best, minimal protection for obscenity.

On the other hand, the Court does not accept government regulations simply because they target sexual expression. Congress often tries to halt the proliferation of sexually explicit material by using minors as the justification, but the Court resists censorship that goes beyond what is necessary to protect children. For example, when Congress targeted Internet pornography by passing the Communications Decency Act of 1996, the Supreme Court ruled that the law was too broad; it regulated adult behavior more than necessary. Then, in 2002, it signaled that even a narrower law targeting pornographers might not meet constitutional standards. Another ruling prevented Congress from banning depictions of youthful sexuality that did not use real minors, because no child was victimized during production.[24]

(text continues on page 380)

Election Voices

DO CAMPUS SPEECH CODES UNDULY RESTRICT FREE SPEECH?

College campuses are supposed to foster creativity and intellectual growth. But since the 1980s, a majority of the nation's colleges and universities have attempted to adopt speech codes that proscribe faculty members and students' uttering offensive words or promoting unacceptable ideas.

Some argue that such codes are essential for intellectual activity to thrive on campus. Racist or sexist language, say proponents of speech codes, only serves to stifle discussion and put many students on edge. Take, for example, the true story of a farm-science professor who used a Playboy centerfold to illustrate different cuts of meat. Is this a legitimate exercise of freedom of expression, or is it offensive and punishable behavior?

Or take another example provided by Sharon Gwyn of Stanford University, who speaks from personal experience:

> *When I was in sixth grade, my teacher gave us the word "slavery" in a spelling test. He recited a sentence to clarify its meaning: "Sharon is lucky she is not in slavery." As my stomach began to lurch, my hands held tighter to my pencil. . . . My teacher merely smiled; he never apologized. . . . If I was hurt in a situation of that level, think of how the person who is the target of a racial epithet must feel.[59]*

A college classroom

Others maintain that offensive language and behavior, though sometimes painful, are part of intellectual growth. Says Jason Shepard, an openly gay student at the University of Wisconsin, "Racism, sexism, homophobia are all parts of our society, whether we like it or not. We can't erect a wall around our university and pretend those things don't exist."[60] Philosophy professor Lester Hunt agrees:

> *Some people, like me, teach subjects that concern all the hot-button areas—race, gender, you name it—and what the [speech] code does is threaten you with punishment if you say the wrong thing. That makes it difficult or impossible to teach these subjects effectively.[61]*

WHAT DO YOU THINK?

1. Should colleges and universities restrict certain types of speech on campus?
2. In 2006, professors and student groups at several colleges and universities generated controversy by displaying Danish cartoons of the Muslim prophet Muhammad that had sparked riots in the Middle East. Muslim students

(continued on next page)

found the images grossly offensive, but one professor justified her display of the cartoons as creating "a teaching moment."[62] With whom do you agree?

For more on free speech issues, see the following Web sites:

Foundation for Individual Rights in Education
www.thefire.org
Nonprofit organization that catalogs and opposes campus speech codes.

Tolerance.org
www.tolerance.org
Sponsored by the Southern Poverty Law Center, Tolerance.org opposes prejudice and intolerance on college campuses and elsewhere.

Freedom of Religion

Two clauses in the First Amendment guarantee religious freedom. Both appear in the same sentence: Congress shall make no law (a) respecting an establishment of religion, or (b) prohibiting the free exercise thereof. The **establishment clause** denies government the power to push religious practices on the citizenry. The **free exercise clause** protects the right of individuals to practice their religion. How the Supreme Court interprets these guarantees often depends on the political and electoral context in which it makes decisions.

The Establishment Clause

Few constitutional phrases have caused more difficulty than the ban on laws "respecting an establishment of religion." As discussed in Chapter 12, the language simply does not convey a clear meaning; judicial interpretation is necessary for the words to offer any protection at all. Perhaps for this reason, the relationship between church and state reveals numerous inconsistencies, sometimes allowing religion and government to mingle, sometimes not.

Federal judges cannot settle on a specific rule for determining when laws cross the line. Liberal judges generally embrace Thomas Jefferson's call for a strict separation of church and state. They prefer to keep government as far away from religion as possible, believing that to overlap the spheres would (1) corrupt churches by introducing political ambitions and (2) invite public officials to legislate moral codes, bullying those of different faiths.

The Lemon Test   In the late 1940s, when the Supreme Court first began probing the meaning of the establishment clause, liberals dominated the bench. Over the next 25 years the Court evolved a particular test for determining whether laws violate the Constitution. It is usually called the **Lemon test** after a 1971 case, *Lemon v. Kurtzman*, although the heart of the rule dates from earlier decisions. The Court (a) required all laws to have clear secular (that is, not religious) purposes, (b) did not permit laws to advance or inhibit either one religion or religion in general, and (c) considered it one sign of a religious establishment if the law entangled public officials with religious institutions or activities.*

Few people openly endorse the Lemon test these days. Even those who prefer a strong division between church and state recognize that federal courts have not done a very good job of applying *Lemon*.[25] Yet no ruling has ever cast out *Lemon* entirely, because its detractors cannot agree on a replacement. Instead, the evolution of case law has forced repeated modifications to how and when federal courts use the test.

The Coercion Test   Conservative judges generally read the establishment clause very narrowly: Government may not coerce citizens into pursuing religious practices. Permitting, encouraging, or even indirectly rewarding religion does not "establish" anything, so the Constitution does not forbid it. Some conservatives, such as Justice Antonin Scalia, openly embrace a government's use of moral judgments to construct law.[26] But religious conservatives have never been able to form a solid Court majority, so they win establishment clause cases only when they are willing to compromise with more moderate justices.

The closest conservatives have ever come to replacing the Lemon test may have been a 1992 case called *Lee v. Weisman*. Deborah Weisman's middle school, like so many public schools around the nation, permitted a prayer at the beginning of its graduation ceremony. Weisman objected to the practice, because it required her (1) to skip the ceremony, despite having earned her place there; (2) to rise and pray with everyone else, contrary to her religious beliefs; or (3) to opt out of the ceremony's prayer, in full view of her fellow students. She argued that the Constitution did not allow public schools to place students in such a position.

Conservatives seemed poised to win their long-running battle to constrict the establishment clause. So many schools featured graduation prayers, and had been doing so for such a long time, that public opinion weighed heavily against Weisman's complaint. Furthermore, Republican presidents had by that time appointed most of the justices on the Court. Conservatives apparently had the votes lined up.

Imagine their dismay when Justice Anthony Kennedy decided to abandon his conservative allies and write a 5-to-4 opinion against them! Kennedy ignored the Lemon test, explaining that Weisman's middle school had failed even if he applied a narrower reading of the establishment clause, one that required coercion.

---

* The significance of the Lemon test's third "prong" has varied over time. Recent modifications have demoted it from the Court's central approach to the establishment clause.

Avoiding the religious exercise would bring damaging peer pressure down on her, either because she skipped graduation or because she did not pray. Kennedy explained that a public institution could not bully a young girl using the force of local opinion.

Conservatives on the Court had lost their chance to unite behind a **coercion test** to replace *Lemon*. Bush appointees John Roberts and Samuel Alito appear skeptical of the Lemon test, but the Court has thus far declined to unite behind an alternative.

Religion in Schools   Public education especially aggravates the controversy surrounding church-state relations. Those who demand a strict wall between church and state generally fear that allowing religion in public schools will become an invitation for communities to promote their preferred faiths.

This fear is not ungrounded. Massachusetts passed the nation's first compulsory-schooling law in 1852 as a response to waves of Catholic immigrants pouring into Boston. The Boston School Committee openly declared that its purpose was to free Catholics from their "moral darkness."[27] As recently as 2000, the Supreme Court prevented a school district in Texas from hosting prayers before sporting events, in part because the District reportedly had worked to convert students by "promoting attendance at a Baptist revival meeting, encouraging membership in religious clubs, chastising children who held minority religious beliefs, and distributing Gideon Bibles on school premises."[28]

On the other hand, mandatory school attendance forces children out of their homes for much of the day. Many religious people believe that worship should be an ongoing part of a child's life, rather than just a diversion compartmentalized to evenings or weekends. They view education as going beyond reading and arithmetic to include teaching morality and values. Public institutions do not permit the type of values-based upbringing that some parents prefer, but often they cannot afford to take their children out of public schools, where children of diverse faiths must mingle. No one has found a feasible way for public schools to accommodate religious exercises without favoring particular forms of religion, nor is it clear that they could provide adequate spiritual guidance.

Evangelical religious groups, concerned by the growing secularization of society, have reacted to Court decisions by advocating an amendment to the Constitution that would allow prayer in schools. A majority of the public have said they support such an amendment,[29] and Republican presidential candidates have generally campaigned in favor of its adoption. But supporters have been unable to win the necessary two-thirds vote in Congress. The Supreme Court has been more responsive, ruling in 1990 that students may form Bible-reading or school prayer clubs if other clubs are allowed to use school property.[30] Banning religious groups while allowing secular ones to organize infringed upon students' rights to free exercise of their religion, a subject to which we now turn.

The Free Exercise Clause

If the establishment clause seems to bar state involvement in religion, the free exercise clause seems to instruct states to accommodate religious practices. This mandate is equally hard to apply, however, for three general reasons: (1) Someone has to decide when a set of beliefs qualifies as a "religion" rather than just a personal preference. (2) Someone has to decide when a law really infringes on core religious exercises rather than just on customs. (3) Someone has to decide what to do when religious beliefs interfere with governmental efforts to protect other constitutional values.

Sorting out these three dilemmas places federal courts in an impossible position. They are not qualified to define religions. Yet allowing elected officials to define them could undercut constitutional protections: Popular faiths would be "religions," while unpopular faiths would be "cults" or merely "philosophies." Allowing individuals to define their own religions, meanwhile, could turn every disagreeable law into a constitutional violation. Imagine the religions that would appear! The Church of No Taxes, the Church of Marijuana Smoking, the Church of Running Red Lights—the possibilities are endless. And the same difficulty arises when determining a religion's core practices. Courts are not qualified to define the central tenets of a faith, but they cannot trust elected officials, church leaders, or individual worshippers to do so either.

The Sherbert Test   On the matter of balancing religious free exercise against other governmental interests, liberals and conservatives once again differ on how stringently to apply the First Amendment. Around the same time they developed

ESTABLISHMENT OR FREE EXERCISE?
First-graders pray in a South Carolina school in 1966. *How does the Supreme Court decide whether such activities constitute state-sponsored religion, or whether they simply allow students to freely exercise their faith?*

the core of the Lemon test, liberals formulated another three-prong formula—the **Sherbert test**—to determine when a law unconstitutionally violates the free exercise clause. The test took formal shape in *Sherbert v. Verner* (1963), a case that focused on whether workers could apply for unemployment benefits if they gave up work because it fell on a holy day. Limits on religiously motivated action, or compulsions to engage in religiously prohibited action, had (a) to promote a secular (that is, nonreligious) goal that was (b) a compelling governmental interest and to do so (c) in the manner least restrictive to religious practices.[31]

The Neutrality Test The Sherbert test had a limited lifespan. Writing for a conservative majority in *Oregon v. Smith* (1990), Justice Scalia threw out *Sherbert* to rule that the free exercise clause did not protect ritual use of the drug peyote by members of the Native American Church. When government passes a neutral, generally applicable law to prevent criminal behavior, Scalia explained, individuals cannot claim a religious exemption. Congress took issue with this **neutrality test**, however, passing an act that protected religious practices even if a seemingly neutral law would prohibit them. Although the Supreme Court ruled that the act applies only to federal government activity, it did decide in 2006 that a Brazil-based church ought to be allowed to use a hallucinogenic tea as a sacrament.[32]

Free Exercise and Public Schools Once again, religious freedom often arises in the context of education policy. The Court protects private religious schools from hostile action by state legislatures. But popular impulses sometimes push the Court to allow interference with religious practices.

Two flag-salute cases provide a good example of how the Court shifts with the times. In 1940, with war breaking out in Europe and patriotic fervor on the rise, the Court upheld a Pennsylvania statute requiring that Jehovah's Witnesses salute the American flag in public school ceremonies, even though their religion forbids revering a government symbol. The Court said that schools could interfere with religious liberty in this case, because saluting the flag promoted "national unity, [which] is the basis of national security."[33] Only one justice dissented.[34]

Just three years later, times had changed. Not only did the earlier flag-salute case stir up extensive mob violence against Jehovah's Witnesses, which brought shame on the Court, but experiences with Nazism lessened American ardor for forced patriotism. "Compulsory unification of opinion," wrote Justice Robert Jackson, when reversing the previous flag-salute ruling, "achieves only the unanimity of the graveyard."[35] Behind him were three justices who had ruled on the opposite side just three years before. Like guarantees of free expression, the religious freedom clauses evolve with public opinion.

Establishment of Religion or Free Exercise? At times judges have been faced with tough decisions that balance the establishment clause against the free exercise clause. The debate over school choice is one such instance. Many Republicans, including President George W. Bush, favor giving vouchers to families that would allow parents to choose to send their children to public schools or private schools—even if the private schools are affiliated with a religion.

Proponents of this system claim that vouchers do not violate the establishment clause because parents, not the government, decide where money gets directed. In fact, they say, the government is promoting free exercise of religion by giving parents a choice they might not otherwise possess. But many Democrats argue that when parochial schools are eligible to receive vouchers, the government is indirectly advancing religion.

The Supreme Court ruled in the 2002 case of *Zelman v. Simmons-Harris* that a small voucher program serving low-income families in Cleveland did not violate the Constitution, even though most students in the program attended private Catholic schools. The Court accepted the voucher advocates' argument that the Ohio parents freely chose whether to send their children to private or public institutions.

The Right to Privacy

The civil liberties discussed so far in this chapter—freedom of expression and freedom of religion—trace back to a specific provision in the Bill of Rights. Not all freedoms recognized by the courts appear in the Constitution, however. Indeed, the Ninth Amendment explicitly recognizes that the people retain rights not listed in the document. The most controversial unlisted right recognized by the Supreme Court is the **right to privacy**.

Privacy, as a legal concept, has evolved over time. Originally, the right to be "left alone" represented an ability to prevent others from spreading details about one's private life. A famous 1890 essay by Samuel Warren and Louis Brandeis publicized the need to protect people from "the evil of invasion of privacy by the newspapers."[36] The word's meaning changed as judges sought a concept to defend personal autonomy, which Americans increasingly valued after World War II. Privacy now means the right to be free of public interference in personal life choices.

Contraception

The modern right to privacy owes its genesis to the Supreme Court's ruling in *Griswold v. Connecticut* (1965).[37] Estelle Griswold, executive director of the Connecticut chapter of Planned Parenthood, was fined $100 for violating a state law prohibiting the use of contraceptives. Justice William O. Douglas did not see any way for government to enforce such a law without intruding on the relationship between husbands and wives, so he declared the law unconstitutional on the basis of "a right of privacy older than the Bill of Rights." His approach to privacy was similar to the old-fashioned concept, because it emphasized keeping personal details out of the public eye. "Would we allow the police to search the sacred precincts of marital bedrooms for telltale signs of the use of contraceptives?" asked Douglas. "The very idea is repulsive to the notions of privacy surrounding the marriage relationship."[38]

A second contraceptives case represented a bigger conceptual leap. This time the Court faced a Massachusetts law that banned the sale of contraceptives rather than their use. The old notion of privacy could not apply here. Governments may not be able to regulate the personal relationships inside a family, but they regulate what businesses sell all the time. So Justice Brennan, who was assigned to write the opinion, sought a new reason for striking down laws against contraception. His solution in *Eisenstadt v. Baird* (1972) was to adapt the "right to be left alone": It no longer merely prevented government from exposing private details, but actually prevented government from trying to influence those details. Privacy had changed to mean personal autonomy rather than just secrecy.[39]

Abortion Rights

When Brennan wrote his *Eisenstadt* opinion, he was thinking about more than just condoms and the pill. He also had his eye turned toward a related set of cases on the Supreme Court docket: those dealing with abortion. Chief Justice Warren Burger had assigned the abortion cases to newly appointed Justice Harry Blackmun, an expert in medical law thought to be mildly conservative. Brennan did not wish to steal the chore away from Blackmun; as the Court's high-profile Catholic justice, he knew that someone else had better announce abortion rights. But Brennan did want to help steer Blackmun to a strong ruling in favor of the right to obtain an abortion. Brennan's approach to privacy in *Eisenstadt* was tailor-made for the issue.[40]

Blackmun's *Roe v. Wade* (1973) decision appeared the next year, guaranteeing at least a partial right of abortion. The case arose out of a request from Norma McCorvey, who used the pseudonym Jane Roe. She asked for a judgment declaring Texas anti-abortion laws unconstitutional. Blackmun grouped the decision of whether to give birth to a fetus under the privacy rubric created by Douglas and Brennan, and allowed state interference only when public interest in the potential life became compelling—that is, when the pregnant woman was close to term.

The *Roe* decision arrived near the end of America's "sexual revolution" and so enjoyed substantial support from parts of the U.S. population. Many others ardently opposed the Supreme Court's decision, which had struck down anti-abortion laws across the nation. *Roe v. Wade* launched a powerful political crusade, the right-to-life movement, dedicated to banning abortion again. Supporters became actively engaged in state and national politics, lobbying legislatures and courts to impose as many restraints on abortion as the courts would allow.

Responding to right-to-life groups, Congress in 1976 enacted legislation prohibiting coverage of abortion costs under government health insurance programs, such as Medicaid. In 1980 the Republican party promised to restore the "right to life," and in subsequent years, Republican presidents began appointing Supreme Court justices expected either to reverse *Roe v. Wade* or to limit its scope. The Court began accepting restrictions on abortion. For example, in 1980 the Court upheld the congressional act prohibiting abortion funding.[41] In 1989 it ruled that states could require the doctor to ascertain the viability of a fetus before permitting an abortion, if the woman were 20 or more weeks pregnant.[42] By 1990 judicial observers believed that four justices on the Supreme Court were prepared to overturn *Roe* and that any new appointment by a Republican president would create the majority needed.

As the right-to-life movement gained momentum and it became more likely that *Roe v. Wade* would be overturned, the right-to-choose movement also gained strength and aggressiveness. By 1984 it was able to secure the Democratic party's commitment to the right-to-choose principle. Both sides of the controversy waited anxiously for the 1992 court decision in *Planned Parenthood v. Casey.*[43] Planned Parenthood had challenged a Pennsylvania law restricting abortion in numerous ways. Right-to-life groups hoped and right-to-choose groups feared that the Court would return authority for abortion law to the states. The majority ultimately decided against taking such a dramatic step, however. Justice O'Connor's opinion explicitly refused to overturn *Roe v. Wade*, although she allowed numerous restrictions on and regulations of the abortion procedure, as long as they did not place an "undue burden" on women trying to exercise their constitutional right.

Either by accident or by design, the Court majority once again adopted a position very close to that of the average American voter. It permitted restrictions endorsed by a majority of voters (such as a requirement that a teenager obtain parental consent) but rejected those most people consider unwarranted (such as a requirement that a married woman obtain the consent of her husband). In 2007, the Court upheld a widely-supported federal law banning a rare and particularly extreme abortion procedure (so-called "partial birth abortion").[44] Even in matters as sensitive as the right of privacy, the Court seems to be influenced by majority opinion.

Gay Rights

There is little doubt that most Americans thought a married couple should be able to use contraceptives, and a large chunk of the U.S. population wanted to liberalize abortion laws. Early privacy cases therefore did not require the Court to stand alone

CELEBRATING A LANDMARK RULING
Activists celebrate the Supreme Court's 2003 ruling in *Lawrence v. Texas,* which declared antisodomy laws unconstitutional. *Which provisions in the Constitution provide the basis for a right to privacy?*

against a large popular majority. In 1986, however, *Bowers v. Hardwick* presented a more difficult constitutional claim: the claim that privacy rights prevented Georgia from prohibiting sodomy between two consenting homosexuals.

The Court declined to buck popular hostility to homosexuality, even though the privacy logic used to allow contraceptives and abortions seemed to apply to intercourse between same-sex adults. Noting that laws against sodomy—that is, anal or oral sex—existed at the founding, the Court majority found no reason to think that privacy rights exempted homosexual behavior from regulation. Not every state took advantage of the Court's weakened stance on privacy rights; many ruled that their state constitutions offered a stronger right to privacy than that found in the U.S. Constitution.[45] But the Court's decision did allow various sexual regulations to stand on the law books, including bans on sodomy of any sort (even between married couples) in 13 states.

Public opinion eventually intervened. In 1986, when *Bowers* was decided, a majority of those surveyed believed that homosexual relations should be outlawed. But by 2001, polls found that Americans favored legalizing homosexual behavior by a margin of 54 to 42 percent. Similarly, 85 percent of people thought gays and lesbians should have equal rights in the workplace—a figure up more than 25 percentage points from the early 1980s. The *Bowers* precedent could not last long. In fact, the 2003 decision of *Lawrence v. Texas* repudiated *Bowers* and extended privacy rights to include sodomy. The Court only achieved a consistent privacy doctrine when the public permitted it.[46]

Criminal Justice

We end where we began: with the criminal justice system. Elections also affect court interpretations of the procedural rights of the accused. Rights of the accused vary with social currents, with the dictates of public opinion. Barriers to criminal arrest and prosecution emerged during a period in which Americans were terribly suspicious of authority, but then they broke down again as the American public tired of the impositions that criminal behavior inflicted on their lives.

Rights of the Accused

The way the criminal justice system treats suspects underwent radical alteration during the 1960s. The Supreme Court, under the leadership of Chief Justice Earl Warren, issued a series of decisions that substantially extended the meaning of the Bill of Rights. It specifically broadened the interpretation of five constitutional provisions, discussed in this section: (a) protection from unreasonable search and seizure, (b) immunity against self-incrimination, (c) right to an impartial jury, (d) right to legal counsel, and (e) protection from double jeopardy. Eventually the Warren Court provoked a backlash among voters, who were angry about criminals "getting off on technicalities." An increasing number of voters began to favor rigorous enforcement of laws and harsh punishments for criminals (see Figure 13.2).

Court procedures soon became a campaign issue, and many who sought office called for tougher law enforcement. Richard Nixon's successful 1968 campaign was the first to provoke what has become known as a "law and order" election. Since then, the issue has arisen in both national and local campaigns. Both mayors Rudolph Giuliani and his successor Michael Bloomberg of New York City were elected partly on the basis of their promises to be tough on criminals. In the 2004 campaign, President Bush, who had presided over numerous executions as governor of Texas, faced Senator John Kerry, who touted his record as a local prosecutor in the 1970s. Both candidates called for tough criminal penalties and for more attention to be paid to the rights of crime victims in legal proceedings.

The Supreme Court has responded to changing political circumstances, tempering its decisions on the rights of the accused without actually overturning

FIGURE 13.2   Most people think courts should be tougher on criminals

Although still strongly in favor of law and order, Americans no longer support tough criminal penalties at the rate they did a decade ago. *Why has support for the death penalty dropped in recent years?*

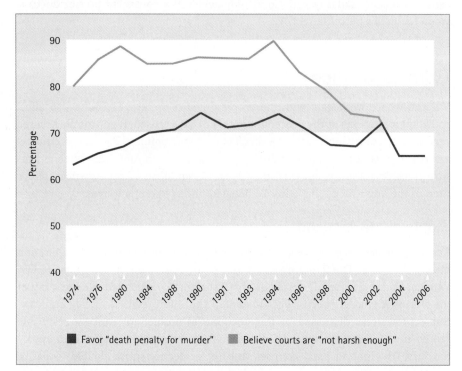

■ Favor "death penalty for murder"   ▨ Believe courts are "not harsh enough"

Source: Benjamin I. Page and Robert Y. Shapiro, *The Rational Public: Fifty Years of Trends in Americans' Policy Preferences* (Chicago: University of Chicago Press, 1992), p. 92; National Opinion Research Center, General Social Survey; Quinnipiac University Poll, February 26–March 3 2003; ABC News/Washington Post Polls., June 23–26, 2005, June 22–25, 2006.

them. One side effect of this stance has been an exceptionally high incarceration rate in the United States (see Figure 13.3).

Search and Seizure   Police may not search homes without a court first granting them a search warrant based on evidence that a crime has probably been committed. The Warren Court established an **exclusionary rule** in *Mapp v. Ohio* (1961): Improperly obtained evidence cannot be presented during a trial.[47] Conservatives on the Court have limited the scope of the exclusionary rule, however. For example, the Court exempted college dormitories from the rule's protection in 1982.[48] Lacking an official warrant may not invalidate police searches conducted in "good faith," according to a line of cases starting with *United States v. Leon* (1984). The Court has relaxed the exclusionary rule when officers use a warrant based on the wrong paperwork and when they accidentally apply a warrant to the wrong person or the wrong apartment.[49]

FIGURE 13.3 A "lock 'em up" mentality?

The United States imprisons a far larger proportion of its citizens than most other industrialized countries do. Arrests in the so-called drug war are a major source of America's large prison population; even limited drug possession can lead to years of incarceration. *Does the United States imprison so many people because law enforcement officials catch more criminals or because the United States is less tolerant of deviant behavior?*

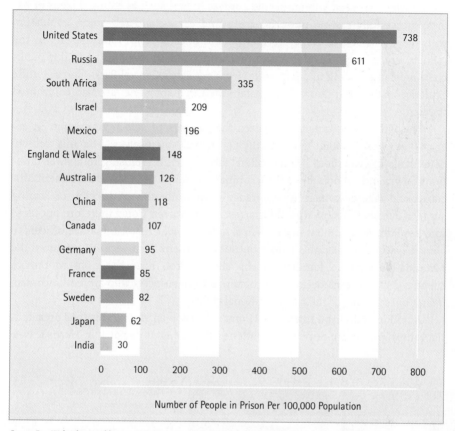

Number of People in Prison Per 100,000 Population

Source: Roy Walmsley, *World Prison Population List* (7th ed.), King's College, London, International Centre for Prison Studies, January 2007.

On the other hand, the Supreme Court has interpreted the guarantee against warrantless searches fairly broadly, to include electronic surveillance such as wiretaps. One recent 5–4 decision, surprising in light of the Court's general sympathy with the war against drugs, defended home owners against sophisticated technologies that can "search" their homes from the outside. The Supreme Court ruled, in *Kyllo v. United States* (2001), that police needed a warrant to scan someone's house with thermal imaging equipment, which is used to detect the presence of halide lamps needed to grow marijuana plants indoors.[50]

Self-Incrimination   People often confess to crimes they have not committed. The reasons for this puzzling behavior no doubt vary: fear or exhaustion during interrogation, the desire to avoid more serious accusations, uncertainty about the implications of an accusation, or the desire for attention or publicity. The most famous example comes from centuries of witch trials in Europe and the Americas, during which accused women would confess to sins such as eating dozens of babies, successfully casting powerful spells and curses, and repeatedly copulating with the devil. The tendency to incriminate oneself falsely still appears in the modern era, though. Several young men confessed, in 1989, to the highly publicized rape and beating of a jogger in New York City's Central Park—but scientific evidence analyzed in 2002 clearly established that someone else had committed the crime.

The Fifth Amendment recognizes the dangers of self-incrimination. It exempts accused persons from testifying against themselves. For this reason, defendants in courtroom dramas often "take the Fifth," refusing to answer questions on grounds of possible self-incrimination. At one time, law enforcement officials could take advantage of ignorance of civil liberties by tricking or scaring suspects into confessing after their arrests. The Warren Court therefore put teeth into the Fifth Amendment in *Miranda v. Arizona* (1966), requiring police officers to alert suspects to their rights before questioning them. This decision produced the **Miranda warning** so familiar in cop shows: "You have the right to remain silent. . . ." Courts exclude evidence obtained from suspects who are not informed, before questioning, of their constitutional rights.

After Richard Nixon made the *Miranda* decision an issue in his 1968 presidential campaign, the Supreme Court softened the ruling. It decided, in *Harris v. New*

THE RIGHT TO REMAIN SILENT
Police officers inform suspects of this and other rights as a result of the *Miranda v. Arizona* case. In reaffirming this ruling, the Supreme Court argued that the warnings are "part of our national culture." *What role does the national culture play in affecting Supreme Court decisions?*

York (1971), that information gathered in violation of the *Miranda* decision may be introduced as evidence when defendants testify on their own behalf. But the Supreme Court declined to throw out *Miranda* in a 2000 decision authored by Chief Justice Rehnquist, usually a hard-liner against rights of the accused. Rehnquist's 7-to-2 decision pointed out that "*Miranda* has become embedded in routine police procedure to the point where the warnings have become part of our national culture."[51]

Impartial Jury   The requirement that a jury be impartial is difficult to meet when crimes become newsworthy, because most potential jurors witness media accounts of the alleged crime before and during the trial. The Warren Court considered these issues in *Sheppard v. Maxwell* (1966), a case in which police accused an influential medical doctor of murdering his wife. (The story became the basis for two television shows and a movie, all called *The Fugitive*.)

Sam Sheppard complained about the excessive news coverage jurors witnessed. Journalists even sat in the courtroom, where they could listen in on Sheppard's conversations with his attorneys.[52] The Supreme Court overturned his conviction and provided guidelines to ensure impartial juries in the future. Judges can postpone trials or transfer them far away from the initial crime to lower public awareness. Timothy McVeigh's trial for the Oklahoma City bombing in 1995, for example, changed "venue" from Oklahoma to Colorado. Judges can "sequester" juries during a trial, keeping them away from external sources of information, as happened with jurors in the O. J. Simpson murder trial. Jurors also should be questioned to screen out those with fixed opinions and should be instructed to rule out any prejudices in the case derived apart from evidence presented in a trial.[53]

Although the Supreme Court has never reversed these constitutional safeguards designed to prevent a biased jury, some later decisions weakened them. The Court's decision in *Nebraska Press Association v. Stuart* (1976) is just one example of how criminal justice law has reflected the country's more conservative mood, as well as a recognition that excluding citizens who stay informed of current events may not be healthy for the jury system. It ruled that "pre-trial publicity—even pervasive, adverse publicity—does not inevitably lead to an unfair trial."[54]

Legal Counsel   The Warren Court ruled in *Gideon v. Wainwright* (1963) that all citizens accused of serious crimes, even the indigent, must have access to proper legal advice. When the accused are too poor to hire attorneys, then the Sixth Amendment right to counsel requires courts to appoint legal representation.

It was easier to enunciate this right than to put it into practice. At one time, courts asked private attorneys to donate their services in order to defend the poor (so-called "pro bono" work). But donating time to help suspected crooks was not popular among members of the legal profession. As a result, states have created the office of **public defender**, an attorney whose full-time responsibility is to provide for the legal defense of indigent criminal suspects.

This solution has its own problems, though. The public trend toward strong anticrime views directly undercuts the right to counsel by influencing the budgets and prestige that accompany the job. The job of a public defender is thankless, pay is low, and defenders must deal with "rotten case after rotten case."[55] From the perspective of the police, defenders simply throw up roadblocks to prevent conviction of the guilty. Talented and ambitious lawyers usually will avoid the job, because defending the accused is politically unpopular and certainly not lucrative.

Double Jeopardy The Warren Court ruled in *Benton v. Maryland* (1969) that states cannot try a person twice for the same offense, thereby placing the defendant in **double jeopardy**. The purpose was to prevent law enforcement officials from wearing someone down by repeated prosecutions.

This rule does not prevent prosecution in both federal and state courts for the same crime, as long as it violates multiple laws. Prosecution by both levels of government is most likely in high-visibility cases, in which political considerations may play a role. For example, when the state of California could not win a conviction of four police officers charged with beating a young black man named Rodney King, federal prosecutors went after the officers and won two convictions. Oklahoma courts tried to pin murder charges on Timothy McVeigh's co-conspirator, Terry Nichols, because a federal jury gave him only life imprisonment for his lesser role in the Oklahoma City bombing.[56]

Capital Punishment

The Eighth Amendment prohibits "cruel and unusual punishment." Convicted criminals may not face torture, grotesque forms of execution such as crucifixion and burning at the stake, or sentences grossly disproportionate to the legal violations committed.

Starting in the nineteenth century, the morality of capital punishment itself came under question. This movement gained widespread support in the 1960s, resulting in a push by various interest groups (such as the American Civil Liberties Union and the National Association for the Advancement of Colored People) to classify executions of any sort as "cruel and unusual."

No Supreme Court majority has ever declared capital punishment, in and of itself, a violation of the Eighth Amendment. On the other hand, at various times the Court has thrown out death penalties when they resulted from a system that imposed capital punishment unfairly or arbitrarily. Executions in the United States virtually halted for 15 years as states grappled to find a constitutional means of applying the death penalty (see Figure 13.4). The Court's opinions initially provided

FIGURE 13.4 Executions in the U.S. 1930–2006

Why do you think executions were more common in the 1930s than they are today?

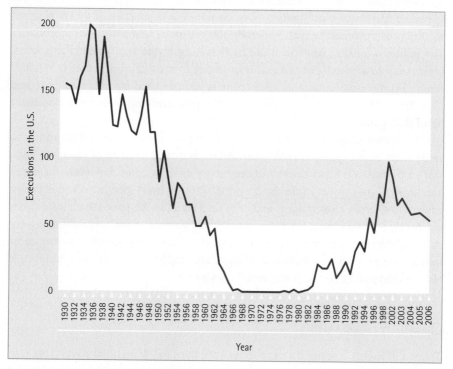

Source: U.S. Department of Justice, Bureau of Justice Statistics, Capital Punishment Statistics, www.ojp.usdoj.gov/bjs/cp.htm, accessed February 4, 2007.

little guidance because justices could not unite behind a majority opinion. The five justices who threw out Georgia's system of capital punishment in 1972, for example, wrote five separate opinions! But the states eventually found capital-punishment procedures that the U.S. Supreme Court would allow.

Executions picked up again in the 1980s. The federal courts reflected public support for law and order, as well as for the death penalty itself, by refusing to block as many capital sentences. The Court also issued various rulings that helped speed up the application of capital sentences. But the issue has never been settled, and public opinion leaves officials with some room to maneuver. In 2002, the Supreme Court gave opponents of the death penalty cause for hope by ruling in *Atkins v. Virginia* that states cannot execute the mentally retarded. In 2005 the Court continued along the same lines by invalidating the death penalty for those who were under the age of 18 when their crimes were committed.[57] The Court has also ruled that only juries may issue death sentences; judges may not.

Rights in Practice: The Plea Bargain

Although those accused of crimes enjoy numerous rights on paper, it is important to realize that these civil liberties often do not exist in practice. If a case is newsworthy, prosecutors and courts generally observe proper constitutional procedures: The public is looking on, and those participating in the trial must take political pressures into account. But the reality of justice in most criminal cases is very different. Hardly anyone accused of a crime is actually tried by a jury. The accused have their rights, to be sure, but most of the time invoking them would do more harm than good.[58]

Trial court judges depend on the willingness of prosecutors and defenders to settle cases before going to trial. The number of people accused of crimes is high, the list of cases on court dockets is seemingly endless, court personnel resources are limited, and court time is precious. Judges must preside over efficient courtrooms, settle cases quickly, and keep dockets short. To speed the criminal justice process, a defender and a prosecutor usually arrange a **plea bargain**—an agreement between prosecution and defense that the accused will admit to having committed a crime, provided that other charges are dropped and a reduced sentence is recommended. That is, most suspects "cop a plea."

CHAPTER SUMMARY

The Bill of Rights remained a dead letter until the Civil War ended slavery, because state governments did not have to honor the Constitution's civil liberties protections. Eventually, though, federal courts used the Fourteenth Amendment's due process clause to protect civil liberties in the states.

Although the founders hoped courts would protect individual rights against majority tyranny, most of the time the Supreme Court follows public opinion. This is true in most areas of constitutional law: free expression, religious freedom, privacy rights, and protection of the accused. Some examples of Court sensitivity to public opinion date back to the early twentieth century, including the Court's fluctuations on the clear and present danger doctrine between war time and peace time and its rapid reversal in the flag-salute cases. But sensitivity to public opinion seems heightened in America's new democracy.

The Warren and early Burger Courts responded to America's postwar liberalism by expanding civil liberties in many areas. The Court embraced free expression as a fundamental freedom central to the democratic system. It evolved three-prong tests to determine when laws violated the First Amendment's establishment clause or free exercise clause. It altered the meaning of privacy to increase personal autonomy and to protect individual decisions from public intervention. And it sought mechanisms to give teeth to constitutional provisions protecting those accused of criminal behavior.

The public has since become more conservative in various respects, and the Court has responded by pulling back somewhat from Warren Court precedents. This retreat is least pronounced for free speech, because several prominent Republican appointees (especially Scalia and Kennedy) continue to defend political expression. But current law on religious freedom no longer follows the Warren Court approach, perhaps most easily remembered as the "Lemon Sherbert" era (after the two tests that dominated the period). Now the United States is stuck with the Lemon, and a modified one at that. Privacy rights provide less protection for abortion than they once did, and they did not shield consenting adults who engaged in sodomy until 2003. Finally, law enforcement officials enjoy increasing power over those suspected of criminal behavior. The country's definition of civil liberties seems to depend as much on the thinking of its citizens as on judicial principles.

KEY TERMS

balancing doctrine, p. 375
civil liberties, p. 372
civil rights amendments, p. 373
clear and present danger doctrine, p. 374
coercion test, p. 381
double jeopardy, p. 393
due process clause, p. 372
establishment clause, p. 378
exclusionary rule, p. 390
free exercise clause, p. 378
fundamental freedoms doctrine, p. 376

Lemon test, p. 380
libel, p. 378
Miranda warning, p. 392
neutrality test, p. 383
obscenity, p. 378
plea bargain, p. 396
prior restraint doctrine, p. 374
public defender, p. 393
right to privacy, p. 385
selective incorporation, p. 373
Sherbert test, p. 383

SUGGESTED READINGS

Abraham, Henry J. and Barbara A. Perry. *Freedom and the Court: Civil Rights and Liberties in the United States*, 8th Edition. Lawrence, KS: University Press of Kansas, 2003. Comprehensive discussion of the Constitution's protections of civil rights and civil liberties.

Garrow, David J. *Liberty and Sexuality: The Right to Privacy and the Making of Roe v. Wade*. Berkeley: University of California Press, 1998. Comprehensive account of the legal debate over abortion before and after *Roe*.

Lewis, Anthony. *Make No Law: The Sullivan Case and the First Amendment*. New York: Random House, 1992. Excellent case study of the politics of the *Sullivan* decision and the evolution of the free-speech doctrine.

Rehnquist, William H. *All the Laws but One: Civil Liberties in Wartime*. New York: Knopf, 1998. The late chief justice of the Supreme Court considers instances in which civil liberties were sacrificed to security needs.

Sandel, Michael J. *Democracy's Discontent: America in Search of a Public Philosophy*. Cambridge, MA: Belknap Press of Harvard University Press, 1996. A readable but sophisticated book arguing that the Supreme Court's approach to civil liberty overemphasizes individual autonomy at the expense of republican principles favoring a community's right to self-government.

Wice, Paul B. *Public Defenders and the American Justice System*. Westport, CT: Praeger, 2005. A detailed case study of public defenders in Newark, NJ shows the role that public defenders play in the modern justice system.

Wilson, James Q. *Thinking About Crime*. New York: Basic Books, 1975. Makes a persuasive, realistic, and conservative case for ways of controlling crime.

ON THE WEB

For more on civil liberties, see the following Web sites:

AMERICAN CIVIL LIBERTIES UNION
www.aclu.org

The sometimes controversial American Civil Liberties Union has a detailed Web site outlining its agenda for promoting civil liberties, as well as describing the history and present status of the law.

FREEDOM FORUM
www.freedomforum.org

The Freedom Forum is an international foundation that promotes freedom of the press and of religion.

ELECTRONIC FRONTIER FOUNDATION (EFF) AND CENTER FOR DEMOCRACY AND TECHNOLOGY (CDT)
www.eff.org
www.cdt.org

Both groups are a useful source of information about free speech and privacy in the computer age.

Civil Rights

ON OCTOBER 23, 2001, ARSHAD CHOWDHURY WALKED INTO THE
San Francisco airport to board a flight back to the northeast. A graduate student in
business at Carnegie Mellon University in Pittsburgh, Chowdhury had been visiting friends in Berkeley over mid-semester break. Little more than a month after
the 9/11 attacks, the airports across the country were on edge, and Chowdhury was

resigned to a bit of extra scrutiny. Although he was an American citizen, his parents had immigrated to the United States in 1967 from Bangladesh, and Chowdhury's dark skin automatically made him suspicious to some people. Still, he could not have anticipated what happened next.

As Chowdhury waited to board, FBI agents, police, and airport security asked him to step aside for additional checks. After satisfying the authorities, he got back in line, only to be told that the Northwest airlines pilot had decided that he would not be allowed onto the aircraft. "People were looking at me, pointing at me, whispering," he said. "I've never felt that way before."[1] As someone who had once worked in the World Trade Center as an investment banker, Chowdhury said he understood that a certain degree of added security was necessary: "The attack on the World Trade Center was an attack on my colleagues, my livelihood, and me. So I endorse increased security at airports."[2] But, he added, he felt unfairly scrutinized. "I don't want this to happen to anybody else."[3] Chowdhury missed his plane, and had to take a later flight escorted by an airline official.[4]

Chowdhury's experience appears to be one example of so-called **racial profiling**, the singling out of certain people for suspicion based on their race or ethnicity. Long a concern regarding police stops of African American motorists, the issue of racial profiling has taken on new meaning in the age of terrorism. The practice has few outright advocates—indeed, the Constitution and congressional enactments prohibit governments and private companies from classifying people on the basis of race or ethnicity except in the most extraordinary cases. But some experts argue that it would be unrealistic not to take race and ethnicity into account—as one of a number of factors—when evaluating threats. "Suspecting people because of who they are rather than what they do is unacceptable," says one commentator. "But ignoring who they are in the course of scrutinizing what they do is equally unacceptable if—as with militant Islam, Italian mafia groups, Russian organized crime, Chinese tongs, etc.—who they are is relevant to the determination of whether they are likely to pose a threat."[5] The public appears to be split about evenly on the issue: in a 2006 poll, 49 percent said it was sometimes justified to use "racial or ethnic profiling" at airport checkpoints, while 46 percent said it was not justified.[6]

After being bumped from his flight, Arshad Chowdhury joined an ACLU lawsuit against four airlines accused of unjustly discriminating on the basis of race or ethnicity. As his case made its way through the court system, Chowdhury graduated from business school and started his own company: a firm that manufactures small "pods" in which weary travelers can take quick naps if, for some reason, they are delayed at the airport.[7]

The debate over racial profiling raises broader questions about America's new democracy. Popular influence may have surged in the U.S. political system, but what does the change mean for people who are members of a minority because of their race, ethnicity, primary language, or sexuality? On the one hand, when elections drive policy, voters decide the nation's future. Minorities are, by definition, smaller than majorities—and so elections could place them at a political disadvantage.*

On the other hand, elections can favor tightly-knit groups whose common concerns prompt them to participate as a bloc. What is more, in very close races such as the presidential elections of 2000 and 2004, the votes of even a small portion of the electorate may constitute the margin of victory. Party leaders, from presidents on down to the smallest precinct organizers, cannot afford to associate with a politician who damages their party's reputation with a distinct voting bloc. For candidates and policy makers, it may be easier to accommodate the passionate demands of a unified and vocal minority than to worry about the mild or divided preferences of a numerical majority. America's new democracy therefore could expand minority influence, compared to a system more insulated from voters.

This chapter grapples with the difficult puzzle of where minorities stand in a system that enhances popular influence. Sometimes minorities thrive in election-driven politics, and sometimes their political goals suffer when the majority rules. Elected officials and ballot-box policies sometimes reflect the preferences, interests, and prejudices of those who enjoy strength in numbers. But sometimes the sensibilities and values of average voters prove friendlier to minorities than what elites or interest groups might have endorsed. And sometimes minorities can operate as swing voters in elections and single-handedly force public officials to pay heed.

By contrast, the least election-driven American institution—the judicial branch—occasionally stands up for minority groups against discriminatory policies. But in most cases the Supreme Court's approach to civil rights follows trends initiated by the public debates and coalition building that make up electoral politics. As Justice Ruth Bader Ginsburg once observed, "With prestige to persuade, but not physical power to enforce, and with a will for self-preservation, the Court generally follows, it does not lead, changes taking place elsewhere in society."[8]

Civil Rights: More Than Just a Race Thing

The terms *civil rights* and *civil liberties* are similar but not identical. Civil liberties are fundamental freedoms that preserve the rights of a free people. **Civil rights** embody the American guarantee to equal treatment under the law—not just for racial groups, as people often assume, but more generally. In Chapter 13 we emphasize how important the due process clause of the Fourteenth Amendment has been to the protection of civil liberties in the United States. An equally important provision in the Fourteenth Amendment guards civil rights. According to the **equal protection clause**, states must give everyone "equal protection of the law."

*This generalization refers to a minority in a statistical sense. Sometimes people use the term minority in a political sense, to mean a "disadvantaged or less-powerful group," in which case women are a "minority" with greater numbers than men.

The equal protection clause is no plainer in meaning than the due process clause. Choice of the word *protection* might suggest that the language applies only to the justice system, requiring that law enforcement officials and the courts defend everyone equally. Yet most interpreters emphasize the word *equal* instead. They read the clause to imply that laws should not make categorical distinctions. Everyone must receive equal *treatment* when government formulates public policy.

But even given this wider understanding, it is not clear exactly how "equal" everyone must be. Almost every law treats some people in one way and others in a different way. Laws regularly distinguish among people on the basis of age, income, health, wealth, criminal history, or place of residence. Some distinguish among people on the basis of race, gender, or sexuality. Obviously, some sorts of categories are acceptable some of the time, and federal judges are the ones who decide (sometimes receiving indirect guidance from civil rights legislation).

Generally, the courts rank various sorts of unequal treatment according to the level of "scrutiny" they deserve. With higher levels of scrutiny, the government must clear a higher bar if it wishes to make distinctions between categories of people. Most forms of government categorization need only pass a *rational basis test*—the legal distinction between two types of people must offer a reasonable way to promote some legitimate government purpose. For example, if a state wishes to place special restrictions on the issuance of driver's licenses to those older than the age of 75, as some have done, it need only provide a reasonable explanation of why different-aged people are treated differently.

Laws receive *strict scrutiny* when they distinguish among people according to a **suspect classification**—which is to say, according to some grouping that has a long history of being used for purposes of discrimination, such as race. State governments or federal agencies responsible for unequal treatment must provide a compelling reason for the differentiation and must explain why their goals were unreachable using less group-conscious legislation. Certain groupings, such as gender, fall between these two extremes. Compared to regular laws, laws distinguishing among people according to these categories receive *heightened scrutiny*, but they need not clear the steep hurdle that suspect-class legislation does. In all three instances, though, the process is the same: Judges decide whether government has good reasons for the categories it uses.

Few voices criticize either the loose interpretation of the word *protection* or varying application of the word *equal* (although the three-tiered "scrutiny" system does have its detractors).[9] Two other questions about how to interpret the Fourteenth Amendment generate much more controversy.[10] The first is over how actively laws must distinguish among people before they fall under scrutiny. A government policy with no direct reference to race—say, for example, a performance test for police academy recruits—might impact two races differently. How should courts decide when indirect sources of unequal treatment represent unconstitutional discrimination? Answers differ.

The second major controversy over the equal protection clause is how to deal with a law that distinguishes among people according to a suspect class but does so to favor rather than harm a minority group. It may be unconstitutional to establish university scholarships available only to Asians or whites.* But can a public university offer money only for blacks, Hispanics, or Native Americans? It may be unconstitutional to shut minority businesses out of receiving government contracts. But can a state government set aside some of its projects exclusively for minority contractors? People clash angrily over whether equal treatment must go both ways when American society itself contains deep inequalities.

The stakes are high in these debates over the equal protection clause. Many minority group members rely on constitutional guarantees to ensure that they obtain equal opportunity. Those outside a minority group, meanwhile, must be on guard to ensure that the claim to equal treatment does not become an excuse for special interests to encroach on their liberties or their own rights to equality before the law. Elected leaders, although sensitive to the demands of minorities, also cannot forget that they are elected by majorities.

Because minorities cannot reliably control the outcome of elections, they have often pursued a legal strategy, bringing apparent civil rights violations to the attention of the courts. But litigation does not always work. Judges, too, are concerned about preserving credibility with majorities. If judges defy public opinion regularly, they may undermine confidence in the courts—and eventually elected officials will replace them.

African Americans and the Importance of Voting Rights

At the end of the Civil War, some southern states enacted "black codes," restrictive laws that applied to newly freed slaves but not to whites. "Persons of color . . . must make annual written contracts for their labor," one of the codes said, adding that if blacks ran away from their "masters," they had to forgo a year's wages.[11] Other codes denied African Americans access to the courts or the right to hold property, except under special circumstances.

Northern abolitionists urged Congress to override these black codes, which they considered thinly disguised attempts to continue slavery. Congress responded by passing the Civil Rights Act of 1866, which gave all citizens "the same right . . . to full and equal benefit of all laws."[12] Both the sentiment and some of the words carried over to the equal protection clause of the Fourteenth Amendment, which won final ratification two years later.

---

*The term white has no basis in genetic traits such as skin, hair, or eye color. Anglo-Saxons, Nordics, Slavs, Arabs, Jews, and many other groups all fall into the "white majority" of the U.S. population.

The federal government enforced its civil rights stance during **Reconstruction**, a period after the Civil War when the federal military still occupied southern states. During this period, blacks exercised their right to vote, a right many white Confederate veterans lacked. In addition, Congress established a Freedman's Bureau, designed to provide the newly freed slaves with education, immediate food relief, and inexpensive land from former plantations.[13]

The close election of 1876 brought Reconstruction to an end. Republican presidential candidate Rutherford B. Hayes claimed victory, but the outcome depended on fraudulent vote counts reported by several states, including three in the South. Politicians trying to resolve the disputed election worked out a compromise. Republicans won the presidency; Democrats won removal of federal troops from the South and control of future southern elections.

Blacks Lose Electoral Power

Within a generation the South had restored many of its old racial patterns.[14] One critical change was that black citizens lost their voting rights, a process that severed the electoral connection between African Americans and their government. State legislatures enacted laws requiring voters to pass literacy tests, meet strict residency requirements, and pay poll taxes to vote. Although the laws themselves used general words, and therefore did not seem to violate equal protection of the law, they clearly targeted blacks and the poor whites who might have allied with them in elections.

These laws became even more discriminatory once local officials began applying them. As the chair of the suffrage committee in Virginia bluntly admitted, "I expect the [literacy] examination with which the black men will be confronted to be inspired by the same spirit that inspires every man in this convention. I do not expect an impartial administration of this clause."[15] States also enacted what became known as a **grandfather clause**, a law that exempted men from voting restrictions if their fathers and grandfathers had voted before the Civil War. Of course, only whites benefited from this exemption.

The most successful restriction on the right to vote was the *white primary*, a nomination election held by the Democratic party that excluded nonwhites from participation. Republicans almost never won southern elections at the time, because of the party's tie to Reconstruction, so Democratic primary winners nearly always took office.[16] This practice, combined with the various voting restrictions, denied former slaves and their descendants a meaningful vote. Only 10 percent of adult African American males were registered in most states of the old Confederacy by 1910.[17]

Once they had been deprived of their voting rights, African Americans lost any leverage they might have had with southern politicians. As a result, legislatures soon began enacting **Jim Crow laws**, state laws that segregated the races from each other.* Jim Crow laws required African Americans to attend segregated schools, sit in separate areas in public trains and buses, eat in different restaurants, and use separate public facilities. These laws were almost universal in the South but appeared in numerous states outside that region as well. Thus, those of African descent entered the twentieth century cut off socially and politically from other Americans.

The Supreme Court initially took a very restrictive view of the Fourteenth Amendment's equal protection clause, and so permitted Jim Crow segregation. Two rulings held particular significance. In a decision given the ironic title the *Civil Rights Cases* (1883), the Court declared the Civil Rights Act of 1875 unconstitutional.[18] This law abolished segregation in restaurants, train stations, and other public places. But the Supreme Court ruled that the equal protection clause only guaranteed equal government policies, not equal treatment by private individuals and businesses (a position called the **state action doctrine**). Congress had no constitutional authority to tell restaurant owners and railroads who could use their property.

The second major Supreme Court decision, *Plessy v. Ferguson* (1896), had even more sweeping consequences. It developed the **separate but equal doctrine**, the principle that segregated facilities passed constitutional muster as long as they were equivalent. Homer Plessy had challenged Louisiana's law requiring racial segregation in buses, railroad cars, and waiting rooms. Plessy argued that his inability to use white facilities denied him equal protection before the law. But the Supreme Court upheld Louisiana's statute, explaining that separating the races did not stamp either with a "badge of inferiority." Only one justice, a Kentuckian, dissented. Justice John Marshall Harlan protested that "our Constitution is color-blind, and

---

* *The name comes from a stereotypical, belittling characterization of African Americans in minstrel shows popular at the time.*

JIM CROW FOUNTAIN
Within a generation after the end of Reconstruction, southern states erected strict social barriers between blacks and whites, as did many states outside the South. People of different races could not attend the same schools, use the same public transportation, or mingle in the same public facilities (such as theaters). *Would Jim Crow laws have been more difficult to maintain if blacks had been able to vote?*

neither knows nor tolerates classes among citizens." Laws enforcing segregation, Harlan argued, clearly violate this ideal.[19]

Blacks Regain Electoral Power

Legally sanctioned segregation remained intact well into the twentieth century. During that time, however, African Americans gained electoral clout by migrating north, to states where they could vote (see Figure 14.1). During both world wars, in particular, northern industrial cities filled labor shortages with blacks from the rural South. Northerners were not much more tolerant of blacks than were southerners. But machine politicians who dominated big-city politics were not fussy about the color or religion of the voters they organized. Any warm body who could walk into a voting booth was worth courting.[20]

By the 1930s, African Americans had used their votes to win small places in the politics of a few big cities. But the biggest political breakthrough for African Americans occurred in 1948, when they appeared to cast the decisive votes that

FIGURE 14.1   Percentage of blacks living outside the South, by decade, 1910 to 2002

The northern migration of blacks greatly increased their electoral clout. *What explains the northern migration of blacks from 1910 to 1970? What explains their recent return to the South?*

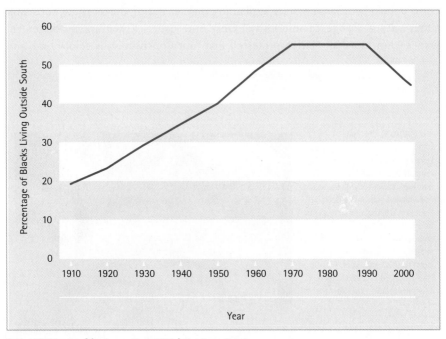

Source: U.S. Bureau of the Census, *Current Population Survey Reports.*

secured Harry Truman's narrow victory in the presidential race. This clout, and the increased rhetorical support Truman gave to civil rights, lent added force to lawsuits that activists began bringing before the federal courts.

Redefining State Action   The legal case against segregation was developed gradually by the National Association for the Advancement of Colored People (NAACP). Founded in 1909 by a group of African American intellectuals and activists, the NAACP chose a courtroom strategy because its leaders feared the inadequacy of black electoral strength. Only 12 percent of the southern black adult population could vote in 1947.[21] Yet a legal strategy without electoral leverage could not be very effective. The NAACP's lead attorney, Thurgood Marshall (who later became the first black Supreme Court justice), initially had few successes.

The NAACP's efforts gained potency as blacks moved north. In several cases the Court proved willing to expand its definition of state action to protect the political and legal rights of Blacks. In an important 1944 case, *Smith v. Allwright*, the Court outlawed the white primary, saying parties were not private organizations but integral parts of a state electoral system.[22] After this decision, black voting in the South gradually increased.

In 1948, the same year blacks helped elect Harry Truman, the Supreme Court took a major step against residential segregation. One tool that whites used to keep African Americans out of their neighborhoods was the **restrictive housing covenant**; a home buyer would sign a contract promising not to sell the property to a black household later. The Court ruled in *Shelley v. Kraemer* (1948) that states could not treat such private agreements as legally binding without violating the equal protection clause.[23] An earlier Court might have seen the covenants as a purely private matter, but by highlighting government enforcement of these agreements, the Court again broadened the scope of the state action doctrine.

Taking the "Separate" Out of "Equal"   The Supreme Court moved much more slowly against the separate but equal doctrine, which helped preserve social inequalities, not just political ones. As late as 1950 the Court passed up several opportunities to overrule the *Plessy* precedent, sensing that the time was not right to take such a controversial stand.[24] The problem was not a lack of sympathetic justices. Rather, the Court feared stepping too far beyond public opinion and losing the policy battle.

NAACP attorneys continued seeking cases that might prompt the Court to overturn *Plessy*. Of the handful they moved to the Court's docket in 1952, one from Kansas eventually took center stage: **Brown v. Board of Education of Topeka** (1954). Oliver Brown had filed a suit arguing that his daughter Linda's all-black school denied her equal protection of the law. The fact that Topeka funded white and black education equivalently made no difference, NAACP lawyers argued; separation was inherently unequal. The Justice Department's Civil Rights Division backed the

NAACP's claim, using strategies developed in collaboration with Justice Felix Frankfurter, a former director of the NAACP.* The Court agreed to hear their arguments and did so in December 1952.

The Supreme Court was still skittish, though. The Court delayed the final decision, scheduling a second round of arguments in 1953. Before they could take place, however, Chief Justice Fred Vinson died of a heart attack. President Eisenhower turned to a popular former governor, Earl Warren, to lead the Court.

Dramatic changes followed Warren's appointment. The Californian approached his appointment not as a former attorney or judge concerned with refining points of law, but as a politician determined to set public policy.[25] To Warren, the South's racial caste system represented an evil that most American voters were willing to exorcize; the Court should not hesitate to alter constitutional precedent as a means of promoting this moral goal. He decided to write the *Brown* opinion himself.

Warren realized how risky it was for the Court to abolish segregated institutions with long histories. To give the ruling additional authority, he wanted a unanimous judgment. He delayed voting on the issue for four months while he worked to persuade reluctant justices. He made compromises: limiting the judgment to schools and leaving flexibility in the ways a school district might remedy a segregated system. Eventually, every justice agreed to sign on.

Warren's opinion in *Brown* built less from law than from social science. Warren cited psychological studies claiming that segregation created a sense of inferiority among black children. One study showed, for example, that black children favored white dolls over black ones.[26] Warren therefore overturned *Plessy* only in the field of education and did not embrace Harlan's sweeping *Plessy* dissent that declared the Constitution "color-blind." Still, the ruling represented a dramatic departure from a system of segregation that from the earliest colonial settlements had organized social life in a large part of the United States.

The Modern Battle for Civil Rights

The *Brown* decision energized civil rights activists around the country. One activist even called the ruling a "new emancipation."[27] The impact on young people and church leaders was particularly noticeable; they formed numerous civil rights organizations and adopted more militant techniques.[28] NAACP activist Rosa Parks, of Montgomery, Alabama, engaged in an extraordinarily successful act of **civil disobedience**—a peaceful violation of a law, designed to dramatize that law's injustice. She refused to vacate her seat in a segregated bus when the driver attempted to expand the white section past her spot. The standoff prompted a bus boycott led by a young Baptist minister, Martin Luther King, Jr., who had recently earned his Ph.D.

---

* For a justice to collaborate with interested parties in a Supreme Court appeal clearly violates today's ethical standards, but there is no indication that Frankfurter saw any problem with sharing notes on an important case. See Howard Ball and Phillip J. Cooper, Of Power and Right (New York: Oxford, 1992), p. 177.

in theology. He was only 27 years old at the time, but he had the resourcefulness necessary to give the event national significance.[29]

The civil rights movement won overwhelmingly sympathetic coverage in the northern press, but it met intense opposition from regional officials.[30] In March 1956, nearly every southern member of Congress signed the Southern Manifesto, committing each official to resist enforcement of the *Brown* decision by "all lawful means."[31] Southern resistance was so consistent and complete that, in the states of the Old Confederacy, few schools desegregated. In the fall of 1964, 10 years after *Brown*, only 2.3 percent of black students in former Confederate states attended integrated schools.[32]

Yet the protests and demonstrations gradually had their effect. For one thing, southern blacks were registering to vote. From 1947 to 1960, the percentage more than doubled from 12 percent to 28 percent. At the same time, African Americans were becoming a more powerful political force in the large industrial states of the North. Presidential candidates had to balance southern resistance against their need for black votes.

John Kennedy's victory over Richard Nixon in the breathtakingly close election of 1960 owed much to his success attracting the black vote. When the campaign began, Kennedy realized that he needed to improve his civil rights credentials, especially because he had won the Democratic nomination by defeating two candidates with stronger records: Hubert Humphrey and Adlai Stevenson. A golden opportunity arose when Birmingham authorities jailed Martin Luther King, Jr. Kennedy placed a well-publicized phone call to Coretta Scott King, expressing sympathy for the plight of her husband. That phone call took on great symbolic

CIVIL RIGHTS ACTIVIST
Did activists or the courts contribute more to the end of formal segregation?

significance and helped mobilize Kennedy's supporters in the black community. He captured enough black votes to win such crucial states as Ohio and Michigan. Once in office, Kennedy proposed new civil rights legislation. To support his efforts, 100,000 black and white demonstrators marched on the Washington Mall in the summer of 1963. Others organized the event, but King emerged as the star, delivering his moving "I Have a Dream" oration from the steps of the Lincoln Memorial. Suddenly, a plurality of Americans viewed civil rights as the country's most important problem.[33] A few months later, Kennedy's assassination generated an unprecedented outpouring of moral commitment to racial justice (see Figure 14.2).

Elected political leaders responded quickly to this transformation in the nation's mood. The new president, Lyndon Baines Johnson (LBJ) of Texas, called upon Congress to memorialize Kennedy by enacting the civil rights bill. After intense debate, majorities of both Republican and Democratic members of Congress voted

FIGURE 14.2   Evaluation of civil rights as the country's most important problem

Many people saw civil rights as an important problem in the wake of the Kennedy assassination and civil rights demonstrations. Today (not shown) only around 3 percent view race relations as the most important problem. *Does this change reflect real progress or a lack of attention to current problems?*

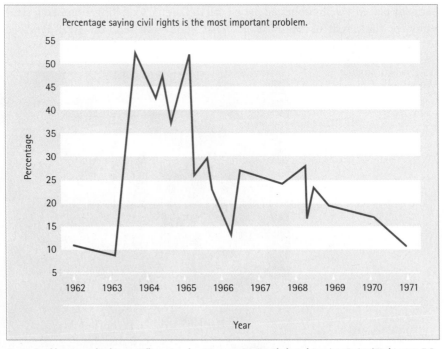

Source: Gerald Jaynes and Robin M. Williams Jr., eds., *A Common Destiny: Blacks and American Society* (Washington, DC: National Academy Press, 1989), p. 224.

to pass the legislation in 1964. The act banned segregation in all places of public accommodation, prohibited the use of federal money to support segregated programs, and created the Equal Employment Opportunity Commission (EEOC) to guard against employment discrimination. From 1964 to 1972, the percentage of black students in southern schools that included whites increased dramatically from 2.3 percent to 91.3 percent.

Buoyed by economic prosperity and his civil rights achievements, LBJ won a sweeping election victory in the fall of 1964. He followed this success by engineering congressional passage of the Voting Rights Act of 1965, which guaranteed African Americans equal access to the polls and, not coincidentally, ensured that more black voters would be able to turn out for Democratic candidates in the future.[34] The percentage of voters among southern black adults jumped upward; by 1992 they were as likely to vote as northern blacks.[35] From 1965 to 2001, the number of black elected officials rose from less than 500 to more than 9,100.[36]

The Public Mood Shifts

Segregation and discrimination did not stop at the South's borders. Most northern blacks lived in racially isolated neighborhoods, sent their children to predominantly black schools, and struggled to get good jobs. Martin Luther King shifted his focus northward after the successes in 1964 and 1965 by mounting a series of demonstrations in Chicago.[37] King broadened his issue concerns, protesting poverty and criticizing the Vietnam War. At the same time, new black leaders such as Malcolm X took a more militant position, affirming black culture and denying the value of integration.

Increasing assertiveness by black leaders changed how the public viewed civil rights. Support for protests dwindled.[38] At the same time, Blacks grew increasingly disenchanted with the slowness of racial change. Leaders began calling for **affirmative action** policies, which are programs designed to enhance opportunities for race- or gender-based minorities by giving them special consideration in recruitment or promotion decisions. Destructive riots broke out in minority neighborhoods, beginning in Los Angeles in 1964 and spreading to other cities over the next three years. King's assassination in the spring of 1968 again set off violent racial disturbances in dozens of cities throughout the country. National guard and army units had to quell wholesale theft and property destruction. The civil rights movement lost its moral authority, and whites began to lose interest in the cause (review Figure 14.2).

Racial issues began to divide the two political parties. When Arizona Senator and presidential candidate Barry Goldwater voted against the Civil Rights Act of 1964, he was among a minority of Republicans to do so. But by 1968, his party started pursuing a "southern strategy" by appealing to those who thought civil rights legislation had gone too far. Meanwhile, blacks solidified their allegiance to the Democratic party.[39] Between 1968 and 1972, the percentage of delegates attending the Democratic convention who were black grew from 6.7 to 14.6 percent (see Figure 14.3).

FIGURE 14.3   Percentage of Black delegates to the national party
conventions

The shifting racial characteristics of party activists reflect similar changes in voter loyalties.
Why has African American participation in Democratic party politics risen dramatically?

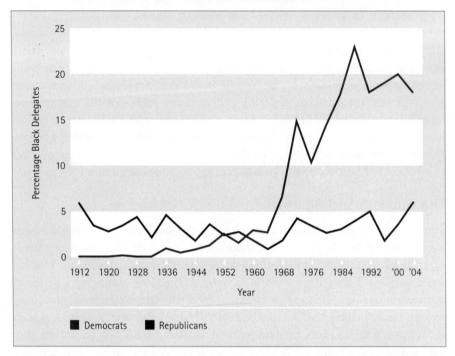

Sources: "The Democratic Delegates," *San Francisco Examiner*, August 27, 1996, p. A9; Robert Zauser, "Small Number of
Black Delegates Illustrates Problem for Republicans," *Philadelphia Inquirer*, August 16, 1996, p. A22; "The 2004 Republican
Delegates," CBS News, www.cbsnews.com/stories/2004/08/28/opinion/polls/main639203.shtml, accessed November 1,
2004; "A Look at the Delegates to the Democratic Convention," CBS News/*New York Times* Poll,
www.cbsnews.com/htdocs/CBSNews_polls/delegates_dems.pdf, accessed November 1, 2004.

African American leaders hoped the federal courts would remain a bulwark
against popular sentiment, but they did not. The Supreme Court distinguished between two types of segregation: *de jure* **segregation**, the separation of races by law
as practiced in the South, and *de facto* **segregation**, separation occurring as the result of private decisions made by individuals. The Court decided that the equal protection clause forbade only Southern-style segregation.

In *Milliken v. Bradley* (1974), for example, the Supreme Court considered the
constitutionality of the *de facto* segregation that plagued northern urban school
districts.[40] A ring of all-white suburban districts surrounded the large African
American population of the city of Detroit, leaving school systems racially distinct. No law required these racially segregated schools—they were a product of
(1) district borders drawn with no apparent discriminatory intent and (2) residen-

tial decisions made by private individuals. Accordingly, the Court declined to invalidate the Detroit-area districts. The Constitution forbids discriminatory policy, wrote Chief Justice Warren Burger, but "does not require any particular racial balance.[41]

The Supreme Court also considered the constitutionality of affirmative action programs in a 1978 case, *Regents of the University of California v. Bakke*. Recruitment policies favoring minorities or women vary in their size and significance. In some cases, these programs consist of nothing more than special advertising and counseling designed to inform disadvantaged groups about available opportunities. At the opposite extreme, some policies establish inflexible **quotas**, or specific numbers of positions reserved for members of disadvantaged groups. The policy under review in *Bakke* was a quota system; the UC–Davis medical school required 16 percent of its entering class to be minority students. Allen Bakke, a Norwegian American, sued after falling just short of admission two years in a row—despite a stronger record than some of the minority applicants who were admitted.[42]

The Supreme Court could not agree on an opinion. Four justices rejected Bakke's claim, arguing that institutions with no history of discrimination could still formulate policies to remedy "societal discrimination." Four other justices would not allow policies that judged applicants differently on the basis of race—whether to help or hurt disadvantaged groups. This left the Court in a 4 to 4 tie, with Justice Lewis Powell sitting in the middle.

Powell, a moderate southerner appointed by President Nixon, supported active attempts to create diversity but knew that explicit quotas lacked public support. He ended up writing an opinion fully supported by no other member of the Court, yet one that has defined constitutional doctrine to this day. It allowed race to play a role in university admissions decisions, with minority applicants favored over others, but forbade unseemly quota systems. Bakke won his case, but universities retained strong affirmative action programs across the nation.

Affirmative action has faced increasing criticism for decades. In 1995, the University of California Board of Regents voted to end the use of race as a factor in its admissions policies, a decision that took on broader significance in the years that followed when the states of California, Florida, Washington, and Texas formally banned race-based preferences in university admissions. But the Court reaffirmed Powell's *Bakke* precedent in 2003, striking down a rigid race-based point system used by the University of Michigan for undergraduate admissions but accepting a less formal affirmative action policy implemented by Michigan's law school. This time the Court managed a narrow but unified majority of five justices in favor of the approach. The need for diversity is so compelling, the Court ruled, universities need not treat everyone equally, at least when there is a "highly individualized, holistic review of each applicant's file" that ensures that admissions are not decided by quotas.[43]

It was an unusual sight for a frigid, snowy day. In mid-February 2004, a small group of University of Colorado students made their way to the north side of campus, set up a table and several signs, and prepared to sell a variety of baked goods to passersby. The group drew a crowd—but not a crowd of customers. More than three dozen students, their mouths duct-taped shut in silent protest, appeared with placards. Others argued with the pastry vendors in exchanges that grew heated at times. "I think it's disgusting," said one student leader, objecting to the event.[93]

The controversial event was a so-called "Affirmative Action Bake Sale," organized by campus Republicans. The price of the cupcakes, donuts, and cookies that the students were selling depended upon the buyer's race. A cookie cost a white student $1, a Hispanic student, 50 cents, while an African American student had to pay a quarter.[94]

By varying prices in this way, the Republicans sought to dramatize their opposition to policies of affirmative action, programs designed to enhance opportunities for race- or gender-based groups that have suffered discrimination in the past. The University of Colorado, by considering race as a factor in admissions decisions, was unfairly classifying applicants by race, argued the protestors. "We're showing [that] the policy of the University of Colorado is racist," said one Republican organizer.[95] Some of their classmates, however, felt the event was ill-conceived. "It is tasteless, what they are doing," said another student.[96]

Protesters converge as the Supreme Court hears an affirmative action case.

Americans as a whole seem just as divided as University of Colorado students over the policy of affirmative action. A poll taken in 2005, for example, found that 50 percent favored it and 42 percent opposed it.[97] Even the Supreme Court crafted a delicate compromise over the issue in a key pair of 2003 cases involving the University of Michigan (*Grutter v. Bollinger* and *Gratz v. Bollinger*). The Court struck down a rigid system of allocating applicants "points" for being a member of a minority group, but allowed a more flexible consideration of race as one of a number of relevant factors.

Supporters of affirmative action say it is necessary to correct systematic inequalities that make it more difficult for members of minority groups to succeed. "Until we create a fair society, we need affirmative action," argues one advocate. "If everyone started equally from the same position, we could end it. But I don't see how anyone can argue that we are there."[98]

Opponents of affirmative action argue that it contradicts the equal protection clause of the 14th Amendment by treating people differently on the basis of race.

AFFIRMATIVE ACTION *(continued)*

As activist Ward Connerly puts it, the program is nothing more than "state sponsored discrimination."[99]

While the Supreme Court has ruled that it is permissible for states to have affirmative action programs under certain conditions, voters in three states have outlawed the practice in statewide referenda: California in 1996, Washington in 1998, and Michigan in 2006. More states may face such votes in the future, as debates over the policy continue.

WHAT DO YOU THINK?

1. Should governments consider race as a factor in making decisions about university admissions, contracting, and other matters?
2. As we discuss in this chapter, the government needs to show a "compelling interest" if race classifications are to stand up to constitutional scrutiny. Universities argue that maintaining a diverse student body constitutes such an interest. Do you think this interest is "compelling" enough?

For more information on affirmative action, see the following Web sites:

Leadership Council on Civil Rights
www.civilrights.org

The LCCR promotes affirmative action, and provides a number of reports and policy briefs.

American Civil Rights Institute
www.acri.org

Founded by anti-affirmative action leader Ward Connerly, this organization presses for state-level bans on affirmative action policies.

Diversity Web
www.diversityweb.org

The Association of American Colleges and Universities maintains this Web site so that schools can share their strategies for ensuring diversity on campus.

Evaluating Racial Progress

Significant problems still beset U.S. blacks. Chief among them is the persistence of unemployment,[44] which creates a high poverty rate in the black community.[45] Teen pregnancy and infant mortality rates are far higher among African Americans than among others.[46] But there is reason for increasing optimism. The percentage of black men and women in professional and managerial positions increased markedly in the decades following the civil rights acts.[47] While in 1960, only 20 percent of African Americans were high school graduates, by 2005, more than 80 percent were.[48] African American poverty rates, while still high, shrank from more than 32 percent to about 25 percent from 1980 to 2004.[49] Blacks have also made electoral gains, winning an increasing number of political offices—sometimes with the

THE SPIRIT OF NEW ORLEANS
After the woeful governmental response to Hurricane Katrina, some civil rights activists charged that racism was to blame. Others said New Orleans residents suffered disproportionately because they were poor. *Would it be easier or more difficult for the government to address "classism" than to address racism?*

direct assistance of electoral laws and sometimes without it.[50] Half a century is a long time to allow injustices to persist in a democratic society, but few nations have moved so quickly to address deep-seated social inequalities.

The Civil Rights of Ethnic Minorities

Congress framed 1960s civil rights legislation to redress unique historical grievances growing out of slavery and the Jim Crow system, and so it dwelt on the position of African Americans in U.S. society. Meanwhile, the Supreme Court has never specifically delineated requirements for a minority group to be eligible for government protection. But after the civil rights movement altered equal protection law, groups representing other ethnic minorities began to make similar civil rights claims. Both Congress and the courts often gave recognition to these groups.

Not all ethnic minorities enjoy the same political standing in American law. For much of U.S. history, Jews faced virulent prejudice and crippling discrimination, including lynchings and synagogue bombings in the twentieth century.[51] Yet Jewish people receive no affirmative protections from government. The degree to which each ethnic minority gains political clout depends in large part on how effectively it mobilizes members in elections. Hispanics and Asian Americans represent influential voting blocs in several large states that are crucial during presidential elections and, accordingly, can exert disproportionate influence on national politics. Only Native Americans rely on their legal position to issue demands on government.

Hispanics

Hispanics (or Latinos) are the fastest-growing minority group in the United States.* In 1980 they made up only 6.4 percent of the U.S. population, but by 2005

---

* Following author Geoffrey Fox, we opt for the less politicized term Hispanic rather than Latino, although we realize the imperfection in either label. See Geoffrey Fox, Hispanic Nation: Culture, Politics, and the Constructing of Identity (Secaucus, NJ: Birch Lane, 1996), pp. 9–14.

they had grown to 14.4 percent, surpassing the 13.4 percent who are African American.[52] Yet Hispanics are only starting to make a significant political impact. Previously, language barriers and the large number of immigrants without citizenship limited their influence. Some new Hispanic immigrants also plan to return to their countries of origin and, therefore, stay out of U.S. politics.[53]

Hispanic voters are much less likely than African Americans to vote as a bloc. Whereas 81 percent of blacks consider themselves Democrats, only 57 percent of Hispanics do.[54] This political diversity is a natural outgrowth of real social and cultural diversity within "the Hispanic nation."[55] Some Hispanics have been Americans for many generations; others are recent arrivals speaking little English. Some are affluent and respected members of their communities; others are migrant laborers living on a pittance. Hispanics come from many different countries. Mexican Americans concentrate in the Southwest, from California to Texas. Puerto Ricans concentrate in northern industrial cities, such as New York. Cuban Americans concentrate in Florida. These disparate groups have little in common, so they share few political concerns.

Activists have worked hard to construct an Hispanic identity. One of the earliest groups to do so was the Mexican American Legal Defense and Education Fund (MALDEF), which has focused on voting, education, and immigration issues. In 1974, in response to MALDEF complaints, the Supreme Court interpreted the 1964 Civil Rights Act to mean that schools must provide special educational programs for those not proficient in the English language.[56] MALDEF and other advocacy groups also argued that voting materials discriminated against linguistic minorities because they appeared only in English. Congress responded in 1982 by requiring foreign-language ballots for any linguistic minority constituting more than 5 percent of a county's population.[57]

Both presidential candidates worked hard to court the Hispanic vote in 2004. President Bush repudiated anti-immigration laws and cited his moderate record on immigration in Texas. He also stressed his support for some bilingual education programs and his opposition to English-only mandates. Democratic presidential candidate John Kerry appealed to Hispanic voters as well, promising to allow undocumented immigrants to earn legal status if they had been in the United States for a long period of time, had been working, and could pass a background check. While most voted for Kerry, George W. Bush received the support of a significant number of Hispanics on Election Day, including majorities of Cuban Americans and Hispanic evangelical Christians.[58] At the start of his second term, Bush appointed Alberto Gonzales as the first Hispanic Attorney General, and in 2006 Bush pressed for an immigration reform law that would create a guest worker program for non-citizens.

Asian Americans

Asian Americans only recently gained a voice in national electoral politics. They constitute just 5 percent of the population, and more than 60 percent are foreign-born.[59]

Like Hispanics, they represent many different nationalities and have differing, even conflicting, foreign policy concerns. Asians vote Republican more often than other minorities do, and they are more likely to oppose affirmative action programs that promote other ethnic groups at their expense.[60]

Yet many Asian Americans worry about anti-immigration sentiment among U.S. voters. Initiatives to require English for government business or to cut off immigrant welfare benefits frequently appear on state ballots. Activists worry that a growth in stereotyping could produce a "chilling effect" on Asian American political participation.[61] Since the 1990s, Asian Americans have become increasingly active at the state and local level, electing key officials to office, organizing cultural celebrations, urging quick responses to anti-Asian slurs and ethnically-motivated violence.[62]

Native Americans

The Bill of Rights does not protect the rights and liberties of Native Americans. At the time of the Constitution's ratification, descendants of indigenous tribes were considered citizens of foreign nations. As one authority on Indian rights put it, "No constitutional protections exist for Indians in either a tribal or an individual sense."[63]

Instead, relations between Native Americans and the government operate under federal laws and treaties signed with American Indian tribes. Over the long course of U.S. history, the government, facing political pressure from those migrating westward, ignored or broke virtually all of the treaties it made with these tribes. Still, the Supreme Court today interprets some of these treaties as binding.[64] As a result, tribal members have certain rights and privileges not available to other groups. For example, Court rulings have given tribes in the Pacific Northwest special rights to fish for salmon. These exemptions can be critical for Native Americans, who suffer from the highest poverty rates of all U.S. racial and ethnic groups.[65]

One economically significant right recognized in recent years has been the authority to offer commercial gambling on tribal property. The Court has said that tribal grounds are governed by federal, not state, law. Federal law does not disallow gambling on tribal grounds except if it is forbidden everywhere within a state. In several cases, tribes have secured political influence using the enormous proceeds from gambling operations.

Congressional legislation has applied most of the Bill of Rights to tribe members. To protect religious freedom, for example, Congress passed the 1978 American Indian Religious Freedom Resolution. Tribal leaders have argued that the resolution gives them special access to traditional religious sites in national parks and other government lands. But the federal courts have interpreted the resolution narrowly, saying it does not make indigenous Americans "supercitizens." Rather, it gives them religious freedoms comparable to those granted other citizens.[66]

Gender, Sexuality, and Civil Rights

"It is in the very nature of ideas to grow in self-awareness, to work out all their implications over time," one constitutional scholar writes. "The very content of the great clauses of the Constitution, their coverage, changes."[67] So it has been with the equal protection clause of the Fourteenth Amendment. Although gender is not mentioned anywhere in the clause, its meaning has evolved to include equal rights for women. But these changes did not take place entirely within the confines of federal courtrooms. They were part of a broad struggle for women's rights, played out as much among the electorate as in the legal arena.

Gender Equality

The first struggle for women's rights focused on voting. Once the Nineteenth Amendment passed in 1920, the women's movement fell dormant for nearly 50 years.[68] Women's groups grew more active in the 1960s, and since then they have achieved three civil rights objectives: equal treatment before the law, protection against sexual harassment, and access to state-funded military academies.

Equality Before the Law As unlikely as it may seem, a conservative southerner, Howard Smith of Virginia, proposed amending Title VII of the Civil Rights Act of 1964 to prohibit discrimination on the basis of sex as well as race, religion, or national origin. The amendment passed overwhelmingly, but activists formed the National Organization for Women (NOW) to ensure that courts would enforce it. They also pushed to ensconce equal treatment in the Constitution, backing the **Equal Rights Amendment (ERA)**, a failed amendment that would have banned gender discrimination.

At first, the ERA seemed destined to sail through the ratification process; it appeared to be an easy way for politicians to secure female votes. Overwhelming congressional majorities passed the ERA in 1972. Within a year a majority of states voted to ratify it.[69] But just before the ERA could join the U.S. Constitution, a resistance movement led by groups of conservative women derailed the effort. Aware of unpopular policies mandated by federal courts in the name of racial equality, the ERA's opponents warned that judges would do the same with constitutional language promising gender equality. They would require government funding of abortions, coed bathrooms, and women in combat.[70] The ERA fell three state legislatures short of the three-fourths required to ratify a constitutional amendment.

As discouraging as the ERA defeat was for its supporters, in retrospect it seems that they achieved their objectives despite losing the ratification fight. The Supreme Court had done little, if anything, to prevent gender discrimination before the ERA campaign. Court opinions changed after Congress voted overwhelmingly in favor of the ERA's passage. Gender equality gained recognition.

Categorizing people by their sex does not receive the same strict scrutiny that racial categories do. Nevertheless, the Supreme Court has ruled that gender discrimination violates the equal protection clause, so gender distinctions receive heightened scrutiny compared to most other legal categories.[71] The Court will rule against a law unless its gender distinctions have "a substantial relationship to an important objective."[72] In part, the Court's cautiousness reflects mixed public feelings about feminism.

The Supreme Court accepted gender distinctions within the military in *Rostker v. Goldberg* (1981). Congress holds broad constitutional powers in military matters, Justice William Rehnquist explained, and "the lack of competence on the part of the courts is marked."[73] The ruling was consistent with the view of a majority of the voters, who favored restricting female participation in combat.[74] As public opinion on the issue shifted, women took on greater roles, serving as military pilots and in so-called "forward support companies" on the battlefield during the Iraq War. Still, official military policy continued to prohibit women from taking direct combat positions.[75]

The Supreme Court also has allowed businesses some latitude when they do not recruit and retain women, as long as a "business necessity" explains their imbalanced personnel practices.[76] The Court initially required those claiming discrimination to disprove the business-necessity argument. Justice Byron White argued in *Ward's Cove Packing Co. v. Atonio* (1989) that Title VII of the Civil Rights Act gave claimants the burden of proof.[77] Women's organizations opposed the ruling, because it is hard for plaintiffs to characterize conclusively what a business needs. The Civil Rights Act of 1991, signed by President George H. W. Bush, shifted the burden of proof to businesses. It was elected officials, not the Court, who took the lead on this issue.

Sexual Harassment   The Supreme Court did not rule on the meaning of sexual harassment in the workplace until *Meritor Savings Bank v. Vinson* (1986).[78] In this case, Michelle Vinson said that sexually abusive language used in her presence had left her psychologically damaged. The Court decided in Vinson's favor, but Justice Rehnquist wrote a narrow opinion implying that harassment would be considered illegal only if it caused real harm. Afterward, sexual harassment became a major political issue, resulting in a large crop of new female elected officials in 1992. Responding to the change in the political atmosphere, the Supreme Court expanded its definition of sexual harassment in the unanimous decision *Harris v. Forklift Systems* (1993).[79]

Teresa Harris worked at Forklift Systems, Inc., a heavy equipment rental firm. Her employer called her derogatory terms, such as "dumb-ass woman." Although Harris complained and her boss promised to restrain his remarks, he subsequently suggested in front of other employees that Harris had slept with a client to obtain a contract. She quit and sued. Although Harris could not show serious psychological damage, Justice Sandra Day O'Connor wrote that Title VII of the Civil Rights Act "comes into play before harassing conduct leads to a nervous breakdown." Justice Ruth Bader Ginsburg went further, arguing in her concurring opinion that discrimination exists whenever it is more difficult for a person of one gender to perform well on a job. Once again, the Supreme Court moved forward in the wake of public pressure.

Single-Sex Schools   Single-sex schools have long been a significant part of American education. As late as the 1950s, well-known private colleges, such as Princeton and Yale, limited their admissions to men. Although these colleges now admit approximately equal numbers of men and women, single-sex education survives at many private women's colleges. These colleges assert that women learn more in an environment where many can assume leadership roles. Hillary Rodham Clinton, who graduated from Wellesley, a Massachusetts women's college, once said: "I am so grateful that I had the chance to go to college at a place where women were valued and nurtured and encouraged."[80] In 2006, in response to such claims, the Bush administration issued new regulations designed to make it easier to establish single-sex public schools.[81]

Despite the claims of those who favor single-sex education, many believe that education separated by gender cannot be equal. The Supreme Court cast doubt on its constitutionality in 1996. In *United States v. Virginia*, the Court ruled that women must be admitted to Virginia Military Institute (VMI), even though the state had recently established a separate military training program for women. The Court said the newly established program for women did not match the history, reputation, and quality of VMI. Justice Scalia, in his dissent, recognized the importance of public opinion on the Court's ruling. He lambasted "this most illiberal Court" because it had "embarked on a course of inscribing one after another of the current preferences of the society . . . into our Basic Law."[82]

Evaluating Women's Rights   Despite many gains, the women's movement has not yet realized all the goals of its civil rights agenda. Sexual harassment remains a burning issue within the military and in many business firms. Only a few women have broken through what is known as the glass ceiling—the invisible barrier that has limited their opportunities for advancement to the highest ranks of politics, business, and the professions. Very few women serve as college presidents, as corporate heads, or as partners in major law firms. Women do hold many important political posts. In 2007, they held one Supreme Court appointment, 16 Senate seats, 73 districts in the House, and nine governorships.

ORCHESTRATING FOREIGN AFFAIRS
Secretary of State Condoleezza Rice, pictured here with acclaimed cellist Yo-Yo Ma, is neither the first woman nor the first African American to call the tune in a major policy area. Yet, as a black woman, Rice has broken ground for her virtuosity conducting foreign affairs—an issue whose leadership historically has been composed of whites and males. *Has Rice's commanding performance in international relations been instrumental in changing how Americans view women and minorities in government services?*

Gays and Lesbians

Some of the most contentious political debates in the late twentieth and early twenty-first centuries surrounded the rights of gays and lesbians. It is no accident that, at the same time, homosexuals engaged in electoral politics more than ever before—especially as campaign contributors. Gay and lesbian donors gave an estimated $3.5 million to the 1992 Clinton campaign, leading Clinton to consider ending a ban on gays in the military, and have remained active in elections ever since.[83] According to one estimate, from 1991 to 2007 the number of openly gay government officials jumped from 49 to more than 350.[84]

At the same time, the country is undergoing an increasingly vocal debate over gay rights, a debate being fought in election and referendum campaigns. The American public believes that gays should have equal rights and in particular equal job opportunities, a belief that is a recent development (see Figure 14.4). Laws barring employment discrimination on the basis of sexual orientation have passed in

FIGURE 14.4   Public opinion on gay rights has changed as gay and lesbian political activism has increased

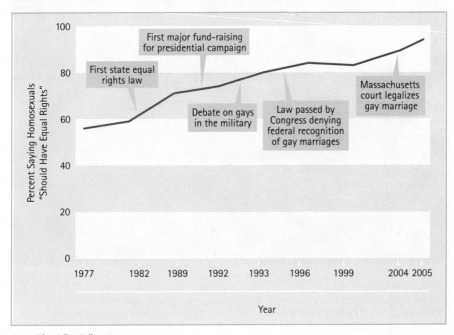

Source: The Gallup Poll, various years.

15 states and have bipartisan support in Congress.[85] In 2000 Vermont became the first state to recognize same-sex civil unions. Finally, the Supreme Court ruled in 2003 that privacy rights prevent states from outlawing sodomy. Justice Kennedy wrote that gays could live their lives with dignity.

But public opinion remains conservative on other issues regarding homosexuality. Large majorities disapprove of same-sex marriages, and 45 states have passed laws or constitutional amendments banning them.[86] In Hawaii, where a state court decision had legalized such unions in 1993, voters overwhelmingly passed a constitutional amendment five years later outlawing them again. Americans also have serious reservations when asked whether gays should be allowed to serve as teachers or youth leaders. The Supreme Court ruled in 2000 that the Boy Scouts had a right to dismiss gay scout leaders because their presence undermines moral and cultural values that the organization seeks to convey to children. President Bush voiced his support for an amendment to the U.S. Constitution defining marriage as a union between a man and a woman after the Massachusetts Supreme Judicial Court ruled in 2004 that the state's constitution protected the right of gays to marry and local officials in other states began marrying gay couples.

FACES OF CHANGING VALUES
Openly affectionate homosexuals may trouble straight America, making public a way of life whose existence many would prefer to ignore. On the other hand, witnessing attractive same-sex couples, such as these couples at a gay pride parade, may lessen the extent to which American citizens view homosexual relationships as unhealthy or abnormal. *Will gays and lesbians escape discrimination faster if they try to be as discreet as possible, or if they become a common sight on America's streets and in American towns?*

Rights of Americans with Disabilities

Disabled people constitute 20 percent of the working-age population.[87] They have an important political advantage that other minorities lack: Every person risks becoming disabled someday, so the rights of disabled people have broad appeal. Yet a troublesome drawback offsets this advantage: The cost of helping people with disabilities can be exorbitant. As of the 2007 fiscal year, the federal government budgets more than $100 billion on Social Security Disability Insurance (SSDI) alone. SSDI is a relatively small program that reaches only about two thirds of those who are unable to work due to a disability, and in many cases fails to lift recipients out of poverty.[88] When insurance costs, additional government programs, lost work hours, and other factors are taken into account, the total cost of disabilities is daunting.

Government began concerning itself with the quality of life for disabled people in the 1960s, around the same time that other minority groups gained their voice in American politics. Previously, programs for the disabled were seen as charitable activities to be supported by private donations. Mentally disabled people were closeted away in "insane asylums" and "homes for the incurable."

Americans held many stereotypes about the extent to which handicaps limited one's abilities.

Rights of the disabled received their first big push not from an interest group, but from one individual. Hugh Gallagher, a wheelchair-bound polio victim, served as a legislative aide to Alaska senator E. L. Bartlett in the mid-1960s. Gallagher constantly faced difficulty using public toilets and gaining access to buildings such as the Library of Congress. At his prodding, Congress in 1968—just four years after the Civil Rights Act—enacted a law requiring that all future public buildings constructed with federal money provide access for the disabled. Similar language appeared in a transportation act in 1970.[89]

Once elected officials responded to the demands of the disabled, the courts became more sensitive. Previously, school officials had denied "retarded" children access to public education on the grounds that they were not mentally competent. But in the early 1970s, federal courts in Pennsylvania and the District of Columbia required that states provide disabled children with equal educational opportunity.[90] These decisions generated a nationwide movement for disabled children, culminating in the passage in 1975 of federal legislation that guaranteed all disabled children educational access.[91]

Encouraged by both judicial and legislative victories, groups representing the physically and mentally disabled became increasingly assertive. They discovered that politicians did not wish to appear insensitive; guarantees of rights for the disabled were much less controversial than those for other minorities. A series of legislative victories in education, transportation, and construction of public buildings culminated in the Americans with Disabilities Act of 1991, signed by President George H. W. Bush. This act made it illegal to deny someone employment because of a disability. Workplaces must adapt to the capacities their employees, when feasible.

Twenty years ago, public toilets for the disabled hardly existed. Sidewalks and staircases had no ramps. Buses and trains were inaccessible to those in wheelchairs. College and university campuses did not accommodate attendance by the physically challenged. Legislative and judicial mandates have produced a sharp change in American society.

CHAPTER SUMMARY

African Americans achieved most of their advances through electoral politics—either directly by exercising their voting rights or indirectly by attracting political support through nonviolent demonstrations.[92] The most notable progress toward racial desegregation occurred as the result of legislation passed in the mid-1960s by bipartisan majorities in Congress. In contrast, the Supreme Court has usually followed the nation's popular moods: denying rights claims late in the nineteenth century, recognizing them after blacks moved north and acquired voting rights, and then pulling back after the civil rights movement lost public support (see Figure 14.5).

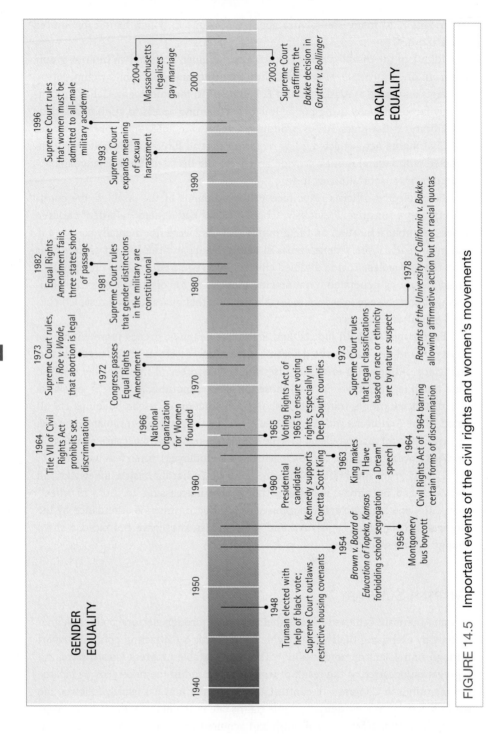

FIGURE 14.5   Important events of the civil rights and women's movements

Warren Court decisions redefined the equal protection clause, which eventually led to a stronger legal position for Hispanics, Asians, and members of other minority groups. Yet getting courts to enforce legal rights relies in part on a group's clout. In general, these groups have only begun to exert their strength in national elections, so they have been slower than blacks to achieve recognition. Often congressional measures, such as the ERA and the Americans with Disabilities Act, signal to the courts when the political mood has changed. Thus, even civil rights respond to public opinion in America's new democracy.

Key Terms

affirmative action, p. 411

Brown v. Board of Education of Topeka, Kansas, p. 407

civil disobedience, p. 408

civil rights, p. 401

de facto segregation, p. 412

de jure segregation, p. 412

equal protection clause, p. 401

Equal Rights Amendment (ERA), p. 419

grandfather clause, p. 404

Jim Crow laws, p. 404

quotas, p. 413

racial profiling, p. 400

Reconstruction, p. 404

restrictive housing covenant, p. 407

separate but equal doctrine, p. 405

state action doctrine, p. 405

suspect classification, p. 402

427

Suggested Readings

Browning, Rufus, Dale Rogers Marshall, and David H. Tabb. *Protest Is Not Enough: The Struggle of Blacks and Hispanics for Equality in Urban Politics.* Berkeley, CA: University of California Press, 1984. Excellent analysis of the importance of electoral politics for black advances.

Lien, Pei-te, M. Margaret Conway and Janelle Wong, *The Politics of Asian Americans: Diversity and Community.* New York: Routledge, 2004. The authors discuss the results of the broadest and most comprehensive survey of Asian-Americans to date.

Deloria, Vine, Jr., and David E. Wilkins. *Tribes, Treaties, and Constitutional Tribulations.* Austin, University of Texas Press, 1999. Discusses the constitutional status of the rights of indigenous peoples.

Garcia, F. Chris, ed. *Pursuing Power: Latinos and the Political System.* Notre Dame, Indiana: University of Notre Dame Press, 1997. A comprehensive series of essays concerning Latino politics.

Riggle, Ellen D. B. and Barry L. Tadlock, eds., *Gays and Lesbians in the Democratic Process: Public Policy, Public Opinion, and Political Representation.* New York: Columbia University Press, 1999. A series of sophisticated essays on gay and lesbian participation in politics.

Rosenberg, Gerald N. *The Hollow Hope: Can Courts Bring About Social Change?* Chicago: University of Chicago Press, 1991. Argues that courts are generally unable to act contrary to majority opinion.

Switzer, Jacqueline Vaughn. *Disabled Rights: American Disability Policy and the Fight for Equality.* Washington, DC: Georgetown University Press, 2003. A political scientist examines the evolution of disability policy and the disability rights movement.

Wolbrecht, Christina. *The Politics of Women's Rights: Parties, Positions, and Change.* Princeton, NJ: Princeton University Press, 2000. Shows how divisions between Democrats and Republicans have been affected by debates over women's rights.

On the Web

For more information on civil rights, see the following Web sites:

U.S. DEPARTMENT OF JUSTICE
www.usdoj.gov
The U.S. Department of Justice's Civil Rights division provides information on its enforcement of existing civil rights law.

U.S. COMMISSION ON CIVIL RIGHTS
www.usccr.gov
Established in 1957, the U.S. Commission on Civil Rights monitors discrimination in many sectors of American society.

NATIONAL ASSOCIATION FOR THE ADVANCEMENT OF COLORED PEOPLE (NAACP)
www.naacp.org
The NAACP is the nation's oldest civil rights organization.

NATIONAL ORGANIZATION FOR WOMEN (NOW)
www.now.org
The country's largest feminist organization, NOW seeks "to take action to bring about equality for all women."

NATIONAL COUNCIL OF LA RAZA
www.nclr.org
The National Council of La Raza monitors issues of concern to Hispanic Americans.

HUMAN RIGHTS CAMPAIGN
www.hrc.org
This is the official Web site for the Human Rights Campaign (a leading gay rights organization).

LEADERSHIP EDUCATION FOR ASIAN PACIFICS, INC.
www.leap.org
Leadership Education for Asian Pacifics, Inc. (LEAP) houses the Asian Pacific American Public Policy Institute, which authors numerous reports on Asian Americans.

NATIONAL COUNCIL ON DISABILITY
www.ncd.gov
The National Council on Disability is an independent federal agency that makes recommendations to the president and Congress regarding Americans with disabilities. The agency's site provides links to other relevant federal agencies, press releases, and in-depth reports.

Public Policy

IN JANUARY 2003, CONGRESSIONAL ANALYSTS AND ADMINISTRA-tion officials predicted that the government would spend significantly more money over the next year than it collected in taxes. Despite record-setting sur-pluses in 1999 and 2000, an economic downturn, terrorist attacks, and tax cuts had sent federal budget figures plunging back into the red. A new Homeland Security Department, increased spending on intelligence gathering and coordination, and the complete federal takeover of airport security, among other measures, had cost the government dearly. The ongoing U.S. presence in Afghanistan and the looming Iraq War promised to deplete federal resources even further. Meanwhile, the so-called "baby boom" generation, born from 1945 to the early 1960s, grew ever closer to retirement. With this large generation due to leave the workforce and rely on social programs for the elderly sometime around 2010, policy experts warned of an unprecedented strain on the federal budget. "The collision course is pretty easy to see," said one economist.[1]

In the face of budget pressures and the impending retirement of the baby boomers, it might have seemed that politicians in Washington would work to raise taxes or reduce spending on ballooning health care and pension programs in order to place the budget back on an even footing. In fact, the opposite occurred. In addition to enacting a significant tax cut in spring 2003, the president and a nearly unanimous Congress supported increased spending on **Medicare**, the government health insurance program for Americans older than 65. In his January State of the Union Address, President George W. Bush promised to "commit an additional $400 billion over the next decade to reform and strengthen Medicare."[2]

Democrats opposed Bush only insofar as they preferred more generous new benefits, as well as limitations on the profits of pharmaceutical companies. While Bush proposed to cover the cost of prescription drugs only for those Medicare recipients who chose to receive coverage through private insurance providers, Democrats pressed for drug coverage for all Medicare enrollees.

By the end of the year, the two parties struck a deal on a compromise plan that would provide limited prescription drug coverage for all elderly Medicare recipi-

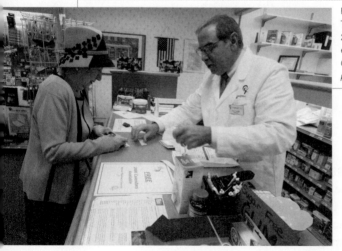

PRESCRIPTION FOR BUDGET DEFICITS? The prescription drug benefit enacted in 2003 wound up being almost twice as expensive as some had claimed. *Why did Congress and the president make this policy such a high priority?*

ents beginning in 2006. Supported by the American Association of Retired Persons (AARP), this bill was criticized as incomplete by some Democratic leaders, but many others saw it as a major victory. As California Democratic senator Dianne Feinstein put it, "I knew in my heart of hearts that the seniors in my great state are going to be better served by this bill than they are today."[3]

When the new policy went into effect in 2006, many seniors, doctors, and pharmacists found the program to be confusing and bureaucratic. Responding to these concerns, members of Congress on both sides of the aisle proposed relaxing deadlines for enrollment and giving money to states to help smooth the transition.[4] Ten-year cost estimates grew from $400 billion to as much as $700 billion, but even in a time of budget deficits, benefits for senior citizens remained secure.[5]

The above example illustrates how policy makers pay close attention to the demands of voters and major interest groups, often at the expense of fiscal discipline. When the nation's elderly drew attention to the rising cost of prescription drugs, politicians could not help but listen to this vocal and politically active group.

The 2004 election campaign showed how careful both parties are to protect programs for the elderly. In a debate devoted to domestic policy issues, George W. Bush and his Democratic challenger John Kerry clashed over the Iraq war, the ongoing global fight against terrorism, and over which candidate had done the most to protect and expand Medicare. "I'm fighting to let Medicare survive," argued Kerry. Bush shot back that he had "led the Congress to reform Medicare so our seniors have got a modern health care system."[6] Elections mold policy in America's new democracy, and when important groups of voters are concerned with particular programs, other policy areas—and budgetary concerns—get short shrift from politicians.

Setting Public Policy

All government programs and regulations are examples of public policy, so we have discussed numerous specific policies in previous chapters (see especially Chapters 3 and 11). Policies generally fall into one of three types: (1) domestic policy, which consists of all government programs and regulations that directly affect those living within the country; (2) economic policy, which indirectly affects those within the country by changing government budgets and the value of a nation's currency; and (3) foreign and defense policy, which involves relations with other nations to preserve national security. However, the distinctions among these three areas of policy are not always sharp and clear. Some domestic policies, such as immigration policy, affect relations with other countries. Some foreign policies, such as trade regulations, have major domestic consequences.

Policy making is a complex, never-ending round of events. To clarify what is often a very messy process, political scientists have divided the policy-making round into six stages (see Figure 15.1):

- *Agenda setting*, deciding which issues government must address.[7] Issues enter the agenda when they reach the notice of public officials. Those issues serious enough to influence voters are most likely to grab attention.
- *Policy deliberation*, the debate over how government should deal with an issue on the agenda.[8] At this stage, groups try to convince leaders that their proposals will win favor with the electorate.
- *Policy enactment*, the passage of a law by public officials at the national, state, or local level. Elected officials who support a law usually expect that doing so will enhance their popularity, although there are celebrated instances when political leaders have knowingly sacrificed their careers to take an unpopular stand.
- *Policy implementation*, the translation of a law into specific government programs.[9] Most laws are flexible, but bureaucrats seldom stray far from the intentions of the legislative branch when doing so might evoke a public backlash.
- *Policy outputs*, the rules and regulations growing out of a program. Beneficiaries usually think well of those responsible for helpful outputs and support them politically. Those who are hurt or neglected by a program may punish the elected officials responsible.

FIGURE 15.1 Policy-making stages

Political scientists break the policy process into six stages.

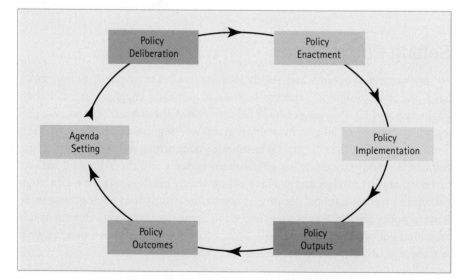

- *Policy outcomes*, the effect of a policy on American society, the economy, or the international sphere.[10] These outcomes often give rise to new issues, which in turn join the policy agenda.

The political forces at work differ from one policy to the next, but electoral incentives nearly always influence how policies pass through the six stages of development. The enactment of the 1996 welfare reform law, **Temporary Assistance for Needy Families (TANF)**, provides one example of the policy process at work.

Bill Clinton placed reform on the policy *agenda* in his 1992 presidential campaign by promising to "end welfare as we know it." Interest groups, policy experts, members of Congress, and the media began *deliberating* how the United States might redesign welfare policy. Congress then *enacted* a law shifting responsibility for welfare policy to state governments, and President Clinton signed the bill. State governments *implemented* new welfare programs in early 1997. As one *output* of the new programs, many families left or were removed from the welfare rolls.

After 10 years under the new law, analysts took stock of policy *outcomes*. Welfare rolls had declined dramatically; from 1996 to 2006, the number of recipients dropped by two thirds.[11] In fact, contrary to expectations, the number of Americans receiving benefits continued to decline even during the economic downturn of 2001 and the slow recovery that followed. Supporters of the reform argued that this proved the policy was a success. But critics charged that this decline during economic hard times was a sign that welfare was not reaching those it was designed to help.[12] In 2006, after considering the outcomes, Congress renewed TANF for five more years, further strengthening work requirements for recipients.[13] Another policy making round had begun.

Domestic Policy

Although the national government originally concentrated on relations with other countries, over the course of more than 200 years it has grown dramatically to influence more and more of daily life in the United States. Social policies set by the national government now affect every stage of American life, from prenatal development in the mother's womb (through nutrition programs and medical regulations) all the way to death (or even after death, if one counts survivor's benefits and inheritance taxes).

A Healthy Place to Grow Old

The generosity of national social policies varies significantly over the course of a lifetime. The primary focus of domestic policy has been to enhance the income and medical care enjoyed by senior citizens, while relatively little money has gone to benefit Americans in the youngest age ranges. The effect of this policy choice shows up in the nation's poverty statistics. From 1970 to 2005, poverty among senior citizens fell from 25 percent to 10.1 percent (see Figure 15.2). During the same period, poverty among children increased from 15 percent to about 18 percent, a rate twice as high as that in most other advanced industrial societies.[14]

Poverty is not just a matter of money; it is a matter of life and death. Of the seven developed countries with the largest economies, the United States has the highest infant mortality rate but the longest life span among senior citizens.[15] As one analyst put it, the United States is the "healthiest place to grow old but the riskiest [in which] to be born."[16]

Benefits for Senior Citizens

The national government has not always worked so hard to finance retirement and medical care for seniors. Poverty among the elderly was so acute during the Great Depression that Congress enacted the Social Security Act of 1935. This legislation created a broad range of social policies, including a welfare program for senior citizens generally known as social security.[17]

FIGURE 15.2   U.S. poverty rates for senior citizens and children, 1970–2005

Poverty rates have fallen for seniors and risen for children.

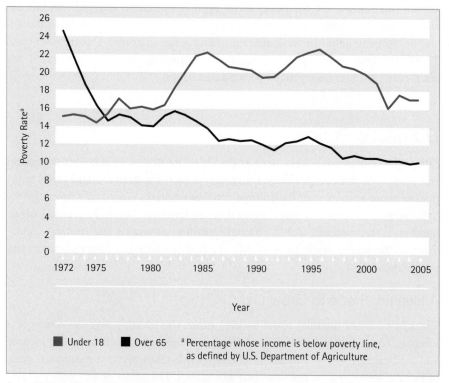

Source: U.S. Census Bureau, *Historical Poverty Tables—People*, Table 3: Poverty Status by Age, Race and Hispanic Origin, www.census.gov/hhes/www/poverty/histpov/hstpov3.html, accessed February 8, 2007.

Social security initially cost the government very little. Benefits were low and life expectancy short. Those reaching age 65 lived, on average, only another 13 to 15 years. Over time both medical improvements and policy changes caused the costs to leap upward. A typical worker retiring at 65 today lives more than 18 years.[18] Congress has also expanded the number of people covered. Benefits have increased in size and cost, including a large hike in 1972 that linked future benefits to the inflation rate. If inflation goes up 10 percent, so does the social security check.[19] And the national government took another substantial step in 1965 by setting up Medicare to subsidize health costs for social security recipients.

The result is that spending on the elderly has grown to dominate the nation's domestic budget. From 1970 to 2005, the amount spent on social programs for senior citizens doubled after adjusting for inflation.* Nor do these benefits go only to the needy. Upon reaching the age of 65, even billionaire Microsoft founder Bill Gates will be eligible to receive a social security check.

Many Americans believe that social security is an insurance program, taking money from able-bodied workers and returning it to them if they live long enough to need it back. This is a myth. Social security operates at a loss, giving far more to the elderly in benefits than they have ever contributed in payroll taxes. For example, a couple with a single average wage earner retiring in 2008 can expect to receive 4.4 percent more in benefits than the worker in the family paid in, even after taking inflation into account.[20] How is this magic possible?[21] It is possible because of a workforce that (1) has been increasingly productive, (2) outnumbers the retired population, and (3) has been willing to bear increasing payroll taxes, including large hikes in 1977 and 1982.[22]

---

* Spending grew from under $10,030 per senior citizen to more than $20,000 in 2005 (based on 2005 dollars).

HIGH-STAKES POLICY
One explanation why aid to the poor receives less public support than aid to senior citizens is that welfare appears to subsidize sins such as sloth, crime, and extramarital sex. Yet many Americans consider gambling a sin, and the elderly are known for their disproportionate presence in casinos. Indeed, some casinos park transports where seniors are known to exchange their social security checks. *Why, then, are the elderly considered so deserving of government handouts?*

The nation's approach to old-age insurance is probably not sustainable. The massive baby boom generation will reach retirement age after 2010, and the number of workers will not keep pace. Nor is worker productivity expected to increase much. Thus, the only way to maintain retirement programs would be to increase payroll taxes substantially. But will the workers of the future be willing to bear taxes sufficient to subsidize retirees at the same level of material comfort as the United States does today? Figure 15.3 illustrates how improbable that is. It projects the payroll tax rates that would be required to sustain current benefits into the future. By 2040, years before today's college students will be old enough to retire, benefits already would demand around 25 percent of taxable payroll. Pessimistically, the price tag could rise to more than half of all payroll money. Will the workers of 2040 give up half of their potential salaries just to take care of the elderly? Not likely.

FIGURE 15.3   Projected cost of social insurance for senior citizens

Costs of programs for senior citizens will rise rapidly in the coming years.

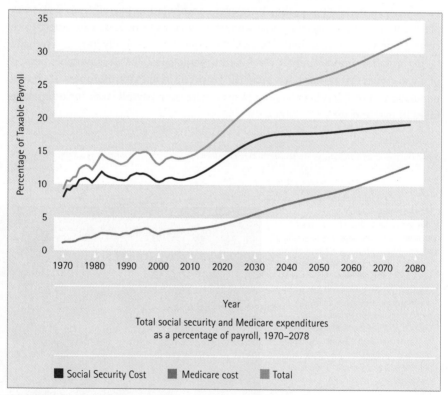

Note: Figures after 2005 are estimates; projections are for an 'intermediate cost' scenario.

Source: U.S. Department of Health and Human Services, Social Security Administration, "Status of the Social Security and Medicare Programs," *A Summary of the 2006 Annual Reports*, www.ssa.gov/OACT/TRSUM/trsummary.html, accessed February 8, 2007.

And the outlook for the future may only be worsening. In a time of moderate economic performance, politicians have not embraced cost-saving proposals. Instead, they moved in the opposite direction, including the implementation of the new prescription drug benefits for the elderly that President Bush and Congress enacted in 2003. These new benefits will result in at least an additional $500 billion in Medicare expenses from 2005 to 2015. Security and reconstruction needs after the 2001 terrorist attacks have also laid claim to social resources, as have the wars in Iraq and Afghanistan.[23]

The Elderly and the Permanent Campaign

Most public officials know better than to question the social security program, even though it is the most costly single item in the entire federal budget. In the early 1980s, President Ronald Reagan suggested offhandedly that Congress might need to place limits on the program's growth. The public backlash was swift and angry, prompting every single senator to condemn the president's idea two days later. Even so, Reagan's remark contributed to his party's loss of the U.S. Senate. Because of this, for many years both Democrats and Republicans saw social security as a perilous program to meddle with. In 2005, when President Bush proposed changing the program to allow workers to place some social security funds in private accounts, even members of his own party were cautious about endorsing the proposal, and the plan went nowhere in Congress. As one analyst put it, challenging social security could be "like standing barefoot in a puddle of water, and sticking your finger in an electric socket."[24]

The politics of Medicare is much the same, making it difficult to hold down program costs. Medicare cost little more than $35 billion in 1970, but by 2007 it had grown to $300 billion.[25] It pays for cutting-edge medical techniques—such as magnetic resonance imaging, bone marrow transfusions, and other high-tech, high-cost procedures. As a result of legislation passed in 2003, it now also pays for some prescription drugs. Adding to the financial burden are the exorbitant penalties that lawsuits extract when health care providers make mistakes, penalties that drive up the fees doctors must charge to cover their malpractice insurance.

Politicians avoid provoking senior citizens because the electoral cost of pleasing them is much lower than the cost of resisting. At a time when overall voter turnout has been declining, senior turnout rates are high and have been climbing. More than 70 percent of Americans older than 65 said they voted in the 2004 presidential election, but only 47 percent of those between the ages of 18 and 24 reported voting.[26] Children cannot vote at all. Senior citizens are also much more likely than young people to back up their votes with other political actions, such as writing letters to officials and contributing money to campaigns.[27]

Upon reaching the age of 50, any person can become a member of the American Association of Retired Persons (AARP) for $12.50 per year. Members qualify for a wide range of discounts worth much more than their annual dues, so more than 35 million people have joined—making AARP the largest interest group in the

United States. AARP employs more than 1,800 people, works with more than 160,000 volunteers, and has an annual budget of $925 million.[28]

Few voters punish elected officials for accommodating AARP demands. In fact, young people are just about as likely to support social security as those older than of 65. They know others who are receiving benefits and hope to do the same some day. Many assume that the elderly are simply receiving funds they originally contributed—and they think that the government is saving their own contributions for them. In fact, nearly nine out of ten Americans between the ages of 18 and 64 say that older Americans have the right amount or too little "influence in this country today."[29] Americans of every age category want political leaders to defend social security (see Figure 15.4).[30]

A Risky Place to be Born

Poor families with children do not receive very good representation in America's new democracy. No association comparable to AARP defends their interests, and neither political party shows much concern for programs that assist them. As a result, government aid to poor families is neither as lavish nor as easy to obtain as that intended for the elderly.

FIGURE 15.4   Both young and old support senior citizens' programs

Why do the young support programs for the elderly even though they do not yet receive benefits from such programs?

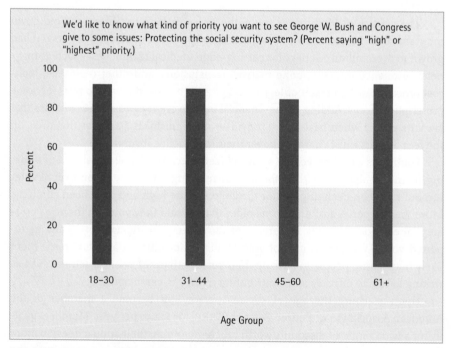

We'd like to know what kind of priority you want to see George W. Bush and Congress give to some issues: Protecting the social security system? (Percent saying "high" or "highest" priority.)

Source: Washington Post/ABC News Poll, January 12–16, 2005.

Benefits for the Poor   More programs assist households with limited income than assist the elderly, but these programs are rarely as generous. Public assistance programs include TANF, food stamps, the Earned Income Tax Credit (EITC), rent subsidies, and Medicaid.

TANF maintains the incomes of poor families. It varies by state but always limits aid to no more than two years in a row and to no more than five years alto · gether. It took the place of a costlier, and highly unpopular, program called **Aid to Families with Dependent Children (AFDC)**, which most Americans knew simply as "welfare." After the end of AFDC, some beneficiaries switched to Supplemental Security Income (SSI). Created in 1972, SSI provides financial assistance to disabled people of low income. As of January 2006, the average monthly benefit for SSI's 6.9 million recipients was $422.[31]

The **Earned Income Tax Credit (EITC)** returns taxes to those who have little income. Initially proposed by Republicans in the early 1970s as a tax rebate that would reward the working poor, EITC was expanded early in the Clinton administration so that even those who have not paid taxes can receive checks. In 2006, a family of four could receive a credit of as much as $4500 a year.[32]

The national government also provides more focused benefits to needy families. **Food stamps** are coupons that can be used to purchase edibles. Enacted by Congress on an experimental basis in the early 1970s, the program has expanded gradually—in part because it is popular with agricultural interests who grow American produce. Low-income families also may receive rent subsidies if they live in designated residences, a program that has helped many minority families leave crime-ridden inner cities and move to the suburbs.

Medicaid covers medical services for the poor. A person becomes eligible only if he or she has no more than a minimal income and few assets other than a home. Medicaid costs have risen almost as rapidly as those for Medicare—from around $13 billion in 1970 to $180 billion in 2006.[33] Because the program covers poor families regardless of age, however, the elderly benefit from Medicaid too. More than one-quarter of all Medicaid costs go to low-income seniors.[34]

Welfare and the Permanent Campaign   The general public varies over time in its support for social welfare policies. Generally, when the economy is strong, people are more likely to blame the poor for their condition and less likely to attribute poverty to circumstances beyond the individual's control.[35] Public opinion also shifts with the current policies. In particular, the welfare issue has become less controversial since the end of AFDC.

Political parties fluctuate on welfare policy in step with public opinion. When the country was building the Great Society in the 1960s and 1970s, Democrats took the lead, but Republicans were not far behind. Republican presidents signed into law several welfare programs for children. President Nixon proposed the food stamp and SSI programs. Republicans proposed, and President Ford signed, the law creating EITC. Republicans in Congress initiated the Medicaid program. As the public mood shifted in a conservative direction, the positions of both parties changed accordingly. In 1995 it was the Republicans who took the lead, proposing cuts in many of the programs they had once sponsored.[36] Although some Democrats opposed the cuts, a majority voted in favor of welfare reform, and President Clinton signed the bill. Today, both parties take credit for the passage of TANF, and the program was renewed without much controversy in 2006.

Seniors Versus Children: A Comparison

The list of public assistance programs helping poor families seems impressive, but actual expenditures are only one-tenth as much as what is spent on the elderly. Federal social programs for the elderly amounted to more than $750 billion in 2005, whereas public assistance programs for poor families with children amounted to little more than $300 billion (see Figure 15.5). This works out to more than $20,500 per person in expenditures for the elderly, but only about $8,800 per person in expenditures for the poor. Government has committed itself to extending the last years of life rather than to enhancing capacities in the first years of life.

Programs for families with children are also more restrictive than programs for senior citizens.[37] They are less likely to provide flexible cash benefits and more likely to provide inflexible goods and services. The elderly receive nearly 64 percent of their benefits in cash,[38] whereas poor families receive only 32 percent that way.[39] Nearly all benefits to the elderly are tied to changes in the cost of living. By contrast, welfare spending generally fails to keep pace with inflation. Average monthly benefits under the main welfare programs, AFDC and later TANF, fell by nearly 60 percent between 1977 and 2003.[40]

The benefits that families receive vary from one state to another. Only EITC benefits are uniform throughout the country. For the other major programs—TANF, food stamps, SSI, housing assistance, and Medicaid—eligibility rules and benefit levels vary from state to state. Variation makes using the programs more confusing and may limit the mobility of the poor.[41] For example, TANF benefits can be five times as much in one state as in another.[42] Senior citizens, by contrast, can move from New Jersey to Florida (or even overseas) without jeopardizing the amount or delivery of their social security checks.

The benefits that poor families with children receive are substitutes for other income. In many states, families are not eligible for income assistance if they have savings of more than $2,000, a car worth more than $5,000, or anything other than a very modest home.[43] The head of the household must visit a government agency and reveal to a government official the family's complete fiscal record. Benefits drop swiftly as a family starts to climb from poverty.[44]

By comparison, senior citizens' benefits supplement the recipient's own resources. Senior citizens may receive their Medicare and social security benefits even if they are working full-time, have savings, earn dividends and interest on their investments, and are homeowners. Before the year 2000, social security

FIGURE 15.5 Federal entitlement expenditures by beneficiary category, 1965–2010

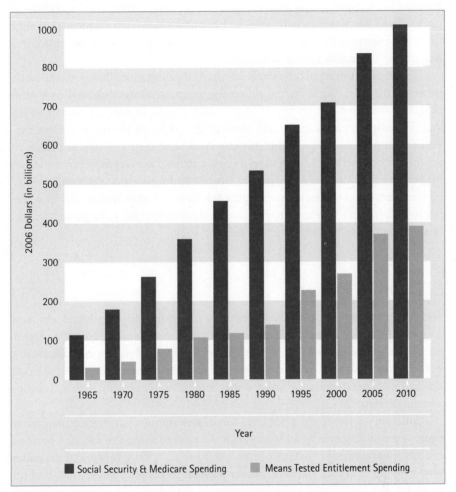

Note: Figures in billions of constant 2006 dollars; figures for 2010 are estimates.

Source: Office of Management and Budget, Budget of the United States, Fiscal Year 2008, Historical Tables, Table 8.2 and Table 8.5.

recipients between 65 and 69 years old lost some benefits if they earned more than $17,000 per year. But Republicans and Democrats in Congress, eager to please elderly voters in an election year, repealed this "earnings penalty" unanimously.[45]

Historically, Americans have supported a large, well-financed education system. This solicitude seems to contradict their relative stinginess toward other programs for young people. Part of the explanation, of course, is that education differs in many ways from other programs oriented toward children. It is primarily funded by local taxes and governed by local leaders, so voters feel closer to the policy's beneficiaries (see Chapter 3). It is not restricted to the poor and so attracts middle-class support. It promotes "equal opportunity" rather than a "culture of poverty" and so coincides with America's political values (see Chapter 4). It cultivates good workers who generate profits and who are less likely to become criminals, and so it benefits society as a whole.

To the extent that public schools fall short of expectations, however, the weaknesses in the educational system reflect the same handicaps that hold back other programs intended to help the young: limited growth in funding, low flexibility, and few budgetary assurances. Like other programs for children, educational policies do not provide cash benefits. Parents must send their children to the school provided for them; they usually cannot choose schools the way Medicare recipients may choose their doctors or hospitals.[46] The public programs available will not supplement family resources, only substitute for them. Citizens lose all the taxes they pay into the school system if they choose to send their children to private schools. In short, public policy strongly favors seniors.

Economic Policy

The U.S. economy is one of the strongest in the world, allowing Americans good wages and a high standard of living. Nevertheless, even wealthy countries experience **business cycles**—periods of economic expansion and rising prices alternating with occasional slowdowns in economic activity called **recessions** (see Figure 15.6). Governments seek economic policies that minimize disruptions such as inflation and unemployment.

Inflation—a rise in the price level—makes consumers pay more money for an equal amount of goods and services, thereby undermining the value of personal savings. **Unemployment**, which occurs when people willing to work at prevailing wages cannot find jobs, harms a smaller number of people—but in ways that can be severe. For a long time, economists thought the two conditions were closely related; lower unemployment eventually created higher inflation, and vice versa.[47] But economists no longer believe the relationship is so close. In fact, President Carter had the misfortune to run for reelection at a time of stagflation, when both inflation and unemployment (stagnation) were high. He suffered a humiliating defeat.

People tend to blame those in charge when times are hard. President George H. W. Bush's popularity ratings plummeted 40 percentage points over two years because of unemployment increases. During the 2004 campaign, Democratic presidential candidate John Kerry blamed Bush's son, George W., for disappointing employment figures during his presidency, as well as for allowing corporations to "outsource" jobs to other countries. Terrible economic times can produce massive election losses for the president's party. The depression of the 1890s ushered in an

FIGURE 15.6 Long-term growth and the business cycle in the United States

Although the general economic trend may be upward over the long run, expansions and recessions that characterize the business cycle can—in the short term—harm both citizens and elected officials.

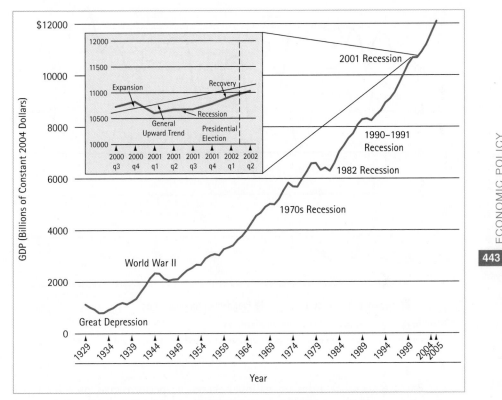

Sources: U.S. Census Bureau, *Statistical Abstract of the United States, 1999*, p. 881, Table 1434; U.S. Department of Commerce, Economics and Statistics Administration, "National Income and Product Accounts," www.bea.gov/dea/dn1.htm, accessed June 12, 2006.

era of Republican dominance, and the Great Depression of the 1930s did the same for the Democrats.

Prosperity, in contrast, strengthens a president's position for reelection (see Figure 15.7). Riding booming economies, Lyndon Johnson trampled Barry Goldwater in 1964, Richard Nixon crushed George McGovern in 1972, Ronald Reagan trounced Walter Mondale in 1984, and Bill Clinton overwhelmed Bob Dole in 1996. Of course, a healthy economy does not guarantee presidential popularity. For example, low unemployment in 2006 did not protect George W. Bush from the Iraq War's unpopularity, and Republicans suffered at the polls as a result. Nonetheless, presidents usually do better electorally when the economy is strong—results that spill over to influence both congressional and state elections.[48]

FIGURE 15.7 Retrospective voting

How Americans feel about the economy influences what they think about the president. *When does the economy not have a major impact on the public's view of the president?*

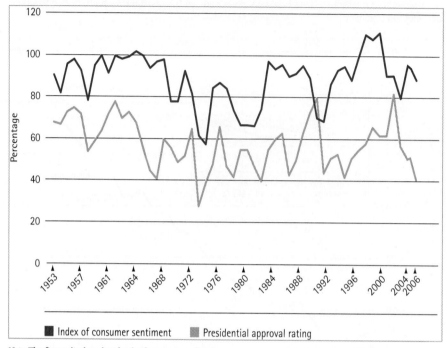

Note: The figure displays data for the first quarter of each year.

Sources: Index of Consumer Sentiment, Surveys of Consumers, University of Michigan; and Gallup polls, various years.

Because so much rides on national economic performance, presidents pay close attention to economic policy. Presidents enjoy little flexibility in dealing with the economy, though. One reason, of course, is that they must compromise with Congress; legislators scrutinize economic proposals closely to see how they would affect voters back home. But members of a school of economic thinking called **monetarism**, which stresses the importance of the money supply, add another important argument about the limits of presidential power. Responsibility for fine-tuning the money supply falls to the Federal Reserve Board (often called the "Fed"), an independent entity at best indirectly influenced by the White House (see Chapter 11).

Monetary policy—whereby the Fed adjusts interest rates and varies the supply of money—is now the government's most important economic tool. When money is cheap, with low interest rates, people borrow more. They invest or spend the money, spurring new productivity and lower unemployment. The weak dollar attracts foreign spending and investments. Conversely, when money is expensive, with high interest rates, people hold on to their money and borrow less.

Inflationary pressures ease. Foreign goods become cheaper for American consumers, siphoning cash out of the overheated economy.

Fiscal Policy

Traditionally, presidents have tried to influence the economy more directly through the federal budget, a policy tool more amendable to political maneuvering. A government's **fiscal policy**, the sum total of taxation and spending in its budget, influences how money passes through a nation's economic system. Government spending usually exceeds revenue, producing a *deficit*. Occasionally, revenue outpaces spending, producing a *surplus*. In either case, fiscal policy influences the speed at which a nation's financial resources change hands.

According to an influential English economist of the 1920s and 1930s, John Maynard Keynes, budget deficits can lift an economy out of a recession. Government spending jump-starts the economy by giving consumers extra money with which to buy goods and services. Following this line of reasoning, which came to be called **Keynesianism**, Franklin Delano Roosevelt broke with the traditional belief in a balanced budget and embraced large deficits during the Great Depression. Officials also use tax cuts to stimulate the economy. In 2003, President Bush won a reduction in taxes on stock dividends, saying that "lower taxes and greater investment will help this economy expand."[49]

Administrations today are much less likely to use fiscal policy as a tool for managing the economy than they were immediately after FDR's New Deal. Aside from the rise of monetarism, three reasons explain the movement away from using fiscal policy: the slowness of the budgetary process, the tendency of elected officials to put off unpopular choices, and the impotence of fiscal tools in the face of a globalized economy.

The Budgetary Process   The federal budgetary process is long and complicated. It starts within the executive branch a year and a half before the beginning of the fiscal year.* Federal agencies submit their budget requests during the summer to the Office of Management and Budget (OMB). During the fall, the OMB reviews requests and modifies them through negotiations with the departments (perhaps under the president's supervision). The Budget and Accounting Act of 1921 requires that Congress receive the president's budget no later than the first Monday in February.

No law requires Congress to pay any attention to what the president recommends. To construct its own budget, Congress generally follows the procedures laid down in the 1974 Budget and Impoundment Control Act. Two budget committees—one in the Senate, one in the House—collect budget proposals from the other congressional committees and construct a resolution specifying the overall

---

* By law, fiscal years and calendar years do not overlap completely. Fiscal year 2007, for example, started on October 1, 2006.

amount that the government will raise and spend in each of the next five years. Congress has met the April 15 deadline for approving a budget resolution only rarely since the deadline went into effect in 1974.[50]

Once the budget resolution is enacted, appropriations subcommittees use its funding targets as a framework for writing 13 detailed appropriations bills. Congress has until October 1, the start of the new fiscal year, to pass these bills. In practice, passage almost never happens on schedule, and parts of the government must operate under continuing resolutions, temporary funding measures passed by Congress to keep the government operating. In 1995, partisan battles forced two extended government shutdowns and left the nation without a budget for nearly four months. In 1998, Congress skipped the budget resolution stage, technically violating the law. And in 2006, Congress adjourned without passing most of the required appropriations bills, forcing the new Congress to cobble together a hasty set of spending measures in early 2007.

Given this complicated process, it is not difficult to understand why fiscal policy is a blunt tool for addressing economic troubles. Fiscal policy changes slowly, especially when different political parties must agree on a budget, whereas economic conditions can fluctuate rapidly.[51] For example, in 1990 the national government approved a tax increase to check inflation, but it did not take effect until the country faced just the opposite problem: unemployment growing out of a recession.

Short-sighted Budgeting   Fiscal policy operates under long-term limits. Several years of deficit spending can run up a serious *debt*—the total quantity of money a government owes. Not only does a large debt tie up lots of borrowed money that otherwise might go toward productive investments, it also commits the government to increasing interest payments on the loans. These sorts of obligations limit how much flexibility the government has to pump up the economy with direct spending. The more debt a nation carries, other things being equal, the higher interest rates that investors demand before they will lend more.

Furthermore, elected officials are quick to spend money they do not have, but they are much less eager to take away taxpayer money without a better justification than the need to slow down the economy! As a result, beginning in the early 1950s, the U.S. government ran up higher and higher deficits, and it did not reverse the trend until a brief period in the 1990s when the national debt's economic impact became too serious to ignore (see Figure 15.8). Policy makers cannot turn to deficit spending to help the economy if they are already running up a large deficit before the economy sours.

Globalization   Fiscal policy rarely seems to work in a globalized economy. Budgetary changes cannot compensate for swings in the value of a nation's currency. The value of money determines the exchange of goods across national borders. When the dollar is particularly valuable, Americans import more. Deficit spending

FIGURE 15.8   The federal deficit or surplus, 1950–2007

What accounts for the large deficits of the 1980s and the sudden surpluses of the late 1990s?

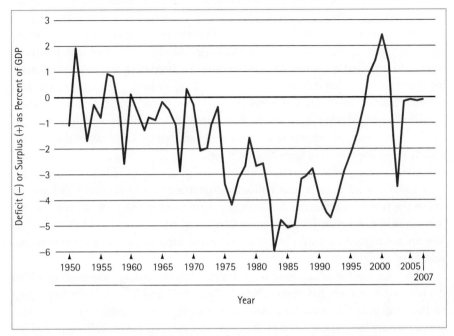

Year

Source: Office of Management and Budget, *The Budget of Fiscal Year 2006, Historical Tables*, p. 22, Table 1.2.

Note: Figures for 2006–2007 are estimates.

cannot increase the circulation of money if the cash it pumps into the economy leaks across national borders. When the dollar is weak, foreigners buy more American goods. High taxes cannot limit inflation if consumers in other countries pump their own assets into the U.S. economy. Investors can shift their assets back and forth in a similar fashion, using their knowledge of a country's economic policies. This sort of behavior dampens the economic impact of fiscal policies.

Globalization also limits the options available to a national government trying to set economic policies independently. Over time, the United States has participated in numerous international agreements that have increased the country's exposure to economic trends outside its borders, creating an "interdependence" among national economies. This trend received its first big push during the Truman administration. International banks were created to lend money to needy countries, United Nations organizations handled world health and refugee problems, and international trade agreements reduced tariffs around the world. In late 1947, for example, 23 countries founded the General Agreement on Tariffs and Trade (GATT). Under the current system, both the tax code and patterns of government spending influence trade with foreign countries—which can result in intense external pressure on national leaders not to implement swift and dramatic policy changes.

The Politics of Taxation

The budget deficit has been a major issue in American politics since the 1980s. When surveyed, voters say they want to reduce the deficit without raising taxes or cutting spending—contradictory demands that elected officials struggle to reconcile. At the turn of the new century, surprisingly robust economic growth produced a surge in expected government revenue, briefly eliminating the deficit and making it possible to either cut taxes, increase spending, or both.[52] The choice was clear to both President Bush and Congress: they cut taxes in early 2001. Although spending also increased after 9/11 due to homeland security needs and international conflicts, this example shows that when weighed against each other, tax cuts are usually more popular than spending increases.

After so many years operating on lean budgets, why wouldn't Americans use their sudden windfall to bolster national programs or start new ones? The answer lies in the popular preference for limited government in the United States, a core part of the nation's political culture (see Chapter 4). Most people think that their tax bills are too high. As a result, tax policy is a major topic of public concern that provokes heated debate.[53]

The total level at which Americans are taxed by the federal government, called the federal tax burden, has risen substantially since World War II. At the beginning of the war, only the wealthiest American families paid income taxes, whereas afterward only the poorest third of the workforce escaped the tax collector.[54] Federal individual income tax receipts rose by more than 60 percent between 1950 and 1970,

THE BELL TOLLS FOR THEE

GRIM TIDINGS

For many Americans, taxation can be as sinister as a gothic horror story. *Why do Americans feel this way if, as Figure 15.9 shows, taxation is low in the United States, relative to other nations?*

relative to the nation's productivity, after which personal income stagnated.[55] Many Americans came to feel that they were paying too much, even though their combined tax burden is still low by international standards (see Figure 15.9).

Nor is opposition to taxation simply a matter of values. For some it is a matter of good sense. Free-market economists, as well as many regular Americans, believe that taxes damage economic performance over the long term. Taxes lessen the incentive that workers and businesses have to increase productivity. Taxes draw wealth out of productive sectors of the economy and distribute it according to political considerations that may have nothing to do with efficiency, logic, or fairness. To antitax thinkers, then, the best way for government to improve social conditions is to stand out of the way of economic progress.

On the other hand, few Americans endorse eliminating national taxes altogether. The debate revolves instead around which taxes to permit and which to scale back or abolish. Organized groups work hard to convert public opinion over to their pet causes. They call on elected officials to use the tax code to encourage some behaviors and discourage others. In response to these pressures, national and state legislators have enacted thousands of **tax preferences**—special treatment that exempts particular types of activity from taxation. These tax loopholes cost the government billions of dollars in forgone revenue. Tax preferences are extremely

FIGURE 15.9   The U.S. tax burden is lower than that in many other democracies

No one likes taxes, but low rates in the United States reflect the American political culture.

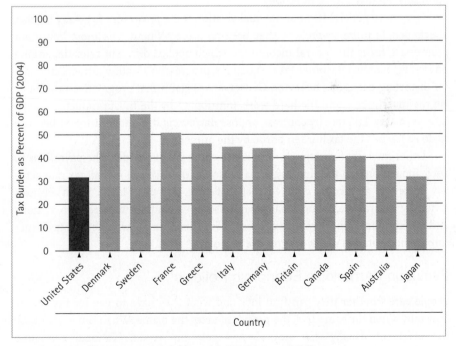

Source: U.S. Bureau of the Census, *Statistical Abstract of the United States, 2006,* Table 1335.

popular with the public or with attentive interest groups. Popular tax preferences include credits for college tuition and deductions for home mortgages and charitable contributions. Analysts have pointed to problems with each of these credits. They fault tuition credits for driving up education costs at the expense of the poor, mortgage deductions for funding oversized homes at the expense of the environment, and charitable deductions because it is hard to tell when a "charity" in fact is providing donors with some kind of hidden product or service. Yet no amount of criticism has dampened enthusiasm for these sacred cows of the tax code.

Furthermore, tax preferences are the classic "slippery slope." Once government grants one to any group, it abandons the principle of neutral taxation and confuses tax law. The policy encourages other groups to lobby for their own preferences, sometimes outside the view of public scrutiny. Moreover, granting preferences to some activities requires higher taxes on everyone else. Tax preferences were a key issue in the 2004 presidential campaign, when Democrat John Kerry accused President Bush of supporting tax breaks that encouraged businesses to move factories overseas. For his part, Bush accused Kerry of opposing tax credits for families and small businesses.

Not all special treatment is favorable. The government also sometimes imposes **sin taxes**, taxes intended to make money from people who engage in unpopular behavior. The most prominent sin taxes target cigarettes and alcohol. Critics of such measures argue that they fall primarily on the poorest segments of the population and fail to have a significant impact on the consumption of addictive products. But governments scrambling for revenue seldom pass up sin taxes as a politically popular source of money.

One more general form of unequal taxation is the *progressive tax*—any tax that affects people more severely as they become more affluent. The most important progressive tax is the federal income tax, which applies different rates depending on family income. Like other tax inequalities, progressive taxation attracts criticism for distorting economic behavior. Conservatives claim that progressive rates punish the investments and the hard work contributed by the most productive members of society. Liberals, by contrast, oppose narrowing differences in rates because to do so lessens the tax burden borne by the affluent.

Other taxes are *regressive*, hitting low-income people harder. The payroll tax in 2007 applied only to the first $97,500 a person earned, so the overall tax rate actually decreased as income climbed past that limit. For this reason, when all taxes levied by federal, state, and local governments—including numerous exceptions and exemptions—are taken into account, it is difficult to say whether the tax structure in the United States is progressive or not.[56]

Evaluating America's Economic Policies

People care whether they can find jobs and what they have to pay for the things they buy. When times are bad, the president takes the blame. When times are good, the president usually—but not always—gets the credit. National economic conditions significantly influence the president's popular standing. To a lesser extent, this is also true of members of Congress and even state-level officials.

Given these political facts of life, presidents accord economic policy top priority. They give the agency responsible for monetary policy, the Federal Reserve, a good deal of independence (see Chapter 11). For half a century, presidents also tried to use fiscal policy to manage the economy. But this approach has lost popularity, in part because it is hard to manipulate, but more so because it seldom works.

The American tax system generally reflects American political culture. The tax system includes numerous progressive taxes as well as tax breaks for individuals who pursue politically popular or influential activities. Yet candidates who push equalizing income attract limited support. Americans seem pleased with the balance in their system between rewarding success and eliminating inequalities—which has helped produce an adaptive economic system with less debt and lower unemployment rates.

Compared to other democracies, the United States is doing a decent job of dealing with its economic difficulties. The size of the national debt ($8.7 trillion in 2007) may be almost unimaginable. Relative to the size of the economy, though, the public debt in the United States is moderate. For example, relative to their productivity, France, Germany, and Canada all have larger national debts than the United States. Japan and Italy have debts nearly twice as large (see Figure 15.10).

FIGURE 15.10   U.S. debt is smaller than the debt of other countries

The U.S. debt is about $8 trillion, but this figure (as a proportion of national productivity) is moderate by international standards.

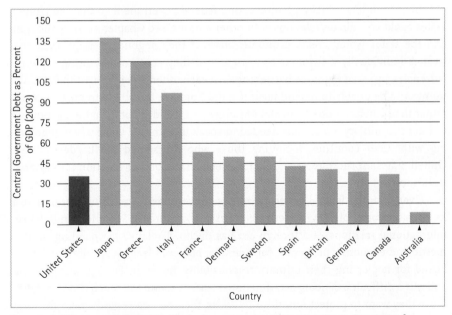

Source: Central Government Debt: Statistical Yearbook, 1994–2003, 2005 Edition, Paris, France, Organisation for Economic Cooperation and Development, 2005.

The United States has done a better job than most countries of incorporating new workers into the economy. In late 2005, for example, the unemployment rate in Western Europe hovered at nearly 10 percent—significantly higher than the 5.1 percent U.S. rate.[57] European countries kept their unemployment rates as low as they did only by using policies that would be unacceptable in the United States. For example, Germany and Switzerland induced so-called guest workers to return to their countries of origin. The United States, by contrast, has increased immigration significantly since the 1980s. Limited regulations and low taxation combined to encourage innovation—including development of high-tech industries such as computer software and biotechnology.

The price of limited government seems to be greater social inequality than is found in other advanced democracies. After declining between 1930 and 1970, inequality rose until, by the beginning of the twenty-first century, it was higher than at any time since the 1930s. Some scholars argue that this rising inequality is to blame for the increasing bitterness and hostility of politics in Washington.[58] Yet public demand for income redistribution is low.[59] The explanation may lie in the necessary trade-off between encouraging prosperity and mandating equality. Americans do not wish to kill the goose that lays the golden eggs. At some point, being relatively poor in a strong economy becomes better than being equal in a weak one.

Foreign and Defense Policy

America's founders initially set up a strong federal government so that the United States could coordinate relations with other nations (see Chapter 2). They thought that the states would create economic chaos if they negotiated trade pacts and treaties individually with other countries, or if they continued printing separate currencies and erecting trade barriers against each other. They thought that the nation would be unable to defend itself if it did not have the ability to raise an army rather than construct one from state militias, and if it did not have the tax powers to fund the military. Americans needed to speak in a unified voice when negotiating with other countries, including those who threatened the borders of the United States. In short, external relations seemed the proper function for national institutions.

Over time the federal government has concentrated less of its attention and its resources on protecting Americans from outside threats. Spending on defense, international relations, and foreign aid has declined relative to spending on domestic and economic programs, for example. National leaders are not entirely to blame for neglecting their primary responsibility, however. Foreign and defense policy is a difficult balancing act. If national leaders spend too much time on it, because they want to protect American interests, then no one rewards them for their

(text continues on page 455)

THE POLITICS OF U.S. ENERGY POLICY

In 2005, Hurricane Katrina and a later hurricane, Rita, disrupted oil rigs near Louisiana and Texas, interrupting the flow of oil from the Gulf of Mexico and sending gasoline prices soaring.[66] As commuters complained, experts argued that the event highlighted the vulnerability of the nation's oil supply to unforeseen events, especially because two-thirds of that oil comes from foreign countries.[67] "If there is a silver lining in this awful cloud," said one advocate, "it's that [Katrina] reminded Americans how vulnerable we are and why we have to end our dangerous addiction to foreign oil."[68]

It is not only vulnerability of the oil supply that Katrina highlighted. The record-breaking hurricane season of 2005 also drew attention to the rising average global temperature, which has now reached a level higher than at any time within the last 400 years.[69] Most of the increase in global temperatures appears to have occurred since industrialization (which began around 1850), suggesting that the 24 billion tons of carbon dioxide (CO_2) and related pollutants produced annually by automobiles, factories, and other industrial sources around the world have caused the atmosphere to trap more solar heat than in previous eras.[70] If global warming continues at its current pace, most scientists predict that within a century habitats will undergo major changes, ice masses at the two poles will melt, and the resulting rise in sea levels will flood coastal areas worldwide. The climbing temperature warms water as well as land, and warmer oceans induce more hurricanes such as Katrina.

Melting icebergs in Disko Bay, Greenland

The U.S. has yet to develop a comprehensive set of policies to mitigate either the vulnerability of the country's energy supply or the rising global temperatures. In 1975, Congress created a strategic petroleum reserve (oil purchased on a regular basis by the government to be held for potential use in times of national crisis). It has also passed two pieces of energy legislation, the first in 1992 and the second in 2005, but few believe the changes enacted were sweeping enough to be truly effective.

Nor has the global warming issue been addressed in a serious way by the larger international community. More than 140 countries have signed the Kyoto Protocol on climate change, a 1997 United Nations-sponsored agreement. Although the protocol asks developed nations to reduce their emissions substantially, it places no limits on countries in the developing world, such as China and India, which are responsible for a growing proportion of the world's pollutants. In 2001, the Bush Administration (which acknowledges that climate change is a serious problem) withdrew from participation, claiming that the treaty is unfair to U.S. industries.

Some experts argue that U.S. policy efforts ought to focus on *increasing the supply of domestic energy resources.* This might include allowing additional oil rigs

(continued on next page)

and refineries in previously protected areas, such as the Alaska National Wildlife Refuge (ANWR), more intensive utilization of coal resources, greater use of biological sources of energy such as ethanol (derived from corn), and, perhaps most importantly, the more extensive use of nuclear energy. They point out that the demand for energy is steadily increasing and any efforts to thwart increasing demand will have serious economic repercussions for the economy as a whole. By reducing dependence on foreign energy sources, this approach is also expected to bolster national security.

Others argue that government should develop policies that reduce the demand for energy by *encouraging conservation*. Many experts believe the best way to cut demand is by placing a higher tax on oil, gas, and other fossil fuels. But, because higher taxes are unpopular, the United States has instead used regulations to try to reduce the demand for energy. Automobile companies must build cars and trucks that get more miles to a gallon of gas. Similarly, home energy appliances—furnaces, hot water heaters, and refrigerators—must now meet efficiency standards. But these regulations have not been as effective as originally anticipated.

Most Americans consider themselves to be environmentalists. But this consensus breaks down when they are asked whether global climate change is a serious problem, and what steps they would be willing to take to address this and other energy policy issues. A majority of Americans say they worry at least "a fair amount" about global warming. They are less certain about what government should do to solve the nation's energy problems.[7]

WHAT DO YOU THINK?

1. What is most important: increasing energy supply or limiting energy demand?
2. Is energy demand better curbed by tighter regulations or higher taxes on gas, oil, or other fossil fuels?
3. Would you be willing to pay higher prices for energy if it reduced dependence on foreign energy sources? If it would slow global warming?
4. Why has neither political party favored a tax increase on gasoline?

For more information on *energy policy*, see the following Web sites:

The Heritage Foundation
www.heritage.org/Research/EnergyandEnvironment

The conservative Heritage Foundation recommends increasing domestic energy supplies.

The Sierra Club
www.sierraclub.org

This environmental group argues for less reliance on oil and more international engagement on climate change.

Realclimate.org
www.realclimate.org

A site created by working climate scientists, commenting on climate-science related news.

House and Senate Energy Committees
  http://energycommerce.house.gov
  http://energy.senate.gov/public

The House Committee on Energy and Commerce and the Senate Committee on Energy and Natural Resources handle most energy-related legislation that passes through Congress.

FOREIGN AND DEFENSE POLICY

preparedness. They suffer on Election Day for "ignoring problems at home." But if an international crisis develops and leaders have not prepared themselves to deal with it quickly and successfully, then they suffer on election Day for being unprepared. In short, national leaders face a double standard: They must protect voters from foreign threats, but they must not spend much time doing it. Under the circumstances, national leaders might even give defense inadequate attention and hope for the best—knowing that if something bad happens, voters may blame the enemy instead of them.

455

In other ways, though, foreign and defense policy is easier for politicians to negotiate than other types of policies. Americans might disagree angrily about which social problems the national government should address, and they may have sharply divided interests on the economic policies that the nation might pursue. But most Americans share the same rough goals and interests for foreign and defense policy. They want a country that is prosperous, safe, and strong. They want enemies defeated and threats averted. They want access to the world's goods and resources. They want international allies, not international enemies.

This basic agreement among Americans of all ideologies and all political parties makes foreign and defense policy less troublesome than other sorts of policies because it is possible to take a stand that pleases just about everybody. It has encouraged Congress to defer to the president, the nation's commander in chief (see Chapter 10), and to create a large foreign policy bureaucracy that enhances the chief executive's ability to gather international intelligence and act on it (see Chapter 11). Most of the policy battles in foreign and defense policy result not from disagreement over basic ideals and interests but, rather, from international decisions that actually affect domestic or economic policy.

Most, but not all. Occasionally Americans do find themselves sharply divided over how their country should deal with outsiders, and not simply because of what might happen back home as a result. A large antiwar movement rose up during the Vietnam conflict, and another peace movement appeared as the Bush administration went to war with Iraq. But even on these rare occasions, Americans do not express differing ideals or differing interests. Rather, sometimes ideals and interests clash in international affairs, and Americans may not be able to decide whether their values or their self-interest should win out.

National Ideals

American foreign policy is shaped by a long-standing tension that exists between American philosophical ideals and the country's practical need to protect its interests. Alexander Hamilton, in the *Federalist Papers*, made the best case for placing the highest priority on practical interests: "No Government [can] give us tranquility and happiness at home, which [does] not possess sufficient stability and strength to make us respectable abroad."[60] President Bush defends the war in Iraq in similarly idealistic terms. "Our actions," he explains, "are guided by a vision. We believe that freedom can advance and change lives." But Bush explains the purpose of freedom in practical terms: "The bitterness and burning hatreds that feed terrorism will fade and die away. America and all the world will be safer when hope has returned to the Middle East."[61]

IDEALISM

George W. Bush argued that the war in Iraq would spread freedom and democracy, while skeptics argued that such a view was unrealistic. *Are Americans more likely to be convinced by idealistic arguments or by arguments about the concrete national interest?*

Over the course of its history, the United States has not been so naïve or innocent that it ignored underlying national interests. The country acquired land and possessions when opportunities were ripe. But more than most nations, the United States has expressed its international goals in missionary language. Liberty, democracy, and inalienable rights are so important to the country's self-definition that they cannot be ignored when framing its relations with other nations. America's early presidents spoke out against European expansion.[62] A century later, the United States fought in two world wars in the name of freedom. When asking Americans to enter World War I, President Woodrow Wilson claimed it was necessary because "the world must be made safe for democracy."[63] When World War II broke out, President Roosevelt asked Americans to fight for four freedoms: free speech, religious freedom, freedom from want, and freedom from fear.[64]

National Interests

Ideals may structure American foreign policy, but that policy also reflects the country's practical self-interests. One of the oldest U.S. foreign policy principles, **isolationism**, is in fact explicitly self-centered. According to this principle, the United States should remain apart from the conflicts taking place among other nations. Isolationists often quote a phrase from George Washington's Farewell Address, made when he retired from the presidency: "'Tis our true policy to steer clear of permanent alliances."[65] For more than a century after Washington made this speech, the United States was, in the words of Winston Churchill, "splendidly isolated."

Isolationism is not so much a philosophy of weakness or of fear as a lack of concern. The United States has always sat an ocean away from the world's other major powers. Wars take place far away. The U.S. mainland last faced foreign invasion in 1814—unless one counts recent terrorist attacks. Limited interest in international affairs has been fed by the country's wartime successes, which have fostered a sense of invincibility. After the War of 1812 and until the Vietnam conflict, the United States had an impressive military record. Most wars ended in overwhelming victories. The United States has suffered few casualties in foreign wars (see Figure 15.11).

In sum, both idealistic and realistic factors help shape American foreign policy. On the one hand, the United States feels responsible for promoting the democratic experiment abroad. Voters do not appreciate presidential sluggishness when children are starving or people are being massacred. On the other hand, the United States, like any other country, has its own interests to protect. Voters become unhappy when the nation enters unnecessary conflicts or appears weak on the world stage. They reward elected officials who, because of their foreign policy activities, achieve important goals—not the least of which is prosperity

FIGURE 15.11   United States lucky in war

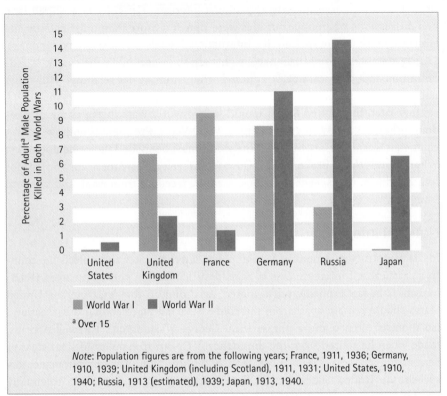

Note: Population figures are from the following years; France, 1911, 1936; Germany, 1910, 1939; United Kingdom (including Scotland), 1911, 1931; United States, 1910, 1940; Russia, 1913 (estimated), 1939; Japan, 1913, 1940.

Sources: R. Ernest Dupuy and Trevor N. Dupuy, *The Harper Encyclopedia of Military History: From 3500 B.C. to the Present* (New York: HarperCollins, 1993); Y. Takenob, *The Japan Year Book: 1919–1920* (Tokyo: Japan Year Book Office, 1921); B. R. Mitchell, *International Historical Statistics: Europe 1750–1988* (New York: Stockton Press, 1992); B. R. Mitchell, *International Historical Statistics of the Americas: 1750–1988* (New York: Stockton Press, 1993); B. R. Mitchell, *International Historical Statistics: Africa and Asia* (New York: New York University Press, 1982); and Raymond E. Zickel, ed., *Soviet Union: A Country Study* (Washington, DC: U.S. Government Printing Office, 1991).

CHAPTER SUMMARY

The elderly enjoy disproportionate influence in the United States, partly because they participate more in American politics, and partly because younger voters endorse the demands that senior citizens place on government. The result is a national budget that, aside from times of crisis, spends 10 times more on the elderly than it spends on other Americans. Furthermore, old-age welfare policies give senior citizens an unmatched amount of privacy and flexibility as they collect their benefits. Domestic policy is not the only policy area influenced by popular preferences, though. Fiscal policy does not work in part because politicians often do not believe they can raise taxes or cut programs to eliminate national debt without suffering electorally. Tax law reflects basic American values, including a preference for prosperity over equality. Presidents must attend to foreign affairs even when they wish to concentrate on domestic policy. A prime example is the way the September

11 terrorist attacks forced President Bush to put his domestic agenda on hold and prompted him to wage a war on terrorism. In sum, the whole scope of public policy illustrates quite starkly this book's central theme: In America's new democracy, elections (or at least the anticipation of them) matter more than they do in most countries—and more than they have for most of the nation's history.

KEY TERMS

Aid to Families with Dependent Children (AFDC), p. 439
business cycles, p. 442
Earned Income Tax Credit (EITC), p. 439
fiscal policy, p. 445
food stamps, p. 439
inflation, p. 442
isolationism, p. 457
Keynesianism, p. 445
Medicaid, p. 439

Medicare, p. 430
monetarism, p. 444
monetary policy, p. 444
recessions, p. 442
sin taxes, p. 450
tax preferences, p. 449
Temporary Assistance for Needy Families (TANF), p. 433
unemployment, p. 442

SUGGESTED READINGS

Daalder, Ivo, and James Lindsay. *America Unbound: The Bush Revolution in Foreign Policy.* Washington, DC: Brookings Institution Press, 2003. Two foreign policy scholars argue that George W. Bush has made dramatic changes in U.S. foreign policy.

Howell, William, and Paul E. Peterson, with Patrick Wolf and David Campbell. *The Education Gap: Vouchers and Urban Public Schools.* Washington, DC: Brookings, 2002. Analysis of school choice initiatives by scholars sympathetic to vouchers.

Huntington, Samuel. *The Clash of Civilizations.* New York: Simon & Schuster, 1996. Argues that future world conflicts will occur between clusters of nations that share a common cultural heritage.

Kingdon, John. *Agenda, Alternatives and Public Policies.* Boston: Little, Brown, 1984. Discusses the policy-making process, paying special attention to how problems become issues on the political agenda.

Slemrod, Joel, and Jon Bakija. *Taxing Ourselves: A Citizen's Guide to the Debate over Taxes* (3rd Edition). Cambridge, MA: MIT Press, 2004. A clear and readable guide to the current tax system.

Stiglitz, Joseph. *The Roaring Nineties: A New History of the World's Most Prosperous Decade.* New York: W. W. Norton & Co., 2003. A Nobel Prize-winning economist critiques recent U.S. economic policy.

ON THE WEB

For more information about public policy, see the following Web sites:

SOCIAL SECURITY ADMINISTRATION
www.ssa.gov
The Social Security Administration (SSA) Web site provides information on the characteristics of the social security program.

HEALTH CARE FINANCING ADMINISTRATION
www.hcfa.hhs.gov
The Health Care Financing Administration (HCFA) administers the Medicare and Medicaid programs.

AMERICAN ASSOCIATION OF RETIRED PEOPLE
www.aarp.org
The American Association of Retired People (AARP) maintains a large Web site describing its volunteer programs and lobbying efforts and offering health and recreation tips for seniors.

SENATE COMMITTEE ON FOREIGN RELATIONS
www.senate.gov/~foreign
The U.S. Senate's Committee on Foreign Relations provides information on treaties presented to the Senate for its approval, as well as on nominations and hearings on foreign policy.

appendix

The Declaration of Independence

In Congress, July 4, 1776

The Unanimous Declaration
of the Thirteen United States of America

When in the course of human events it becomes necessary for one people to dissolve the political bonds which have connected them with another, and to assume, among the powers of the earth, the separate and equal station to which the Laws of Nature and of Nature's God entitle them, a decent respect to the opinions of mankind requires that they should declare the causes which impel them to the separation.

We hold these truths to be self-evident, that all men are created equal, that they are endowed by their Creator with certain unalienable Rights, that among these are Life, Liberty and the pursuit of Happiness. That to secure these rights, Governments are instituted among Men, deriving their just powers from the consent of the governed. That whenever any Form of Government becomes destructive of these ends, it is the Right of the People to alter or to abolish it, and to institute new Government, laying its foundation on such principles and organizing its powers in such form, as to them shall seem most likely to effect their Safety and Happiness. Prudence, indeed, will dictate that Governments long established should not be changed for light and transient causes; and accordingly all experience hath shown that mankind are more disposed to suffer, while evils are sufferable, than to right themselves by abolishing the forms to which they are accustomed. But when a long train of abuses and usurpations, pursuing invariably the same Object evinces a design to reduce them under absolute Despotism, it is their right, it is their duty, to throw off such Government, and to provide new Guards for their future security.

Such has been the patient sufferance of these Colonies; and such is now the necessity which constrains them to alter their former Systems of Government. The history of the present King of Great Britain is a history of repeated injuries and usurpations, all having in direct object the establishment of an absolute Tyranny over these States. To prove this, let Facts be submitted to a candid world.

He has refused his Assent to Laws, the most wholesome and necessary for the public good.

He has forbidden his Governors to pass Laws of immediate and pressing importance, unless suspended in their operation till his Assent should be obtained; and when so suspended, he has utterly neglected to attend to them.

He has refused to pass other Laws for the accommodation of large districts of people, unless those people would relinquish the right of Representation in the Legislature, a right inestimable to them and formidable to tyrants only.

He has called together legislative bodies at places unusual, uncomfortable, and distant from the depository of their Public Records, for the sole purpose of fatiguing them into compliance with his measures.

He has dissolved Representative Houses repeatedly, for opposing with manly firmness his invasions on the rights of the people.

He has refused for a long time, after such dissolutions, to cause others to be elected; whereby the Legislative Powers, incapable of Annihilation, have returned to the People at large for their exercise, the State remaining in the meantime exposed to all the dangers of invasion from without, and convulsions within.

He has endeavored to prevent the population of these States; for that purpose obstructing the Laws of Naturalization of Foreigners; refusing to pass others to encourage their migration hither, and raising the conditions of new Appropriations of Lands.

He has obstructed the Administration of Justice, by refusing his Assent to Laws for establishing Judiciary powers.

He has made Judges dependent on his Will alone, for the tenure of their offices, and the amount and payment of their salaries.

He has erected a multitude of New Offices, and sent hither swarms of Officers to harass our people, and eat out their substance.

He has kept among us, in times of peace, Standing Armies without the Consent of our legislatures.

He has affected to render the Military independent of and superior to the Civil power.

He has combined with others to subject us to a jurisdiction foreign to our constitution, and unacknowledged by our laws, giving his Assent to their Acts of pretended Legislation:

For quartering large bodies of armed troops among us:

For protecting them, by a mock Trial, from punishment for any Murders which they should commit on the Inhabitants of these States:

For cutting off our Trade with all parts of the world:

For imposing Taxes on us without our Consent:

For depriving us in many cases, of the benefits of Trial by Jury:

For transporting us beyond Seas to be tried for pretended offences:

For abolishing the free System of English Laws in a neighboring Province, establishing therein an Arbitrary government, and enlarging its Boundaries so as to render it at once an example and fit instrument for introducing the same absolute rule into these Colonies:

For taking away our Charters, abolishing our most valuable Laws, and altering fundamentally the Forms of our Governments:

For suspending our own Legislatures, and declaring themselves invested with power to legislate for us in all cases whatsoever.

He has abdicated Government here, by declaring us out of his Protection and waging War against us.

He has plundered our seas, ravaged our Coasts, burnt our towns, and destroyed the lives of our people.

He is at this time transporting large Armies of foreign Mercenaries to compleat the works of death, desolation and tyranny, already begun with circumstances of Cruelty and perfidy scarcely paralleled in the most barbarous ages, and totally unworthy the Head of a civilized nation.

He has constrained our fellow Citizens taken Captive on the high Seas to bear Arms against their Country, to become the executioners of their friends and Brethren, or to fall themselves by their Hands.

He has excited domestic insurrections amongst us, and has endeavored to bring on the inhabitants of our frontiers, the merciless Indian Savages, whose known rule of warfare, is an undistinguished destruction of all ages, sexes and conditions.

In every stage of these Oppressions We have Petitioned for Redress in the most humble terms: Our repeated Petitions have been answered only by repeated injury: A Prince, whose character is thus marked by every act which may define a Tyrant, is unfit to be the ruler of a free people.

Nor have We been wanting in attention to our British brethren. We have warned them from time to time of attempts by their legislature to extend an unwarrantable jurisdiction over us. We have reminded them of the circumstances of our emigration and settlement here. We have appealed to their native justice and magnanimity; and we have conjured them by the ties of our common kindred to disavow these usurpations, which would inevitably interrupt our connections and correspondence. They too have been deaf to the voice of justice and consanguinity. We must, therefore, acquiesce in the necessity, which denounces our Separation, and hold them, as we hold the rest of mankind, Enemies in War, in Peace Friends.

We, therefore, the Representatives of the United States of America, in General Congress, Assembled, appealing to the Supreme Judge of the world for the rectitude of our intentions, do, in the Name, and by Authority of the good People of these Colonies, solemnly publish and declare, That these United Colonies are, and of Right ought to be Free and Independent States; that they are Absolved from all Allegiance to the British Crown, and that all political connection between them and the State of Great Britain, is and ought to be totally dissolved: and that as Free and Independent States, they have full power to levy War, conclude Peace, contract Alliances, establish Commerce, and to do all other Acts and Things which Independent States may of right do. And for the support of this Declaration, with a firm reliance on the protection of divine Providence, we mutually pledge to each other our Lives, our Fortunes and our sacred Honor.

JOHN HANCOCK

New Hampshire	Massachusetts Bay	Rhode Island
Josiah Bartlett,	Saml. Adams,	Step. Hopkins,
Wm. Whipple,	John Adams,	William Ellery.
Matthew Thornton.	Robt. Treat Paine,	
	Elbridge Gerry.	

Connecticut
Roger Sherman,
Samuel Huntington,
Wm. Williams,
Oliver Wolcott.

New York
Wm. Floyd,
Phil. Livingston,
Frans. Lewis,
Lewis Morris.

New Jersey
Richd. Stockton,
In. Witherspoon,
Fras. Hopkinson,
John Hart,
Abra. Clark.

Pennsylvania
Robt. Morris,
Benjamin Rush,

Benjamin Franklin,
John Morton,
Geo. Clymer,
Jas. Smith,
Geo. Taylor,
James Wilson,
Geo. Ross.

Delaware
Caesar Rodney,
Geo. Read,
Tho. M'kean.

Maryland
Samuel Chase,
Wm. Paca,
Thos. Stone,
Charles Caroll of
    Carollton.

Georgia
Button Gwinnett,

Lyman Hall,
Geo. Walton.

Virginia
George Wythe,
Richard Henry Lee,
Th. Jefferson,
Benjamin Harrison,
Thos. Nelson, jr.,
Francis Lightfoot Lee,
Carter Braxton.

North Carolina
Wm. Hooper,
Joseph Hewes,
John Penn.

South Carolina
Edward Rutledge,
Thos. Heyward, Junr.,
Thomas Lynch, jnr.,
Arthur Middleton.

The Constitution of the United States of America

Preamble

WE THE PEOPLE of the United States, in Order to form a more perfect Union, establish Justice, insure domestic Tranquility, provide for the common defence, promote the general Welfare, and secure the Blessings of Liberty to ourselves and our Posterity, do ordain and establish this Constitution for the United States of America.

Article I

Section 1

All legislative Powers herein granted shall be vested in a Congress of the United States, which shall consist of a Senate and House of Representatives.

Section 2

The House of Representatives shall be composed of Members chosen every second Year by the People of the several States, and the Electors in each State shall have the Qualifications requisite for Electors of the most numerous Branch of the State Legislature.

No person shall be a Representative who shall not have attained to the Age of twenty five Years, and been seven Years a Citizen of the United States, and who shall not, when elected, be an Inhabitant of that State in which he shall be chosen.

Representatives and direct Taxes shall be apportioned among the several States which may be included within this Union, according to their respective Numbers which shall be determined by adding to the whole Number of free Persons, including those bound to Service for a Term of Years, and excluding Indians not taxed, three fifths of all other Persons. The actual Enumeration shall be made within three Years after the first Meeting of the Congress of the United States, and within every subsequent Term of ten Years, in such Manner as they shall by Law direct. The Number of Representatives shall not exceed one for every thirty Thousand, but each State shall have at Least one Representative; and until such enumeration shall be made, the State of New Hampshire shall be entitled to chuse three, Massachusetts eight, Rhode-Island and Providence Plantations one, Connecticut five, New-York six, New Jersey four, Pennsylvania eight, Delaware one, Maryland six, Virginia ten, North Carolina five, South Carolina five, and Georgia three.

When vacancies happen in the Representation from any State, the Executive Authority thereof shall issue Writs of Election to fill such Vacancies.

The House of Representatives shall chuse their speaker and other Officers; and shall have the sole Power of Impeachment.

Section 3

The Senate of the United States shall be composed of two Senators from each State chosen by the Legislature thereof, for six Years; and each Senator shall have one Vote.

Immediately after they shall be assembled in Consequence of the first Election, they shall be divided as equally as may be into three Classes. The Seats of the Senators of the first Class shall be vacated at the Expiration of the second year, of the second Class at the Expiration of the fourth Year, and of the third Class at the Expiration of the sixth Year, so that one third may be chosen every second Year and if Vacancies happen by Resignation, or otherwise, during the Recess of the Legislature of any State, the Executive thereof may make temporary Appointments until the next Meeting of the Legislature, which shall then fill such Vacancies.

No Person shall be a Senator who shall not have attained to the Age of thirty Years, and been nine Years a Citizen of the United States, and who shall not, when elected, be an Inhabitant of that State for which he shall be chosen.

The Vice President of the United States shall be President of the Senate, but shall have no Vote, unless they be equally divided.

The Senate shall chuse their other Officers, and also a President pro tempore, in the Absence of the Vice President, or when he shall exercise the Office of President of the United States.

The Senate shall have the sole Power to try all Impeachments. When sitting for that Purpose, they shall be on Oath or Affirmation. When the President of the United States is tried, the Chief Justice shall preside: And no Person shall be convicted without the Concurrence of two thirds of the Members present.

Judgment in Cases of Impeachment shall not extend further than to removal from Office, and disqualification to hold and enjoy any Office of honor, Trust or Profit under the United States; but the Party convicted shall nevertheless be liable and subject to Indictment, Trial, Judgment and Punishment, according to Law.

Section 4

The Times, Places and Manner of holding Elections for Senators and Representatives, shall be prescribed in each State by the Legislature thereof; but the Congress may at any time by law make or alter such Regulations, except as to the Places of chusing Senators.

The Congress shall assemble at least once in every Year, and such Meeting shall be on the first Monday in December, unless they shall by Law appoint a different Day.

Section 5

Each House shall be the Judge of the Elections, Returns and Qualifications of its own Members, and a Majority of each shall constitute a Quorum to do Business; but a smaller Number may adjourn from day to day, and may be authorized to compel the Attendance of absent Members, in such Manner, and under such Penalties as each House may provide.

Each House may determine the Rules of its Proceedings, punish its Members for disorderly Behaviour, and with the Concurrence of two thirds, expel a Member.

Each House shall keep a journal of its Proceedings, and from time to time publish the same, excepting such Parts as may in their judgment require Secrecy; and the Yeas and Nays of the Members of either House on any question shall, at the Desire of one fifth of those present, be entered on the Journal.

Neither House, during the Session of Congress, shall, without the Consent of the other, adjourn for more than three days, nor to any other Place than that in which the two Houses shall be sitting.

Section 6

The Senators and Representatives shall receive a Compensation for their Services, to be ascertained by Law, and paid out of the Treasury of the United States. They shall in all Cases, except Treason, Felony and Breach of the Peace, be privileged from Arrest during their Attendance at the Session of their respective Houses, and in going to and returning from the same; and for any Speech or Debate in either House, they shall not be questioned in any other Place.

No Senator or Representative shall, during the Time for which he was elected, be appointed to any civil Office under the Authority of the United States, which shall have been created, or the Emoluments whereof shall have been encreased during such time; and no Person holding any Office under the United States, shall be a Member of either House during his Continuance in Office.

Section 7

All Bills for raising Revenue shall originate in the House of Representatives; but the Senate may propose or concur with Amendments as on other Bills.

Every Bill which shall have passed the House of Representatives and the Senate, shall, before it become a Law, be presented to the President of the United States; If he approve he shall sign it, but if not he shall return it, with his Objections to that House in which it shall have originated, who shall enter the Objections at large on their journal, and proceed to reconsider it. If after such Reconsideration two thirds of that House shall agree to pass the Bill, it shall be sent, together with the Objections, to the other House, by which it shall likewise be reconsidered, and if approved by two thirds of that House, it shall become a Law. But in all such Cases the Votes of both Houses shall be determined by Yeas and Nays, and the Names of the Persons voting for and against the Bill shall be entered on the Journal of each House respectively. If any Bill shall not be returned by the President within ten Days (Sundays excepted) after it shall have been presented to him, the Same shall be a Law, in like Manner as if he had signed it, unless the Congress by their Adjournment prevent its Return, in which Case it shall not be a Law.

Every Order, Resolution, or Vote to which the Concurrence of the Senate and House of Representatives may be necessary (except on a question of Adjournment) shall be presented to the President of the United States; and before the Same shall take Effect, shall be approved by him, or being disapproved by him, shall be repassed by two thirds of the Senate and House of Representatives, according to the Rules and Limitations prescribed in the Case of a Bill.

Section 8

The Congress shall have Power To lay and collect Taxes, Duties, Imposts and Excises, to pay the Debts and provide for the common Defence and general Welfare of the United States; but all Duties, Imposts and Excises shall be uniform throughout the United States;

To borrow Money on the credit of the United States;

To regulate Commerce with foreign Nations, and among the several States, and with the Indian Tribes;

To establish an uniform Rule of Naturalization, and uniform Laws on the subject of Bankruptcies throughout the United States;

To coin Money, regulate the Value thereof, and of foreign Coin, and fix the Standard of Weights and Measures;

To provide for the Punishment of counterfeiting the Securities and current Coin of the United States;

To establish Post Offices and post Roads;

To promote the Progress of Science and useful Arts, by securing for limited Times to Authors and Inventors the exclusive Right to their respective Writings and Discoveries;

To constitute Tribunals inferior to the supreme Court;

To define and punish Piracies and Felonies committed on the high Seas, and Offences against the Law of Nations;

To declare War, grant Letters of Marque and Reprisal, and make Rules concerning Captures on Land and Water;

To raise and support Armies, but no Appropriation of Money to that Use shall be for a longer Term than two Years;

To provide and maintain a Navy;

To make Rules for the Government and Regulation of the land and naval Forces;

To provide for calling forth the Militia to execute the Laws of the Union, suppress Insurrections and repel Invasions;

To provide for organizing, arming, and disciplining, the Militia, and for governing such Part of them as may be employed in the Service of the United States, reserving to the States respectively, the Appointment of the Officers, and the Authority of training the Militia according to the discipline prescribed by Congress;

To exercise exclusive Legislation in all Cases whatsoever, over such District (not exceeding ten Miles square) as may, by Cession of particular States, and the Acceptance of Congress, become the Seat of the Government of the United States, and to exercise like Authority over all Places purchased by the Consent of the

Legislature of the State in which the Same shall be for the Erection of Forts, Magazines, Arsenals, dock-Yards, and other needful Buildings;—And

To make all Laws which shall be necessary and proper for carrying into Execution the foregoing Powers, and all other Powers vested by this Constitution in the Government of the United States, or in any Department or Officer thereof.

Section 9

The Migration or Importation of such Persons as any of the States now existing shall think proper to admit, shall not be prohibited by the Congress prior to the Year one thousand eight hundred and eight, but a Tax or duty may be imposed on such Importation, not exceeding ten dollars for each Person.

The Privilege of the Writ of Habeas Corpus shall not be suspended, unless when in Cases of Rebellion or Invasion the public Safety may require it.

No Bill of Attainder or ex post facto Law shall be passed.

No Capitation, or other direct, Tax shall be laid, unless in Proportion to the Census or Enumeration herein before directed to be taken.

No Tax or Duty shall be laid on Articles exported from any State.

No Preference shall be given by any Regulation of Commerce or Revenue to the Ports of one State over those of another; nor shall Vessels bound to, or from, one State, be obliged to enter, clear, or pay Duties in another.

No Money shall be drawn from the Treasury, but in Consequence of Appropriations made by Law; and a regular Statement and Account of the Receipts and Expenditures of all public Money shall be published from time to time.

No Title of Nobility shall be granted by the United States: And no Person holding any Office of Profit or Trust under them, shall, without the Consent of the Congress, accept of any present, Emolument, Office, or Title, of any kind whatever, from any King, Prince, or foreign State.

Section 10

No state shall enter into any Treaty, Alliance, or Confederation; grant Letters of Marque and Reprisal; coin Money; emit Bills of Credit; make any Thing but gold and silver Coin a Tender in Payment of Debts; pass any Bill of Attainder, ex post facto Law, or Law impairing the Obligation of Contracts, or grant any Title of Nobility.

No State shall, without the Consent of the Congress, lay any Imposts or Duties on Imports or Exports, except what may be absolutely necessary for executing its inspection Laws: and the net Produce of all Duties and Imposts, laid by any State on Imports or Exports, shall be for the Use of the Treasury of the United States, and all such Laws shall be subject to the Revision and Control of the Congress.

No State shall, without the Consent of Congress, lay any Duty of Tonnage, keep Troops, or Ships of War in time of Peace, enter into any Agreement or Compact with another State, or with a foreign Power, or engage in War, unless actually invaded, or in such imminent Danger as will not admit of delay.

Article II

Section 1

The executive Power shall be vested in a President of the United States of America. He shall hold his Office during the Term of four Years, and, together with the Vice President, chosen for the same Term, be elected as follows.

Each State shall appoint, in such Manner as the Legislature thereof may direct, a Number of Electors, equal to the whole Number of Senators and Representatives to which the State may be entitled in the Congress; but no Senator or Representative, or Person holding an Office of Trust or Profit under the United States, shall be appointed an Elector.

The Electors shall meet in their respective States, and vote by Ballot for two Persons, of whom one at least shall not be an Inhabitant of the same State with themselves. And they shall make a List of all the Persons voted for, and, of the Number of Votes for each; which List they shall sign and certify, and transmit sealed to the Seat of the Government of the United States, directed to the President of the Senate. The President of the Senate shall, in the Presence of the Senate and House of Representatives, open all the Certificates, and the Votes shall then be counted. The Person having the greatest Number of Votes shall be the President, if such Number be a Majority of the whole Number of Electors appointed; and if there be more than one who have such Majority, and have an equal Number of Votes, then the House of Representatives shall immediately chuse by Ballot one of them for President; and if no Person have a Majority, then from the five highest on the List the said House shall in like Manner chuse the President. But in chusing the President, the Votes shall be taken by States, the Representation from each State having one Vote; A quorum for this Purpose shall consist of a Member or Members from two thirds of the States, and a Majority of all the States shall be necessary to a Choice. In every Case, after the Choice of the President, the Person having the greatest Number of Votes of the Electors shall be the Vice President. But if there should remain two or more who have equal Votes, the Senate shall chuse from them by Ballot the Vice President.

The Congress may determine the Time of chusing the Electors, and the Day on which they shall give their Votes; which Day shall be the same throughout the United States.

No Person except a natural born Citizen, or a Citizen of the United States, at the time of the Adoption of this Constitution, shall be eligible to the Office of President; neither shall any Person be eligible to that Office who shall not have attained to the Age of thirty five Years, and been fourteen Years a Resident within the United States.

In Case of the Removal of the President from Office, or of his Death, Resignation, or Inability to discharge the Powers and Duties of the said Office, the Same shall devolve on the Vice President, and the Congress may by Law provide for the Case of Removal, Death, Resignation or Inability, both of the President and Vice President, declaring what Officer shall then act as President, and such Officer shall act accordingly, until the Disability be removed, or a President shall be elected.

The President shall, at stated Times, receive for his Services, a Compensation, which shall neither be encreased nor diminished during the Period for which he shall have been elected, and he shall not receive within that Period any other Emolument from the United States, or any of them.

Before he enter on the Execution of his Office, he shall take the following Oath or Affirmation—"I do solemnly swear (or affirm) that I will faithfully execute the Office of President of the United States, and will to the best of my Ability, preserve, protect and defend the Constitution of the United States."

Section 2

The President shall be Commander in Chief of the Army, and Navy of the United States, and of the Militia of the several States, when called into the actual Service of the United States; he may require the Opinion, in writing, of the principal Officer in each of the executive Departments, upon any Subject relating to the Duties of their respective Offices, and he shall have Power to grant Reprieves and Pardons for Offences against the United States, except in Cases of Impeachment.

He shall have Power, by and with the Advice and Consent of the Senate, to make Treaties, provided two thirds of the Senators present concur; and he shall nominate, and by and with the Advice and Consent of the Senate, shall appoint Ambassadors, other public Ministers and Consuls, Judges of the supreme Court, and all other Officers of the United States, whose Appointments are not herein otherwise provided for, and which shall be established by Law: but the Congress may by Law vest the Appointment of such inferior Officers, as they think proper, in the President alone, in the Courts of Law, or in the Heads of Departments.

The President shall have Power to fill up all Vacancies that may happen during the Recess of the Senate, by granting Commissions which shall expire at the end of their next Session.

Section 3

He shall from time to time give to the Congress Information of the State of the Union, and recommend to their Consideration such Measures as he shall judge necessary and expedient; he may, on extraordinary Occasions, convene both Houses, or either of them, and in Case of Disagreement between them, with Respect to the Time of Adjournment, he may adjourn them to such Time as he shall think proper; he shall receive Ambassadors and other public Ministers; he shall take Care that the Laws be faithfully executed, and shall Commission all the Officers of the United States.

Section 4

The President, Vice President and all civil Officers of the United States, shall be removed from Office on Impeachment for, and Conviction of, Treason, Bribery, or other high Crimes and Misdemeanors.

Article III

Section 1

The judicial Power of the United States, shall be vested in one supreme Court, and in such inferior Courts as the Congress may from time to time ordain and establish. The Judges, both of the supreme and inferior Courts, shall hold their Offices during good Behaviour, and shall, at stated Times, receive for their Services, a Compensation, which shall not be diminished during their Continuance in Office.

Section 2

The judicial Power shall extend to all Cases, in Law and Equity, arising under this Constitution, the Laws of the United States, and Treaties made, or which shall be made, under their Authority;—to all Cases affecting Ambassadors, other public Ministers and Consuls;—to all Cases of admiralty and maritime Jurisdiction;—to Controversies to which the United States shall be a Party;—to Controversies between two or more States;—between a State and Citizens of another State;—between Citizens of different States,—between Citizens of the same State claiming Lands under Grants of different States,—and between a State, or the Citizens thereof, and foreign States, Citizens of Subjects.

In all Cases affecting Ambassadors, other public Ministers and Consuls, and those in which a State shall be Party, the supreme Court shall have original Jurisdiction. In all the other Cases before mentioned, the supreme Court shall have appellate Jurisdiction, both as to Law and Fact, with such Exceptions, and under such Regulations as the Congress shall make.

The Trial of all Crimes, except in Cases of Impeachment, shall be by Jury; and such Trial shall be held in the State where the said Crimes shall have been committed; but when not committed within any State, the Trial shall be at such Place or Places as the Congress may by Law have directed.

Section 3

Treason against the United States, shall consist only in levying War against them, or in adhering to their Enemies, giving them Aid and Comfort. No Person shall be convicted of Treason unless on the Testimony of two Witnesses to the same overt Act, or on Confession in open Court.

The Congress shall have Power to declare the Punishment of Treason, but no Attainder of Treason shall work Corruption of Blood, or Forfeiture except during the Life of the Person attainted.

Article IV

Section 1

Full Faith and Credit shall be given in each State to the public Acts, Records, and judicial Proceedings of every other State. And the Congress may by general Laws prescribe the Manner in which such Acts, Records and Proceedings shall be proved, and the Effect thereof.

Section 2

The Citizens of each State shall be entitled to all Privileges and Immunities of Citizens in the several States.

A Person charged in any State with Treason, Felony, or other Crime, who shall flee from Justice, and be found in another State, shall on Demand of the executive Authority of the State from which he fled, be delivered up, to be removed to the State having Jurisdiction of the Crime.

No Person held to Service or Labour in one State under the Laws thereof, escaping into another, shall, in Consequence of any Law or Regulation therein, be discharged from such Service or Labour, but shall be delivered up on Claim of the Party to whom such Service or Labour may be due.

Section 3

New States may be admitted by the Congress into this Union; but no new State shall be formed or erected within the Jurisdiction of any other State; nor any State be formed by the Junction of two or more States, or Parts of States, without the Consent of the Legislatures of the States concerned as well as of the Congress.

The Congress shall have Power to dispose of and make all needful Rules and Regulations respecting the Territory or other Property belonging to the United States; and nothing in this Constitution shall be so construed as to Prejudice any Claims of the United States, or of any particular State.

Section 4

The United States shall guarantee to every State in this Union a Republican Form of Government, and shall protect each of them against Invasion, and on Application of the Legislature, or of the Executive (when the Legislature cannot be convened) against domestic Violence.

Article V

The Congress, whenever two thirds of both Houses shall deem it necessary, shall propose Amendments to this Constitution, or, on the Application of the Legislatures of two thirds of the several States, shall call a Convention for proposing Amendments, which, in either Case, shall be valid to all Intents and Purposes, as Part of this Constitution, when ratified by the Legislatures of three fourths of the several States, or by Conventions in three fourths thereof, as the one or the other Mode of Ratification may be proposed by the Congress; Provided that no Amendment which may be made prior to the Year One thousand eight hundred and eight shall in any Manner affect the first and fourth Clauses in the Ninth Section of the first Article; and that no State, without its Consent, shall be deprived of its equal Suffrage in the Senate.

Article VI

All Debts contracted and Engagements entered into, before the Adoption of this Constitution, shall be as valid against the United States under this Constitution, as under the Confederation.

This Constitution, and the laws of the United States which shall be made in Pursuance thereof; and all Treaties made, or which shall be made, under the Authority of the United States, shall be the supreme Law of the Land; and the Judges in every State shall be bound thereby, any Thing in the Constitution or Laws of any State to the Contrary notwithstanding.

The Senators and Representatives before mentioned, and the Members of the several State Legislatures, and all executive and judicial Officers, both of the United States and of the several States, shall be bound by Oath or Affirmation, to support this Constitution; but no religious Test shall ever be required as a Qualification to any Office or public Trust under the United States.

Article VII

The Ratification of the Conventions of nine States, shall be sufficient for the Establishment of this Constitution between the States so ratifying the Same.

Done in Convention by the Unanimous Consent of the States present the Seventeenth Day of September in the Year of our Lord one thousand seven hundred and Eighty seven and of the Independence of the United States of America the Twelfth. In witness whereof we have hereunto subscribed our Names,

Go. WASHINGTON
Presid't. and deputy from Virginia

Attest
WILLIAM JACKSON
Secretary

Articles in addition to, and amendment of the Constitution of the United States of America, proposed by Congress and ratified by the Legislatures of the several states, pursuant to the Fifth Article of the original Constitution.

(The first ten amendments were passed by Congress on September 25, 1789, and were ratified on December 15, 1791.)

Amendment I

Congress shall make no law respecting an establishment of religion, or prohibiting the free exercise thereof; or abridging the freedom of speech, or of the press; or the right of the people peaceably to assemble, and to petition the Government for a redress of grievances.

Amendment II

A well regulated Militia, being necessary to the security of a free State, the right of the people to keep and bear Arms, shall not be infringed.

Amendment III

No Soldier shall, in time of peace be quartered in any house, without the consent of the Owner, nor in time of war, but in a manner to be prescribed by law.

Amendment IV

The right of the people to be secure in their persons, houses, papers, and effects, against unreasonable searches and seizures, shall not be violated, and no warrants shall issue, but upon probable cause, supported by Oath or affirmation, and particularly describing the place to be searched, and the persons or things to be seized.

Amendment V

No person shall be held to answer for a capital, or otherwise infamous crime, unless on a presentment or indictment of a Grand Jury, except in cases arising in the land or naval forces, or in the Militia, when in actual service in time of War or public danger; nor shall any person be subject for the same offence to be twice put in jeopardy of life or limb; nor shall be compelled in any criminal case to be a witness against himself, nor be deprived of life, liberty, or property, without due process of law; nor shall private property be taken for public use, without just compensation.

Amendment VI

In all criminal prosecutions, the accused shall enjoy the right to a speedy and public trial, by an impartial jury of the State and district wherein the crime shall have been committed, which district shall have been previously ascertained by law, and to be informed of the nature and cause of the accusation; to be confronted with the witnesses against him; to have compulsory process for obtaining witnesses in his favor, and to have the assistance of counsel for his defence.

Amendment VII

In Suits at common law, where the value in controversy shall exceed twenty dollars, the right of trial by jury shall be preserved, and no fact tried by a jury, shall be otherwise re-examined in any Court of the United States, than according to the rules of the common law.

Amendment VIII

Excessive bail shall not be required, nor excessive fines imposed, nor cruel and unusual punishments inflicted.

Amendment IX

The enumeration in the Constitution, of certain rights, shall not be construed to deny or disparage others retained by the people.

Amendment X

The powers not delegated to the United States by the Constitution, nor prohibited by it to the States, are reserved to the States respectively, or to the people.

Amendment XI
[Ratified on February 7, 1795]

The Judicial power of the United States shall not be construed to extend to any suit in law or equity, commenced or prosecuted against one of the United States by Citizens of another State, or by Citizens or Subjects of any Foreign State.

Amendment XII
[Ratified on June 15, 1804]

The Electors shall meet in their respective states, and vote by ballot for President and Vice-President, one of whom, at least, shall not be an inhabitant of the same state with themselves; they shall name in their ballots the person voted for as President, and in distinct ballots the person voted for as Vice-President, and they shall make distinct lists of all persons voted for as President, and of all persons voted for as Vice-President, and of the number of votes for each, which lists they shall sign and certify, and transmit sealed to the seat of the government of the United States, directed to the President of the Senate;—The President of the Senate shall, in the presence of the Senate and House of Representatives, open all the certificates and the votes shall then be counted;—The person having the greatest number of votes for President, shall be the President, if such number be a majority of the whole number of Electors appointed; and if no person have such majority; then from the persons having the highest numbers not exceeding three on the list of those voted for as President, the House of Representatives shall choose immediately, by ballot, the President. But in choosing the President, the votes shall be taken by states, the representation from each state having one vote; a quorum for this purpose shall consist of a member or members from two-thirds of the states, and a majority of all the states shall be necessary to a choice. And if the House of Representatives shall not choose a President whenever the right of choice shall devolve upon them, before the fourth day of March next following, then the Vice-President shall act as President, as in the case of the death or other constitutional disability of the President.—The person having the greatest number of votes as Vice-President, shall be the Vice-President, if such number be a majority of the whole number of Electors appointed, and if no person have a majority, then from the two highest numbers on the list, the Senate shall choose the Vice-

President; a quorum for the purpose shall consist of two-thirds of the whole number of Senators, and a majority of the whole number shall be necessary to a choice. But no person constitutionally ineligible to the office of President shall be eligible to that of Vice-President of the United States.

Amendment XIII
[Ratified on December 6, 1865]

Section 1
Neither slavery nor involuntary servitude, except as a punishment for crime whereof the party shall have been duly convicted, shall exist within the United States, or any place subject to their jurisdiction.

Section 2
Congress shall have power to enforce this article by appropriate legislation.

Amendment XIV
[Ratified on July 9, 1868]

Section 1
All persons born or naturalized in the United States, and subject to the jurisdiction thereof, are citizens of the United States and of the State wherein they reside. No State shall make or enforce any law which shall abridge the privileges or immunities of citizens of the United States; nor shall any State deprive any person of life, liberty, or property, without due process of law; nor deny to any person within its jurisdiction the equal protection of the laws.

Section 2
Representatives shall be apportioned among the several States according to their respective numbers, counting the whole number of persons in each State, excluding Indians not taxed. But when the right to vote at any election for the choice of electors for President and Vice President of the United States, Representatives in Congress, the Executive and Judicial officers of a State, or the members of the Legislature thereof, is denied to any of the male inhabitants of such State, being twenty-one years of age, and citizens of the United States, or in any way abridged, except for participation in rebellion, or other crime, the basis of representation therein shall be reduced in the proportion which the number of such male citizens shall bear to the whole number of male citizens twenty-one years of age in such State.

Section 3
No person shall be a Senator or Representative in Congress, or elector of President and Vice President, or hold any office, civil or military, under the United States, or under any State, who, having previously taken an oath, as a member of Congress, or as an officer of the United States, or as a member of any State legislature, or as an executive or judicial officer of any State, to support the Constitution of the

United States, shall have engaged in insurrection or rebellion against the same, or given aid or comfort to the enemies thereof. But Congress may by a vote of two-thirds of each House, remove such disability.

Section 4
The validity of the public debt of the United States, authorized by law, including debts incurred for payment of pensions and bounties for services in suppressing insurrection or rebellion, shall not be questioned. But neither the United States nor any State shall assume or pay any debt or obligation incurred in aid of insurrection or rebellion against the United States, or any claim for the loss or emancipation of any slave, but all such debts, obligations and claims shall be held illegal and void.

Section 5
The Congress shall have power to enforce, by appropriate legislation, the provisions of this article.

Amendment XV
[Ratified on February 3, 1870]

Section 1
The right of citizens of the United States to vote shall not be denied or abridged by the United States or by any State on account of race, color, or previous condition of servitude.

Section 2
The Congress shall have power to enforce this article by appropriate legislation.

Amendment XVI
[Ratified on February 3, 1913]

The Congress shall have power to lay and collect taxes on incomes, from whatever source derived, without apportionment among the several States, and without regard to any census or enumeration.

Amendment XVII
[Ratified on April 8, 1913]

The Senate of the United States shall be composed of two Senators from each State, elected by the people thereof, for six years; and each Senator shall have one vote. The electors in each State shall have the qualifications requisite for electors of the most numerous branch of the State legislatures.

When vacancies happen in the representation of any State in the Senate, the executive authority of such State shall issue writs of election to fill such vacancies: Provided, That the legislature of any State may empower the executive thereof to make temporary appointments until the people fill the vacancies by election as the legislature may direct.

This amendment shall not be so construed as to affect the election or term of any Senator chosen before it becomes valid as part of the Constitution.

Amendment XVIII
[Ratified on January 16, 1919]

Section 1
After one year from the ratification of this article the manufacture, sale, or transportation of intoxicating liquors within, the importation thereof into, or the exportation thereof from the United States and all territory subject to the jurisdiction thereof for beverage purposes is hereby prohibited.

Section 2
The Congress and the several States shall have concurrent power to enforce this article by appropriate legislation.

Section 3
This article shall be inoperative unless it shall have been ratified as an amendment to the Constitution by the legislatures of the several States, as provided in the Constitution, within seven years from the date of the submission hereof to the States by the Congress.

Amendment XIX
[Ratified on August 18, 1920]

The right of citizens of the United States to vote shall not be denied or abridged by the United States or by any State on account of sex.

Congress shall have power to enforce this article by appropriate legislation.

Amendment XX
[Ratified on February 6, 1933]

Section 1
The terms of the President and Vice President shall end at noon on the 20th day of January, and the terms of Senators and Representatives at noon on the 3d day of January, of the years in which such terms would have ended if this article had not been ratified; and the terms of their successors shall then begin.

Section 2
The Congress shall assemble at least once in every year, and such meeting shall begin at noon on the 3d day of January, unless they shall by law appoint a different day.

Section 3
If, at the time fixed for the beginning of the term of the President, the President elect shall have died, the Vice President elect shall become President. If a President shall not have been chosen before the time fixed for the beginning of his term, or if the President elect shall have failed to qualify, then the Vice President elect shall

act as President until a President shall have qualified; and the Congress may by law provide for the case wherein neither a President elect nor a Vice President elect shall have qualified, declaring who shall then act as President, or the manner in which one who is to act shall be selected, and such person shall act accordingly until a President or Vice President shall have qualified.

Section 4
The Congress may by law provide for the case of the death of any of the persons from whom the House of Representatives may choose a President whenever the rights of choice shall have devolved upon them, and for the case of the death of any of the persons from whom the Senate may choose a Vice President whenever the right of choice shall have devolved upon them.

Section 5
Sections 1 and 2 shall take effect on the 15th day of October following the ratification of this article.

Section 6
This article shall be inoperative unless it shall have been ratified as an amendment to the Constitution by the legislatures of three-fourths of the several States within seven years from the date of its submission.

Amendment XXI
[Ratified on December 5, 1933]

Section 1
The eighteenth article of amendment to the Constitution of the United States is hereby repealed.

Section 2
The transportation or importation into any State, Territory, or possession of the United States for delivery or use therein of intoxicating liquors, in violation of the laws thereof, is hereby prohibited.

Section 3
This article shall be inoperative unless it shall have been ratified as an amendment to the Constitution by conventions in the several States, as provided in the Constitution, within seven years from the date of the submission hereof to the States by the Congress.

Amendment XXII
[Ratified on February 27, 1951]

No person shall be elected to the office of the President more than twice, and no person who has held the office of President, or acted as President, for more than two years of a term to which some other person was elected President shall be elected to the office of the President more than once. But this Article shall not apply to any person holding the office of President when this Article was proposed by the Congress, and shall not prevent any person who may be holding the office of President, or acting as President, during the term within which this Article becomes operative from holding the office of President or acting as President during the remainder of such term.

Amendment XXIII
[Ratified on March 29, 1961]

Section 1
The District constituting the seat of Government of the United States shall appoint in such manner as the Congress may direct:

A number of electors of President and Vice President equal to the whole number of Senators and Representatives in Congress to which the District would be entitled if it were a State, but in no event more than the least populous State; they shall be in addition to those appointed by the States, but they shall be considered, for the purposes of the election of President and Vice President, to be electors appointed by a State; and they shall meet in the District and perform such duties as provided by the twelfth article of amendment.

Section 2
The Congress shall have power to enforce this article by appropriate legislation.

Amendment XXIV
[Ratified on January 23, 1964]

Section 1
The right of citizens of the United States to vote in any primary or other election for President or Vice President, for electors for President or Vice President, or for Senator or Representative in Congress, shall not be denied or abridged by the United States or any State by reason of failure to pay any poll tax or other tax.

Section 2
The Congress shall have power to enforce this article by appropriate legislation.

Amendment XXV
[Ratified on February 10, 1967]

Section 1
In case of the removal of the President from office or of his death or resignation, the Vice President shall become President.

Section 2

Whenever there is a vacancy in the office of the Vice President, the President shall nominate a Vice President who shall take office upon confirmation by a majority vote of both Houses of Congress.

Section 3

Whenever the President transmits to the President pro tempore of the Senate and the Speaker of the House of Representatives his written declaration that he is unable to discharge the powers and duties of his office, and until he transmits to them a written declaration to the contrary, such powers and duties shall be discharged by the Vice President as Acting President.

Section 4

Whenever the Vice President and a majority of either the principal officers of the executive departments or of such other body as Congress may by law provide, transmit to the President pro tempore of the Senate and the Speaker of the House of Representatives their written declaration that the President is unable to discharge the powers and duties of his office, the Vice President shall immediately assume the powers and duties of the office as Acting President.

Thereafter, when the President transmits to the President pro tempore of the Senate and the Speaker of the House of Representatives his written declaration that no inability exists, he shall resume the powers and duties of his office unless the Vice President and a majority of either the principal officers of the executive department or of such other body as Congress may by law provide, transmit within four days to the President pro tempore of the Senate and the Speaker of the House of Representatives their written declaration that the President is unable to discharge the powers and duties of his office. Thereupon Congress shall decide the issue, assembling within forty-eight hours for that purpose if not in session. If the Congress, within twenty-one days after receipt of the latter written declaration, or, if Congress is not in session, within twenty-one days after Congress is required to assemble, determines by two-thirds vote of both Houses that the President is unable to discharge the powers and duties of his office, the Vice President shall continue to discharge the same as Acting President; otherwise, the President shall resume the powers and duties of his office.

Amendment XXVI
[Ratified on July 1, 1971]

Section 1

The right of citizens of the United States, who are eighteen years of age or older, to vote shall not be denied or abridged by the United States or by any State on account of age.

Section 2

The Congress shall have power to enforce this article by appropriate legislation.

Amendment XXVII
[Ratified on May 7, 1992]

No law varying the compensation for the services of Senators and Representatives shall take effect until an election of Representatives shall have intervened.

The Federalist No. 10

November 22, 1787
James Madison

TO THE PEOPLE OF THE STATE OF NEW YORK.

Among the numerous advantages promised by a well constructed Union, none deserves to be more accurately developed than its tendency to break and control the violence of faction. The friend of popular governments, never finds himself so much alarmed for their character and fate, as when he contemplates their propensity to this dangerous vice. He will not fail therefore to set a due value on any plan which, without violating the principles to which he is attached, provides a proper cure for it. The instability, injustice and confusion introduced into the public councils, have in truth been the mortal diseases under which popular governments have every where perished; as they continue to be the favorite and fruitful topics from which the adversaries to liberty derive their most specious declamations. The valuable improvements made by the American Constitutions on the popular models, both ancient and modern, cannot certainly be too much admired; but it would be an unwarrantable partiality, to contend that they have as effectually obviated the danger on this side as was wished and expected. Complaints are every where heard from our most considerate and virtuous citizens, equally the friends of public and private faith, and of public and personal liberty; that our governments are too unstable; that the public good is disregarded in the conflicts of rival parties; and that measures are too often decided, not according to the rules of justice, and the rights of the minor party; but by the superior force of an interested and over-bearing majority. However anxiously we may wish that these complaints had no foundation, the evidence of known facts will not permit us to deny that they are in some degree true. It will be found indeed, on a candid review of our situation, that some of the distresses under which we labor, have been erroneously charged on the operation of our governments; but it will be found, at the same time, that other causes will not alone account for many of our heaviest misfortunes; and particularly, for that prevailing and increasing distrust of public engagements, and alarm for private rights, which are echoed from one end of the continent to the other. These must be chiefly, if not wholly, effects of the unsteadiness and injustice, with which a factious spirit has tainted our public administrations.

By a faction I understand a number of citizens, whether amounting to a majority or minority of the whole, who are united and actuated by some common impulse of passion, or of interest, adverse to the rights of other citizens, or to the permanent and aggregate interests of the community.

There are two methods of curing the mischiefs of faction: the one, by removing its causes; the other, by controlling its effects.

There are again two methods of removing the causes of faction: the one by destroying the liberty which is essential to its existence; the other, by giving to every citizen the same opinions, the same passions, and the same interests.

It could never be more truly said than of the first remedy, that it is worse than the disease. Liberty is to faction, what air is to fire, an aliment without which it instantly expires. But it could not be a less folly to abolish liberty, which is essential to political life, because it nourishes faction, than it would be to wish the annihilation of air, which is essential to animal life, because it imparts to fire its destructive agency.

The second expedient is as impracticable, as the first would be unwise. As long as the reason of man continues fallible, and he is at liberty to exercise it, different opinions will be formed. As long as the connection subsists between his reason and his self-love, his opinions and his passions will have a reciprocal influence on each other; and the former will be objects to which the latter will attach themselves. The diversity in the faculties of men from which the rights of property originate, is not less an insuperable obstacle to a uniformity of interests. The protection of these faculties is the first object of Government. From the protection of different and unequal faculties of acquiring property, the possession of different degrees and kinds of property immediately results: and from the influence of these on the sentiments and views of the respective proprietors, ensues a division of the society into different interests and parties.

The latent causes of faction are thus sown in the nature of man; and we see them every where brought into different degrees of activity, according to the different circumstances of civil society. A zeal for different opinions concerning religion, concerning Government and many other points, as well of speculation as of practice; an attachment to different leaders ambitiously contending for preeminence and power; or to persons of other descriptions whose fortunes have been interesting to the human passions, have in turn divided mankind into parties, inflamed them with mutual animosity, and rendered them much more disposed to vex and oppress each other, than to cooperate for their common good. So strong is this propensity of mankind to fall into mutual animosities, that where no substantial occasion presents itself, the most frivolous and fanciful distinctions have been sufficient to kindle their unfriendly passions, and excite their most violent conflicts. But the most common and durable source of factions, has been the various and unequal distribution of property. Those who hold, and those who are without property, have ever formed distinct interests in society. Those who are creditors, and those who are debtors, fall under a like discrimination. A landed interest, a manufacturing interest, a mercantile interest, a monied interest, with many lesser interests, grow up of necessity in civilized nations, and divide them into different classes, actuated by different sentiments and views. The regulation of these various and interfering interests forms the principal task of modern Legislation, and involves the spirit of party and faction in the necessary and ordinary operations of Government.

No man is allowed to be a judge in his own cause; because his interest would certainly bias his judgment, and, not improbably, corrupt his integrity. With equal, nay with greater reason, a body of men, are unfit to be both judges and parties, at the same time; yet, what are many of the most important acts of legislation, but so many judicial determinations, not indeed concerning the rights of single persons, but concerning the rights of large bodies of citizens, and what are the different classes of legislators, but advocates and parties to the causes which they determine? Is a law proposed concerning private debts? It is a question to which the creditors are parties on one side, and the debtors on the other. Justice ought to hold the balance between them. Yet the parties are and must be themselves the judges; and the most numerous party, or, in other words, the most powerful faction must be expected to prevail. Shall domestic manufactures be encouraged, and in what degree, by restrictions on foreign manufactures? are questions which would be differently decided by the landed and the manufacturing classes; and probably by neither, with a sole regard to justice and the public good. The apportionment of taxes on the various descriptions of property, is an act which seems to require the most exact impartiality; yet, there is perhaps no legislative act in which greater opportunity and temptation are given to a predominant party, to trample on the rules of justice. Every shilling with which they over-burden the inferior number, is a shilling saved to their own pockets.

It is in vain to say, that enlightened statesmen will be able to adjust these clashing interests, and render them all subservient to the public good. Enlightened statesmen will not always be at the helm: Nor, in many cases, can such an adjustment be made at all, without taking into view indirect and remote considerations, which will rarely prevail over the immediate interest which one party may find in disregarding the rights of another, or the good of the whole.

The inference to which we are brought, is, that the causes of faction cannot be removed; and that relief is only to be sought in the means of controlling its effects.

If a faction consists of less than a majority, relief is supplied by the republican principle, which enables the majority to defeat its sinister views by regular vote: It may clog the administration, it may convulse the society; but it will be unable to execute and mask its violence under the forms of the Constitution. When a majority is included in a faction, the form of popular government on the other hand enables it to sacrifice to its ruling passion or interest, both the public good and the rights of other citizens. To secure the public good, and private rights, against the danger of such a faction, and at the same time to preserve the spirit and the form of popular government, is then the great object to which our enquiries are directed: Let me add that it is the great desideratum, by which alone this form of government can be rescued from the opprobrium under which it has so long labored, and be recommended to the esteem and adoption of mankind.

By what means is this object attainable? Evidently by one of two only. Either the existence of the same passion or interest in a majority at the same time, must be prevented; or the majority, having such co-existent passion or interest, must be rendered, by their number and local situation, unable to concert and carry into effect schemes of oppression. If the impulse and the opportunity be suffered to coincide, we well know that neither moral nor religious motives can be relied on as an adequate control. They are not found to be such on the injustice and violence of individuals, and lose their efficacy in proportion to the number combined together; that is, in proportion as their efficacy becomes needful.

From this view of the subject, it may be concluded, that a pure Democracy, by which I mean, a Society, consisting of a small number of citizens, who assemble and administer the Government in person, can admit of no cure for the mischiefs of faction. A common passion or interest will, in almost every case, be felt by a majority of the whole; a communication and concert results from the form of Government itself; and there is nothing to check the inducements to sacrifice the weaker party, or an obnoxious individual. Hence it is, that such Democracies have ever been spectacles of turbulence and contention; have ever been found incompatible with personal security, or the rights of property; and have in general been as short in their lives, as they have been violent in their deaths. Theoretic politicians, who have patronized this species of Government, have erroneously supposed, that by reducing mankind to a perfect equality in their political rights, they would, at the same time, be perfectly equalized and assimilated in their possessions, their opinions, and their passions.

A republic, by which I mean a government in which the scheme of representation takes place, opens a different prospect, and promises the cure for which we are seeking. Let us examine the points in which it varies from pure democracy, and we shall comprehend both the nature of the cure and the efficacy which it must derive from the union.

The two great points of difference, between a democracy and a republic, are, first, the delegation of the government, in the latter, to a small number of citizens, elected by the rest; secondly, the greater number of citizens, and greater sphere of country, over which the latter may be extended.

The effect of the first difference is, on the one hand, to refine and enlarge the public views, by passing them through the medium of a chosen body of citizens, whose wisdom may best discern the true interest of their country, and whose patriotism and love of justice, will be least likely to sacrifice it to temporary or partial considerations. Under such a regulation, it may well happen, that the public voice, pronounced by the representatives of the people, will be more consonant to the public good, than if pronounced by the people themselves, convened for the purpose. On the other hand the effect may be inverted. Men of factious tempers, of local prejudices, or of sinister designs, may by intrigue, by corruption, or by other means, first obtain the suffrages, and then betray the interest of the people. The question resulting is, whether small or extensive republics are most favorable to the election of proper guardians of the public weal, and it is clearly decided in favor of the latter by two obvious considerations.

In the first place, it is to be remarked that, however small the republic may be, the representatives must be raised to a certain number, in order to guard against the cabals of a few; and that however large it may be, they must be limited to a certain number, in order to guard against the confusion of a multitude. Hence, the number of representatives in the two cases not being in proportion to that of the constituents, and being proportionally greatest in the small republic, it follows, that if the proportion of fit characters be not less in the large than in the small republic, the former will present a greater option, and consequently a greater probability of a fit choice.

In the next place, as each Representative will be chosen by a greater number of citizens in the large than in the small Republic, it will be more difficult for unworthy candidates to practise with success the vicious arts, by which elections are too often carried; and the suffrages of the people being more free, will be more likely to center on men who possess the most attractive merit, and the most diffusive and established characters.

It must be confessed, that in this, as in most other cases, there is a mean, on both sides of which inconveniences will be found to lie. By enlarging too much the number of electors, you render the representatives too little acquainted with all their local circumstances and lesser interests; as by reducing it too much, you render him unduly attached to these, and too little fit to comprehend and pursue great and national objects. The Federal Constitution forms a happy combination in this respect; the great and aggregate interests being referred to the national, the local and particular, to the state legislatures.

The other point of difference is, the greater number of citizens and extent of territory which may be brought within the compass of Republican, than of Democratic Government; and it is this circumstance principally which renders factious combinations less to be dreaded in the former, than in the latter. The smaller the society, the fewer probably will be the distinct parties and interests composing it; the fewer the distinct parties and interests, the more frequently will a majority be found of the same party; and the smaller the number of individuals composing a majority, and the smaller the compass within which they are placed, the more easily will they concert and execute their plans of oppression. Extend the sphere, and you take in a greater variety of parties and interests; you make it less probable that a majority of the whole will have a common motive to invade the rights of other citizens; or if such a common motive exists, it will be more difficult for all who feel it to discover their own strength, and to act in unison with each other. Besides other impediments, it may be remarked, that where there is a consciousness of unjust or dishonorable purposes, communication is always checked by distrust, in proportion to the number whose concurrence is necessary.

Hence it clearly appears, that the same advantage, which a Republic has over a Democracy, in controlling the effects of faction, is enjoyed by a large over a small Republic—is enjoyed by the Union over the States composing it. Does this advantage consist in the substitution of Representatives, whose enlightened views and virtuous sentiments render them superior to local prejudices, and to schemes of injustice? It will not be denied, that the Representation of the Union will be most likely to possess these requisite endowments. Does it consist in the greater security afforded by a greater variety of parties, against the event of any one party being able to outnumber and oppress the rest? In an equal degree does the increased variety of parties, comprised within the Union, increase this security? Does it, in fine, consist in the greater obstacles opposed to the concert and accomplishment of the secret wishes of an unjust and interested majority? Here, again, the extent of the Union gives it the most palpable advantage.

The influence of factious leaders may kindle a flame within their particular States, but will be unable to spread a general conflagration through the other States: a religious sect, may degenerate into a political faction in a part of the Confederacy but the variety of sects dispersed over the entire face of it, must secure the national Councils against any danger from that source: a rage for paper money, for an abolition of debts, for an equal division of property, or for any other improper or wicked project, will be less apt to pervade the whole body of the Union, than a particular member of it; in the same proportion as such a malady is more likely to taint a particular county or district, than an entire State.

In the extent and proper structure of the Union, therefore, we behold a Republican remedy for the diseases most incident to Republican Government. And according to the degree of pleasure and pride, we feel in being Republicans, ought to be our zeal in cherishing the spirit, and supporting the character of Federalists.

PUBLIUS

The Federalist No. 51

February 6, 1788
James Madison

TO THE PEOPLE OF THE STATE OF NEW YORK.

To what expedient then shall we finally resort for maintaining in practice the necessary partition of power among the several departments, as laid down in the constitution? The only answer that can be given is, that as all these exterior provisions are found to be inadequate, the defect must be supplied, by so contriving the interior structure of the government, as that its several constituent parts may, by their mutual relations, be the means of keeping each other in their proper places. Without presuming to undertake a full development of this important idea, I will hazard a few general observations, which may perhaps place it in a clearer light, and enable us to form a more correct judgment of the principles and structure of the government planned by the convention.

In order to lay a due foundation for that separate and distinct exercise of the different powers of government, which to a certain extent, is admitted on all hands to be essential to the preservation of liberty, it is evident that each department should have a will of its own; and consequently should be so constituted, that the members of each should have as little agency as possible in the appointment of the members of the others. Were this principle rigorously adhered to, it would require that all the appointments for the supreme executive, legislative, and judiciary magistracies, should be drawn from the same fountain of authority, the people, through channels, having no communication whatever with one another. Perhaps such a plan of constructing the several departments would be less difficult in practice than it may in contemplation appear. Some difficulties however, and some additional expense, would attend the execution of it. Some deviations therefore from the principle must be admitted. In the constitution of the judiciary department in particular, it might be inexpedient to insist rigorously on the principle; first, because peculiar qualifications being essential in the members, the primary consideration ought to be to select that mode of choice, which best secures these qualifications; secondly, because the permanent tenure by which the appointments are held in that department, must soon destroy all sense of dependence on the authority conferring them.

It is equally evident that the members of each department should be as little dependent as possible on those of the others, for the emoluments annexed to their offices. Were the executive magistrate, or the judges, not independent of the legislature in this particular, their independence in every other would be merely nominal.

But the great security against a gradual concentration of the several powers in the same department, consists in giving to those who administer each department, the necessary constitutional means, and personal motives, to resist encroachments of the others. The provision for defense must in this, as in all other cases, be made commensurate to the danger of attack. Ambition must be made to counteract ambition. The interest of the man must be connected with the constitutional right of the place. It may be a reflection on human nature, that such devices should be necessary to control the abuses of government. But what is government itself but the greatest of all reflections on human nature? If men were angels, no government would be necessary. If angels were to govern men, neither external nor internal controls on government would be necessary. In framing a government which is to be administered by men over men, the great difficulty lies in this: You must first enable the government to control the governed; and in the next place, oblige it to control itself. A dependence on the people is no doubt the primary control on the government; but experience has taught mankind the necessity of auxiliary precautions.

This policy of supplying by opposite and rival interests, the defect of better motives, might be traced through the whole system of human affairs, private as well as public. We see it particularly displayed in all the subordinate distributions of power; where the constant aim is to divide and arrange the several offices in such a manner as that each may be a check on the other; that the private interest of every individual, may be a sentinel over the public rights. These inventions of prudence cannot be less requisite in the distribution of the supreme powers of the state.

But it is not possible to give to each department an equal power of self defense. In republican government the legislative authority, necessarily, predominates. The remedy for this inconveniency is, to divide the legislature into different branches; and to render them by different modes of election, and different principles of action, as little connected with each other, as the nature of their common functions, and their common dependence on the society, will admit. It may even be necessary to guard against dangerous encroachments by still further precautions. As the weight of the legislative authority requires that it should be thus divided, the weakness of the executive may require, on the other hand, that it should be fortified. An absolute negative, on the legislature, appears at first view to be the natural defense with which the executive magistrate should be armed. But perhaps it would be neither altogether safe, nor alone sufficient. On ordinary occasions, it might not be exerted with the requisite firmness; and on extraordinary occasions, it might be perfidiously abused. May not this defect of an absolute negative be supplied, by some qualified connection between this weaker department, and the weaker branch of the stronger department, by which the latter may be led to support the constitutional rights of the former, without being too much detached from the rights of its own department?

If the principles on which these observations are founded be just, as I persuade myself they are, and they be applied as a criterion, to the several state constitutions, and to the federal constitution, it will be found, that if the latter does not perfectly correspond with them, the former are infinitely less able to bear such a test.

There are moreover two considerations particularly applicable to the federal system of America, which place that system in a very interesting point of view.

First. In a single republic, all the power surrendered by the people, is submitted to the administration of a single government; and usurpations are guarded against by a division of the government into distinct and separate departments. In the compound republic of America, the power surrendered by the people, is first divided between two distinct governments, and then the portion allotted to each, subdivided among distinct and separate departments. Hence a double security arises to the rights of the people. The different governments will control each other; at the same time that each will be controlled by itself.

Second. It is of great importance in a republic, not only to guard the society against the oppression of its rulers; but to guard one part of the society against the injustice of the other part. Different interests necessarily exist in different classes of citizens. If a majority be united by a common interest, the rights of the minority will be insecure. There are but two methods of providing against this evil: The one by creating a will in the community independent of the majority, that is, of the society itself, the other by comprehending in the society so many separate descriptions of citizens, as will render an unjust combination of a majority of the whole, very improbable, if not impracticable. The first method prevails in all governments possessing an hereditary or self appointed authority. This at best is but a precarious security; because a power independent of the society may as well espouse the unjust views of the major, as the rightful interests, of the minor party, and may possibly be turned against both parties. The second method will be exemplified in the federal republic of the United States. While all authority in it will be derived from and dependent on the society, the society itself will be broken into so many parts, interests and classes of citizens, that the rights of individuals or of the minority, will be in little danger from interested combinations of the majority. In a free government, the security for civil rights must be the same as for religious rights. It consists in the one case in the multiplicity of interests, and in the other, in the multiplicity of sects. The degree of security in both cases will depend on the number of interests and sects; and this may be presumed to depend on the extent of country and number of people comprehended under the same government. This view of the subject must particularly recommend a proper federal system to all the sincere and considerate friends of republican government: Since it shows that in exact proportion as the territory of the union may be formed into more circumscribed confederacies or states, oppressive combinations of a majority will be facilitated, the best security under the republican form, for the rights of every class of citizens, will be diminished; and consequently, the stability and independence of some member of the government, the only other security, must be proportionally increased. Justice is the end of government. It is the end of civil society. It ever has been, and ever will be pursued, until it be obtained, or until liberty be lost in the pursuit. In a society under the forms of which the stronger faction can readily unite and oppress the weaker, anarchy may as truly be said to reign, as in a state of nature where the weaker individual is not secured against the violence of the stronger: And as in the latter state even the stronger individuals are prompted by the uncertainty of their condition, to submit to a government which may protect the weak as well as themselves: So in the former state, will the more powerful factions or parties be gradually induced by a like motive, to wish for a government which will protect all parties, the weaker as well as the more powerful. It can be little doubted, that if the state of Rhode Island was separated from the confederacy, and left to itself, the insecurity of rights under the popular form of government within such narrow limits, would be displayed by such reiterated oppressions of factious majorities, that some power altogether independent of the people would soon be called for by the voice of the very factions whose misrule had proved the necessity of it. In the extended republic of the United States, and among the great variety of interests, parties and sects which it embraces, a coalition of a majority of the whole society could seldom take place on any other principles than those of justice and the general good; and there being thus less danger to a minor from the will of the major party, there must be less pretext also, to provide for the security of the former, by introducing into the government a will not dependent on the latter; or in other words, a will independent of the society itself. It is no less certain than it is important, notwithstanding the contrary opinions which have been entertained, that the larger the society, provided it lie within a practicable sphere, the more duly capable it will be of self government. And happily for the republican cause, the practicable sphere may be carried to a very great extent, by a judicious modification and mixture of the federal principle.

PUBLIUS

Presidents of the United States

President	Year	Party	Most Noteworthy Event
George Washington	1789–1797	Federalist	Establishment of Federal Judiciary
John Adams	1797–1801	Federalist	Alien-Sedition Acts
Thomas Jefferson	1801–1809	Dem.-Republican	First President to Defeat Incumbent/Louisiana Purchase
James Madison	1809–1817	Dem.-Republican	War of 1812
James Monroe	1817–1825	Dem.-Republican	Monroe Doctrine/ Missouri Compromise
John Quincy Adams	1825–1829	Dem.-Republican	Elected by "King Caucus"
Andrew Jackson	1829–1837	Democratic	Set up Spoils System
Martin Van Buren	1837–1841	Democratic	Competitive Parties Established
William H. Harrison	1841	Whig	Universal White Male Suffrage
John Tyler	1841–1845	Whig	Texas Annexed
James K. Polk	1845–1849	Democratic	Mexican-American War
Zachary Taylor	1849–1850	Whig	California Gold Rush
Millard Fillmore	1850–1853	Whig	Compromise of 1850
Franklin Pierce	1853–1857	Democratic	Republican Party Formed
James Buchanan	1857–1861	Democratic	Dred Scott Decision
Abraham Lincoln	1861–1865	Republican	Civil War
Andrew Johnson	1865–1869	Dem. (Unionist)	First Impeachment of President
Ulysses S. Grant	1869–1877	Republican	Reconstruction of South
Rutherford B. Hayes	1877–1881	Republican	End of Reconstruction
James A. Garfield	1881	Republican	Assassinated by Job-seeker
Chester A. Arthur	1881–1885	Republican	Civil Service Reform
Grover Cleveland	1885–1889	Democratic	Casts 102 Vetoes in One Year
Benjamin Harrison	1889–1893	Republican	McKinley Law Raises Tarrifs
Grover Cleveland	1893–1897	Democratic	Depression/Pullman Strike
William McKinley	1897–1901	Republican	Spanish-American War
Theodore Roosevelt	1901–1909	Republican	Conservation/Panama Canal
William H. Taft	1909–1913	Republican	Judicial Reform
Woodrow Wilson	1913–1921	Democratic	Progressive Reforms/ World War I
Warren G. Harding	1921–1923	Republican	Return to Normalcy

(continued)

Presidents of the United States

President	Year	Party	Most Noteworthy Event
Calvin Coolidge	1923–1929	Republican	Cuts Taxes/Promotes Business
Herbert C. Hoover	1929–1933	Republican	Great Depression
Franklin D. Roosevelt	1933–1945	Democratic	New Deal/ World War II
Harry S. Truman	1945–1953	Democratic	Beginning of Cold War
Dwight D. Eisenhower	1953–1961	Republican	End of Korean War
John F. Kennedy	1961–1963	Democratic	Cuban Missile Crisis
Lyndon B. Johnson	1963–1969	Democratic	Great Society/Vietnam War
Richard M. Nixon	1969–1974	Republican	Watergate Scandal
Gerald R. Ford	1974–1977	Republican	War Powers Resolution
James Earl Carter	1977–1981	Democratic	Iranian Hostage Crisis
Ronald Reagan	1981–1989	Republican	Tax Cut/ Expenditure Cuts
George H. W. Bush	1989–1993	Republican	End of Cold War/Persian Gulf War
William J. Clinton	1993–2001	Democratic	Deficit Reduction
George W. Bush	2001–	Republican	War on Terror

Note: Refer to www.ablongman.com/fiorina

glossary

A

affirmative action   Programs designed to enhance opportunities for groups that have suffered discrimination in the past. (Chapter 14)

agenda setting   Occurs when the media affect the issues and problems people think about. (Chapter 5)

Aid to Families with Dependent Children (AFDC)   Public assistance program established in 1935 as part of the Social Security Act and replaced in 1996. (Chapter 15)

ambassador   The head of a diplomatic delegation to a major foreign country. (Chapter 11)

Anti-Federalists   Those who opposed ratification of the Constitution. (Chapter 2)

appropriations process   Process of providing funding for governmental activities and programs that have been authorized. (Chapter 9)

Articles of Confederation   The "league of friendship" under which the American colonies operated during and immediately after the Revolutionary War, until ratification of the U.S. Constitution in 1789. (Chapter 2)

authorization process   Term given to the process of providing statutory authority for a government program activity; does not provide funding for the project. (Chapter 9)

B

balancing doctrine   The principle enunciated by the courts that freedom of speech must be balanced against other competing public interests. (Chapter 13)

Bay of Pigs   Location of CIA-supported effort by Cuban exiles in 1961 to invade Cuba and overthrow Fidel Castro. (Chapter 11)

beltway insider   Person living in the Washington metropolitan area who is engaged in, or well informed about, national politics and government. (Chapter 10)

bicameral   A legislature that contains two chambers. (Chapter 9)

Bill of Rights   The first ten amendments to the U.S. Constitution. Promised by the framers to overcome resistance to the new Constitution, and compiled by

James Madison, they list some of the most important civil liberties protected in the United States. (Chapter 2)

block grant   Federal grant to a state and/or local government that imposes minimal restrictions on the use of funds. (Chapter 3)

brief   Written arguments presented to a court by lawyers on behalf of clients. (Chapter 12)

Brown v. Board of Education of Topeka, Kansas   Supreme Court decision (1954) declaring racial segregation in schools unconstitutional. (Chapter 14)

bully pulpit   A description of the presidency emphasizing opportunities to preach to voters on behalf of good policy. (Chapter 10)

bureaucracy   Hierarchical organization designed to perform a particular set of tasks. (Chapter 11)

business cycle   The alternation of periods of economic growth with periods of economic slowdown. (Chapter 15)

C

Cabinet   Top administration officials; mostly heads of executive branch departments. (Chapter 10)

categorical grant   Federal grant to a state and/or local government that imposes programmatic restrictions on the use of funds. (Chapter 3)

caucus   Either a meeting to choose delegates to a state or national convention or a collection of like-minded legislators. (Chapters 7, 9)

checks and balances   Limits that one branch of government places on another because they have different interests, preventing an abuse of power. (Chapter 1)

chief of staff   Head of White House staff, usually in continuous contact with the president. (Chapter 10)

circuit court of appeals   Court to which decisions by federal district courts are appealed. (Chapter 12)

civic republicanism   A political philosophy that emphasizes the obligation of citizens to act virtuously in pursuit of the common good. (Chapter 4)

civil code   Laws regulating relations among individuals. Alleged violators are sued by presumed victims, who ask courts to award damages and otherwise offer relief. (Chapter 12)

civil disobedience   A peaceful violation of law designed to dramatize injustice. (Chapter 14)

civil liberties   Fundamental freedoms that protect a people from their government. (Chapter 13)

civil rights   Guarantees to equal treatment under the law. (Chapter 14)

civil rights amendments   The Thirteenth, Fourteenth, and Fifteenth Amendments to the U.S. Constitution, designed to abolish slavery and secure rights for freemen. (Chapter 13)

civil service   A system that protects government employees from losing their jobs when elected offices change hands. (Chapter 11)

class action suit   Suit brought on behalf of all individuals in a particular category, whether or not they are actually participating in the suit. (Chapter 12)

classical liberalism   A belief in freedom, individualism, equality, and small government that characterized many, if not most, of the nation's founders. It grew from the social, political, and religious changes of the Enlightenment period. (Chapter 4)

clear and present danger doctrine   The principle that people should have freedom of speech unless their language poses a direct threat that lawmakers have the authority to prevent. (Chapter 13)

closed primaries   Primaries in which only party members can vote—and vote only in the party in which they are registered. (Chapter 7)

cloture   Motion to end debate; requires 60 votes to pass. (Chapter 9)

coattails   Positive electoral effect of a popular presidential candidate on congressional candidates of the party. (Chapter 7)

coercion test   Alternative to the Lemon test preferred by conservative judges defining a religious establishment as an instance when government coerces citizens into following religious practices or punishes those who do not. (Chapter 13)

Cold War   The 43-year period (1946–1989) during which the United States and the Soviet Union threatened one another with mutual destruction. (Chapter 11)

commerce clause   Constitutional provision that gives Congress power to regulate commerce "among the states." (Chapter 3)

communitarianism   A modern revival of the civic republican tradition that characterized some of the nation's founders. It defines freedom not as individual rights and liberties, but as the rights of a community's members to seek the good life using political institutions. (Chapter 4)

compositional effect   A change in the behavior of a group that arises from a change in membership rather than a change in the behavior of individuals in the group. (Chapter 6)

concurring opinion   A written opinion prepared by judges who vote with the majority but who wish to disagree with or elaborate on some aspect of the majority opinion. (Chapter 12)

conference committee   Group of representatives from both the House and the Senate who iron out the differences between the two chambers' versions of a bill or resolution. (Chapter 9)

conservatism   A word that differs in meaning depending on the time and place, but in modern America it generally refers to those who prefer to (1) limit government activity in economic affairs, (2) use government to promote morality, (3) allow states wide latitude in shaping social policies, and (4) use foreign policy aggressively to promote national-security interests. (Chapter 4)

constituency   Those legally entitled to vote for a public official. (Chapter 1)

constituency service   The work a member of Congress performs to win federal funds for the state or district and to help constituents deal with federal agencies. (Chapter 9)

constituents   The voters that an elected official represents before the government, who as a group are often called the representative's "constituency." May refer to everyone who constitutes an elected official's jurisdiction rather than only those who actually voted. (Chapter 5)

containment   U.S. policy that attempted to stop the spread of communism in the expectation that this system of government would eventually collapse on its own. (Chapter 11)

cooperative federalism   The theory that all levels of government can work together to solve common problems. (Chapter 3)

criminal code   Laws regulating relations between individuals and society. Alleged violators are prosecuted by government. (Chapter 12)

critical election   Election that marks the emergence of a new, lasting alignment of partisan support within the electorate. (Chapter 8)

D

Declaration of Independence   Document signed in 1776 declaring the United States to be a country independent of Great Britain. (Chapter 2)

de facto **segregation**   Segregation that occurs as the result of private decisions. (Chapter 14)

defendant   One accused of violating the civil or criminal code. (Chapter 12)

de jure **segregation**   Segregation that is legally sanctioned. (Chapter 14)

delegate   Role a representative plays when following the wishes of those who have elected him or her. (Chapter 9)

democracy   System in which governmental power is widely shared. (Chapter 1)

department   Organizational unit into which many federal agencies are grouped. (Chapter 11)

devolution   Return of governmental responsibilities to states and localities. (Chapter 3)

direct democracy   System in which ordinary people make all the laws themselves. (Chapter 1)

direct mail   Computer-generated letters, faxes, and other communications to people who might be sympathetic to an appeal for money or support. (Chapter 8)

dissenting opinion   Written opinion presenting the reasoning of judges who vote against the majority. (Chapter 12)

distributive theory   Theory predicting that a legislature's members will serve on the committees most important for delivering benefits to their constituents. (Chapter 9)

district attorney   Person responsible for prosecuting criminal cases. (Chapter 12)

district court   The lowest tier of the judicial system where most federal cases initially appear. (Chapter 12)

divided government   Said to exist when no single party controls the presidency and both houses of Congress. (Chapter 8)

double jeopardy   Fifth Amendment provision that prohibits prosecution for the same offense twice. (Chapters 12, 13)

dual sovereignty   A theory of federalism by which both the national and state governments have final authority over their own policy domains. (Chapter 3)

due process clause   Clause found in the Fifth and Fourteenth Amendments to the Constitution that forbids deprivation of life, liberty, or property without due process of law. (Chapter 13)

E

Earned Income Tax Credit (EITC)   Provision that returns tax payments to those who have little income. (Chapter 15)

elastic clause   An alternate name for the U.S. Constitution's "necessary and proper clause" that stresses how flexibly courts have interpreted the language to reconcile it with congressional activities. (Chapter 3)

Electoral College   The formal name for the electors selected by each U.S. state during presidential elections to cast the state's official "electoral votes." Presidential candidates must win a majority in the Electoral College or the election goes to the U.S. House of Representatives. (Chapter 2)

electoral vote   Votes cast for a presidential candidate, with each state receiving one vote for each of its members of the House of Representatives and one vote for each of its senators. (Chapter 7)

embassy The structure that houses ambassadors and their diplomatic aides in the capital cities of many foreign countries. (Chapter 11)

equal protection clause Fourteenth Amendment clause specifying that no state can deny any of its people equal protection under the law. (Chapter 14)

Equal Rights Amendment (ERA) Failed constitutional amendment to ban gender discrimination. (Chapter 14)

equal-time rule Promulgated by the FCC, rule that required any station selling time to a candidate to sell time to other candidates at comparable rates. (Chapter 11)

establishment clause Clause that denies government the power to favor religion or to establish any single religious practice as superior. (Chapter 13)

exclusionary rule The rule that evidence obtained improperly may not be introduced in a trial. (Chapter 13)

executive agreement Agreement with foreign countries that requires only a presidential signature. (Chapter 10)

Executive Office of the President (EOP) Agency that houses both top coordinating offices closely connected to the president; contains the White House office. (Chapter 10)

executive order A presidential directive that has the force of law. (Chapter 10)

executive privilege The right of members of the executive branch to have private communications among themselves that need not be shared with Congress. (Chapter 10)

F

fairness doctrine Promulgated by the FCC, policy that required stations to carry some public affairs programming and to balance the points of view expressed. (Chapter 11)

Federal Reserve System The country's central bank, which executes monetary policy by manipulating the supply of funds that lower banks can lend. (Chapter 11)

federalism Division of sovereignty between at least two different levels of government. (Chapter 3)

Federalist Papers Essays that were written in support of the Constitution's ratification and have become a classic argument for the American constitutional system. (Chapter 2)

Federalists Those who campaigned on behalf of the Constitution. (Chapter 2)

filibuster Delaying tactic by which senators refuse to allow legislation to be considered, usually by speaking indefinitely. (Chapter 9)

filing deadline   The latest date on which a candidate for office may file official papers or pay required fees to state election officials. (Chapter 7)

fiscal policy   The sum total of government taxing and spending decisions. (Chapter 15)

floor   Term for an entire congressional chamber; usually used when bills have left committee and moved to a vote of the full membership. (Chapter 9)

food stamps   Public assistance program providing recipients with stamps that can be used to purchase food. (Chapter 15)

foreign service   Diplomats who staff U.S. embassies and consulates. (Chapter 11)

framing   Stating of an argument in such a way as to emphasize one set of considerations and deemphasize others. (Chapter 5)

franchise   The right to vote. (Chapter 6)

frank   Free mailing privileges enjoyed by members of Congress when communicating with constituents. (Chapter 9)

free exercise clause   Clause that protects the right of individuals to practice their religion. (Chapter 13)

free-rider problem   Barrier to collective action that arises when people can enjoy the benefits of group activity without contributing their limited share of the costs. (Chapter 8)

fundamental freedoms doctrine (preferred freedoms doctrine)   Court doctrine stating that some liberties are fundamental to the preservation of democratic practice—the freedoms of speech, press, assembly, and religion—are to be scrutinized by the courts more closely than other legislation. (Chapter 13)

G

general election   Final election that selects the office holder. (Chapter 1)

gerrymandering   Drawing of boundary lines of congressional districts in order to confer an advantage on some partisan or political interest. (Chapter 7)

GOP   Grand Old Party (Republican). (Chapter 1)

government corporation   Independent organization created by Congress to fulfill functions related to business. (Chapter 11)

grandfather clause   Racially restrictive provision of certain southern laws after Reconstruction permitting a man to vote if his grandfather could have voted. (Chapter 14)

H

Hatch Act   Law enacted in 1939 prohibiting federal employees from engaging in political campaigning and solicitation. (Chapter 11)

honeymoon   The first several months of a presidency, when reporters are more forgiving than usual, Congress more inclined to be cooperative, and the public receptive to new approaches. (Chapter 10)

horse-race coverage   The tendency of news organizations to emphasize who is winning and losing when they cover elections, rather than covering the issues prominent in the elections. (Chapter 5)

I

ideology   System of beliefs in which one or more organizing principles connect the individual's views on a wide range of issues. (Chapters 4, 5)

impeachment   Recommendation by a majority of the House of Representatives that a president, other executive-branch official, or judge of the federal courts be removed from office; removal depends on a two-thirds vote of the Senate. (Chapter 10)

incumbency advantage   The electoral advantage a candidate enjoys by virtue of being an incumbent, over and above his or her other personal and political characteristics. (Chapter 7)

incumbent   The politician who currently holds an elective office and therefore may enjoy an "incumbency advantage" over challengers when running for reelection. (Chapter 7)

independent agencies   Agencies that have quasi-judicial responsibilities. (Chapter 11)

independent counsel   Originally called special prosecutor, legal officer appointed by a court to investigate allegations of criminal activity against high-ranking members of the executive branch. Law expired in 1999. (Chapter 10)

inflation   A sustained rise in the price level such that people need more money to purchase the same amount of goods and services. (Chapter 15)

information cost   The time and mental effort required to absorb and store information, whether from conversations, personal experiences, or the media. (Chapter 5)

informational theory   Theory that sees committees as means of providing reliable information about the actual consequences of the legislation that members could adopt. (Chapter 9)

initiative   Proposed laws or state constitutional amendments placed on the ballot via citizen petition. (Chapter 1)

Iran–Contra affair   An allegedly illegal diversion of funds from the sale of arms to Iran to a guerrilla group in Nicaragua. (Chapter 11)

iron curtain   Armed barrier during the Cold War that prevented movement across national borders between communist Eastern Europe and democratic Western Europe. (Chapter 11)

iron triangle   A congressional committee, bureaucratic agency, and allied interest groups who combine to dominate policy making in some specified policy area. (Chapter 8)

isolationism   A foreign policy that keeps the United States separate from the conflicts taking place among other nations. (Chapter 15)

issue network   A loose constellation of larger numbers of committees, agencies, and interest groups active in a particular policy area. (Chapter 8)

issue public   Group of people particularly affected by or concerned with a specific issue. (Chapter 5)

J

Jim Crow laws   Segregation laws passed after Reconstruction. (Chapter 14)

Joint Chiefs of Staff   The heads of all the military services, together with a chair and vice-chair nominated by the president and confirmed by the Senate. (Chapter 11)

judicial activism   Doctrine that indicates the principles of *stare decisis* and legislative deference should sometimes be sacrificed in order to adapt the Constitution to changing conditions. (Chapter 12)

judicial restraint   Doctrine that indicates courts should, if at all possible, avoid overturning a prior court decision or legislative act. (Chapter 12)

judicial review   Court authority to declare null and void laws of Congress and of state legislatures on the grounds that they violate the Constitution. (Chapters 2, 12)

justices   The nine judges who make up the U.S. Supreme Court. (Chapter 12)

K

Keynesianism   Economic policy based on the belief that governments can control the economy by running deficits to expand it and surpluses to contract it. (Chapter 15)

L

law clerk   Young, influential aide to a Supreme Court justice. (Chapter 12)

Lemon test   Three-part test developed in the early 1960s and formalized in 1971; determines whether a law violates the Constitution's establishment clause. (Chapter 13)

libel   False statement damaging to someone's reputation. (Chapter 13)

liberalism   A philosophy that elevates and empowers the individual as opposed to religious, hereditary, governmental, or other forms of authority. (Chapter 4)

libertarianism   A modern revival of the classical liberal tradition that character-ized many, if not most, of the nation's founders. It favors small government in all areas of public policy, not just in some public-policy areas. (Chapter 4)

line-item veto   Power of most governors to reject specific components of legisla-tion rather than reject entire bills. (Chapter 3)

lobbying   Attempts by interest group representatives to influence the decisions of government officials directly. (Chapter 8)

logrolling   Colloquial term given to politicians' trading of favors, votes, or gener-alized support for each other's proposals. (Chapter 9)

M

machine   A highly organized party under the control of a boss, based on patron-age and control of government activities. (Chapter 8)

Marbury v. Madison   Supreme Court decision (1803) in which the court first exer-cised the power of judicial review. (Chapter 12)

markup   Process in which a committee or subcommittee considers and revises a bill that has been introduced. (Chapter 9)

mass media   Means of communication that are technologically capable of reach-ing most people and economically affordable to most. (Chapter 5)

mass public   Ordinary people for whom politics is a peripheral concern. (Chapter 5)

matching funds   Public moneys (from $3 checkoffs on income tax returns) that the FEC distributes to primary candidates. (Chapter 7)

McCulloch v. Maryland   Decision of 1819 in which the Supreme Court declared unconstitutional the state's power to tax a federal government entity. (Chapter 3)

measurement error   Polling error that arises from questioning rather than sam-pling. (Chapter 5)

Medicaid   Program that provides medical care to those of low income. (Chapter 15)

Medicare   Program that provides medical benefits to Social Security recipients. (Chapter 15)

midterm loss   When the president's party loses seats in Congress during the off-year election, which failed to happen only twice in the twentieth century: 1934 and 1998. (Chapter 7)

Miranda warning   The specific words used by police officers to inform accused persons of their constitutional rights; necessary before questioning suspects. (Chapter 13)

mobilization The efforts of parties, groups, and activists to encourage their supporters to participate in politics. (Chapter 6)

monetarism An economic school of thought that rejects Keynesianism, arguing that the money supply is the most important influence on the economy. (Chapter 15)

monetary policy The actions taken by government to affect the level of interest rates by varying the supply of money. (Chapter 15)

mugwumps A group of civil service reformers organized in the 1880s who maintained that government officials should be chosen on a merit basis. (Chapter 11)

multiple referrals Practice of party leaders who give more than one committee responsibility for considering a bill. (Chapter 9)

N

natural rights Fundamental rights such as life, liberty, and property to which classical liberals considered all people entitled and therefore upon which legitimate governments could not infringe. (Chapter 2)

necessary and proper clause Constitutional clause that gives Congress the power to take all actions that are "necessary and proper" to the carrying out of its delegated powers. Also known as the elastic clause. (Chapters 2, 3)

neutrality test Test allowing restrictions on the exercise of religion when they are part of a neutral criminal law generally applied to the population. Replaced the Sherbert test. (Chapter 13)

New Deal Programs created by Franklin Roosevelt's administration that expanded the power of the federal government over economic affairs. (Chapter 3)

new media Cable and satellite TV, the fax, e-mail, and the Internet—the consequences of the technological advances of the past few decades. (Chapters 5, 12)

nullification A doctrine that gives states the authority to declare acts of Congress unconstitutional. (Chapter 3)

O

obscenity Publicly offensive language or portrayals with no redeeming social value. (Chapter 13)

Office of Management and Budget (OMB) Agency responsible for coordinating the work of departments and agencies of the executive branch. (Chapter 10)

open primaries Primaries in which any registered voter can vote in any party's primary. (Chapter 7)

open seat A House or Senate race with no incumbent (because of death or retirement). (Chapter 7)

opinion of the court   A court's written explanation for its decision. (Chapter 12)

override   Congressional passage of a bill by a two-thirds vote over the president's veto. (Chapter 10)

P

party identification   A person's subjective feeling of affiliation with a party. (Chapter 7)

patronage   Jobs, contracts, or favors in exchange for their political support. Widely practiced in the eighteenth and nineteenth centuries and continues to present day. (Chapters 2, 8, 11)

Pendleton Act   Legislation in 1881 creating the Civil Service Commission. (Chapter 11)

permanent campaign   Term describing the tendency for election campaigns to begin as soon as the last election has ended and for the line between electioneering and governing to disappear. (Chapter 1)

plaintiff   One who brings legal charges against another. (Chapter 12)

plea bargain   Agreement between prosecution and defense that the accused will admit having committed a crime, provided that other charges are dropped or the recommended sentence shortened. (Chapter 13)

plenary session   Activities of a court in which all judges participate. (Chapter 12)

pocket veto   Presidential veto after congressional adjournment, executed merely by not signing a bill into law. (Chapter 10)

political action committee (PAC)   Specialized organization for raising and contributing campaign funds. (Chapter 8)

political culture   Collection of beliefs and values about government. (Chapter 4)

political efficacy   The belief that one can make a difference in politics. (Chapter 5)

political elite   Activists and officeholders who are deeply interested in and knowledgeable about politics. (Chapter 5)

political entrepreneurs   People willing to assume the costs of forming and maintaining an organization even when others may free ride on them. (Chapter 8)

popular vote   The total vote cast for a presidential candidate nationwide. (Chapter 7)

pork-barrel spending   Government spending that a group considers unneeded or wasteful. (Chapter 9)

precedent   Previous court decision or ruling applicable to a particular case. (Chapter 11)

primary election   Preliminary election that narrows the number of candidates by determining who will be the party nominees in the general election. (Chapters 1, 7)

priming What occurs when the media affect the standards people use to evaluate political figures or the severity of a problem. (Chapter 5)

prior restraint doctrine Legal doctrine that gives individuals the right to publish without prior restraint—that is, without first submitting material to a government censor. (Chapter 13)

proportional representation (PR) An electoral system that assigns legislative seats in a manner roughly proportional to the number of votes each party received. (Chapter 7)

public defender Attorney whose full-time responsibilities are to provide for the legal defense of indigent criminal suspects. (Chapter 13)

public goods Goods that you can enjoy without contributing. (Chapter 8)

Q

quota Specific number of positions set aside for a specific group; said by the Supreme Court to be unconstitutional. (Chapter 14)

R

"rally 'round the flag" effect The tendency for the public to back presidents in moments of crisis. (Chapter 10)

random sample A representative subset of a larger group, chosen in such a way that each member of the group had roughly the same chance of being selected. (Chapter 5)

realignment Arrangement that ccurs when the pattern of group support for political parties shifts in a significant and lasting way, such as in the latter half of the twentieth century, when the white South shifted from Democratic to Republican. (Chapter 8)

reapportionment The redrawing of state legislative and congressional districts that occurs after each decennial census. (Chapter 3, Chapter 7)

recall election Attempt to remove an official from office before the completion of the term. (Chapter 1)

recession A slowdown in economic activity, officially defined as a decline that persists for two quarters (six months). (Chapter 15)

Reconstruction Period after the Civil War when southern states were subject to a federal military presence. (Chapter 14)

redistricting Drawing of new boundaries of congressional districts. (Chapter 7)

referenda Laws or state constitutional amendments that are proposed by a legislative body but do not go into effect unless the required number of voters approve it. (Chapter 1)

registered voters   Those legally eligible to vote who have registered in accordance with the requirements prevailing in their states and localites. (Chapter 6)

remand   To send a case to a lower court to determine the best way of implementing the higher court's decision. (Chapter 12)

remedy   Court-ordered action designed to compensate plaintiffs for wrongs they have suffered. (Chapter 12)

republic   See direct democracy. (Chapter 1)

restrictive housing covenant   Legal promise by home buyers that they would not resell to black households; enforcement declared unconstitutional by Supreme Court. (Chapter 14)

retrospective voting   Voting on the basis of the past performance. (Chapter 7)

riders   Budgetary laws and regulations that are tucked inside other budget bills so that they have a better chance of passing than a separate bill because of the chaotic nature of the budgetary process. (Chapter 9)

right to privacy   Right to keep free of government interference those aspects of one's personal life that do not affect others. (Chapter 13)

roll-call vote   A congressional vote in which the specific choice of each member is recorded, allowing constituents to learn how their representative voted. (Chapter 9)

rule   Specification of the terms and conditions under which a bill or resolution will be considered on the floor of the House—in particular, how long debate will last, how time will be allocated, and the number and type of amendments that will be in order. (Chapter 9)

S

safe seat   A congressional district almost guaranteed to elect either a Democrat or a Republican because the distribution of partisans is so lopsided. (Chapter 7)

sampling error   The error that arises in public opinion surveys as a result of relying on a representative but small sample of the larger population. (Chapter 5)

select committee   Temporary Congressional committee appointed to deal with a specific issue or problem. (Chapter 9)

selection bias   The error that occurs when a sample systematically includes or excludes people with certain attitudes. (Chapter 5)

selective benefits   Side benefits of belonging to an organization that are limited to contributing members of the organization. (Chapter 8)

selective incorporation   The case-by-case incorporation, by the courts, of the Bill of Rights into the due process clause of the Fourteenth Amendment. (Chapter 13)

selective perception   The tendency of listeners, such as a media audience, to distort a message so that they hear what they already believe or hear what they want to hear. (Chapter 5)

senatorial courtesy   An informal rule that the Senate will not confirm nominees within or from a state unless they have the approval of the senior senator of the state from the president's party. (Chapters 11, 12)

seniority   Congressional practice by which the majority party member with the longest continuous service on a committee becomes the chair. (Chapter 9)

separate but equal doctrine   Obsolete rule stating that racial segregation did not violate the equal protection clause as long as the facilities were equivalent. (Chapter 14)

separation of powers   A system of government in which different institutions exercise different components of governmental power. (Chapter 2)

Shays's Rebellion   Uprising in western Massachusetts in 1786 led by Revolutionary War captain Daniel Shays. (Chapter 2)

Sherbert test   Three-part test formalized in the early 1960s but overruled in 1990 that determined whether a law violates the Constitution's free exercise clause. (Chapter 13)

sin tax   Tax intended to discourage unwanted behavior. (Chapter 15)

single-issue voter   Voter for whom one issue is so important that it determines which political candidates attract his or her votes or campaign activism. (Chapter 5)

single-member, simple plurality (SMSP) system   Electoral system in which the country is divided into geographic districts, and the candidates who win the most votes within their districts are elected. (Chapter 7)

social connectedness   The degree to which individuals are integrated into society—families, churches, neighborhoods, groups, and so forth. (Chapter 6)

social-contract theory   An approach to political philosophy starting from the hypothetical assumption that there was a time before society or before government, and that people accepted such innovations as part of a contract in which they gained some sort of guarantee as the terms of cooperating. (Chapter 2)

social issues   Issues such as obscenity, feminism, gay rights, capital punishment, and prayer in schools that reflect personal values more than economic interests. (Chapter 6)

social movement   Broad-based demand for government action on some problem or issue, such as civil rights for blacks and women or environmental protection. (Chapter 8)

socializing agent   A person or institution that teaches social values and political attitudes. (Chapter 5)

soft money   Campaign funds that are spent on a candidate's behalf by an interest group or political party but that the candidate does not receive or coordinate directly. (Chapter 7)

solicitor general   Government official responsible for presenting before the courts the position of the presidential administration. (Chapter 12)

sovereign immunity   The legal doctrine protecting states from lawsuits filed under national legislation. (Chapter 3)

Speaker of the House   The presiding officer of the House of Representatives; normally, the Speaker is the leader of the majority party. (Chapter 9)

spending clause   Constitutional provision that gives Congress the power to collect taxes to provide for the general welfare. (Chapter 3)

spoils system   A system of government employment in which workers are hired on the basis of party loyalty. (Chapter 11)

sponsor   Representative or senator who introduces a bill or resolution. (Chapter 9)

standing committee   Committee with fixed membership and jurisdiction, continuing from Congress to Congress. (Chapter 9)

stare decisis   In court rulings, remaining consistent with precedents. (Chapter 12)

state action doctrine   Rule stating that only the actions of state and local governments, not those of private individuals, must conform to the equal protection clause. (Chapter 14)

State of the Union address   Annual speech delivered by the president in fulfillment of the constitutional obligation of reporting to Congress on the state of the Union. (Chapter 10)

statutory interpretation   The judicial act of applying laws to particular cases. (Chapter 12)

suffrage   Another term for the right to vote. (Chapter 6)

supremacy clause   Part of the Constitution that says the Constitution is the "supreme Law of the Land," to which all judges are bound. (Chapters 2, 3)

suspect classification   Categorization of a particular group that will be strictly scrutinized by the courts to see whether its use is unconstitutional. (Chapter 14)

suspension of the rules   Fast-track procedure for considering bills and resolutions in the House; debate is limited to 40 minutes, no amendments are in order, and a two-thirds majority is required for passage. (Chapter 9)

T

tariffs   Taxes on imported goods. (Chapter 2)

tax preferences   Special tax treatment received by certain activities, property, or investments. (Chapter 15)

Temporary Assistance for Needy Families (TANF)   Reformed welfare program established by Congress in 1996. (Chapter 15)

three-fifths compromise   Constitutional provision that counted each slave as three-fifths of a person when calculating representation in the House of Representatives; repealed by the Fourteenth Amendment. (Chapter 2)

ticket splitting   Occurs when a voter chooses candidates from multiple parties. (Chapter 8)

transition   The period after a presidential candidate has won the November election but before the candidate assumes office as president on January 20. (Chapter 10)

treaties   Official agreements with foreign countries ratified by the Senate. (Chapter 10)

trustees   Role a representative plays when acting in accordance with his or her own best judgment. (Chapter 9)

two-presidency theory   Idea that a president has so much more power in foreign affairs than in domestic policy that there are two presidencies. (Chapter 10)

U

U.S. attorney   Person responsible for prosecuting violations of the federal criminal code. (Chapter 12)

unanimous-consent agreement   Agreement that sets forth the terms according to which the Senate will consider a bill; these are individually negotiated by the leadership for each bill. (Chapter 9)

unemployment   When people who are willing to work at the prevailing wage cannot get jobs. (Chapter 15)

unfunded mandates   Federal regulations that impose burdens on state and local governments without appropriating enough money to cover costs. (Chapter 3)

V

veto   Executive rejection of legislation, which usually may be overridden by a supermajority in the legislature. (Chapter 10)

Virginia Plan   James Madison's rough draft of the U.S. Constitution, especially his proposal that states would receive representation in the national legislature proportional to their population sizes. (Chapter 2)

voting-age population All people in the United States over the age of 18. (Chapter 6)

W

War Powers Resolution Congressional resolution in 1973 requiring the president to notify Congress formally upon ordering U.S. troops into military action. (Chapter 10)

whips Members of Congress who serve as informational channels between the leadership and the rank and file. (Chapter 9)

White House Office Political appointees who work directly for the president, many of whom occupy offices in the White House. (Chapter 10)

winner-take-all voting Any voting procedure in which the side with the most votes gets all of the seats or delegates at stake. (Chapter 7)

writ of *certiorari* (cert) A document issued by the Supreme Court indicating that the Court will review a decision made by a lower court. (Chapter 12)

Y

yeoman Independent farmers who made up approximately four-fifths of the U.S. population at the time of the founding and who tended to embrace a radical version of revolutionary ideals such as "liberty" and "equality." (Chapter 2)

endnotes

Preface

1. On the limited importance of elections, see for example the string of works by Benjamin Ginsberg, including an influential book with Martin Shefter, *Politics By Other Means: The Declining Importance of Elections in America* (New York: Basic, 1990). On the dominance of elites, see the running textbook series by Thomas R. Dye, including listed in their first editions *Who's Running America?* (Englewood Cliffs, NJ: Prentice-Hall, 1976) and, with L. Harmon Ziegler, *The Irony of Democracy* (Belmont, CA: Wadsworth, 1970).

2. Morris P. Fiorina, Paul E. Peterson, Bertram Johnson, and William G. Mayer, *The New American Democracy*, 5th ed. (New York: Longman, 2007).

3. *Ibid.*

Chapter 1

1. John F. Harris, "Campaign Promises Aside, It's Politics As Usual," *Washington Post Weekly Edition* (July 2–8, 2001): 11.

2. Evelyn Nieves, "Heinz Kerry's Campaign Balancing Act," *Washington Post*, September 12, 2004: A1; *New York Times*, "Political Family Rules," August 1, 2004: Section D, page 10.

3. See, for example: Wayne Barrett, "The Crusader," *New York Times Book Review*, Part R p. 4, July 30, 2006; Rupert Cornwell, "The Face that Fits is the One Nobody Knows," *Independent on Sunday* (London), June 25, 2006, p. 42.

4. American National Election Studies cumulative data file 1948–2002, University of Michigan.

5. H. H. Gerth and C. W. Mills, trans., *From Max Weber* (New York: Oxford University Press, 1946), p. 78.

6. Thomas Hobbes, *Leviathan* (New York: Dutton, 1973), p. 65.

7. Henning, *Wit and Wisdom*, p. 89.

8. "Federalist No. 51. " See the Appendix to this book.

9. Giovanni Sartori, *The Theory of Democracy Revisited* (Chatham, NJ: Chatham House, 1987); Carole Pateman, *Participation and Democratic Theory* (New York: Cambridge University Press, 1970).

10. Angus Campbell, Philip E. Converse, Warren E. Miller, and Donald E. Stokes, *The American Voter* (New York: Wiley, 1960); Deborah R. Hensler and Carl P. Hensler, *Evaluating Nuclear Power* (Santa Monica, CA: Rand Corporation, 1979), p. 106; David Magleby, *Direct Legislation* (Baltimore: Johns Hopkins University Press, 1984), p. 144; Barbara S. Gamble, "Putting Civil Rights to a Popular Vote," *American Journal of Political Science* 41 (1997): 245–269.

11. John Adams, *The Political Writings of John Adams*, George Peek, Jr., ed. (New York: Macmillan, 1985), p. 89.

12. "Half a Million Voters' Choices," *Governing* 8, No. 7 (April 1995): 15.

13. Herbert Jacob and Kenneth Vines, "Courts," in Virginia Gray, Herbert Jacob, and Kenneth Vines, eds., *Politics in the American States*, 4th ed. (Boston: Little, Brown, 1983), p. 238.

14. Professor Richard Murray, as reported by Professor Jay Greene, personal communication, April 10, 1997.

15. Initiative and Referendum Institute, www.iandrinstitute.org, accessed August 21, 2006.

16. Susan A. Macmanus, *Young v. Old* (Boulder, CO: Westview Press, 1996), Ch. 2.

17. Sidney Blumenthal, *The Permanent Campaign* (New York: Simon & Schuster, 1982).

18. Ron Faucheux, "2008: A Democratic Odyssey," *Campaigns & Elections*, February 2005, p. 9.

19. Hugh Heclo, "The Permanent Campaign," in *Campaigning to Govern or Governing to Campaign?* eds. Thomas Mann and Norman Ornstein (Washington, DC: Brookings, 2000).

20. Frank Sorauf, *Political Parties in the American System* (Boston: Little, Brown, 1964); and Martin Wattenberg, *The Decline of American Political Parties, 1952–1984* (Cambridge, MA: Harvard University Press, 1986).

21. Carolyn Lochhead, "GOP Rebels Keep Bush's Tax Cut Bill on the Ropes," *San Francisco Chronicle*, May 14, 2003, p. A1.

22. The average winning campaign cost $87,000 in 1976 ($288,800 in 2004 dollars), while the average winning campaign cost about $1 million in 2004. Joseph E. Cantor, "Campaign Finance," CRS Issue Brief for Congress, IB87020, Updated May 4, 2006, p. 2.

23. Calculation based on $7 million average winning Senate campaign. See Cantor, p. 2.

24. "Spending Soars in Gubernatorial Races," SouthNow Update, March 13, 2003, available at www.southnow.org, accessed August 21, 2006.

25. Terry Moe, "The Politics of Bureaucratic Structure," in John Chubb and Paul Peterson, eds., *Can the Government Govern?* (Washington, DC: Brookings, 1989), pp. 267–329.

26. John Dewey, as quoted in Marone, *The Democratic Wish*, p. 322.

27. R. Douglas Arnold, *The Logic of Congressional Action* (New Haven, CT: Yale University Press, 1990).

28. "A League of Evil," *The Economist* 352, Issue 8136 (September 11, 1999): 7.

29. Human Rights Watch, "Country Summary: North Korea" January 2006, available at http://hrw.org, accessed August 21, 2006.

30. Henning, *Wit and Wisdom*, p. 94.

31. *Ibid.*, p. 58.

32. Howard Wolfson, senior adviser to Senator Hillary Rodham Clinton, quoted in Ryan Lizza, "The YouTube Election," *New York Times*, August 20, 2006, Section 4, p. 1.

33. See "I & R Factsheet Number One," The Initiative and Referendum Institute, available at www.iandrinstitute.org, accessed August 22, 2006.

34. National Conference of State Legislatures database, available at www.ncsl.org, accessed August 22, 2006.

35. Grover Norquist, President, Americans for Tax Reform, quoted in "Statements Regarding the Initiative and Referendum Process," Initiative and Referendum Institute, available at www.iandrinstitute.org, accessed August 22, 2006.

36. Elisabeth Gerber, "Legislative Response to the Threat of Popular Initiatives," *American Journal of Political Science*, 40:1 (February 1996): 99–128; Mark A. Smith, "The Contingent Effects of Ballot Initiatives and Candidate Races on Turnout," *American Journal of Political Science*, 45:3 (July 2001): 700–706; Mark A. Smith, "Ballot Initiatives and the Democratic Citizen," *Journal of Politics*, 64:3 (August 2002): 892–903.

37. On this last point, see Barbara Gamble, "Putting Civil Rights to a Popular Vote," *American Journal of Political Science* 41:1 (January 1997): 245–269.

38. David Broder, *Democracy Derailed: Initiative Campaigns and the Power of Money* (Orlando, FL: Harcourt, 2000), p. 5.

Chapter 2

1. Details for the Shays' Rebellion story come primarily from David P. Szatmary, *Shays' Rebellion* (Amherst: University of Massachusetts Press, 1980); and Merrill Jensen, *The New Nation* (New York: Vintage, 1965).

2. Szatmary, *Shays' Rebellion*, p. 36.

3. *Ibid.*, p. 82.

4. James W. Loewen, *Lies My Teacher Taught Me* (New York: New Press, 1995), Ch. 3.

5. Greg Smith, *Beer* (New York, Avon, 1995), p. 52.

6. An interesting discussion of Locke's influence on Jefferson appears in David Freeman Hawke, *A Transaction of Free Men* (New York: Da Capo, 1989), pp. 50, 148–151. Originally published in 1964.

7. Robert J. Dinkin, *Voting in Revolutionary America* (Westport, CT: Greenwood Press, 1982); and Robert J. Dinkin, *Voting in Provincial America* (Westport, CT: Greenwood Press, 1977).

8. Willi Paul Adams, *The First American Constitutions* (Chapel Hill, NC: University of North Carolina Press, 1980), pp. 245, 308–311.

9. Thomas A. Bailey, *The American Pageant* (Boston: D.C. Heath, 1956), p. 136.

10. Henry Moyer, *A Son of Thunder: Patrick Henry and the American Republic* (New York: Grove Press, 1991), p. 370.

11. Jensen, *The New Nation*, p. 33.

12. Gordon S. Wood, *The Creation of the American Republic, 1776–1787* (Chapel Hill: University of North Carolina Press, 1969), pp. 396–403; Szatmary, *Shays' Rebellion*, p. 77; Hawke, *Transaction of Free Men*, p. 112.

13. Charles A. Beard, *An Economic Interpretation of the Constitution of the United States* (New York: Free Press, 1913).

14. John P. Roche, "The Founding Fathers: A Reform Caucus in Action," *American Political Science Review* 55 (December 1961): 799–816.

15. Robert E. Brown, *Charles Beard and the Constitution* (Princeton, NJ: Princeton University Press, 1956); and Forrest McDonald, *We the People* (Chicago: University of Chicago Press, 1958).

16. Max Farrand, *The Framing of the Constitution of the United States* (New Haven, CT: Yale University Press, 1913), p. 113.

17. Thornton Anderson, *Creating the Constitution* (University Park: Pennsylvania State University Press, 1993).

18. Herbert J. Storing, ed., *The Complete Anti-Federalist: Maryland and Virginia and the South*, Vol. 5 (Chicago: University of Chicago Press, 1981), p. 210.

19. Henry Steele Commager, ed., *Documents of American History* (New York: Appleton, 1958), p. 104.

20. Joseph J. Ellis, "Welcome to 2004, President Washington," *Newsweek* (November 1, 2004): 31.

21. Barry Latzer, *Death Penalty Cases: Leading U.S. Supreme Court cases on Capital Punishment* (Boston, MA: Butterworth-Heinemann, 1998), p. 2.

22. "Facts About the Death Penalty," Death Penalty Information Center, May 12, 2006, www.deathpenaltyinfo.org/FactSheet.pdf, accessed May 25, 2006; for more details on the federal death penalty, see The Federal Death Penalty System: A Statistical Survey, 1988–2000 (Washington, DC: U.S. Department of Justice, September 12, 2000), available at www.usdoj.gov/dag/pubdoc/dpsurvey.html, accessed July 15, 2002.

23. Amnesty International, "Facts and Figures About the Death Penalty," March 2002, available at http://web.amnesty.org/pages/deathpenalty-facts-eng, accessed May 25, 2006.

24. *Gregg v. Georgia*, 428 U.S. 153 (1976).

25. Maryland halted executions from 2002 to 2003; Illinois from 2000 to the present (2006), New Jersey in 2006. See "Uncertain Justice: Efforts to Determine Whether a State Has Executed an Innocent Man Reflect the Country's Growing Unease with Capital Punishment," *Houston Chronicle*, January 24, 2006, p. B8.

26. Quoted in John Aloysius Farrell, "Lethal Dilemma: Five of the Prisoners Scheduled for Execution in Texas Early Next Year Will Highlight Gov. George W. Bush's Death Penalty Role," *Boston Globe*, December 19, 1999, p. A1.

27. ABC News/Washington Post Poll, June 22, 2006.

28. *Atkins v. Virginia*, 536 U.S. 304 (2002) (execution of mentally ill prohibited); and *Roper v. Simmons*, 543 U.S. 551 (2005) (death penalty for minors prohibited).

Chapter 3

1. Evan Thomas, "The Lost City; What Went Wrong: Devastating a Swath of South, Katrina Plunged New Orleans into Agony," *Newsweek*, Sept. 12, 2005, p. 42.

2. Editorial, "Politics May Doom New Orleans," *San Francisco Chronicle*, Aug. 25, 2006, p. B10.

3. For estimates of job losses and property damage, see Douglas Holtz-Eakin, Director, Congressional Budget Office, "CBO Testimony: Macroeconomic and Budgetary Effects of Hurricanes Katrina and Rita," testimony before the Committee on the Budget, U.S. House of Representatives, Oct. 6, 2005, available at www.cbo.gov/ftpdocs/66xx/doc6684/10-06-Hurricanes.pdf, accessed Jan. 15, 2006; and Congressional Budget Office, "The Macroeconomic and Budgetary Effects of Hurricanes Katrina and Rita: An Update," Sept. 29, 2005, available at www.cbo.gov/ftpdocs/66xx/doc6669/09-29-EffectsOfHurricanes.pdf, accessed January 15, 2006.

4. Mark Fischetti, "Drowning New Orleans," *Scientific American*, Oct. 2001: 76–85.

5. Fischetti, p. 85.

6. Robert Block, Amy Schatz, Gary Fields, and Christopher Cooper, "Behind Poor Katrina Response, a Long Chain of Weak Links," *Wall Street Journal*, Sept. 6, 2005, p. A1.

7. Eric Lipton, Christopher Drew, Scott Shane, and David Rohde, "Breakdowns Marked Path from Hurricane to Anarchy," *New York Times*, Sept. 11, 2005, p. 1.

8. See, for example: Office of Senator Trent Lott (R-MS), "Senator Lott Demands Help for Katrina Victims," press release, Sept. 5, 2005, http://lott.senate.gov/index.cfm?FuseAction=PressReleases.Detail&PressRelease_id=187&Month=9&Year=2005, accessed Sept. 6, 2005; Robert Block, Amy Schatz, Gary Fields, and Christopher Cooper, "Behind Poor Katrina Response, a Long Chain of Weak Links," *Wall Street Journal*, Sept. 6, 2005, p. A1; Spencer S. Hsu and Susan B. Glasser, "FEMA Director Singled Out by Response Critics," *Washington Post*, Sept. 6, 2005, p. A1.

9. Spencer S. Hsu, "Brown Defends FEMA's Efforts," *Washington Post*, Sept. 28, 2005, p. A1.

10. Jere Longman and Sewell Chan, "Flooding Recedes in New Orleans; U.S. Inquiry Is Set," *New York Times*, Sept. 7, 2005, p. 1.

11. Alexis de Tocqueville, *Democracy in America*, Vol. I, ed. Philips Bradley (New York: Knopf, 1945), p. 169.

12. *Board of Trustees of the University of Alabama v. Garrett*, 99-1240 (2001).

13. Stephen Henderson, "Family Leave Covers State Employees, Justices Rule," *Lexington Herald-Leader* (May 28, 2003): p. A1.

14. *McCulloch v. Maryland* (1819), 4 Wheaton 316.

15. *Ibid.*

16. *Wickard v. Filburn*, 317 U.S. 111 (1942).

17. *Helvering v. Davis*, 301 U.S. 619 (1937).

18. Stephen Gettinger, "Congress Clears Drunk Driving Legislation," *CQ Weekly*, June 30, 1984: 1557.

19. *South Dakota v. Dole*, 483 U.S. 203 (1987).

20. Lynn A. Baker, "Conditional Federal Spending and States' Rights," *Annals of the American Academy of Political and Social Science* 574 (March 2001): 105.

21. Morton Grodzins, *The American System*, ed. Daniel J. Elazar (Chicago: Rand McNally, 1966).

22. Calculated from data in Ester Fuchs, *Mayors and Money* (Chicago: University of Chicago Press, 1992), p. 210.

23. *Congressional Record*, July 16, 2003: S9476–7.

24. Jeffrey L. Pressman and Aaron Wildavsky, *Implementation*, 3rd ed. (Berkeley: University of California Press, 1984); Eugene Bardach, *The Implementation Game*, 4th ed. (Cambridge, MA: MIT Press, 1982).

25. Theresa Funiciello, *Tyranny of Kindness* (New York: Atlantic Monthly Press, 1993).

26. Murray Evans, "Cities' Leaders Describe Budget Woes," Associated Press, June 7, 2003. Also see Gregory S. Lashutka, "Local Rebellion," *Commonsense* 1 (Summer 1994): 66.

27. Alan Greenblatt, "The Washington Offensive," *Governing*, January 2005: 26.

28. *New York v. United States*, 505 U.S. 144 (1992).

29. *Printz v. U.S.*, 521 U.S. 98 (1997).

30. David Osborne, *Laboratories of Democracy* (Boston: Harvard Business School Press, 1991).

31. Frances Stokes Berry and William D. Berry, "State Lottery Adoptions as Policy Innovations: An Event History Analysis," *American Political Science Review*, 84:2 (June, 1990): 395–415.

32. Calculated from *Statistical Abstract of the United States, 2006*, Tables 437 and 654. Data are expressed in 2005 dollars and combine expenditures by state and local governments.

33. Paul E. Peterson, *The Price of Federalism* (Washington, DC: Brookings, 1995), p. 105.

34. The Council of State Governments, *The Book of the States: 2004 Edition* (Lexington, KY: Council of State Governments), Tables 3. 2 and 3. 9, pp. 78–80; 94–95; Peter Hecht, "Most Take Pay Hikes in Capitol," *Sacramento Bee*, Dec. 6, 2005, p. A1.

35. Thad Kousser, quoted in Alan Greenblatt, "The Truth About Term Limits," *Governing*, January 2006: 24–26.

36. Morris Fiorina, *Divided Government* (New York: Macmillan, 1992).

37. Thad Beyle, "Being Governor," in Carl E. Van Horn, ed., *The State of the States*, 2nd ed. (Washington, DC: Brookings, 1993).

38. Douglas Turner, "Governors Issue Call for States to Get Share of Anti-Terror Funding," *Buffalo News*, Dec. 6, 2001, p. A10.

39. *Baker v. Carr*, 369 U.S. 186 (1962); *Reynolds v. Sims*, 377 U.S. 533 (1964).

40. See Gordon E. Baker, *The Reapportionment Revolution* (New York: Random House, 1966); and Timothy G. O'Rourke, *The Impact of Reapportionment* (New Brunswick, NJ: Transaction Books, 1980).

41. John Sanko, "Boundary Map Favors Democrats," *Rocky Mountain News*, Nov. 28, 2001, p. 23A.

42. *League of United Latin American Citizens et al. v. Perry*, No. 05-204 (2006).

43. Matea Gold, "Gov-Elect Rolls Up His Sleeves on Budget," *Los Angeles Times*, Oct. 22, 2003, p. 1.

44. Jodi Wilgoren, "With Deadline Near, States Are in Budget Discord," *New York Times*, June 27, 2003, p. A14.

45. In addition to the specific cites below, the story of higher education story draws on two David Broder columns from the *Washington Post Weekly Edition*: "Talk vs. Action" (August 20–26, 2001): p. 4; "A Matter of Money" (May 6–12, 2002): p. 4.

46. Robert E. Pierre, "The Budget Squeeze," *Washington Post Weekly Edition* (March 25–31, 2002): p. 6.

47. Robert R. Alford and Eugene C. Lee, "Voting Turnout in American Cities," *American Political Science Review* 62 (1968): 796–813.

48. Statistical Abstract of the United States, 1992, Table 22.

49. Gallup Poll, Sept. 12–15, 2005.

50. "Money to Burn," *The Economist* 328, Issue 7824 (August 14, 1993): 23.

51. Amy Pyle, "Bond Backers Weigh Second Try," *Los Angeles Times* (March 24, 2000): p. A3; Randal C. Archibold, "School Budgets," *New York Times* (May 21, 2001): p. B1; Iver Peterson, "As Taxes Rise, Suburbs Work to Keep Elderly," *New York Times* (Feb. 27, 2001): p. A1; Martha Groves and Duke Helfand, "Schools Prepare Fresh Set of Bond Issues," *Los Angeles Times* (Nov. 9, 2000): p. A3; Martha Groves, "Voters Ready to Give Vouchers a Drubbing," *Los Angeles Times* (Oct. 26, 2000): p. A3; and Lisa Frazier, "In Bowie, 'White Angst' Bubbles Beneath Secession Movement," *Washington Post* (Oct. 26, 2000): p. M2.

52. The Gallup Organization, Roper Center for Public Opinion Research Database, Question ID Numbers USGALLUP. 870. Q005A; USGALLUP. 99JNE25R11E.

53. Eric A Hanushek, "School Resources and Student Performance," in *Does Money Matter?* ed. Gary Burtless (Washington, DC: Brookings, 1996), pp. 43–73.

54. Author's calculation, based on *Digest of Education Statistics, 2000*, National Center for Education Statistics, March 2000, Table 158 (public school revenues); and *Statistical Abstract of the United States: 2001*, Table 640 (GDP figures).

55. Author's calculation, based on *Digest of Education Statistics, 2000*, National Center for Education Statistics, March 2000, Table 75; and *Statistical Abstract of the United States, 2001*, Table 647. Average teacher salaries compared with national per capita personal income, 1970–1999.

56. For the 1970–1971 school year, an average of $4,682 (in constant 2004–2005 dollars) was spent per pupil in public elementary and secondary schools. For the 2002–2003 school year, the average per pupil expenditure had raised to $9,788 (also in constant 2004–2005 dollars). U.S. Department of Education, Institute of Education Sciences, National Center for Education Statistics, *Digest of Education Statistics*, 2005, Table 162: Total and current expenditure per pupil in public elementary and secondary schools: Selected years, 1919–1920 through 2002–2003.

57. U.S. Department of Education, Institute of Education Sciences, National Center for Education Statistics, *NAEP 2004 Trends in Academic Progress Three Decades of Student Performance*

in *Reading and Mathematics*, July 2005; and U.S. Department of Education, Institute of Education Sciences, National Center for Education Statistics, *NAEP 1999 Trends in Academic Progress: Three Decades of Student Performance*, Aug. 2000.

58. Voucher programs only offered to students with disabilities are excluded from this discussion because they are not justified on the same grounds.

59. In addition, Ohio has enacted a pilot voucher program that will begin its operations in 2006–07; and Vermont and Maine have voucher-like tuitioning programs, which provide scholarships to children residing in districts without public schools to attend either a secular private school or a public school in another district.

60. About 14,200 students made use of the voucher program in Milwaukee, 5,700 in Cleveland, 733 in Florida, and 1,090 in Washington, D.C. These calculations do not include enrollment in vouchers offered only to students with disabilities or the recently enacted pilot program in Ohio.

61. According to the Center for Education Reform, in 2005–06 there were 3,617 charter schools serving 1,074,809 students. The National Center for Education Statistics projected that in the fall of 2005 48. 4 millions of students would enroll in one of the public elementary and secondary schools in the country. Sources: Center for Education Reform, "National Charter School Data At-a-Glance," and U.S. Department of Education, "Digest of Education Statistics, 2005," Table 1.

62. Alveda C. King, niece of Dr. Martin Luther King, in "Fighting for School Choice: It's a Civil Right" op-ed published by the *Wall Street Journal*, Sept. 11, 1997.

63. Americans United for the Separation of Church and State, "Vouchers/Religions School Funding," position statement available at www.au.org/site/ PageServer?pagename=issues_vouchers, accessed Sept. 4, 2006.

64. Results may also depend on where a question is placed in a survey. On this topic, read the exchange the authors of the poll and Stanford professor Terry Moe: Terry M. Moe, "Cooking the Questions?" *Education Next* (Spring 2002): 71–77; Lowell C. Rose and Alec M. Gallup, "Responsible Polling," *Education Next* (Fall 2002): 73–76; and Terry M. Moe, "Dodging the Questions," *Education Next* (Fall 2002): 77–81.

Chapter 4

1. Karen Breslau, "Hate Crime: He Wasn't Afraid," *Newsweek* (October 15, 2001): 8.
1. *Los Angeles Times*, "Rights and the New Reality" (September 21, 2002): part 2, p. 22.
3. Sam Howe Verhovek, "Americans Give in to Racial Profiling," *New York Times* (September 23, 2001): p. 1A; Sandra Tan, "Change of Heart," *The Buffalo News* (October 22, 2001): p. A1.
4. American Arab Anti-Discrimination Committee, press release, September 21, 2001.
6. Mary Jordan, "It's Harder to Cross the Mexican Border," *Washington Post Weekly Edition*, June 3–9, 2002, p. 17; Anne Hull, "A New Anxiety," *Washington Post Weekly Edition*, Dec. 3–9, 2002, p. 9.
7. Shannon McCaffrey, "Justice Report: Immigrants Held after 9/11 Abused," Knight Ridder News Service, June 3, 2003; "Fewer Foreign Students," *Lexington* (KY) *Herald-Leader*, Nov. 3, 2003, p. A3; David J. Jefferson, "Stopped at the Border," *Newsweek*, October 14, 2002: 59.
7. For background, video clips, and photographs, go to www.jainternment.org/.
8. Elizabeth Becker, "All White, All Christian, and Divided by Diversity," *New York Times*, June 10, 2001, Section 4, p. 7.

9. Brian Faler, "Lawmakers Under Fire for Comments Deemed Insensitive," *Washington Post* (Feb. 10, 2003): p. A5.

10. Carl J. Friedrich, *Problems of the American Public Service* (New York: McGraw-Hill, 1935), p. 12.

11. John A. Garrity and Peter Gay, eds., *The Columbia History of the World* (New York: Harper & Row, 1972), p. 673.

12. Garrity and Gay, eds., *Columbia History of the World*, pp. 669–670.

13. Israel Zangwill, *The Melting Pot* (New York: Macmillan, 1912, ©1909).

14. Quoted in Marc Shell, "Babel in America; Or, The Politics of Language Diversity in the United States," *Critical Inquiry* 20 (1993): 109.

15. Richard McCormick, "Ethno-Cultural Interpretations of Nineteenth-Century American Voting Behavior," *Political Science Quarterly* 89 (1974): 351–377.

16. Richard Wayman, "Wisconsin Ethnic Groups and the Election of 1890," *Wisconsin Magazine of History* 51 (1968): 273. More generally, see Paul Kleppner, *The Third Electoral System, 1853–1892: Parties, Voters, and Political Cultures* (Chapel Hill: University of North Carolina Press, 1979).

17. See Oscar Handlin, *Race and Nationality in American Life* (Boston: Little, Brown, 1957), p. 95.

18. Madison Grant, *The Passing of the Great Race* (New York: Scribner's, 1916), pp. 80–81.

19. *Abstracts of Reports of the Immigration Commission* (Washington, DC: Government Printing Office, Vol. 1, 1911). See pp. 229, 244–265.

20. John Miller, "Chinese Exclusion Act," *Congressional Record–Senate 1882*, 13, Pt. 2: 1484–1485.

21. J. Morgan Kousser, *The Shaping of Southern Politics* (New Haven, CT: Yale University Press, 1974).

22. Seymour Martin Lipset and Earl Raab, *The Politics of Unreason* (New York: Harper & Row, 1970), p. 111.

23. Henry Cabot Lodge, "Immigration Restriction," *Congressional Record—Senate 1896*, 28, Pt. 3: 2817.

24. "Emergency" immigration restrictions passed in 1921 were fine-tuned and formalized in the National Origins Act of 1924 and the National Origins Quota Act of 1929.

25. Department of Homeland Security, Office of Immigration Statistics, *2005 Yearbook of Immigration Statistics*, September 2006, Table 1.

26. Department of Homeland Security, Office of Immigration Statistics, *2005 Yearbook of Immigration Statistics*, September 2006, Table 2.

27. Federation for American Immigration Reform, "How Many Illegal Aliens?" updated February 2005, available at www.fairus.org/ImmigrationIssueCenters/ImmigrationIssueCenters.cfm?ID=1183&c=13, accessed March 23, 2005.

28. Caroline J. Tolbert and Rodney E. Hero, "Race/Ethnicity and Direct Democracy: An Analysis of California's Illegal Immigration Initiative," *Journal of Politics* 58 (1996): 806–818.

29. George Borhas, "The New Economics of Immigration," *The Atlantic Monthly* (November 1996): 72–80.

30. National Research Council, *The New Americans: Economic, Demographic, and Fiscal Effects of Immigration* (Washington, DC: National Academy Press, 1977), Chs. 4–6.

31. David Kennedy, "Can We Still Afford to Be a Nation of Immigrants?" *The Atlantic Monthly* (November 1996): 67.

32. Arthur Schlesinger, Jr., *The Disuniting of America* (Knoxville, TN: Whittle, 1991); Samuel Huntington, *Who Are We? The Challenges to America's National Identity* (New York: Simon & Schuster, 2004).

33. Louis Hartz, *The Liberal Tradition in America* (New York: Harcourt, 1955).

34. On Madison's pessimistic view of human nature, see Richard Matthews, *If Men Were Angels* (Lawrence, KS: University of Kansas Press, 1995), especially Ch. 3.

35. Ayn Rand, *The Virtue of Selfishness: A New Concept of Egoism*, New American Library (New York: Signet, 1964), pp. 80–91.

36. Bernard Bailyn, *The Ideological Origins of the American Revolution* (Cambridge, MA: Harvard University Press, 1967).

37. Gordon Wood, *The Creation of the American Republic* (New York: Norton, 1972); and J. G. A. Pocock, *The Machiavellian Moment* (Princeton, NJ: Princeton University Press, 1975).

38. Michael J. Sandel, *Democracy's Discontent: American in Search of a Public Philosophy* (Cambridge, MA: Belknap Press of Harvard University Press, 1996).

39. Rogers Smith, "Beyond Tocqueville, Myrdal and Hartz: The Multiple Traditions in America," *American Political Science Review* 87 (1993): 549–566. These inconsistencies were not lost on earlier thinkers, to be sure. Recall Jefferson's pessimistic predictions in his *Notes on the State of Virginia 1781–1785*. Also see Alexis de Tocqueville, *Democracy in America*, ed. J. P. Mayer (New York: Harper, 1969), pp. 340–363.

40. Samuel Huntington, *American Politics: The Promise of Disharmony* (Cambridge, MA: Harvard University Press, 1981).

41. Everett Carl Ladd, *The American Ideology* (Storrs, CT: The Roper Center, 1994), p. 79.

42. I. A. Lewis and William Schneider, "Hard Times: The Public on Poverty," *Public Opinion* 8 (June–July 1985): 2–8, 59–60.

43. "Income Tax Irritation," *Public Perspective* 1, No. 5 (July–August, 1990): 86.

44. Stanley Feldman, "Structure and Consistency in Public Opinion: The Role of Core Beliefs and Values," *American Journal of Political Science* 32 (1988): 416–440.

45. Alexis de Tocqueville, *Democracy in America*, ed. J. P. Mayer (New York: HarperPerennial, 1969), p. 506.

46. Madison, "Federalist No. 10." See the Appendix to this book.

47. Krissah Williams, "Rich, Poor and Making Ends Meet," *Washington Post Weekly Edition*, July 9–15, 2001, p. 34.

48. Paul Krugman, *Peddling Prosperity* (New York: Norton, 1994), Ch. 5.

49. Karl Mannheim, *Ideology and Utopia* (New York: Harcourt, 1936), pp. 55–79.

50. Hartz, *The Liberal Tradition*, p. 89.

51. Frederick Jackson Turner, *The Frontier in American History* (New York: Holt, 1920).

52. For a discussion, see Seymour Martin Lipset, "Why No Socialism in the United States?" in Seweryn Bialer and Sophia Sluzar, eds., *Sources of Contemporary Radicalism* (New York: Westview Press, 1977).

53. Sven Steinmo, "American Exceptionalism Reconsidered," in Lawrence C. Dodd and Calvin Jillson, eds., *The Dynamics of American Politics* (Boulder, CO: Westview, 1994), pp. 106–131.

54. For a sympathetic description of the trials and ordeals of the immigrants, see Oscar Handlin, *The Uprooted*, 2nd ed. (Boston: Little, Brown, 1973).

55. Abstracts of Reports of the Immigration Commission, U.S. Immigration Commission, 1911, p. 170.

56. Studies by the Center for Immigration Reform often report costs: www.cis.org/topics/costs.html.

57. Carolyn Lockhead, "Economists Support Entry of Educated Foreigners," *San Francisco Chronicle*, April 26, 2006, p. A4.

58. Quoted in Peter Slevin, "Town's-Eye View of Immigration Debate," *Washington Post*, April 3, 2006, p. A01.

59. Peter Brown, "Immigration Costs More than Thought," *Orlando Sentinel*, Oct. 14, 2005.

60. Victor Davis Hanson, *Mexifornia*.

61. Oscar Avila and Hugh Dellios, "Mexican Expatriate Voter Drive Comes up Far Short," *Chicago Tribune*, Jan. 13, 2006.

62. Thomas Elias, ""Lack of Attendance at Forum Speaks Volumes," *The Unon.com*, December 9, 2005.

63. Peter Brown, "Democrats are Split on Immigration, Too," *RealClearPolitics*, April 3, 2006. Mort Kondracke, "Bush Must Talk Sense to Republicans on Immigration, *RealClearPoltics*, January 10, 2006.

64. NBC News/*Wall Street Journal*, April 21–24, 2006; AP/IPSO poll, March 28–30, 2006.

65. Gallup Poll, April 7–9, 2006.

66. FOX News/Opinion Dynamics poll, April 4–5, 2006.

67. NBC News/*Wall Street Journal*, April 21–24, 2006.

Chapter 5

1. John E. Mueller, *War, Presidents, and Public Opinion* (New York: Wiley, 1973). See also Mueller's update of his thesis to cover the Iraq War, "The Iraq Syndrome," *Foreign Affairs*, November/December 2005.

2. On whether the war was "worth fighting" see ABC News/*Washington Post* poll, January 23–26, 2006; on Bush's handling of war, see Gallup poll, January 20–22, 2006.

3. V. O. Key, *Public Opinion and American Democracy* (New York: Knopf, 1961).

4. Carl Friedrich, *Man and His Government* (New York: McGraw-Hill, 1963), pp. 199–215.

5. Robert Hess and Judith Horney, *The Development of Political Attitudes in Children* (Garden City, NY: Doubleday, 1967).

6. Elizabeth Cook, Ted Jelen, and Clyde Wilcox, *Between Two Absolutes: Public Opinion and the Politics of Abortion* (Boulder, CO: Westview Press, 1992).

7. For a survey of positive and negative findings, see Jack Citrin and Donald Green, "The Self-Interest Motive in American Public Opinion," *Research in Micropolitics* Vol. 3 (Greenwich, CT: JAI Press, 1993), pp. 1–28.

8. Douglas Hibbs, *The American Political Economy* (Cambridge, MA: Harvard University Press, 1987), Ch. 5.

9. Jennifer A. Lindholm, Alexander W. Astin, Linda J. Sax, and William S. Korn, *The American College Teacher: National Norms for the 2001–2002 HERI Faculty Survey* (Los Angeles, CA: Higher Education Research Institute). Also, Karl Zinsmeister, "The Shame of America's One-Party Campuses," *American Enterprise Online* (September 2002), but see Martin Plissner, "Flunking Statistics," *American Prospect Online* 13 (December 30, 2002).

10. Norman Nie, Jane Junn, and Kenneth Stehlik-Barry, *Education and Democratic Citizenship in America* (Chicago: University of Chicago Press, 1996).

11. John G. Geer, *From Tea Leaves to Opinion Polls: A Theory of Democratic Leadership* (New York: Columbia University Press, 1996).

12. Details on how these polls are conducted appear in D. Stephen Voss, Andrew Gelman, and Gary King, "Preelection Survey Methodology: Details from Eight Polling Organizations, 1988 and 1992," *Public Opinion Quarterly* 59 (Spring 1995): 98–132.

13. Don Van Natta, Jr., "Polling's 'Dirty Little Secret': No Response," *New York Times* (November 21, 1999, Sect. 4): pp. A1, A16.

14. John Brehm, *The Phantom Respondents* (Ann Arbor, MI: University of Michigan Press, 1993), Ch. 2. www.exit-poll.net, accessed February 19, 2005.

15. Craig Gilbert, "Feingold Clicks with Blog Fans," *Milwaukee Journal Sentinel*, February 27, 2006, p. 1.

16. Jon Krosnick and Matthew Barent, "Comparisons of Party Identification and Policy Preferences: The Impact of Survey Question Format," *American Journal of Political Science* 37 (1993): 941–964.

17. For a full discussion, see David Moore and Frank Newport, "Misreading the Public: The Case of the Holocaust Poll," *Public Perspective* 5 (March/April 1994): 28–30; and Tom Smith, "Review: The Holocaust Denial Controversy," *Public Opinion Quarterly* 59 (1995): 269–295. D. Stephen Voss and Penny Miller present two other instances in which a double negative apparently caused many people to misreport their policy preferences in "Following a False Trail: The Hunt for White Backlash in Kentucky's 1996 Desegregation Vote," *State Politics and Policy Quarterly* 1 (2001): 63–82.

18. National Opinion Research Center, General Social Survey 2004.

19. National Opinion Research Center, General Social Survey, 2004.

20. Gallup Poll, June 8–12, 2005.

21. "Abortion: Overview of a Complex Opinion," *The Public Perspective* (November/December, 1989): 19, 20.

22. "Abortion," *The American Enterprise* 6, Issue 4 (July/August 1995): 107.

23. Cook, Jelen, and Wilcox, *Between Two Absolutes*, Ch. 2.

24. Tamar Lewin, "Study Points to Increase in Tolerance of Ethnicity," *New York Times* (Jan. 8, 1992): p. A12.

25. "Majority of 18–29-year-olds Think Bush Favors Reinstating the Draft, Annenberg Data Shows," National Annenberg Election Survey, press release, October 8, 2004.

26. Anthony Downs, *An Economic Theory of Democracy* (New York: Harper & Row, 1957), Chs. 11–13.

27. Morris P. Fiorina, "Information and Rationality in Elections," in John Ferejohn and James Kuklinski, eds., *Information and Democratic Processes* (Urbana: University of Illinois Press, 1990), pp. 329–342.

28. John Krosnick, "Government Policy and Citizen Passion: A Study of Issue Publics in Contemporary America," *Political Behavior* 12 (1990): 59–92; and Peter Natchez and Irvin Bupp, "Candidates, Issues, and Voters," *Public Policy* 1 (1968): 409–437.

29. The inhalation form of anthrax is more likely to be fatal. Henry J. Kaiser Family Foundation poll conducted by Princeton Survey Research Associates, November 29–December 2, 2001. See also Markus Prior, "Political Knowledge after September 11," *PS: Political Science and Politics*, 35:3 (September 2002): 523–529.

30. Anthony Downs, "Up and Down with Ecology—The Issue Attention Cycle," *The Public Interest* 28 (1972): 38–50.

31. Fiorina, "Information and Rationality."

32. Philip Converse, "The Nature of Belief Systems in Mass Publics," in David Apter, ed., *Ideology and Discontent* (New York: Free Press, 1964), pp. 206–261.

33. National Election Studies, 1972–2004.

34. James A. Davis, "Changeable Weather in a Cooling Climate Atop the Liberal Plateau," *Public Opinion Quarterly* 56 (1992): 261–306; and Morris P. Fiorina, "The Reagan Years: Turn-

ing to the Right or Groping Toward the Middle?" in Barry Cooper, Allan Kornberg, and William Mishler, eds., *The Resurgence of Conservatism in Anglo-American Democracies* (Durham, NC: Duke University Press, 1988), pp. 430–459.

35. "Public Expects GOP Miracles," *Times-Mirror News Release*, Dec. 8, 1994; CNN, "Gallup Poll: 50 Percent Americans Support, 33 Percent Oppose, Bush Tax Plan," February 27, 2001.

36. Samuel Stouffer, *Communism, Conformity, and Civil Liberties* (New York: Doubleday, 1955); and James Prothro and Charles Grigg, "Fundamental Principles of Democracy: Bases of Agreement and Disagreement," *Journal of Politics* 22 (1960): 176–194.

37. For evidence that people's opinions reflect a smaller number of "core beliefs" that may conflict with each other or situational characteristics, see Stanley Feldman, "Structure and Consistency in Public Opinion: The Role of Core Beliefs and Values," *American Journal of Public Opinion* 32 (1988): 416–440; and Stanley Feldman and John Zaller, "A Simple Theory of the Survey Response: Answering Questions versus Revealing Preferences," *American Journal of Political Science* 36 (1992): 579–616.

38. On the effects of posing political conflicts as matters of conflicting rights, see Mary Anne Glendon, *Rights Talk: The Impoverishment of Political Discourse* (New York: Free Press, 1991).

39. All quotations are from John F. Harris, "Campaign Promises Aside, It's Politics as Usual: Policy Shifts, Internal Debates—The Bush White House Looks a Lot Like the Clinton One," *Washington Post Weekly Edition* (July 2–8, 2001): p. 11.

40. Dan Carney, "House GOP Embrace of Gun Curbs Not Yet Lock, Stock and Barrel, CQ *Weekly* 57 (May 29, 1999): 1267.

41. Dan Carney, "Beyond Guns and Violence: A Battle for House Control," *CQ Weekly* 57 (June 1999): 1426–1432.

42. Kathy Keily, "After Failed Gun Legislation, Political Finger Pointing Begins," *USA Today* (June 21, 1999): p. 14A.

43. ABC News/*Washington Post* poll of August 30–September 2, 1999.

44. Benjamin Page and Robert Shapiro, *The Rational Public* (Chicago: University of Chicago Press, 1992).

45. James Stimson, "A Macro Theory of Information Flow," in John Ferejohn and James Kuklinski, eds., *Information and Democratic Processes* (Urbana: University of Illinois Press, 1990), pp. 345–368.

46. Arthur Lupia, "Shortcuts versus Encyclopedias: Information and Voting Behavior in California Insurance Reform Elections," *American Political Science Review* 88 (1994): 63–76.

47. James Stimson, *Public Opinion in America: Moods, Cycles, and Swings* (Boulder, CO: Westview Press, 1991).

48. Pew Research Center for the People and the Press, "Online Papers Modestly Boost Newspaper Readership," Washington, DC: Pew Research Center, July 30, 2006, p. 2.

49. William Mayer, "Trends in Media Usage," *Public Opinion Quarterly* 57 (1993): 597, 610.

50. For example, Doris Graber, *Mass Media and American Politics* (Washington, DC: CQ Press, 1993), Ch. 7.

51. Russell Neuman, Marion Just, and Ann Crigler, *Common Knowledge: News and the Construction of Political Meaning* (Chicago: University of Chicago Press, 1992); and Jeffrey Mondak, "Newspapers and Political Awareness," *American Journal of Political Science* 39 (1995): 513–527.

52. Pew Research Center on the People and the Press, "How Journalists See Journalists in 2004," Washington, DC: Pew Research Center, p. 24.

53. William Schneider and I. A. Lewis, "Views on the News," *Public Opinion* 8 (August/September 1985): 6–11; and "Ordinary Americans More Cynical Than Journalists: News Media Differs with Public and Leaders on Watchdog Issues" (Washington, DC: Times-Mirror Center on People and the Press, May 22, 1995).

54. Tim Groseclose and David Milyo, "A Measure of Media Bias," *Quarterly Journal of Economics* 120:4 (November 2005), pp. 1191–1237.

55. Calculated by authors from data in "Daily Show Viewers Knowledgeable About Presidential Campaign, National Annenberg Election Survey Shows," Annenberg Public Policy Center, University of Pennsylvania, September 21, 2004, Table D, p. 8.

56. S. Robert Lichter, Stanley Rothman, and Linda S. Lichter, *The Media Elite: America's New Powerbrokers* (New York: Hastings House, 1990).

57. John Leo, "A Surprising Jog to the Right," *U.S. News & World Report*, November 24, 2003: p. 64.

58. Larry Sabato, *Feeding Frenzy* (New York: Simon & Schuster, 1991).

59. A widely cited study of what constitutes news is provided by Herbert Gans, *Deciding What's News: A Case Study of CBS Evening News, NBC Nightly News, Newsweek and Time* (New York: Vintage, 1979).

60. John David Rausch, Jr., "The Pathology of Politics: Government, Press, and Scandal," *Extensions: A Publication of the Carl Albert Congressional Research and Studies Center* (Norman, OK: Carl Albert Congressional Research and Studies Center, Fall 1990), pp. 11–12.

61. A Gallup survey of former Nieman Journalism Fellows found that more than three-quarters believe that traditional journalism is being replaced by tabloid journalism. See *The State of the Public Media Today* (Cambridge, MA: Nieman Foundation, April 1995).

62. Marc Peyser, "Red, White, and Funny," *Newsweek*, January 5, 2004, p. 77.

63. Mark Weisbrot, "Shirking Journalistic Duty," Knight Ridder/Tribune News Service, May 13, 2003; Greg Dyke, quoted in *Newsweek*, May 5, 2003, p. 25; and Howard Kurtz, "What's Blue and White and Red All Over?" *Washington Post Weekly Edition*, December 13–19, 2001: 34.

64. Michael Robinson and Margaret Sheehan, *Over the Wire and on TV* (New York: Russell Sage, 1983), Doris Graber, *Mass Media and American Politics*, 6th ed. (Washington, DC: CQ Press, 2002), Ch. 9.

65. S. Robert Lichter and Daniel Amundson, "Less News Is Worse News: Television News Coverage of Congress, 1972–92," in Thomas Mann and Norman Ornstein, eds., *Congress, the Press, and the Public* (Washington, DC: American Enterprise Institute, 1994), pp. 131–140.

66. Shanto Iyengar, *Is Anyone Responsible?* (Chicago: University of Chicago Press, 1991).

67. Lichter and Amundson, "Less News Is Worse News."

68. Thomas Patterson, *Out of Order* (New York: Knopf, 1993), Ch. 2.

69. Kiku Adatto, *Picture Perfect* (New York: Basic Books, 1993), Ch. 25; Daniel C. Hallin, "Sound Bite News: Television Coverage of Elections, 1968-1988," *Journal of Communication*, 42(2), Spring, 1992, pp. 5–24; "Election Newswatch: Campaign 2004," Center for Media & Public Affairs, www.cmpa.com.

70. Elihu Katz and Jacob Feldman, "The Debates in the Light of Research: A Survey of Surveys," in Sidney Kraus, ed., *The Great Debates* (Bloomington: University of Indiana Press, 1962), pp. 173–223.

71. Annenberg Public Policy Center, National Annenberg Election Survey "Voters Learned Positions on Issues Since Presidential Debates; Kerry Improves Slightly on Traits, Annenberg Data Show," www.annenbergpublicpolicycenter.org/naes/2004_03_%20Voters-and-the-issues_10-23_pr.pdf, accessed February 20, 2005.

72. Alison Carper, "Paint-by-Numbers Journalism: How Reader Surveys and Focus Groups Subvert a Democratic Press," discussion paper D–19, Barone Center on the Press, Politics and Public Policy, Harvard University Kennedy School of Government, April 1995.

73. Dave Barry, "Scandal Sheep," *Boston Globe Magazine* (March 15, 1998): pp. 12–13.

74. William Kornhauser, *The Politics of Mass Society* (New York: Free Press, 1959).

75. An example is the study of the 1940 presidential campaign reported in Paul Lazarsfeld, Bernard Berelson, and Hazel Gaudet, *The People's Choice* (New York: Columbia University Press, 1948).

76. Joseph Klapper, *The Effects of Mass Communication* (New York: Free Press, 1960).

77. Presentation by Steven Livingston at the John F. Kennedy School of Government, Harvard University, March 1996.

78. Robert Rotberg and Thomas Weiss, eds., *From Massacres to Genocide* (Washington, DC: Brookings, 1996).

79. Bernard Cohen, *The Press and Foreign Policy* (Princeton, NJ: Princeton University Press, 1963), p. 13.

80. M. McCombs and D. Shaw, "The Evolution of Agenda-Setting: Twenty-Five Years in the Marketplace of Ideas," *Journal of Communications* 43 (1993): 58–67.

81. Steven Livingston and Todd Eachus, "Humanitarian Crises and U.S. Foreign Policy: Somalia and the CNN Effect Reconsidered," *Political Communication* 12 (1995): 413–429.

82. Shanto Iyengar and Donald Kinder, *News That Matters: Television and American Opinion* (Chicago: University of Chicago Press, 1987).

83. Jon Krosnick and Laura Brannon, "The Impact of the Gulf War on the Ingredients of Presidential Evaluations," *American Political Science Review* 87 (1993): 963–975.

84. The most extensive study of framing is Iyengar, *Is Anyone Responsible?*

85. Iyengar and Kinder, *News That Matters*, Chs. 6, 10.

86. John Zaller, *The Nature and Origins of Mass Opinion* (New York: Cambridge University Press, 1992).

87. Bernard Cohen, *The Press and Foreign Policy*. See also Lutz Erbring, Edie Goldenberg, and Arthur Miller, "Front-Page News and Real-World Clues: A New Look at Agenda-Setting by the Media," *American Journal of Political Science* 24 (1980): 16–49.

88. Frank Luther Mott, *American Journalism* (New York: Macmillan, 1950).

89. Samuel Kernell, *Going Public: New Strategies of Presidential Leadership* (Washington, DC: CQ Press, 1986). Compare Mel Laracey, "The Presidential Newspaper: The Forgotten Way of Going Public," manuscript, Harvard University, 1993.

90. Mott, *American Journalism*, p. 216.

91. Gannett also owns 21 television stations. "Washington Post 200: Gannett Co." www.washingtonpost.com/wp-srv/business/post200/2005/GCI.html, accessed September 20, 2006.

92. William Safire, "Media Mergers Limit Information Flow," New York Times News Service, January 22, 2003.

93. The 1999 annual radio station survey by M Street Corporation of Nashville, www.mstreet.net; 1999 annual radio station survey by M Street Corporation of Nashville, www.mstreet.net; Tom Humphrey, "Talk Radio is Major Player in Tennessee Political Wars," *Knoxville* (TN) *News-Sentinel*, July 19, 2002, p. A1; David Hinkley, "Rush & Sean Tops in Talk," New York *Daily News*, December 10, 2005, p. 72; Arian Campo-Flores and Evan Thomas, "Rehabbing Rush" *Newsweek*, May 8, 2006, p. 26.

94. Mary Ann Watson, *The Expanding Vista: American Television in the Kennedy Years* (New York: Oxford University Press, 1990), p. 76.

95. For cable statistics see National Cable and Telecommunications Association, 2006 Industry Overview, www.ncta.com/, accessed September 20, 2006, p. 6; for network television news statistics, see The Project for Excellence in Journalism, "The State of the News Media, 2006," www.stateofthenewsmedia.org/, accessed September 20, 2006.

96. The Project for Excellence in Journalism, "The State of the News Media, 2006," www.stateofthenewsmedia.org/, accessed September 20, 2006.

97. Marc Peyser, "Red, White, and Funny," *Newsweek*, January 5, 2004, pp. 71–77.

98. Pew Research Center Poll, March 17–21, 2004.

99. The Project for Excellence in Journalism, "The State of the News Media, 2006," www.stateofthenewsmedia.org/, accessed September 20, 2006.

100. Eve Gerber, "Six Arguments for Online Fund Raising," *Slate* (January 18, 2000), www.slate.com/id/73270, accessed April 11, 2005; and Lindsey Arent, "Candidates Eye Check Republic," *Wired News* (January 13, 2000), www.wired.com/news/politics/0,1283,32994,00.html, accessed April 11, 2005.

101. *New York Times v. U.S.* 403 U.S. 713 (1971).

102. *Ibid.*

103. Eric Lichtblau and James Risen, "Bank Data Sifted in Secret by U.S. To Block Terrorism," *New York Times*, June 23, 2006, p. A1.

104. *Ibid.*

Chapter 6

1. Michael D. Shear, "Virginia Sizzling with Election Fever," *Washington Post*, October 24, 2004, p. C7.

2. Darrel Rowland, "Campaigns Hope Personal Contacts Win Voters One by One," *Columbus Dispatch*, August 26, 2004, p. 1A.

3. Robert D. McFadden, "Record Turnout Forecast; Vote Drives Intensify," *New York Times*, November 2, 2004, p. A1.

4. McFadden.

5. According to the National Election Studies, 35 percent of Americans reported being contacted by a party in 2000; 43 percent reported such a contact in 2004.

6. All of the statistics in this paragraph are taken from the final report of the Committee for the Study of the American Electorate, available at http://election04.ssrc.org/research/csae_2004_final_report.pdf.

7. Benjamin Barber, *Strong Democracy: Participatory Politics for a New Age* (Berkeley: University of California Press, 1984), p. xiii.

8. Jeff Jacoby, "Making It Too Easy to Vote," *Boston Globe* (July 18, 1996): p. A15.

9. John Aldrich, *Why Parties?* (Chicago: University of Chicago Press, 1995), pp. 106–107.

11. Chilton Williamson, *American Suffrage from Property to Democracy: 1760–1860* (Princeton, NJ: Princeton University Press, 1960); and Alexander Keyssar, *The Right to Vote* (New York: Basic Books, 2000), p. 29.

11. *Ibid.*, p. 277.

12. "18-Year-Old Vote: Constitutional Amendment Cleared," *Congressional Quarterly Almanac* (Washington, DC: Congressional Quarterly, 1972), pp. 475–477.

13. For a comparative study of the American and Swiss suffrage movements, see Lee Ann Banaszak, *Why Movements Succeed or Fail* (Princeton, NJ: Princeton University Press, 1996).

14. Howard Rosenthal and Subrata Sen, "Electoral Participation in the French Fifth Republic," *American Political Science Review* 67 (1973): 29–54.

15. "Election Results for the U.S. President, the U.S. Senate, and the House of Representatives, 2004," Federal Election Commission, Washington, DC, May, 2005, p. 36.

16. Raymond E. Wolfinger and Steven J. Rosenstone, *Who Votes?* (New Haven, CT: Yale University Press, 1980), p. 116.

17. Ruy Teixeira, *The Disappearing American Voter* (Washington, DC: Brookings, 1992), p. 10.

18. "Can the Black Vote Hold Up? *The Economist* (April 3, 1999): 24.

19. Martha Angle, "Low Voter Turnout Prompts Concern on Hill," *Congressional Quarterly Weekly Report* (April 2, 1988): 864; and Stephen Bennett, "The Uses and Abuses of Registration and Turnout Data," *PS: Political Science and Politics* 23 (1990): 166–171.

20. Stephen Knack, "Drivers Wanted: Motor Voter and the Election of 1996," *PS: Political Science and Politics* 32 (1999): 237–243; Michael Martinez and David Hill, "Did Motor Voter Work? *American Politics Quarterly* 27 (1999): 296–315; and Robert D. Brown and Justin Wedeking, "People Who Have Their Tickets But Do Not Use Them: 'Motor-Voter,' Registration, and Turnout Revisited," *American Politics Research* 34:4 (July 2006), pp. 479–504.

21. Wolfinger and Rosenstone, *Who Votes?* p. 88.

22. Richard Hasen, "Voting Without Law," *University of Pennsylvania Law Review* 144 (1996): 2135–2179.

23. Mark Franklin, "Electoral Engineering and Cross-National Turnout Differences: What Role for Compulsory Voting?" *British Journal of Political Science* 29 (1999): 205.

24. Richard Boyd, "Decline of U.S. Voter Turnout: Structural Explanations," *American Politics Quarterly* 9 (1981): 133–159.

25. Stephen Knack, "The Voter Participation Effects of Selecting Jurors from Registration Lists," Working Paper No. 91–10, University of Maryland, Department of Economics; and J. Eric Oliver and Raymond Wolfinger, "Jury Aversion and Voter Registration," paper presented at the 1997 Annual Meeting of the American Political Science Association, Washington, D.C.

26. G. Bingham Powell, "American Voter Turnout in Comparative Perspective," *American Political Science Review* 80 (1986): 17–43; and Robert Jackman, "Political Institutions and Voter Turnout in the Industrial Democracies," *American Political Science Review* 81 (1987): 405–423.

27. Steven J. Rosenstone and John Mark Hansen, *Mobilization, Participation, and Democracy* (New York: Macmillan, 1993), pp. 63–70. There is some conflict between their figures and those reported by Sidney Verba, Kay Lehman Schlozman, and Henry E. Brady in *Voice and Equality: Civic Volunteerism in American Politics* (Cambridge, MA: Harvard University Press, 1995), pp. 69–74. Part of the explanation may be that the survey items relied on by Rosenstone and Hansen generally have more specific referents (such as this year's elections), whereas the items relied on by Verba, Schlozman, and Brady ask more generally about activity in the last year or two years. Thus, the Verba, Schlozman, and Brady figures may reflect the increasing number of opportunities.

28. Jack Citrin, "Comment: The Political Relevance of Trust in Government," *American Political Science Review* 68 (1974): 973–988.

29. Teixeira, *The Disappearing American Voter*, p. 49.

30. "Politics Brief: Is There a Crisis?" *The Economist* (July 17, 1999): 50.

31. Rosenstone and Hansen, *Mobilization, Participation, and Democracy*, Ch. 2.

32. Jeffrey Jones, "Does Bringing Out the Candidate Bring Out the Votes?" *American Politics Quarterly* 26 (1998): 406.

33. John Milholland, "The Danger Point in American Politics," *North American Review* 164 (1897).

34. Wolfinger and Rosenstone, *Who Votes?* p. 101.

35. John Ferejohn and Morris Fiorina, "The Paradox of Not Voting: A Decision Theoretic Analysis," *American Political Science Review* 68 (1974): 525–535.

36. Anthony Downs, *An Economic Theory of Democracy* (New York: Harper & Row, 1957), Ch. 14.

37. Richard Brody, "The Puzzle of Political Participation in America," in Anthony King, ed., *The New American Political System* (Washington, DC: American Enterprise Institute, 1978), pp. 287–324; and Paul Abramson and John Aldrich, "The Decline of Electoral Participation in America," *American Political Science Review* 76 (1982): 502–521.

38. Rosenstone and Hansen, *Mobilization, Participation, and Democracy*, p. 183.

39. Marshall Ganz, "Motor Voter or Motivated Voter," *The American Prospect* (September–October, 1996): 46–48; Marshall Ganz, "Voters in the Crosshairs," *The American Prospect* (Winter 1994): 100–109; and Michael Scherer, "Campaign Finance Reform School," *Columbia Journalism Review* (September/October 2002): 54; David S. Broder, "Shoe-Leather Politicking," *Washington Post Weekly Edition*, June 25–July 1, 2001: p. 4.

40. Stephen Knack, "Civic Norms, Social Sanctions, and Voter Turnout," *Rationality and Society* 4 (1992): 133–156.

41. Warren Miller, "The Puzzle Transformed: Explaining Declining Turnout," *Political Behavior* 14 (1992): 1–43.

42. Rosenstone and Hansen, *Mobilization, Participation, and Democracy*, Ch. 7; and Teixeira, *The Disappearing American Voter*, Ch. 2.

43. Eric Uslaner, "Faith, Hope, and Charity: Social Capital, Trust, and Collective Action" (College Park, MD: University of Maryland, unpublished manuscript).

44. For detailed analyses of the relationship between demographic characteristics and voting, see Wolfinger and Rosenstone, *Who Votes?*, and Rosenstone and Hansen, *Mobilization, Participation, and Democracy*, Ch. 5.

45. Sidney Verba and Norman Nie, *Participation in America: Political Democracy and Social Equality* (New York: Harper & Row, 1972), pp. 170–171; and Wolfinger and Rosenstone, *Who Votes?* p. 90.

46. Rosenstone and Hansen, *Mobilization, Participation, and Democracy in America*, Ch. 5.

47. On language and political participation, see Verba, Schlozman, and Brady, *Voice and Equality*.

48. Russell Dalton, *Citizen Politics in Western Democracies* (Chatham, NJ: Chatham House, 1988), pp. 51–52.

49. Herbert Tingsten, *Political Behavior: Studies in Election Statistics* (London: King & Son, 1937), pp. 225–226.

50. "The Democratic Distemper," *The Public Interest* 41 (1975), pp. 36–37.

51. Quoted in Seymour Martin Lipset, *Political Man* (New York: Anchor, 1963), p. 228, note 90.

52. George Will, "In Defense of Nonvoting," in George Will, ed., *The Morning After* (New York: Free Press, 1986), p. 229.

53. Joseph Carroll and Frank Newport, "A Quarter of Americans Say Iraq Nation's Most Important Problem; But Americans Still More Likely to Name Economic Issues as Top Prob-

lem Facing Country," Gallup Poll News Service, April 15, 2004; Tom W. Smith, "America's Most Important Problem: A Trend Analysis, 1946–1976," *Public Opinion Quarterly* (1980): 164–180; and "America's Most Important Problems: Part I," *Public Opinion Quarterly* (1985): 264–274.

54. Frank M. Bryan, *Real Democracy: The New England Town Meeting and How it Works*, (Chicago: The University of Chicago Press, 2004).

55. Stephen Bennett and David Resnick, "The Implications of Nonvoting for Democracy in the United States," *American Journal of Political Science* 34 (1990): 771–802.

56. U.S. Bureau of the Census, *Current Population Reports*, P20–485, Table B. For a general discussion, see Peverill Squire, Raymond Wolfinger, and David Glass, "Residential Mobility and Voter Turnout," *American Political Science Review* 81 (1987): 45–65.

57. Contact with officials, contributions, rallies, campaign work: National Election Studies, 2004 data; Petition: Civic and Political Health of the Nation Survey, Center for Information and Research on Civic Learning and Engagement, April 4–May 20, 2002.

58. David Nexon, "Asymmetry in the Political System: Occasional Activists in the Democratic and Republican Parties, 1956–1964," *American Political Science Review* 65 (1971): 716–730; and Warren Miller and M. Kent Jennings, *Parties in Transition* (New York: Russell Sage, 1986), Ch. 2.

59. See Martin P. Wattenberg, *Is Voting for Young People?* (New York: Pearson Longman, 2006), Chs. 1–3.

60. Arend Lijphart, "Unequal Participation: Democracy's Unresolved Dilemma," *American Political Science Review* 91 (March 1997): 2.

61. On the point that a "floor" in participation may be necessary, see Sidney Verba, Norman H. Nie, and Jae-On Kim, *Participation and Political Equality* (New York: Cambridge University Press, 1978).

62. For an argument that increased voter participation would have changed the results in 2000 and in the 1994 midterm elections, see Martin P. Wattenberg, *Where Have All the Voters Gone?* (Cambridge, MA: Harvard University Press, 2002), Ch. 5.

63. For an argument about how this might be done, see Lisa Hill, "Low Voter Turnout in the United States: Is Compulsory Voting a Viable Solution?" *Journal of Theoretical Politics* Vol. 18. No. 2 (April 2006): 207–232.

Chapter 7

1. Pradnya Joshi, "Wall Street Looks for Clear Winner," *New York Newsday*, November 2, 2004, p. A42.

2. Dan Balz and David Broder, "Election Day Dawns with Unpredictability," *Washington Post*, November 2, 2004, p. A1.

3. Mike Littwin, "It's almost over (maybe); But one thing is sure: It's been a scream," *Rocky Mountain News*, November 2, 2004, p. 28A.

4. Steve Schultze, "Bush Derides Rival," *Milwaukee Journal-Sentinel*, October 16, 2004, p. A1.

5. Tucker Carlson, "CNN Live Event/Special 12:00 AM EST, November 3, 2004," CNN Transcript.

6. Andrew Gelman and Gary King, "Why Are American Presidential Election Campaign Polls So Variable When Votes Are So Predictable?" *British Journal of Political Science* 23 (1993): 409–451; Dan B. Thomas and Larry R. Baas, "The Postelection Campaign: Competing Constructions of the Clinton Victory in 1992," *Journal of Politics* 58 (1996): 309–331; and Richard

Morin, "The True Political Puppeteers," *Washington Post Weekly Edition* (February 20–26, 1989): p. 37.

7. American National Election Studies, University of Michigan.

8. Although the general notion of "partisanship" has been around for centuries, the social-psychological concept of party ID was advanced in the pioneering work of Angus Campbell, Philip Converse, Warren Miller, and Donald Stokes, *The American Voter* (New York: Wiley, 1960), Chs. 6–7.

9. Donald Philip Green and Bradley Palmquist, "How Stable Is Party Identification?" *Political Behavior* 16 (1994): 437–466.

10. Morris Fiorina, *Retrospective Voting in American National Elections* (New Haven, CT: Yale University Press, 1981); and Michael MacKuen, Robert Erikson, and James Stimson, "Macropartisanship," *American Political Science Review* 83 (1989): 1125–1142. On the latter piece, though, see Donald Green, Bradley Palmquist, and Eric Schickler, "Macropartisanship: A Replication and Critique," *American Political Science Review* 92 (1998): 883–899.

11. Bruce E. Keith et al., *The Myth of the Independent Voter* (Berkeley, CA: University of California Press, 1992).

12. Jane Mansbridge, "Myth and Reality: The ERA and the Gender Gap in the 1980 Election," *Public Opinion Quarterly* 49 (1985): 164–178.

13. Emily Stoper, "The Gender Gap Concealed and Revealed," *Journal of Political Science* 17 (1989): 50–62; and Tom Smith, "Gender and Attitudes Toward Violence," *Public Opinion Quarterly* 48 (1984): 384–396; Karen M. Kaufmann, "The Gender Gap," PS: *Political Science and Politics* 39:3 (July 2006): 447–453.

14. For discussions, see Pamela Conover, "Feminists and the Gender Gap," *Journal of Politics* 50 (1988): 985–1010; and Elizabeth Cook and Clyde Wilcox, "Feminism and the Gender Gap—A Second Look," *Journal of Politics* 53 (1991): 1111–1122.

15. This was first noted by Herbert Weisberg, "The Demographics of a New Voting Gap: Marital Differences in American Voting Behavior," *Public Opinion Quarterly* 51 (1987): 335–343.

16. "Where the Parties Are Today," *The Public Perspective* 5, No. 3 (March/April 1994): 78–79; and "Which Party Is Better on Which Issues?" *The Public Perspective* 7, No. 4 (June/July 1996): 65.

17. Fiorina, *Retrospective Voting*.

18. Scott Teeter, "Public Opinion in 1984," and Gerald Pomper, "The Presidential Election," both in Gerald Pomper et al., *The Election of 1984* (Chatham, NJ: Chatham House, 1985).

19. Samuel Popkin, *The Reasoning Voter* (Chicago: University of Chicago Press, 1991), pp. 60–67.

20. The classic demonstration in Chapter 8 of Campbell et al.'s *The American Voter* almost certainly overstates the case. Balanced treatments of policy issues in recent campaigns appear in the series of *Change and Continuity* volumes by Paul Abramson, John Aldrich, and David Rohde, published by CQ Press.

21. Benjamin Page and Richard Brody, "Policy Voting and the Electoral Process: The Vietnam War Issue," *American Political Science Review* 66 (1972): 979–995.

22. Edward Carmines and James Stimson, "The Two Faces of Issue Voting," *American Political Science Review* 74 (1980): 78–91.

23. CNN Transcript, "Bush, Kerry Debate Domestic Policies," October 14, 2004, www.cnn.com/2004/ALLPOLITICS/10/13/debate.transcript/, accessed February 26, 2005.

24. Donald Stokes, "Some Dynamic Elements of Contests for the Presidency," *American Political Science Review* 60 (1966): 19–28.

25. Fiorina, *Retrospective Voting*, pp. 150–153; and Andrew Kohut, "The Vox Pop on Mala-props," *Washington Post Weekly Edition* (October 2, 2000): p. 22.

26. On the failure of incumbency to provide a complete explanation of Democratic domi-nance during this era, see Morris Fiorina, *Divided Government*, 2nd ed. (Boston: Allyn & Bacon, 1996), pp. 18–23. D. Stephen Voss and David Lublin offer evidence of a candidate overstating her own incumbency advantage in "Black Incumbents, White Districts: An Appraisal of the 1996 Congressional Elections," *American Politics Research* 29 (2001): 141–182. Ironically, that candidate lost her party primary in 2002.

27. Norman Ornstein, Thomas Mann, and Michael Malbin, *Vital Statistics on Congress, 1998–2000* (Washington, DC: American Enterprise Institute, 2000).

28. Robert Erikson, "Malapportionment, Gerrymandering and Party Fortunes in Congres-sional Elections," *American Political Science Review* 66 (1972): 1234–1245. Gary King and Andrew Gelman, "Systemic Consequences of Incumbency Advantage in U.S. House Elec-tions," *American Journal of Political Science* 35 (1991): 110–138.

29. Gary W. Cox and Jonathan N. Katz, *Elbridge Gerry's Salamander: The Electoral Consequences of the Reapportionment Revolution* (New York: Cambridge University Press, 2002).

30. Morris P. Fiorina, "*Keystone* Reconsidered," in Lawrence C. Dodd and Bruce Oppen-heimer, *Congress Reconsidered*, 8th ed. (Washington, DC: CQ Press, 2005), pp. 159–179.

31. John Ferejohn and Randall Calvert, "Presidential Coattails in Historical Perspective," *American Journal of Political Science* 28 (1984): 127–146.

32. Fiorina, *Divided Government*, p. 14.

33. *Ibid.*, pp. 135–139.

34. Ronald Keith Gaddie and Charles S. Bullock, III, *Elections to Open Seats in the U.S. House: Where the Action Is* (Lanham, MD: Rowman and Littlefield, 2000), pp. 4–5, 24–35; and David Lublin and D. Stephen Voss, "Boll-Weevil Blues," *American Review of Politics* 22 (2000): 427–450.

35. Jon Healey, "Projects Are His Project," *Congressional Quarterly Weekly Report* (September 21, 1996): 2672. Also see Jonathan Salant, "Some Republicans Turned Away from Leadership," *Congressional Quarterly Weekly Report* (December 7, 1996): 3352–3354; and Andrew Taylor, "GOP Pet Projects Give Boost to Shaky Incumbents," *Congressional Quarterly Weekly Report* (August 3, 1996): 2169–2173.

36. Federal Election Commission, "Party Financial Activity Summarized for the 2004 Elec-tion Cycle," (Washington, DC: Federal Election Commission), press release, March 2, 2005 (corrected on March 15, 2005), www.fec.gov/press/press2005/20050302party/Party2004final.html, accessed April 24, 2005.

37. David Rohde, *Parties and Leaders in the Postreform House* (Chicago: University of Chicago Press, 1991); Keith T. Poole and Howard Rosenthal, *Congress: A Political-Economic History of Roll Call Voting* (New York: Oxford University Press, 1997); Jon Bond and Richard Fleisher, *Polarized Politics: Congress and the President in a Partisan Era* (Washington, DC: CQ Press, 2000); Richard Fleisher and Jon Bond, "The Shrinking Middle in the U.S. Congress," *British Journal of Political Science* 34, No. 3 (July 2004): 429–451.

38. Wisconsin Advertising Project, "One Billion Dollars Spent on Political Television Adver-tising, Says New Report," press release, December 5, 2002.

39. Max Farrand, ed., *The Records of the Federal Convention of 1787* (New Haven, CT: Yale Uni-versity Press, 1966), Vol. 1, p. 151.

40. Based on the average incumbent's expenditure of $6,536,018, as reported by www.opensecrets.org.

41. See the overview in R. Douglas Arnold, *Congress, the Press, and Political Accountability* (Princeton: Princeton University Press, 2004), pp. 58–60. Coverage of Senators in many local newspapers is about equal to that of Representatives, but Senators have an advantage in national media as well as in newspapers that cover four or more congressional districts.

42. James Campbell, "When Have Presidential Campaigns Decided Election Outcomes?" paper presented at the 1999 Annual Meeting of the American Political Science Association, Sept. 2–5, Atlanta.

43. See Thomas Holbrook, *Do Campaigns Matter?* (Thousand Oaks, CA: Sage, 1996).

44. For a discussion, see Marjorie Hershey, "The Campaign and the Media," in Gerald Pomper et al., *The Election of 1988* (Chatham, NJ: Chatham House, 1989), Ch. 3.

45. To qualify, a candidate must raise $5,000 in each of 20 states, in donations not exceeding $250 each. A candidate loses eligibility if he or she receives less than 10 percent of the vote in two successive primaries.

46. Thomas B. Edsall and Juliet Eilperin, "PAC Attack II," *Washington Post* (August 18, 2002): p. B02.

47. George F. Will, "Checkout for an Undemocratic Checkoff," *Washington Post*, September 28, 2006, p. A23.

48. During the last two months of the presidential campaigns of 1976 to 1988, about 40 percent of the lead stories on the CBS evening news were about the election, as were 20 percent of all the stories reported. See Steven J. Rosenstone and John Mark Hansen, *Mobilization, Participation, and Democracy in America* (New York: Macmillan, 1993), p. 178, n. 26.

49. www.politicalmoneyline.com, accessed February 26, 2005.

50. Thomas Patterson and Robert McClure, *The Unseeing Eye: The Myth of Television Power in National Elections* (New York: Putnam, 1976); and Darrel West, Air Wars: Television Advertising in Election Campaigns, 1952–1992 (Washington, DC: Congressional Quarterly, 1993).

51. Edwin Diamond and Stephen Bates, *The Spot,* 3rd ed. (Cambridge, MA: MIT Press, 1992); and Craig Brians and Martin Wattenberg, "Campaign Issue Knowledge and Salience: Comparing Reception from TV Commercials, TV News, and Newspapers," *American Journal of Political Science* 40 (1996): 172–193.

52. Ken Goldstein and Joel Rivlin, Political Advertising in the 2002 Elections, (Madison, WI: Wisconsin Advertising Project, 2003), Chapter 4, available at www.polisci.wisc.edu/tvadvertising/Political%20Advertising%20in%20the%202002%20Elections.htm, accessed February 27, 2005.

53. Federal Election Commission (www.fec.gov) and www.opensecrets.org.

54. Gary Jacobson, "Practical Consequences of Campaign Finance Reform: An Incumbent Protection Act?" *Public Policy* 42 (1976): 1–32.

55. Gary Jacobson, *Money in Congressional Elections* (New Haven, CT: Yale University Press, 1980).

56. Jacobson, *Politics of Congressional Elections,* p. 40; Kenneth Bickers and Robert Stein, "The Electoral Dynamics of the Federal Pork Barrel," *American Journal of Political Science* 40 (1996): 1300–1326.

57. Dave Barry, "Direct Deposit," *Boston Globe Magazine* (November 30, 1997): 12–13.

58. Charles Lane, "Kohl Train," *The New Republic* (February 14, 2000): 17.

59. Richard Katz, "Party Organizations and Finance," in Lawrence LeDuc, Richard Niemi, and Pippa Norris, eds., *Comparing Democracies* (Thousand Oaks, CA: Sage, 1996), pp. 129–132.

60. Howard Margolis, "The Banzhaf Fallacy," *American Journal of Political Science* 27 (1983): 321–326; George Rabinowitz and Stuart Elaine MacDonald, "The Power of the States in U.S.

Presidential Elections," *American Political Science Review* 80 (1986): 65–87; and James C. Garand and T. Wayne Parent, "Representation, Swing, and Bias in U.S. Presidential Elections, 1872–1988," *American Journal of Political Science* 35 (1991): 1011–1031.

61. For a discussion, see Nelson Polsby and Aaron Wildavsky, *Presidential Elections*, 10th ed. (Chatham, NJ: Chatham House, 2000), pp. 245–253.

62. Frederick D. Weil, "The Sources and Structure of Legitimation in Western Democracies," *American Sociological Review* 54 (1989): 682–706; and Frederick D. Weil, "Political Culture, Political Structure and Democracy: The Case of Legitimation and Opposition Structure," in Frederick D. Weil, ed., *Research on Democracy and Society, Vol. 2, Political Culture and Political Structure: Theoretical and Empirical Studies* (Greenwich, CT: JAI Press, 1994).

63. "Fresh Light on Primary Colors," *The Economist* 338, Issue 7954 (February 24, 1996): 23.

64. A good current description of the caucus system can be found in William Mayer, "Caucuses: How They Work, What Difference They Make," in William Mayer, ed., *In Pursuit of the White House* (Chatham, NJ: Chatham House, 1996).

65. On the history of the presidential primary, see James Davis, *Springboard to the White House* (New York: Crowell, 1967).

66. John Kessel, *The Goldwater Coalition* (Indianapolis, IN: Bobbs-Merrill, 1968), Ch. 3.

67. Nelson Polsby, *Consequences of Party Reform* (New York: Oxford University Press, 1983), Ch. 1.

68. For a participant observer's account of the post-1968 reforms, see Austin Ranney, *Curing the Mischiefs of Faction* (Berkeley, CA: University of California Press, 1975).

69. On primary dynamics, see John Aldrich, *Before the Convention* (Chicago: University of Chicago Press, 1980); and Larry Bartels, *Presidential Primaries and the Dynamics of Public Choice* (Princeton, NJ: Princeton University Press, 1988).

70. John Haskell, *Fundamentally Flawed* (Lanham, MD: Rowman and Littlefield, 1996).

71. Pew Research Center for the People and the Press, "It's Still Too Early for the Voters," www.people-press.org/june99rpt.htm.

72. Pew Research Center Poll, June 3–13, 2004.

73. Susan Page, "Debate's Flaw: No One's Watching," *USA Today*, October 24, 2003, p. 5A.

74. Larry Sabato, "Presidential Nominations: The Front-Loaded Frenzy of '96," in Larry Sabato, ed., *Toward the Millennium: The Elections of 1996* (Boston: Allyn & Bacon, 1997), pp. 37–91.

75. "A Good Fight Draws a Crowd," *New York Times* (March 12, 2000): Section 4, p. 5.

76. See John G. Geer, *Nominating Presidents* (New York: Greenwood Press, 1989), Ch. 2; and Barbara Norander, "Nomination Choices: Caucus and Primary Outcomes, 1976–1988," *American Journal of Political Science* 37 (1993): 343–364.

77. See, for example, the ABC News/*Washington Post* poll of August 30–September 2, 1999.

78. Thomas Patterson, *Out of Order* (New York: Vintage, 1994), p. 74.

79. "Once Again, 2 Small States Warp Political Process, *USA Today* (January 24, 2000): p. 18A.

80. Adam Nagourney, "Democrats Set Primary Calendar and Penalties," *New York Times*, August 20, 2006, p. 18.

81. Patterson, *Out of Order*, p. 82.

82. Most research finds only small electoral impacts for the vice-presidential nominees. See Steven Rosenstone, *Forecasting Presidential Elections* (New Haven, CT: Yale University Press, 1983), pp. 64–66, 87–88.

83. "Congressional Primary Schedule," *Congressional Quarterly Weekly Report* (January 1, 2000): 16–17.

84. William G. Mayer and Andrew E. Busch, *The Front-Loading Problem in Presidential Nominations* (Washington, DC: Brookings Institution Press, 2003), 85.

85. See Stephen G. Wright, "Voter Turnout in Runoff Elections," *Journal of Politics* 51 (May 1989): 385–96; and Charles S. Bullock III and Loch K. Johnson, *Runoff Elections in the United States* (Chapel Hill: University of North Carolina Press, 1992), Ch. 6.

86. On this last point, see James W. Davis, *U.S. Presidential Primaries and the Caucus-Convention System: A Sourcebook* (Westport, CN: Greenwood, 1977), pp. 202–203.

Chapter 8

1. Derek Bok, *The State of the Nation* (Cambridge, MA: Harvard University Press), pp. 235–255.

2. "OECD Health Care Data 2006: How Does the U.S. Compare?" Organisation for Economic Cooperation and Development, www.oecd.org/dataoecd/29/52/36960035.pdf, accessed October 28, 2006.

3. "Income Climbs, Poverty Stabilizes, Uninsured Rate Increases," United States Bureau of the Census, press release, August 29, 2006, www.census.gov/Press-Release/www/releases/archives/income_wealth/007419. html, accessed October 28, 2006.

4. *Ibid.*

5. *Ibid.*

6. Gallup Poll, September 7–10, 2006 (health care costs); Associated Press/Ipsos poll, September 11–13, 2006 (important issue).

7. Haynes Johnson and David Broder, *The System* (Boston: Little, Brown, 1996), p. 81.

8. *Ibid.*, p. 205.

9. Helen Dewar and Amy Goldstein, "Partisan Bickering Is a Side Effect," *Washington Post Weekly Edition* (July 22–28, 2002): p. 14.

10. Details come from Terence Samuel, "Taking Care of, Ahem, Business," *U.S. News & World Report* (December 1, 2003), 24; Ron Hutcheson, "'Explosion of Spending' Rattles Bush's Image," Knight Ridder, December 4, 2003; George Will, "Conservatism, Um, *Evolving*," *Newsweek* (December 8, 2003), 110.

11. Steven Rosenstone, Roy Behr, and Edward Lazarus, *Third Parties in America* (Princeton, NJ: Princeton University Press, 1981).

12. V. O. Key Jr., "A Theory of Critical Elections," *Journal of Politics* 17 (1955): 3–18; Walter Dean Burnham, *Critical Elections and the Mainsprings of American Politics* (New York: Norton, 1970); James Sundquist, *Dynamics of the Party System*, rev. ed. (Washington, DC: Brookings, 1983).

13. David R. Mayhew, *Electoral Realignments* (New Haven, CT: Yale, 2002).

14. George Johnson, *Architects of Fear* (Los Angeles: Tarcher/Houghton Mifflin, 1983), p. 59.

15. Paul Kleppner, *The Third Electoral System, 1853–1892* (Chapel Hill: University of North Carolina Press, 1979).

16. Charles Stewart and Barry Weingast, "Stacking the Senate, Changing the Nation," *Studies in American Political Development* 6 (1992): 223–271.

17. Michael McGerr, *The Decline of Popular Politics* (New York: Oxford University Press, 1986).

18. George Brown Tindall, *America* (New York: Norton, 1984), p. 1025.

19. Stanley Lebergott, *The Americans* (New York: Norton, 1984), Ch. 34.

20. Joel Silbey, "Beyond Realignment and Realignment Theory," in *The End of Realignment?*, ed. Byron Shafer (Madison: University of Wisconsin Press, 1991), pp. 3–23.

21. "In Quotes," *U.S. News & World Report* (November 17, 2003), 10.

22. Martin Wattenberg, *The Decline of American Political Parties, 1952–1992* (Cambridge, MA: Harvard University Press, 1994).

23. E. E. Schattschneider, *Party Government* (New York: Farrar and Rinehart, 1942), p. 1.

24. American Political Science Association, "Toward a More Responsible Two-Party System," *Supplement to the American Political Science Review* 44 (1950).

25. See, for example, James Campbell, *The Presidential Pulse of Congressional Elections* (Lexington: University Press of Kentucky, 1993).

26. Juliet Eilperin, "GOP, Trying to Expand, Aids Black Candidates," *Washington Post*, July 16, 2000, p. A6.

27. White House Web site section on Social Security, www.whitehouse.gov/infocus/social-security/, accessed April 24, 2004.

28. Morris Fiorina, *Divided Government*, 2nd ed. (Boston: Allyn & Bacon, 1996), pp. 107–110.

29. Julius Turner, *Party and Constituency* (Baltimore, MD: Johns Hopkins University Press, 1951).

30. James MacGregor Burns, *The Deadlock of Democracy* (Englewood Cliffs, NJ: Prentice Hall, 1964).

31. Thomas Weko, *The Politicizing Presidency* (Lawrence: University of Kansas Press, 1995), p. 161.

32. Stephen Skowronek, *Building a New American State* (New York: Cambridge University Press, 1992), p. 69.

33. Tom Baxter, "Grass-Roots Politics Flourishes on Internet," *Atlanta Journal-Constitution*, October 2, 2006, p. 1A.

34. Cornelius Cotter, James Gibson, John Bibby, and Robert Huckshorn, *Party Organizations in American Politics* (New York: Praeger, 1984).

35. Robert Dahl, *Dilemmas of Pluralist Democracy* (New Haven, CT: Yale University Press, 1982).

36. There is some controversy about how to measure group membership. See Frank Baumgartner and Jack Walker, "Survey Research and Membership in Voluntary Associations," *American Journal of Political Science* 32 (1988): 908–928; Tom Smith, "Trends in Voluntary Group Membership: Comments on Baumgartner and Walker," *American Journal of Political Science* 34 (1990): 646–661; and Baumgartner and Walker, "Response to Smith's 'Trends in Voluntary Group Membership,'" *American Journal of Political Science* 34 (1990): 662–670.

37. Alexis de Tocqueville, *Democracy in America*, ed. J. P. Mayer (New York: HarperPerennial, 1969), p. 513.

38. Robert Wiebe, *The Search for Order, 1877–1920* (New York: Hill and Wang, 1967).

39. Kay Schlozman and John Tierney, *Organized Interests and American Democracy* (New York: Harper & Row, 1981), p. 75.

40. James Q. Wilson, *Political Organizations* (New York: Basic Books, 1973), Ch. 3.

41. Mancur Olson, *The Logic of Collective Action* (Cambridge, MA: Harvard University Press, 1965).

42. See www.unicefusa.org (viewed May 19, 2006).

43. Richard Wagner, "Pressure Groups and Political Entrepreneurs," *Papers in Nonmarket Decision Making* 1 (1966): 161–170; Terry Moe, *The Organization of Interests* (Chicago: University of Chicago Press, 1980), Chs. 3–4.

44. Walker, Mobilizing Interest Groups, pp. 98–99.

45. Lobbying expenditures data from www.politicalmoneyline.com, accessed October 28, 2006.

46. Carl Weiser, "Enforcement of Law Almost Non-existent," *USA Today* (November 16, 1999): p. 11A.

47. Jeffrey H. Birnbaum, "The Road to Riches is Called K Street," *Washington Post*, June 22, 2005, p. A1.

48. Lobbyist Michael Bromberg, quoted in Eleanor Clift and Tom Brazaitis, *War Without Bloodshed* (New York: Scribner, 1996), p. 100.

49. The Christian Coalition claims 2 million members, and MoveOn.org claims 3 million, although these figures may be overestimates. See www.cc.org, www.moveon.org.

50. Peter Odegard, *Pressure Politics* (New York: Columbia University Press, 1928), p. 76.

51. Ross Baker, *The New Fat Cats* (New York: Priority Press, 1989); and Eliza Carney, "PAC Men," *National Journal* Vol. 26, Issue 40 (October 1, 1994): 2268–2273.

52. See Edward Epstein, "Business and Labor Under the Federal Election Campaign Act of 1971," in Michael Malbin, ed., *Parties, Interest Groups, and Campaign Finance Laws* (Washington, DC: American Enterprise Institute, 1980), pp. 107–151.

53. Jeff Zeleny and Aron Pilhofer, "Democrats Get Late Donations from Business," *New York Times*, October 28, 2006, p. 1.

54. Richard Hall and Frank Wayman, "Buying Time," *American Political Science Review* 84 (1990): 797–820.

55. www.opensecrets.org, 527 data available at http://opensecrets.org/527s/ 527new.asp?cycle=2004, accessed April 24, 2005.

56. Andrew McFarland, *Common Cause* (Chatham, NJ: Chatham House, 1984), pp. 74–81.

57. R. Shep Melnick, *Between the Lines* (Washington, DC: Brookings Institution, 1994).

58. Hugh Graham and Ted Gurr, *The History of Violence in America* (New York: Bantam, 1969).

59. Jonathan Rauch, *Demosclerosis* (New York: Random House, 1994).

60. Philip Stern, *The Best Congress Money Can Buy* (New York: Pantheon, 1988).

61. J. Leiper Freeman, *The Political Process*, rev. ed. (New York: Random House, 1965); Grant McConnell, *Private Power and American Democracy* (New York: Knopf, 1966); and Theodore Lowi, *The End of Liberalism* (New York: Norton, 1969).

62. Richard A. Oppel, Jr. "A point man on corporate change," *New York Times*, July 14, 2002, Section 3, p. 2.

63. Hugh Heclo, "Issue Networks and the Executive Establishment," in Anthony King, ed., *The New American Political System* (Washington, DC: Brookings, 1978), pp. 87–124.

64. Robert Salisbury, John Heinz, Robert Nelson, and Edward Laumann, "Triangles, Networks, and Hollow Cores," in Mark Petracca, ed., *The Politics of Interests* (Boulder, CO: Westview Press, 1992), pp. 130–149.

65. Schlozman and Tierney, *Organized Interests and American Democracy*, pp. 314–317.

66. Henry Brady, Sidney Verba, and Kay Schlozman, "Beyond SES," *American Political Science Review* 89 (1995): 271–294.

67. John Hibbing and Elizabeth Theiss-Morse, *Congress as Public Enemy* (New York: Cambridge University Press, 1995), pp. 63–65, 147.

68. Peter Aranson and Peter Ordeshook, "A Prolegomenon to a Theory of the Failure of Representative Democracy," in Peter Aranson and Peter Ordeshook, eds., *American Re-evolution* (Tucson, AR: University of Arizona, 1977), pp. 23–46.

69. Jane Mansbridge, *Why We Lost the ERA* (Chicago: University of Chicago Press, 1986), p. 73.

70. Shailagh Murray and Allan Lengel, "The Legal Woes of Rep. Jefferson," *Washington Post*, February 16, 2006, p. A1.

71. "Lobbying FAQ: What is Permissible? Out of Bounds? Punishable?" Center for Public Integrity, www.publicintegrity.org/lobby/report.aspx?aid=775, accessed October 28, 2006.

72. Jonathan E. Kaplan, "Lobbying Reform Targeted at DeLay, Abramoff Issues," *The Hill*, April 21, 2005, www.hillnews.com/thehill/export/TheHill/News/Frontpage/042105/delay.html; Public Citizen —— Clean Up Washington, "Summary Comparison of Lobby Reform Proposals," www.cleanupwashington.org/lobbying/page.cfm?pageid=55, accessed October 28, 2006.

73. Chuck Henning, *The Wit and Wisdom of Politics* (Golden, CO: Fulcrum Publishing, 1992), p. 137.

Chapter 9

1. Martin O'Malley, Mayor of Baltimore, Maryland, "Testimony on Behalf of the U.S. Conference of Mayors before the Committee on Appropriations, United States Senate, on 'Homeland Security,'" April 10, 2002, p. 1.

2. Kate O'Beirne, "Introducing Pork-Barrel Homeland Security: A Little Here, a Lot There," *National Review*, August 11, 2003.

3. Veronique de Rugy, "Homeland Security Pork," *Washington Times*, August 1, 2005.

4. These and other examples appear in Rich Lowry, "Homeland Pork," *National Review Online*, July 19, 2005. JoAnn Wypijewski, "Homeland Security on the Range," *MotherJones.com*, March/April, 2006. Veronique de Rugy and Nick Gillespie, "America's Fleecing in the Name of Security," *SFGate.com*, February 19, 2006.

5. O'Beirne, "Introducing Pork-Barrel Homeland Security."

6. George H. Mayer, *The Republican Party, 1854–1966*, 2nd ed. (New York: Oxford University Press, 1967).

7. Charles Jones, "Joseph G. Cannon and Howard W. Smith," *Journal of Politics* 30 (1968): 617–646.

8. Barbara Sinclair, *Majority Leadership in the U.S. House* (Baltimore, MD: Johns Hopkins University Press, 1983).

9. Juliet Eilperin, "The Making of 'Madam Whip,'" *Washington Post Weekly Edition* (January 14–20, 2002): pp. 6–8.

10. For a full discussion, see Steven S. Smith and Marcus Flathman, "Managing the Senate Floor," *Legislative Studies Quarterly* 14 (1989): 349–374.

11. Gerald Gamm and Kenneth Shepsle, "Emergence of Legislative Institutions," *Legislative Studies Quarterly* 14 (1989): 39–66; and Joseph Cooper, *The Origins of the Standing Committees and the Development of the Modern House* (Houston: Rice University Studies, 1970).

12. Mark Ferber, "The Formation of the Democratic Study Group," in Nelson Polsby, ed., *Congressional Behavior* (New York: Random House, 1971), pp. 249–267.

13. "Democrats Oust Hebert, Poage; Adopt Reforms," *Congressional Quarterly Weekly Report* (January 18, 1975): 114.

14. Norman Ornstein, "Causes and Consequences of Congressional Change," in Norman Ornstein, ed., *Congress in Change* (New York: Praeger, 1975), pp. 88–114; and Roger Davidson and Walter Oleszek, *Congress Against Itself* (Bloomington: Indiana University Press, 1977).

15. Gary Cox and Matthew McCubbins, *Legislative Leviathan* (Berkeley: University of California Press, 1993).

16. David King, *Turf Wars* (Chicago: University of Chicago Press, 1997).

17. John Ferejohn, *Pork Barrel Politics* (Stanford, CA: Stanford University Press, 1974); and R. Douglas Arnold, *Congress and the Bureaucracy* (New Haven, CT: Yale University Press, 1979).

18. Keith Krehbiel, *Information and Legislative Organization* (Ann Arbor: University of Michigan Press, 1991).

19. Committee on House Administration, "109th Congress Congressional Member Organizations (CMOs)," http://cha.house.gov/oversight/109cmo.htm, accessed December 23, 2006.

20. Susan Webb Hammond, *Congressional Caucuses in National Policy Making* (Baltimore, MD: Johns Hopkins University Press, 2001).

21. United States Department of Commerce, Bureau of the Census, *Statistical Abstract of the United States*, 2007, Table 483.

22. Jeffrey Talbert, Bryan Jones, and Frank Baumgartner, "Nonlegislative Hearings and Policy Change in Congress," *American Journal of Political Science* 39 (1995): 391–392.

23. For a treatment of conference committees, see Stephen Van Beek, *Post-Passage Politics* (Pittsburgh, PA: University of Pittsburgh Press, 1995).

24. Richard Munson, *The Cardinals of Capitol Hill* (New York: Grove Press, 1993).

25. Dan Morgan, "Along for the Rider," *Washington Post Weekly Edition* (August 19–25, 2002), p. 15.

26. James Young, *The Washington Community, 1800–1828* (New York: Harcourt, 1966), Ch. 2.

27. From the very beginning, southern members of Congress stayed longer than northerners. Morris Fiorina, David Rohde, and Peter Wissel, "Historical Change in House Turnover," in Norman Ornstein, ed., *Congress in Change* (New York: Praeger, 1975), pp. 34–38.

28. Robert Struble, Jr., "House Turnover and the Principle of Rotation," *Political Science Quarterly* 94 (1979–1980): 660.

29. Douglas Price, "The Congressional Career—Then and Now," in Nelson Polsby, ed., *Congressional Behavior* (New York: Random House, 1971), pp. 14–27.

30. Glenn Parker, *Homeward Bound* (Pittsburgh, PA: University of Pittsburgh Press, 1986); Juliet Eilperin, "The House Member as Perpetual Commuter," *Washington Post Weekly Edition* (September 10–16, 2001): 29.

31. John G. Geer, *From Tea Leaves to Opinion Polls* (New York: Columbia University Press, 1996).

32. Heinz Eulau, "Changing Views of Representation," in Heinz Eulau and John Wahlke, eds., *The Politics of Representation* (Beverly Hills, CA: Sage, 1978), pp. 31–53.

33. Morris Fiorina, *Congress—Keystone of the Washington Establishment*, 2nd ed. (New Haven, CT: Yale University Press, 1989).

34. "Budget Stuffers," *U.S. News & World Report* (December 6, 2004), 16.

35. Fiorina, *Congress*, Ch. 10. See also Bruce Cain, John Ferejohn, and Morris Fiorina, *The Personal Vote* (Cambridge, MA: Harvard University Press, 1987), Ch. 2.

36. Ornstein, Mann, and Malbin, *Vital Statistics*, pp. 126, 130.

37. Morris Fiorina, "Congressmen and Their Constituents: 1958 and 1978," in Dennis Hale, ed., *The United States Congress* (Leominster, MA: Eusey Press, 1982), pp. 33–64.

38. Maureen Fan, "Finding a Congressional Job is Tougher Than Ever," *Washington Post Weekly Edition* (September 20–26, 2004): p. 15.

39. Richard H. Shapiro, *Frontline Management* (Washington, DC: Congressional Management Foundation, 1989), p. 94.

40. Ornstein, Mann, and Malbin, *Vital Statistics*, pp. 67–68.

41. Gary Jacobson, *The Politics of Congressional Elections*, 4th ed. (New York: Longman, 1997).

42. Barbara Sinclair, *Legislators, Leaders, and Lawmaking* (Baltimore, MD: Johns Hopkins University Press, 1995); David Rohde, *Parties and Leaders in the Postreform House* (Chicago: University of Chicago Press, 1991).

43. Jim Drinkard, "Confident Candidates Share Campaign Wealth," *USA Today* (April 19, 2000): p. 10A.

44. George F. Will, "Devil's Island! Guillotines!" *Newsweek* (December 10, 2001), 84.

45. Harrison Donnelly, "Reagan Opposition Threatens EDA Development Program," *CQ Weekly* 40 (1982): 2295–2296.

46. Chuck Henning, *The Wit and Wisdom of Politics* (Golden, CO: Fulcrum, 1992), p. 39; "Perspectives," *Newsweek* (November 17, 2003): 21.

47. John Hibbing and Elizabeth Theiss-Morse, *Congress as Public Enemy* (New York: Cambridge University Press, 1995), Ch. 2.

48. Richard Fenno, "If, As Ralph Nader Says, Congress Is the 'Broken Branch,' How Come We Love Our Congressmen So Much?" in Norman Ornstein, ed., *Congress in Change* (New York: Praeger, 1975), pp. 277–287.

49. Richard Fenno, *Home Style* (Boston: Little, Brown, 1978), p. 168.

50. Glenn Parker and Roger Davidson, "Why Do Americans Love Their Congressman So Much More Than Their Congress? *Legislative Studies Quarterly* 4 (1979): 52–61.

51. Richard Hall and Frank Wayman, "Buying Time," *American Political Science Review* 84 (1990): 797–820.

52. Sandy Streeter, "Earmarks and Limitations in Appropriations Bills," *CRS Report for Congress, 98-518,* December 7, 2004.

53. Ronald Utt, "A Primer on Lobbyists, Earmarks, and Congressional Reform," *The Heritage Foundation, Backgrounder #1924.* April 27, 2006, p. 3.

54. Rebecca Clarren, "A Bridge to Nowhere," http://dir.salon.com/story/news/feature/200-5/08/09/bridges/index.html.

55. "Up to their Earmarks," www.washingtonpost.com/wp-dyn/content/graphic/2006/01/27/GR2006012700168.html.

56. Diana Evans, *Greasing the Wheels* (New York: Cambridge University Press, 2004).

Chapter 10

1. "President Bush Delivers State of the Union Address," www.whitehouse.gov/news/releases/2006/01/20060131-10. html, accessed March 15, 2006.

2. President George W. Bush, "Remarks Following a Tour of United Solar Ovonic in Auburn Hills, Michigan," February 20, 2006, *Weekly Compilation of Presidential Documents*, week ending Friday, February 24, 2006, pp. 296–297.

3. Paul Blustein, "Some in Congress Object to Arab Port Operator," *Washington Post*, February 17, 2006, p. A11.

4. *CQ Weekly*, Vote Studies, various years.

5. Dan Froomkin, "When the Trust is Gone," WashingtonPost.com, February 22, 2006, www.washingtonpost.com/wp-dyn/content/blog/2006/02/22/BL2006022201449.html, accessed March 15, 2006.

6. "President Addresses National Newspaper Conference," www.whitehouse.gov/news/releases/2006/03/20060310-2.html, accessed March 15, 2006.

7. Elisabeth Bumiller and David E. Sanger, "Bush is Business as Usual Despite Party Blunders," *New York Times*, March 12, 2006, p. 20.

8. Richard Neustadt, *Presidential Power and the Modern Presidents* (New York: Free Press, 1990).

9. Paul C. Light, *The True Size of Government* (Washington, DC: Brookings Institution Press, 1999), p. 1.

10. Tome Brune and William Douglas, "Reinvention Reality: Gore Boasts REGO Success, But Critics See New Problems," *Newsday* (July 17, 2000): p. A5.

11. Terry Moe, "The Politicized Presidency," in John Chubb and Paul E. Peterson, eds., *The New Direction in American Politics* (Washington, DC: Brookings, 1985).

12. Mark Peterson, *Legislating Together: The White House and Capitol Hill from Eisenhower to Reagan* (Cambridge, MA: Harvard), p. 157.

13. Richard E. Neustadt, *Presidential Power and the Modern Presidents* (New York: Free Press, 1990), p. 29.

14. James S. Young, *The Washington Community 1800–1828* (New York: Columbia University Press, 1966).

15. Benjamin Ginsberg and Martin Shefter, *Politics by Other Means: The Declining Importance of Elections in America* (New York: Basic Books, 1990).

16. Thomas Bailey, *The American Pageant* (Boston: D. C. Heath, 1956), p. 669.

17. Samuel Kernell, *Going Public* (Washington, DC: CQ Press, 1986).

18. Daniel Stid, *The Statesmanship of Woodrow Wilson: Responsible Government Under the Constitution* (Lawrence: University Press of Kansas, 1998), Ch. 6.

19. Neustadt, *Presidential Power*, p. 274.

20. George W. Bush, State of the Union Address, January 28, 2003, Washington, DC: White House Office of the Press Secretary, www.whitehouse.gov/news/releases/2003/01/20030128-19. html, accessed January 8, 2004.

21. Jonathan Weisman, "Thomas Questions Dividend Tax Cuts," *Washington Post*, January 28, 2003, p. A4.

22. Jeffrey Tulis, *The Rhetorical Presidency* (Princeton, NJ: Princeton University Press, 1987), Ch. 3.

23. *Ibid.*

24. John W. Kingdon, *Agendas, Alternatives and Public Policies* (Boston: Little, Brown, 1981).

25. Harry McPherson, *A Political Education* (Boston: Little, Brown, 1972), p. 268, as quoted in Paul C. Light, *The President's Agenda: Domestic Policy Choice from Kennedy to Reagan* (Baltimore, MD: Johns Hopkins University Press, 1991), p. 13.

26. Stephen Hess, *Organizing the Presidency* (Washington, DC: Brookings, 1988), pp. 11–18.

27. Herbert Kaufman, *The Administrative Behavior of Federal Bureau Chiefs* (Washington, DC: Brookings, 1981), p. 183, n. 8.

28. Hugh Heclo, "OMB and the Presidency—the Problem of 'Neutral Competence,'" *Public Interest* 38 (Winter 1975): 80–98; and Karen Hult, "Advising the President," in George C. Edwards, John H. Kessel, and Bert A. Rockman, *Researching the Presidency: Vital Questions, New Approaches* (Pittsburgh, PA: University of Pittsburgh Press, 1992), p. 126.

29. David Stockman, *The Triumph of Politics* (New York: Harper & Row, 1986).

30. Haynes Johnson and David Broder, *The System: The American Way of Politics at the Breaking Point* (Boston: Little, Brown, 1996), p. 116.

31. Norman C. Thomas, Joseph A. Pika, and Richard A. Watson, *The Politics of the Presidency*, 3rd ed. (Washington, DC: CQ Press, 1993), p. 204.

32. Nick Anderson "Deal on Media Could Bring Passage of Spending Bill," *Los Angeles Times*, November 25, 2003, p. 23; Bill Miller, "Senators Take Up Homeland Security; Bush Strengthens Veto Threat," *Washington Post*, September 5, 2002, p. A29.

33. As quoted in James P. Pfiffner, *The Modern Presidency* (New York: St. Martin's, 1994), p. 114.

34. James L. Sundquist, *The Decline and Resurgence of Congress* (Washington, DC: Brookings, 1981), p. 93.

35. *United States v. Belmont*, 301 U.S. 324 (1937).

36. U.S. Department of State, *Treaties in Force*, 2004 (Washington, DC: U.S. Department of State, 2004), available at www.state.gov/documents/organization/38542. pdf, p. 1.

37. *United States v. Curtiss-Wright Export Corporation*, 299 U.S. 304 (1936).

38. *Youngstown Sheet & Tube Co. v. Sawyer*, 343 U.S. 579 (1952).

39. Joint Resolution of Congress, H.J. RES 1145 August 7, 1964.

40. *United States v. Belmont*, 301 U.S. 324 (1936); Harold Bruff and Peter Shane, *The Law of Presidential Powers: Cases and Materials* (Durham, NC: Carolina Academic Press, 1988), p. 88; and Joseph Paige, *The Law Nobody Knows: Enlargement of the Constitution—Treaties and Executive Orders* (New York: Vantage Press, 1977), p. 63.

41. William Howell, "The President's Powers of Unilateral Action: The Strategic Advantages of Acting Alone," Stanford University Dissertation, 1999.

42. Louis Fisher, *Constitutional Conflicts Between Congress and the President,* 3rd ed. rev. (Lawrence: University of Kansas, 1991), p. 154.

43. *United States v. Nixon*, 418 U.S. 683 (1974).

44. Michael Doyle, "U.S. Sues U.S. Over Cheney Files," *Chicago Sun-Times*, February 24, 2001, p. 21.

45. Walter Bagehot, *The English Constitution* (London: Fantana, 1993).

46. Stanley Elkins and Eric McKitrick, *Age of Federalism* (New York: Oxford University Press, 1993), p. 48.

47. Doris Kearns Goodwin, *No Ordinary Time: Franklin and Eleanor Roosevelt: The Home Front in World War II* (New York: Simon & Schuster, 1994).

48. Bert Rockman, "Leadership Style and the Clinton Presidency," in Colin Campbell and Bert Rockman, eds., *The Clinton Presidency: First Appraisals* (Chatham, NJ: Chatham House, 1996), pp. 334–336.

49. David Johnston, "With Counsel Law Expiring, Attorney General Takes Reins," *New York Times*, June 30, 1999, p. A1.

50. John Hart, *The Presidential Branch: From Washington to Clinton*, 2nd ed. (Chatham, NJ: Chatham House, 1995), pp. 26–30.

51. See Matthew Dickinson, *Bitter Harvest: FDR, Presidential Power, and the Growth of the Presidential Branch* (New York: Cambridge University Press, 1997).

52. Paul Quirk, "Presidential Competence," in Michael Nelson, ed., *The Presidency and the Political System*, 4th ed. (Washington, DC: CQ Press, 1994), pp. 171–221; and John P. Burke, *The Institutional Presidency* (Baltimore, MD: Johns Hopkins University Press, 1992), pp. 40–42.

53. Colin Campbell, "Management in a Sandbox," in Colin Campbell and Bert A. Rockman, Eds. *The Clinton Presidency: First Appraisals* (New York: Chatham House, 1995), p. 60.

54. Charles O. Jones, "Campaigning to Govern: The Clinton Style," in Campbell and Rockman, *The Clinton Presidency*, p. 16.

55. Terry Moe, "The Politicized Presidency," in Chubb and Peterson, *New Direction in American Politics*; and Andrew Rudalevige, "The President's Program and the Politicized Presidency," paper presented at the Annual Meeting of the American Political Science Association, Atlanta, GA, September 2–5, 1999.

56. "Ex-Aide Insists White House Put Politics above Policy," *New York Times*, December 2, 2002, p. A16.

57. Peter Baker, "Senior White House Staff May be Wearing Down," *Washington Post*, March 13, 2006, p. A4.

58. Jack Mitchell, *Executive Privilege: Two Centuries of White House Scandals* (New York: Hippocrene Books, 1992), pp. 89–90.

59. John Farrell, "Embattled Security Official Quits, Calls Getting FBI Files a 'Mistake,'" *Boston Globe*, June 27, 1996, p. A-12.

60. Niccolo Machiavelli, *The Prince*, Translated by Harvey C. Mansfield, Jr. (Chicago: University of Chicago Press, 1985), Ch. 14, pp. 58–60.

61. Aaron Wildavsky, "The Two Presidencies [1965]," in Steven A. Shull, *The Two Presidencies: A Quarter Century Assessment* (Chicago: Nelson Hall, 1991), pp. 11–25.

62. Wildavsky, "The Two Presidencies," p. 17.

63. Barry M. Blechman, *The Politics of National Security: Congress and U.S. Defense Policy* (New York: Oxford University Press, 1990); Duane M. Oldfield and Aaron Wildavsky, "Reconsidering the Two Presidencies," in Steve A. Shull, ed., *The Two Presidencies: A Quarter Century Assessment* (Chicago: Nelson Hall, 1991), pp. 181–90; Thomas Franck and Edward Weisband, *Foreign Policy by Congress* (New York: Oxford University Press, 1979); Thomas E. Mann, ed., *A Question of Balance: The President, the Congress and Foreign Policy* (Washington, DC: Brookings, 1990); and Stephen R. Weissman, *A Culture of Deference: Congress's Failure of Leadership in Foreign Policy* (New York: Basic Books, 1955).

64. James Baker, III, with Thomas M. DeFrank, *The Politics of Diplomacy: Revolution, War, and Peace, 1989–1992* (New York: Putnam, 1995), p. 116.

65. *Statistical Abstract of the United States, 2007* (Washington, DC: U.S. Government Printing Office, 2006), Table 1279.

66. Wildavsky, "The Two Presidencies," p. 16.

67. *Ibid.*, p. 15.

68. John E. Mueller, *War, Presidents and Public Opinion* (New York: Wiley, 1973); and Gary King and Lyn Ragsdale, *The Elusive Executive: Discovering Statistical Patterns in the Presidency* (Washington, DC: CQ Press, 1988).

69. Mueller, *War, Presidents and Public Opinion*.

70. Paul Brace and Barbara Hinckley, *Follow the Leader: Opinion Polls and the Modern Presidents* (New York: Basic Books, 1992), p. 33.

71. George F. Kennan, "Somalia, Through a Glass Darkly," *New York Times*, September 30, 1993, p. A25.

72. Laura King and Fayed abu Shammalah, "Israel Kills New Leader of Hamas," *Los Angeles Times*, April 18, 2004, p. A1; Patrick McMahon, "Terrorism Stirs Jews in USA to Activism," *USA Today*, June 25, 2002, p. 13A.

73. Council on Foreign Relations, "Backgrounder: Hamas," Updated June 14, 2006, www.cfr.org/publication/8968/, accessed June 15, 2006.

74. U. S. Bureau of the Census, *Statistical Abstract of the United States: 2006*, Table 71.

75. American Israel Public Affairs Committee, www.aipac.org, accessed June 14, 2006.

76. John J. Mearsheimer and Stephen M. Walt, "The Israel Lobby and U.S. Foreign Policy," Harvard University, John F. Kennedy School of Government, Faculty Working Paper RWP06-011, March 2006, p. 1.

77. Harvard University Law Professor Alan Dershowitz, quoted in Michael Powell, "Academic Paper Stirs Debate," *Washington Post*, April 3, 2006, p. A3.

78. This is especially true if the establishment of such a state would lead to an end to terrorism. Fully 74 percent say "favor" when asked the question "Do you favor or oppose the establishment of an independent Palestinian state on the West Bank if the Palestinian government demonstrates that it can end the suicide bombings in Israel?" Gallup poll, June 21–23, 2002.

Chapter 11

1. Dan Eggen and Cheryl W. Thompson, "The Tip of the INS Iceberg," *Washington Post Weekly Edition*, January 7–13, 2002, p. 6.

2. James Bamford, "Too Much, Not Enough; The Biggest Intelligence Agency Ought to Know Better," *Washington Post*, June 2, 2002, p. B1.

3. John Donnelly, "U.S. Security Aspects Familiar to Some," *Boston Globe*, September 12, 2001, p. A9.

4. United States Commission on National Security in the 21st Century, "Road Map for National Security: Imperative for Change," Final Draft Report, Washington, DC: January 31, 2001, p. x.

5. Richard Simon and Charles Piller, "Security Chief Must Battle Bureaucracy," *Los Angeles Times*, October 8, 2001, p. A9.

6. Alison Mitchell, "Dispute Erupts on Ridge's Needs for His Job," *New York Times*, November 4, 2001, p. B7.

7. James Gerstenzong, "Response to Terror: Bush Proposes a Cabinet-Level Homeland Security Department," *Los Angeles Times*, June 7, 2002, p. A1.

8. Harry Truman, *Memoirs, Vol. 2: Years of Trial and Hope* (Garden City, NY: Doubleday, 1956), p. 51.

9. David Von Drehle and Mike Allen, "Bush Plan's Underground Architects," *Washington Post*, June 9, 2002, p. A1.

10. Adriel Bettelheim, "Lawmakers with a List of Concerns Are Sure to Add Strings to Bush Proposal," *CQ Weekly* (June 15, 2002): 1577.

11. Nick Anderson and Richard Simon, "Democrats Attack Item in Bush's Security Plan," *Los Angeles Times*, June 21, 2002, p. A26.

12. "Daschle Says Bush Attack Politicizes Debate," *Seattle Post-Intelligencer*, September 26, 2002, p. A1; and Jim VandeHei, "Daschle Angered by Bush Statement," *Washington Post*, September 26, 2002, p. A1.

13. Tod Lindberg, "The Homeland Security Two-fer," *Weekly Standard*, June 24, 2002, p. I3.

14. See, for example, Theodore Lowi, *The End of Liberalism* (New York: Norton, 1969); and Jonathan Rauch, *Demosclerosis* (New York: Times Books, 1994).

15. CNN/*USA Today*, Gallup Poll, June 7–10, 2002.

16. Ann McFeatters, "Homeland Security Failing to Meet Challenge," *Pittsburgh Post-Gazette*, December 2, 2004, p. A11. See also John Mintz, "Infighting Cited at Homeland Security," *Washington Post*, February 2, 2005, p. A1.

17. David Lightman, "Homeland Security Choice Warned, Confirmed," *Hartford Courant*, February 16, 2005, p. A1.

18. Committee on Government Reform and Oversight, U.S. House of Representatives, *U.S. Government Policy and Supporting Positions ("Plum Book")* (Washington, DC: U.S. Government Printing Office, 1996).

19. General Accounting Office, *Government Corporations: Profiles of Existing Government Corporations* (GAO/GGD-96-14) (Washington, DC: General Accounting Office, 1995).

20. Lyn Ragsdale, "Studying the Presidency: Why Presidents Need Political Scientists," in Michael Nelson, ed., *The Presidency and the Political System*, 5th ed. (Washington, DC: CQ Press, 1998), p. 50.

21. Max Weber, *Essays in Sociology* (New York: Oxford University Press, 1958); and Max Weber, *Economy and Society* (Berkeley, CA: University of California Press, 1978).

22. Chuck Henning, *The Wit and Wisdom of Politics: Expanded Edition* (Golden, CO: Fulcrum Publishing, 1992), p. 92.

23. James Q. Wilson, "The Bureaucracy Problem," *The Public Interest* No. 6 (Winter 1967): 3–9.

24. Graham Allison, *Essence of Decision: Explaining the Cuban Missile Crisis* (Boston: Little, Brown, 1971), Ch. 3.

25. Tom McGinty and Dan Fagin, "One Tangled Web; Experts Agree: Nation's Electric System Aging, Byzantine," *Newsday*, November 17, 2003, p. A6.

26. Barton Gellman and Dana Milbank, "Blackout Causes Mass Disruption; Millions Struggle without Power from New York to Toronto to Detroit," *Washington Post*, August 15, 2003, p. A1.

27. Laurence J. Peter, as quoted in Chuck Henning, *The Wit and Wisdom of Politics: Expanded Edition* (Golden, CO: Fulcrum Publishing, 1992), p. 16.

28. William A. Niskanen, *Bureaucracy and Representative Government* (Chicago: Aldine-Atherton, 1971), Chs. 2–4.

29. Aaron Wildavsky, *The New Politics of the Budgetary Process* (Boston: Little, Brown, 1988), pp. 84–85.

30. Tony Perry, "Forest Service Official Defends Cedar Fire Response," *Los Angeles Times*, November 8, 2003, p. B14.

31. Michael Lipsky, Street Level Bureaucracy: Dilemmas of the Individual in Public Service (New York: Russell Sage, 1980).

32. Kaufman, *Red Tape*, p. 434.

33. James Young, *The Washington Community 1800–1828* (New York: Harcourt, 1966), p. 49. Ellipses deleted.

34. John Bartlett, *Familiar Quotations: Revised and Enlarged*, 15th ed. (Boston: Little, Brown, 1980), p. 455.

35. Seymour J. Mandelbaum, *Boss Tweed's New York* (New York: Wiley, 1965).

36. As quoted in Henning, *Wit and Wisdom*, p. 11.

37. A. James Reichley, *The Life of the Parties* (New York: Free Press, 1992), pp. 157–158.

38. Robert Dahl, *Who Governs?* (New Haven, CT: Yale University Press, 1961); Raymond E. Wolfinger, *The Politics of Progress* (Englewood Cliffs, NJ: Prentice-Hall, 1974), Ch. 4; Edward Banfield and James Q. Wilson, *City Politics* (New York: Random House, 1963); and Robert K. Merton, *Social Theory and Social Structure* (Glencoe, IL: Free Press, 1957), pp. 71–81.

39. Quoted in Reichley, *Life of the Parties*, p. 212.

40. Paul E. Peterson, *The Politics of School Reform, 1870–1940* (Chicago: University of Chicago Press, 1985), pp. 86–87.

41. Rufus P. Browning, Dale Rogers Marshall, and David H. Tabb, *Protest Is Not Enough: The Struggle of Blacks and Hispanics for Equality in Urban Politics* (Berkeley, CA: University of California Press, 1984), Ch. 5.

42. Alben W. Barkley, vice president of the United States, 1949–1953, as quoted in Henning, *Wit and Wisdom*, p. 17.

43. Paul Light, *Thickening Government* (Washington, DC: The Brookings Institution, 1995), p. 9, Table 1-2; Paul Light, "The Changing Shape of Government," Brookings Institution Policy Brief 45 (Washington, DC: The Brookings Institution, February 1999), p. 1; and "Urgent Business for America: Revitalizing the Federal Government for the 21st Century," Report of the National Commission on the Public Service (the "Volcker Commission"), January 2003, p. 18.

44. Paul Light, *Thickening Government: Federal Hierarchy and the Diffusion of Accountability* (Washington, DC: Brookings, 1995), Ch. 1.

45. G. Calvin MacKenzie, "The Presidential Appointment Process: Historical Development, Contemporary Operations, Current Issues," background paper for the Twentieth Century Fund Panel on Presidential Appointments, March 1, 1994, p. 1.

46. "Urgent Business for America: Revitalizing the Federal Government for the 21st Century," Report of the National Commission on the Public Service (the "Volcker Commission"), January 2003, p. 1.

47. *Wall Street Journal*, February 9, 1994, p. A1.

48. Council for Excellence in Government survey, March 2004, reprinted in Partnership for Public Service, "Poll Watch: Public Opinion on Public Service," PPS-05-03, May 2, 2005, www.ourpublicservice.org/usr_doc/PPS-05-03. pdf, accessed March 29, 2006.

49. See *New York Times*, September 5, 1993: Sec. I, p. 39.

50. Beryl A. Radin and Willis D. Hawley, *The Politics of Federal Reorganization: Creating the U.S. Department of Education* (New York: Pergamon Press, 1988).

51. Dick Kirschten, "Congress," GovExec.com, April 1, 1999 available at www.govexec.com/features/0499/0499congress.htm, accessed May 6, 2005.

52. Graeme Browning, "Fiscal Fission," *National Journal* 28, No. 23 (June 8, 1996): 1259; and Jeffrey Brainard and Marie Borrego, "Academic Pork Barrel Tops $2 billion for the First Time," *Chronicle of Higher Education* 50 (September 26, 2003): 18.

53. Bill McAllister, "Byrd's Big Prize: Bringing Home the FBI," *Washington Post*, March 13, 1991, p. A1.

54. Joel Aberbach, *Keeping a Watchful Eye* (Washington, DC: The Brookings Institution, 1990), p. 38; Policy Agendas Project, University of Washington, www.policyagendas.org, hearings-data.

55. Policy Agendas Project.

56. R. Shep Melnick, *Between the Lines* (Washington, DC: Brookings).

57. Judy Keen, "Bush, Lay Kept Emotional Distance," *USA Today*, February 26, 2002, p. 6A; Joseph Kahn, "Contract Offers Look at How Global Played Influence Game," *New York Times*, February 28, 2002, p. C1.

58. Michael E. Kanell, "Business Scandals: Bush Official Seeks 'Severe' Action," *Atlanta Journal Constitution*, July 12, 2002, p. 5D.

59. Patrick Wolf, "What History Advises About Reinventing Government," Ph.D. dissertation, Department of Government, Harvard University, 1996.

60. John DiIulio, *No Escape: The Future of American Corrections* (New York: Basic Books, 1991), pp. 19–26.

61. James A. Morone, *The Democratic Wish: Popular Participation and the Limits of American Government* (New York: Basic Books, 1990).

62. Francis Rourke, "Executive Secrecy: Change and Continuity," in Rourke, *Bureaucratic Power in National Policy Making*, pp. 536–537.

63. *Ibid.*

64. *Ibid.*

65. Albert B. Crenshaw, "IRS Overhaul Set for Passage; Measure Gives Taxpayers New Rights, Includes Capital Gains Break," *Washington Post*, June 25, 1998, p. A1.

66. Martha Derthick, *Agency Under Stress: The Social Security Administration in American Government* (Washington, DC: Brookings Institution, 1990) p. 87.

67. Former Bureau of the Budget Director Kermit Gordon, as quoted in Kaufman, *Administrative Behavior*, p. 443.

68. Paul J. Quirk, "Food and Drug Administration," in James Q. Wilson, *The Politics of Regulation* (New York: Basic Books, 1980), p. 199.

69. Terry Moe, "The Politics of Bureaucratic Structure," in John E. Chubb and Paul E. Peterson, *Can the Government Govern?* (Washington, DC: Brookings, 1988).

70. Sandra Blakeslee, "Expert Warned that Mad Cow Was Imminent," *New York Times*, December 25, 2003, p. A1; and Denise Grady, "U.S. Issues Safety Rules to Protect Food From Mad Cow Disease," *New York Times*, December 31, 2003, p. A1.

71. *Heart of Atlanta Motel v. United States*, 379 U.S. 241 (1964); and *United States v. South-Eastern Underwriters Association*, 322 U.S. 533 (1944).

72. Paul Attewell and Dean R. Gerstein, "Government Policy and Local Practice," *American Sociological Review* 44 (1979): 311–327. For a banking example, see John T. Woolley, "Conflict Among Regulators and the Hypothesis of Congressional Dominance," *Journal of Politics* 55 (1993): 102–103.

73. Marc K. Landy, Marc J. Roberts, and Stephen R. Thomas, *The Environmental Protection Agency: Asking the Wrong Questions from Nixon to Clinton*, expanded ed. (New York: Oxford University Press, 1994).

74. Kenneth Meier, *Regulation: Politics, Bureaucracy, and Economics* (New York: St. Martin's Press, 1985).

75. Martha Derthick and Paul Quirk, *The Politics of Deregulation* (Washington, DC: Brookings, 1985); and Mark C. Rom, *Public Spirit in the Thrift Tragedy* (Pittsburgh, PA: University of Pittsburgh Press, 1996).

76. H. Craig Petersen, *Business and Government*, 2nd ed. (New York: Harper & Row, 1985), p. 198.

77. Kelly Yamanouchi, "Deregulator Eyes Airlines' Evolution," *Denver Post*, February 18, 2006, p. C1.

78. Marver H. Bernstein, *Regulating Business by Independent Commission* (Princeton, NJ: Princeton University Press, 1955); Harold Seidman, *Politics, Position and Power: The Dynamics of Federal Organization*, 2nd ed. (New York: Oxford University Press, 1975); George J. Stigler, "The Theory of Economic Regulation," *Bell Journal of Economics and Management Science* 2 (Spring 1971): 3–21; Terry Moe, "Regulatory Performance and Presidential Administration," *American Journal of Political Science* 16 (1982): 197–224; and B. R. Weingast and M. J. Moran, "Bureaucratic Discretion or Congressional Control? Regulatory Policymaking by the Federal Trade Commission," *Journal of Political Economy* 91 (1983): 765–800; and B. R. Weingast, "The Congressional-Bureaucratic System: A Principal–Agent Perspective (with Application to the SEC)," *Public Choice* 44, 1 (1984): 147–191.

79. Robyn Meredith, "Credit Unions Help Finance a Bid for Reinstatement by a Dismissed Federal Regulator," *New York Times*, July 20, 1996, p. A7; and United States Court of Appeals for the District of Columbia Circuit, November 22, 1996, No. 96–5193.

80. Frank Ahrens, "FCC Aims to Speed Evaluation of Indecency Complaints," *Washington Post*, February 9, 2005, p. E1.

81. Scott Shepard, "Broadcast Decency Bill Clears House," *Atlanta Journal-Constitution*, February 17, 2005, p. E1.

82. Address at Westminster College, Fulton, Missouri, March 5, 1946, as reprinted in John Bartlett, *Familiar Quotations* (Boston: Little, Brown, 1980), p. 746.

83. George Marshall, secretary of state under Harry Truman, as quoted in Alexander De Conde, "George C. Marshall," in Norman A. Graebner, ed., *An Uncertain Tradition: American Secretaries of State in the Twentieth Century* (New York: McGraw Hill, 1961), p. 252.

84. Barry Rubin, *Secrets of State: The State Department and the Struggle Over U.S. Foreign Policy* (New York: Oxford University Press, 1985), p. 64.

85. Stephen Holmes, "What Russia Teaches Us Now; How Weak States Threaten Freedom," *The American Prospect* (July–August 1997): 30.

86. Donald H. Rumsfeld, "Defense for the 21st Century," *Washington Post*, May 22, 2003, p. A35.

87. Michael R. Gordon and Bernard E. Trainor, *Cobra II: The Inside Story of the Invasion and Occupation of Iraq* (New York: Random House, 2006), p. 4.

88. Barbara Slavin and Dave Moniz, "How Peace in Iraq Became So Elusive," *USA Today*, July 22, 2003, p. 1A.

89. Loch K. Johnson, *America's Secret Power* (New York: Oxford University Press, 1989), Ch. 2.

90. Johnson, *America's Secret Power*; and Rhodri Jeffreys-Johnes, *The CIA and American Democracy* (New Haven, CT: Yale University Press, 1989).

91. Rubin, *Secrets of State*, p. 50.

92. As quoted in Robert Pastor, "Disagreeing on Latin America," in Paul E. Peterson, ed., *The President, the Congress, and the Making of Foreign Policy* (Norman, OK: Oklahoma University Press, 1994), p. 217.

93. Donald Kettl, *Leadership at the Fed* (New Haven, CT: Yale University Press, 1986).

94. John M. Berry, "Where's the Rebound? The Fed, Increasingly Concerned That Its Rate Cuts Haven't Worked, Is Poised to Act Again," *Washington Post Weekly Edition*, June 25–July 1, 2001, p. 18.

95. *Annual Report: Budget Review, 2006* (Washington, DC: Board of Governors of the Federal Reserve System, 2006), p. 1.

96. *90th Annual Report, 2003* (Washington, DC: Board of Governors of the Federal Reserve System, 2004), Statistical Tables, Table 5.

97. James Livingston, *Origins of the Federal Reserve System* (Ithaca, NY: Cornell University Press, 1986).

98. John Woolley, *Monetary Politics: The Federal Reserve and the Politics of Monetary Policy* (New York: Cambridge University Press, 1984).

99. Douglas Hibbs, "The Partisan Model of Macroeconomic Cycles: More Theory and Evidence for the United States," *Economics and Politics* 6 (1994): 1–23.

100. Edward Tufte, *Political Control of the Economy* (Princeton, NJ: Princeton University Press, 1978), Ch. 2.

101. William Greider, *Secrets of the Temple: How the Federal Reserve Runs the Country* (New York: Simon & Schuster, 1987).

102. Michael Schrage, "It's Time to Put a Transaction Tax on Credit Card Purchases," *Washington Post*, October 17, 1990, p. F3.

103. Michael Prowse, "Hat Trick for Alan: Greenspan Wins Another Term at the Fed Despite White House Fears that Tight Monetary Politics are Depressing Growth," *Financial Times*, February 26, 1996, p. 18.

104. Jennifer A. Dlouhy, "U.S. Terror Alert System to Be Revamped," *Houston Chronicle*, May 15, 2005, p. A18.

105. Clark Kent Ervin, "Homeland Security's Intelligence Gap," *New York Times*, July 17, 2005: Section 4, p. 12.

106. Seth Borenstein, "Disaster Response Fixes Pushed; Homeland Security Chief Set to Face Critics," *Pittsburgh Post-Gazette*, February 14, 2006, p. A8.

107. Michael Chertoff, Secretary of Homeland Security, Remarks at the National Newspaper Association's Annual Government Affairs Conference, Washington, D.C., March 9, 2006.

108. Thomas Frank, "Terror Warnings not Coordinated," *Newsday*, May 28, 2004, p. A4.

109. Michael Crowley, "Playing Defense," *The New Republic*, March 15, 2004, p. 17.

Chapter 12

1. "The Second Bush-Kerry Presidential Debate," Washington University, St. Louis, MO, October 8, 2004, Transcript from Commission on Presidential Debates, www.debates.org/pages/trans2004c.html, accessed April 29, 2006.

2. Robin Toner, "After a Brief Shock, Advocates Quickly Mobilize," *New York Times*, July 2, 2005, p. A2.

3. Douglas Jehl, "At White House, Surprise is Borne out in Name Only," *New York Times*, July 2, 2005, p. A2.

4. Peter Baker and Jo Becker, "Court Watchers are Resigned to Wait," *Washington Post*, July 9, 2005, p. A7.

5. Dahlia Lithwick, "Confirmation Report: Oh the Humanity!" Slate.com, September 14, 2005, http://slate.msn.com/?id=2126131&entry/2126220/nav=tap1/, accessed September 15, 2005.

6. For example, Gallup/CNN/*USA Today* poll, September 16–18, 2005: 60 percent support confirmation.

7. Carolyn Lochhead, "Key Senator Backs Roberts — Focus Turns to Next Pick," *San Francisco Chronicle*, September 22, 2005, p. A1.

8. Charles Babington and Peter Baker, "Roberts Confirmed as 17th Chief Justice," *Washington Post*, September 30, 2005, p. A1.

9. Chuck Henning, *The Wit and Wisdom of Politics* (Golden, CO: Fulcrum Publishing, 1992) p. 108.

10. Richard A. Serrano, "Alito's Sole Trial Before a Jury was A Gamble that Paid Off," *Los Angeles Times*, November 14, 2005, p. A11.

11. Linda Greenhouse, "Legacy of a Term," *New York Times*, July 3, 1996, p. A1.

12. H. W. Perry, Jr., *Deciding to Decide: Agenda Setting in the United States Supreme Court* (Cambridge, MA: Harvard University Press, 1991), p. 27.

13. "Judicial Business of the United States Courts, 2003," Washington, DC: Administrative Office of the U.S. Courts, 2003, www.uscourts.gov/judbususc/judbus.html, accessed March 9, 2005.

14. Perry, pp. 218–219.

15. Perry, p. 99.

16. *Zelman v. Simmons-Harris*, No. 00-1751 536 U.S. 639 (2002).

17. Simon, *Advice and Consent* (Washington, DC: National Press Books, 1992), p. 128.

18. As quoted in Henning, *Wit and Wisdom*, p. 106.

19. John C. Jeffries, Jr., *Justice Lewis F. Powell, Jr: A Biography* (New York: Scribner, 1994), pp. 245–247.

20. Bob Woodward and Scott Armstrong, *The Brethren: Inside the Supreme Court* (New York: Simon and Schuster, 1979), pp. 126, 286–287, 297–298, 311.

21. *Parts and Electric Motors, Inc. v. Sterling Electric Inc.* 866 F. 2d 228 (7th Cir. 1988).

22. Jones and Uelmen, *Supreme Folly*, p. 114.

23. Hart Pomerantz, as quoted in Henning, *Wit and Wisdom*, p. 250.

24. *Harris v. Forklift Systems, Inc.*, 510 U.S. 17 (1993).

25. Jeffries, *Justice Lewis F. Powell, Jr.*, p. 323.

26. Jones and Uelmen, *Supreme Folly*, p. 146.

27. Woodward and Armstrong, *The Brethren*, pp. 71, 199.

28. Linda Cohen and Matthew Spitzer, "The Government Litigant Advantage: Implications for the Law," *Florida State University Law Review* 28 (Fall 2000): 391.

29. Jeffrey A. Segal, "*Amicus Curiae* Briefs by the Solicitor General During the Warren and Burger Courts: A Research Note," *Western Political Quarterly* 41 (March 1988): 135–144.

30. Perry, *Deciding to Decide*, p. 71.

31. Perry, *Deciding to Decide*; and Bernard Schwartz, *A History of the Supreme Court* (New York: Oxford University Press, 1993), Ch. 16.

32. Joan Biskupic and Elder Witt, *Guide to the U.S. Supreme Court*, 3rd ed., Vol. II (Washington, DC: CQ Press, 1997), p. 832.

33. Myron Levin and Henry Weinstein, "Big Tobacco Must Pay Damages in Florida Case," *Los Angeles Times*, April 8, 2000, p. A1.

34. Dirk Johnson, "City of Deep Pockets," *Newsweek*, December 15, 2003: 45; Abram Chayes, "The Role of the Judge in Public Law Litigation," *Harvard Law Review* 89 (May 1976): 1281–1316.

35. Dirk Johnson, "City of Deep Pockets," *Newsweek*, December 15, 2003: 45; Alexis de Tocqueville, *Democracy in America*, J. P. Mayer, ed. (New York: Harper, 1988), p. 270.

36. Robert J. Samuelson, "Delegating Democracy: Government by Litigation Has Become Increasingly Popular," *Newsweek* (June 12, 2000): 59; and "Perspectives," *Newsweek* (May 29, 2000): 19.

37. As quoted in Henning, *Wit and Wisdom*, p. 107.

38. David O'Brien, "Background Paper," in Twentieth Century Fund, *Judicial Roulette* (New York: Priority Press, 1988), p. 37; Sheldon Goldman, "Unpicking Pickering in 2002: Some Thoughts on the Politics of Lower Federal Court Selection and Confirmation," *U.C. Davis Law Review* 36: 695 (February 2003), p. 707.

39. Robert Carp, Ronald Stidham, and Kenneth L. Manning, *Judicial Process in America*, 6th Edition (Washington, DC: CQ Press, 2004), Table 7-1, p. 163.

40. Simon, *Advice and Consent*, p. 275.

41. Henry J. Abraham, *Justices and Presidents: A Political History of Appointments to the Supreme Court*, 3rd ed. (New York: Oxford University Press, 1992).

42. Lyle Denniston, "Court Nominee Withdraws in Senate Battle, Democrats Prevail by Way of Filibuster," *Boston Globe*, September 5, 2003, p. A2.

43. Stephen L. Carter, "Looking for Law in All the Wrong Places," *Manhattan Lawyer* (September 1990): 20.

44. Michael McGough, "Frist Tries to End Debate on Alito's Nomination," *Pittsburgh Post-Gazette*, January 27, 2006, p. A8.

457. Ethan Bronner, *Battle for Justice: How the Bork Nomination Shook America* (New York: Norton, 1989), pp. 158–159.

46. Robert G. McCloskey, *The American Supreme Court* (Chicago: University of Chicago Press, 1960), p. 14.

47. Marbury's story is drawn primarily from Jean Edward Smith, *John Marshall: Definer of a Nation* (New York: Holt, 1996), Ch. 13, as well as the case itself, *Marbury v. Madison*, 5 U.S. 137 (1803).

48. *Lochner v. New York*, 198 U.S. 45 (1905).

49. University of Wisconsin Law School, "Supreme Court Justice Scalia Speaks at Law School," *Law School News* (March 2001, accessed at www.law.wisc.edu/news/main.asp on July 30, 2001).

50. Jeffrey A. Segal and Albert D. Cover, "Ideological Values and the Votes of U.S. Supreme Court Justices," *American Political Science Review* 83 (June 1989): 557–565.

51. Woodward and Armstrong, *The Brethren*, p. 193.

52. Institute for Justice, *State of the Supreme Court 2000: The Justices' Record on Individual Liberties* (Washington, DC: Institute for Justice, 2000, accessed at www.ij.org/PDF_folder/supreme_court_report.pdf on August 13, 2001).

53. Joan Biskupic, "The Rehnquist Court," *Washington Post*, May 25, 1999, p. B3.

54. *Lynch v. Donnelly*, 465 U.S. 668 (1984); and *County of Allegheny v. ACLU*, 492 U.S. 573 (1989).

55. *City of Erie v. Pap's A. M.*, tdba "Kandyland" 529 U.S. 277 (2000).

56. Jeffrey Toobin, "Swing Shift: How Anthony Kennedy's Passion for Foreign Law Could Change the Supreme Court," *New Yorker*, September 12, 2005, www.newyorker.com/fact/content/articles/050912fa_fact.

57. *Schechter Poultry Corp. v. United States*, 295 U.S. 495 (1935).

58. Congressional Research Service, Library of Congress, *The Constitution of the United States of America: Analysis and Interpretation, 2004 Supplement* (Washington, DC: Government Printing Office, 2004).

59. James A. Stimson, Michael B. Mackuen, and Robert S. Erikson, "Dynamic Representation," *American Political Science Review* 89 (1995): 555. Also see William Mishler and Reginald S. Sheehan, "The Supreme Court as a Counter-Majoritarian Institution? The Impact of Public Opinion on Supreme Court Decisions," *American Political Science Review* 87 (1993): 87–101; and Helmut Norpoth and Jeffery Segal, "Popular Influence on Supreme Court Decisions," *American Political Science Review* 88 (1994): 711–724.

60. *Massachusetts v. Environmental Protection Agency*, No. 05-1120 (2007).

61. As quoted by Austin Ranney, "Peltason Created a New Way to Look at What Judges Do," *Public Affairs Report*, Institute of Governmental Studies, 36, No. 6 (November 1995): p. 7.

62. R. Shep Melnick, *Between the Lines* (Washington, DC: Brookings, 1994), Ch. 1.

63. C. Herman Pritchett, *The American Constitution* (New York: McGraw-Hill, 1959), p. 99.

64. Lee Epstein and Thomas G. Walker, *Constitutional Law for a Changing America: Rights, Liberties, and Justice*, 3rd ed. (Washington, DC: Congressional Quarterly, 1998), pp. 200–201.

65. Los Angeles County District Attorney's Office, http://da.co.la.ca.us/oview.htm, accessed April 23, 2006.

66. Robert A. Carp, Ronald Stidham, and Kenneth L. Manning, *Judicial Process in America*, 6th ed. (Washington, DC: CQ Press, 2004), p. 100.

67. "Investigate, Then Prosecute; Bungled Lewis Trial: Atlanta Prosecutors, Police Rushed to Indict Before They Had All the Evidence," *Baltimore Sun*, June 14, 2000, p. 22A.

68. Cynthia Tucker, "My Opinion; Murder Acquittals: Running for Glory, Fulton DA Fumbles." *Atlanta Constitution*, June 14, 2000, p. 14A.

69. Herbert Jacob and Kenneth Vines, "Courts," in Virginia Gray, Herbert Jacob, and Kenneth Vines, eds., *Politics in the American States: A Comparative Analysis*, 4th ed. (Boston: Little, Brown, 1983), p. 238.

70. Melinda Gann Hall, "Justices as Representatives: Elections and Judicial Politics in the American States," *American Politics Quarterly* 23 (October 1995): 485–503.

71. Jacob and Vines, "Courts," p. 239.

72. Zach Patton, "Robe Warriors," *Governing*, March 2006: p. 34.

73. As quoted in Pritchett, *The American Constitution*, pp. 65, 215.

74. Congressional Research Service, Library of Congress, *The Constitution of the United States of America: Analysis and Interpretation, 2004 Supplement* (Washington, DC: Government Printing Office, 2004).

75. *In re Chapman*, 16 U.S. 661 (1897).

76. See "The Case for Partisan Judicial Elections," Federalist Society White Paper, www.fed-soc.org/Publications/White%20Papers/judicialelection.htm, accessed February 2, 2007.

77. Melinda Gann Hall, "Justices as Representatives: Elections and Judicial Politics in the American States," *American Politics Quarterly* 23 (October 1995): 485–503.

78. Henry R. Glick, "Courts: Politics and the Judicial Process," in Virginia Gray and Russell L. Hanson, Eds. *Politics in the American States: A Comparative Analysis*, 8th ed. (Washington, DC: CQ Press, 2004), p. 240.

79. Jessica Garrison, "Politics Creeps into Judge Races," *Los Angeles Times*, October 25, 2006, p. B3.

Chapter 13

1. Kevin Whitelaw & Chitra Ragavan, "A Good Spy is Hard to Find," *U.S. News and World Report*, November 22, 2004, p. 59.

2. Patrick Radden Keefe, "Can Network Theory Thwart Terrorists?" *New York Times Magazine*, March 12, 2006, p. 16.

3. James Bamford, *Body of Secrets: Anatomy of the Ultra-Secret National Security Agency*, New York: Random House, 2001, p. 428–429.

4. James Risen and Eric Lichtblau, "Bush Lets U.S. Spy on Callers Without Courts," *New York Times*, December 16, 2005, p. 1; Brian Ross, "NSA Whistleblower Alleges Illegal Spying," ABCNews.com, January 10, 2006, http://abcnews.go.com/WNT/Investigation/story?id=1491889, accessed May 13, 2006.

5. Eric Lichtblau and Adam Liptak, "Bush and His Senior Aides Press On in Legal Defense for Wiretapping Program," *New York Times*, January 28, 2006, p. 13.

6. Leslie Cauley, "NSA Has Massive Database of Americans' Phone Calls; 3 Telecoms Help Government Collect Billions of Domestic Records," *USA Today*, May 11, 2006, p. 1A.

7. Richard A. Falkenrath, "The Right Call on Phone Records," *Washington Post*, May 13, 2006, p. A17.

8. Greg Miller, "New Furor over NSA Phone Logs," *Los Angeles Times*, May 12, 2006, p. A1.

9. Paul Taylor, "Qwest Snubbed 'Illegal' Call for Details of Phone Records," *Financial Times*, May 13, 2006, p. 1.

10. Richard Sisk, "They Know Who We're Calling," *New York Daily News*, May 12, 2006, p. 7.

11. *Ibid.*

12. Arthur M. Schlesinger, *Prelude to Independence: The Newspaper War on Britain, 1764–1776* (New York: Knopf, 1958), p. 299.

13. Michael W. McConnell, "Establishment and Disestablishment at the Founding, Part I, Establishment of Religion," 44 *William and Mary Law Review* 2105, April 2003, pp. 2157–2159.

14. *Barron v. Baltimore*, 1833, as quoted in C. Herman Pritchett, *Constitutional Civil Liberties* (Englewood Cliffs, NJ: Prentice-Hall, 1984), p. 6.

15. *Stromberg v. California*, 283 U.S. 359 (1931).

16. *United States v. Carolene Products Co.*, 304 U.S. 144 (1938).

17. George Anastaplo, as quoted in Robert Justin Goldstein, *Political Repression in Modern America: From 1870 to 1976* (Champaign, IL: University of Illinois Press, 2001), p. 532.

18. *Papish v. the Board of Curators of the University of Missouri*, 410 U.S. 667 (1973).

19. *New York Times Co. v. United States*, 403 U.S. 713 (1971).

20. Robert Goldstein, *Saving "Old Glory": The History of the Desecration Controversy* (Boulder, CO: Westview Press, 1995).

21. *Texas v. Johnson*, 491 U.S. 397 (1989).

22. *United States v. Eichman*, 496 U.S. 310 (1990).

23. *Jenkins v. Georgia*, 418 U.S. 153 (1974).

24. Linda Greenhouse, "Court, 9–0, Upholds State Laws Prohibiting Assisted Suicide, Protects Speech on Internet," *New York Times*, June 27, 1997, p. A1; *Ashcroft v. American Civil Liberties Union*, 535 U.S. 564 (2004).

25. Michael W. McConnell, "Stuck with a Lemon: A New Test for Establishment Clause Cases Would Help Ease Current Confusion," *ABA Journal* 83 (February 1997): 46–47.

26. Scalia concurrence, *City of Erie v. Pap's* A. M., *"Kandyland,"* (98-1161) 529 U.S. 277 (2000).

27. As quoted in Charles L. Glenn, Jr., *The Myth of the Common School* (Amherst, MA: University of Massachusetts Press, 1987), p. 84.

28. *Sante Fe Independent School District v. Doe*, (99-62) 530 U.S. 290 (2000).

29. Benjamin I. Page and Robert Y. Shapiro, *The Rational Public: Fifty Years of Trends in Americans' Policy Preferences* (Chicago: University of Chicago Press, 1992), p. 113.

30. *Board of Education of the Westside Community Schools v. Mergens*, 496 U.S. 226 (1990).

31. *Sherbert v. Verner*, 374 U.S. 398 (1963).

32. *Gonzales v. UDV*, 546 U.S. 418 (2006).

33. C. Herman Pritchett, *The American Constitution* (New York: McGraw-Hill, 1959), p. 477.

34. James F. Simon, *The Antagonists: Hugo Black, Felix Frankfurter and Civil Liberties in Modern America* (New York: Simon & Schuster, 1989), pp. 106–114.

35. Pritchett, *The American Constitution*, p. 478.

36. Samuel Warren and Louis Brandeis, "The Right to Privacy," *Harvard Law Review* 4 (1890): 193–220.

37. *Griswold v. Connecticut*, 381 U.S. 479 (1965).

38. *Ibid.*

39. Michael J. Sandel, *Democracy's Discontent: American in Search of a Public Philosophy* (Cambridge, MA: Belknap Press of Harvard University Press, 1996), pp. 93–94.

40. Bob Woodward and Scott Armstrong, *The Brethren: Inside the Supreme Court* (New York: Simon & Schuster, 1979), pp. 198–206.

41. *Harris v. McRae*, 448 U.S. 297 (1980).

42. *Webster v. Reproductive Health Services*, 492 U.S. 490 (1989).

43. *Planned Parenthood v. Casey*, 505 U.S. 833 (1992).

44. *Gonzales v. Carhart*, No. 05-380 (2007).

45. Pamela Coyle, "Second State Court Overturns Sodomy Law," *New Orleans Times–Picayune* (March 18, 1999): p. A1; and Amy Argetsinger, "Maryland Judge's Ruling Protects Private, Consensual Sex Acts," *Washington Post*, January 20, 1999, p. B8.

46. "The Gallup Poll: Social and Economic Indicators—Homosexual Relations," accessed at www.gallup.com/poll/indicators/indhomsexual.asp on March 22, 2000.

47. *Mapp v. Ohio*, 367 U.S. 643 (1961).

48. *Washington v. Chrisman*, 455 U.S. 1 (1982), p. 182.

49. John C. Domino, *Civil Rights and Liberties in the 21st Century* (New York: Longman), pp. 176–177.

50. *Kyllo v. United States*, (99-8508) 533 U.S. 27 (2001).

51. *Dickerson v. United States*, 530 U.S. 428 (2000).

52. Pritchett, *Constitutional Civil Liberties*, p. 78.

53. *Sheppard v. Maxwell*, 384 U.S. 333 (1966).

54. *Nebraska Press Association v. Stuart*, 427 U.S. 539 (1976).

55. Lisa J. McIntyre, *The Public Defender: The Practice of Law in the Shadows of Repute* (Chicago: University of Chicago Press, 1987), p. 162.

56. Toni Locy, "Okla. Trial for Nichols Rethought: New Prosecutor Reviewing Options," *USA Today*, June 19, 2001, p. 6A.

57. *Roper v. Simmons*, 03-633 (2005).

58. Casper, *American Criminal Justice: The Defendant's Perspective* (Englewood Cliffs, NJ: Prentice-Hall, 1972); and Jerome Skolnick, *Justice Without Trial* (New York: Wiley, 1966).

59. *New York Times*, May 12, 1989, p. B12.

60. Mitchell Zuckoff, "A New Word on Speech Codes; One School That Led Way Is Rethinking Its Rules," *Boston Globe*, October 21, 1998, p. A1. See also, Tom Mashberg, "Debates Rage on Campus Over Free-Speech Rules," *Boston Herald*, October 31, 1999, p. 1.

61. Zuckoff, p. A1.

62. Nat Hentoff, "'Free Speech' Cries Ring Hollow on College Campuses and Beyond," *USA Today*, April 19, 2006, p. 11A.

Chapter 14

1. Stephanie Stoughton, "Fighting Terror, Security vs. Discrimination; Fliers See Bias as Pilots Move to Bump Them," *Boston Globe*, November 11, 2001, p. A1.

2. American Civil Liberties Union of Northern California, "Caught in the Backlash: Arshad Chowdhury, Pittsburgh, Pennsylvania," www.aclunc.org/911/backlash/chowdhury.html, accessed May 20, 2006.

3. Harriet Chiang, "ACLU sues airlines for discrimination after September 11," *San Francisco Chronicle*, June 5, 2002, p. A16.

4. American Civil Liberties Union of Northern California, "Caught in the Backlash: Arshad Chowdhury, Pittsburgh, Pennsylvania," www.aclunc.org/911/backlash/chowdhury.html, accessed May 20, 2006.

5. Andrew C. McCarthy, "Garden State Variety Profiling Hysteria," National Review Online, www.defenddemocracy.org//in_the_media/in_the_media_show.htm?doc_id=302808, accessed May 20, 2006.

6. CBS News/*New York Times* poll, August 17–21, 2006.

7. Terese Loeb Kreuzer, "Now I Lay Me Down to Sleep, in a Pod, at the Airport," *New York Times*, April 12, 2005, p. C6.

8. Ruth Bader Ginsburg, "Employment of the Constitution to Advance the Equal Status of Men and Women," in Shlomo Slonim, ed., *The Constitutional Bases of Political and Social Change in the United States* (New York: Praeger, 1990), p. 188.

9. Robert F. Nagel, *Constitutional Cultures: The Mentality and Consequences of Judicial Review* (Berkeley, CA: University of California Press, 1989), Chs. 5–6.

10. Philip Converse, "The Nature of Belief Systems in Mass Publics," in David E. Apter, *Ideology and Discontent* (New York: Free Press, 1964), pp. 206–261.

11. John D. Hicks, *The American Nation* (Cambridge, MA: Riverside Press, 1949), p. 21.

12. 42 U.S. Code Chapter 21, Section 1981.

13. Eric Foner, *A Short History of Reconstruction* (New York: Harper & Row, 1990).

14. Richard M. Valelly, "National Parties and Racial Disfranchisement," in Paul E. Peterson, ed., *Classifying by Race* (Princeton, NJ: Princeton University Press, 1995), pp. 188–216.

15. U.S. Commission on Civil Rights, *Report of the Commission on Civil Rights* (Washington, DC: U.S. Government Printing Office, 1959), p. 32. Ellipses deleted.

16. V. O. Key Jr., *Southern Politics* (New York: Random House, 1949).

17. J. Morgan Kousser, *The Shaping of Southern Politics: Suffrage Restriction and the Establishment of the One-Party South, 1880–1910* (New Haven, CT: Yale University Press, 1974), p. 61.

18. *Civil Rights Cases*, 109 U.S. 3 (1883).

19. *Plessy v. Ferguson*, 163 U.S. 537 (1896).

20. Edward Banfield and James Q. Wilson, *City Politics* (New York: Vintage Books, 1963); and James Q. Wilson, *Negro Politics* (New York: Free Press, 1960). For caveats, see Steven P. Erie, *Rainbow's End: Irish-Americans and the Dilemmas of Urban Machine Politics, 1840–1985* (Berkeley, CA: University of California Press, 1990).

21. Gerald N. Rosenberg, *The Hollow Hope: Can Courts Bring About Social Change?* (Chicago: University of Chicago Press, 1991), p. 61.

22. *Smith v. Allwright*, 321 U.S. 649 (1944).

23. *Shelley v. Kraemer*, 334 U.S. 1 (1948).

24. Howard Ball and Phillip J. Cooper, *Of Power and Right: Hugo Black, William O. Douglas, and America's Constitutional Revolution* (New York: Oxford University Press, 1992), p. 172.

25. Bob Woodward and Scott Armstrong, *The Brethren: Inside the Supreme Court* (New York: Simon & Schuster, 1979), Prologue.

26. *Brown v. Board of Education*, 347 U.S. 483 (1954), note 11. The citation of six psychological and sociological studies in this note led Herbert Garfinkel to charge that the Court was making decisions on the basis of sociology, not law. "Social Science Evidence and the School Segregation Cases," *Journal of Politics* 21 (February 1959): 37–59. Kenneth B. Clark, "Effect of Prejudice and Discrimination on Personality Development" (Midcentury White House Conference on Children and Youth 1950, as cited in note 11 to *Brown*).

27. Henry Lee Moon, "New Emancipation," in Herbert Aptheker, ed. *A Documentary History of the Negro People in the United States*, 6, (New York: Citadel Press, 1993) pp. 200–203.

28. A. D. Morris, *Origins of the Civil Rights Movement: Black Communities Organizing for Change* (New York: Free Press, 1984).

29. *Ibid.*, pp. 51–63.

30. Michael Lipsky, "Protest as a Political Resource," *American Political Science Review* 62 (December 1968): 1144–1158.

31. University of Georgia, Carl Vinson Institute of Government, "Historical Documents Related to Georgia," accessed at www.cviog.uga.edu/Projects/gainfo/gahisdoc.htm on April 6, 2000.

32. Rosenberg, *The Hollow Hope*, p. 50.

33. Gerald D. Jaynes and Robin M. Williams, Jr., eds., *A Common Destiny: Blacks and American Society* (Washington, DC: National Academy Press, 1989), p. 224.

34. Patricia Gurin, Shirley Hatchett, and James S. Jackson, *Hope and Independence: Blacks' Response to Electoral and Party Politics* (New York: Russell Sage, 1989), pp. 42–49.

35. Jaynes and Williams, *A Common Destiny*, p. 233.

36. Joint Center for Political and Economic Studies, *Focus* (Washington, DC: Joint Center for Political and Economic Studies 1993); and David A. Bositis, *Black Elected Officials: A Statistical Summary, 2001* (Washington, DC: Joint Center for Political and Economic Studies, 2002), p. 3.

37. William J. Grimshaw, *Bitter Fruit: Black Politics and the Chicago Machine, 1931–1991* (Chicago: University of Chicago Press, 1992).

38. Gary Orfield, *The Reconstruction of Southern Education: The Schools and the 1964 Civil Rights Act* (New York: Wiley, 1969); and Jennifer Hochschild, *The New American Dilemma* (New Haven, CT: Yale University Press, 1984).

39. Katherine Tate, *From Protest to Politics* (Cambridge, MA: Harvard University Press, 1993), Ch. 8.

40. *Milliken v. Bradley*, 418 U.S. 717 (1974); 433 U.S. 267 (1977).

41. *Milliken v. Bradley*, 418 U.S. 717 (1974).

42. *Regents of the University of California v. Bakke*, 438 U.S. 265 (1978).

43. *Grutter v. Bollinger*, 02-241 (2003).

44. U.S. Bureau of the Census, *Statistical Abstract of the United States, 1999* (Washington, DC: U.S. Government Printing Office, 1999), Table 760.

45. U.S. Bureau of the Census, *Statistical Abstract of the United States, 1999*, Table 680; and Amitabh Chandra, "Is the Convergence in the Racial Wage Gap Illusory?" *American Economic Review* 90 (2000).

46. U.S. Bureau of the Census, *Statistical Abstract of the United States, 1999*, Tables 99 and 133.

47. Jaynes and Williams, *A Common Destiny*, p. 313.

48. U.S. Bureau of the Census, *Statistical Abstract of the United States, 2007*, Table 214.

49. United States Bureau of the Census, Statistical Abstract of the United States, 2007, Table 692; U.S. Bureau of the Census, Current Population Survey, *Annual Demographic Survey, March Supplement*, 2005, Table POV01.

50. Lisa Handley and Bernard Grofman, "The Impact of the Voting Rights Act on Minority Representation: Black Officeholding in Southern State Legislatures," in Chandler Davidson and Bernard Grofman, eds., *Quiet Revolution in the South: The Impact of the Voting Rights Act, 1965–1990* (Princeton, NJ: Princeton University Press, 1994), pp. 335–350; Margaret Edds, *Claiming the Dream: The Victorious Campaign of Douglas Wilder of Virginia* (Chapel Hill, NC: Algonquin Books, 1990); and D. Stephen Voss and David Lublin, "Black Incumbents, White

Districts: An Appraisal of the 1996 Congressional Elections," *American Politics Research* 29 (2001): 141–182.

51. Frederic Cople Jaher, *A Scapegoat in the Wilderness: The Origins and Rise of Anti-Semitism in America* (Cambridge, MA: Harvard University Press, 1994); Leonard Dinnerstein, *Anti-Semitism in America* (New York: Oxford, 1994); and Jack Nelson, *Terror in the Night: The Klan's Campaign Against the Jews* (New York: Simon & Schuster, 1993).

52. U.S. Bureau of the Census, Population Estimates, www.census.gov/popest/estimates.php, accessed February 7, 2007.

53. Michael Jones-Correa, *Between Two Nations: The Political Predicament of Latinos in New York City* (Ithaca, NY: Cornell University Press, 1998).

54. National Election Studies 2004 for blacks; for Latinos, figure based on 2006 National Latino Survey, The Latino Coalition, www.thelatinocoalition.com/news/2006/2006NationalLatinoSurvey-Topline.pdf, accessed February 7, 2007, those who answered "don't vote" excluded from analysis.

55. Geoffrey Fox, *Hispanic Nation: Culture, Politics, and the Constructing of Identity* (Secaucus, NJ: Birch Lane, 1996).

56. *Lau v. Nichols*, 414 U.S. 563 (1974).

57. Bernard Grofman, Lisa Handley, and Richard G. Niemi, *Minority Representation and the Quest for Voting Equality* (New York: Cambridge University Press, 1992), pp. 16–25. Also see Thomas Weyr, *Hispanic U.S.A.: Breaking the Melting Pot* (New York: Harper, 1959); and Peter Skerry, *Mexican Americans: The Ambivalent Minority* (New York: Free Press, 1993).

58. David L. Leal, Matt A. Barreto, Jongho Lee, and Rodolfo O. de la Garza, "The Latino Vote in the 2004 Election," *PS: Political Science and Politics* (January 2005): 41–49.

59. U.S. Bureau of the Census, Population Estimates, www.census.gov/popest/estimates.php, accessed February 7, 2007; U.S. Bureau of the Census, *Statistical Abstract of the United States, 2007*, Table 47.

60. Stanley Karnow and Nancy Yoshihara, *Asian Americans in Transition* (New York: Asia Society, 1992).

61. Asian Pacific American Institute for Congressional Studies, "Statement from APA Community Organizations," accessed at www.apaics.org/statement.html on April 10, 2000.

62. Amit R. Paley, "A Date with Tradition: Chinese New Year Ushers in Quest for Official Holiday Recognition," *Washington Post*, January 29, 2006, p. C1; Errol Louis, "Strength in Numbers: John Liu galvanizes the city's Asian community to quash bias," *New York Daily News*, May 16, 2006, p. 31.

63. Vine Deloria, Jr., "The Distinctive Status of Indian Rights," in Peter Iverson, ed., *The Plains Indians of the Twentieth Century* (Norman, OK: University of Oklahoma Press, 1985), p. 241.

64. *Ibid.*, pp. 237–248.

65. U.S. Department of Commerce, Bureau of the Census, *Poverty in the United States: 2000*, Current Population Reports P60-214, Washington, DC: Government Printing Office, September 2001, p. 7, Table B.

66. Deloria, "The Distinctive Status of Indian Rights," p. 237.

67. John Agresto, *The Supreme Court and Constitutional Democracy* (Ithaca, NY: Cornell University Press, 1984), pp. 148–149.

68. Theda Skocpol, *Protecting Soldiers and Mothers: The Political Origins of Social Policy in the United States* (Cambridge, MA: Harvard University Press, 1992); and Sara Evans, *Personal Politics: The Roots of Women's Liberation in the Civil Rights Movement and the New Left* (New York: Knopf, 1979).

69. Nancy McGlen and Karen O'Conner, *Women's Rights: The Struggle for Equality in the Nineteenth and Twentieth Centuries* (New York: Praeger, 1983), Ch. 9.

70. Jane J. Mansbridge, *Why We Lost the ERA* (Chicago: University of Chicago Press, 1986).

71. *Craig v. Boren*, 429 U.S. 190 (1976).

72. Ruth Bader Ginsburg, "Employment of the Constitution to Advance the Equal Status of Men and Women," in Shlomo Slonim, ed. *The Constitutional Bases of Political and Social Change* (New York: Praeger, 1990), p. 191.

73. *Rostker v. Goldberg*, 453 U.S. 57 (1981).

74. Mansbridge, *Why We Lost the ERA*, Ch. 7.

75. Bryan Bender, "Army Secretary Rejects Change in Policy on Women in Combat," *Boston Globe*, January 29, 2005, p. A11; Gallup poll, December 14–16, 2001, showing that 52% of Americans favor women "serving as ground combat troops."

76. *Watson v. Fort Worth Bank & Trust*, 487 U.S. 977 (1988) at 997–999; *New York City Transit Authority v. Beazer*, 440 U.S. 568 (1979) at 587, no 31; and *Griggs v. Duke Power*, 401 U.S. 424 (1971) at 432.

77. *Wards Cove Packing Co. v. Atonio*, 490 U.S. 642 (1989).

78. *Meritor Savings Bank v. Vinson*, 477 U.S. 57 (1986).

79. *Harris v. Forklift Systems*, 510 U.S. 17 (1993).

80. "Hillary's Class," *Frontline* (PBS television broadcast, No. 15, 1994), as cited in Karla Cooper-Boggs, "The Link Between Private and Public Single-Sex Colleges: Will Wellesley Stand or Fall with the Citadel?" *Indiana Law Review* 29 (1995): 137.

81. "Bush Aims to Ease Coeducation Rules for Public Schools," *Los Angeles Times*, March 4, 2004, p. A9; Diana Jean Schemo, "Change in Federal Rules Backs Single-Sex Public Education," *New York Times*, October 25, 2006, p. A1.

82. *United States v. Virginia*, 116 SCt 2264 (1996).

83. Shawn Zeller, "Gay Rites: Giving to Democrats," *National Journal* (May 8, 1999): 1241.

84. Data from the Gay and Lesbian Victory Fund, www.victoryfund.org, accessed February 7, 2007.

85. Deb Price, "Gays Need Democrats to Win 2000 Elections," *Detroit News*, November 1, 1999, p. A7; and Human Rights Campaign, accessed at www.hrc.org on February 18, 2005.

86. Human Rights Campaign, www.hrc.org, accessed February 7, 2007.

87. White House Office, "Fulfilling America's Promise to Americans with Disabilities," www.whitehouse.gov/news/freedominitiative/freedominitiative.html, accessed May 20, 2006.

88. U.S. Social Security Administration, "The Fiscal Year 2008 Budget Press Release," February 5, 2007, accessed at www.ssa.gov/budget/2008bud.pdf; Congressional Budget Office, *Disability and Retirement: The Early Exit of Baby Boomers From the Labor Force* (Washington, DC: Congressional Budget Office, November, 2004), Tables 2, 4, 5.

89. Robert A. Katzman, *Institutional Disability: The Saga of Transportation Policy for the Disabled* (Washington, DC: Brookings, 1986).

90. Frederick J. Weintraub, ed., *Public Policy and the Education of Exceptional Children* (Washington, DC: Council for Exceptional Children, 1976).

91. Paul E. Peterson, "Background Paper," in *Twentieth Century Fund, Making the Grade: Report of the Twentieth Century Fund Task Force on Federal Elementary and Secondary Education Policy* (New York: Twentieth Century Fund, 1983), Ch. 5.

92. Rufus Browning, Dale Rogers Marshall, and David H. Tabb, *Protest Is Not Enough: The Struggle of Blacks and Hispanics for Equality in Urban Politics* (Berkeley, CA: University of California Press, 1984).

93. Berny Morson, "CU Cookie Caper Gets a Stale Reception; 'Affirmative Action Bake Sale' Met With Protest, Discussion," *Rocky Mountain News*, February 12, 2004, p. 6A.

94. Meagan Balink, "Will Students Buy at the 'Bake Sale?'" *Colorado Daily* February 10, 2004.

95. Morson, p. 6A.

969. Balink.

97. Gallup Poll, June 6–25, 2005.

98. Bob Laird, former director of undergraduate admissions, University of California, Berkeley, quoted in Leslie Fulbright, "Connerly Gearing up for Wider Crusade," *San Francisco Chronicle*, December 14, 2006, p. A1.

99. Quoted in Fulbright, *ibid.*

Chapter 15

1. Jonathan Weisman, "Deficit Projections Soar with Bush Stimulus Plan; Economists Say a Record Shortfall is Likely," *Washington Post*, January 10, 2003, p. A1.

2. "President Delivers 'State of the Union,'" (The White House: Washington DC, January 28, 2003), www.whitehouse.gov/news/releases/2003/01/20030128-19. html, accessed March 30, 2004.

3. Carolyn Lochhead, "Medicare Bill Gives GOP Win on Dems' Turf," *San Francisco Chronicle*, November 26, 2003, p. A4.

4. Robert J. McCarthy, "Clinton Calls for Changes in Drug Plan," *Buffalo News*, January 23, 2006, p. B1; Robert Pear, "In Medicare Debate, Massaging the Facts," *New York Times*, May 23, 2006, p. A4.

5. Vicki Kemper, "Secrecy Probed in Medicare Plan Cost Estimates," *Los Angeles Times*, March 20, 2004, p. A24; Joseph Antos, "Medicare and the Prescription Drug Benefit: Increased Pressure for Reform," Testimony before the United States Senate, Committee on Homeland Security and Governmental Affairs, Subcommittee on Federal Financial Management, Government Information, and International Security, September 22, 2005.

6. Commission on Presidential Debates, "The Second Bush-Kerry Presidential Debate," transcript, October 8, 2004, www.debates.org/pages/trans2004c.html, accessed March 11, 2005.

7. Clarke Canfield, "Prescription Drugs Take Center Stage for Fall Elections in States with Many Elderly People," Associated Press, August 2, 2002.

8. Arthur Maass, *Congress and the Common Good* (New York: Basic Books, 1983).

9. Eugene Bardach, *The Implementation Game*, 4th ed. (Cambridge, MA: MIT Press, 1982); and Jeffrey L. Pressman and Aaron Wildavsky, *Implementation*, 3rd ed. (Berkeley, CA: University of California Press, 1984).

10. Thomas R. Dye, *Politics, Economics and the Public: Policy Outcomes in the American States* (Chicago: Rand McNally, 1966).

11. Department of Health and Human Services, Office of Family Assistance, "TANF Recipients as of 1/10/07" www.acf.hhs.gov/programs/ofa/caseload/2006/tanf_recipients.htm, accessed February 8, 2007.

12. Amy Goldstein, "Forgotten Issues; Welfare Reform's Progress Is Stalled," *Washington Post*, June 1, 2000, p. A1; Robert Pear, "Despite Sluggish Economy, Welfare Rolls Actually Fell," *New York Times*, March 22, 2004, p. A21.

13. Jonathan Weisman, "Budget Cuts Pass by a Slim Margin; Poor, Elderly, and Students to Feel the Pinch," *Washington Post*, February 2, 2006, p. A1.

14. Timothy Smeeding, Michael O'Higgins, and Lee Rainwater, eds., *Poverty, Inequality and Income Distribution in Comparative Perspective* (New York: Harvester Wheatsheaf, 1990); and Lee Rainwater and Timothy M. Smeeding, "Doing Poorly: The Real Income of American Children in a Comparative Perspective," working paper no. 127, Maxwell School of Citizenship and Public Affairs, Syracuse University, Syracuse, NY, August 1995.

15. United States Bureau of the Census, International Data Base, www.census.gov/ipc/www/idbnew.html, accessed May 26, 2006, Table 10; CIA World Factbook 2006, www.cia.gov/cia/publications/factbook/index.html, accessed May 26, 2006. Infant mortality data are from 2006; GDP data from 2005.

16. Neil Howe and Richard Jackson, *Entitlements and the Aging of America* (Washington, DC: National Taxpayers Union Foundation, 1994).

17. Martha Derthick, *Policymaking for Social Security* (Washington, DC: Brookings, 1979); and Theda Skocpol, *Protecting Soldiers and Mothers: The Politics of Social Provision in the United States* (Cambridge, MA: Harvard University Press, 1993).

18. "Life Expectancy for Social Security," Social Security Administration, /www.ssa.gov/history/lifeexpect.html, accessed May 26, 2006; U.S. Department of Health and Human Services, National Center for Health Statistics, *Health, United States, 2005, with Chartbook on Trends in the Health of Americans*, National Center for Health Statistics, 2005, Table 27.

19. R. Kent Weaver, *Automatic Government: The Politics of Indexation* (Washington, DC: Brookings, 1988).

20. Orlo Nichols, Michael Clingman, and Alice Wade, *Internal Real Rates of Return Under the OASDI Program for Hypothetical Workers*, Social Security Administration, Office of the Chief Actuary (Baltimore, MD: March 2005) Table 1.

21. Because these figures are in constant dollars, one should not compare social security benefits directly to other possible forms of investment.

22. *Boston Globe*, December 27, 1994, p. A70.

23. John F. Harris and Glenn Kessler, "Who Shrank the Surplus? Both Sides Place Blame as the Effects of a Slow Economy and a Tax Cut Set In," *Washington Post Weekly Edition*, July 16–22, 2001, p. 6.

24. Charlie Cook, quoted in Marc Sandalow, "Retirement Overhaul Plan Tests Bush's Political Capital," *San Francisco Chronicle*, March 6, 2005, p. A1.

25. 1970 figure is expressed in 2005 dollars. *Budget of the United States Government, Fiscal Year 2008, Historical Tables* (Washington, DC: Office of Management and Budget, 2004), Table 8. 6, p. 148. These figures reflect the total cost of Medicare, minus premiums paid by patients.

26. Department of Commerce, U.S. Bureau of the Census, *Current Population Reports, Voting and Registration in the Election of November 2004*, Washington DC: U.S. Government Printing Office (March 2006, Table B).

27. Susan A. MacManus, with Patricia A. Turner, *Young v. Old: Generational Combat in the 21st Century* (Boulder, CO: Westview Press, 1996), pp. 60, 141.

28. Employment information, membership and volunteer numbers, "AARP: Making the Most of Life After 50" accessed at www.aarp.org/leadership/Articles/a2003-01-13-aarphistory.html on March 11, 2005; and budget figures2005 AARP *Annual Report*, p. 22.

29. AARP *Images of Aging in America 2004*, March 2006, Figure 4. 4, p. 56.

30. Survey by the Luntz Research Companies/Mark A. Siegal and Associates, September 8–10, 1994; and *The Public Perspective: People, Opinions, & Polls* (February/March 1995).

31. *2006 SSI Annual Report* (Washington, DC: Social Security Administration, 2006), p. v.

32. Internal Revenue Service, "2006 1040A Instructions," Earned Income Credit (EIC) Table, p. 45.

33. *Budget of the United States Government, Fiscal Year 2008, Historical Tables,* Table 16. 1, p. 322.

34. Medicaid budget figure from Office of Management & Budget, Budget for Fiscal Year 2006, Historical Tables, Table 16. 1. Percentage of monies going for services to the elderly in fiscal year 1993. Marilyn Werber Serafini, "Pinching Pennies," *National Journal* 27/37 (September 16, 1995): 2273. Also see Mark Rom, "Health and Welfare in the American States," *Politics in the American States,* 6th ed., Virginia Gray and Herbert Jacob, eds. (Washington, DC: CQ Press, 1995).

35. *Public Perspective* (February/March 1995): p. 39; and *The Gallup Poll,* accessed at www.gallup.com on July 24, 2000.

36. Jeff Shear, "The Credit Card," *National Journal* 27/32 (August 12, 1995): 2056–2058; and Marilyn W. Serafini, "Turning Up the Heat," *National Journal* 27/32 (August 12, 1995): 2051–2055.

37. Paul E. Peterson, "An Immodest Proposal," *Daedalus* 121 (Fall 1992): 151–174.

38. U.S. House of Representatives, Committee on Ways and Means, Overview of Entitlement Programs: Background Material and Data on Programs Within the Jurisdiction of the Committee on Ways and Means (otherwise known as the 2004 Green Book) (Washington, DC: U.S. Government Printing Office, 2004), Table I-5, p. I-9. All subsequent references to this document in this chapter will be simply to the Green Book. They refer to the 2004 edition.

39. Green Book, Table I-5, p. I-9.

40. *Changes in Participation in Means-Tested Programs* (Washington, DC: Congressional Budget Office, April 20, 2005), p. 6.

41. Paul E. Peterson and Mark Rom, *Welfare Magnets: A New Case for a National Standard* (Washington, DC: Brookings, 1990).

42. U.S. Department of Health and Human Services, Office of Family Assistance, *Temporary Assistance for Needy Families (TANF), Sixth Annual Report to Congress,* November 2004, Table C, p. I-11.

43. Rules vary widely by state. See U.S. Department of Health and Human Services, Administration for Children and Families, *Temporary Assistance to Needy Families, Third Annual Report to Congress,* August, 2000, pp. 207–210.

44. Green Book, Table 12, p. 1212.

45. "Social Security Penalty on Earnings Is Repealed," *Los Angeles Times,* April 8, 2000, p. A14.

46. David K. Kirkpatrick, *Choice in Schooling: A Case for Tuition Vouchers* (Chicago: Loyola University Press, 1990); and Terry Moe, ed., *Private Vouchers* (Stanford, CA: Hoover Institution Press, 1995).

47. A. W. Phillips, "The Relationship Between Unemployment and the Rate of Change of Money Wage Rates in the United Kingdom 1862–1957," *Economica* 25 (1958): 283–299.

48. For a summary of the relevant literature, see Fiorina, "Elections and Economics in the 1980s." Also see John Chubb, "Institutions, the Economy, and the Dynamics of State Elections," *American Political Science Review* 82 (1988): 133–154; and Dennis Simon, Charles Ostrom, and Robin Marra, "The President, Referendum Voting, and Subnational Elections in the United States," *American Political Science Review* 85 (1991): 1177–1192.

49. George W. Bush, State of the Union Address, January 28, 2003, www.whitehouse.gov/news/releases/2003/01/20030128-19. html, accessed April 1, 2004.

50. The following summary account is drawn from Allen Schick, *The Federal Budget* (Washington, DC: Brookings, 1995); and Steven Smith, *The American Congress* (Boston, MA: Houghton Mifflin, 1995), Ch. 11.

51. Bruce Oppenheimer, "The Importance of Elections in a Strong Congressional Party Era: The Effect of Unified v. Divided Government," manuscript, 1995.

52. *Budget and Economic Outlook, Fiscal Years 2000–2009* (Washington, DC: Congressional Budget Office, January 1999).

53. David Bradford, *Untangling the Income Tax* (Cambridge, MA: Harvard University Press, 1986); and surveys by the National Opinion Research Center.

54. Ballard C. Campbell, *The Growth of American Government: Governance from the Cleveland Era to the Present* (Bloomington: Indiana University Press, 1995), p. 181.

55. Calculated by authors from U.S. Bureau of the Census, *Statistical Abstract of the United States, 1999*, Tables 1434 and 1443.

56. Howard Schuman, *Politics and the Budget*, 3rd ed. (Englewood Cliffs, NJ: Prentice-Hall, 1992), p. 121.

57. Organisation for Economic Cooperation and Development, *OECD In Figures 2006–2007*, p. 36.

58. Nolan McCarty, Keith Poole, and Howard Rosenthal, *Polarized America: The Dance of Ideology and Unequal Riches* (Cambridge, MA: MIT Press, 2006).

59. For a critical survey, see Paul Krugman, *Peddling Prosperity* (New York: Norton, 1994), Ch. 5.

60. Speech at the Constitutional Convention, as quoted in Hans J. Morgenthau, *Politics Among Nations*, 4th ed. (New York: Knopf, 1966), p. 12.

61. George W. Bush, "Remarks by the President on Iraq and the War on Terror," United States Army War College, Carlisle, PA, May 24, 2004.

62. See, for example, the Monroe Doctrine, which was articulated in the President's Message to Congress in 1823. Available at the U.S. Department of State's Web site: http://usinfo.state.gov/use/infousa/facts/democrac/50. htm, Accessed May 6, 2005,.

63. Address to Congress, asking for a declaration of war, April 2, 1917, as reprinted in Bartlett, *Familiar Quotations*, p. 682.

64. Carl B. Swisher, *American Constitutional Development*, 2nd ed. (Boston: Houghton Mifflin, 1958), pp. 992–993.

65. George Washington, *Farewell Address*, September 17, 1796, as quoted in Bartlett, *Familiar Quotations*, p. 379.

66. American Automobile Association data, available at www.fuelgagereport.com, accessed June 22, 2006.

67. "Monthly Energy Review, May 2006," United States Department of Energy, Energy Information Administration, www.eia.doe.gov/emeu/mer/pdf/pages/sec1_15. pdf, accessed June 22, 2006, Table 1. 7.

68. Griff Witte, "Another Look at Fuel Efficiency," *Washington Post*, September 6, 2005, p. D3.

69. Committee on Surface Temperature Reconstructions for the Last 2000 Years, National Research Council, *Surface Temperature Reconstructions for the Last 2000 Years* (Washington, DC: National Academy of Sciences, 2006), Figure S-1.

70. John R. Justus and Susan Fletcher, *Global Climate Change* (Washington, DC: Congressional Research Service), CRS Report for Congress IB89005, Updated May 12, 2006, p. 2.

71. Gallup Poll, March 13–16, 2006.

photo credits

Chapter 1

Page 5: Ken Cedeno/Corbis; **7:** Mathew Cavanaugh/epa/Corbis; **8:** AFP/Getty Images; **11:** DeLaurentis/The Kobal Collection; **13:** Porter Gifford/Getty Images News; **15:** Phil Klein/Corbis.

Chapter 2

Page 33: Ahmad Masood/Reuters/Corbis; **34:** Colonial Williamsburg Foundation; **36:** Joe Raedle/Getty Images News; **38:** Bob Daemmerich/Corbis Sygma.

Chapter 3

Page 46: Gerardo Mora/epa/Corbis; **50:** Dan Lamont/Corbis; **60:;** Signe Wilkinson © 2003 Washington Post Writers Group. Reprinted with permission.; **64:** Tom and Dee Ann McCarthy/Corbis.

Chapter 4

Page 73: Copley News Service; **75:** Bettmann/Corbis; **80:** Steve Shapiro/Corbis; **81:** David Butow/Corbis/Saba; **97:** Eric Miller/Reuters/Corbis.

Chapter 5

 Page 126: Michael Brown/Getty Images News; **128:** Charleston Gazette/ZUMA; **129:** Win McNamee/Getty Images News; **132:** Bruno Stevens/Cosmos/Aurora.

Chapter 6

Page 149: Fabrice Coffrini/AFP/Getty Images; **156:** George Skadding/Time & Life Pictures/ Getty Images; **163:** Mike Simons/Corbis.

Chapter 7

Page 168: TOLES © 2004 The Washington Post. Reprinted with permission of Universal Press Syndicate.; **172:** Alex Wong/Getty Images News; **173:** Mark Peterson/Redux Pictures; **180 (top):** Joe Heller © Green Bay Press Gazette; **180 (bottom):** Nick Anderson © 2004 Washington Post Writers Group. Reprinted with permission.; **189:** Thompson/Detroit Free Press; **193:** Brooks Kraft/Corbis; **198:** Jim Young/Reuters/Corbis.

Chapter 8

Page 211: Justin Sullivan/Getty Images; **213:** Jim Young/Reuters/Corbis; **220:** David Burnett/Contact Press Images; **224:** Jaimie Rose/Getty Images News.

Chapter 9

Chapter 10

Chapter 11

Chapter 12

Chapter 13

Chapter 14

Chapter 15

name index

Page numbers with an *f* or *t* indicate figures or tables, respectively.

Abramoff, Jack, 223–225
Acheson, Dean, 326
Adams, John, 10, 25, 43, 204, 207, 351
Adams, John Quincy, 144
Adams, Samuel, 25, 38, 49
Alexander, Lamar, 54–56
Alito, Samuel, 340, 350, 356, 356*f*, 382
Allen, George, 171*f*
Anderson, John B., 205*t*
Aristotle, 7–8, 160
Arthur, Chester A., 310

Baez, Joan, 370
Bagehot, Walter, 282
Baird, Zoe, 312
Baker, James, 293
Bakke, Allen, 413
Baltimore, Lord, 74
Barber, Benjamin, 143
Barber, James, 294
Barry, Dave, 131, 184, 261
Bartlett, Dan, 288*f*
Bernanke, Benjamin, 330, 330*f*
Black, Hugo, 354, 373
Blackmun, Harry, 356, 386
Blair, Tony, 12
Blanco, Katherine, 46–47
Bloomberg, Michael, 390
Boesky, Ivan, 340
Bolton, Joshua, 274, 288, 288*f*
Bork, Robert H., 349, 350
Brandeis, Louis, 385
Brennan, William, 36, 386
Breyer, Stephen, 356, 356*f*
Broder, David, 15
Brown, Linda, 407
Brown, Michael, 47
Brown, Oliver, 407
Brownlow, Louis, 286, 288
Bryan, William Jennings, 209, 210
Buchanan, Patrick, 205*t*
Burger, Warren E., 345, 347, 356, 386, 396, 413
Burr, Aaron, 204
Bush, George H. W.

Americans with Disabilities Act signed by, 425
campaigns of, 179
Cheney under, 284
civil rights policy of, 420
economy and, 133, 269, 331, 442
on flag burning, 377
judicial appointments of, 347–348, 347*f*, 348*f*
popularity of, 133, 134*f*, 267*f*
Supreme Court appointment of, 350
Bush, George W.
abortion policy of, 173
Arab Americans supported by, 72
Arab–Israeli policy of, 292
budgetary policy of, 254–255, 274
and bureaucracy, 300–303
campaign finance by, 181
as chief of state, 283, 283*f*
as commander-in-chief, 280*f*, 281
context for, 295
creation of Department of Homeland
    Security, 300–303
criminal justice policy of, 390
death penalty supported by, 36
debates with Kerry, 130–131
Defense Department under, 326–327
Democratic opposition to, 242
Dubai Ports World and, 266, 276
economy and, 442–443
education reform initiative of, 4, 53, 54–56
2000 election of, 3–4, 104, 142, 185–187, 211
2004 election of, 4–6
battleground states in, 188
criminal justice issues in, 390
debates in, 130–131
economy and, 442–443
Hispanic voters in, 417
media coverage of, 123–124, 129
nomination process for, 192
predictions of results, 165–168
public's knowledge in, 111
speculation about 2008 during, 13
tax policy in, 450
voter turnout in, 142–143, 158
energy policy of, 265–266
executive agreements of, 278, 279*f*
executive order of, 281
on gay marriage, 423

568

subject index

Page numbers with an *f* or *t* indicate figures or tables, respectively.

anti-terrorism funding, 237–239, 238*f*
appeals courts, 340, 341*f*
appointment power, presidential, 276
apportionment, 59, 188–190, 189*f*
Appropriations Committee
    House, 242–244, 243*t*
    Senate, 243*t*, 244
appropriations process, 252–253
Arab American(s)
    backlash against, 71–73
    patriotism of, 97*f*
Arab American Institute, 293
Arab–Israeli conflict, 291–293
Arkansas, school shooting in, 117
Article I of Constitution, 239–240
Articles of Confederation, 30–32
    abandonment of, 32–33
    versus Constitution, 42–43, 42*t*
Asian Americans, 417–418, 427
Asian immigrants, 78, 79, 97, 418
assembly, freedom of, 374
Association of American Colleges and
    Universities, 415
Atkins v. Virginia, 395
Australia, compulsory voting in, 148, 149
Austria, rise of fascism in, 158
authorization process, 252

balancing doctrine, 375–376
Ballot Initiatives Strategy Center, 16
Bank of the United States, 49
banking, international, 447
Barron v. Baltimore, 373
battleground states, 188
Bay of Pigs, 327–328
Belgium, compulsory voting in, 149
beliefs, formation of, 101–102
beltway insiders, 294
benefits, government
    by beneficiary category, 441*f*
    for elderly, 434–437, 441–442
    for poor, 439–441
Benton v. Maryland, 394
bias
    in media, 122–125
        ideological, 123–124
        professional, 125
        story selection, 124–125
    in polls, 104–110
bicameral legislature, 240
bigotry, immigration and, 71–73, 77–78
big-three networks, 124, 137
Bill of Rights, 25–26, 34–35, 40–41, 85, 371–373, 418
bill-to-law process, 249–253, 250*f*
"black codes," 403
blacks. *See* African Americans
block grants, 52–53

"blogs," 16
"blue laws," 76
Border Patrol, 301
bosses, party, 14
Boston Tea Party, 28
bottom-up reform, of bureaucracy, 310–311
Bowers v. Hardwick, 388
Boy Scouts, and gay rights, 423
"bridges to nowhere," 247–248
briefs, 342
Brown v. Board of Education of Topeka, 407–408, 409
Brownlow Committee, 287
"buckrakers," 123
Budget and Accounting Act of 1921, 445
Budget and Impoundment Control Act of 1974, 445
Budget Committee, House, 243*t*, 244
budget committees, 445–446
budget crisis, in state governments, 59–60, 60*f*
budgetary politics, congressional, 252–253,
    314–315, 445–446
budgetary power, presidential, 274
budgetary process, 445–446
Bull Moose Party, 209
bully pulpit, 272
Bureau of Alcohol, Tobacco and Firearms
    (BATF), 313–314
bureaucracy, 299–334
    agency reorganization in, 313–314
    American, 309–311
        bottom-up reform of, 310–311
        difficult beginnings of, 309
        patronage in, 309–310
    budgetary control of, 314–315
    caution by, 319
    change in, 302–303, 307
    civil service in, 310–311
    coercion by, 318–319
    compromised capacity of, 319
    Congress and, 304, 312–315
    creation of new department, 299–303
    elections and, 317–319
    employment growth in, 305–306, 306*f*
    expansionary tendencies of, 307, 319
    foreign policy institutions in, 325–329
    "go native," 315
    ideal, 304–305
    impossibility of tasks for, 308
    interest groups and, 304, 315–317, 323–324
    legislative details on, 314, 319
    legislative oversight of, 315
    monetary policy set by, 329–332
    outside influences on, 311–319
    performance of, difficulty in measuring, 307
    policy environments of, 332
    policy implementation by, 320–332, 432–433
    political appointees in, 310–311
    political power of, 304

Criminal Justice Legal Foundation, 37
criminal trials
    federal, 339–340, 339*t*
    state, 360–361
critical elections, 206
"cruel and unusual punishment," 36–37, 394–395
C-SPAN, 16
Cuba, CIA operation against, 327–328
Cuban Americans
    support for Bush (George W.), 417
    and U. S. policy toward Cuba, 293
Cuban immigrants, 79, 97
culture, political. *See* political culture
Customs Service, 300
cynical argument, on voter turnout, 159
cynicism, 6–7, 10

The Daily Show, 138
de facto segregation, 412–413
de jure segregation, 412–413
death penalty. *See* capital punishment
Death Penalty Information Center, 37
deaths, attributed to governments, 20
debates, presidential, 130–131
debt, national, 446, 451, 451*f*
debtors, in Shays' Rebellion, 24–25
decentralization, 54–56
Declaration of Independence, 28
    classical liberalism of, 85, 93
    signers of, 25
    social-contract theory and, 27, 28, 29*t*
defendant, 339
Defense Department, 277*t*, 326–327
defense policy, 332, 431, 452–457
defense spending, 327, 328*f*
deficits, 445–448, 447*f*
Delaware, Constitution ratified by, 40*t*
delegates, 260–261
democracy
    America's new, 10–21
    Churchill on, 21
    direct, 11–12, 15–16
    elections as driving force of, 5–6, 12–13
    laboratories of, states as, 57
    mass, birth of, 144–145
    media as component of, 135
    more, in pervasive elections, 19–20
    number and frequency of elections in, 10–13
    origin of word, 8
    popular influence in, 9–10
    popular model of, 9
    representative, 8–9
    responsible model of, 9, 15
    unique conception of, 6–10
    voting as fundamental form of, 143
    weak institutions in, 7–8
Democracy in America (de Tocqueville), 218

Democratic-Republicans, 144, 206*t*, 207, 351–352
Democrats
    activists' influence on, 195, 196*f*
    African American support of, 169, 169*t*, 207,
        210, 211*f*, 411, 412*f*
    and centralized government, 54
    and civil rights, 210, 404, 410–411
    in Civil War and Reconstruction, 206*t*, 208–209
    in Congress, 240–242, 255–257, 256*f*, 257*f*
    congressional races of, 176–177
    and Department of Homeland Security, 302–303
    in divided government, 58, 58*f*, 206*t*, 210–212
    family/children as, 101
    and federal grants, 52–53
    and Federal Reserve Board, 331
    and health care, 202–203, 430–431
    history of, 14, 204–212
    ideology of, 14
    and immigration, 81–82
    in Industrial Republican era, 206*t*, 209–210
    Jacksonian, 206*t*, 207–208
    Jeffersonian, 206*t*, 207, 351–352
    journalists as, 123
    and judicial appointments, 347–350, 347*f*, 348*f*
    loyalty to, 169–170, 169*t*, 174, 174*f*
    New Deal, 210
    nomination process of, 190–199
    opposition to Bush (George W.), 242
    PAC donations to, 226
    patronage politics of, 310
    and reapportionment, 59
    and senior citizen benefits, 437–438
    and social programs, 439–440
    in state government, 58, 58*f*
    and Supreme Court, 336–337
    voter turnout and, 142–143, 155, 160
    Web site of, 232
    and women's suffrage, 146
    women's support of, 170, 170*f*
    yellow-dog, 169
"demosclerosis," 228
Dennis v. United States, 376
departments, 304. *See also* bureaucracy; *specific*
    departments
deregulation, 322–323
Detroit, school segregation in, 412–413
devolution, 54–56
diminishing returns, in campaign spending, 184
direct action, 229
direct democracy, 11–12, 15–16
    versus checks and balances, 15
    Web resources on, 16
direct mail, 228
disabilities, Americans with, 424–425
disaster planning and response, 45–47, 46*f*, 52,
    237–239
dissenting opinions, 343–344, 344*f*

fiscal policy, 445–447
Fish and Wildlife Service, 322
527 Committees, 4–5, 227–228
flag burning, as free speech, 377–378
flag-salute cases, 384
floor, of Congress, 240, 251–252
Florida
    2000 presidential election in, 4, 104
    2004 presidential election in, 166, 188
    affirmative action in, 413
    class action lawsuit in, 346
    immigrants to, 79, 84
Food and Drug Administration (FDA), 314, 319
food stamps, 439
foreign and defense policy, 332, 431, 452–457
    Congress' self-denying ordinance in, 293
    interest groups and, 293
    national ideals and, 456–457
    national interests and, 457–458
    presidential opportunity in, 290–293
Foreign Intelligence Surveillance Act (FISA), 371
foreign policy institutions, 325–329
Foreign Relations Committee, House and
    Senate, 242, 243t
foreign service, 326
Forest Service, 307
Foundation for Individual Rights in Education, 380
Founding Fathers, 25, 41
four freedoms, 457
Fourteenth Amendment
    due process clause of, 373, 401
    equal protection clause of, 401–403, 405,
        414–415, 419, 427
framing, by media, 133
franchise (right to vote), 143–146
    African American, 78, 144, 157f, 158
        grandfather clause and, 404
        loss of, 404–405
        modern struggle for, 408–411
        post-Civil War, 403–404
        regaining in migration north, 406–407, 406f
        white primary and, 404, 407
    extension of, 145, 145f
    women's, 145, 145f, 146, 419
frank (free postage), 254
free exercise clause, 380, 383–385
    neutrality test of, 384
    and public schools, 384
    Sherbert test of, 383–384
Free Soil Party, 205t, 208
free speech, 355, 374–378
    balancing doctrine and, 375–376
    clear and present danger doctrine and, 374–375
    at colleges and universities, 376, 379–380
    evolution of doctrine, 374–378
    fundamental freedoms doctrine and, 376–377
    limitations on, 378

Mill's defense of, 374
    public opinion on, 376, 377f
    symbolic, 377–378
Freedman's Bureau, 404
Freedom Forum, 398
freedom of expression, 355, 374–378. See also free
    speech
Freedom of Information Act of 1967, 318
freedom of press
    in Bill of Rights, 374
    versus impartial jury, 393
    versus national security, 126–127
    prior restraint doctrine and, 126–127, 374
freedom of religion, 353, 355, 380–385, 418
    coercion test of, 381–382
    conservative interpretation of, 381–382
    establishment clause and, 355, 380–382
    free exercise clause and, 380, 383–385
    Lemon test of, 380–381
    liberal interpretation of, 380–381
    neutrality test of, 384
    and school vouchers, 384–385
    in schools, 381–382, 383f, 384
    Sherbert test of, 383–384
free-rider problem, 220–223
French Canadian immigrants, 76
"friend of the court," 229, 345
frontier, and political culture, 95–96
"front-loaded" primaries, 192–194
The Fugitive, 393
fundamental freedoms doctrine, 376–377

Gallup poll, 103, 159–160
gambling
    by elderly, 435f
    on Native American property, 418
gay marriage, 15, 423
gay rights, 85, 387–389, 388f, 422–423, 423f, 424f
Gazette of the United States, 135
gender and civil rights, 419–420
gender gap, 170, 170f, 171t
General Agreement on Tariffs and Trade
    (GATT), 447
general election, 11
general-election campaign, financing of,
    182–183
Geneva Conventions, 312
geography, and party loyalties, 169, 169t
Georgia
    capital punishment in, 395
    Constitution ratified by, 40t
    court system of, 360–361
    school shooting in, 117
German Americans, during World War I, 72
German immigrants, 76–77
Germany, rise of fascism in, 158
gerrymandering, 189

random sample, 103
rational basis test, 402
Realclimage.org, 454
realignment, 205–206
reapportionment, 59, 188–190, 189f
recall election, 11, 15–16, 228
recessions, 442, 443f
recommend, presidential power to, 272–273
Reconstruction, 208–209, 404
Red Scare, 78, 375–376, 375f
red tape, 308
redistricting, 59, 188–190, 189f
referenda, 11–12, 15–16
Reform Party, 204, 205t
Regents of the University of California v. Bakke, 413
registered voters, 148
regressive tax, 450
regulation, 320–324
    court interpretations of, 322
    decrease in (deregulation), 322–323
    of electronic media, 324
    history of, 321
    independent agencies in, 323–324, 323t
    interest groups and, 323–324, 323t
    politics of, 321–322
    zone of acceptance in, 322
religion
    and abortion, 102
    conflict over, 75–76
    freedom of. *See* freedom of religion
    of immigrants, 76–77
    and party loyalties, 169, 169t
    in schools, 381–382, 383f, 384
remands, 344
remedy, Supreme Court, 344–345
representative democracy, 8–9
republic, 8–9
republicanism, civic, 85
Republicans
    and abortion, 387
    activists' influence on, 195, 196f
    and affirmative action, 414
    Bush's (George W.) support from, 213
    and civil rights, 410–411
    in Civil War and Reconstruction, 206t, 208–209
    in Congress, 240–242, 255–257, 256f
    congressional races of, 176–177
    and decentralization, 54–56
    in divided government, 58, 58f, 206t, 210–212
    family/child identification as, 101
    and federal grants, 52–53
    and Federal Reserve Board, 331
    and health care, 202–203
    history of, 14, 204–212
    ideology of, 14
    and immigration, 81–82

in Industrial Republican system, 206t, 209–210
    and judicial appointments, 347–350, 347f, 348f
    loyalty to, 169–170, 169t
    L-shaped state support for, 186, 187f
    in New Deal, 206t, 210
    nomination process of, 190–199
    opposition to Clinton, 242
    and reapportionment, 59
    on school prayer, 382
    and senior citizen benefits, 437–438
    and social programs, 439–440
    "southern strategy" of, 411
    in state government, 58, 58f
    voter turnout and, 142–143, 155, 160
    Web site of, 232
    and women's suffrage, 146
residential segregation, 407
responsible model of democracy, 9, 15
restraint
    judicial, 357
    prior, 126–127, 374
restrictive housing covenant, 407
restrictive rule, for bill, 251
results, equality of, 90–91
"retail politics," 192
retrospective voting, 171–172, 444f
Revolutionary War
    aftermath of, 23–25
    influence on Constitution, 28–29
Rhode Island, Constitution ratified by, 40t, 41
riders, 252
right or right wing, 14
"right to life," 387
right to privacy, 385. *See also* privacy rights
right to vote. *See* voting rights
rights. *See* civil liberties; civil rights
Rita, Hurricane, 453
Rocky Mountain Llama and Alpaca Association, 218
Roe v. Wade
    constitutional interpretation in, 354
    controversy over, 358
    privacy rights and, 386–387
    public opinion polls on, 107–110, 109f
roll-call vote, 253–254
Roper Center for Public Opinion Research, 140
Roper Starch Worldwide, 105–106
Rostker v. Goldberg, 420
rule, for bill, 251
Rules Committee
    House, 242–244, 243t, 244, 251
    Senate, 243t, 244
Rwanda, media coverage of, 132

safe seats, 174
same-sex unions, 15, 423

social movement, 222–223
Social Security, 51, 434–437, 441–442
  earnings penalty in, 442
  operation at loss, 435
  politics of, 437–438
  privatization of, 437
  projected costs of, 436, 436f
  support for, 438, 438f
Social Security Act of 1935, 434
Social Security Disability Insurance (SSDI), 424
social-contract theory, 27, 28, 29t, 84–85
socialism, American disinterest in, 95–96
socializing agent, 101–102
socioeconomic status
  and party loyalties, 169, 169t
  and voter turnout, 157–158, 157f, 160
sodomy law, 387–388, 388f, 423
soft money, 181, 182f
solicitor general, 345, 365
solidary benefits, 220, 220f
Somalia, media coverage of, 132
Sons of Liberty, 28
sources of information, 120–122, 121f
South Carolina
  Constitution ratified by, 40t
  primary of, 197
South Dakota v. Dole, 51
South Park, 124
Southern Manifesto, 409
Southern Poverty Law Center, 380
"southern strategy," 411
sovereign immunity, 49
Speaker of the House, 240–241
special interests. *See* interest groups
special prosecutors, 286
speech, freedom of. *See* free speech
speech-making, presidential, 270–272, 271f
spending clause, 49, 51
spoils system, 216, 309–310
sponsor, of bill, 249
Sportsmen's Caucus, 246, 249
spying, domestic, 370–372, 370f
Stamp Act, 28
standing committees, 242, 243t
stare decisis, 343
state, chief of, 282–284, 284f
state action doctrine, 405, 407
state courts, 360–363
  federal courts and, 361–363
  trial, 360–361
State Department, 277t, 325–326
state elections, 10, 14
state governments, 56–61
  budget crisis in, 59–60, 60f
  divided, 58, 58f
  economic action by, 59–60
  education financing by, 57

expenditures by, 57
federal grants to, 52–54, 53f
grants to local government, 57
immigration impact on, 80, 83–84
as laboratories of democracy, 57
political competition in, 58
powers granted by Constitution, 47, 48t
reapportionment in, 59
trade missions of, 59
trust in, 62f
unfunded mandates to, 54–56
variation in responsibilities, 57–58
veto power in, 59
state legislatures, 56–58
  professionalism of, 57–58
  term limits in, 58
State of the Union address, 272
states rights
  versus Constitution, 26
  court decisions on, 48–51
  decentralization and, 54–56
States' Rights Democratic Party, 205t
statistics, country-to-country comparison of, 21
statutory interpretation, 359
story selection, media bias in, 124–125
strategic petroleum reserve, 453
strict constructionists, 355
strict scrutiny, of suspect classification, 402
Stromberg v. California, 375
suffrage (right to vote), 143–146
  African American, 78, 144, 157f, 158
    grandfather clause and, 404
    loss of, 404–405
    modern struggle for, 408–411
    post-Civil War, 403–404
    regaining in migration north, 406–407, 406f
    white primary and, 404, 407
  extension of, 145, 145f
  women's, 145, 145f, 146, 419
sunshine laws, 318
Supplemental Security Income (SSI), 439
supremacy clause, 35, 49
Supreme Court, 335–360
  on 2000 presidential election, 4
  on abortion, 354, 386–387
  on affirmative action, 413–415
  appointments to, 335–337, 347–350, 348–350, 349f
  on capital punishment, 394–395
  certs by, 341–342
  checks on power of, 359–360
  chief justice of, 336–337, 340, 345
  on civil rights, 401, 419–420, 423
  clerks of, 346
  in Constitution, 338
  on contraception, 385–386
  on criminal justice, 389–396
  on decentralization, 56

additional titles of interest

Note to Instructors: Any of these Penguin-Putnam, Inc., titles can be packaged with this book at a special discount. Contact your local Longman sales representative for details on how to create a Penguin–Putnam, Inc. Value Package.

Stephen E. Ambrose, *Rise to Globalism*

Alexis De Tocqueville (edited by
Richard D. Heffner), *Democracy in America*

The Federalist Papers
(edited by Clinton Rossiter and
new introduction by Charles R. Kesler)

Al Gore, *Earth in the Balance*

Peter Irons, *The Courage of Their Convictions*

Martin Luther King, Jr., *Why We Can't Wait*

Philip B. Kunhardt and Peter W. Kunhardt, *The American President*

Joe McGinniss, *Selling of the President*

David Osborne and Ted Gaebler, *Reinventing Government*

Thomas Paine, *Common Sense*

William L. Riordan, *Plunkitt of Tammany Hall*

Upton Sinclair, *The Jungle*

Harriet Beecher Stowe, *Uncle Tom's Cabin*

Stephen Waldman, *The Bill*

Juan Williams (introduction by Julian Bond), *Eyes on the Prize*